Praise for Best Places® Guidebooks

"Best Places *are the best regional restaurant and guide books in America.*"
—THE SEATTLE TIMES

"Best Places *covers must-see portions of the West Coast with style and authority.
In-the-know locals offer thorough info on restaurants, lodgings, and the sights.*"
—NATIONAL GEOGRAPHIC TRAVELER

"*Travelers swear by the recommendations in the* Best Places *guidebooks.*"
—SUNSET MAGAZINE

"*Still the region's undisputed heavyweight champ of guidebooks.*"
—SEATTLE POST-INTELLIGENCER

"*Known for their frank yet chatty tone.*"
—PUBLISHERS WEEKLY

"*For travel collections covering the Northwest, the* Best Places
series takes precedence over all similar guides."
—BOOKLIST

"Best Places Vancouver *is a cure-all to the lost-in-the-big-city blues.*"
—AMAZON.COM

"*Funny, conversational writing and clever sidebars make*
Best Places Vancouver *an enjoyable read.*"
—VANCOUVER MAGAZINE

"*Not only the best travel guide in the region, but maybe one of the most definitive
guides in the country, which many look forward to with the anticipation usually
sparked by a best-selling novel. A browser's delight,* Best Places Northwest
should be chained to dashboards throughout the Northwest."
—THE OREGONIAN

"*Visitors to Washington, Oregon, and British Columbia would do well to
pick up* Best Places Northwest *for an exhaustive review of food and lodging
in the region. . . . An indispensable glove-compartment companion.*"
—TRAVEL AND LEISURE

TRUST THE LOCALS

The original insiders' guides, written by local experts

EVERY PLACE STAR-RATED & RECOMMENDED

★★★★   The very best in the region

★★★   Distinguished; many outstanding features

★★   Excellent; some wonderful qualities

★   A good place

HELPFUL ICONS
Watch for these quick-reference symbols throughout the book:

 FAMILY FUN

 GOOD VALUE

 ROMANTIC

 EDITORS' CHOICE

BEST PLACES®

VANCOUVER

The Locals' Guide to the Best Restaurants,
Lodgings, Sights, Shopping, and More!

917.11
BEST PL
2009

Edited by
KASEY WILSON

EDITION 5

SASQUATCH BOOKS
SEATTLE

This book is dedicated to Eli, Amelia, and Julien. ★★★★

Printed in the United States of America
Published by Sasquatch Books
Distributed by PGW/Perseus

Fifth edition
15 14 13 12 11 10 09   9 8 7 6 5 4 3 2 1

ISBN-13: 978-1-57061-561-0
ISBN-10: 1-57061-561-6
ISSN: 1095-9807

Project editor: Rachelle Longé
Cover photograph: Photodisc Photography / Getty Images
Cover design: Rosebud Eustace
Interior design: Scott Taylor/FILTER/Talent
Interior composition: Sarah Plein
Maps: Lisa Brower/GreenEye Design
Indexer: Michael Ferreira

SPECIAL SALES

Best Places guidebooks are available at special discounts on bulk purchases for corporate, club, or organization sales promotions, premiums, and gifts. For more information, contact your local bookseller or Special Sales, Best Places Guidebooks, 119 South Main Street, Suite 400, Seattle, Washington 98104, 800/775-0817.

SASQUATCH BOOKS
119 South Main Street, Suite 400
Seattle, WA 98104
(206) 467-4300
www.sasquatchbooks.com
custserv@sasquatchbooks.com

CONTENTS

Introduction and Acknowledgments, **ix**

Contributors, **x**

About Best Places Guidebooks, **xi**

How to Use This Book, **xii**

    Best Places Star Ratings, **xii**

PLANNING A TRIP   **1**

How to Get Here, **2**

When to Visit, **9**

General Costs, **10**

Tips for Special Travellers, **13**

Web Information, **17**

    Vancouver Through Time, **6**

    Favourite Books about Vancouver, **14**

LAY OF THE CITY   **19**

Orientation, **20**

Visitor Information, **21**

Getting Around, **22**

Essentials, **27**

Local Resources, **34**

Important Telephone Numbers, **37**

    Buddha in a Hotel and Other Places of Worship, **28**

RESTAURANTS   **39**

Restaurants by Star Rating, **40**

Restaurants by Neighbourhood, **42**

Restaurants by Food and Other Features, **45**

Top 200 Restaurants, **51**

    Cocktail Culture, **58**

    Bubble Tea, **74**

    Sayonara, Sushi Place—Hello, Izakaya!, **87**

    Vancouver's Best Dim Sum and Then Some, **94**

    Brood Food: Kid-Friendly Dining, **106**

    Tea Party: What's Brewing in Vancouver?, **118**

LODGINGS   **129**

Downtown/West End, **130**

North Shore, **137**

Airport Area, **138**

    Have Pet, Will Travel, **132**

CONTENTS

EXPLORING   139

Top 20 Attractions, 140

Neighbourhoods, 161

Museums, 166

Galleries, 170

Gardens, 173

Parks and Beaches, 174

Organized Tours, 180

Top 20 Attractions, 141

Serious Architecture, 148

The Richmond Oval, 164

The Green Party: Farmers Markets, 178

SHOPPING   185

Shopping Areas and Malls, 186

Shops from A to Z, 190

Neighbourhood Watch: South Main, 192

The Silk Road, 206

Vintage Chic, 210

Asian Purveyors, 216

PERFORMING ARTS   225

Theatre, 226

Classical Music and Opera, 230

Dance, 233

Film, 237

Literature, 239

Creative Collaborations: See Seven, 229

City Arts and Lectures, 234

NIGHTLIFE   241

Nightlife by Neighbourhood, 242

Nightlife by Feature, 243

Nightlife, 245

Music and Clubs, 246

Bars, Pubs, and Taverns, 254

Lounges, 258

Coffee, Tea, and Dessert, 263

After Hours, 249

Where to Eat if You're a Night Crawler, 260

RECREATION 267

Outdoor Activities, **268**

Spectator Sports, **301**

The Great Indoors, **270**

The Perfect Fit, **276**

Glamping, **282**

The Bald Eagle—That Great BC Symbol, **288**

Squamish: Going to the Extremes, **296**

2010 Winter Olympics in Vancouver, **302**

VICTORIA AND BEYOND 305

How to Get Here, **306**

Orientation, **308**

Visitor Information, **308**

Getting Around, **309**

Tours of Victoria and the Region, **310**

Restaurants, **311**

Lodgings, **315**

Top 10 Attractions, **318**

Shopping, **325**

Performing Arts, **326**

Festivals, **327**

Beyond Victoria, **328**

Sooke, **328**

Sidney and the Saanich Peninsula, **331**

Malahat, **331**

Cowichan Valley, **332**

Duncan, **333**

Salt Spring Island, **333**

Tofino and Long Beach, **334**

Ghostly Victoria, **311**

Vancouver Island Three-Day Tour, **323**

WHISTLER 337

How to Get Here, **338**

Orientation, **341**

Visitor Information, **343**

Getting Around, **343**

Restaurants, **344**

Lodgings, **351**

Exploring, **355**

WHISTLER *continued*

Shopping, **357**

Nightlife, **357**

Recreation, **358**

The Lure of the Rings, **342**

The 2010 Winter Olympics, **354**

Fresh Tracks, **359**

OKANAGAN VALLEY   363

How to Get Here, **364**

Orientation, **364**

Visitor Information, **366**

Kelowna and Beyond, **366**

Penticton and Naramata, **367**

Oliver and Osoyoos, **367**

Okanagan Valley Wine Country, **368**

Restaurants, **373**

Lodgings, **378**

Romancing the Desert, **368**

Three One-Day Okanagan Wine-Tasting Tours, **370**

Vineyard Dining: Your Guide to the Best Winery Restaurants, **376**

INDEX   381

LIST OF MAPS

Victoria, **307**

Whistler, **339**

Okanagan Valley, **365**

Introduction and Acknowledgments

Vancouver's calling card has always been its outdoor spirit. As a cosmopolitan city fashioned on the edge of a rain forest, this boomtown continues to burst with ever-developing character as soaring cranes fill the skyline for the 2010 Winter Olympics. Adventure and the discovery of gold may have once lured the masses west, but today, it is the city's food that has sparked the new gold rush. The mother lode of ingredients comes from the Pacific Ocean and the "I'll do it my way" farmers who sell local and organic produce to Vancouver's gifted cooks. Besides our home-grown talent, international chefs are being seduced by the city and the scenery, and are staking their claim. Given the city's best culinary establishments, innovative dining trends, wine bars, food blogs, an Iron Chef, and immeasurable attention to ambience, visitors and locals anticipate and explore new taste sensations, novel presentations, and a fresh scene.

With all that taste-testing, it's no wonder walking, biking, and jogging are a way of life here, and they are the best ways to explore the neighbourhoods. Crisscross old warehouse districts; climb mountains, comb the beaches, scour the shops; hunt down the local farmers markets; indulge your senses with art, theatre, and museums; and reward yourself at the end of the day with a glass (or two) of superlative Okanagan Valley wines poured by a nose-y sommelier. Then party into the wee hours of the morning at the many lounges, clubs, and pubs. Stunning scenery and diverse attractions are just a short drive away. Whistler (Vancouver's partner for the 2010 Olympics) provides a cornucopia of activities year-round, while Victoria, the genteel capital of BC, attracts garden lovers. No matter your age or taste, there's a nugget of pleasure just waiting to be unearthed within these pages.

Many people contributed to *Best Places Vancouver* in many different ways. My thanks to Anthony Gismondi, Erin Guppy, Mark Laba, editor/pal Murray McMillan, Lynne McNamara, Jane Mundy, Karen Rusk, and Jim Tobler.

It's been wonderful working with the extraordinary Sasquatch team again, including acquisitions editor Terence Maikels, project editor Rachelle Longé, production coordinator Sarah Plein, copy editor Kris Fulsaas, and proofreader Diane Sepanski. That's five down!

And last, but always first—Jeff, Pam, Karen Meagan, and Jason.

—Kasey Wilson

Contributors

Editor **KASEY WILSON** counts this latest edition as her fifth time editing *Best Places Vancouver*. An award-winning food and travel writer, broadcaster, and author, Wilson is food editor of *Wine Access* magazine and produces and co-hosts a weekly radio show on Talk 1410 AM for CTVglobemedia. Her articles have appeared in *National Geographic Traveler*, *Bon Appétit*, and *Gastronomica*. Wilson is a member of the Society of American Travel Writers and the Association of Food Journalists.

SARAH BANCROFT, who wrote the Shopping chapter, is the editor in chief and co-founder of Daily Dose Media, publisher of daily online magazines in several Canadian cities, including Vancouver (www.vitaminv.ca).

Ski Whistler's powder all day, eat all night—that made the perfect assignment for sports-obsessed gastronome **LUCY HYSLOP**, a British transplant who swapped London for Vancouver in 2000. The former chief features editor of the *Vancouver Sun*, Lucy still writes for the metropolitan daily, as well as the *Daily Telegraph Magazine*, *Globe and Mail*, *Vancouver*, and *BC Business* magazines.

JOIE ALVARO KENT is certain that there's a baby picture of her somewhere with a spoon in one hand and a pen in the other. A freelance food writer, her work has been published in *Vancouver* and *EAT* magazines.

ARLENE KROEKER is a Vancouver-based freelance writer and weekly food columnist for the *Richmond Review*. She created and hosts "Life Tastes Great," a series of cooking workshops to promote West Coast chefs and cuisine. As a director of the Terranova Schoolyard Project, she connects kids with gardens.

TARA LEE feels incredibly fortunate to be able to combine her love of words with her passion for food. She is a Vancouver-based freelance writer whose work has appeared in such publications as *Globe and Mail*, *Ottawa Citizen*, and the *Vancouver Sun*. She holds a PhD in Asian Canadian Literature and teaches in the English Department at the University of British Columbia.

After showing an aptitude for gluttony at an early age, **LEE MAN**'s eating skills and appetite were further sharpened while living in Hong Kong, Shanghai, and San Francisco. With an emphasis on Asian cuisine, Lee's food writing has appeared in numerous Vancouver-based publications and international travel guides.

Performing Arts contributor **SHERRY MCGARVIE** is a freelance grant writer, proofreader, and copy editor, when not at her day job with Vancouver's largest talent agency.

PETER MORGAN is the president of Morgan:Newsletters and a former editor of *BC Business Magazine*. He also publishes a daily subscriber-based newsletter, Morgan:News:2010, about the business and management side of the 2010 Winter Olympics.

JOANNE SASVARI is a Vancouver-based writer who covers food, travel, fashion, drink, and other lifestyle topics for a variety of publications. She is also the author of the culinary-travel book *Paprika: A Spicy Memoir from Hungary* (CanWest Books, 2006).

After spending six years in Vancouver's tourism and hospitality industry, **TARA SCHMIDT** now works for *Western Living* and *Vancouver* magazines but still stays up till dawn researching Vancouver's nightlife.

SHELORA SHELDAN is a food and travel writer based in Victoria. Her work has appeared in *Northwest Palate*, *Western Living*, and *Wine Access* magazines.

JOHN SCHREINER is Canada's most prolific author of wine books. He has written 12 since 1984, including the bestsellers *British Columbia Wine Country*, *The Wineries of British Columbia*, and *John Schreiner's Okanagan Wine Tour Guide*. He juggled his passion for wine with a 40-year career as a business writer for the *Financial Post* until retiring in 2001 to devote himself totally to wine.

IAN WALKER, author of the Recreation chapter, is one of the luckiest men in the world. Not only is he an extreme and adventure sports writer for the *Vancouver Sun*, but he is also married to rock star Bif Naked.

About Best Places® Guidebooks

People trust us. Best Places guidebooks, which have been published continuously since 1975, represent one of the most respected regional travel series in the country. Our reviewers know their territory and seek out the very best a city or region has to offer. We are able to provide tough, candid reports about places that have rested too long on their laurels, and to delight in new places that deserve recognition. We describe the true strengths, foibles, and unique characteristics of each establishment listed.

Best Places Vancouver is written by and for locals, and is therefore coveted by travellers. It's written for people who live here and who enjoy exploring the city's bounty and its out-of-the-way places of high character and individualism. It is these very characteristics that make *Best Places Vancouver* ideal for tourists, too. The best places in and around the city are the ones that denizens favor: independently owned establishments of good value, touched with local history, run by lively individuals, and graced with natural beauty. With this fifth edition of *Best Places Vancouver*, travellers will find the information they need: where to go and when; what to order; which rooms to request (and which to avoid); where the best music, art, nightlife, shopping, and other attractions are; and how to find the city's hidden secrets.

NOTE: *The reviews in this edition are based on information available at press time and are subject to change. Readers are advised that places listed in previous editions may have closed or changed management, or may no longer be recommended by this series. The editors welcome information conveyed by users of this book. A report form is provided at the end of the book, and feedback is also welcome via e-mail: BPFeedback@sasquatchbooks.com.*

BEST PLACES® STAR RATINGS

Any travel guide that rates establishments is inherently subjective—and Best Places is no exception. We rely on our professional experience, yes, but also on a gut feeling. And, occasionally, we even give in to a soft spot for a favourite neighbourhood hangout. Our star-rating system is not simply a checklist; it's judgmental, critical, sometimes fickle, and highly personal.

For each new edition, we send local food and travel experts out to review restaurants and lodgings and then rate them on a scale of one to four, based on uniqueness, loyalty of local clientele, performance measured against the establishment's goals, excellence of cooking, cleanliness, value, and professionalism of service. That doesn't mean a one-star establishment isn't worth dining or sleeping at—far from it. When we say that all the places listed in our books are recommended, we mean it. That one-star pizza joint may be just the ticket for the end of a whirlwind day of shopping with the kids. But if you're planning something more special, the star ratings can help you choose an eatery or hotel

How to Use This Book

This book is divided into 12 chapters covering a wide range of establishments, destinations, and activities in and around Vancouver. All evaluations are based on reports from local and travelling inspectors. Final judgments are made by the editors. **EVERY PLACE FEATURED IN THIS BOOK IS RECOMMENDED.**

STAR RATINGS *(for Restaurants and Lodgings only)* Restaurants and lodgings are rated on a scale of one to four stars (with half stars in between), based on uniqueness, loyalty of local clientele, performance measured against the establishment's goals, excellence of cooking, cleanliness, value, and professionalism of service. Reviews are listed alphabetically, and every place is recommended.

★★★★	The very best in the region
★★★	Distinguished; many outstanding features
★★	Excellent; some wonderful qualities
★	A good place
UNRATED	New or undergoing major changes

(For more on how we rate places, see "Best Places Star Ratings," above.)

PRICE RANGE *(for Restaurants and Lodgings only)* Prices for restaurants are based primarily on dinner for two, including dessert, tax, and tip, but no alcohol. Prices for lodgings are based on peak season rates for one night's lodging for two people (i.e., double occupancy). Peak season is typically Memorial Day to Labour

that will wow your new clients or be a stunning, romantic place to celebrate an anniversary or impress a first date.

We award four-star ratings sparingly, reserving them for what we consider truly the best. And once an establishment has earned our highest rating, everyone's expectations seem to rise. Readers often write us letters specifically to point out the faults in four-star establishments. With changes in chefs, management, styles, and trends, it's always easier to get knocked off the pedestal than to ascend it. Three-star establishments, on the other hand, seem to generate healthy praise. They exhibit outstanding qualities, and we get lots of love letters about them. The difference between two and three stars can sometimes be a very fine line. Two-star establishments are doing a good, solid job and gaining attention, while one-star places are often dependable spots that have been around forever.

The restaurants and lodgings described in this book have earned their stars from hard work and good service (and good food). They're proud to be included in this book—look for our Best Places sticker in their windows. And we're proud to honor them in this, the fifth edition of *Best Places Vancouver*.

Day; off-season rates vary but can sometimes be significantly less. Call ahead to verify, as all prices are subject to change. **ALL PRICES ARE GIVEN IN CANADIAN DOLLARS.**

$$$$	Very expensive (more than $125 for dinner for two; more than $250 for one night's lodging for two)
$$$	Expensive (between $85 and $125 for dinner for two; between $150 and $250 for one night's lodging for two)
$$	Moderate (between $35 and $85 for dinner for two; between $85 and $150 for one night's lodging for two)
$	Inexpensive (less than $35 for dinner for two; less than $85 for one night's lodging for two)

RESERVATIONS *(for Restaurants only)* We used one of the following terms for our reservations policy: reservations required, reservations recommended, no reservations. "No reservations" means either reservations are not necessary or are not accepted.

PARKING We've indicated a variety of options for parking in the facts lines at the end of reviews as appropriate.

ADDRESSES AND PHONE NUMBERS Every attempt has been made to provide accurate information on an establishment's location and phone number, but it's always a good idea to call ahead and confirm. For establishments with two or more locations, we try to provide information on the original or most recommended branches.

CREDIT CARDS Credit cards are abbreviated in this book as follows: American Express (AE); Carte Blanche (CB); Diners Club (DC); Discover (DIS); Japanese credit card (JCB); MasterCard (MC); Visa (V).

CHEQUES AND DEBIT CARDS Vancouver is ahead of the world when it comes to using electronic cash at retailers and restaurants. Debit cards can be used in virtually all retail shops and restaurants in Greater Vancouver, and cheques are nearly obsolete. ATMs are also located throughout high-volume areas of the city and at most bank branches. We have indicated whenever possible whether an establishment accepts cheques and debit cards.

E-MAIL AND WEB SITE ADDRESSES Web sites or e-mail addresses for establishments have been included where available. Please note that the Web is a fluid and evolving medium, and that Web pages are often "under construction"—or, as with all time-sensitive information, may no longer be valid.

MAP INDICATORS The letter-and-number codes appearing at the end of most listings refer to coordinates on the fold-out map included in the front of the book. Coordinates with letters A–M (e.g., D7) refer to the Greater Vancouver map; coordinates with letters N–Z (V7) refer to the Downtown Vancouver map on the flip side. If an establishment does not have a map code listed, its location falls beyond the boundaries of these maps.

HELPFUL ICONS Watch for these quick-reference symbols throughout the book:

 FAMILY FUN Places that are fun, easy, and great for kids.

 GOOD VALUE While not necessarily cheap, these places offer a good deal within the context of the area.

 ROMANTIC These spots offer candlelight, atmosphere, intimacy, or other romantic qualities—kisses and proposals are encouraged!

 EDITORS' CHOICE These are places that are unique and special to the city, such as a restaurant owned by a beloved local chef or a tourist attraction recognized around the globe.

 Appears after listings for establishments that have wheelchair-accessible facilities.

INDEXES In addition to a general index at the back of the book, there are five specialized indexes: restaurants are indexed by star rating, neighbourhood, and food and other features at the beginning of the Restaurants chapter; nightspots are indexed by neighbourhood and feature at the beginning of the Nightlife chapter.

READER REPORTS At the end of the book is a report form. We receive hundreds of reports from readers suggesting new places or agreeing or disagreeing with our assessments. They greatly help in our evaluations, and we encourage you to respond.

PLANNING A TRIP

PLANNING A TRIP

How to Get Here

BY PLANE

VANCOUVER INTERNATIONAL AIRPORT (604/207-7077; www.yvr.ca; map: B5) is a major international airport with daily flights to every continent. (A travel tip: If your luggage is destined for Vancouver, make sure the tag on it has "YVR" as the airport code.) The spacious modern airport is located 15 kilometres (9 miles) south of downtown on Sea Island. The major airlines of Canada, the United States, Asia, and Europe fly into Vancouver, providing regular service to more than 40 cities around the world. Annually, the airport handles more than 17 million passengers. The International Air Transport Association of Geneva recognized the Vancouver International Airport with an Eagle Award for outstanding performance in customer satisfaction, cost efficiency, and continuous improvement.

After passing through the **CANADA CUSTOMS** checkpoint, travellers arriving from the United States and overseas enter the international terminal's reception lobby. The lobby has a tourist information counter, foreign-exchange kiosks, banking services, and access to ground transportation into the city and beyond. Porters and free baggage carts are available in both terminals. Guests are greeted with large, bright signs displaying pictograms and multiple languages. For advice and basic directions, newcomers can turn to an army of about 200 **GREEN COATS**, volunteer goodwill ambassadors for the airport authority who are found throughout the terminal.

In 2007, changes to passenger and visitor services include 24-hour customer care in the international arrivals area and inside the Customs Hall. Also available are easily identifiable, terminal-wide access to translation services, 24-hour medical response, and messaging service from the Customs Hall to the public greeting area. The airport has installed 22 "eMillennium" Internet-access pay phones throughout the terminal. The "eMillenium" offers high-speed Internet and e-mail connection for 35 cents per minute. High-speed Internet and e-mail access is available via your mobile computer.

Several car rental agencies are located on the ground floor of the three-level parkade; these include **ALAMO** (604/231-1400), **AVIS** (604/606-2847), **BUDGET** (604/668-7000), **DOLLAR** (604/606-1656), **HERTZ** (604/606-3700), **NATIONAL CAR RENTAL** (604/273-3121), and **THRIFTY** (604/606-1666). **ENTERPRISE** (604/303-1117) has a shuttle to its off-site facility on parking level P1. **DISCOUNT** (604/207-8180) is off-site and offers pickup service.

Convenient short-term and long-term **PARKING** is available by the half hour in the parkade across from the terminal. The main level (P1) is for short-term parking up to a maximum of four hours ($2.75 per half hour for self-serve, $3.25 with cashier service). The maximum daily charge on the second and third levels (P2 and P3) is $17; for the week, it's $102. An "economy" parking lot offers value-priced parking within walking distance of the terminal: $2.75 per half hour, $13 per day, $78 per week, $198 per month. The long-term parking lot is located farther from the terminals but offers complimentary 24-hour shuttle service and the lowest-priced parking: $10.83 per day, $70.40 per week. **PARK 'N FLY** (6380 Miller Rd, Richmond; 604/270-9476; www.parknfly.ca) is an off-site service that offers valet parking and shuttle service to the airport for $15.95 per day, $79.95 per week, $319.80 per month.

GATEWAY VALET AND CONCIERGE (604/303-3415), the airport's 24-hour valet service, allows patrons to drive right up to the terminal entrances and leave the car with a valet chauffeur, who will park the car in a secure, on-site compound. Not only that, they will also do your errands at no additional charge. This unique service covers everything from dry cleaning, automotive care (provided you've arranged an appointment with your dealer), picking up flowers or alcohol, or any other request you might have. For international flights, the Gateway Valet drop-off and pickup spot is by the entrance to the international departures level at the Fairmont Airport Hotel. Domestic travellers can drop off their vehicles on the domestic departures level in front of Air Canada. The cost is $25 for the first day, $19 for each subsequent day; weekly rates are $90. Car detailing is available from $34.95.

AIR CANADA (888/247-2262; www.aircanada.com), the largest carrier in Canada, moves people and freight all over British Columbia and internationally through its regional subsidiaries. With more than 70 years of aviation service, Air Canada has repeatedly been voted best airline by a variety of travel publications. Any travel agent can help you with an airline reservation.

The major airlines of the United States, Asia, and Europe also operate facilities at Vancouver International Airport. For a listing of current **ARRIVALS** and **DEPARTURES**, visit www.yvr.ca.

Airport Transportation

The **CANADA LINE** (www.canadaline.ca), an automated, rail-based rapid transit service, is scheduled to begin service in November 2009, in time for the 2010 Winter Olympics. The Canada Line carries passengers from the airport to the Waterfront Station in downtown Vancouver, with 13 stations along the route. (Three additional stations are in Richmond.) Trains are expected to leave every six minutes, and the travel time will be 26 minutes to downtown.

TAXIS, shuttles, limousines, and public transit are all available curbside in front of the terminals to take you anywhere in the city. Taxis from the airport to downtown cost about $30. A 30-minute ride will take you through the Marpole neighbourhood (a favourite with university students), the grand old Shaughnessy neighbourhood, and the exclusive shopping strip of South Granville on your way downtown. For about half the price ($13.50 one-way, $21 round-trip, with discount rates for children, seniors, and families), you can catch the **YVR AIRPORTER** (604/946-8866 or 800/668-3141;

www.yvrairporter.com). The distinctive green buses pull up outside the arrivals level of the terminals about once every 30 minutes. The service operates 8:30am–9:45pm daily, stopping at approximately 20 downtown hotels. Reservations are not required.

Alternatively, board **TRANSLINK**'s 424-Airport bus (604/953-3333 for schedule info; www.translink.bc.ca), which offers connections to the downtown core. The fare is $3.75, $2.50 after 6:30pm; make sure you have exact coin fare, since TransLink drivers do not carry change. Board outside the terminals, ask for a transfer (good for 90 minutes), and get off at Airport Station bus terminal. Transfer to 98 B-Line to get downtown in 40 minutes. If you want a scenic 1-hour, 30-minute tour of the city, use your transfer to board the 100-22nd Street bus at the Airport Station bus terminal and disembark at the 22nd Street SkyTrain station in New Westminster, where you can then use your transfer to ride the SkyTrain rail transit system into downtown (see Getting Around in the Lay of the City chapter).

PERIMETER TRANSPORTATION'S WHISTLER EXPRESS (604/266-5386 or 877/317-7788; www.perimeterbus.com) shuttles travellers by bus to Squamish for $40 or to the Whistler ski resort for $67, nine times a day between 8:30am and 11:30pm. The **SNOWBUS** (604/685-7669 or 866/766-9287; www.snowbus.ca) provides daily transportation during the ski season between the airport or downtown Vancouver and Whistler. Fee for one way from the airport is $55.94, return is $74.95. **QUICK SHUTTLE** (604/940-4428 or 800/665-2122; www.quickcoach.com) operates a service between downtown Vancouver, the Vancouver International Airport, and three locations in Washington state—Bellingham Airport, downtown Seattle, and Seattle-Tacoma International Airport—five times daily. A one-way ticket to downtown Seattle is $36, $49 to Sea-Tac Airport.

Smaller Aircraft

If you need a quick link to or from Victoria, the province's capital, you can take advantage of daily flights offered by **HELIJET AIRWAYS** (800/665-4354; www.helijet.com) between downtown Vancouver harbour heliport or Vancouver International Airport and Victoria Harbour. Regular one-way cost of the half-hour flight is $229.

HARBOUR AIR SEAPLANES (800/665-0212; www.harbour-air.com), North America's first carbon-neutral airline, and **WEST COAST AIR** (800/347-2222; www.westcoastair.com) both serve Vancouver, Victoria, and other coastal communities. Scenic tours and charters are available, as well as scheduled flights.

Private aircraft are welcome at Vancouver International's south terminal, but those coming from the United States or overseas should call **CANADA CUSTOMS** (888/226-7277) at least 2 hours but not more than 48 hours prior to arrival to clear their entry into Canada. For the current listing of airports of entry throughout BC, visit www.cbsa.gc.ca.

Seaplanes

Vancouver is one of the few major international airports to also operate a floatplane facility. For many communities along the province's rugged Pacific Coast, year-round floatplane access is more economical than it is to build facilities for conventional wheeled aircraft. Other seaplane connections to Vancouver are detailed under Air Tours in the Exploring chapter.

BY BUS

Located just east of the downtown core near the intersection of Main Street and Terminal Avenue, the weathered but still graceful facade of **PACIFIC CENTRAL STATION** (1150 Station St; map:V6) welcomes travellers to the local terminus of several bus and rail services. The station is well served by taxis and public transit. City buses and SkyTrain, Vancouver's high-speed rail transit service, are only a block away.

Bus lines operating from Pacific Central Station include **GREYHOUND** (800/661-8747; www.greyhound.ca) and **PACIFIC COACH LINES** (604/662-8074; www.pacificcoach.com). Greyhound operates five trips daily between Vancouver and Seattle, with connections in Seattle to other U.S. points. The Greyhound depot in Bellingham, Washington, offers a convenient link to ferries travelling north to Alaska. Pacific Coach Lines operates a modern, Greyhound-like bus service between Vancouver and Victoria via BC Ferries. Connections are available in downtown Victoria for points throughout Vancouver Island. Although most people board at Pacific Central Station, you can arrange to be picked up or dropped off at the airport or at specific city bus stops along the route in Vancouver, Richmond, or Victoria and its suburbs.

Pacific Coach Line buses depart Vancouver and Victoria for the Tsawwassen (pronounced "SWAH-sehn") and Swartz Bay ferry terminals about an hour before each ferry departure. Since the ferries adjust their schedules seasonally, it is wise to verify departure times prior to travelling. The round-trip fare of $73.50 per person includes the ferry ride. While aboard the ferry, you are free to go anywhere passengers are allowed on the ship. Shortly before docking, the ferry crew makes an announcement asking bus passengers to return to their coach; your driver will explain the procedure in detail before you board the ferry. The total travel time, one way, is about three hours (see Getting Around in the Lay of the City chapter).

BY FERRY

Vancouver is surrounded by water on three sides, but no large passenger ferries dock within the city. **BC FERRIES** (250/386-3431; 888/223-3779; www.bcferries.com) provides year-round service on 25 routes throughout coastal BC, including a minimum of eight daily sailings (more than a dozen in summer) between Tsawwassen, a town named after a local Native tribe that's located about a half-hour drive south of the city, and Swartz Bay, on Vancouver Island near Sidney, a town that's a similar distance from downtown Victoria. Travel time, city centre to city centre, is about three hours; 90 minutes of that is on

VANCOUVER THROUGH TIME

16,000–11,000 BCE: Ancestors of the native Squamish, Burrard, Tsleil-Waututh, Musqueam (Xw'muthk'i'um), Tsawwassen, Coquitlam (Kwayhquitlam), Katzie, and Semiahmoo bands—all Coast Salish people—arrive and establish settlements in and around the beaches and forests at the mouth of a big river emptying into a vast ocean.

1792: British explorer Captain George Vancouver arrives on the West Coast, where he surveys Puget Sound, Burrard Inlet, and the island that will later bear his name.

1808: Simon Fraser, a U.S.-born explorer and fur trader, arrives at the village of Musqueam by following an overland route along a river he thinks is the Columbia. The river he navigated is later named for him.

1827: The Hudson's Bay Company builds a trading post on the Fraser River, the first permanent, non-Native settlement in the area. Since 1893, the company has occupied one corner of Georgia and Granville in Vancouver's downtown core, and it's still trading.

1858: The news that there is gold on the banks of the Fraser River brings about 25,000 prospectors.

1859: A talkative chap nicknamed "Gassy Jack" Deighton opens a saloon on the shore of Burrard Inlet. It becomes so popular, a community builds up around the place and calls itself Gastown.

1869: A 2½-hectare (6-acre) townsite, including Gastown, is incorporated as the town of Granville, named after the colonial secretary of the time.

1886: Granville is incorporated as the City of Vancouver. The first mayor is real estate agent M. A. McLean. On June 13, a brushfire goes wild and burns the city to the ground in less than 30 minutes. McLean starts rebuilding in a matter of days.

1887: The Canadian Pacific Railway's first train arrives; Vancouver is the terminus of the first transcontinental trip.

1898: The Nine O'Clock Gun is placed at Brockton Point. People still set their watches by it.

1908: The University of British Columbia opens its doors. Today there are nearly 45,000 full- and part-time students.

1909: The Dominion Trust Building, the city's first skyscraper, opens at Hastings and Cambie streets.

1911: Canada's first artificial ice rink, the Arena, opens. People immediately begin skating around the edge counterclockwise.

1936: The new City Hall at 12th Avenue and Cambie Street is dedicated. It still looks like it belongs in Gotham City.

1939: The Lions Gate Bridge is officially opened by King George VI and Queen Elizabeth II. Built so a real estate company could sell the property it had bought on the North Shore, the bridge was engineered to last about 50 years.

1954: At Empire Stadium, Roger Bannister and John Landry run the "Miracle Mile" in less than four minutes.

1958: The Second Narrows Bridge collapses, killing 18 workmen and one rescue worker.

1964: The Beatles come to town.

1967: The first of many anti–Vietnam War protests takes place.

1970: The Vancouver Canucks play their first National Hockey League game.

1979: The Vancouver Whitecaps win the North American Soccer League championship.

1980: One-legged runner Terry Fox begins his cross-Canada "Marathon of Hope."

1983: BC Place Stadium inflates, becoming the world's largest air-supported dome, with 60,000 seats.

1985: Rick Hansen begins his around-the-world "Man in Motion" tour by wheelchair.

1986: Vancouver's centennial is marked by the transportation fair Expo 86, the largest special-category world exposition ever staged in North America.

1994: The Vancouver Canucks reach the Stanley Cup finals but lose in the final moments of the game. Disappointed fans riot in downtown Vancouver.

1998: Ross Rebagliati, a local Whistler 'boarder, wins gold in the new men's giant slalom snowboard event at the Nagano Winter Olympics. The medal is stripped after Ross tests positive for marijuana, then it's given back after Ross explains he's a victim of secondhand Whistler party smoke.

2000: Ujjal Dosanjh wins leadership of BC's New Democratic Party (NDP) and becomes the first Indo-Canadian premier in Canada.

2003: On Canada Day, July 1, Vancouver is selected as the Host City for 2010 Olympic and Paralympic Winter Games. GM Place broadcasts the announcement live to a sold-out crowd.

2006: Vancouver's famous Stanley Park loses more than 1,000 trees after storms batter the West Coast with near-hurricane-force winds. Trees, including a 200-year-old hemlock, are uprooted or snap off and block trails and roads. Cleanup and restoration will take years.

—Kasey Wilson

the ferry trip. All fares are one way and are subject to increase; rates for passengers are $14.25, cars are $47.15.

Other sailings go from Tsawwassen or Horseshoe Bay, northwest of Vancouver, to the city of Nanaimo, the Sunshine Coast, and the Gulf Islands. The ferries provide a pleasant cruise through spectacular scenery and offer amenities that include a cafeteria and (on some) buffet dining room, snack bar, gift shop, newsstand, and promenade decks. Foot passengers can take either **WEST VANCOUVER TRANSIT** (604/985-7777) to the Horseshoe Bay terminal or a **TRANSLINK BUS** (604/953-3333) to Tsawwassen, or travel via **PACIFIC COACH LINES** (604/662-8074), which goes to Victoria, Nanaimo, and the Sunshine Coast.

BY TRAIN

VIA RAIL (1150 Station St; 888/842-7245; www.viarail.ca; map:V6) is Canada's national passenger rail service. The *Canadian*, the transcontinental train, travels between Toronto and Vancouver, with stops in Sudbury Junction, Ontario; Winnipeg, Manitoba; Saskatoon, Saskatchewan; Edmonton and Jasper, Alberta; and Kamloops, BC. The *Canadian* leaves Vancouver on Fridays, Sundays, and Tuesdays and leaves Toronto on Tuesdays, Thursdays, and Saturdays. The entire journey takes three days: If you leave Toronto on, say, Tuesday at midday, you'll arrive in Vancouver on Friday morning. Two classes are offered aboard the *Canadian*: first class ("Silver & Blue") and economy ("Comfort").

AMTRAK (1150 Station St; 800/872-7245; www.amtrak.com; map:V6) is the American passenger train service, and part of Amtrak's Pacific Northwest route system services Vancouver from Oregon and Washington states. Trains travel daily between Seattle and Vancouver. The starting fare is $30 one way, subject to change.

ROCKY MOUNTAINEER (1755 Cottrell St; 604/606-7245 or 877/460-3200; www.rockymountaineer.com; map:Y7) has three routes—between Vancouver and Banff or Calgary, between Vancouver and Jasper, and between Whistler and Jasper. The tourist train winds through the heart of the Canadian Rockies three times per week, with added trips between Vancouver and Whistler. The all-daylight, two-day train journey offers two levels of service: Redleaf (one level, glass windows, meals served at your seat) and Goldleaf (dome car with dining room).

BY CAR

Two major highways connect Greater Vancouver to the rest of British Columbia, the rest of Canada, and the United States, offering drivers a panorama of farmland, towns, cities, and mountains. **HIGHWAY 99**, the main highway connecting Vancouver to Seattle and the rest of Washington state, leads south from the city across the fertile delta at the mouth of the Fraser River and connects with Interstate 5. The approximately three-hour drive between Vancouver and Seattle crosses the international boundary at Blaine, Washington.

Highway 99 also connects Vancouver to the ski resort town of Whistler, about a two-hour drive north of the city. Offering some stunning views of the Coast Mountains, the stretch of highway has been dubbed the "Sea-to-Sky Highway." From Whistler, Highway 99 arcs northeastward into the province's interior, joining Highway 97, the main north-south highway in BC, just north of Cache Creek.

HIGHWAY 1, the **TRANS-CANADA HIGHWAY**, winds through the Lower Mainland, up the Fraser River Valley, and east across the rest of Canada. Highway 97 junctions at Cache Creek, and Highway 5 (the Yellowhead) intersects at Kamloops. The Trans-Canada crosses the Rocky Mountains through the historic Rogers and Kicking Horse passes, passing through Revelstoke and Golden, BC, and Banff, Alberta.

RUSH HOUR in Vancouver starts about 7am and tangles up traffic until about 9:30am, Monday through Friday. In the afternoon, it starts about 3pm and ends about 6:30pm. You can get regular updates (800/550-4997, cell *4997; www.drivebc.ca) on **ROAD CONDITIONS** in the Vancouver area and across the province.

When to Visit

Keep in mind that airfares, hotel rates, and admission fees are often lower from November through February. Expect the city to be inundated with athletes and spectators for the 2010 Winter Olympics February 12–28, followed by the Paralympic Games March 12–21. Hotel accommodation and many restaurants will be fully booked in advance.

WEATHER

While the rest of Canada suffers from long winters, British Columbia, blessed by a temperate maritime climate, has become known as "Lotus Land." Vancouver's weather is the mildest in Canada, thanks to ocean currents and major weather patterns that bring warm, moist air in waves from the Pacific year-round. Spring comes early, with flowers generally in full bloom by early March. July and August are the warmest months. Late-summer and autumn days—through October—tend to be warm and sunny, with the odd day of showers. Winter is the rainy season, which starts about November and tapers off about March, but the rain usually falls as showers or drizzle. Heavy continuous downpours are rare, as are thunderstorms and strong winds. Of course, the amount of rain is what makes the Douglas fir trees grow so large on the mountainsides readily visible from Vancouver and what causes the area to look so lush to many visitors. If it's going to snow—and most of the time it doesn't—it will usually snow in late December or early January. Higher elevations experience the precipitation as snow, translating into excellent skiing on the area's three major ski hills during the winter. July, August, and September are the driest months.

AVERAGE DAILY HIGH TEMPERATURES

Month	Celsius	Fahrenheit
JANUARY	5	42
FEBRUARY	7	44
MARCH	10	50
APRIL	14	58
MAY	18	65
JUNE	21	69
JULY	23	74
AUGUST	23	74
SEPTEMBER	18	65
OCTOBER	14	58
NOVEMBER	9	48
DECEMBER	6	43

Source: Tourism Vancouver

TIME

Vancouver is on **PACIFIC STANDARD TIME** (PST), the same as the American states of Washington, Oregon, and California. Residents enjoy long daylight hours in summer, with sunrises before 6am and sunsets as late as 10pm.

WHAT TO BRING

The best clothes for summer are lightweight shirts or blouses, shorts or pants, and a rain jacket. For fall and winter, bring the type of clothing you can layer, including long-sleeved shirts or blouses, as well as a heavier layer, such as a sweater or jacket. Pack an umbrella, a pair of waterproof shoes, and a rain jacket. Clothing is casual in virtually all parts of the city; even the most expensive restaurants allow patrons to wear jeans, and none require men to wear ties.

General Costs

British Columbians have worked hard to rebuild the economic prosperity of the province after a period of economic doldrums in the 1990s. The BC economy has long been based on the province's rich endowment of natural resources, primarily forestry, mining (including oil and gas), and fishing (including aquaculture). In recent years, the economy has diversified, supported by non-resource-based activities such as film and high-technology industries (including software and biotechnology). Tourism, which has always contributed significantly to the economy, in 2006 ranked as the third-largest moneymaker in the province, after wood/paper and energy products. Since 2001, tourism has been affected by several factors: September 11, 2001; the war in Iraq; severe acute respiratory syndrome (SARS) and bovine spongiform encephalopathy (BSE); forest fires in the interior of the province; the weakened American dollar; and higher-than-expected gas prices. Despite these events, tourism has continued to grow, and in 2006, 23.1 million overnight visitors travelled to the province and spent $10.2 billion.

British Columbia's population of a little more than 4 million continues to grow more diverse, with a steady influx of newcomers from other parts of Canada and around the world. The role of immigration in population growth continues, and in 2006, BC welcomed 44,000 immigrants from 180 countries or regions, with China (26 percent) as the top source country for immigration in BC, followed by India (14 percent) and the Philippines (9 percent). Only a small percentage of immigrants arrived from Europe, although historically, Europeans formed the bulk of immigration.

CURRENCY

The Canadian dollar is constantly being measured against its U.S. counterpart because as neighbours both countries form the world's largest trading partnership. In fall 2007, the Canadian dollar reached parity with the American dollar. The last time the Canadian dollar was at the US$1 mark was 1976. Demand for Canadian oil, natural gas, and other natural resources in markets such as China has pushed up the value of the Canadian dollar. The rise in the dollar is a boon for Canadians planning trips to the United States, as well as for cross-border and online shoppers. Conversely, U.S. visitors to Canada find their money buys less than it used to.

Most Greater Vancouver firms accept U.S. dollars, and they usually offer reasonable **EXCHANGE RATES** (see the Foreign Visitors section under Tips for Special Travellers in this chapter). American coins work in most vending machines, as Canadian coins resemble American coins of similar value. For instance, an American and a Canadian quarter look similar and can usually be used interchangeably in vending machines, as can dimes, nickels, and pennies—but don't expect to get an exchange rate when paying with coins. The Canadian dollar itself is no longer paper; it's a relatively large gold-coloured coin nicknamed the "loonie" because it features the loon, an aquatic bird, on its face. A distinctive two-tone $2 coin, a bit bigger and heavier than the $1 coin, goes by the nickname "toonie" (or "twoonie") because it rhymes with "loonie." Retailers say visitors often have trouble remembering which coin is what value, but here's a simple method: The $1 is one colour, the $2 is two colours.

Vancouver is ahead of the world when it comes to using **ELECTRONIC CASH** at retailers and restaurants. Debit cards can be used in virtually all retail shops and restaurants—even fast-food eateries—in Greater Vancouver. Cash machines (ATMs) are located throughout high-volume areas of the city and usually at each bank branch. **MAJOR CREDIT CARDS**, particularly Visa and MasterCard, are accepted virtually everywhere. American Express, Diners Club, and Discover charge cards are accepted only at major retail locations and restaurants.

VISITOR TAXES AND GRATUITIES

Three levels of taxation affect visitors to Vancouver. On the sale of most goods and the provision of most services, a 7 percent **PROVINCIAL SALES TAX** (PST) and a separate 5 percent **FEDERAL GOODS AND SERVICES TAX** (GST) are levied. Even though governments claim they are trying to keep things simple, there are lots of untaxed exemptions, particularly when it comes to food. Typically, no tax is charged on food unless it's prepared food or food in small portions. Children's clothing is usually PST-exempt. PST on liquor is 10 percent instead of 7 percent. PST is not charged on accommodation; instead, a 10 percent **ACCOMMODATION TAX** appears on hotel and motel bills. By law, retailers must show whether they are including the GST when they show prices, and the tax must be shown separately on bills or receipts. By convention, most prices shown are before tax; taxi fares (which include GST) are the notable exception, because it's more practical to pay the amount shown on the meter.

GRATUITIES are not mandatory for most services rendered, but tips of 10 to 20 percent on the pretax amount are encouraged when above-average service is encountered. An easy formula is to triple the GST (federal tax) to equal 15 percent. Add a little, and you have a decent tip on the pretax bill. It is courteous to tip hotel staff from $1 to $5 depending on the service provided, such as baggage delivery ($5 per bag at top hotels) or room service. It's best to leave chambermaids a tip of from $1 to $5 ($5 per day at top hotels).

AVERAGE COSTS FOR LODGING AND FOOD

Double room:	
INEXPENSIVE	**$60–$80**
MODERATE	**$80–$180**
EXPENSIVE	**$180 AND UP**
Lunch for one:	
INEXPENSIVE	**$6–$12**
MODERATE	**$12–$20**
EXPENSIVE	**$20 AND UP**
Beverages in a restaurant:	
GLASS OF WINE	**$6–$15**
PINT OF BEER	**$5.50**
COCA-COLA	**$1.50**
BOTTLED WATER	**$2.00**
GRANDE LATTE	**$3.70**
Other common items:	
MOVIE TICKET	**$10–$12**
TAXI PER KILOMETRE	**$1.58**
16 OZ. SMOKED SOCKEYE SALMON	**$20.00**
VANCOUVER SOUVENIR T-SHIRT	**$15–$20**

Tips for Special Travellers

FAMILIES WITH CHILDREN

In an emergency, call 911, 24 hours a day. For answers to questions about your child's health, growth, or development, call the **BC CHILDREN'S HOSPITAL** (4880 Oak St; 604/875-2345). If you think your child has swallowed a toxic substance, call the **POISON CONTROL CENTRE** (604/682-5050). *West Coast Families* is an award-winning monthly publication (604/249-2866) full of event listings and information for parents, available free at most bookstores, children's retailers, community centres, and other locations throughout the Vancouver area, as well as online (www.westcoastfamilies.com). Another useful free magazine, published nine times a year, is *BC Parent* (604/221-0366; www.bcparent.ca).

If notified in advance, most major hotels can arrange for child care. Travelling to special sights or events with kids is not a problem; children 4 years and younger ride free on TransLink.

Watch for this icon throughout the book: **♜♜**. It indicates places and activities that are great for families.

SENIORS

SENIORS ONE-STOP INFORMATION LINE (604/983-3303) and **INFORM VANCOUVER** (604/875-6381) provide information about programmes and services available to seniors in the Vancouver area. Seniors 65 and over with valid proof of age are eligible for concession fares on TransLink vehicles; they vary according to time of day and distance travelled. On weekdays before 6:30pm, senior fares are as follows: one zone $1.75, two zones $2.50, three zones $3.50. After 6:30pm and on weekends and holidays, the fare is a standard $1.75. A FareSaver book of 10 tickets is $16, and a day pass offering unlimited travel is $7. All can be purchased at "FareDealers," identified by a decal in windows of retail stores, such as Safeway, 7-Eleven, and some gas stations.

PEOPLE WITH DISABILITIES

BC is home to more disabled people per capita than any other province in Canada, thanks to its mild climate and its efforts to accommodate the needs of residents and visitors. Most buses and businesses are wheelchair accessible, and a wide range of community and recreational services are available. Resource groups include the **BC PARAPLEGIC ASSOCIATION** (604/324-3611 or 877/324-3611; www.bcpara.org), the **BC MOBILITY OPPORTUNITY SOCIETY** (604/688-6464, ext. 126; www.reachdisability.org/bcmoss), the **CANADIAN NATIONAL INSTITUTE FOR THE BLIND** (604/431-2020, or TTY 604/431-2131; www.cnib.ca), and the **WESTERN INSTITUTE FOR THE DEAF AND HARD OF HEARING** (604/736-7391, or TTY 604/736-2527; www.widhh.com).

Exterior door-to-door transportation in lift-equipped vans is available for passengers in wheelchairs and others with restricted mobility who are

FAVOURITE BOOKS ABOUT VANCOUVER

City Making in Paradise: Nine Decisions That Saved Greater Vancouver Livability, by Mike Harcourt, et al. (Douglas & McIntyre, 2007)

City of Glass, by Douglas Coupland (Douglas & McIntyre, 2000)

Drive around Vancouver & BC: Your Guide to Great Drives, by Maxine Cass (Thomas Cook Publications, 2007)

Frommer's Vancouver with Kids, by Eve Lazarus (Frommers, 2001)

Great Walks of Vancouver: The Lower Mainland at Your Feet, by Charles Clapham (Granville Island Publishing, 2004)

Kids' Vancouver: Things to See and Things to Do for Kids of Every Age, by Victoria Bushnell (Raincoast Books, 2000)

The 100-Mile Diet: A Year of Local Eating, by Alisa Smith and J. B. MacKinnon (Random House, 2007)

Stanley Park's Secret: The Forgotten Families of Whoi Whoi, Kanaka Ranch, and Brockton Point, by Jean Barman (Vancouver Harbour Publishing, 2005)

Vancouver: Representing the Postmodern City, by Paul Delany (Arsenal Pulp Press, 1994)

Vancouver: Secrets of the City, by Shawn Blore and *Vancouver Magazine* (Arsenal Pulp Press, 2000)

Vancouver Short Stories, by Carole Gerson (UBC Press, 1983)

Vancouver Then & Now, by Chuck Davis (Magic Light Productions, 2001)

Vancouver Walks: Discovering City Heritage, by Michael Kluckner and John Atkin (Stellar Press, 2003)

—Arlene Kroeker

already registered users in any part of Canada or the United States through **HANDYDART** (604/430-2692), a contracted service of TransLink. The basic fare is $2.50; a FareSaver book of 10 tickets is available for $19, a monthly pass for $73. **VANCOUVER TAXI** (604/871-1111) also carries passengers in wheelchairs, at no additional charge to the regular fare.

WOMEN

Vancouver is a safe city for female travellers, but extra precautions are always wise at night, especially in the city's many parks. Women should also be wary in the old commercial district of Downtown East Side, east of Cambie Street and north of Hastings Street; though relatively safe during the day, the area takes on a more lurid cast in the evening. The **RAPE RELIEF AND WOMEN'S SHELTER** (604/872-8212) and **RAPE CRISIS CENTRE** (604/255-6344) are available to assist victims of rape and abuse. For health and reproductive services, call **PLANNED PARENTHOOD** (604/731-4252).

GAYS AND LESBIANS

Vancouver has the largest gay population in Western Canada, which is centred around two distinctly different neighbourhoods: the West End and Commercial Drive, both with a variety of restaurants, coffee shops, pubs, and boutiques catering to gays and lesbians. The West End is an exciting urban residential area long established as friendly to its gay population and mainly centred around Davie and Denman streets. **DELANY'S ON DENMAN** (1105 Denman St; 604/662-3344; map:P2) and **MELRICHES** (1244 Davie St; 604/689-5282; map:Q4) are cool coffee spots and meeting places for the gay and lesbian crowd. Davie Street between Burrard and Broughton streets, internationally renowned as Davie Village, is a short strip that hosts gay-friendly cafes, martini lounges, a piano bar, nightclubs, sports bars, pubs, and restaurants, anchored for over 25 years by the city's gay bookstore, **LITTLE SISTER'S BOOK & ART EMPORIUM** (1238 Davie St; 604/669-1753; map:Q4). For club options, see the Nightlife chapter.

Commercial Drive is an East Side neighbourhood fuelled by pool halls that pay homage to Portuguese emperors and cafes that tune into Italian and Brazilian football matches. The drive, once the centre for the Portuguese and Italian immigrant communities, is today a hive of world-beat culture, particularly of the revolutionary kind. Old men sip espressos to warm up for their bocce-ball games, rubbing shoulders with the pierced, the punk, and the tattooed at local cafes. Hand drumming and guitar strumming are popular pastimes here, as is the consumption of some of the best coffee in the city. Try the **CALABRIA** (1745 Commercial Dr; 604/253-7017; map:Z6) and enjoy the scene and coffee steam with the local counterculture. Among the authentic Italian delis and coffee joints, you'll find pink-triangle shops and services, including the popular **WOMYNS' WARE** (896 Commercial Dr; 604/254-2543; map:Z5) and **THE KISS STORE** (2512 Watson St; 604/675-9972; map:V7). **FLYGIRL** (www.flygirlproductions.com) and **CREMA PRODUCTIONS** (www.cremaproductions.com) host popular lesbian parties throughout the year; check Web sites for schedule and venue information.

Xtra West (604/684-9696), a free gay and lesbian publication, lists events, clubs, and community groups; it's available throughout the city. Visitors may also wish to drop by the **CENTRE** (1170 Bute St; 604/684-5307; map:Q4), which offers a library, or call **PRIDELINE** from 7pm to 10pm (604/684-6869). Gay businesses and services are listed in the **GLBA DIRECTORY**, published by the Gay and Lesbian Business Association of British Columbia (604/739-4522; www.glba.org) and available free in many stores.

Gay culture also thrives outdoors. Clothing-optional **WRECK BEACH**, off Marine Drive below the University of British Columbia, is a Vancouver tradition frequented by everyone, gay or otherwise. Or head to **LEES TRAIL** near Second Beach in Stanley Park. In the summer months, lesbians head up Highway 99 to the beach at **LIONS BAY**. Gay bashing is uncommon but not extinct. If you are in danger, call 911; report incidents by leaving a message on the **BASHLINE** (604/899-6203).

The **VANCOUVER PRIDE PARADE** (604/687-0955; www.vancouverpride. ca), held the first weekend of August, is not just a party for gays and lesbians, it's a celebration of diversity, and anybody who shares the "life is a cabaret" spirit will feel right at home. Parties, tea dances, and cruises culminate with the attendance of more than 300,000 people to watch the noontime parade of colourful floats, contingents of drag queens, and gay cops that moves down Denman Street to Beach Avenue, finally gathering for a mass celebration at Sunset Beach on English Bay.

The **QUEER FILM FESTIVAL** (www.outonscreen.com) runs for 11 days in August. As the largest queer arts event in Western Canada and the second-largest film festival in Vancouver, it has, for more than 20 years, showcased international and local films representing the diversity of gay, lesbian, bisexual, and transgender experiences from around the world.

Every year an estimated 2,500 people from all corners of the globe participate in weeklong events on and off the slopes in early February during **WINTERPRIDE** at Whistler (604/288-7218; www.gaywhistler.com).

FOREIGN VISITORS

Vancouver is a cosmopolitan port city offering a wide range of services to international visitors. Several exchange firms have locations downtown, including the **INTERNATIONAL SECURITIES EXCHANGE** (1169 Robson St; 604/683-9666; map:R3), **INTER CURRENCY EXCHANGE CORPORATION** (300-609 W Hastings St; 604/688-8668; map:U4), and **VANCOUVER BULLION AND CURRENCY EXCHANGE** (120-800 W Pender St; 604/685-1008; 2576 Granville St; 604/739-3997; www.vbce.info; map:T3, D3). Banks are also able to exchange many currencies, and most businesses accept U.S. dollars (though at varying exchange rates, sometimes significantly different from the rate posted at banks and exchange offices).

Many translation services operate in Vancouver. For names of accredited translators who will best serve your needs, contact the **SOCIETY OF TRANSLATORS AND INTERPRETERS OF BC** (604/684-2940; www.stibc.org). The **COLLEGE OF PHYSICIANS AND SURGEONS** (604/733-7758; www.cpsbc. ca/cps) provides a list of multilingual doctors, and some transit and taxi drivers are familiar with Asian languages.

For customs information and services, call **CANADA CUSTOMS** (800/461-9999 within Canada, or 204/983-3500 or 506/636-5064 outside Canada; www.cbsa.gc.ca). There are no embassies in Vancouver, but the city hosts more than 60 consulates.

PET OWNERS

Vancouver, with its glorious views, green grass, and miles of beaches, is dog heaven—as long as you use a leash. Your year-round best bets for **OFF-LEASH EXERCISE** are Pacific Spirit Regional Park (the University of British Columbia Endowment Lands), particularly nice in the summer as the big trees keep it cool, and Ambleside Dog Park behind Park Royal Shopping Centre in West

Vancouver. The privileges are earned, so scoop your pooch's waste. Certain Vancouver parks (www.vancouver.ca/parks/info/dogparks) offer specific off-leash times. For more information concerning parks, doggie day care, and dog walkers, visit www.raincitydogs.com, a guide for Vancouver dogs.

Visitors to Vancouver will delight in the fact that the **FOUR SEASONS HOTEL** (791 W Georgia St; 604/689-9333; map:S3) not only welcomes dogs but has a "Pet Friendly Programme," including a handmade dog bowl by a local ceramic artist, biscuits (with recipe card) made in the hotel's bakery, and bottled Evian water. At the **FOUR SEASONS HOTEL IN WHISTLER** (4591 Blackcomb Wy, Whistler; 604/935-3400; www.fourseasons.com/whistler), staff will lay out a corner in the room with a bed for your dog or cat, fresh biscuits made in-house, a bowl, a map of trails to hike with your dog, and a pet menu—for your pooch, "best friend's breakfast" (scrambled eggs with rice), or for your cat, "eye of the tiger" (scrambled eggs with smoked salmon).

Pets are welcome at the **FAIRMONT VANCOUVER HOTEL** (900 W Georgia St; 604/684-3131; map:S3) and the **FAIRMONT VANCOUVER AIRPORT** (3111 Grant McConachie Wy, Richmond; 604/207-5200; map:C6). The extra charge of $25 includes a welcome mat in the room, a pet dish, welcome treats, a toy, and information on pet activities.

For more on accommodation, see Marg Meikle's *Dog City: Vancouver* (Raincoast Books, 2000), which also covers resources from doo to don'ts, photographers to psychics, and taxis to training.

Dirty dog? Skunked dog? Bad hair day? **IT'S STILL A DOG'S LIFE** (3428 W Broadway; 604/739-3647; www.itsstilladogslife.com; map:C3) offers a self- or full-serve dog wash, grooming, and 911 Skunk Kit.

Need pet day care? Dogs must have all standard shots and kennel cough vaccination. In the downtown area, **LAUNDERDOG DAYCARE** (1064 Davie St; 604/685-2306; map:R4) offers day care and grooming. **THE DOGHOUSE** has two locations: one for all-size dogs (2425 Manitoba, at W 8th; 604/708-6100; map:V7), and another for small dogs only (105-1833 Anderson St, entrance to Granville Island; 604/737-7500; map:Q6).

Does your dog deserve a serious treat? Birthday cakes, personalized dog bones, and assorted homemade goodies are available from **THREE DOG BAKERY** (2186 W 4th Ave; 604/737-3647; www.threedog.ca; map:N7).

Web Information

Vancouver is home to some of North America's most active animation, Internet, and software development firms. Vancouver remains a beehive of activity, with Yaletown in particular the base for many internationally recognized tech companies, including Tantalus, eTunnels, and Blast Radius. A number of good Web sites disseminate current information on Vancouver. They include the **MAIN PORTAL SITE** (www.mybc.com), with movie reviews, sports events, and local news, and the content-rich **INFORMATION SITE** (www.vancouver.about.com). The hub of technology news for Vancouver is www.bctechnology.com.

LAY OF THE CITY

LAY OF THE CITY

Orientation

Hold your right hand out, palm up and thumb out, so your thumb points straight ahead, away from your body. That's what the city of Vancouver looks like from above. Your thumb is a peninsula jutting into the middle of the large **BURRARD INLET**, nearly splitting the inlet in half, and Vancouver's downtown core is the lower half of your thumb. To the north, in the direction your thumb is pointing, are Vancouver's trademark mountains—Cypress, Grouse, and Hollyburn—with their forested slopes, caps of clouds, and, in the fall, winter, and spring, snowy peaks. At their base, just beyond your thumbnail, are the suburbs of **NORTH VANCOUVER** and **WEST VANCOUVER**, gathered like petticoats skirting the bottom of these peaks. The rest of Vancouver, which is primarily residential (except for business and retail sections along main thoroughfares), is on your palm.

That may sound like quite a handful, but so is Vancouver. It's actually an extensive group of cities built on an ancient river delta that was formed, squished, pushed, and squashed by the Ice Age glaciers. The entire Lower Mainland, which encompasses Greater Vancouver and the once rural but now bustling Fraser Valley to the east, has been built up on the outflow remnants of a vast, roaring river that burst out of central British Columbia tens of thousands of years ago during the ice age. The delta's geological origins made for rich, forested land, which became a magnet for settlers after the interior gold rush ended in the middle of the 19th century. Since then the population, economics, and politics of the region have molded the delta's communities until they now form one giant metropolitan area.

The suburban communities of **BURNABY** and **NEW WESTMINSTER**, once separate cities in their own right and still maintaining their own urban governments, lie to the east of Vancouver, but only a map and the occasional road sign will let you know where their city limits begin. Along the south edge of Vancouver is the North Arm of the Fraser River. It borders the north edge of the delta of the mighty **FRASER**, one of the world's largest rivers. Big as it is, it's only a remnant of the river that once flowed into a pristine fjord when the glaciers held sway. The delta's islands are now the huge suburbs of **RICHMOND, DELTA**, and **SURREY**. The city of Richmond is on Lulu Island, defined by the North and South arms of the Fraser River, and Vancouver International Airport is on Sea Island.

Hold out your palm again. Remember that the lower part of your thumb represents Vancouver's downtown core. On the left side of it is Vancouver's heavily populated **WEST END**, a forest of apartment buildings on a grid of streets that have been retrofitted to keep traffic from roaring through the neighbourhood. In the lower-middle part of your thumb is the business centre of the city, with skyscrapers up to 48 floors high. On the right side of your thumb is what's called the **DOWNTOWN EAST SIDE**, a blue-collar docks-and-warehouse area with a skid row and flophouse core. All along the lower-right edge of your thumb is waterfront docks.

At your thumb's pad and tip is **STANLEY PARK**, a 405-hectare (1,000-acre) forest of lush green pines, firs, and cedars interspersed with wonderful paths and meadows. On the left edge of your thumb, where Stanley Park meets the West End, is a rambling shoreline fronted by apartments, readily accessible public beaches, parks, and walking paths that, as they get to the base of your thumb, skirt the north shore of False Creek, an inlet packed with yachts, restaurants, and high-rise condos. Right at the eastern end of False Creek is the big, can't-miss-it, sparkly bubble that houses **SCIENCE WORLD** (1455 Quebec St; 604/443-7443; www. scienceworld.bc.ca; map:V5), a great place for the whole family to learn about science. Vancouver has an extensive network of parks that allow public access to the waterfront via large, well-lit, paving-stone paths. Many of these parks and paths, which wrap around much of the downtown waterfront, were built only in the past two or three decades. They make for a pleasant outing by foot or bike.

On the west side of the city (we're on your palm now) is an area called **KITSI-LANO**. Chockablock with friendly folk, it retains in its funky retail stores a whiff of the hippie culture that infiltrated it in the 1960s. The sprawling campus of the **UNIVERSITY OF BRITISH COLUMBIA** (UBC; www.ubc.ca), a city-within-a-city of almost 45,000 full- and part-time students during most of the year, is at the far western tip of Vancouver (and your fingertips), about 20 minutes from downtown Vancouver. Officially—that is, legally—it's not actually part of Vancouver, but everybody except City Hall bureaucrats pretends it is. To the east of the university is **KERRISDALE**, the affluent West Side of Vancouver. If you're going to tony Kerrisdale, take your credit cards. (Don't confuse Vancouver's West Side with the West End or West Vancouver; they are three entirely different areas.) The working-class area of **EAST VANCOUVER** (there's only one East Van) is east of an invisible line that runs the length of Main Street as it cuts south through the city (across your palm from the very interior base of your thumb). Chinatown can be found around Main and Pender. A blue-collar area of East Van called **LITTLE ITALY** is just to the east of **CHINATOWN**, north and south of the fascinating intersection of First Avenue and Commercial Drive. **SOUTH VANCOUVER** is a combination of ethnic areas, including Punjabi Market, along 49th Avenue between Fraser and Main. It's located at about the middle of your palm.

And that's the lay of your hand, er, Vancouver.

Visitor Information

Whether you're looking to climb Grouse Mountain, plan an evening out, or just go to the mall, ask a passerby for advice. Vancouverites pride themselves on knowing their city well, and most will be able at least to steer you in the right direction. Otherwise, the **VANCOUVER TOURIST INFO CENTRE** (200 Burrard St; 604/683-2000; www.tourismvancouver.com; map:T2) offers a wealth of information about the city, including tickets and events, attractions and adventures.

Getting Around

BY BUS

Although many Vancouver-area residents prefer to drive, the public transit system is one of the most effective ways to get around the city. **TRANSLINK** (604/953-3333; www.translink.bc.ca) covers more than 1,800 square kilometres (695 square miles) of service area with three forms of transit: bus, SeaBus, and SkyTrain. In 2009, service on the CanadaLine is scheduled to begin, carrying passengers from the airport into downtown Vancouver (see Airport Transportation in the Planning a Trip chapter). Detailed information and transit maps are available at all visitor information centres, public libraries, city halls, a lot of magazine stores, and most ticket sellers.

The current fare schedule, applicable to all three forms of transportation, is based on the number of zones traveled, as follows: one zone $2.50, two zones $3.75, three zones $5. The off-peak fare, in effect through all zones after 6:30pm weekdays, on weekends, and on holidays, is $2.50. The concession fare, available to students and senior citizens with valid ID, is as follows: one zone $1.75, two zones $2.50, three zones $3.50. A transfer, available from drivers at the time you pay your fare, is good for 90 minutes in any direction on any service. Businesses identified by a special "FareDealer" decal sell tickets and passes: The most common retailers are Safeway supermarkets and 7-Eleven convenience stores. Validation machines at SkyTrain and SeaBus stations sell tickets and can make change for bills up to $20. Ticket booklets called FareSavers ($19 for 10 tickets in one zone) and $9 day passes, which are great for visitors, are also available. Drivers are helpful, but they accept only exact change, tickets for the correct amount, or valid transfers.

BY SKYTRAIN

SKYTRAIN, Vancouver's fast, modern, and efficient rapid transit system, is elevated on its own special tracks for most of its route, and stops are linked to the bus system. The world's longest automated light rapid transit moves along a 49.5-kilometre (31-mile) route, making 33 stops as it runs from the downtown core through Vancouver, across Burnaby through New Westminster, and across the Fraser River to the Whalley area of Surrey. The new **MILLENNIUM LINE** takes a northern route to New Westminster. The **CANADALINE** is scheduled to begin service in late 2009, in time for the 2010 Olympics, and will route from the Vancouver Airport to downtown and Richmond Centre. All the SkyTrain stations have elevators (except Granville station, map:S4, one of four stations in the downtown core), and most have escalators. The other downtown stations are Waterfront (map:U2), Burrard (map:S3), and Stadium (map:T5). In the downtown core, the SkyTrain becomes a subway. The system is entirely computerized, with no drivers; proponents liken it to a horizontal elevator. The train cars, which can run individually or, typically, in batches of four, use a special electromagnetic system of propulsion, which gives the SkyTrain its distinctive sound. Trains run every 2–8 minutes. The last SkyTrain service out of downtown is scheduled at 1:15am; from New Westminster into downtown at 12:09am; from Surrey into downtown at 12:38am. Service from downtown resumes at 5:35am. On weekends, the trains run every 3–8 minutes. Saturdays, the trains start running from downtown at 6:50am; Sundays at 7:50am with the last train leaving downtown at 12:30am on Saturdays and 11:30pm on Sundays and holidays. Service from Surrey begins at 6:08am Saturdays, 7:08am Sundays and holidays, with the last train into downtown leaving Surrey at 12:38am Saturdays and 11:38pm Sundays and holidays.

BY SEABUS

SEABUS is the only integrated marine bus system in the world. The SeaBuses are double-ended catamaran ferries that carry up to 400 foot-passengers across Burrard Inlet between Vancouver's Waterfront station in the downtown core (north foot of Granville St; map:U2) and North Vancouver's Lonsdale Quay (south foot of Lonsdale Ave; map:E1). At either end, the terminals link directly to the regular bus system; on the Vancouver side, the terminal is also adjacent to stations for the SkyTrain and the West Coast Express, a regional commuter rail service (see By Train in this chapter). The SeaBus is wheelchair accessible, and bikes can be strapped into special racks onboard. The spectacular ride—you cruise around huge freighters and busy tugboats across one of the world's most impressive harbours, against a backdrop of tree-clad mountains and shining skyscrapers—takes 12 minutes.

The SeaBus runs every 15 minutes weekdays from about 6am to 6:30pm, then every half hour until 1:22am. Service on Saturdays is every half hour until 10:16am, then every 15 minutes until 6:46pm, at which time it reverts to half-hourly sailings. On Sundays and holidays, service is only at quarter after and quarter to the hour, 8:16am–11:16pm. If exact timing is crucial, double-check with the transit information line (604/953-3333) or the Web site (www.translink.bc.ca), which can also outline possible connections to your destination with other forms of transit.

BY CAR

Unique among major North American centres, Vancouver has no freeways within its city limits—that's what the suburbs are for, in the opinion of many Vancouverites—so traffic tends to move less than briskly during busy times. City engineers and even a few brave politicians have talked about building freeways, but plans get shot down by residents of the proposed location whenever the topic comes up. **RUSH HOURS**, which are particularly heavy and getting heavier, are from about 7am to 9:30am and 3pm to 6:30pm, Monday through Friday. Weekend mornings can be quiet; however, shoppers downtown on sunny Saturday or Sunday afternoons or avid hockey fans on weekday or weekend evenings can often make it seem like rush hour. Fortunately, you don't really need a car to get around, unless you're planning a trip outside the main areas of the city.

The **BC AUTOMOBILE ASSOCIATION** is the local affiliate of the Canadian Automobile Association; two branches are located on the West Side (999 W Broadway; 604/268-5600, cell *222, or 800/CAA-HELP; www.bcaa.com; map:R8; and 2347 W 41st Ave; 604/268-5800; map:C4). There are no downtown locations. For 24-hour roadside assistance, call 604/293-2222.

Several **RENTAL CAR AGENCIES** are located downtown, and some offer pickup and drop-off service:

AVIS (757 Hornby St; 604/606-2868 or 800/879-2847; www.avis.com; map:S3)

BUDGET (99 W Pender St; 604/683-5666 or 800/268-8900; www.budget. ca; map:V4; and 416 W Georgia St; 604/668-7000; map:T4)

ENTERPRISE (1250 Granville St; 604/688-5500 or 800/736-8222; www. enterprise.ca; map:R5; and 550 Bute St; 604/689-7377; map:S2)

HERTZ (1128 Seymour St; 604/606-4711 or 800/654-3131; www.hertz. ca; map:S5; and 999 Canada Pl Wy; 604/604-4711; map:T2; and Renaissance Hotel Harbourside, 1133 W Hastings St; 604/606-4770; map:S2)

NATIONAL CAR RENTAL (1130 W Georgia St; 604/609-7150 or 800/227-7368; www.nationalcar.ca; map:R3)

THRIFTY (1400 Robson St; 604/681-4869; www.thrifty.com; map:R2; and 413 Seymour St; 604/606-1666; map:T3)

Downtown **PARKING** is available on the street (except during rush hour as marked), in lots, or at parkades. The lots and parkades are relatively expensive—they range from $1.50 per half hour to $3 per 20 minutes—and varied metered curbside parking rates are in effect 9am–8pm. Most allow 2 hours' parking. (Beware: The streets are regularly patrolled by meter readers.) Good news for those who want to reduce the relatively low risk of car thefts and break-ins: Many lots and parkades are now patrolled by parking guards.

If your car has disappeared from where you left it, first find out if it was towed. Vancouver City Hall has a contract with **UNITOW** (1717 Vernon Dr; 604/659-1255; map:Y7), so call there if you parked on a city street. If your car was on a private parking lot, call **BUSTERS** (104 E 1st Ave; 604/685-8181; map:V6) or **DRAKE'S TOWING** (1553 Powell St; 604/251-3344; map: Z6). All three companies provide 24-hour towing within Vancouver. If none has your wheels, call 911 and report the missing car to the police. According to 2006 statistics, an average of 48 cars per day were reported stolen, with Royal Canadian Mounted Police and municipal police recovering 93 percent of them.

You can buy road maps at most newsstands, convenience stores, drugstores, and bookstores. If you're heading into more remote areas of the province, **INTERNATIONAL TRAVEL MAPS AND BOOKS** (530 W Broadway; 604/879-3621; www.itmb.com; map:V7) and the **GEOLOGICAL SURVEY OF CANADA** (625 Robson St; 604/666-0529; map:S4) sell detailed topographic maps.

BY TAXI AND LIMOUSINE

If anything, Vancouver may be a city of too many cabs. The phone book lists 15 taxi companies of various pedigrees, whose drivers must meet a set of standards formulated, in part, by the city's tourism groups. All drivers accept either Visa or MasterCard, and many take American Express, but cash is the preferred payment method. Four main companies serve downtown—and they'll take you to the surrounding communities. **YELLOW CAB COMPANY** (604/681-1111 or 800/898-8294; www.yellowcabvancouver.ca), with the largest fleet, has been around since 1921, but you can also depend on **BLACK TOP** and **CHECKER CABS** (604/733-3333 or 604/731-1111), **MACLURE'S CABS** (604/683-6666), and **VANCOUVER TAXI** (604/871-1111; www.vancouvertaxi.com). Vancouver Taxi specializes in wheelchair-accessible cabs, but all of the firms accommodate passengers with wheelchairs if you mention the requirement to the dispatcher when you call in. The fare is $1.58 per kilometre, plus a $2.70 flag or service charge.

If you'd rather pay by the hour and go first class, **STAR LIMOUSINE SERVICE** (604/685-5600; www.starlimousine.com), which has been around for more than 20 years, has a fleet of more than 24 limousines. Another company offering prompt, luxurious service for more than 20 years is **LIMOJET** (604/273-1331; www.limojetgold.com).

BY BICYCLE

Cycling is a popular method of getting to work in Vancouver, but you won't find a stream of cyclists negotiating rush-hour traffic. Most people still opt to drive a car, take the bus, or find some other means of getting to the office. Part of the reason is that there are few bike lanes into the downtown core. On the other hand, 240.5 kilometres (149 miles) of bike paths wind through the city centre and surrounding areas, including 55 kilometres (34 miles) in **PACIFIC SPIRIT REGIONAL PARK** (map:B3) on the edge of the University of British Columbia campus. The city of Vancouver has done quite a bit to encourage bike travel on and off roads, and it has established a comprehensive bike route network, featuring routes designed so bikes can share the road with cars. The city has also instituted some bicycle-activated signals, made some changes to the pavement, and given bicycles priority at some stop signs, traffic circles, traffic diversions, and medians. Fortunately—or unfortunately, depending on your point of view—these measures also reduce motor vehicle speed and volume.

Numerous **BIKE ROUTES** include the Adanac Bikeway, the BC Parkway, the Cassiar Bikeway, the Cypress Bikeway, the Fraser Lands, the Heather Bikeway, the Lakewood Bikeway, the Midtown and Ridgeway bikeways, the Mosaic Bikeway, the Off-Broadway Bikeway, the Ontario Bikeway, Pender Street, the Portside Bikeway, the Seaside Bicycle Route, the SW Marine Drive Bikeway, the Sunrise Bikeway, and the TransCanada Trail. The east sidewalk of the **CAMBIE STREET BRIDGE** (map:T6) is also an official bike route. On the Burrard Bridge, cyclists on the pedestrian sidewalk pedal in the same direction as vehicle traffic. Contact the **BICYCLE HOTLINE** (604/871-6070; www.city.vancouver.bc.ca) for details or pick up a free map of bike routes at **CITY HALL** (453 W 12th Ave; map:D3), community centres, and bike shops.

The Seaside Bike Route is one of the most popular and scenic bike routes in the city. It's also shared in part with pedestrians and in-line skaters, which makes it one of the most crowded routes in Vancouver. The route begins at the **STANLEY PARK SEAWALL** (map:D1), where cyclists must ride in a counterclockwise direction. The Seawall passes by the Brockton Point totem poles, under the Lions Gate Bridge, by Siwash Rock and Second and Third beaches to English Bay. Separated bicycle and pedestrian paths wind through English Bay and Sunset beaches, through the newly developed former Expo lands to Science World. From Science World, cyclists use a combination of roadways passing by Granville Island (where a Trans-Canada Trail pavilion is located), through Vanier and Kitsilano parks and Jericho and Locarno beaches before coming to the end of the route at **SPANISH BANK WEST** (map:B2).

The car-versus-bike debate hasn't yet conceded all to bike riders, even on designated bike routes. Bicyclists still have to yield to pedestrians and watch for schoolchildren crossing the routes, and they are supposed to obey all other rules of the road—although quite a number of cyclists seem to disdain such regulations. In addition, cyclists are not allowed to wear headphones that cover both ears, and safety helmets, headlights, and taillights are required by law. Safety jackets, the kind that cover arms and have reflective tape on them, are recommended but optional. If you're thinking you'll just skip that helmet, forget it. About 80 police officers and a half-dozen parking-meter staff are on bikes instead of in squad cars, and they all enforce bike regulations.

Many bike rental facilities (which also rent bike safety equipment) cluster around Stanley Park; the most popular are **SPOKES BICYCLE RENTAL & ESPRESSO BAR** (1798 W Georgia St; 604/688-5141; www.vancouverbikerental.com; map:Q2) and **BIKES 'N' BLADES** (718 Denman St; 604/602-9899; map:Q2). Outside the downtown core, drop in at the **RECKLESS BIKE STORES** (110 Davie St; 604/648-2600; www.rektek.com; map:S5; and 1810 Fir St at 2nd Ave; 604/731-2420; map:P7). They offer delivery and pickup of rental bikes (for a small fee) to and from your hotel.

VANCOUVER BY CYCLE (604/730-1032; www.vancouver-tour.citybycycle.com) offers daily tours of the Seawall, starting at Stanley Park and making their way through Yaletown and on to the Aquabus (bikes are boarded too), which cruises to Granville Island. Cyclists can pedal the island at their leisure before everyone heads back downtown. The $69 fee includes bike and helmet rental as well as commentary along the way.

Public bike racks are conveniently located throughout the downtown area, but bring a shackle-style U-lock if you plan to stop and shop or walk around. For additional information on biking in the city, see Bicycling in the Recreation chapter.

BY TRAIN

During the first half of the 20th century, passenger trains were a common way to get to and from Vancouver, but the advent of cars, buses, and aircraft travel sounded the death knell for many of those passenger trains. Now most of the trains arriving in Vancouver carry freight only. For information on trains in and out of Vancouver, see How to Get Here in the Planning a Trip chapter.

Within the city, the **WEST COAST EXPRESS** (Waterfront Station; 604/488-8906 or 800/570-7245; www.westcoastexpress.com; map:T3) operates a weekday commuter rail service between Mission in the Fraser Valley and Waterfront Station in downtown Vancouver that offers various amenities, including cappuccino bars. Five morning trains head west from Mission beginning at 5:27am. Eastbound service begins in the afternoon and ends with the last departure from Waterfront Station at 6:20pm. Fare to Mission is $11.25 one way, $21 round-trip. Interurban rates, as well as weekly and monthly passes, are also available.

Essentials

BUSINESS, COPY, AND MESSENGER SERVICES

Most hotels have a business centre on the premises, but if you're not at a hotel or can't wait till its copying and printing services open up in the morning, head over to any of four **FEDEX KINKO'S** (1900 W Broadway; 604/734-2679; map:O7; 789 W Pender; 604/685-3338; map:T3; 4361 Kingsway, Burnaby; 604/430-1700; map:G4; 811-5300 No. 3 Rd, Richmond; 604/303-0144; map:D7; www.fedexkinkos.ca).

To get your documents on their way pronto within the Greater Vancouver area, call **NOVEX COURIER** (604/278-1935), **PDX COURIER** (604/684-3336), or **FLASH COURIER** (604/689-3278) for fast, reliable service.

Offices and meeting spaces in a professional atmosphere and with the necessary administrative and communications services are available at a number of downtown locations. **INSIGNIA INTERNATIONAL** (500-666 Burrard St; 604/688-9276; map:R5), **ALLIANCE** (900-555 Burrard St; 604/692-2800; map:S3), and **SUITE 400 EXECUTIVE OFFICES AND SECRETARIAL SERVICES** (400-850 W Hastings St; 604/687-5516; map:T3) all offer short- and long-term rentals. For a more casual approach in a beautiful setting, **WORKSPACE** (400-21 Water St; 604/637-2252; www.abetterplacetowork.com; map:V3) in Gastown has meeting rooms, a lounge, and a cafe. Professional simultaneous translation services are available from **ISTS** (1475 E Georgia St; 604/255-1151; www.ists.com; map:Z4).

COMPUTER REPAIRS AND RENTALS

COMPUKITS (6 E 2nd Ave; 604/879-9288; map:E2) and the **CSC COMPUTER SERVICE CENTRE** (310 Brooksbank Ave, North Vancouver; 604/980-6373; map:F1) service the major lines of hardware. Need to rent? **COMPUKITS** can

BUDDHA IN A HOTEL AND OTHER PLACES OF WORSHIP

Vancouver has some of the nicest places to pray.

CHRIST CHURCH ANGLICAN CATHEDRAL (690 Burrard St; 604/682-3848; map:S3), built in 1889, is the oldest Vancouver church. When banks and office towers moved in, even the diocese wanted to bring on the wrecking ball. Heritage planners intervened, and today the building is also a heavenly setting for string quartet recitals and Shakespearean plays.

Oak Street is the heart of the local Jewish community: the orthodox **SCHARA TZEDECK** (3476 Oak St; 604/736-7607; map:D3) and the conservative **BETH ISRAEL** (4350 Oak St; 604/731-4161; map:D3) draw the biggest crowds on Friday nights.

On a quiet street just north of Broadway, the tiny square edifice of **JAMIA MASJID** (655 W 8th Ave; 604/803-7344; map:R7) is where Muslims of Pakistani origin gather for weekly prayers. Older, larger, and considerably more ornate, **MASJID AT-TAQWA** (12407 72nd Ave, Surrey; 604/591-7601; map:J7) is the local centre for adherents of the Sunni tradition.

help you out, or try **CENTRAL COMPUTER** (105-1425 W Pender St; 604/684-4545; map:R2), which rents IBM and peripheral systems with delivery and setup service. Apple Computer dealers **WESTWORLD COMPUTERS** (1368 W Broadway; 604/732-4499; www.westworld.ca; map:Q7) and **MAC STATION** (101-1014 Homer St; 604/606-6227; www.macstation.com; map:S5) provide service, support, and information. **FEDEX KINKO'S** (see Business, Copy, and Messenger Services in this chapter) rents Mac and PC stations for in-store use. **OFFICEWIDE LTD.** (14 W 7th Ave; 604/681-4800; map:V7) rents copiers and office furniture by the day, week, or month. Staff members are accommodating and friendly—and they deliver, too!

DRY CLEANERS AND LAUNDROMATS

The **VALETOR** has helped Vancouverites keep their clothes clean for the past 50 years with five locations throughout the city, including one downtown at the **BAY** (W Georgia and Granville sts; 604/681-6211; map:S4). **SCOTTY'S ONE HOUR CLEANERS** (834 Thurlow St; 604/685-7732; map:R3) offers good service and a professional job. **WHEELY CLEAN** (604/816-8721;www. wheelyclean.ca) will pick up and deliver dry cleaning to your home or downtown office at reasonable rates. **WOODMAN'S CLEANERS** (Bentall Centre, 101-505 Burrard St; 604/684-6622; map:S3; and Royal Centre, 1055 W Georgia St; 604/684-3623; map:S3) offers same-day dry cleaning or shirt laundry, as well as alterations and repairs.

The congregation of the **UNITARIAN CHURCH OF VANCOUVER** (949 W 49th Ave; 604/261-7204; map:C3) prides itself on intellectual enrichment and religious pluralism.

The **KHALSA DIWAN SOCIETY'S GURDWARA SAHIB** (8000 Ross St; 604/324-2010; map:G4), designed by renowned local architect Arthur Erickson, has entrances on each side to signify that people from all points of the world are welcome.

The multidomed **HARE KRISHNA TEMPLE** (5462 SE Marine Dr, Burnaby; 604/433-9728; map:G4) claims one of the largest congregations in North America, drawing up to 10,000 on high holy days.

The Radisson President is the only hotel in the Western Hemisphere that is home to a genuine **BUDDHIST TEMPLE** (8181 Cambie Rd, Richmond; 604/273-0369; map:E6); visitors enjoy a free vegetarian lunch after services. Bonsai plants and leaping dragons at the **INTERNATIONAL BUDDHIST SOCIETY TEMPLE** (9160 Steveston Hwy, Richmond; 604/274-2822; map:C7) grace what is perhaps the most impressive example of Ming architecture in Canada.

—Noel Hulsman

Self-serve Laundromats are few and far between downtown, but you can find a full range of cleaning services seven days a week at the **DAVIE LAUNDROMAT** (1061 Davie St; 604/683-9706; map:Q5). Several Laundromats are situated across English Bay in the Kitsilano neighbourhood (all of which have drop-off services), including the **GOLD COIN LAUNDRY** (3496 W Broadway; 604/739-0598; map:C2), which claims to be the largest coin Laundromat in western Canada.

GROCERY STORES

In addition to numerous produce shops, bakeries, and butcher shops, Greater Vancouver is fed by three major chain grocers: **CANADA SAFEWAY** (1641 Davie St; map:Q3; and 1766 Robson St; www.safeway.ca; map:Q2), **OVERWAITEA/SAVE-ON-FOODS** (2308 Cambie St; www.saveonfoods.com; map:T7), and **IGA MARKETPLACE** (909 Burrard St; www.marketplaceiga.com; map:R4). For cutting-edge foodstuffs—including farmers market–style produce displays, specialty breads flown in from France, prepared luxe meals, and a wine bar and restaurant—**URBAN FARE** in Yaletown (177 Davie St at Pacific; 604/975-7550; www.urbanfare.com; map:S6) and **COAL HARBOUR** (305 Bute St; 604/669-5831; map:S2) is the stylish stop for grocery shopping. It's open 6am to midnight, seven days a week. **SUPERVALU** (1255 Davie St; 604/684-9530 or 604/688-0911; www.supervalu.com; map:Q4) is open almost 24 hours, closing from 3–6am. Organic food stores include **CAPERS** (1675 Robson St; 604/687-5288; map:Q2; and 2285 W 4th; 604/739-6676;

map:N7; and 3277 Cambie St; 604/909-2988; map:D3; and 2496 Marine Dr, West Vancouver; 604/925-3316) and **CHOICES** (1202 Richards St; 604/633-2392; map:S5; and 3493 Cambie St; 604/875-0099; map:D3; and 2627 16th Ave; 604-736-0009; map:C3). The international chain **WHOLE FOODS MARKET** can be found in West Vancouver (929 Main St; 604/678-0500; www.wholefoodsmarket.com). For wholesale grocery shopping, there's **COSTCO** (605 Expo Blvd; 604/622-5050; www.costco.ca; map:U4).

GYMS

To keep yourself toned, drop in at **DENMAN FITNESS** (1731 Comox St; 604/688-2484; www.denmanfitness.com; map:P2) or **WORLD GYM** (1676 Robson St; 604/915-3032; www.worldgymvancouver.com; map:Q2). For a monthly fee, enjoy the benefits of the **STEVE NASH SPORTS CLUB** (610 Granville St; 604/682-5213; www.stevenashsportsclub.com; map:S3), where state-of-the-art equipment, cycling, yoga, an Internet lounge, a juice bar, massage therapists, saunas, and a Nike pro shop await.

HOSPITALS AND MEDICAL-DENTAL SERVICES

We hope you don't need the information in this section, but we provide it just in case.

The two largest hospitals are **VANCOUVER GENERAL HOSPITAL** (899 W 12th Ave; 604/875-4111; www.vanhosp.bc.ca; map:D2), atop what's locally called Fairview Slopes overlooking the downtown core, and **ST. PAUL'S HOSPITAL,** in the city's heavily populated West End (1081 Burrard St; 604/682-2344, or 604/806-8011 patient information; map:R4). The University of British Columbia campus on Point Grey is home to the **UNIVERSITY HOSPITAL** (2211 Westbrook Mall; 604/822-7121; map:A2).

Walk-in clinics, with no appointment necessary, include **CAREPOINT MEDICAL CENTRES** (1175 Denman St; 604/681-5338; map:P3; and 5138 Joyce St; 604/436-0800; map:F3; and 1623 Commercial Dr; 604/254-5554; map:Z6), **MAPLE MEDICAL CLINIC** (103-2025 W Broadway; 604/730-9769; map:C3), **MEDICENTRE** (Bentall Centre, 1055 Dunsmuir St; 604/683-8138; map:S3), and **ROYAL CENTRE MEDICAL** (238-1055 W Georgia St; 604/682-6886; map: S3). The **COLLEGE OF PHYSICIANS AND SURGEONS OF BC** (1807 W 10th Ave; 604/733-7758; map:C3) has a list of doctors accepting patients.

WEST COAST DENTAL CLINICS welcome walk-ins and dental emergencies: **PACIFIC CENTRE DENTAL** (701 W Georgia St; 604/669-1016; map:S4), **MAX DENTAL** (90 Smithe St; 604/609-2020; map:T5), **DENTAL CLINIC @ ROBSON** (301-1525 Robson St; 604/683/6565; map:Q2), and **COAL HARBOUR DENTAL** (45-200 Granville St; 604/696-9299; map:T3).

LEGAL SERVICES

The local branch of the Canadian Bar Association operates the free **DIAL-A-LAW SERVICE** (604/687-4680 or 800/565-5297), a library of recorded messages on various topics. The **LAW STUDENTS' LEGAL ADVICE PROGRAM**

(604/822-5791) offers a free consultation service, and the **LAWYER REFERRAL SERVICE** (604/687-3221) advises people seeking legal representation.

MAJOR BANKS

All the major Canadian banks and many foreign financial institutions provide a full range of financial services, including foreign exchange. Dozens of ATMs are also scattered throughout the downtown core. Standard banking hours are 9:30am–4:30pm, with extended hours, including weekends, at some banks and branches.

PETS AND STRAY ANIMALS

If puss or pooch gets sick while in Vancouver, call the **WEST END VETERINARY CLINIC** (1788 Alberni St; 604/685-4535; map:Q1), the **VANCOUVER VETERINARY HOSPITAL** (1541 Kingsway; 604/876-2231; map:E3), or the **ANIMAL CLINIC** (1635 W 4th Ave; 604/738-7600; map:P7). **VANCOUVER ANIMAL EMERGENCY CLINIC** (1590 W 4th Ave; 604/734-5104; map:P7) offers 24-hour care. For bird patients, contact the **NIGHT OWL BIRD HOSPITAL** (1675 W 3rd Ave; 604/734-5100; map:P7).

Lost pets could end up at the **CITY ANIMAL CONTROL HOME** (1280 Raymur Ave; 604/871-6888; map:E2) or the **VANCOUVER SOCIETY FOR THE PREVENTION OF CRUELTY TO ANIMALS ANIMAL HOSPITAL** (1205 E 7th Ave; 604/879-3571; map:Y7). In addition to a shelter, the society also operates the **BC SPCA GROOM SHOP** (604/709-4658). An excellent resource for dog owners visiting the city is *Dog City: Vancouver* by Marg Meikle (Raincoast, 2000). Also see Tips for Special Travellers in the Planning a Trip chapter.

PHARMACIES

Shopper's Drug Mart and London Drugs (nine locations in Vancouver) both have locations throughout Greater Vancouver; they are mini–department stores as well as full-fledged and extensive pharmacies. Four **SHOPPER'S DRUG MARTS** located downtown and in Vancouver's West Side are open until midnight (1006 Homer St; 604/669-0330; map:S4; and 1020 Denman St; 604/681-3411; map:P2; and 4326 Dunbar St; 604/732-8855; map:B3; and 2947 Granville St; 604/738-3107; map:D3; www.shoppersdrugmart. ca). Three are open 24 hours a day, seven days a week (2302 W 4th Ave; 604/738-3138; map:C2; and 885 W Broadway; 604/708-1135; map:S7; and 1125 Davie St; 604/669-2424; map:D4). Three **LONDON DRUGS** are located downtown (1650 Davie St; 604/448-4850; map:P3; and 710 Granville St; 604/448-4802; map:S3; and 1187 Robson St; 604/448-4819; map:R3; www. londondrugs.com).

PHOTOGRAPHY EQUIPMENT AND SERVICES

Local camera buffs—and those still needing quick, reliable film processing—head to **LENS & SHUTTER** (2912 W Broadway; 604/736-3461 or 888/736-3461; www.lensandshutter.com; map:C2). **DUNNE AND RUNDLE**, another alternative, also does repairs at their location in the Bentall Centre (595 Burrard St; 604/681-9254 or 888/999-1929; www.dunneandrundle.com; map:S3). The three downtown locations of **LONDON DRUGS** (see Pharmacies in this chapter) have an exceptional selection of moderately priced cameras at competitive prices and also offer good prices on video transfers from film, slides, and photos.

POLICE AND SAFETY

In **EMERGENCY** situations, dial 911. For fire and ambulance, typical response times are 3–5 minutes; for police, it depends on the situation, but 3 minutes is typical for an emergency. For **NONEMERGENCY** situations, call 604/717-3321. There are two police stations: The old one is in the rough section of town at 312 Main Street (map:V3), and the newer main one is at 2120 Cambie Street at Sixth Avenue (map:T7).

Greater Vancouver is among the safest cities in the world for residents as well as visitors. Men can safely walk in any area of the city at any time of the day or night, but should be wary in the skid row areas of Hastings Street (three blocks either side of Main St; map:V4). It is extremely unlikely that women, even if alone, would be attacked in these areas, which are well patrolled, well lit, and usually quite busy, but women are much more likely than men to be approached, panhandled, or hassled. Women should also avoid the several blocks of the red-light district that establishes itself in the late afternoon and evening along the three blocks of Hastings Street either side of Main (map:V4).

Most panhandlers are courteous and focus on the downtown core and malls. Pickpockets are not a great concern either, but drug-driven "smash-and-grabs" in cars and homes are known to happen. Hotels, especially in the downtown core, are fairly protective, but one should not leave personal property of any value in a vehicle, especially not if it can be seen by passersby. Cars in park-and-ride lots near public transit are particularly vulnerable to thieves.

POST OFFICE

The federal government owns the independent national company **CANADA POST**, which has a monopoly on moving letter mail in the country. Canada Post's main post office is a big, one-block square building in downtown Vancouver (349 W Georgia St; map:T4). Located across the street from Library Square, it is one of two outlets the national postal service operates in the downtown core. The other is in the **BENTALL CENTRE** (595 Burrard St; 604/482-4296; map:S3). Both have philatelic counters. Standard first-class postal rates, not including the 5 percent federal sales tax, are 52 cents within Canada, 93 cents to the United States, and $1.55 overseas. Mail bound outside

Canada and requiring more than $5 postage is GST exempt at the time of mailing (see Visitor Taxes and Gratuities in the Planning a Trip chapter). Please note the obvious—but sometimes overlooked—point that all postage on mail that goes through the Canadian postal system must be Canadian.

PUBLIC RESTROOMS

All of the major malls in Greater Vancouver have public facilities, and some large stores, such as the Bay and Chapters, have restrooms open to the public. Downtown, the most accessible public restrooms are located on the Howe Street level of the **PACIFIC CENTRE** (700 W Georgia St to 777 Dunsmuir St; map:S4) and the ground level of the **BENTALL SHOPPING CENTRE** (595 Burrard St; map:S4).

SPAS AND SALONS

Given the healthy Vancouver lifestyle, it's no wonder that day spas flourish here. **ABSOLUTE SPA** (www.absolutespa.com), winner of more than 30 awards and continually rated by Vancouverites as the best spa, has five locations: the **CENTURY** (1015 Burrard St; 604/684-2772; map:R4), celebrities' choice for a spa, offers a full range of services to primp and pamper, with complimentary spa cuisine; **FAIRMONT HOTEL VANCOUVER** (900 W Georgia St; 604/648-2909; map:S3), a popular and convenient location for the downtown professional and the frequent traveller, boasts the first spa designed for men; **ABSOLUTE SPA & SALON YVR** (Domestic Arrivals, Level 1 at Vancouver International Airport; 604/278-2514; map:C5) offers travellers a full-service salon, as well as a steam shower and massage spa suite for those with short layovers; the **FAIRMONT AIRPORT HOTEL** (International Terminal at Vancouver International Airport; 604/248-2772; map:C5) also offers hotel guests, airline employees, other travellers, and the general public private sleep chambers (no appointment necessary); and the newest location, at **RIVER ROCK CASINO RESORT** (8811 River Rd, Richmond; 604/273-1895; map:D5).

SPA UTOPIA at the Pan Pacific (999 Canada Pl; 604/641-1351; www.spautopia.ca; map:T2) also offers spa suites—residential-style rooms with personal attendants, waterfall showers and infinity-edged showers, fireplaces, and spectacular vistas.

Numerous other aestheticians and hair stylists are located in downtown Vancouver. Some of the city's top salons are **SUKI'S** (206-1030 W Georgia St; 604/687-8805; map:S3; and 1805 W 1st Ave; 604/732-9101; map:O6; and 3157 Granville St; 604/738-7713; map:D3) and **STYLE LAB** (851 Beatty St; 604/331-6991; map:T5). For more listings, see Skin and Hair Care in the Shopping chapter.

YOGA

Vancouver embraces yoga—from Lululemon wear to yoga studios on (almost) every block. **BIKRAM'S YOGA** has three locations (including 101-1650 Alberni St; 604/662-7722; www.bikramyogavancouver.com; map:Q2).

FLOW YOGA (1409 W Pender St; 604/682-3569; www.flowyogavancouver. com; map:R2) offers a view of the mountains and Coal Harbour. Find six forms of yoga teaching and more than 100 classes a week at SEMPERVIVA (200-1333 Johnstone St, Granville Island; 604/739-2009; www.semperviva. com; map:Q6; and 2608 W Broadway; map:C3). Check with your hotel: many offer their own yoga programmes; for example, Pacific Palisades offers an in-room yoga kit and 24-hour yoga programming on the TV.

Local Resources

NEWSPAPERS AND MAGAZINES

The *Vancouver Sun* (604/605-2111; www.canada.com/vancouversun), the city's main English-language daily, is published every morning except Sunday. The *Province* (604/605-2222; www.canada.com/theprovince) is a tabloid newspaper, and its mandate is flashy, headline-grabbing journalism with an emphasis on sports and entertainment. Both are part of CanWest Global Communications, which owns papers in most major cities across Canada, as well as one of the country's national newspapers, the *National Post* (416/383-2300; www.nationalpost.com). The other national paper is the well-respected *Globe and Mail* (416/585-5000; www.theglobeandmail.com). Both nationals publish Monday through Saturday.

The *Georgia Straight* (604/730-7000; www.straight.com) is a free entertainment weekly published on Thursdays. *Vancouver*, the city magazine published 10 times a year, offers restaurant reviews, fashion and style reviews, and insights on the latest happenings around town. *Business in Vancouver* (604/688-2398; www.biv.com) is Vancouver's weekly business tabloid—and an excellent paper. *CityFood* (604/737-7845; www.cityfood.com) and *EAT Magazine* (250/384-9042; www.eatmagazine.ca) are free insider's guides to cooking and dining.

There aren't many cities that have more daily ethnic newspapers than mainstream publications, as Vancouver does. The city has three daily Chinese-language newspapers: *Sing Tao* (604/321-1111), *Ming Pao* (604/231-8998), and the *World Journal* (604/876-1338).

PUBLIC LIBRARIES

The Vancouver Public Library's main branch is in dramatic LIBRARY SQUARE (350 W Georgia St; 604/331-3600; map:T4), one of the city's architectural landmarks; the strength and breadth of its multifloor collection reflect the value the city puts on reading. The bright, spacious building, designed by world-renowned architect Moshe Safdie, is open Monday through Thursday 10am–9pm, Friday and Saturday 10am–9pm, and Sunday noon to 5pm. Twenty-one other library branches are located throughout the city, all offering a wide selection of books, magazines, and audio and video recordings. All branches are closed on holidays.

RADIO AND TV

Vancouver's radio airwaves are crowded with AM and FM stations that range from opera each Saturday afternoon on **CBC-FM** (which the CBC calls "CBC Radio Two") to the in-your-face rap and hip-hop of **CO-OP RADIO**. There are many channels out there that are mainstream in music, talk, arts, and current affairs. **CKNW** is western Canada's most popular radio station, and it has been thus for decades, thanks in part to excellent and thorough news and sports coverage and, for the past two decades, open-line shows. Multi-cultural and Chinese-language stations—**CHKG**, **CKYE**, and **CHMB**—thrive in their particular niche. **CBC-AM** (which the CBC calls "CBC Radio One") is commercial-free public radio with a patented series of 10-minute interviews for much of its programming. For up-to-the-minute food and wine news, tune into award-winning journalists Anthony Gismondi and Kasey Wilson (this book's editor) during "Tony & Kasey's Buzz on Food & Wine" on Talk 1410 AM Vancouver from noon to 1pm every Saturday.

RADIO STATIONS

600 AM	UNFORGETTABLE 600-AM	ADULT FAVOURITES
690 AM	CBC-AM (RADIO ONE)	NEWS/TALK
980 AM	CKNW-AM	NEWS/SPORTS
1040 AM	THE TEAM-AM	ALL SPORTS
1130 AM	CKWX-AM	NEWS/WEATHER
1320 AM	CHMB-AM	CHINESE RADIO
1410 AM	TALK 1410 AM	ALL TALK
1470 AM	FAIRCHILD-AM	CHINESE RADIO
93.1 FM	CKYE RED-FM	ETHNIC RADIO
93.7 FM	JR-FM	COUNTRY
95.3 FM	Z-95-FM	POP
96.1 FM	CHKG-FM	CANTONESE RADIO
96.9 FM	JACK-FM	RETRO
99.3 FM	THE FOX-FM	ROCK
101.1 FM	ROCK 101-FM	CLASSIC ROCK
102.7 FM	CO-OP-FM	ALTERNATIVE
103.5 FM	QM-FM	EASY LISTENING
105.7 FM	CBC-FM (RADIO TWO)	CLASSICAL/ARTS

TELEVISION STATIONS

3	CBUT-2	CBC ENGLISH
7	CBC-F-26	CBUFT (CBC FRENCH)
9	CIVT-32	CTV
11	CHAN-8	GLOBAL
13	CKVU-10	CITYTV
15	KIRO-7	CBS

16	KING-5	NBC
21	KOMO-4	ABC
26	NW	CBC NEWSWORLD
27	KCTS-9	PBS
33	CNN	CNN

INTERNET ACCESS

Most major hotels offer the option of Internet access with double phone lines in guest rooms, and several have business centres with computers (see the Lodgings chapter). Public library branches allow patrons to access the Internet on a limited number of terminals. Try surfing at **FEDEX KINKO'S** (1900 W Broadway; 604/734-2679), **INTERNET COFFEE** (1104 Davie St; 604/682-6668; map:Q4), **GLOBAL INTERNET** (779 Denman St; 604/633-9389; map:Q2), **BLENZ** (1201 Robson St; 604/669-4848; map:R3), and the **LONDON DRUGS** branch at the corner of Granville and Georgia (map:S3).

UNIVERSITIES

You won't have to study hard to find the **UNIVERSITY OF BRITISH COLUMBIA** (604/822-2211; www.ubc.ca; map:A2). Founded in 1908, it's the oldest university in the province. The campus, perched on Point Grey overlooking Burrard Inlet, is one of the most attractive in Canada, offering amazing vistas of sea, mountains, and sky. It's also a bustling centre of research and learning in the humanities and sciences, with an excellent library collection. It's not the only postsecondary institution in town, though: **SIMON FRASER UNIVERSITY** (8888 University Dr, Burnaby; 604/291-3111; www.sfu.ca; map:I2) has a campus downtown at **HARBOUR CENTRE** (515 W Hastings St; 604/291-5000; map:T3) in Gastown, and **REGENT COLLEGE** (5800 University Blvd; 604/224-3245; map:A2) on the UBC campus is well known in Christian circles for its theological teaching. The **BC INSTITUTE OF TECHNOLOGY** (3700 Willingdon Ave, Burnaby; 604/434-5734; map:G3), which produces skilled high-technology grads, also has a campus downtown (555 Seymour St; 604/412-7777; map:T4). Recognized internationally in art, media, and design, the **EMILY CARR INSTITUTE OF ART AND DESIGN** (1399 Johnston St, Granville Island; 604/844-3800; map:Q6) is one of the oldest institutes in BC. The Greater Vancouver area also has its share of colleges, including **CAPILANO COLLEGE** (2055 Purcell Wy, North Vancouver; 604/986-1911; map:F1), **DOUGLAS COLLEGE** (700 Royal Ave, New Westminster; 604/527-5400; map:I5), and **LANGARA COLLEGE** (100 W 49th Ave; 604/323-5511; map:D4.

Important Telephone Numbers

All telephone numbers in the Lower Mainland require 10 digits, beginning with
either 604 or 778.

EMERGENCIES—POLICE, FIRE, AMBULANCE	911
EMERGENCIES—COAST GUARD	800/567-5111
NONEMERGENCY—POLICE	604/717-3321
AIDS VANCOUVER HELP LINE	604/893-2222
ALCOHOLICS ANONYMOUS	604/434-3933
ANIMAL CARE (SPCA)	604/879-7721
ANIMAL EMERGENCY (SPCA)	604-879-7343
ANIMAL EMERGENCY CLINIC	604/734-5104
ANIMAL POUND	604/871-6888
BCAA	604/268-5600
BCAA EMERGENCY ROAD SERVICE (24 HOURS)	604/293-2222
BC FERRIES	888/223-3779
BETTER BUSINESS BUREAU	604/682-2711
BUS, SEABUS, SKYTRAIN SCHEDULE INFO	604/953-3333
CANADA CUSTOMS	800/461-9999
CANADIAN BLOOD SERVICES	604/879-6001
CITIZENSHIP AND IMMIGRATION	604/666-8155
CRIMESTOPPERS (ANONYMOUS POLICE CRIME-TIP LINE)	604/669-TIPS
CRISIS CENTRE	604/872-3311
CUSTOMS (CANADA)	800/461-9999
CUSTOMS (U.S.)	604/278-1825
DIRECTORY ASSISTANCE (95 CENTS PER CALL)	411
DOMESTIC VIOLENCE HOTLINE /	
BATTERED WOMEN'S SUPPORT SERVICES	604/687-1867
GREYHOUND CANADA SCHEDULE INFO	604/683-8133
INDUSTRY CANADA	604/666-5000
INFORMATION SERVICES VANCOUVER	604/875-6381, 604/875-0885 (TTY)
KIDS HELP LINE	800/668-6868
LEGAL SERVICES	604/687-4680
MISSING PERSONS	604/717-3535
PASSPORTS	800/567-6868
PLANNED PARENTHOOD	604/731-4252
POISON CONTROL CENTRE	604/682-5050
POST OFFICE INFORMATION	800/267-1177
POSTAL CODE INFORMATION	900/565-2633
RAPE CRISIS CENTRE	604/255-6344
RAPE RELIEF	604/872-8212
ROAD CONDITIONS	800/550-4997
ROYAL CANADIAN MOUNTED POLICE ADMINISTRATION	604/264-3111
SENIORS INFORMATION (VANCOUVER)	604/684-8171
SKI REPORT	604/986-6262
SUICIDE PREVENTION	604/872-3311

TICKETMASTER	604/280-4444
TOURISM OKANAGAN	800/567-2275
TOURISM WHISTLER	877/991-9988
VANCOUVER BOARD OF TRADE	604/681-2111
VANCOUVER CITY HALL	604/873-7011
VANCOUVER CITY POLICE ADMINISTRATION	604/717-3535
VANCOUVER HEALTH DEPARTMENT	604/736-2033
VANCOUVER PARKS AND RECREATION BOARD	604/257-8400
VANCOUVER PUBLIC LIBRARY	604/331-3603
VANCOUVER TOURIST INFO CENTRE	604/683-2000
VIA RAIL	888/842-7245
VITAL STATISTICS (BIRTH, MARRIAGE, DEATH CERTIFICATES)	604/660-2937
WEATHER	604/664-9010
WOMEN'S SHELTER	604/872-8212
YMCA	604/681-9622
YWCA	604/895-5800

RESTAURANTS

RESTAURANTS

Restaurants by Star Rating

★★★★

Bishop's
West

★★★★½

Blue Water Cafe + Raw Bar
C Restaurant
Cioppino's Mediterranean
   Grill & Enoteca
Pear Tree, The
Tojo's
Vij's

★★★

Aurora Bistro
Bacchus Restaurant
   & Piano Lounge
Bin 941 Tapas Parlour
Bin 942 Tapas Parlour
Chambar Belgian
   Restaurant
Chow
CinCin Ristorante & Bar
Cru
Dan Japanese Restaurant
Five Sails Restaurant
Fuel Restaurant
Gastropod
Gotham Steakhouse
   & Cocktail Bar
Il Giardino di Umberto
Kingyo
Kirin Mandarin Restaurant
La Belle Auberge
La Régalade French Bistro
La Terrazza

Le Crocodile
Lift
Morton's the Steakhouse
Moustache Café
Okada Sushi Japanese
   Restaurant
Parkside
Quattro on Fourth
Salmon House, The
Sea Harbour Seafood
   Restaurant
Spice Islands Indonesian
   Restaurant
Thomas Haas Patisserie
   and Café
Trattoria Italian Kitchen
William Tell Restaurant,
   The
YEW Restaurant + Bar
Yoshi Japanese Restaurant
Zen Japanese Restaurant
Zest Japanese Cuisine

★★½

Akbar's Own Dining
   Lounge
Beach House, The
Beyond Restaurant
   and Lounge
Boneta
Cactus Club Cafe
Cannery Seafood
   House, The
Coast Restaurant
Cobre
Diva at the Met

Earls
Elixir
Fish House in Stanley
   Park, The
Fraîche
Globe@YVR
Glowbal Grill & Satay Bar
Goldfish Pacific Kitchen
Hapa Izakaya
Hart House Restaurant
Hermitage, The
Herons Restaurant
Imperial Chinese
   Seafood Restaurant
Italian Kitchen
La Buca
La Cucina Italiana
Mangia e Bevi Ristorante
Memphis Blues Barbeque
   House
Mistral French Bistro
Nu
Phnom Penh
Pied-à-Terre
Provence Marinaside
Provence Mediterranean
   Grill
Raincity Grill
Rinconcito Salvadoreño
   Restaurant
Salt Tasting Room
Sanafir
Shore Club, The
So.Cial at Le Magasin
Sun Sui Wah Seafood
   Restaurant

Toshi Sushi
Uva Wine Bar /
  Cibo Trattoria
Yuji's Japanese Tapas
Zakkushi Charcoal
  Grill Diner

 ★★

Aqua Riva
Ashiana Tandoori
  Restaurant
Au Petit Café
Banana Leaf Malaysian
  Cuisine
Bistro Pastis
Bistrot Bistro
Bridges Seafood
  Restaurant
Brix Restaurant
Café Kathmandu
Cascade Room, The
Chen's Shanghai Restaurant
Chill Winston Restaurant
  & Lounge
Chutney Villa
Crave
Delilah's Restaurant and Bar
Doña Cata Mexican Foods
East Is East / Chai Gallery
Flying Beaver
Go Fish!
Gramercy Grill
Griffins
Gusto di Quattro
Hanwoori Korean
  Restaurant
Horizons Restaurant
Ho Yuen Kee
Irish Heather, The /
  Shebeen Whisk(e)y
  House
Joe Fortes Seafood
  & Chop House

Kamei Royale Japanese
  Restaurant
Kitanoya Guu
Landmark Hot Pot House
La Piazza Dario
  Ristorante Italiano
Le Gavroche
Le Marrakech
  Moroccan Bistro
Lime Japanese Cuisine
Lolita's South of the
  Border Cantina
Montri's Thai Restaurant
Nat's New York Pizzeria
Ningtu Restaurant
Northern Delicacy
Octopus Garden
  Restaurant
Pho Thai Hoa
Pinkys Steakhouse
Rekados
Rodney's Oyster House
Saltlik
Sciué Italian Bakery Caffé
Shanghai Chinese Bistro
Simply Thai
Smoking Dog Bistro, The
Splitz Grill
Stella's Tap and Tapas Bar
Suvai Restaurant
Tapastree Restaurant
Tomato Fresh Food Café
Trafalgars Bistro
Tramonto at the River
  Rock Casino Resort
Vij's Rangoli
Wild Rice

★★

Benkei Ramen Noodle Shop
Dai Tung Chinese
  Restaurant

Fiddlehead Joe's Eatery
  & Bar
Hal Mae Jang Mo Jib
Kintaro Handmade
  Tonkotsu Ramen
Motomachi Shokudo
Original Tandoori Kitchen
Osteria Napoli Ristoranté
Pondok Indonesia
SalaThai Thai Restaurant
Sawasdee Thai Restaurant
Tropika
Zen Fine Chinese Cuisine

★

Ajisai Sushi Bar
American Grille, The
Annapurna
Café de Paris
Cardero's
Chao Phraya Thai
  Restaurant
Congee Noodle House
Ellie Tropical Cuisine
Ezogiku Noodle Cafe
Fisherman's Terrace
  Seafood Restaurant
Floata Seafood Restaurant
Fritz European Fry House
Grand View Szechuan
  Restaurant
Green Basil Thai
  Restaurant
Gyoza King
Habit Lounge
Hon's Wun-Tun House
Hy's Encore
Incendio
Incendio West
Josephine's Restaurant
  and Catering
Jules Bistro

Kim Phung Vietnamese
   Restaurant
La Bretagne Crêperie
Legendary Noodles
Marcello Pizzeria &
   Ristorante
Me & Julio
Noodle Box, The
Nyala African Cuisine
Pajo's
Plan B Lounge and Eatery
Planet Veg

Red Onion, The
Rocky Mountain Flatbread
   Company
Salty Tongue Urban Deli
Sandy's Cuisine
Sophie's Cosmic Cafe
Spice Alley Korean
   Restaurant & Bar
Steamworks Brewing Co.
Steamworks
   TransContinental
Steveston Pizza Co.

Subeez Cafe
Taco Shack, The
Tomahawk Restaurant
Vogue Chinese Cuisine
White Spot
Won More Szechuan
   Cuisine

UNRATED
DB Bistro Moderne
Lumière with
   Daniel Boulud

Restaurants by Neighbourhood

BURNABY
Green Basil Thai
   Restaurant
Hanwoori Korean
   Restaurant
Hart House Restaurant
Horizons Restaurant
Pear Tree, The

CHINATOWN
Floata Seafood Restaurant
Hon's Wun-Tun House
Phnom Penh
Wild Rice

DELTA
Cactus Club Cafe

DOWNTOWN
Aqua Riva
Bacchus Restaurant
   & Piano Lounge
Beyond Restaurant
   and Lounge
C Restaurant
Cactus Club Cafe
Cardero's

Chambar Belgian
   Restaurant
CinCin Ristorante & Bar
Diva at the Met
Earls
Fiddlehead Joe's Eatery
   & Bar
Five Sails Restaurant
Fritz European Fry House
Gotham Steakhouse
   & Cocktail Bar
Griffins
Gyoza King
Hal Mae Jang Mo Jib
Hapa Izakaya
Hermitage, The
Herons Restaurant
Hy's Encore
Il Giardino di Umberto
Imperial Chinese Seafood
   Restaurant
Italian Kitchen
Joe Fortes Seafood
   & Chop House
Kamei Royale Japanese
   Restaurant

Kirin Mandarin Restaurant
Kitanoya Guu
La Bretagne Crêperie
Le Crocodile
Le Gavroche
Lift
Morton's the Steakhouse
Nu
Okada Sushi Japanese
   Restaurant
Parkside
SalaThai Thai Restaurant
Saltlik
Sanafir
Sciué Italian Bakery Caffé
Shanghai Chinese Bistro
Shore Club, The
Spice Alley Korean
   Restaurant & Bar
Tropika
Uva Wine Bar /
   Cibo Trattoria
White Spot
William Tell Restaurant,
   The
YEW Restaurant + Bar

EAST VANCOUVER

Ashiana Tandoori
   Restaurant
Au Petit Café
Aurora Bistro
Café Kathmandu
Cannery Seafood
   House, The
Cascade Room, The
Chutney Villa
Congee Noodle House
Crave
Dai Tung Chinese
   Restaurant
Doña Cata Mexican Foods
East Is East
Grand View Szechuan
   Restaurant
Habit Lounge
Ho Yuen Kee
Josephine's Restaurant
   and Catering
Kim Phung Vietnamese
   Restaurant
La Piazza Dario Ristorante
   Italiano
Lime Japanese Cuisine
Marcello Pizzeria
   & Ristorante
Me & Julio
Memphis Blues Barbeque
   House
Ningtu Restaurant
Nyala African Cuisine
Original Tandoori Kitchen
Osteria Napoli Ristorante
Pho Thai Hoa
Pondok Indonesia
Rekados
Rinconcito Salvadoreño
   Restaurant
Sandy's Cuisine
Sawasdee Thai Restaurant

Splitz Grill
Stella's Tap and Tapas Bar
Sun Sui Wah Seafood
   Restaurant
Toshi Sushi

GASTOWN

Boneta
Chill Winston Restaurant
   & Lounge
Cobre
Incendio
Irish Heather, The
Jules Bistro
Kitanoya Guu
Le Marrakech
   Moroccan Bistro
Salt Tasting Room
Salty Tongue Urban Deli
So.Cial at Le Magasin
Steamworks Brewing Co.
Steamworks
   TransContinental

GRANVILLE ISLAND

Bridges Seafood
   Restaurant

LADNER

La Belle Auberge

NEW WEST

Hon's Wun-Tun House

NORTH VANCOUVER

Cactus Club Cafe
Gusto di Quattro
La Cucina Italiana
Memphis Blues Barbeque
   House
Moustache Café
Thomas Haas Patisserie
   and Café
Tomahawk Restaurant

PORT COQUITLAM

Cactus Club Cafe
Earls

RICHMOND

American Grille, The
Chen's Shanghai Restaurant
Ellie Tropical Cuisine
Fisherman's Terrace
   Seafood Restaurant
Flying Beaver
Globe@YVR
Hal Mae Jang Mo Jib
Hon's Wun-Tun House
Kirin Mandarin Restaurant
Kitanoya Guu
Northern Delicacy
Pajo's
Sea Harbour Seafood
   Restaurant
Steveston Pizza Co.
Sun Sui Wah Seafood
   Restaurant
Tramonto at the River
   Rock Casino Resort
Tropika
Vogue Chinese Cuisine
Zen Fine Chinese Cuisine

SURREY

Cactus Club Cafe
Earls

WEST END

Banana Leaf Malaysian
   Cuisine
Benkei Ramen Noodle Shop
Café de Paris
Delilah's Restaurant
   and Bar
Ezogiku Noodle Cafe
Fish House in Stanley
   Park, The
Hon's Wun-Tun House

43

Kingyo
Kintaro Handmade
    Tonkotsu Ramen
Legendary Noodles
Lolita's South of the
    Border Cantina
Motomachi Shokudo
Nat's New York Pizzeria
Raincity Grill
Tapastree Restaurant
Won More Szechuan
    Cuisine
Yoshi Japanese Restaurant
Zakkushi Charcoal
    Grill Diner

WEST SIDE

Ajisai Sushi Bar
Akbar's Own Dining
    Lounge
Annapurna
Banana Leaf Malaysian
    Cuisine
Bin 941 Tapas Parlour
Bin 942 Tapas Parlour
Bishop's
Bistro Pastis
Bistrot Bistro
Cactus Club Cafe
Chao Phraya Thai
    Restaurant
Chow
Cru
Dan Japanese Restaurant
DB Bistro Moderne
Earls
East Is East / Chai Gallery
Fuel Restaurant

Gastropod
Go Fish!
Gramercy Grill
Hapa Izakaya
Incendio West
Kirin Mandarin Restaurant
La Buca
Landmark Hot Pot House
Lumière with
    Daniel Boulud
Mistral French Bistro
Montri's Thai Restaurant
Nat's New York Pizzeria
Noodle Box, The
Octopus Garden
    Restaurant
Pied-à-Terre
Planet Veg
Provence Mediterranean
    Grill
Quattro on Fourth
Red Onion, The
Rocky Mountain Flatbread
    Company
SalaThai Thai Restaurant
Smoking Dog Bistro, The
Sophie's Cosmic Cafe
Spice Islands Indonesian
    Restaurant
Suvai Restaurant
Taco Shack, The
Tojo's
Tomato Fresh Food Café
Trafalgars Bistro
Trattoria Italian Kitchen
Tropika
Vij's

Vij's Rangoli
West
Yuji's Japanese Tapas
Zakkushi Charcoal
    Grill Diner
Zest Japanese Cuisine

WEST VANCOUVER

Beach House, The
Cactus Club Cafe
Earls
Fraîche
La Régalade French Bistro
Mangia e Bevi Ristorante
Salmon House, The
Zen Japanese Restaurant

WHITE ROCK

Earls

YALETOWN

Blue Water Cafe + Raw Bar
Brix Restaurant
Cactus Club Cafe
Cioppino's Mediterranean
    Grill & Enoteca
Coast Restaurant
Elixir
Glowbal Grill & Satay Bar
Goldfish Pacific Kitchen
La Terrazza
Pinkys Steakhouse
Plan B Lounge and Eatery
Provence Marinaside
Rodney's Oyster House
Simply Thai
Subeez Cafe

Restaurants by Food and Other Features

AFRICAN
Nyala African Cuisine

AMERICAS
Cobre
Doña Cata Mexican Foods
Lolita's South of the
   Border Cantina
Me & Julio
Rinconcito Salvadoreño
   Restaurant
Taco Shack, The

BARBEQUE
Memphis Blues Barbeque
   House

BREAKFAST
American Grille, The
Bacchus Restaurant
   & Piano Lounge
Beyond Restaurant
   and Lounge
Congee Noodle House
Diva at the Met
Elixir
Floata Seafood Restaurant
Globe@YVR
Griffins
Herons Restaurant
Ho Yuen Kee
La Bretagne Crêperie
Sciué Italian Bakery Caffé
So.Cial at Le Magasin
Sophie's Cosmic Cafe
Thomas Haas Patisserie
   and Café
Tomahawk Restaurant
Tomato Fresh Food Café
White Spot
YEW Restaurant + Bar

BREAKFAST, ALL DAY
Sophie's Cosmic Cafe
Tomahawk Restaurant

BRUNCH
Aurora Bistro
Bacchus Restaurant
   & Piano Lounge
Beach House, The
Beyond Restaurant
   and Lounge
Bistro Pastis
Bridges Seafood
   Restaurant
Chill Winston Restaurant
   & Lounge
Chutney Villa
Crave
Diva at the Met
Elixir
Fiddlehead Joe's Eatery
   & Bar
Fish House at Stanley
   Park, The
Fraîche
Globe@YVR
Glowbal Grill & Satay Bar
Gramercy Grill
Griffins
Hart House Restaurant
Herons Restaurant
Horizons Restaurant
Joe Fortes Seafood
   & Chop House
Lift
Lolita's South of the
   Border Cantina /
   Me & Julio
Provence Marinaside

Provence Mediterranean
   Grill
Raincity Grill
Salmon House, The
So.Cial at Le Magasin
Sophie's Cosmic Cafe
Stella's Tap and Tapas Bar
Subeez Cafe
Suvai Restaurant
Tomato Fresh Food Cafe
Trafalgars Bistro
William Tell Restaurant,
   The
YEW Restaurant + Bar

BURGERS
Cactus Club Cafe
Cascade Room, The
DB Bistro Moderne
Earls
Flying Beaver
Red Onion, The
Sophie's Cosmic Cafe
Splitz Grill
Steamworks Brewing Co.
Steamworks
   TransContinental
Subeez Cafe
Tomahawk Restaurant
White Spot

CHINESE (CASUAL)
Chen's Shanghai Restaurant
Congee Noodle House
Dai Tung Chinese
   Restaurant
Floata Seafood Restaurant
Grand View Szechuan
   Restaurant
Hon's Wun-Tun House
Ho Yuen Kee

Landmark Hot Pot House
Legendary Noodles
Ningtu Restaurant
Northern Delicacy
Won More Szechuan
  Cuisine

CHINESE (FINE DINING)

Fisherman's Terrace
  Seafood Restaurant
Imperial Chinese Seafood
  Restaurant
Kirin Mandarin Restaurant
Sea Harbour Seafood
  Restaurant
Shanghai Chinese Bistro
Sun Sui Wah Seafood
  Restaurant
Vogue Chinese Cuisine
Wild Rice
Zen Fine Chinese Cuisine

CONTEMPORARY WEST COAST

Aqua Riva
Aurora Bistro
Beyond Restaurant
  and Lounge
Bin 941 Tapas Parlour
Bin 942 Tapas Parlour
Bishop's
Blue Water Cafe + Raw Bar
Boneta
Bridges Seafood
  Restaurant
Brix Restaurant
C Restaurant
Cardero's
Cascade Room, The
Chill Winston Restaurant
  & Lounge
Chow
Crave

Delilah's Restaurant
  and Bar
Diva at the Met
Elixir
Fiddlehead Joe's Eatery
  & Bar
Fish House in Stanley
  Park, The
Five Sails Restaurant
Fraîche
Fuel Restaurant
Gastropod
Globe@YVR
Glowbal Grill & Satay Bar
Goldfish Pacific Kitchen
Gramercy Grill
Habit Lounge
Hart House Restaurant
Herons Restaurant
Horizons Restaurant
Lift
Moustache Café
Nu
Parkside
Pear Tree, The
Plan B Lounge and Eatery
Raincity Grill
Salmon House, The
So.Cial at Le Magasin
Suvai Restaurant
Tapastree Restaurant
Tomato Fresh Food Café
Trafalgars Bistro
West
YEW Restaurant + Bar

DESSERTS

Bacchus Restaurant
  & Piano Lounge
CinCin Ristorante & Bar
Elixir
Thomas Haas Patisserie
  and Café

Trafalgars Bistro
William Tell Restaurant,
  The
YEW Restaurant + Bar

DIM SUM

Chen's Shanghai
  Restaurant
Dai Tung Chinese
  Restaurant
Fisherman's Terrace
  Seafood Restaurant
Floata Seafood Restaurant
Hon's Wun-Tun House
Imperial Chinese Seafood
  Restaurant
Kirin Mandarin Restaurant
Sea Harbour Seafood
  Restaurant
Shanghai Chinese Bistro
Sun Sui Wah Seafood
  Restaurant

EDITORS' CHOICE

Beach House, The
Bishop's
Blue Water Cafe + Raw Bar
Bridges Seafood
  Restaurant
C Restaurant
Chambar Belgian
  Restaurant
Cioppino's Mediterranean
  Grill & Enoteca
Fish House in Stanley
  Park, The
Five Sails Restaurant
Fuel Restaurant
Hapa Izakaya
Kirin Mandarin Restaurant
Lift
Pear Tree, The
Phnom Penh Restaurant
Raincity Grill

Rodney's Oyster House
Salmon House, The
Salt Tasting Room
Sea Harbour Seafood
   Restaurant
Thomas Haas Patisserie
   and Café
Tojo's
Tomato Fresh Food Café
Trattoria Italian Kitchen
Vij's
Vij's Rangoli
West
YEW Restaurant + Bar
Yoshi Japanese Restaurant

FAMILY

Doña Cata Mexican Foods
Incendio
Incendio West
Marcello Pizzeria
   & Ristorante
Nat's New York Pizzeria
Pajo's
Red Onion, The
Rinconcito Salvadoreño
   Restaurant
Rocky Mountain Flatbread
   Company
Sophie's Cosmic Cafe
Thomas Haas Patisserie
   and Café
Tomato Fresh Food Café

FILIPINO

Josephine's Restaurant
   and Catering
Rekados
Sandy's Cuisine

FRENCH

Bacchus Restaurant
   & Piano Lounge
Bistro Pastis

Bistrot Bistro
Café de Paris
DB Bistro Moderne
Elixir
The Hermitage
Jules Bistro
La Belle Auberge
La Bretagne Crêperie
La Régalade French Bistro
Le Crocodile
Le Gavroche
Lumière with
   Daniel Boulud
Mistral French Bistro
Moustache Café
Parkside
Pied-à-Terre
Provence Marinaside
Provence Mediterranean
   Grill
Smoking Dog Bistro, The
William Tell Restaurant,
   The

GOOD VALUE

Akbar's Own Dining
   Lounge
Au Petit Café
Benkei Ramen Noodle Shop
Beyond Restaurant
   and Lounge
Bin 941 Tapas Parlour
Bin 942 Tapas Parlour
Congee Noodle House
Cru
Doña Cata Mexican Foods
Ezogiku Noodle Cafe
Floata Seafood Restaurant
Go Fish!
Gyoza King
Hon's Wun-Tun House
Incendio
Incendio West

Josephine's Restaurant
   and Catering
Kim Phung Vietnamese
   Restaurant
Kintaro Handmade
   Tonkotsu Ramen
Kitanoya Guu
La Bretagne Crêperie
La Régalade French Bistro
Legendary Noodles
Memphis Blues Barbeque
   House
Motomachi Shokudo
Moustache Café
Ningtu Restaurant
Nyala African Cuisine
Pajo's
Rinconcito Salvadoreño
   Restaurant
Sciué Italian Bakery Caffé
Sophie's Cosmic Cafe
Splitz Grill
Taco Shack, The
Thomas Haas Patisserie
   and Café
Trattoria Italian Kitchen
Zakkushi Charcoal
   Grill Diner

GOURMET TAKEOUT

Provence Marinaside
Provence Mediterranean
   Grill
Sciué Italian Bakery Caffé
So.Cial at Le Magasin
Vij's
Vij's Rangoli

INDIAN

Akbar's Own Dining
   Lounge
Annapurna
Ashiana Tandoori
   Restaurant

Café Kathmandu
Chutney Villa
East Is East / Chai Gallery
Original Tandoori Kitchen
Planet Veg
Vij's
Vij's Rangoli

INDONESIAN

Pondok Indonesia
Spice Islands Indonesian
    Restaurant

ITALIAN

Cibo Trattoria
CinCin Ristorante & Bar
Gusto di Quattro
Il Giardino di Umberto
Incendio
Incendio West
Italian Kitchen
La Buca
La Cucina Italiana
La Piazza Dario Ristorante
    Italiano
La Terrazza
Mangia e Bevi Ristorante
Marcello Pizzaria
    & Ristorante
Osteria Napoli Ristorante
Quattro on Fourth
Sciué Italian Bakery Caffé
Tramonto at the River
    Rock Casino Resort
Trattoria Italian Kitchen

IZAKAYA (JAPANESE SMALL PLATES)

Hapa Izakaya
Kingyo
Kitanoya Guu
Lime Japanese Cuisine

JAPANESE

Ajisai Sushi Bar
Benkei Ramen Noodle Shop
Dan Japanese Restaurant
Ezogiku Noodle Cafe
Gyoza King
Hapa Izakaya
Kamei Royale Japanese
    Restaurant
Kingyo
Kintaro Handmade
    Tonkotsu Ramen
Kitanoya Guu
Lime Japanese Cuisine
Motomachi Shokudo
Octopus Garden
    Restaurant
Okada Sushi Japanese
    Restaurant
Tojo's
Toshi Sushi
Yoshi Japanese Restaurant
Yuji's Japanese Tapas
Zakkushi Charcoal
    Grill Diner
Zen Japanese Restaurant
Zest Japanese Cuisine

KITSCHY

Lolita's South of the
    Border Cantina
Osteria Napoli Ristorante
Sophie's Cosmic Cafe
Tomahawk Restaurant

KOREAN

Hal Mae Jang Mo Jib
Hanwoori Korean
    Restaurant
Spice Alley Korean
    Restaurant & Bar

LATE NIGHT

Bin 941 Tapas Parlour
Bin 942 Tapas Parlour
Brix Restaurant
Chill Winston Restaurant
    & Lounge
CinCin Ristorante & Bar
Congee Noodle House
Fritz European Fry House
Glowbal Grill & Satay Bar
Gyoza King
Hal Mae Jang Mo Jib
Ho Yuen Kee
Kingyo
Lime Japanese Cuisine
Sanafir
Spice Alley Korean
    Restaurant & Bar
Subeez Cafe
Uva Wine Bar

MIDDLE EAST

Le Marrakech
    Moroccan Bistro
Sanafir

MALAYSIAN

Banana Leaf Malaysian
    Cuisine
Ellie Tropical Cuisine
Noodle Box, The
Tropika

MEXICAN

Doña Cata Mexican Foods
Lolita's South of the
    Border Cantina
Me & Julio
Taco Shack, The

OUTDOOR DINING

Beach House, The
Blue Water Cafe + Raw Bar
Bridges Seafood Restaurant

Brix Restaurant
C Restaurant
Cardero's
Chill Winston Restaurant
& Lounge
CinCin Ristorante & Bar
Cioppino's Meditterranean
Grill & Enoteca
Coast Restaurant
Crave
Earls
Fiddlehead Joe's Eatery
& Bar
Fish House in Stanley
Park, The
Flying Beaver
Glowbal Grill & Satay Bar
Go Fish!
Gotham Steakhouse
& Cocktail Bar
Hart House Restaurant
Hermitage, The
Il Giardino di Umberto
Incendio
Incendio West
Joe Fortes Seafood
& Chop House
Jules Bistro
La Bretagne Crêperie
La Terrazza
Lift
Nu
Pajo's
Parkside
Raincity Grill
Sciué Italian Bakery Caffé
Smoking Dog Bistro, The
So.Cial at Le Magasin
Spice Alley Korean
Restaurant & Bar
Steamworks Brewing Co.
Stella's Tap and Tapas Bar
Tapastree Restaurant

Trafalgars Bistro
Tramonto at the River
Rock Casino Resort
Trattoria Italian Kitchen
Zen Japanese Restaurant

OYSTERS

Blue Water Cafe + Raw Bar
Cannery Seafood
House, The
Joe Fortes Seafood
& Chop House
Rodney's Oyster House
Salmon House, The
So.Cial at Le Magasin

PIZZA

Earls
Flying Beaver
Incendio
Incendio West
Italian Kitchen
Marcello Pizzeria
& Ristorante
Nat's New York Pizzeria
Rocky Mountain Flatbread
Company
Steamworks Brewing Co.
Steamworks
TransContinental
Steveston Pizza Co.
Trattoria Italian Kitchen

POST-THEATRE
MENUS

Bin 941 Tapas Parlour
Bin 942 Tapas Parlour
Brix Restaurant
Chambar Belgian
Restaurant
Cobre
Sanafir
Subeez Cafe
Uva Wine Bar

William Tell Restaurant,
The
YEW Restaurant + Bar

ROMANTIC

Bacchus Restaurant
& Piano Lounge
Bin 941 Tapas Parlour
Bin 942 Tapas Parlour
Brix Restaurant
C Restaurant
Cru
Delilah's Restaurant
and Bar
Five Sails Restaurant
Fraîche
La Gavroche
La Terrazza
Lift
Lumière with
Daniel Boulud
Nu
Parkside
Pear Tree, The

SEAFOOD

Ajisai Sushi Bar
Blue Water Cafe + Raw Bar
Bridges Seafood
Restaurant
C Restaurant
Cannery Seafood
House, The
Cardero's
Coast Restaurant
Dan Japanese Restaurant
Fish House in Stanley
Park, The
Go Fish!
Imperial Chinese Seafood
Restaurant
Joe Fortes Seafood
& Chop House

Kamei Royale Japanese
Restaurant
Kingyo
Kirin Mandarin Restaurant
Kitanoya Guu
Lime Japanese Cuisine
Octopus Garden
Restaurant
Okada Sushi Japanese
Restaurant
Pajo's
Pear Tree, The
Provence Marinaside
Raincity Grill
Rodney's Oyster House
Salmon House, The
Sea Harbour Seafood
Restaurant
Shore Club, The
So.Cial at Le Magasin
Sun Sui Wah Seafood
Restaurant
Tojo's
Toshi Sushi
West
Yoshi Japanese Restaurant
Yuji's Japanese Tapas
Zen Fine Chinese Cuisine
Zen Japanese Restaurant
Zest Japanese Cuisine

SMALL PLATES

Bin 941 Tapas Parlour
Bin 942 Tapas Parlour
Brix Restaurant
Chill Winston Restaurant
& Lounge
Cobre
Cru
Elixir
Glowbal Grill & Satay Bar
Goldfish Pacific Kitchen
Habit Lounge

Hapa Izakaya
Kingyo
Kitanoya Gu
Lift
Lime Japanese Cuisine
Lolita's South of the
Border Cantina
Me & Julio
Nu
Plan B Lounge and Eatery
Rekados
Salt Tasting Room
Sanafir
Stella's Tap and Tapas Bar
Tapastree Restaurant
Uva Wine Bar
Wild Rice
YEW Restaurant + Bar
Yuji's Japanese Tapas

SOUP/SALAD/ SANDWICH

Irish Heather, The / Salty
Tongue Urban Deli
Planet Veg
Sciué Italian Bakery Caffé
So.Cial at Le Magasin
Thomas Haas Patisserie
and Café

STEAK

American Grille, The
Gotham Steakhouse
& Cocktail Bar
Griffins
Hy's Encore
Morton's the Steakhouse
Pinkys Steakhouse
Saltlik
Shore Club, The
Steamworks Brewing Co.
Steamworks
TransContinental

SUSHI

Ajisai Sushi Bar
Blue Water Cafe + Raw Bar
Dan Japanese Restaurant
Kamei Royale Japanese
Restaurant
Lime Japanese Cuisine
Octopus Garden
Restaurant
Okada Sushi Japanese
Restaurant
Tojo's
Toshi Sushi
Yuji's Japanese Tapas
Zen Japanese Restaurant
Zest Japanese Cuisine

THAI

Chao Phraya Thai
Restaurant
Green Basil Thai
Restaurant
Montri's Thai Restaurant
SalaThai Thai Restaurant
Sawasdee Thai Restaurant
Simply Thai
Tropika

VEGETARIAN

Annapurna
Hon's Wun-Tun
House (Robson
Street location)
Planet Veg

VIETNAMESE

Au Petit Café
Kim Phung Vietnamese
Restaurant
Phnom Penh
Pho Thai Hoa

VIEW

Aqua Riva
Beach House, The
Bridges Seafood
   Restaurant
C Restaurant
Cannery Seafood
   House, The
Cardero's
Fiddlehead Joe's Eatery
   & Bar
Fish House in Stanley
   Park, The
Five Sails Restaurant
Flying Beaver
Fraîche
Go Fish!
Hart House Restaurant
Horizons Restaurant
Le Gavroche
Lift

Nu
Pajo's
Raincity Grill
Salmon House, The
Tramonto at the River
   Rock Casino Resort

WINE SAVVY

Aurora Bistro
Bishop's
Blue Water Cafe + Raw Bar
C Restaurant
Cannery Seafood
   House, The
CinCin Ristorante & Bar
Cioppino's Mediterranean
   Grill & Enoteca
Coast Restaurant
Cobre
Cru
DB Bistro Moderne

Earls
Globe@YVR
Glowbal Grill & Satay Bar
Goldfish Pacific Kitchen
Gusto di Quattro
Hart House Restaurant
Herons Restaurant
Italian Kitchen
La Terrazza
Le Gavroche
Lumière with
   Daniel Boulud
Parkside
Quattro on Fourth
Raincity Grill
Salmon House, The
Sanafir
Trattoria Italian Kitchen
Uva Wine Bar
West
YEW Restaurant + Bar

TOP 200 RESTAURANTS

Ajisai Sushi Bar / ★

2081 W 42ND AVE, WEST SIDE; 604/266-1428

Despite being tucked in the quiet breezeway of a retail development, Ajisai has attracted an enthusiastic clientele in tony Kerrisdale. The encyclopedic menu of nigiri and sushi rolls is impressive not only for its size but also for adhering to traditional techniques. Authentic ingredients such as sticky natto (fermented soybeans) and slippery grated *yamaimo* (mountain potato) are prominently featured. The *una kyu* roll contrasts cool cucumber against savoury *unagi* (freshwater eel). Cornflakes add playful crunch to the spicy, and slightly misnamed, crispy hot tuna roll. Though cooked food selections are limited, the grilled black cod is exemplary with salty-sweet miso glazing wonderfully succulent fish. While the small space makes it difficult for large groups to be seated quickly, the speedy service helps minimize wait times. *$–$$; MC, V; no debit cards; lunch Tues–Sat, dinner Tues–Sun; no alcohol; no reservations; self-parking; map:C4.* &

Akbar's Own Dining Lounge / ★★☆

1905 W BROADWAY, WEST SIDE; 604/736-8180

If the wait is too long at Vij's (see review), head down the street to Akbar's—you won't be disappointed. From the kitchen, chef Kan proves his mastery of Northern Indian cuisine by cooking authentic Kashmiri and Mughlai dishes with puffy breads and delicately balanced spices and flavours. Shrimp pakoras, zingy with ginger and green chiles, are crunchily wrapped in sesame-seed batter. Lamb tikka has an equally surprising overcoat: a batter that hints at tandoori. Particularly good are the fiery prawn vindaloo or the more subtle prawn Kashmiri, cooked with butter, tomatoes, apples, and cream. The biryanis, heady with saffron and shot through with your choice of chicken, lamb, prawns, or vegetables, are exceptional. Vegetarian dishes include the irresistible *alu gobi*—chopped cauliflower and potato. A bonus is the wine list that's been designed to pair perfectly with the food. *$$; AE, MC, V; debit cards; lunch Mon–Fri, dinner Mon–Sat; full bar; no reservations; street parking; map:O7.* ♿

The American Grille / ★

7571 WESTMINSTER HWY (MARRIOTT HOTEL), RICHMOND; 604/232-2804

Located in the centre of Richmond, the American Grille offers a reprieve from the hundreds of Asian restaurants in the vicinity. The room, wrapped in wood, fabric, and warm tones, with floor-to-ceiling windows, welcomes locals and visitors alike. Chef Shane Lamb stepped into the kitchen in 2007 and introduced his Alberta roots to the menu. While steak dominates, the West Coast is represented with entrées such as pan-seared wild salmon with grilled fennel and lemon tomato preserve. In honor of clientele from Texas and California, chef Lamb offers his version of Southern fried chicken. The devoted and expertly trained waitstaff contributes to the restaurant's success. Focus is on BC wines. *$$$; AE, MC, V; debit cards; breakfast, lunch, dinner every day; full bar; reservations recommended; www.marriott.com; self-parking; map:C6.* ♿

Annapurna / ★

1812 W 4TH AVE, WEST SIDE; 604/736-5959

Annapurna was the first restaurant in the Lower Mainland to tap into the most highly developed vegetarian cuisine in the world. Every non-meat-eater who has opened a menu at an Indian restaurant only to see the same standard meatless dishes just one too many times is going to like Annapurna a lot. There are unfamiliar dishes to try, and some of them—such as *baigan bharta* (eggplant), a blend of smoky grilled, mashed eggplant with onions and tomatoes—are especially good. Service is casual. The small dining room has a ringside view of a busy intersection at Burrard and Fourth Avenue. *$; MC, V; debit cards; dinner every day; full bar; no reservations; www.annapurna vegetarian.com; street parking; map:O7.* ♿

Aqua Riva / ★★

200 GRANVILLE ST (ENTRANCE OFF HOWE ST), DOWNTOWN; 604/683-5599

Like its siblings, The Salmon House and Horizons, Aqua Riva boasts an outstanding view of the harbour, and being adjacent to Canada Place, it takes in the North Shore mountains, too. Generous portions of tapas, alder-grilled salmon, wood-fired pizzas, spit-roasted chicken, and slow-smoked barbecued ribs are served up by unfailingly friendly waitstaff. The stunning decor is especially soothing when you're settled into a booth with Dana Irving's Art Deco wraparound mural above you. Aqua Riva is very popular for lunch with the crowd that inhabits the adjacent office towers and with tourists from area hotels. The New World wine list features an impressive array of British Columbia wines. *$$$; AE, MC, V; debit cards; lunch Mon–Fri, dinner every day; full bar; reservations recommended; www.aquariva.com; self-parking; map:O7.* &

Ashiana Tandoori Restaurant / ★★

1440 KINGSWAY, EAST VANCOUVER; 604/874-5060

Devoted neighbourhood regulars have been enjoying Rick and Sonia Takhar's north Indian cuisine for over 25 years. Served sizzling on cast-iron platters, tandoori dishes are the house specialty. Peshawari lamb tikka is superb: fragrant chunks of meat are tender from a marinade of yogurt, garlic, ginger, and ground aromatic spices. Better known as butter chicken, *murgh makhani* is creamy and sweet in contrast to the deep, multilayered richness of Kashmiri lamb *rogan josh* that finishes with a sharp heat. Wipe your plate clean with chunks torn from an onion-and-coriander-stuffed tandoori *kulcha*. *$$; MC, V; debit cards; lunch Tues–Sun, dinner every day; full bar; no reservations; www.ashianatandoori.com; street parking; map:E3.* &

Au Petit Café / ★★

4851 MAIN ST, EAST VANCOUVER; 604/873-3328

Comfy home-style cooking keeps this miniature restaurant packed with satisfied diners. The insanely crusty baguettes used for the *bahn mi* (Vietnamese subs) are supplied by one of Vancouver's most established French bakeries. The coveted sandwiches sell out daily, so order early to avoid disappointment (the meatball *banh mi* is a favourite). French influences work their way into an aromatic stew of luscious chunks of beef, carrots, and tomatoes, though the soft pieces of tendon let you know you are still eating Asian cuisine. Served with perfect jasmine rice or crackling bread, the slow-simmered flavours will have you sighing with contentment. Run by the most civilized restaurant family imaginable, the service is efficient yet genuinely friendly. *$; cash only; dinner Thurs–Tues; no alcohol; no reservations; self-parking; map:E4.* &

Aurora Bistro / ★★★

2420 MAIN ST, EAST VANCOUVER; 604/873-9944

In this minimalist modern storefront, an anchor in the redeveloping and energetic Main Street 'hood, chef/owner Jeff Van Geest serves creative dishes emphasizing Pacific Northwest ingredients to a casually trendy crowd. On the inventive market-fresh menu, you might find bison carpaccio, spot prawns with grilled watermelon, or crispy white spring salmon served with cedar jelly. The ever-changing BC-only wine list is one of the best in the city. At brunch, locals line up for the five-spice doughnuts with maple syrup. *$$$; AE, MC, V; debit cards; lunch Mon–Fri, dinner every day, brunch Sat–Sun; full bar; reservations recommended; www.aurorabistro.ca; street parking; map:V7.*

Bacchus Restaurant & Piano Lounge / ★★★

**845 HORNBY ST (WEDGEWOOD HOTEL),
DOWNTOWN; 604/608-5319**

This elegant retreat in one of the city's best hotels hums with legal beagles from the neighbouring courthouse and local businesspeople by day. But in the evening—with its burgundy velvet benches, soft piano music, and servers who cater to your every whim—it lives up to its billing as the "most romantic restaurant in Vancouver." The changing French-influenced menu might include squab with tortellini of its own leg, wild salmon poached in extra virgin olive oil, or braised oxtail with Jerusalem artichoke purée. Afternoon tea (2–4pm on weekends) in front of the fireplace hits the spot, with finger sandwiches followed by tea pastries and freshly baked scones with Devon clotted cream, swished down by your favourite blend. Hope that the panna cotta with Summerland Bing cherries happens to be on the menu or surrender to the chocolate fondant with prunes and Armagnac ice cream. Best of all, Bacchus offers superb French cheese and fine wines. *$$$$; AE, MC, V; debit cards; breakfast, lunch, dinner every day, brunch Sat–Sun; full bar; reservations recommended; www.wedgewoodhotel.com; valet parking; map:S4.* &

Banana Leaf Malaysian Cuisine / ★★

820 W BROADWAY, WEST SIDE (AND BRANCHES); 604/731-6333

A perennial winner of local restaurant awards, Banana Leaf has been a Vancouver favourite since 1995. Of the trio, the Broadway location takes top marks for menu selection and consistency in both service and execution of Malaysian cuisine, a dramatic confluence of flavours from across Southeast Asia. *Roti canai*, light and flaky layered bread accompanied by a sweet curry dipping sauce, is a winning lead. Signature dishes include sambal green beans tossed with tomatoes and prawns and *rendang* boneless beef shank curry with a deep, rich heat. However, it's the Singapore chile crab that has a cultlike following—invariably, it leaves you licking your fingers and wanting more. The wine list is short and simple, but an icy bottle of Tiger beer is your best bet for putting a damper on the spice. *$$; AE, MC, V; debit cards; lunch, dinner every day; full bar; reservations recommended; www.bananaleaf-vancouver. com; street parking; map:D3.* &

The Beach House / ★★☆

150 25TH ST, WEST VANCOUVER; 604/922-1414

On sunny days, this waterside favourite offers unequalled water views from its year-round heated patio. Misty nights, when dining is accompanied by the basso profundo of distant foghorns, it's just as appealing. Lovingly restored, the green, shake-clad heritage building that first opened as a teahouse in 1912 sits only metres from the waters of Dundarave Beach. Recommended dishes include any pasta, halibut-and-chips at lunch, and osso buco at dinner. There's an impressive wine list, which features many good wines by the glass, the best of BC estate wineries, an excellent mix of U.S. West Coast varietals, and a sizable number of bottles from around the world. *$$$; AE, MC, V; debit cards; lunch Mon–Sat, dinner every day, brunch Sun; full bar; reservations recommended; www.atthebeachhouse.com; free parking.* &

Benkei Ramen Noodle Shop / ★★

1741 ROBSON ST, WEST END; 604/688-6980

Benkei holds its own as one of the newer contenders in this local hot zone of ramen joints. The air is redolent of simmering broth, enticing you to tuck into a bowl of your own. Choose among three types of broth: chicken consommé shoyu is the lightest; shio, tonkatsu broth made from slow-simmered pork bones, is glossy and rich; miso combines the pork and chicken broths. Concoct your own slurptastic soup from a list of toppings that includes green onion, boiled egg, spinach, and butter, the latter a surprisingly traditional add-on with corn. *Chasiu onigiri*, nori-wrapped triangles of rice surrounding chunks of barbecued pork, placates your stomach until soup arrives, and a side order of kimchee brightens your palate. *$; MC, V; debit cards; lunch, dinner Fri–Wed; no alcohol; no reservations; street parking; map:Q2.* &

Beyond Restaurant and Lounge / ★★★

**1015 BURRARD ST (CENTURY PLAZA HOTEL),
DOWNTOWN; 604/684-3474**

Locals who remember the dowdy old Century Plaza will be delighted by its cool, contemporary makeover, while visitors who have already discovered it may not realize that they've stumbled across one of the best-kept secrets in town. That applies to the chicly colorful decor, of course, but even more so to the dining room, where chef Paul Marshall's excellent, elegant West Coast cuisine emphasizes local flavours. Best of all are the prices: a whole rack of tender lamb costs just $29, while a seafood chowder bursting with salmon and shellfish in Pernod broth is only $7. There's some serious talent behind the bar, too, with the creative mixology of Chris Brown, winner of the prestigious 2007 Giffard International Cocktail Competition. *$$–$$$; AE, DC, MC, V; debit cards; breakfast, lunch, dinner every day, brunch Sun; full bar; no reservations; www.beyondrestaurant.com; valet parking; map:R4.* &

Bin 941 Tapas Parlour / ★★★
Bin 942 Tapas Parlour / ★★★

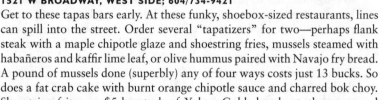

941 DAVIE ST, WEST SIDE; 604/683-1246
1521 W BROADWAY, WEST SIDE; 604/734-9421

Get to these tapas bars early. At these funky, shoebox-sized restaurants, lines can spill into the street. Order several "tapatizers" for two—perhaps flank steak with a maple chipotle glaze and shoestring fries, mussels steamed with habañeros and kaffir lime leaf, or olive hummus paired with Navajo fry bread. A pound of mussels done (superbly) any of four ways costs just 13 bucks. So does a fat crab cake with burnt orange chipotle sauce and charred bok choy. Shoestring frites—a $5 haystack of Yukon Golds hand-cut, then seasoned after frying—are the city's best-tasting potato bargain. A seat at 941's kitchen bar adds a free lesson in artful plate presentation. A savvy, well-conceived wine list. *$$; MC, V; debit cards; dinner every day; beer, wine, and liqueurs; no reservations; www.bin941.com; street parking; map:R5 and P8.* &

Bishop's / ★★★★

2183 W 4TH AVE, WEST SIDE; 604/738-2025

John Bishop was a pioneer on Fourth Avenue long before it became the West Side's hippest food corridor. He's a fanatic about local and seasonal ingredients: what his 40-seat restaurant serves is almost 100 percent organic. Chef Andrea Carlson's recent arrival and her haute barnyard-ish menu has brought new excitement to Bishop's. Her meticulously sourced dishes rely on ingredients that move from field to table with few stops in between, and partnerships with farmers mean many ingredients are grown or raised exclusively for the restaurant. (The kitchen even butchers whole animals and makes charcuterie.) Start your feast with petite Kumamotos and a sake-pear granité that takes the oyster experience to a new level, or a cool summertime soup of green garlic and Warba potato garnished with Dungeness crab. Standouts include a Pacific octopus terrine with a fava tip and baby fennel salad, and a tender Polderside duck breast paired with a duck confit empanada. For dessert, invoke childhood memories with the Maralumi chocolate bar. Want elegance? Choose the rhubarb cream tart. Manager Abel Jacinto oversees an eclectic list of fine wines with an emphasis on half bottles. *$$$$; AE, MC, V; debit cards; dinner every day (closed 2 weeks in Jan); full bar; reservations required; www.bishopsonline.com; street parking; map:O7.* &

Bistro Pastis / ★★

2153 W 4TH AVE, WEST SIDE; 604/731-5020

Autumnal colours, disarming elegance, and the flavours of Paris greet you in this classic French bistro. Locals adore the unassuming ambience and a menu that breathes new life into time-honored tradition. Warm up with French onion soup gratiné and then tuck into a simple salad of endive, double-smoked bacon, and poached free-range egg. If you can resist the steak tartare, order the 8-ounce triple-A Canadian New York steak with pommes frites and peppercorn sauce. Lighter options include grilled halibut with chanterelle and asparagus barley risotto, as well as pan-seared arctic char with wild rice and sautéed artichokes. Daily specials, like the coq au vin, are also highly recommended. Have a glass of pastis as you mull over the many French wine selections. *$$$; AE, MC, V; debit cards; lunch Tues–Fri, dinner Tues–Sun, brunch Sat–Sun; full bar; reservations recommended; www.bistropastis.com; street parking; map:N7.* &

Bistrot Bistro / ★★

1961 W 4TH AVE, WEST SIDE; 604/732-0004
Be prepared to sup on deliciously executed bistro fare in a simple yet elegant room. Co-owner Valerie Devin is the consummate hostess, guiding you through a menu that takes its inspiration from well-loved French classics. Begin with a 1-pound portion of tender mussels marinière or the warm onion Gruyère tart, and then settle in to enjoy one of the ample mains. The fisherman's stew pot is a generous mélange of snapper, shrimp, scallops, and clams, while the rabbit, in a white wine–cream sauce, is rich and intensely flavoured. Sides of gratin dauphinois and ratatouille can be ordered separately. The wine list features mainly French selections, with a few BC favourites. *$$–$$$; MC, V; debit cards; dinner Tues–Sun; beer and wine; reservations recommended; www.bistrotbistro.com; street parking; map:O7.* &

Blue Water Cafe + Raw Bar / ★★★½

1095 HAMILTON ST, YALETOWN; 604/688-8078
Nobody nets the ocean's bounty better than inventive chef Frank Pabst. He knows and loves fish, even the "unsung heroes," the yet-to-be-overexposed delicacies from the Pacific, such as green sea urchins. Spend an evening "barhopping" in this converted Yaletown warehouse turned posh seafood restaurant. First stop: The main bar, to slurp Cortes Island oysters and sip British Columbia's Blue Mountain Brut. Next stop: The raw bar, for Yoshi's wild salmon sashimi with chilled sake. Finally, settle into a plush banquette for the formidable seafood tower or one of Pabst's underdogs. The wine list is extensive, with a good selection of BC's best wines. Service is flawless. *$$$$; AE, MC, V; debit cards; dinner every day (also lunch in Dec); full bar; reservations recommended; www.bluewatercafe.net; street and valet parking; map:S5.* &

Boneta / ★★½

I W CORDOVA ST, GASTOWN; 604/684-1844
Imagination and hard work have turned this airy but neglected room into possibly the coolest and friendliest hangout in Gastown. Boneta's young partners bring high spirits and a good dose of experience gained in some of Vancouver's best restaurants. This marriage of playfulness and discipline is evident in the food. A starter of stuffed squid, shrimp, tomato chutney, and house-made harissa sparkles with refinement. Roasted duck breast with couscous balances sophistication and comfort. The exuberant desserts incorporate elements such as passion fruit foams, lime marshmallows, and Sichuan spices. A deft wine list provides smartly delicious choices while the cocktails are a real standout,

---

COCKTAIL CULTURE

Vancouver has had a fondness for a well-shaken drink ever since the Sylvia Hotel opened the city's first cocktail lounge in the 1950s. Back in the 1980s and early '90s, in fact, Delilah's set a North American standard with its extensive list of creative cocktails. Today Vancouver is once again leading the way, this time with its passion for local, seasonal ingredients. In the last few years, a handful of local mixologists have made Vancouver a world leader in handcrafted cocktails. Sure, you can still find plenty of places serving premade margarita mixes and "'tini" drinks. But more and more, you can find passionate bartenders shaking and stirring classically inspired cocktails made with juices squeezed à la minute and housemade infusions based on seasonal, organic produce. If you're look-ing for a drink—a real drink—here's where to go, and who'll be wielding the cocktail shaker:

BLUE WATER CAFE + RAW BAR (1095 Hamilton St; 604/688-8078)

What's new and in season? Whatever it is, Ron Oliver will find a way to work it into a fresh, lively concoction that may seem unexpected but works as well as any classic. www.bluewatercafe.net.

BONETA (1 W Cordova St; 604/684-1844)

This funky Gastown eatery is home to Vancouver's cocktail all-star team of Mark Brand, Steve Da Cruz, Chris Stearns, and Justin Tisdall. Try something crazy and new from the "tribute list" of cocktails created in honor of the

---

expertly mixed by some of the best bartenders in the city. *$$–$$$; AE, MC, V; debit cards; lunch Fri, dinner Tues–Sat; beer and wine; reservations recom-mended; www.boneta.ca; self-parking; map:U4.* ㅎ

Bridges Seafood Restaurant / ★★

1696 DURANLEAU ST, GRANVILLE ISLAND; 604/687-4400

This popular Granville Island destination is actually three restaurants in one: a cozy pub and casual bistro on the main floor, and an elegant fine-dining res-taurant upstairs. Seafood is the focus here, ranging from the bistro's smoked-salmon pizza and seafood Caesar salad to the restaurant's fusiony fare, such as pan-seared Alaskan sablefish with green Thai coconut curry butter and mango cilantro salsa. But the best reason to come here is the patio. On sunny afternoons, Vancouverites and visitors alike flock to the massive—and mas-sively popular—umbrella-decked space, where the people-watching is almost as spectacular as the views of False Creek and the North Shore mountains. *$$–$$$$; AE, E, MC, V; debit cards; lunch, dinner every day, brunch Sun; full bar; reservations recommended (dining room); www.bridgesrestaurant.com; self-parking; map:Q6.* ㅎ

best bartenders around the city, or get the guys to mix up a batch of classics such as the Ramos gin fizz or Sazerac. *www.boneta.ca.*

THE CASCADE ROOM (2616 Main St; 604/709-8650)

Nick Devine has put together the city's largest cocktail list, comprised of dozens of forgotten classics including flips, sours, daisies, and crustas. But Devine still finds time to create a fresh, new daily drink based on whatever's in season—or whatever it is you fancy. *www.thecascade.ca.*

CHAMBAR BELGIAN RESTAURANT (562 Beatty St; 604/879-7119)

Chambar really glammed up Vancouver's cocktail scene with some of the city's most celebrated bartenders. Look for exciting, exotic flavour combinations that really work. *www.chambar.com.*

WEST (2881 Granville St; 604/738-8938)

What are you having for dinner? Tell Dave Wolowidnyk, and he'll create a cocktail to pair with it. Better yet, sit at the bar and let Vancouver's most loquacious cocktail raconteur entertain you with his stories. *www.westrestaurant.com.*

YEW RESTAURANT + BAR AT THE FOUR SEASONS HOTEL
(791 W Georgia St; 604/689-9333)

This recently renovated room features soaring ceilings, chic decor, and see-and-be-seen seating. But the real action is behind the bar, where a talented team craft classic and new cocktails with care and precision. *www.fourseasons.com.*

—Joanne Sasvari

Brix Restaurant / ★★

1138 HOMER ST, YALETOWN; 604/915-9463

Many a kiss has been stolen in the restaurant's outdoor courtyard, where flickering candlelight and charming seclusion lend an air of romance. With its late-night hours and quietly elegant interiors, Brix is a favourite with locals and cross-town partygoers looking for an escape from the trendy pulse of Yaletown. Mains include pan-seared Alaskan sablefish, Alberta bison rib-eye, and beef short-rib pasta, while the small plates range from smoked wild sockeye salmon crepes to a pound of fresh Salt Spring Island mussels. Once you're satiated, head downstairs to George Lounge, where the cocktails and the crowd will keep you buzzing into the night. *$$–$$$; AE, MC, V; debit cards; dinner Mon–Sat; full bar; reservations recommended; www.brix vancouver.com; valet parking Thurs–Sat; map:S5.* &

C Restaurant / ★★★½

2-1600 HOWE ST, DOWNTOWN; 604/681-1164

In a city with no shortage of trendy newcomers, Harry Kambolis's decade-old C Restaurant continues to rise above the competition with food that is devotedly local, sustainable, and nothing short of a work of art. The ambience alone is unbeatable—cool and modern, with a glass front and patio gazing across False Creek to Granville Island. But it's the food that continues to draw raves. Executive chef Rob Clark made sustainable seafood fashionable before the cognoscenti had even heard of the Monterey Bay Aquarium. He and chef de cuisine Quang Dang have also made it delicious: cauliflower soup comes with a briny slab of sea urchin, sablefish is basted with black olives, seared Bayne Sound scallops are wrapped in their signature octopus bacon, salmon is served with pine mushroom ravioli. Unexpected local ingredients like Granville Island sake lees make regular appearances, and the wine list is eclectic and extensive. Best bet: Put yourself in Clark and Dang's competent hands and order whatever is fresh that day. *$$$$; AE, DC, E, MC, V; debit cards; lunch Mon–Fri, dinner every day; full bar; reservations recommended; www.crestaurant.com; valet parking; map:Q6.*

Cactus Club Cafe / ★★½

575 W BROADWAY ST, WEST SIDE (AND BRANCHES); 604/714-6000

This successful chain has captured the middle dining ground with its crowd-wooing formula of reasonable prices, casual luxe interiors, and a bevy of serving beauties. Now, with Rob Feenie (formerly of Lumière and Feenie's fame) at the helm as "Food Concept Architect," expect some of the Iron Chef's classics, as well as new creations, to make an appearance on the menu. Loyal fans already love the butternut squash ravioli and sake-miso-marinated sablefish. Overall, the menu features some innovative twists while still feeling very familiar to less adventurous palates. Asian influences inflect dishes like the favourite spicy chicken with sweet chile glaze and scallions, or the Sichuan beans with onions and serrano peppers. Otherwise, expect the gamut of burgers, pastas, steak, and seafood options. Crowds flock for the hand-squeezed lime margaritas and the signature locally brewed beers. *$$; AE, MC, V; debit cards; lunch, dinner every day; full bar; no reservations; www.cactusclubcafe. com; street parking; map:P7.* ⚊

Café de Paris / ★

751 DENMAN ST, WEST END; 604/687-1418

Since this cozy French bistro opened in 1977, it's been a favourite with diners for its hearty interpretations of such traditional fare as gooey French onion soup and savoury cassoulet, as well as its award-winning wine list. On its best days, it's like a tiny taste of Paris plunked down on busy Denman. Its table d'hôte menu is still a good deal, as is the annual fall wild game festival. However, since the departure of chef Scott Kidd, some of the sizzle has gone out of the kitchen, and the spotty service is occasionally reminiscent of one of the few things about Paris that is not so *merveilleux*. Still, the fries—authentic, crispy-tender frites—are the best in the city, and not to be missed under any circumstances. *$$$; AE, MC, V; debit cards; lunch Mon–Fri, dinner every day; full bar; reservations recommended; www.cafedeparisbistro.com; street parking; map:Q2.* &

Café Kathmandu / ★★

2779 COMMERCIAL DR, EAST VANCOUVER; 604/879-9909
Fueled by a desire to increase awareness of his native country's culture and cuisine, in 2005 Abi Sharma opened Vancouver's only Nepali restaurant. He warmly welcomes guests to this peaceful room bathed in traditional Buddhist colours of saffron yellow and sky blue. Its walls are adorned with striking photographs of Nepal's people and landscape, prayer flags draping the ceiling. A concise menu showcases the culinary influences of India, Tibet, and China on this simple, subtly flavoured fare. Lead off with *choilaa*, tender chunks of pork or chicken brightly flavoured with lemon, garlic, and cilantro. Or tickle your taste buds with *bhatmaas*, crunchy toasted soybeans enlivened by garlic and ginger. Curries are softer and more elegant than their Indian cousins; *khasi ko masu* is tender goat meat simmered in a rich, hearty sauce. Vegetarians won't go wanting with dishes such as *kaauli*, turmeric-infused cauliflower with fenugreek potatoes, and *quaanti*, mixed sprouted beans simmered with roasted coriander and dried Himalayan chives. Close out your meal with a soothing cup of spiced *chiyaa* (chai). *$; MC, V; debit cards; dinner Tues–Sun; full bar; no reservations; www.cafekathmandu.com; street parking; map:E3.* &

The Cannery Seafood House / ★★★☆

2205 COMMISSIONER ST, EAST VANCOUVER; 604/254-9606
For fresh, straightforward seafood, it's worth the trek to this relatively remote east-end dockside location. Due to port security, access from downtown is via Clark Drive and through a security checkpoint. The restaurant itself looks modest, but the interior boasts expansive water and mountain views. You'll find a baker's dozen of high-quality seafood dishes on the fresh sheet, including delicate arctic char, juicy grilled swordfish, and meaty ahi tuna. Salmon Wellington has been a house specialty since 1971; it's still a winner, but so is the smoked BC black cod, aka sablefish. Those who don't go for fish are catered to with house-smoked rack of lamb and filet mignon. The award-winning wine list is one of the city's best. Service is friendly and enthusiastic. *$$$; AE, MC, V; debit cards; lunch Mon–Fri, dinner every day; full bar; reservations recommended; www.canneryseafood.com; self-parking; map:F2.* &

Cardero's / ★

1583 COAL HARBOUR QUAY, DOWNTOWN; 604/669-7666
Get a seat on the coveted patio, and take in the sparkling views of Burrard Inlet and the joggers making their way along the winding Coal Harbour seawall. The nautical-themed decor takes its cue from a kitchen that specializes in seafood, as well as "chops and a wok." Seared sesame-crusted BC albacore tuna with wasabi and soy, and the crispy wok squid with zingy

garlic chile seasoning, both make for great starters. Specialties include the soy- and brown sugar–glazed wild Pacific salmon baked on a cedar plank in a wood oven, and the double-cut, wild pepper–crusted pork chops with sage sun-dried cranberry sauce. Enjoy a glass of BC Gewürtztraminer before going for a pint at the adjoining Marine Pub. *$$–$$$; AE, MC, V; debit cards; lunch, dinner every day; full bar; reservations recommended; www.vancouver dine.com/carderos/home.html; valet and street parking; map:R2.* &

The Cascade Room / ★★

2616 MAIN ST, EAST VANCOUVER; 604/709-8650

Named after one of Vancouver's original brews, this restaurant/lounge is an ideal nighttime spot for some fabulous drinks and good eats. The room is all quirky chic—retro booths and banquettes, deep red wallpaper accents, whimsical hanging lamps. The owners of the next-door Habit continue with casual options for unassuming dining in this new venture. Appetizers include spiced calamari with smoked paprika breading, as well as crisp cod and potato cakes with curried yam ragout and crème fraîche. The kitchen also does a solid job with Moroccan lamb pizza, as well as a classic beef burger with hand-cut fries. Be sure to check out the finely crafted cocktails from talented mixologist Nick Devine and savvy wine selections. *$$; MC, V; debit cards; dinner every day; full bar; no reservations; www.thecascade.ca; street parking; map:E3.* &

Chambar Belgian Restaurant / ★★★

562 BEATTY ST, DOWNTOWN; 604/879-7119

Karri and chef Nico Schuermans opened this gorgeous room in 2005 and, almost overnight, became the darlings of the dining scene. Their success continues unabated, primarily because the restaurant offers stylish, tightly wrought cuisine alongside impeccable service. The vibe is hip and confident, from the exposed brick walls and crimson palette to the discerning diners who sit at the bar. Although initially Schuermans focused on his native Belgian cuisine, more recently he has been pushing his own culinary envelope. Menu highlights include tender charred baby octopus with an avocado and *aji* vinaigrette; braised lamb shank with honey, figs, cinnamon, and cilantro; and slow-roasted venison loin and sausage with forest mushroom ragout. And don't forget to indulge in a glass of Belgian beer over your moules frites. The smart wine list has strong French showings. Tip: If you're in the neighbourhood, make sure to visit their next-door Café Medina, where the best breakfast and brunch in the city can be found. *$$$; AE, MC, V; debit cards; dinner every day; full bar; reservations recommended; www.chambar.com; valet and street parking; map:U4.* &

Chao Phraya Thai Restaurant / ★

2325 CAMBIE ST, WEST SIDE; 604/732-3939

Despite the incongruous faux Mediterranean decor, authentic Thai cuisine is found at this Fairview Slopes favourite. Bargain-priced weekday lunch specials make for inexpensive midday meals, but the comprehensive dinner menu features dishes like *moo pad bai gra-pow*, spicy minced pork with hot chile and fresh basil, and a palate-scorching salad of green mango and green papaya tossed in a tangy lime vinaigrette. *Tung choy* is a simple stir-fry of morning glory leaves with soy sauce and garlic, a contrast to the coconut-milk creaminess of *gaeng ka-ri*, mild yellow curry with your choice of meat. Curb the capsaicin count with Coconut Surprise, refreshing coconut water brought to your table in its shell, together with a long-handled spoon for scooping out the lightly sweet, tender meat. *$–$$; MC, V; debit cards; lunch, dinner every day; full bar; no reservations; street parking; map:T7.* &

Chen's Shanghai Restaurant / ★★

8095 PARK RD, RICHMOND; 604/304-8288
The big attractions here are the rustic house-made dumplings and pastries. The *xiao long bao* (soup dumplings) are arguably the best in the city. Swollen with rich, clear broth (the soup is inside the dumpling), they are served with dark Chinese vinegar and ginger dipping sauces. Hold the parcel in a soup spoon and gently sip while trying not to scald your tongue. Lush, flaky daikon (radish) pastries are spiked with ham. The spicy *dan dan* noodles are dressed in a peanut sauce that packs surprising heat. Though desserts are not a Chinese cuisine forte, the red bean spring rolls provide an elegant finish, while the bittersweet black sesame pastries are worth a visit in their own right. This popular restaurant can get very busy, so sharing a large table may be a necessity. All the better to see what other diners have ordered. *$–$$; cash only; lunch, dinner Thurs–Tues; no alcohol; no reservations; self-parking; map:D6.* &

Chill Winston Restaurant & Lounge / ★★

3 ALEXANDER ST, GASTOWN; 604/288-9575
Chill Winston is laid-back and sexy in a grown-up way. Low-slung black leather chairs are set against a sleek black bar. Candlelight is punctuated by pools of light from chic designer fixtures. An island kitchen has foodie front-row seats for chef John Jesten's culinary calisthenics. And, perhaps best of all, some of Vancouver's premier alfresco patio dining is here at Gassy Jack's Maple Leaf Square, the nexus of Gastown's cobblestone streets. The menu dictum encourages diners to "order lots . . . and share it all," focusing on solidly executed seasonal comfort food. Meals are covered round the clock: their brunch menu promises "lazy Sunday morningish deliciousness," and weekday lunches offer soups and salads to accompany top-notch sandwiches. Dinner service features small plates such as wild sockeye salmon and Dungeness crab tempura rolled together with daikon and enoki mushrooms, ideal finger fare to accompany a selection from the extensive list of cocktails and wines by the glass. Larger dishes include a Half Duck, a duo of confit leg and oven-roasted breast in a Grand Marnier jus, perfectly paired with thoroughly addictive butter-poached pancetta potatoes. Despite their self-indulgent monikers—case in point, Mercury the Winged Messenger—desserts are not to be missed. *$$; AE, MC, V; debit cards; lunch, dinner every day, brunch Sun; full bar; reservations recommended; www.chillwinston.ca; street parking; map:V3.* &

Chow / ★★★

3121 GRANVILLE ST, WEST SIDE; 604/608-2469

Chef Jean-Christophe Poirier, formerly of Lumière and Montreal's Toqué, has brought a chic, lively dining energy to the South Granville neighbourhood. Mingle with friends at the modish bar and lounge area, then make your way to the adjoining and equally sleek dining corridor. Poirier adapts his French culinary sensibilities to West Coast abundance, exactingly sourcing fresh, organic ingredients from local suppliers. Pan-seared Vancouver Island scallops with house-made garganelli pasta, baby oyster mushrooms, and smoky bacon exemplify a simple yet expert attention to flavours. The organic duck breast, tagliatelle pasta, sweet garlic purée, and rosemary duck jus melds deft execution with the finest-quality ingredients. The wine list has excellent local showings, and the reinvented classic cocktails are well worth sampling. *$$–$$$; AE, JCB, MC, V; debit cards; dinner every day; full bar; reservations recommended; www.chow-restaurant.com; street and self-parking; map:D3.* &

Chutney Villa / ★★

147 E BROADWAY, EAST VANCOUVER; 604/872-2228

The saffron and olive walls of this casual room are adorned with antique Indian carvings, a warm backdrop complementing Chindi Varardarajulu's fiery South Indian dishes. Unlike northern Punjabi fare, this regional cuisine's complex range of flavours incorporates whole spices in addition to ground and significantly ups the heat quotient. *Tiffins* are perfect for lighter meals—choices include delicately crisped *masala dosa* or lamb-stuffed *murtabak*, paratha filled with cinnamon- and star anise–braised lamb. Accompanying house-made chutneys change daily; a selection of two sweet and two savoury/spicy options might feature pear banana, coconut, and onion. Those with heartier appetites won't be left wanting after tucking into a *taali*: a cavalcade of seven dishes and dessert served atop a banana leaf, with entrées such as Mysore lamb cooked in Chettinad spices. *$; MC, V; debit cards; lunch, dinner Wed–Mon, brunch Sat–Sun; beer and wine; no reservations; www.chutneyvilla. com; street parking; map:E3.* &

CinCin Ristorante & Bar / ★★★

1154 ROBSON ST, DOWNTOWN; 604/688-7338

From the Mediterranean-inspired decor to the wood-fired open kitchen, this bustling room exudes warmth. The crowd-pleasing menu combines Italian influences with West Coast flavours. Be sure to order the antipasto platter; then, among the pastas, you might try aged biodynamic risotto with squash, speck (an Italian bacon), and stracchino cheese. Other options include Kurobuta pork tenderloin with savoy cabbage and a licorice reduction, roasted lamb saddle with mint and spinach tortellini, or a simple pizza topped with wild mushrooms and pecorino. Enjoy a cocktail at the bar, have a light meal in the lounge (till midnight), or dine on the heated garden terrace overlooking Robson Street. Surrender to pastry chef Thierry Busset's pear charlotte and petits fours. Wine takes centre stage with an award-winning 1,300-label cellar, and it's good value because of a reduced mark-up. *$$$$; AE, MC, V; debit cards; dinner every day; full bar; reservations recommended; www.cincin. net; valet parking; map:R3.* &

Cioppino's Mediterranean Grill & Enoteca / ★★★☆

1133 HAMILTON ST, YALETOWN; 604/688-7466

It takes just one visit to the celebrity-studded Cioppino's to acquire an addiction to chef Pino Posteraro's Mediterranean dishes—and, of course, his $2.5 million wine cellar. The talented and passionate Posteraro named this sunny Yaletown restaurant as a pun, melding his name with San Francisco's delicious seafood stew, cioppino. His French-inspired Mediterranean cooking and wine-pairing ability is an almost perfect marriage. Signature creations—grilled calamari with mushrooms, sage, and black olives; linguine with lobster; free-range chicken with Sauternes-mustard sauce—have earned him a loyal following in his side-by-side pair of Yaletown restaurants. Stick to a tasting menu ($55 and up), and you'll have one of the most brilliant meals in town. For dessert, indulge in the "soft"-heart chocolate cake with vanilla custard and ice cream, caramelized pear tarte Tatin, or *limoncello* cheesecake with lime-tequila sorbet. Next door, the Enoteca (604/685-8462) is a low-key wine bar with a rotisserie. *$$$$; AE, MC, V; debit cards; lunch Mon–Fri, dinner Mon–Sat (closed spring break); full bar; reservations recommended; www.cioppinosyaletown.com; street and valet parking; map:S4.* &

Coast Restaurant / ★★★☆

1257 HAMILTON ST, YALETOWN; 604/685-5010

Sibling to Glowbal Grill and Italian Kitchen (see review), Coast is a posh seafood restaurant offering simply prepared fish from around the world. You can hide in a booth on the upper level favoured by celebrities, lounge on the patio, or sit around the 12-seat communal grill watching chef Josh Wolfe prepare your dinner. While he chops, simmers, and sautés—everything from sashimi-grade ahi tuna to Dungeness crab and venison—diners pepper him with questions and talk amongst themselves. There's a 17-foot wall of wine offering more than 2,700 local and international choices. At press time a new location was planned for 2009. *$$$; MC, V; debit cards; dinner every day; full bar; reservations recommended; www.coastrestaurant.ca; valet parking Thurs–Sat; map:S5.* &

Cobre / ★★★☆

52 POWELL ST, GASTOWN; 604/669-2396

The name of this Gastown restaurant means "copper" in Spanish, which accounts for the copper ceiling scoops radiating from the open kitchen. Start in the sexy bar, where they muddle gently priced mojitos and Latino-themed cocktails like there's no *mañana*. Chef Stuart Irwin, who had a Mexican mother-in-law, is a fiesta-fired follower of neuvo Latino and a longtime exponent of tapas dining (Wild Rice, Bin 941 Tapas Parlour). In his latest kitchen, he serves up a greatest hits list of the Latin larder—small plates of sprightly seafood ceviches, a comforting oxtail posole, lush Dungeness arepas, and trios of tacos with pulled duck, salmon, or pork saddle. Jason Kelly's hip wine list leans toward the Southern Hemisphere—perfect pairings for the Latino offerings. *$$–$$$; AE, MC, V; debit cards; dinner every day; full bar; reservations recommended; www.cobrerestaurant.com; street parking; map:V3.*

Congee Noodle House / ★

141 E BROADWAY, EAST VANCOUVER; 604/879-8221
Though the decor is bare bones, the extensive menu and warming Cantonese noodle-house fare attract diners from all over the city. The expertly handled house specialty, congee (rice broth), is cooked to a creamy finish with a choice of ingredients. The sliced fish congee is remarkably elegant with fresh seafood flavours, while the Hong Kong–style minced beef congee is soothing comfort in a bowl. Tender braised beef brisket scented with star anise tops snappy al dente noodles and soup. Shredded pork and bean sprouts chow mein is served with crispy Hong Kong–style noodles, and the dry beef fried rice noodles (chow fun) arrives wok-hot and savoury. Blanched gai lan (Chinese broccoli) with an oyster-flavoured sauce rounds out the meal. Late-night dining brings out a traditional small plates menu as well as an interesting cast of characters. *$; cash only; breakfast–late night every day; no alcohol; no reservations; street and self-parking; map:D2.* ⌖

Crave / ★★

3941 MAIN ST, EAST VANCOUVER; 604/872-3663
Imagine a modest, cozy neighbourhood spot where the food is unassuming yet confidently executed, where the ambience is polished yet at ease enough for a group of friends to chatter over flickering candlelight. The kitchen playfully re-creates the familiar in dishes that don't stint on flavour or ingredient quality. Start with the buttermilk fried chicken cobb salad, the popcorn shrimp with creamy chile sauce, or the "shorty" poutine with truffle Parmesan frites and short-rib jus. Mains are also dependable takes on classic favourites, from sun-dried tomato and basil meat loaf with green peppercorn sauce to "shorty" rigatoni with beef short-rib tomato ragout and pecorino cheese. Brunch items, like whole-wheat challah French toast and the Dungeness crab cake benny, are perfect on a balmy day on their outdoor patio. The wine list is modest, with a few select BC and Californian showings. At press time a new location had opened in West Vancouver. *$$–$$$; AE, MC, V; debit cards; lunch Tues–Fri, dinner Tues–Sun, brunch Sat–Sun; full bar; no reservations; www.craveonmain.ca; street parking; map:E3.* ⌖

Cru / ★★★

1459 W BROADWAY, WEST SIDE; 604/677-4111
The focus at the aptly named Cru, an inviting restaurant done in warm coffee and butterscotch hues, is food and wine pairing. Each item on the

imaginative menu is color-coded to match the wines (all sold by the glass). There's a three-course prix-fixe meal, but we recommend grazing through the casual small plates that come in two sizes. The Caesar salad is a signature dish, and Cru serves some of the best duck confit in town. Another good choice is the bruschetta trio: with fig and walnut tapenade; marinated peppers, fennel, and pine nuts; and white beans with sage. *$$; AE, MC, V; debit cards; dinner every day; full bar; reservations recommended; www.cru. ca; street parking; map:C2.* &

Dai Tung Chinese Restaurant / ★★☆

108-1050 KINGSWAY, EAST VANCOUVER; 604/872-2268
With traditional dim sum carts rapidly disappearing in Vancouver, here midday diners are often shoulder to shoulder in the foyer as they willingly queue up for old-school service and value. Corn and prawn *har gow* are delicate, flowerlike steamed dumplings, the sweetness of each ingredient playing off of the other. Deep-fried squid is deftly prepared, remarkably light and crispy with a garlic and chile kick. And be sure to check the menu for Dai Tung's signature dish: "wind sand"—organic free-range chicken served cold-poached and delicately spiced. It's cash only at lunchtime, but your wallet will barely feel the hit at this popular standby. *$–$$; MC, V; debit cards; lunch, dinner every day; full bar; reservations recommended; self-parking; map:E3.* &

Dan Japanese Restaurant / ★★★

2511 W BROADWAY, WEST SIDE; 604/677-6930
Finesse and hospitality are the mantra here, and simple dishes sparkle. Tamago sushi (egg omelet) blossoms with eggy richness, sweet mirin, and the clean brininess of dashi stock. Red tuna sushi is lovingly cut and laid out so that the grain of the fish is perfectly set off. Asparagus tempura is the epitome of pale, crisp lightness, a hallmark of sure-handed cooking. Charred and savoury grilled pork cheeks are lifted by a vivid chile ponzu sauce. *Dan* means "warmth," and the welcoming staff and open kitchen certainly add to the easy mood. Look to the specials board for sake recommendations, including local artisan sakes. *$$–$$$; AE, MC, V; debit cards; dinner Wed–Mon; beer and wine; no reservations; self-parking; map:C2.* &

DB Bistro Moderne / UNRATED

2563 W BROADWAY, WEST SIDE; 604/739-7115
There is a sister restaurant in New York, where the now-iconic DB burger was created—spawning a legion of imitators—and, yes, you'll find a version of it here. You'll also find a West Coast version, which is, in fact, vegetarian. This is just one example of the creativity Daniel Boulud and executive chef Stepahne Istel are bringing—literally—to the table. Roasted black cod with a brandade, herb, and bacon crust with potatoes paysanne, razor clams, and cockles in chowder is one example of the approachable yet innovative meals. Next door is the re-invented Lumière with Daniel Boulud, but DB Bistro Moderne is worth a visit or two all its own. It is the epitome of creative, hearty

(and always convivial) bistro cuisine—a contemporary interpretation of an ageless classic. *$$$; AE, DC, MC, V; debit cards; lunch, dinner every day; full bar; reservations recommended; self-parking; map:C2.*

Delilah's Restaurant and Bar / ★★

1789 COMOX ST, WEST END; 604/687-3424

The combination of elegant decadence, campy fun, and delicious food has made Delilah's a West End institution and a rite of passage for local foodies. Diners tick boxes on the ambitious menu for a two- or four-course meal. Recent standouts include a lush cauliflower soup with Cambozola, an intense porcini-dusted bison carpaccio, and a sunny cioppino with fresh seafood. Delilah's is a temple to the martini, and the inventive cocktail menu is second to none. The whimsically named lemon-infused Edsel and the darkly raspberry Ruby Slipper are seriously made and seriously potent. The red velvet banquettes and art nouveau lamps will have you imagining 1930s underground Paris; the top-notch service staff provide just the right amount of impish humor. *$$–$$$; AE, DC, MC, V; debit cards; dinner Tues–Sun; full bar; reservations recommended; www.delilahs.ca; self-parking; map:P3.* &

Diva at the Met / ★★★⯪

645 HOWE ST (METROPOLITAN HOTEL), DOWNTOWN; 604/602-7788

This diva may not be grabbing the headlines that some of her flashier sisters do, but that's all the more reason to enjoy her cool, airy design and executive chef Dino Renaerts's exquisite cuisine. Look for beautifully constructed, seasonal-ingredient-driven dishes such as truffled celeriac agnolotti or pheasant breast wrapped in Tyrolean bacon. Desserts play almost as big a starring role at Diva—they're by North Vancouver's award-winning Thomas Haas, considered one of the best pastry chefs in North America (see review of Thomas Haas Patisserie)—and make for a perfect post-theatre pick-me-up. The wide selection of Pacific Northwest wines provides a perfect supporting cast. And don't even think about skipping Diva's breakfast or brunch, which features dishes such as smoked black cod and poached eggs or citrus maple croissant French toast. It just might be the best brekkie in the city, definitely worth a round of applause of its own. *$$$–$$$$; AE, DC, JCB, MC, V; debit cards; breakfast, lunch, dinner every day, brunch Sat–Sun; full bar; reservations recommended; www.metropolitan.com/diva; valet parking; map:S3.* &

Doña Cata Mexican Foods / ★★

5076 VICTORIA DR, EAST VANCOUVER; 604/436-2232

The room may be small and plain, but the food in this authentic, family-run taqueria more than makes up for any shortcomings in ambience. Back home in Mexico, cook and co-owner Brenda Castrejon's grandmother ran a famous taqueria, and it's clear Castrejon inherited her skills in the kitchen. She prepares seven succulent fillings for tacos, slow-cooked spiced meats such as the carnitas (pork), *longaniza* (sausage), and *bistec* (beef), which can be paired with any of eight different housemade salsas, including chipotle, green tomato, and *chile de arbol*. Everything is freshly made, the flavours bright, the experience as authentic as you can get this far north. Longtime fans of this award-winning eatery will be pleased to note that in its new location, Doña Cata now offers beer and margaritas. *$–$$; MC, V; debit cards; lunch, dinner Tues–Sun; full bar; no reservations; street parking; map:F4.*

Earls / ★★☆

1601 W BROADWAY, WEST SIDE (AND BRANCHES); 604/736-5663
The kingpin of casual fine dining in Vancouver, Earls continues to win the hearts of dining crowds with its accessible yet inventive menu and trendy, dressed-down vibe. Although the extensive menu features reliable standbys like burgers, pizza, and pasta, it also boasts signature entrées such as steaks and chops, as well as Asian-inspired wok options including *jeera* chicken curry or Hunan kung pao. Monthly features showcase seasonal offerings as well as the latest test-kitchen creations. Attractive and enthusiastic servers move at lightning speed, ready with a smile and another pitcher of the Albino Rhino honey lager. The one-price wine list is consistently lauded for its good value and savvy selections. During peak times, be prepared to wait for a seat in the dining room or on the patio. *$$; AE, MC, V; debit cards; lunch, dinner every day; full bar; no reservations; www.earls.ca; street parking; map:P7.* &

East Is East / Chai Gallery / ★★

3243 W BROADWAY, WEST SIDE; 604/734-5881
4413 MAIN ST, EAST VANCOUVER; 604/879-2020
Flickering candlelight, low-slung tables, and tapestries adorning the walls transport you a world away to a tiny stall deep in the heart of a Moroccan souk. Sip on a comforting cup of chai while perusing the menu of organic fare that traces the Silk Road from Istanbul to Calcutta. For truly inspired feasting, share an Eastern Plate with a friend: dhal soup, salad, roti, and either coconut or Afghan rice, along with two choices from main dishes including organic lamb kebabs and mango butter squash. Those with lighter appetites can opt for an exotically named roti roll, perhaps a Silk Route (grilled wild salmon, green onion, and fresh tomatoes) or Gandhi's Breakfast (spinach, mushroom, and green onion). Wash it all down with a healthful shake, fruit smoothie, or yogurt lassi—the Himalayan High is a flavourful blend of mango, pistachio, cardamom, and rosewater. The takeout window at the Kitsilano location and its smaller Main Street counterpart serves roti rolls and drinks to go. Just upstairs from the West Broadway address, Chai Gallery offers buffet-style Ayurvedic dining and nightly live entertainment ranging from flamenco and belly dancing to classical Persian and Indian music. *$–$$; AE, MC, V; debit cards; lunch, dinner every day, dinner Wed–Mon (Chai Gallery); no alcohol; reservations recommended; www.eastiseast.ca; street parking; map:C2, E3.* &

Elixir / ★★☆

350 DAVIE ST (OPUS HOTEL), YALETOWN; 604/642-0557

If executive chef Don Letendre is in the kitchen at this brasserie-style bar and restaurant, you'll be treated to exemplary modern French cooking inspired by West Coast ingredients. Reserve a corner table in the red velvet room—it's one of the most intimate spaces in the city. For starters, Letendre prepares a porcini and sunchoke velouté and drops in a croquette of foie gras and chestnut—it's so rich and refined, you'd think you were in France. Inventive mains include roasted sablefish (aka Alaskan black cod) with miso in a soba dashi broth and spice-rubbed venison loin with bitter chocolate sauce. For dessert, Elixir's version of coffee and Kahlúa cheesecake tames the usual cloying sweetness of standard cheesecakes. Service under the humorous maître d' Mikel Kanter is spot-on. There's a good selection of Champagnes and wines by the glass on the local and international wine list. The O-bites menu offers globally inspired small plates in the Opus Bar. Elixir is also a good choice for brunch in Yaletown. *$$$; AE, MC, V; debit cards; breakfast, lunch, dinner every day, brunch Sat–Sun; full bar; reservations recommended; www.elixir vancouver.ca; valet parking; map:S5.*

Ellie Tropical Cuisine / ★

1111-3779 SEXSMITH RD, RICHMOND; 604/232-0999

A pair of faux palm trees stand like sentries flanking the door. A quartet of massive M. C. Escher prints adorns the bright yellow and chartreuse walls. Tucked away in a nondescript strip mall, this quirky, casual eatery with its steady music feed of Canto-pop serves Malaysian and Taiwanese dishes at bargain prices. Start off with a few sticks of chicken satay, scented with ginger and lemongrass and accompanied by a chunky dipping sauce, or a plate of Malaysian-style lemon chicken, crunchy, deep-fried goodness piled high with a stack of sliced onions and sweet chile sauce. For those seeking a starch fix, noodle dishes abound, among them Singaporean *mee siam* and Malay *hokkien mee*. But, really, it's all about the *laksa*, the curry *laksa* a steaming bowl of coconut-rich broth laden with seafood, tofu, and cilantro. *$–$$; cash only; lunch, dinner Tues–Sun; no alcohol; reservations recommended; self-parking; map:D5.* &

Ezogiku Noodle Cafe / ★

1329 ROBSON ST, WEST END (AND BRANCHES); 604/685-8606

With 40 years of ramen history in Tokyo, Ezogiku was one of the first restaurants to introduce Vancouver to the pleasures of slurping noodles and soup. Order the miso ramen, and treat yourself to a huge bowl of snappy noodles, napa cabbage, and pork in a soothingly rich broth. For a little more, add expertly made gyoza to your noodle meal. Ramen additions to consider include spicy kimchee, curry, and *p-torro*, otherwise known as pork belly. Toppings such as corn, butter, or a shoyu hard-boiled egg can also be added to create a noodle bowl that would make Dagwood proud. Fried rice and Japanese-style curry dishes are available for the noodle-averse. The service is friendly and impressively efficient. *$; cash only; lunch, dinner every day; no alcohol; no reservations; self-parking; map:R3.* ⅃

Fiddlehead Joe's Eatery & Bar / ★★☆

1-1012 BEACH AVE, DOWNTOWN; 604/688-1969
Perched at the entrance to False Creek across from Granville Island, Fiddlehead Joe's sits on prime people-watching real estate as one of the few restaurants along the seawall with patio seating. Rollerbladers whiz by, dodging the joggers and dog walkers, Aquabuses putt to and fro across the creek—ample mealtime entertainment for those lucky enough to snag an outdoor table. Sunny weekends are invariably busy with diners looking to get their brunch on, but the serious eating starts after dark. The dinner menu blends Asian inspiration with West Coast bistro fare in selections such as seared ahi tuna with marinated mushrooms in a miso broth and porcini-grilled beef tenderloin with crab rémoulade. Give the namesake fiddleheads a try; tossed with smoked bacon, they're available as a side dish. Creative desserts may include white-chocolate bread pudding with pistachio and black pepper ice cream. *$$; AE, MC, V; debit cards; lunch, dinner every day, brunch Sat–Sun, holidays; full bar; reservations recommended; www.fiddleheadjoeseatery.com; street parking; map:Q5.* ⅃

Fisherman's Terrace Seafood Restaurant / ★

UNIT 3580 ABERDEEN MALL, 4151 HAZELBRIDGE WAY, RICHMOND; 604/303-9739
This room with bright, modern decor plays host to boisterous Chinese families happily dining together. Though dinner service is available, dim sum lunch is the meal of choice. The extensive à la carte menu features classics such as shrimp dumplings (*har gow*) and sticky rice steamed in bamboo leaves. More adventurous offerings include steamed pork neck meat in a spicy XO sauce (made from chiles and dried seafood), mixed mushrooms wrapped in delicate steamed rice rolls, and pan-fried egg tofu with contrasting smooth and crisp textures. The fried rice with egg whites and *conpoy* (dried scallops) is light and elegant, and the warm egg tarts are coddled in an incredibly flaky crust. *$$; AE, MC, V; debit cards; lunch, dinner every day; beer and wine; reservations recommended; self-parking; map:D5.* ⅃

The Fish House in Stanley Park / ★★★☆

8901 STANLEY PARK DR (ENTRANCE TO STANLEY PARK), WEST END; 604/681-7275
This historic building nestled amidst the gardens of Vancouver's lush Stanley Park wouldn't have to try very hard to attract the crowds. It's to the credit of chef (and prolific cookbook author) Karen Barnaby's excellent food that the draw goes far beyond the gorgeous patio view and tourist-attraction setting. As the name would suggest, the main event here is the seafood, from the fresh bivalves at the oyster bar to the prawns flamed tableside in ouzo to the daily fresh fish. Most dishes are prepared simply, allowing their natural

flavours to shine through, and Barnaby includes mostly Oceanwise (sustainable) seafood on the menu. The Fish House also serves a charming afternoon tea daily, and the Sunday brunch is one of the best in the city. *$$–$$$; AE, MC, V; debit cards; lunch Mon–Sat, afternoon tea, dinner every day, brunch Sun; full bar; reservations recommended; www.fishhousestanleypark.com; self-parking; map:O2.* ⑆

Five Sails Restaurant / ★★★

410-999 CANADA PL, DOWNTOWN; 604/844-2855

Husband-and-wife team chef Ernst Dorfler and Gerry Sayer have assumed the reins of this former Pan Pacific Hotel space, transforming it into a sweeping room with breathtaking sightlines of the Canada Place building's five sails and Vancouver's harbour and coastal mountains. Intimate banquettes, elegant table seating, and warm neutral tones all suit the muted light that enters through the floor-to-ceiling windows. The menu draws upon Dorfler's classical European culinary training, while still celebrating the local and the seasonal. Favourites include half a grilled Atlantic lobster with weathervane scallops, Pacific prawns, and fresh catch of the day; Fraser Valley duck done three different ways; and homemade red *kurri* squash and goat cheese ravioli. The six-course chef's tasting menu ($110) is a great way to put yourself in Dorfler's capable hands. The wine list boasts a strong old-world base alongside a sizable local presence. *$$$–$$$$; AE, DC, JCB, MC, V; debit cards; dinner every day; full bar; reservations recommended; www.fivesails.ca; self-parking; map:T2.* ⑆

Floata Seafood Restaurant / ★

400-180 KEEFER ST, CHINATOWN; 604/602-0368

The cavernous interiors here have been home to many celebrations, including an annual Chinese New Year–Robbie Burns Day mashup that could happen only in Vancouver. Floata is the last true dim sum palace in Chinatown, with a menu that packs almost 80 choices. Along with standards such as steamed shrimp dumplings and *shui mai* (pork dumplings), the more adventurous can sample steamed curried baby squid, panfried lotus paste, and eels in black bean sauce. Chicken and local cured sausage (*lap cheong*) rice hot pot is classic Chinese comfort food, while the warm egg tarts provide a satisfyingly sweet finish. The clientele of old-school Chinatown characters adds gentle charm, and the friendly and engaging servers provide good guidance. *$$; AE, MC, V; no debit cards; breakfast, lunch, dinner every day; beer and wine; reservations recommended; www.floata.com; self-parking; map:V4.* ⑆

Flying Beaver / ★★

4760 INGLIS DR, RICHMOND; 604/273-0278

Remember the sitcom *Wings*? Well, Flying Beaver is similar, with the Harbour Air terminal on one side and the restaurant on the other. The large stone fireplace, long wooden bar, rafters and beams, and mounted salmon might get you thinking you've flown into a fishing camp. Locals, as well as flight crews and airline employees, head through the rustic-style restaurant to the glass-enclosed heated patio, where they sip their microbrews and watch the seaplanes land and depart. With the emphasis on West Coast pub food, the halibut and BC wild salmon burger are most popular, but individual pizzas, teriyaki wings, and beef dip come a close second. *$$; AE, MC, V; debit cards; lunch, dinner every day; full bar; reservations recommended; www.markjamesgroup.com/flyingbeaver. html; self-parking; map:C6.* &

Fraîche / ★★☆

2240 CHIPPENDALE RD, WEST VANCOUVER; 604/925-7595
Set on a lofty perch amongst some of West Vancouver's toniest addresses, Fraîche enjoys a breathtakingly expansive view of the city and glittering ocean below. The mood is warm and relaxed, an understated palette of earth tones creating a soothing milieu. Chef and co-owner Wayne Martin serves a menu of "renewed classics," upscale comfort food with a nod to seasonal, regionally sourced ingredients: organic chicken noodle soup and grilled bone-in New York steak are perfect examples. The grilled milk-fed veal chop is Fred Flintstone–sized, served over a horseradish potato galette with black trumpet mushrooms and a lush reduction sauce. Martin is equally deft with seafood, evident in dishes such as arctic char accompanied by caramelized onion, bacon, and Brie ravioli. Desserts are executed with skill and panache. Reminiscent of a 3 Musketeers, the chocolate malt bar pairs impossibly creamy ganache with the textural counterpoint of a crisp feuilletine crust. Co-owner Mary Ann Masney's concise wine list is smartly chosen. *$$$–$$$$; MC, V; debit cards; dinner Tues–Sun, brunch Sat–Sun; full bar; reservations recommended; www.fraicherestaurant.ca; self-parking.* &

Fritz European Fry House / ★

718 DAVIE ST, DOWNTOWN; 604/684-0811
Satisfy those late french fry cravings until 3am (Mondays till 8pm) at the Fritz European Fry House. Crispy takeout fries are served in paper cones and accompanied by a choice of one of 13 dips. The crowd favourites seem to be the garlic lover's mayo and the mango chutney curry mayo, which are outstanding. The king cone of fries here is the Montreal-style poutine, dripping with cheese curds from St. Albert, Ontario, and hot gravy. Portions range in size from mini to large. There's a wooden bench along one wall in case you want to dine in, complete with holes cut in the armrests for holding your cone of fries. *$; V; debit cards; lunch, dinner every day; no alcohol; no reservations; street parking; map:R5.*

Fuel Restaurant / ★★★

1944 W 4TH AVE, WEST SIDE; 604/288-7905
Large picture windows spotlight cooks busily prepping the bounty of ingredients that will wow diners during service. The room conveys simple elegance, just like the food itself. Chef Robert Belcham is a culinary artist, creating dishes that are in homage to local abundance. An heirloom beetroot and

BUBBLE TEA

Testimony to the strong, vibrant Asian cultural presence in Vancouver is the popularity of bubble tea cafes alongside the many coffee-chain giants that dominate the city.

The drink, which originated in Taiwan, is a frothy, shaken-up mixture of black tea, milk, honey, and fruit flavours that is highly addictive after the first sip. Purists go for these milky teas, while others opt for slushes that are blended smoothies of honey, milk, sugar, fresh fruit, and juices. More unusual versions with taro, red bean, and chestnut, highly popular among Asian customers, are also well worth a try. What makes bubble tea most distinctive are the tapioca pearls that you can thoughtfully chew on after slurping them with your extra-wide straw. Some people claim that they interrupt the drinking experience, but, frankly, it's no fun without them! Many places also offer coconut jelly, pudding, or grass jelly (made from a member of the mint family) as alternatives to the tapioca.

There are a ton of options in the city for getting your bubble tea fix. The Starbucks of bubble tea, **BUBBLE WORLD** (7980 Granville St, West Side and branches; 604/263-6031), is a consistently solid bet, especially with standout pineapple milk slush and lychee green tea options. Other popular Vancouver

butter lettuce salad with house-made ricotta, firewood honey, and lime is an expert showcasing of ingredients. Mains are equally impressive, from the Redbro organic chicken with de puy lentils, cheese curds, pancetta, and lemon to the organic pork with savoy cabbage, spiced crispy potatoes, and preserved ramps. Opt for the chef's designed four- to six-course dinners for an even more individualized experience. Co-owner and sommelier Tom Doughty carefully assembles a wine list that also takes its cue from seasonal shifts. *$$$–$$$$; AE, DC, MC, V; debit cards; lunch Mon–Fri, dinner every day; full bar; reservations recommended; www.fuelrestaurant.ca; street parking; map:O7.* &

Gastropod / ★★★
1938 W 4TH AVE, WEST SIDE; 604/730-5579
This recently opened Kitsilano room is the embodiment of casual elegance, with its light wood accents and white linen tabletops. Young chef Angus An, formerly of Montreal's Toqué and New York's JoJo, already has garnered a loyal following for his modern version of haute cuisine. Dishes are innovative and ingredient driven, showcasing An's talent with flavours and techniques. Begin with the venison cannelloni—Nicola Valley venison bolognese, ricotta, celeriac, and Parmigiano-Reggiano—before sampling the Fraser Valley organic lamb with Stuttgart onion purée, turnips, and tortellini, or the organic sous vide chicken breast and roasted thigh with garlic purée, daikon,

picks are the **DRAGON BALL TEA HOUSE** (1007 W King Edward, West Side; 604/738-3198), **OASIS BUBBLE TEA** (2076 W 41st Ave, West Side; 604/606-0688), **KAT'S TEA HUT** (6519 Victoria Dr, East Side; 604/326-0008), and **YUEN YUEN CAFE** (5890 Cambie St, West Side; 604/322-1020), which the customers love for its coconut milk tea and mango milk tea.

For the true bubble tea adventure, head over to Richmond, where small cafes tucked in neon-lit strip malls buzz with activity into the wee hours of the night. These establishments range from the charmingly eccentric to the impressively stylish. A favourite by far is **PEARL CASTLE** (1128-3779 Sexsmith Rd; 604/270-3939), where chic female staff circulate in the sleek room, serving strawberry milk tea and oolong milk tea, along with authentic Taiwanese dishes such as satay pork and fried noodles, fried fish cakes, and hot-pot beef brisket. Some other Richmond highlights include **TAPIOCA EXPRESS** (1438-8388 Capstan Wy; 604/278-4998) and **BUBBLE KING** (1110-8788 McKim Wy; 604/279-5464). And for a truly quirky experience, try out **GOGO TEA CAFE** (270-8788 McKim Wy; 604/244-7336), where servers dressed in Sailor Moon–esque outfits serve drinks and great snacks in a trendy lounge environment. Before you know it, you'll be substituting your daily latte for the quintessential Asian hangout drink.

—Tara Lee

and Asian pesto. During the summer, the restaurant sources from its own local herb and vegetable gardens. The wine list also does an expert job of showcasing regional offerings. *$$$–$$$$; AE, JCB, MC, V; debit cards; dinner every day; full bar; reservations recommended; www.gastropod.ca; street parking; map:O7.* &

Globe@YVR / ★★☆

3111 GRANT MCCONACHIE WY (FAIRMONT VANCOUVER AIRPORT), RICHMOND; 604/248-3281
In-the-know travellers prefer this light-flooded, in-terminal restaurant, bar, and lounge (with comfy settees and sofas) to the airlines' first-class lounge because of its attentively executed food and creative libations. A monthly fresh sheet reflects seasons, but pan-roasted halibut, rare seared albacore tuna, roasted BC bison tenderloin, and seared wild sockeye salmon with pearl couscous are available, accompanied by Hazelmere Farm organic produce. The extensive wine list focuses on elusive BC gems, including Blue Mountain and La Frenz, and there's a good draught beer and scotch list. Globe@YVR will validate parking for three hours after 5:30pm on P2, P3, or the economy lot. *$$$; AE, MC, V; debit cards; breakfast, lunch, dinner every day, brunch Sat–Sun; full bar; reservations recommended; www.fairmont.com/vancouver airport; valet and self-parking; map:D5.* &

Glowbal Grill & Satay Bar / ★★☆

1079 MAINLAND ST, YALETOWN; 604/602-0835
This hip, happening spot is an ideal place to go for late-night drinks or small-plate nibblies like the signature satays. The decor is '60s sleek and chic, perfect for showing off the pretty people at the bar. Service and food quality can be inconsistent, but when the kitchen and waitstaff are on, this is one of the best hangouts in town. Get a table outside for a view of the pretty Yaletown crowds. Under new executive chef John Crook, the world fusion menu is taking a slight detour toward the Mediterranean, with plenty of pasta and paella. But the yummy (if not exactly authentic) satays keep up the global cred: Kobe meatball, seven-spice ahi tuna, tequila lamb, or barbecued baby octopus. While the cocktails are the show, the wine list also has some standout selections. *$$–$$$; AE, MC, V; no debit cards; lunch Mon–Fri, dinner every day, brunch Sat–Sun; full bar; reservations recommended; www.glowbalgrill.com; valet parking; map:S5.*

Go Fish! / ★★

1505 W 1ST AVE, WEST SIDE; 604/730-5040
Gord Martin, chef/owner of Bin 941 and Bin 942 Tapas Parlours (see review), opened this fish shack on False Creek, a short stroll from Granville Island, and fish-and-chips has never been the same. The menu is simple: a few fresh fish dishes, paired with a tangy Asian-style slaw or fries. There are only a handful of tables, all outside, so you might have to take your meal to go. Primarily a lunch venue, closing times here vary; call to confirm. *$; cash only; lunch, dinner Tues–Sun; no alcohol; no reservations; self-parking; map:P6.*

Goldfish Pacific Kitchen / ★★☆

1118 MAINLAND ST, YALETOWN; 604/689-8318 OR 888/689-8318
Goldfish, with its lavish bar with a dramatic marble backdrop and two elegant private rooms for more intimate dining occasions, is as sleek as its clientele. The kitchen adopts a modern approach to Asian cuisine, creating dishes that are ideal for sharing over an after-work fusion cocktail. Experiment with tastes and textures by sampling the crisp vegetable spring rolls wrapped with mint and lettuce leaf accompaniments. Then move on to the tender grilled short ribs with roasted peanuts before ending with the pan-seared arctic char with kaffir lime coconut sauce and snow pear salad with lychee raspberry dressing. Sides, like the bacon fried rice with scallions, garlic, and fried quail eggs, round out the meal. The extensive wine list includes some solid reserve selections. *$$–$$$; AE, MC, V; no debit cards; lunch Mon–Fri, dinner every day; full bar; reservations recommended; www.goldfishkitchen. com; valet parking; map:S5.* &

Gotham Steakhouse & Cocktail Bar / ★★★

615 SEYMOUR ST, DOWNTOWN; 604/605-8282
Meat is the main course in this power dining room downtown, where the steaks may be even more beautiful than the people. From the New York strip

to the splendid 24-ounce porterhouse, it's a cattle drive for the taste buds. Vegetables are à la carte, so you can share mashed potatoes, creamed spinach, or crispy french fries. For sheer entertainment value, take a seat at the bar and do some of the best people-watching in Vancouver. Beware: This place prices under the assumption that everyone has a Swiss bank account. The spacious outdoor patio has a fireplace. *$$$$; AE, DC, MC, V; debit cards; dinner every day; full bar; reservations recommended; www.gothamsteakhouse.com; valet parking; map:T4.* &

Gramercy Grill / ★★

2685 ARBUTUS ST, WEST SIDE; 604/730-5666
Experience a little bit of Manhattan in Vancouver's West Side. Dark wood paneling and flickering candlelight make for a sophisticated and welcoming interior. Warm service exudes a quiet, knowledgeable efficiency. Dishes are equally elegant, from a delicate puff pastry tart with wild mushrooms, herbed goat cheese, and balsamic caramel to a beef carpaccio with truffle purée aioli, fried capers, and shaved Parmesan. Be prepared to sup well on the braised lamb shank with mashed potatoes, basil pesto–tomato compote, and red wine jus or the roasted trout fillet with almonds, capers, and brown butter. The lengthy wine list traverses the globe with solid picks per variety. *$$–$$$; AE, MC, V; debit cards; lunch Mon–Fri, dinner every day, brunch Sat–Sun; full bar; reservations recommended; street and self-parking; map:C3.* &

Grand View Szechuan Restaurant / ★

4181 FRASER ST, EAST VANCOUVER; 604/879-8885
Once a mainstay on the Broadway corridor, the Grand View's move to the Fraser Street rise hasn't deterred regulars from seeking their fix of crispy-skin chicken with "spicy nutty sauce." Smaller than the previous digs, it's still a cheerful room warmed by sunny yellow walls and owner Debbie Sum's bright smile. Menu favourites include hot and sour soup, almost a meal in itself, and dangerously addictive General Tao spicy chicken. Forgo the combination dinners and keep an eye on the specials board for prawns with XO sauce and fresh crab in hot garlic sauce. An extensive "vegetarian delights" menu features meatless versions of dishes such as kung pao "chicken" with peanuts or *ma bao* tofu. Wipe your plate clean with chunks of a shredded (silver thread) roll, either steamed or deep-fried. *$–$$; MC, V; debit cards; lunch Tues–Sat, dinner Tues–Sun; beer and wine; no reservations; www.grandviewrestaurant.com; street parking; map:E3.* &

Green Basil Thai Restaurant / ★

4623 KINGSWAY, BURNABY; 604/439-1919
Green Basil Thai is a welcome respite from the Metrotown corridor's hustle and bustle. Awash in mango and tamarind hues, the decor of this relaxed, stylish room is punctuated with dark wood accents and touches of Thai art. Midday diners pack the house for bargain-priced lunch specials, but those in the know come back to explore the sizable dinner menu. Forget anything that

Mom ever said about eating with your hands, and kick-start your taste buds with the duck lettuce wrap. Follow up with *phat see iw,* a delectable jumble of rice noodles, eggs, cabbage, and broccoli together with your choice of meat. And stretch your culinary boundaries with ostrich *gaeng dang* (red curry), its heat softened by coconut milk and the surprising addition of lychees. *$$; MC, V; debit cards; lunch, dinner every day; full bar; no reservations; www. greenbasilthai.com; street parking; map:G4.* &

Griffins / ★★

900 W GEORGIA ST (FAIRMONT HOTEL VANCOUVER), DOWNTOWN; 604/684-3131

This bright, airy brasserie in the iconic Fairmont Hotel Vancouver is a solid choice after a day of strolling on bustling Robson Street. The menu features time-honored starters such as onion soup au gratin, Caesar salad, and Pacific seafood chowder with tomato Pernod broth. Also of note are signature cuts, including the 15-ounce sterling rib eye with market vegetables, roast shallot mashed potatoes, and Madagascar peppercorn sauce. Undoubtedly, the biggest draws are the signature appetizer buffet, with a wide array of Pacific Northwest seafood, and the sumptuous dessert buffet for those with an insatiable sweet tooth. Sunday's buffet brunch is ideal for fuelling up on breakfast favourites. The wine list strikes a balance between local and imported selections. *$$–$$$; AE, DC, DIS, JCB, MC, V; debit cards; breakfast, lunch, dinner every day, brunch Sat–Sun; full bar; reservations recommended; www.fairmont. com/hotelvancouver; valet and self-parking; map:S3.* &

Gyoza King / ★

1508 ROBSON ST, DOWNTOWN; 604/669-8278

Gyoza King serves two dozen varieties of gyoza: fried dumplings filled with prawns, pork, or vegetables along with ginger, scallions, and garlic, served with a soy dipping sauce. This casual hangout, which is perennially packed with Japanese students, also makes sushi, udon noodle soups, katsudon (breaded pork cutlet over rice), and a hearty soup called *o-den.* Sit at the bar or at the low front table for a good view of the chef in action. There are western-style tables as well. The other pluses here are late hours, reasonable prices, a very courteous staff, and a good selection of beers. *$; AE, MC, V; debit cards; lunch Sat–Sun, dinner every day; beer and wine; reservations recommended; street parking; map:S4.*

Habit Lounge / ★

2610 MAIN ST, EAST VANCOUVER; 604/877-8582

"Make it a habit to share," the menu says. Indeed, this retro chic room, with plenty of design whimsy, is a great spot for chatting with good company over small bites. Indulge in modern comfort food by having a plate of sweet carrot and Brie piroshkis with caramelized onions and chive sour cream. Then, when you want to feel slightly more virtuous, order the grilled vegetable lasagne or the crispy glazed tofu with mushrooms and spinach. While the wine list is select, the beer list is quite extensive. *$$; AE, MC, V; debit cards; dinner every day; full bar; no reservations; www.habitlounge.ca; street parking; map:E3.* &

Hal Mae Jang Mo Jib / ★★☆

1719 ROBSON ST, DOWNTOWN; 604/642-0712
8320 ALEXANDRA ST, RICHMOND; 604/233-0712
3200-4151 HAZELBRIDGE WY, RICHMOND; 604/273-0712
Modeled after a traditional beer house in Seoul's university district, the Robson Street location is packed until the wee hours with those seeking hearty traditional Korean fare. Get through a rainy day with a bowl of *ssuk uh soon doo boo*; served in a clay hot pot, it's a thick and spicy soup with a mile-long ingredient list that includes soft tofu, beef, pork, and assorted seafood. Dolsot bibimbap offers a cavalcade of flavours: preserved vegetables, beef, a fried egg, and house-made hot chile paste on steamed rice, all meant to be mixed together and crisped in a hot stone bowl. When in Richmond, skip the food court outlet in Aberdeen Centre and head instead to the homey Alderbridge location. *$–$$; AE, MC, V; debit cards; lunch, dinner every day; beer and wine; reservations recommended; street parking; map:Q2, D6, D6.* &

Hanwoori Korean Restaurant / ★★

5740 IMPERIAL ST, BURNABY; 604/439-0815
The food here is so lovingly home style, you half expect elderly Korean ladies to come out and pinch your cheeks. Chile heat is underpinned with real flavours coaxed from careful cooking in the *jeyuk bossam*, a comforting dish of steamed pork belly, napa cabbage, and kimchee. *Gom tang* (beef broth and rice) is fortifying, soothing, and warming. *Mul naeng myun* (buckwheat in chilled broth) garnished with pear slices, cucumber, and hard-boiled egg awakens the summer appetite. The deep-fried chicken with chile sauce is perfect with a cold beer or a glass of seriously potent *soju*, Korean distilled rice wine. The nondescript location, tucked beside an auto repair shop, hides a spotlessly clean wooden interior with warm and friendly service. *$$; MC, V; debit cards; lunch, dinner every day; beer and wine; reservations recommended; self-parking; map:H4.* &

Hapa Izakaya / ★★★

1479 ROBSON ST, DOWNTOWN; 604/689-4272
1516 YEW ST, WEST SIDE; 604/738-4272
The gorgeously sophisticated room makes you feel like a movie star even before you sit down. The food and warm service balances polish with a good dose of fun. *Hapa* is a play on words, meaning literally "leaf" but also slang for "half," in reference to the part-Japanese owners and the cross-culture-influenced menu; *izakaya* are Japanese small plates. Lively *negitoro* is served with soft thick slices of garlic bread. The *om* rice bowl is a comforting mix of egg, chicken, and spicy tomato sauce. Press the rice mixture against the side of the sizzling Korean-style stone bowls to maximize toasty tidbits. Finish with

almond-scented, soft, creamy *annin* tofu, topped with that most Canadian of ingredients: dark maple syrup. *$$–$$$; AE, MC, V; debit cards (no debit cards at Yew St location); dinner every day; beer and wine; reservations recommended (no reservations at Robson St location 6–8pm); www.hapaizakaya. com; self-parking; map:R3, N6.* &

Hart House Restaurant / ★★☆

6664 DEER LAKE AVE, BURNABY; 604/298-4278

This elegant heritage Tudor with its lakeside gardens and graceful gazebo is an ideal place for a celebration brunch or afternoon wedding. Thanks to new chef Dennis Peckham, formerly of Lumière and the French Laundry, it's also an excellent place for fine West Coast dining. All the classics are here, but each is prepared with a fresh flash of inspiration—black pepper mignonette with the oysters, pickled fennel with the smoked salmon, and Panang red curry with the crab cakes, for instance. Mains lean toward upscale comfort food, such as the savoury braised beef short ribs, chicken breast with truffled mashed potatoes, and luscious mac and cheese made with aged fromage. No big surprises—but deft touches, a remarkable wine list, a gorgeous garden patio, and great skill in the kitchen make this beautiful spot a must-visit dining destination. *$$–$$$; AE, MC, V; debit cards; lunch Tues–Fri, dinner Tues–Sun, brunch Sun; full bar; reservations recommended; www.harthouserestaurant. com; self-parking; map:H3.* &

The Hermitage / ★★☆

115-1025 ROBSON ST, DOWNTOWN; 604/689-3237

The Hermitage offers an intimate dining experience and a polished professional staff. Chef/owner Hervé Martin (who was once chef to the late King Leopold of Belgium) holds strongly to his French roots. The appetizer of foie gras sautéed with Armagnac is perfectly prepared, and the sweetbreads and kidneys in a bordelaise sauce are as rich and satisfying as any in the city. A bowl of West Coast bouillabaisse is dense with local fish and shellfish, and the lobster ravioli ($18) with vanilla beurre blanc is sublime. More than 300 wines (some from his sister's vineyard in Burgundy) reflect Martin's eye for high-quality, good-value producers. Although the Hermitage (as its name implies) may be hidden, it's well worth looking for. *$$–$$$; AE, MC, V; debit cards; lunch Mon–Fri, dinner every day; full bar; reservations required; www. thehermitagevancouver.com; street parking; map:S3.* &

Herons Restaurant / ★★☆

900 CANADA PL WY (WATERFRONT CENTRE HOTEL),
DOWNTOWN; 604/691-1991

This hotel restaurant is one of the city's best-kept secrets, with the inspired cooking of talented chef Shannon Wrightson. The 2,100-square-foot rooftop herb garden determines the fresh sheet: start with the duo of smoked salmon on a blini and Sichuan pepper confit salad, and move on to lavender-crusted goat cheese croquettes or the roasted rack of lamb paired with an oven-dried tomato and pine nut ragout. Cap the feast with a Thomas Haas dessert, or say cheese with a local artisanal plate. The wine list starts in the friendly $30 range with BC wines but also includes sought-after international producers. Accommodating service warms the room despite its lack of intimacy. *$$$; AE, MC, V; debit cards; breakfast, lunch, dinner every day, brunch Sun; full bar; reservations recommended; www.fairmont.com/waterfront; valet parking; map:T3.* &

Hon's Wun-Tun House / ★

1339 ROBSON ST, DOWNTOWN (AND BRANCHES); 604/685-0871
By serving the just plain good, basic Chinese specialties you'd find in hundreds of street-corner restaurants in Hong Kong, and by keeping prices to a comfortable minimum, this onetime small and steamy Chinatown noodle house has now become something of a restaurant empire, with five branches located all over the Lower Mainland. One of the keys to Hon's success is that all the locations are unpretentious and comfortable. Dishes are prepared before your eyes in open kitchens. (Robson Street has a separate vegetarian kitchen.) Wonton is just one of the more than 90 varieties of soup available, and there's a seemingly endless list of noodle specialties. The trademark potsticker dumplings, fried or steamed, are justly famous. They also offer delivery, takeout, and a full line of frozen dim sum. One more thing: You'll be happy to know that those addictive candied walnuts are available on your way out. *$; MC, V; debit cards (dine-in only); lunch, dinner every day; beer and wine; no reservations; www.hons.ca; street parking; map:V4.*

Horizons Restaurant / ★★

100 CENTENNIAL WY, BURNABY; 604/299-1155
You may need a map to find this place near the top of Burnaby Mountain, and when you do, the weather had better be clear or you'll miss the main attraction: a view of Burrard Inlet, the North Shore mountains, Stanley Park, the Strait of Georgia, and of course, the city itself. The menu features traditional native green alder–smoked and alder-grilled oysters and salmon, a perennial favourite, but other temptations include unique maple-roasted salmon and a cider-cured pork tenderloin. The impressive wine list features mostly BC wines. *$$$; AE, MC, V; debit cards; lunch Mon–Sat, dinner every day, brunch Sun; full bar; reservations recommended; www.horizonsrestaurant. com; self-parking; map:I2.*

Ho Yuen Kee / ★★

6836 FRASER ST, EAST VANCOUVER; 604/324-8855
Save the airfare and visit Ho Yuen Kee to get a dose of real Hong Kong–style family dining. The room is unrepentantly loud, and the decor is a puzzling mix of baroque chairs and scuffed tables, but the food is undeniably delicious. The encyclopedic menu includes standouts such as steamed live Dungeness crab with plump sticky rice, possibly the best crab dish in the city. Tender beef brisket is served in a hot pot of clear consommé, fragrant with star anise. The

sweet ginger double-boiled milk is full of fresh, hot ginger bite that aids the digestion. The waitstaff have clearly skipped charm school, but the service is fast and efficient right up to the midnight closing time. *$–$$; V; no debit cards; breakfast, lunch, dinner every day; beer only; reservations recommended; self-parking; map:E4.* &

Hy's Encore / ★

637 HORNBY ST, DOWNTOWN; 604/683-7671
Trends may come and go, but don't expect Hy Aisenstat's vintage steak house to go changing for anyone. In many ways, that's a good thing: There's always room for tangy tableside Caesar salad, gooey cheese toast, and great big hunks of seared red meat. But with the plethora of new steak houses opening around town, it may be time to update things just slightly with the addition of some top-quality organic, range-fed, and/or grass-fed beef. In the meantime, just sit back with a classic martini and, like countless other well-sated guests, enjoy the retro men's-club vibe of Vancouver's most authentic steak house. *$$–$$$; AE, MC, V; debit cards; lunch Mon–Fri, dinner every day; full bar; reservations recommended; www.hyssteakhouse.com; valet parking; map:S4.*

Il Giardino di Umberto / ★★★

1382 HORNBY ST, DOWNTOWN; 604/669-2422
At some point, everyone who's anyone wanders through the Tuscan-villa decor of Umberto Menghi's Il Giardino. Menghi is one of Canada's best-known restaurateurs, the man who taught Vancouverites to cook Italian through his five cookbooks and taught them to enjoy *la dolce vita* through his various restaurants and Tuscan cooking school, Villa Delia. Il Giardino is the one that has stood the test of time, which is why the beautiful people can still be seen improving the view in the lovely garden patio. The emphasis is on pasta and hearty meat dishes such as osso buco with saffron risotto, and the tiramisu can't be beat. The service is amongst the best in the city, so even if you aren't really one of the glitterati, by the end of the night you'll feel as if you could be. Plus, the wine list offers impeccable Italian selections. *$$$–$$$$; AE, MC, V; debit cards; lunch Mon–Fri, dinner Mon–Sat; full bar; reservations recommended; www.umberto.com; valet parking; map:S5.*

Imperial Chinese Seafood Restaurant / ★★★

MAIN FLOOR, MARINE BUILDING, 355 BURRARD ST, DOWNTOWN; 604/688-8191
This downtown dim sum temple has been in business for more than 20 years, with flawless execution and authenticity. Five full-time dim sum chefs produce everything from scratch and ensure optimal freshness. Steamed shrimp dumplings are packed with juicy shrimp enveloped in a translucent skin. Steamed minced beef rice rolls are punched up with chopped cilantro. Deep-fried banana shrimp rolls may sound odd but are deliciously addictive. Ordering is generally done à la carte, but servers will bring trays of hot dim sum for you to sample. The soaring Art Deco room buzzes with power lunchers and elegant

Japanese tourists. The service is friendly and informed but can be forward, so turn your dim sum ticket face down to be left in peace. *$$; DC, MC, V; no debit cards; lunch, dinner every day; beer and wine; lunch reservations recommended; www.imperialrest.com; self-parking; map:T3.* ᕕ

Incendio / ★
Incendio West / ★

103 COLUMBIA ST, GASTOWN; 604/688-8694
2118 BURRARD ST, WEST SIDE; 604/736-2220

If you have a craving for big pasta with big flavours, park yourself here and reach for your twirling fork. Decor at both locations is simple and the service speedy—perfect for a hearty meal after an afternoon exploring Gastown or for a quick bite before a film at the cinemas next door. The menu concept is simple: Pick your sauce (carbonara, ragù, pesto, etc.), then your type of pasta, and prepare to feast Italian style. The excellent pizzas are well worth a slice (or two) if you like traditional thin crust made crisp and smoky from the wood-fired brick oven. While the wine list is relatively small, the beer selections are quite extensive and perfect for a drink on the patio. *$$; AE, MC, V; debit cards; lunch Mon–Fri, dinner every day; beer and wine; no reservations; www.incendio.ca; street parking; map:V3, O7.* ᕕ

The Irish Heather / Shebeen Whisk(e)y House / ★★
Salty Tongue Urban Deli / ★

217 CARRALL ST, GASTOWN; 604/688-9779

If you're yearning for a touch of the Emerald Isle, look no further than the Irish Heather, where proprietors Sean, Erin, and Roisin Heather have created a truly authentic Celtic experience. Pull up a stool at the bar and sip on a freshly pulled pint of Irish draught while perusing the menu of soulful fare. Popular choices include traditional bangers and mash with local handmade sausages, rich Guinness-braised steak pot pie, and a hearty platter of Mike Vitow's artisan corned beef with horseradish mashed potatoes and parsley cream sauce. Across a private courtyard, the Shebeen Whisk(e)y House stocks British Columbia's largest selection of Irish single malts, scotch, bourbons, and ryes. Hot-smoked Jameson-cured salmon served with onion marmalade and brown bread is an ideal accompaniment for your choice of spirits. Next door, the Salty Tongue Urban Deli offers quick meals in hand—design your own sandwich from a selection of organic breads and specialty meats. Taking its moniker from rock star Bono's self-proclaimed cussing prowess, this neighbourhood lunch spot also stocks its shelves with specialty comestibles, all the fixings for picnics to go. *$–$$; MC, V; debit cards; lunch, dinner every day; full bar; reservations recommended; street parking; www.irishheather.com; map:V3.* ᕕ

Italian Kitchen / ★★★

1037 ALBERNI ST, DOWNTOWN; 604/687-2858

Restaurant kingpins Emad Yacoub and Jack Lamont (of Glowbal Grill, Coast, Sanafir) oversee the sleek downtown Italian. There's an open kitchen and a 60-foot-long white marble bar on the ground floor named "D.O.C." (There's also a second bar upstairs.) The clientele is a vibrant mix of young professionals eager to relax. We're talking about conviviality, vivified by peerless platters of antipasto, pastas, and mains meant to be shared. Chef Ryan Gauthier deftly combines flavours: osso buco risotto, zucchini blossoms stuffed with *burrata*, and a caprese salad that shines when heirloom tomatoes are in season; an imported gas-fired brick oven flaunts crisp pizza crusts with savoury toppings. You'll also see why the spaghetti with Kobe meatballs (hijacked from Glowbal Grill) has caused such a stir. The cellar is stocked with solid Italian vintages and new- and old-world offerings. Kudos to GM Robert Byford and his enthusiastic staff. *$$$; MC, V; debit cards; lunch Mon–Fri, dinner every day; full bar; reservations recommended; www. theitaliankitchen.ca; street parking; map:S3.* &

Joe Fortes Seafood & Chop House / ★★

777 THURLOW ST, DOWNTOWN; 604/669-1940 OR 877/669-JOES

Don't be surprised to see John Cleese or Steven Tyler from the rock group Aerosmith sitting at the bar of the heated rooftop garden. Joe Fortes— named for the city's best-loved lifeguard—has a kind of high-energy, uptown-chophouse feel to it and is one of the city's hippest watering holes. The draw is more than the horseshoe-shaped bar, where martinis and single-malt scotch are in equal demand. It's the oyster bar, too, dispensing dozens of faultlessly fresh varieties, all sold individually. Sipping, schmoozing, and sampling (starters include a salmon trio, carpaccio, and Joe's $145 seafood tower) often segue seamlessly into the dinner hour. The fresh fish is a constant lure; order the chef's trio of grilled seafood, and $29 gets you your choice of shark, red snapper, salmon, halibut, mahi mahi, sea bass, or swordfish. Attentive service (ask for Frenchy) and a solid wine list round out the allure. *$$$–$$$$; AE, MC, V; debit cards; lunch Mon–Fri, dinner every day, brunch Sat–Sun; full bar; reservations recommended; www.joefortes.ca; valet and street parking; map:G3.* &

Josephine's Restaurant and Catering / ★

2650 MAIN ST, EAST VANCOUVER; 604/876-8785

Service at this casual Filipino restaurant is cafeteria style, or *turo-turo*, literally translated as "point-point" to your food items of choice. Budget-conscious diners form lengthy lineups at lunch and dinner hour for the bargain-priced combination plate: just $7.75 buys you a bowl of *sinigang na bangus* (tamarind-flavoured sour soup with milkfish, amped up with green chiles) together with generous servings of rice and two main dishes. *Lechon paksiw* is a solid choice, a sweet-and-sour stew of pork that's first roasted and then slow-simmered to tenderness. Round out that combination with *lumpiang prito*, a deep-fried vegetarian spring roll, or *kalderetang baka*, a tomato-based beef stew with potatoes. Save space for sweets, perhaps some rich, smooth cassava cake or crispy *turon*, a fried dessert spring roll filled with ripe banana and jackfruit and drizzled with caramelized sugar. *$; MC, V; debit cards; lunch, dinner every day; no alcohol; no reservations; street parking; map:E3.* &

Jules Bistro / ★

216 ABBOTT ST, GASTOWN; 604/669-0033

Feel yourself whisked away to France in this quintessential Parisian bistro. Crystal chandeliers, exposed brick, and smart black-and-white mosaic tiled floors all add to the charm of this bustling room. Ask for a seat on the patio to take in the Gastown scenery. The menu cheerfully adheres to the classics, from escargots de Bourgogne and salade niçoise to cassoulet Toulousain and moules frites. Make sure to reserve (or make) space for a final indulgence: sour cherry clafoutis or vanilla crème brûlée that would make Amelie swoon. An especial deal is the nightly three-course prix fixe for $23 that includes a bistro salad, steak or salmon frites, and a silky chocolate terrine. The reasonably priced wine list leans toward the French and the local. *$$–$$$; AE, MC, V; debit cards; lunch, dinner Tues–Sat; full bar; reservations recommended; www.julesbistro.ca; street parking; map:U3.*

Kamei Royale Japanese Restaurant / ★★

211-1030 W GEORGIA ST, DOWNTOWN; 604/687-8588

Kamei Royale was one of the city's first high-end Japanese restaurants, and it's where many Vancouverites had their first taste of sushi. The handsome room remains incredibly popular with appreciative diners enjoying well-executed food. Gleaming fresh hamachi and salmon sushi are cut and presented with skill and attention. The buttery softness of beef *tataki* is served with brightly tart soy vinaigrette. Outsized sushi rolls draped with mango slices add a touch of *izakaya* playfulness to the menu. The friendly sushi-bar team works with awe-inspiring precision, and while the waitstaff can seem a little harried, service is quick and efficient. *$$–$$$; AE, JCB, MC, V; debit cards; lunch, dinner every day; beer and wine; reservations recommended; self-parking; map:S3.* &

Kim Phung Vietnamese Restaurant / ★

5764 VICTORIA DR, EAST VANCOUVER; 604/327-4490

The comforting fragrance of simmering broth is an instant reminder that it's not about the ambience as you step into this oddly decorated bare-bones eatery. For many Vancouverites, this quirky East Side restaurant is home to the city's best Vietnamese noodle soup, known as pho. Those not in a soup mood can quell their appetites with *goi cuon*, fresh salad rolls of shrimp and Vietnamese pâté, or *bun thit nuong*, grilled pork served atop vermicelli with green salad. But make no mistake about it: Pho is the headliner on this playbill. *Pho tai bo vien* is a good choice for neophytes: redolent with star anise, it features rare beef and meatballs over a tangle of rice noodles. An accompanying plate of bean sprouts, green chiles, Thai basil, and lime leaves the garnish duties to you. *$; cash only; lunch, dinner Thurs–Tues; no alcohol; no reservations; street parking; map:F3.*

Kingyo / ★★★

871 DENMAN ST, WEST END; 604/608-1677

Step through heavy, rustic doors, and shouts of "*Irrashimase!*" echo through the restaurant in rollicking welcome. You'll feel as though you've entered the courtyard of an elegant Japanese home: a clay-tiled roof tops the bar, an elegant stand of bamboo graces the long communal table, and traditional wood carvings adorn the walls. A relative newcomer to Vancouver's dining scene, Kingyo has won numerous awards right out of the starting block, garnering both local and national accolades. Whet your appetite with a yuzu tea Lime Soda cocktail while you peruse the *izakaya* (small plates) menu, featuring playful flavour combinations that are deftly executed with subtlety and finesse. The *ebi* tempura rice ball is jewel-like in its simplicity: succulent, lightly battered prawn tempura and salmon roe rest atop an impossibly lacy sheet of nori (dried seaweed). Chicken kara age is crisp-fried chunks of chicken accompanied by three kinds of salt for dipping, and the yuzu jalapeño pasta is a piquant tangle of spaghettini with bacon and tiny dried anchovies that add a subtle punch of flavour. Round out your meal with creamy almond tofu, delicately flavoured and incredibly smooth. Open late, Kingyo is a favourite haunt of both hungry night owls and local chefs after shift. *$$; MC, V; debit cards; dinner every day; full bar; reservations recommended; street parking; map:Q2.* &

Kintaro Handmade Tonkotsu Ramen / ★★☆
Motomachi Shokudo / ★★☆

788 DENMAN ST, WEST END; 604/682-7568
740 DENMAN ST, WEST END; 604/609-0310

Summer or winter, the line snakes out the door as noodle devotees queue up patiently for what's arguably the city's quintessential bowl of ramen. The Kintaro soup ritual begins with selecting your flavour of tonkatsu, or pork-bone broth, and then choosing the level of fattiness: either rich (ridiculously indulgent), medium, or light. Follow suit with either fat or lean pork. Servers' comments are politely punctuated by "Thank you for waiting"— however, precious few minutes elapse before a bathtub-sized bowl of steaming handmade ramen appears before you. Available only on Saturdays, Forest Fire Ramen with pork, spinach, and burnt scallions in chicken stock is a surefire panacea for Vancouver's rainy-day blues. In contrast to the pork-based Tokyo-style ramen served at Kintaro, chef/owner Daiji Matsubara has opted for a lighter, more health-conscious approach at Motomachi Shokudo, located just a half block north. As with its sister restaurant, your flavour choices are threefold: miso, shio with all-natural imported salt, and shoyu with unpasteurized raw soy sauce. Here, however, the broth is chicken-based and the focus is on organic ingredients. *$; no credit cards; debit cards; lunch, dinner Tues–Sun; beer only; no reservations; street parking; map:Q2.* &

SAYONARA, SUSHI PALACE—HELLO, IZAKAYA!

Upscale izakayas are the new wave of Japanese dining: The first thing you hear is a boisterous welcome cry. Don't walk in craving California rolls (there aren't any). And don't look for the tatami room decor that has turned myriad Japanese restaurants into cultural clichés.

Izakaya means "eat-drink place." In Japan, they are after-work destinations usually catering to blue-collar workers (men only). The first to open in Vancouver back in 1993 were modest, down-and-dirty, Japanese-style pubs—tiny places with cheap wooden tables, dispensing a wide array of affordable snacks to home-sick kids studying English. Now they've moved upmarket, refining flavours and expanding bar offerings from beer and sake to scores of wines by the glass.

Izakayas are quickly replacing the sushi palaces of yore with a simple ploy: inventive mini-dishes paired with hipster ambiance. The establishments are ultra-modern, bustling (often noisy), and energized by a young clientele seeking robust meals for reasonable prices.

The upscale izakaya was born in 2003, when Justin Ault, a Japanese Canadian, unveiled **HAPA IZAKAYA** (see review) on Robson Street and reinterpreted traditional pub food. In a high-tech room with low-slung tables, he pioneered "tapanese"—inspired tapas-style plates such as mackerel blowtorched tableside and beef tataki. Four years later, he opened a second location in Kitsilano, one of the city's liveliest neighbourhoods.

At the humble **GYOZA KING** (see review), pork gyoza with crisp skins emerge from the kitchen frequently to serve after-hours chefs and line cooks until 1:30am. At Guu Japanese Bars you might as well be in Tokyo ordering the rustic dishes such as *butabara* (grilled pork belly) and *onigiri* (rice balls).

—Kasey Wilson

Kirin Mandarin Restaurant / ★★★

102-1166 ALBERNI ST, DOWNTOWN (AND BRANCHES); 604/682-8833

The delicious high standards at this award-winning restaurant group is one of the reasons why Vancouver's Chinese food scene is considered the best in North America. The emphasis is on the light and fresh flavours of high-end Hong Kong–style dining. At dinner, look to the specials menu for seasonal dishes that in winter may include a rich bone-in lamb hot pot spiked with fermented tofu, or braised mushrooms with mixed vegetables in warmer months. Dungeness crab tossed with spicy garlic is available year-round, and for a real splash, try the lobster with Sichuan spices. The dim sum lunch menu also reflects seasonality, with highlights including asparagus and scallop rice rolls, crispy vegetarian spring rolls, and whole fried local smelts with spicy salt. Service is polished and quick if not always solicitous. *$$–$$$; AE, MC, V (Alberni St location only); debit cards; lunch, dinner every day; beer and wine; reservations recommended; www.kirinrestaurant.com; self-parking; map:S3.* &

Kitanoya Guu / ★★

838 THURLOW ST, DOWNTOWN (AND BRANCHES); 604/685-8817
At this friendly trio of *izakayas* (Japanese small-plates restaurants), you can sample the hottest Asian trend: tapanese. The Thurlow Street location is handy for a lunchtime shopping break, while the Water Street branch (in a converted Gastown warehouse) is the most stylish. Locals flock to the tiny storefront on Robson though, for the best food. Don't miss the kimchee udon (noodles with cod roe and cabbage), the kabocha *karokke* (an egg coated with squash, then fried), or the grilled yellowtail cheeks. *$; AE, MC, V; debit cards; lunch Mon–Sat (Thurlow location), dinner every day; beer and sake; reservations recommended; www.guu-izakaya.com/thurlow.html; street parking; map:R3.*

La Belle Auberge / ★★★

4856 48TH AVE, LADNER; 604/946-7717
Thirty minutes from Vancouver, famed chef/owner Bruno Marti serves creative French-style cuisine at this century-old Victorian manse in Ladner. Marti is well known to Vancouverites as a member and coach of the gold medal–winning teams at the Culinary Olympics. Choose the table d'hôte, pricey but worth it for choices such as poached arctic char, bison pot-au-feu or free-range chicken with morels. The wine list is well rounded with Pacific Northwest and international wines. *$$$; AE, MC, V; debit cards; dinner Tues–Sat; full bar; reservations recommended; www.labelleauberge.com; self-parking.* &

La Bretagne Crêperie / ★

795 JERVIS ST, DOWNTOWN; 604/688-5989
This wee slice of Brittany, just off the main Robson Street thoroughfare, draws the crowds with its affordable and addictively delicious crepes. The *crepe fromant*, made with organic white flour, arrives delicate and paper-thin while the *galette sarazin*, made with organic buckwheat flour, is a slightly heartier, equally satisfying alternative. Favourites include a sweet-and-savoury apple, cinnamon, and Swiss cheese version; the *sarladaise* with duck confit, onion, potato, and white sauce; and, finally, the peanut butter and banana crepe with melted Belgian chocolate. Plus, the cherry on top is the chance to practise your French on the servers as you enjoy a glass of French vin from the menu. A seat on their compact raised patio is ideal for a lazy weekend breakfast. *$; AE, DC, MC, V; debit cards; breakfast, lunch Tues–Sun, dinner Wed–Sat; beer and wine; reservations recommended; street parking; map:R3.* &

La Buca / ★★☆

4025 MACDONALD ST, WEST SIDE; 604/730-6988
Italian for "hole-in-the-wall," La Buca is more casual than Andrey Durbach's formal Parkside restaurant. The low-key Kitsilano location is more New York than Vancouver—it's a narrow 32-seater, so don't linger too long. Durbach's kitchen uses a basic arsenal of Italian ingredients—olive oil, garlic, balsamic vinegar, tomatoes, wine, Parmesan, prosciutto—to great effect. The menu ranges from chicken livers wrapped in prosciutto to daily fresh fish, crowd-pleasing classic house-made pastas, and hearty mains of pot roast lamb and boneless rabbit. Order the garlic bread and finish with a plate of biscotti. *$$– $$$; MC, V; debit cards; dinner every day; full bar; reservations recommended; www.labuca.ca; street parking; map:C3.*

La Cucina Italiana / ★★☆

1509 MARINE DR, NORTH VANCOUVER; 604/986-1334
What a delight it is to discover this charmingly rustic eatery in the midst of an unpromising strip of car dealerships! It's a simple and attractive place, with a menu featuring many of the usual players in Italian cuisine. Whether it's the spaghetti with tomatoes and fresh basil, the bresaola (air-dried beef) appetizer, a perfectly grilled veal chop, or homemade marsala ice cream, everything is prepared with a light, fastidious hand. It's clear there is some serious love going on in the kitchen—and that goes for the small but well-edited wine list, too. *$$; AE, DC, MC, V; debit cards; lunch Mon–Fri, dinner Mon–Sat; full bar; reservations recommended; street parking; map:E1.* &

Landmark Hot Pot House / ★★

4023 CAMBIE ST, WEST SIDE; 604/872-2868
Open flames and hot liquids usually do not figure into kid-friendly dining, but hot pots are incredibly popular with Asian families looking to chase away the winter chills. Diners cook their own food in tabletop pots heated by inset gas burners. Concoct your own dipping sauce from soy, sesame, and chile sauces. You can select up to two broths per pot; clear stocks allow the flavours of the ingredients to shine through, while spicy broths, such as Sichuan, add zing. The well-marbled beef needs only a quick dip to bring out its best; lobster emerges sweet and succulent. Watercress adds green freshness, and the deliciously enriched soup is perfect for noodles. The '80s decor is lovingly worn, and the waitstaff provides excellent help. *$$–$$$; MC, V; debit cards; dinner every day; beer and wine; reservations recommended; self-parking; map:D3.* &

La Piazza Dario Ristorante Italiano / ★★

3075 SLOCAN ST (ITALIAN CULTURAL CENTRE),
EAST VANCOUVER; 604/430-2195
Located in the Italian Cultural Centre, Dario's is not an upstart trendy restaurant. An antipasto station displays the day's offerings and splits the room in two. Tropical plants and floral displays complete the comfortable

89

illusion of dining in a courtyard. The large menu bucks the trends in favour of familiar favourites: spaghetti with red or white clam sauce, veal with lemon and white wine sauce, risotto with mushrooms and chicken in Gorgonzola sauce. The small bar extends into a floor-to-ceiling wall of wine, highlighting the restaurant's inventory of local and many old Italian vintages. Service is mature, understated, and seamlessly orchestrated. *$$; AE, MC, V; debit cards; lunch Mon–Fri, dinner every day; full bar; reservations recommended; www. lapiazzadario.bc.ca; self-parking; map:F3.* &

La Régalade French Bistro / ★★★

103-2232 MARINE DR, WEST VANCOUVER; 604/921-2228
West Vancouverites line up to get into the tiny, crowded La Régalade, and they're happy to do it. The food in this family-run, country-style French bistro is simply superb—homey, hearty daubes, braises, roasts, and terrines. Behind the stove is chef/owner Alain Rayé, while his wife, Brigitte, greets guests up front and their son Steeve makes nostalgic pastries such as floating island, profiteroles, and an apple tart that's so intense it tastes like candy. Each day brings a vast list of seasonal specials—butter-tender veal cheeks braised with tomatoes, for instance, or peppery rabbit with Dijon mustard. Still, it's Rayé's treatment of traditional dishes such as boeuf bourguignonne that has guests coming back again and again—that, and the prices, which are almost too reasonable to believe. *$$–$$$; MC, V; debit cards; lunch Tues–Fri, dinner Tues–Sat; full bar; reservations recommended; www.laregalade.com; street parking.* &

La Terrazza / ★★★

1088 CAMBIE ST, YALETOWN; 604/899-4449
La Terrazza lives up to its name: in warm weather, a row of French doors opens onto a large terrace, which adds an alfresco atmosphere to the inside tables. Chef Gennaro Iorio's cuisine is inventive, modern northern Italian. Start with the seared Quebec foie gras on poached pear, toasted brioche, and late-harvest wine reduction, or the extraordinary, juicy boneless short ribs. The pasta dishes are simple yet inspired, including house-made tortellini and chewy little *strozzapreti* ("priest stranglers") bolognese. The service is discreet yet attentive, and the wine list leans toward traditional producers, but upstart regions and innovative winemakers abound. *$$$; AE, MC, V; debit cards; lunch (Dec only), dinner every day; full bar; reservations recommended; www. laterrazza.ca; valet and street parking; map:T5.* &

Le Crocodile / ★★★

100-909 BURRARD ST, DOWNTOWN; 604/669-4298
Le Crocodile ages like a grande dame: classic and elegant—that's French-born chef/owner Michel Jacob's graceful downtown restaurant. Everyone orders Jacob's savoury onion tart and his Dover sole in a beurre blanc, but other classics, such as garlic-sautéed frogs' legs, double-cut veal chop, and sweetbreads with tarragon all pay their respects to tradition. The professional service,

European atmosphere, and mostly French wine list make a meal at Le Croco-dile an event. *$$$–$$$$; AE, DC, MC, V; debit cards; lunch Mon–Fri, dinner Mon–Sat; full bar; reservations recommended; www.lecrocodilerestaurant. com; valet parking; map:R4.* ♿

Le Gavroche / ★★

1616 ALBERNI ST, DOWNTOWN; 604/685-3924

For 30 years, Le Gavroche has been inviting guests to fall in love, both with each other and with its West Coast–influenced French cuisine. In part that's due to the attentive hospitality of owner Manuel Ferreira, not to mention his remarkable, award-winning 34,000-bottle wine cellar. Guests will also be seduced by the ambience of this refurbished heritage house with its fireplaces, shadowy nooks, and mountain views. Look for dishes based on traditional techniques and regional ingredients—quail stuffed with wild rice, smoked salmon with seaweed caviar, diver scallops with white beans—or simply succumb to the pleasures of the tasting menu. A meal here isn't just a fling, but the beginning of a long and beautiful love affair. *$$$; AE, DC, JCB, MC, V; debit cards; lunch Mon–Fri, dinner every day; full bar; reservations recommended; www.legavroche.ca; street parking; map:Q2.*

Le Marrakech Moroccan Bistro / ★★

52 ALEXANDER ST, GASTOWN; 604/688-3714

Get transported to exotic Morocco in this richly embroidered room. Color-ful tapestries, decorative lanterns, and servers garbed in traditional costume complete the inviting journey. After washing your hands in fragrant rosewa-ter, start with an order of the *kefta meshouiya*, a grilled mutton kebab with a mint, blueberry, and dried fruit salad. Then enjoy the braised lamb shank tagine with quince or *la casserole d'essaouira*, a flavourful mélange of ling cod, mussels, prawns, scallops, and *merguez* sausage in a saffron tomato broth. The *m'hanncha*, toasted almond paste in *brique* pastry with orange blossom honey and nougat, is a nice finish to the meal, especially with a cup of sweet-ened mint tea. Moroccan and Lebanese wine selections are well worth a sip. *$$–$$$; AE, DC, MC, V; debit cards; lunch Mon–Fri, dinner Mon–Sat; full bar; reservations recommended; www.lemarrakech.ca; valet and street park-ing; map:V3.*

Legendary Noodles / ★

**1074 DENMAN STREET, WEST END
(AND BRANCHES); 604/669-8551**

Stepping into this cozy space on a cold, rainy day, you feel as though you're in one of the tiny noodle and dumpling shops that dot the side streets of Beijing. The decor and food lean toward the rustic; amazingly, almost all of the noodle dishes are hand-pulled to order. Start with the garlicky potato salad, surprisingly crunchy potato shreds tossed in a zingy vinaigrette. The crispy, chewy green onion cakes are also made to order, served with a peanut dipping sauce. The lamb shank hand-pulled-noodle soup is warming, clean flavoured, and filling. Infused with flowers and wolfberries, a glass of the house tea soothes and aids digestion. Service is a little absentminded, but that's authentic too. *$; MC, V; debit cards; lunch, dinner every day; beer only; no reservations; self-parking; map:P3.*

Lift / ★★★

333 MENCHIONS MEWS, DOWNTOWN; 604/689-5438

Lift is that rarest of breeds: a view restaurant with good food. Perched above the bobbing yachts of the Coal Harbour Marina, this sleekly modern restaurant offers spectacular vistas of Stanley Park and the North Shore mountains. Of course, the well-heeled crowd may just be too busy checking out the surgically enhanced beauties gathered on the upstairs patio to take in the natural beauty around them. Adding to the stylish ambience is chef Scott Kidd's chic cuisine with a strong emphasis on local ingredients. Try the Aldergrove pheasant breast stuffed with smoked salmon and duxelles, or the roasted *sake kasu* sea bass. Indecisive diners may prefer the smaller "whet plates" of duck confit, seared foie gras, or five-spice quail breast. *$$$; AE, MC, V; debit cards; lunch Mon–Fri, dinner every day, brunch Sat–Sun; full bar; reservations recommended; www.liftbarandgrill.com; valet parking; map:R1.* &

Lime Japanese Cuisine / ★★

1130 COMMERCIAL DR, EAST VANCOUVER; 604/215-1130

Lime, with its seemingly incongruous pairing of live entertainment and meticulously executed Japanese cuisine, is a refreshing addition to "the Drive." The interior decor is an equally unexpected yet successful juxtaposition of rustic wooden tables with sleek leather chairs and hammered stainless steel ringing the sushi bar. Head chef Masaaki Kudo runs a tight ship, his skillful craftsmanship evident in small plates such as the *toro* stack: an artful arrangement of tuna belly slices, lightly dressed and delicately topped with a quail egg over a jumble of sliced green onions. Crispy avocado croquettes are skewered wonders, a textural contrast of creamy avocado and mozzarella jacketed in a crunchy rice-crisp skin. The smartly chosen wine list is BC-centric, while signature cocktails have a refreshing Asian twist: the Kakuro Royal is a delightful mix of pomegranate liqueur and *prosecco*. Stay, sip, and snack into the wee hours while enjoying the nightly show, but remember that there's a cover charge in effect. *$$; AE, MC, V; debit cards; dinner Tues–Sun; full bar; reservations recommended; www.limerestaurant.ca; street parking; map:E2.* &

Lolita's South of the Border Cantina / ★★
Me & Julio / ★

1326 DAVIE ST, WEST END; 604/696-9996
2095 COMMERCIAL DR, EAST VANCOUVER; 604/696-9997

In a city starved for Mexican food, the sister-and-brother team of Lila and Jaison Gaylie have brought exuberant *nuevo latino* cooking to an appreciative audience. Lolita's slow-cooked brisket *taquitos* spiked with pico de gallo is beefy heaven. The crisply seared halibut taco is served with a mango salsa. Cocktails are a heady blend of rum or vodka with fresh, juicy fruits. The tightly packed room mixes surfer girl chic, tiki kitsch, and cantina glow. Over at little-brother restaurant Me & Julio, there is more elbow room but the same cosy vibe. Carne asada tacos are brightened with pickled papayas, while the seafood soup is sharp with lime. Reflecting the Gaylies' stint with local tapas pioneer Bin 941 Tapas Parlour, there is an emphasis on shareable small plates. Along with mixed cocktails, there is an enticing array of tequilas to sample straight up. The servers are just as young and fresh-faced as the clientele. *$$–$$$; MC, V; debit cards; dinner every day, brunch Sat–Sun, holidays (Me & Julio); beer and wine; no reservations; www.lolitasrestaurant. com; www.meandjulio.ca; self-parking; map:Q4, Z7.* &

Lumière with Daniel Boulud / UNRATED

2551 W BROADWAY, WEST SIDE; 604/739-8185

Scheduled to re-open at press time, Lumière will be a phoenix rising from the flame. Gone is founding-chef Robert Feenie. Daniel Boulud (of the French-countryside approach to fine dining in New York, Palm Beach, Las Vegas, and Beijing) now has the helm, along with executive chef Dale MacKay. Dining in any of Boulud's establishments is a rhapsody of classical dishes with sublime contemporary touches—imaginative and fulsome food. A tasting menu is available, but there are splendid à la carte options. While some signature dishes are modeled after those in his eponymous flagship in New York, Boulud says his focus is "seasonal, local ingredients, farm-to-table dining." Dungeness crab salad with Granny Smith apples, celery root, and toasted hazelnuts is one tantalizing example. The prowess of the chef's Dinex Group will be at Lumière's disposal, making this yet another opportunity for local diners to experience some of the world's best cooking, right here at home. *$$$$; AE, DC, MC, V; debit cards; dinner Tues–Sun; full bar; reservations recommended; www.relaischateaux.com; valet parking; map:C2.*

Mangia e Bevi Ristorante / ★★☆

2222 MARINE DR, WEST VANCOUVER; 604/922-8333

Since it opened in spring 2007, Mangia e Bevi has managed to create a perfect balance of the formal and casual—it's a warmly elegant space with friendly but correct service, an accommodating wine list, and a menu that will satisfy your appetite for both simple food and fancier fare. Chef Rob Parrott hails from the more experimental kitchen of Gusto di Quattro, but here he's sticking to traditional Italian cuisine, and guests are all the better for it. Start with the antipasto, a three-tiered tower of everything from risotto cakes to prosciutto-wrapped arugula. Then dive into tagliolini with sinfully rich truffled porcini cream sauce or savoury wild boar bolognese. If you can manage a *secondo* after that, try the tender veal tenderloin stuffed with Gorgonzola. Whatever you order, though, expect to bring some home with you. *$$–$$$; AE, MC, V; debit cards; lunch Mon–Fri, dinner every day; full bar; reservations recommended; www.mangiaebevi.ca; street parking.* &

VANCOUVER'S BEST DIM SUM AND THEN SOME

Unabashedly loud, boisterous, and family friendly, dim sum lunch is the perfect way to sample a wide variety of Chinese dishes. Producing first-class dim sum is labour intensive and requires specialized chefs who do nothing but create these little masterpieces. In Vancouver, cart service has been mostly replaced by tick-box menus that ensure optimal freshness. Though menu descriptions can border on cryptic, waitstaff are usually happy to provide guidance. Try a variety of preparations: steamed, deep-fried, pan-seared, and braised. It is common practice to round out the meal with chow mein or fried rice.

Don't forget that tea is an integral part of the meal; choose a lovely floral jasmine tea for lighter summer fare or a robust iron Buddha for richer cold-weather dishes. But really, let your stomach be your guide, and you won't go very wrong.

Here are some of the best purveyors who make everything in-house and take freshness seriously.

CHEN'S SHANGHAI RESTAURANT (8095 Park Rd, Richmond; 604/304-8288)

Northern-style restaurants also offer their version of dim sum, snack-sized dumplings, and savouries. The steamed *xiao long bao* (pork soup dumplings) are among the best anywhere, and the sweet black-sesame pastries are sophisticated.

GINGERI CHINESE CUISINE (323-5300 No 3 Rd, Richmond; 604/278-6006)

Dim sum here is the epitome of clean and fresh flavours. The kalbi ribs steamed in a red wine sauce are full of beefy succulence. Rice served with a selection of broths provides a satisfying and healthy finish to your dim sum meal.

Marcello Pizzeria & Ristorante / ★

1404 COMMERICAL DR, EAST VANCOUVER; 604/215-7760

This spot is made for a night out with the family when the kids want oodles of noodles and plenty of meat sauce. The lineup often snakes out the door as diners wait for a coveted seat amidst the pseudo-Italian rustic decor and the bustling pace of the room. The menu doesn't throw any curveballs, just generous portions of fresh, homemade pasta and thin-crust wood-fired-oven pizza. A word to the wise: Unless you are famished, opt for a small plate of the pasta—such as the spaghetti carbonara or *tagliatelle al pomodoro*—and start with a simple caprese salad or a few of the antipasti selections. With a glass of Italian vino, you may just forget how full you really are. *$$; MC, V;*

GOLDEN SWAN RESTAURANT (5380 Victoria, East Vancouver; 604/321-6621)

With its cart service, superbright lighting, and insanely loud crowds, the atmosphere here is pure old-school dim sum palace. The bold and stronger-flavoured offerings such as deep-fried squid and pan-seared turnip cakes are particularly good. Egg tarts are sweetly warm and flaky.

IMPERIAL CHINESE SEAFOOD RESTAURANT (main floor, Marine Bldg, 355 Burrard St, Downtown; 604/688-8191)

Despite the mostly non-Chinese clientele, the authenticity level here is off the charts. Deep-fried crab claws, usually banquet fare, make a welcome dim sum appearance. Steamed curried baby cuttlefish are tender and sweet, and the crispy fried wontons are a guilty treat. In addition to the tick-box menu, trays of hot dim sum are brought by for further sampling. www.imperialrest.com.

KIRIN MANDARIN RESTAURANT (102-1166 Alberni St, Downtown, and branches; 604/682-8833)

Seasonality and lightness are the bywords here. The spring rolls are breathtakingly crisp, and the *har gow* (shrimp dumplings) are textbook plump and sweet. The feather-light scallop and egg-white fried rice will completely redefine your expectations of this classic standby. www.kirinrestaurant.com.

SUN SUI WAH SEAFOOD RESTAURANT (3888 Main St, East Vancouver; 604/872-8822 and 102-4940 No 3 Rd, Richmond; 604/273-8208)

Long a champion of local and exotic seafood, Sun Sui Wah embellishes dim sum with Dungeness crab, slivers of shark's fin, and sprinkles of tobiko roe. The rice rolls are delicate and tender, and the baked tapioca pudding is the best in the city. Cart service is available at the Main Street location on weekends. www.sunsuiwah.com.

—Lee Man

no debit cards; lunch, dinner every day; full bar; reservations for parties of 4 or more; street parking; map:Z6. ♿

Memphis Blues Barbeque House / ★★★

1342 COMMERCIAL DR, EAST VANCOUVER; 604/215-2599
1629 LONSDALE AVE, NORTH VANCOUVER; 604/929-3699

Get your butt here early. All the Memphis favourites—ribs, beef brisket, pulled pork, rib ends, and smoked sausage—are perfectly prepared with sides of coleslaw, corn bread, potato salad or fries, and barbecue-pit beans. All items can be had on their own, ranging from $13.95 for a half slab of ribs to $19.95 for a combo plate of any two meats (sides included). The brisket is unsurpassed, spread out in thick, meltingly tender slices. Tender and juicy Cornish game hen, as the signature dish, definitely deserves its John Hancock. The Memphis Feast ($34.95) features every kind of meat plus all the fixins'; the Elvis Platter, $66, is double the Memphis Feast. And if that isn't enough, you can pre-order the Priscilla, $125, to feed 10–12. Park Heffelfinger posts a wine list selected to whistle Dixie with smoked pork treats. Service is minimal—order at the counter and listen carefully, 'cause you gotta pick it up. *$$; AE, MC, V; debit cards; lunch, dinner every day; beer and wine; no reservations; www.memphisbluesbbq.com; street parking; map:C2.*

Mistral French Bistro / ★★☆

2585 W BROADWAY, WEST SIDE; 604/733-0046
Take a bite of the pissaladière (a thin-crusted tart of onions, olives, and anchovies) at this sunny Kitsilano bistro, and you may feel transported to the south of France. Chef/owner Jean-Yves Benoit prepares a menu of Provençal classics, while his wife, Minna, adds her own sunshine to the small dining room. Duck lovers can share the platter of rillettes, pâté, and smoked duck breast, and the hearty cassoulet is comfort food, rain or shine. The dark chocolate mousse, the lemon tart, or the Brie with pears makes a suitably classic ending. *$$$; AE, MC, V; debit cards; lunch Tues–Sat, dinner Mon–Sat; full bar; reservations recommended; www.mistralbistro.ca; street parking; map:C2.*

Montri's Thai Restaurant / ★★

3629 W BROADWAY, WEST SIDE; 604/738-9888
Look past the dated mishmash of decor and somewhat stiff service to focus instead on some of Vancouver's most authentic Thai cuisine. Though namesake Montri Rattanaraj is no longer at the helm, the fiery fare is still certain to please even the most die-hard capsaicin junkie—a five-chile count on the heat meter "is for addicts, masochists, and Thai nationals." Awaken your palate with *yum-nua*, a cold salad of smoky charbroiled beef jumbled together with tomato, lettuce, onion, chile, and mint in a tangy lime dressing. Pad thai, the quintessential noodle dish, is second to none, with excellent depth of wok flavour. Muslim-style *mus-a-mun* curry, available with either chicken or beef, delivers a soft, sweet heat with notes of tamarind and lemongrass. But don't reach for a glass of water to quell the flames: Thailand's Singha beer is a far more effective extinguisher. *$$; MC, V; debit cards; dinner Tues–Sun; full bar; reservations recommended; www.montri-thai.com; street parking; map:C2.* &

Morton's the Steakhouse / ★★★

750 W CORDOVA ST, DOWNTOWN; 604/915-5105
Secluded in the basement of the Sinclair Centre, this men's-club bomb shelter has all the trappings you'd want if the big one did go off: U.S. luxury, built like a Cadillac. Jumbo shrimp cocktails feature prawns the size of pinky fingers. Skip the hockey puck–size beefsteak tomato salad, unless they're buying heirloom tomatoes. Prime USDA beef awaits you ringside. The portly porterhouse is so tender you won't need the monster-size serrated

steak knife (for sale at six for $75). Request the prime rib—it impresses, too (especially as lunch for the following two days). Skip the baked potato and order the lyonnaise and creamed spinach. End with a bang and indulge in the Godiva hot chocolate cake. The wine list is big, and the prices are bigger. *$$$$; AE, DC, MC, V; debit cards; dinner Mon–Sat; full bar; reservations recommended; www.mortons.com; valet parking; map:T3.* &

Moustache Café / ★★★

129 W 2ND ST, NORTH VANCOUVER; 604/987-8461
The beloved old Moustache Café has a new chef, new owner, new location, and brand-new style—but it's still creating the kind of flavourful, Mediterranean-influenced West Coast cuisine that won its loyal following in the first place. From the tiny old house on busy Marine Drive, Moustache has moved into spacious modern digs in the condo valley of Lower Lonsdale. It's all airy, linear, and elegant, with a chic bar area and bright open kitchen, the kind of stylish place North Vancouver has long been awaiting. At the helm is chef/owner Geoff Lundholm, who brings serious skill and passion to the kitchen. Dishes change daily, but his salads are always a revelation—tender golden and purple beets with chèvre or duck confit, for instance—and his crisp duck breast glazed with honey is one of the best in the city, as is the luscious, made-to-order tarte Tatin. Best of all, the wine list features a remarkable selection of inexpensive but interesting choices. *$$$; AE, DC, MC, V; debit cards; dinner Tues–Sun; full bar; reservations recommended; www. moustachecafe.ca; street parking; map:E1.* &

Nat's New York Pizzeria / ★★

2684 W BROADWAY, WEST SIDE; 604/737-0707
1080 DENMAN ST, WEST END; 604/642-0777
Nat and Franco Bastone learned how to create Naples-style pizza at their uncle's pie parlor in Yonkers and, along with their wise-cracking staff, now serve some of the best thin-crust pizza around. Pull up a chair under the Big Apple memorabilia and sink your teeth into a slice loaded with chorizo and mushrooms or artichokes and pesto. Kids and teens love it here; the West Broadway location gets jammed at noon with students from nearby Kitsilano High, where Nat himself went to school. *$; MC, V; debit cards; lunch, dinner every day; no alcohol; no reservations; www.natspizza.com; street parking; map:C3, P2.*

Ningtu Restaurant / ★★

2130 KINGSWAY, EAST VANCOUVER; 604/438-6669
Relaxed home-style Shanghainese cooking keeps this neighbourhood gem full of happy diners. Salty and sour notes are used to bring out fresh, bright flavours. Fish fillets, fried in a nori-streaked batter and served with robust dark vinegar, are crisply delicious. *Edamame* beans tossed with pickled vegetables and tofu strips are light and savoury. Chilled marinated beef sandwiched in a flaky sesame pastry tastes like a Chinese take on pastrami. For something

that will charm the kids, try the hot crispy rice (*wo bah*) served with a choice of sauces, tossed together tableside for pyrotechnic sizzle. The service is warm and friendly, and the menu includes helpful pictures. *$$; cash and debit cards only; lunch, dinner every day; beer and wine; reservations recommended (minimum reservation for 8 at lunch); self-parking; map:F3.* ⅃

The Noodle Box / ★

1-1867 W 4TH AVE, WEST SIDE; 604/734-1310

In keeping with its cheerful food-cart beginnings in Victoria, this eatery's spirit of fun and adventure prevails. The clang and sizzle of wok cooking greet you as soon as you enter the energetic space. The heady flavours of Southeast Asia are sampled, remixed, and spun into dishes that smartly combine depth of spice and fresh ingredients. Singapore curry is gently warm with coconut milk, cashew nuts, rice noodles, and your choice of protein. The ginger heat of Cambodian jungle curry is lifted and soothed by mango and lime. Child- and vegan-friendly options help keep the whole family happy. *$$; AE, MC, V; debit cards; lunch, dinner every day; beer and wine; no reservations; www.thenoodlebox.net; self-parking; map:O7.* ⅃

Northern Delicacy / ★★

UNIT 2788, ABERDEEN CENTRE, 4151 HAZELBRIDGE WY, RICHMOND; 604/233-7050

Shanghainese- and Northern Chinese–style robustness is updated and served in a refined and modern space. Drunken chicken, poached with wine, is served chilled to enhance the silken texture of the dish. The salty charcuterie flavours of the succulent tea-smoked duck are perfect with the soft steamed bun. Rice, steamed with salted pork belly and chopped bok choy, is pure comfort food, and the steamed pork dumplings are a juicy dream. For a hit of heat, try the richly delicious noodles in hot and sour soup. The comprehensive, elegant, and easy-to-follow menu features a wide selection of small plates for easy sampling. Service follows the Hong Kong model of speed over charm. *$$; AE, MC, V; debit cards; lunch, dinner every day; beer and wine; reservations recommended; www.northern-delicacy.com; self-parking; map:D5.* ⅃

Nu / ★★★

1661 GRANVILLE ST, DOWNTOWN; 604/646-4668

Part 1980s cruise-ship aesthetic, part futuristic-lounge vibe, this room with a view (of False Creek) is boldly and stylishly design-forward. The room's streamlined curves mirror the stripped-down approach to the cuisine that uses "naked" flavours in cleanly wrought West Coast–inspired dishes. Plating is equally unadorned, with all of the focus on the quality of ingredients and their execution. Like its sister restaurant, C, Nu prides itself on its ethical and sustainable sourcing from local farmers and producers. Signature starts include standout small plates like chèvre-stuffed chicken wings and BC albacore tuna tartare, while principal plates tempt: seared Bayne scallops with confit of pork belly; pan-roasted lamb sirloin with mint-crusted peas and roasted parsnips; feta cannelloni. Make sure to request a seat on the wrap-around patio, cocktail or glass of BC's finest in hand. *$$$; AE, MC, V; debit cards; lunch, dinner every day; full bar; reservations recommended; www. whatisnu.com; self-parking; map:Q6.* &

Nyala African Cuisine / ★

4148 MAIN ST, EAST VANCOUVER; 604/876-9919
If you're planning dinner with a crowd, you can't go wrong with this lively African eatery in the trendy South Main area. (The former Kitsilano fave changed neighbourhoods two years ago.) The bright room decorated with quirky African artifacts is warm and welcoming, and so is the spicy fragrance in the air. Guests can enjoy savoury simmered meat (chicken, lamb, goat, venison) or vegetables, along with traditional South African biltong and *boerwors* and a variety of spicy condiments. There are plenty of vegetarian options, too. Everything is served in the Ethiopian style, without forks or spoons but with chunks of *injera* flatbread to scoop up the food from communal platters. Entertaining—and delicious, too. *$; AE, MC, V; debit cards; dinner every day; full bar; reservations recommended; www.nyala.com; self-parking; map:E4.* &

Octopus Garden Restaurant / ★★

1995 CORNWALL AVE, WEST SIDE; 604/734-8971
Witty and imaginative Japanese cooking grounded by top-notch ingredients and disciplined technique keep well-heeled Kitsilano natives coming back for more. The playful dragon roll combines perfectly seasoned rice, ripe avocados, and *unagi* tempura into a luscious perfect storm. The classic tuna roll balances spicy heat with the natural sweetness of red tuna, then raises the stakes with crunchy tobiko and tempura bits. Delicious. The bluefin tuna *toro* sashimi is expertly sliced and heartbreakingly lush. Consult the daily specials for the best of seasonal offerings. If you can't decide, give yourself over to one of the *omakase* (chef's choice) menus. The cosy, warm room and friendly service reflect the generosity of the cooking. *$$–$$$; AE, JCB, MC, V; debit cards; dinner Thurs–Tues; beer and wine; reservations recommended; www. octopusgarden.ca; self-parking; map:N6.* &

Okada Sushi Japanese Restaurant / ★★★

M101-888 NELSON ST, 2ND FLOOR, DOWNTOWN; 604/899-3266
Tucked away on the second floor, Okada is a hidden treasure worth seeking out. You are rewarded with a remarkably tranquil view and some of the finest Japanese food in the city. Though lunch service is available, dinner is the real star, with a daily sheet of incredibly fresh seafood and cleanly wrought traditional dishes. Pristine wild sockeye salmon comes straight from nearby waters. Prized local wild matsutake mushrooms are elegantly served in iron teapots with a fragrant clear broth, brightened by a squeeze of lime. Whole Japanese snapper braised in salty-sweet soy sauce is home cooking raised to a higher plane. Familiar gyozas are the picture of crisp freshness and pan-seared

flavour. Finish with a warmly satisfying bowl of *chazuke*, rice with green tea and various toppings. *$$–$$$; AE, JCB, MC, V; debit cards; lunch Mon–Fri, dinner Mon–Sat; beer and wine; no reservations; www.okadasushi.com; self-parking; map:R5.* &

Original Tandoori Kitchen / ★ ★☆

689 E 65TH AVE, EAST VANCOUVER; 604/327-8900
The Original Tandoori K. King has changed its name to the Original Tandoori Kitchen. Don't be confused by the Tandoori King around the corner. A feud between two brothers led to this royal battle that borders on a saga, but it's the Original Tandoori Kitchen that plays a raga on the taste buds. Tender lamb *seekh* kebab, chicken tikka, and rich, layered breads from the Tandoori's oven are addictive, as is the smoky eggplant, roasted whole over the wood fire in the tandoor before being mashed and seasoned. Order a side of mango chutney for dipping. Cool off with a Kingfisher beer. Delivery and takeout too. *$$; AE, MC, V; debit cards; lunch, dinner every day; beer and wine; no reservations; street parking; map:E4.*

Osteria Napoli Ristoranté / ★ ★☆

1660 RENFREW ST, EAST VANCOUVER; 604/255-6441
Replete with silk grape vines hanging from the ceiling, murals adorning the walls, and the requisite keyboard player singing "That's Amore," Osteria Napoli has been serving chef/owner Joe Briffa's old-school Italian fare for more than 20 years. Service is warm and personable at this cozy, unpretentious restaurant where large families from the neighbourhood often gather for weekend dinners. Monthly on Sunday evenings, porchetta is the main attraction, bells ringing as a glorious roast suckling pig is paraded through the restaurant before being carved. The essence of late summer in a bowl, chef Briffa's tomato sauce is the basis for simple traditional dishes such as *spaghetti alla Siciliana* with eggplant and a fiery kick, or *capone alla marinara*, red snapper baked together with white wine, capers, and olives. *$$; AE, MC, V; debit cards; dinner every day; full bar; reservations recommended; www.osterianapoli.com; street parking; map:F2.* &

Pajo's / ★

BAYVIEW AND 3RD ST, RICHMOND (AND BRANCHES); 604/272-1588
Open year-round, unless incessant rain showers dampen the spirits, this place is where to come for fish-and-chips. Select from fresh-as-can-be cod, salmon, and halibut, or dive into shrimp skewers, crab cakes, hamburgers, hot dogs, and poutine. Fries are chipped in-house. The original Pajo's floats on the Fraser River amidst a slew of fishing boats. Settle into a wooden chair, plunk your cone of fries into the hole cut in the armrest, and watch out for greedy seagulls. The second location, just a few blocks away, is grounded at Garry Point Park. If you don't want your fish deep fried, no problem—they are happy to grill it for you. Afterward, stroll off the tartar sauce by

walking the paths around the water's edge. *$; cash, debit cards only; lunch, dinner every day (depending on weather); no alcohol; no reservations; www. pajos.com; street parking; map:B7.*

Parkside / ★★★

1906 HARO ST, DOWNTOWN; 604/683-6912

It doesn't get any more romantic than holding hands under table No. 10 at Parkside. With a $65 prix fixe menu created by chef Andrey Durbach (of La Buca and Pied-à-Terre fame), the food is even more fabulous than the ambience. After all, this is where local chefs head for a top-of-the-line meal. Choose a libation from the inventive cocktail list or from an extensive old-world and regional wine list. The seasonal French and Mediterranean menu may include a starter of handmade fresh herb fettuccine or seared foie gras with a carmelized onion *tartelette*, mains of first-of-the-season halibut or lamb tenderloin niçoise, and for dessert *fromage frais* cannelloni with strawberry sorbet or a silky lemon tart brûlée. To go with the summer breeze on the patio, try heirloom tomato salad with Dungeness bisque. Service is exceptionally polite. *$$$$; MC, V; debit cards; dinner Wed–Sun; full bar; reservations recommended; www.parksiderestaurant.ca; valet parking; map:P2.*

The Pear Tree / ★★★☆

4120 E HASTINGS ST, BURNABY; 604/299-2772

Chef Scott Jaeger creates an array of dishes, grounded in classics but executed with finesse, at what is probably the best neighbourhood restaurant in the Vancouver area. His charming wife and business partner, Stephanie, adds a refined touch to the service in this recently remodeled stylish, casual, and romantic space. Seafood receives skillful handling: Jaeger's lobster "cappuccino" and pan-seared trout are not to be missed. At $55–$65, the three-course table d'hôte is an unbeatable bargain. The international wine list is food-friendly. *$$$; AE, MC, V; debit cards; dinner every day; full bar; reservations recommended; valet parking; map:G2.* &

Phnom Penh / ★★☆

244 E GEORGIA ST, CHINATOWN; 604/682-5777

The Hyunh family's award-winning restaurant has attained cultlike status amongst those seeking top-notch Cambodian and Vietnamese fare, even garnering nods from culinary notables Anthony Bourdain and Julia Child. Devotees sit elbow to elbow at peak dining hours, anxious to tuck into an order of Phnom Penh's signature spicy garlic squid or deep-fried chicken wings. Served with a piquant lemon-pepper dip and sprinkled with toasted garlic chips, these dishes deliver a rollicking cavalcade of flavour. Sweet and citrusy green papaya salad is another standout, tossed with julienned carrot, prawns, and warmed strips of beef jerky. Meat lovers will delight in paper-thin slices of rare carpaccio-style butter beef, served in a flowerlike fan beneath fresh cilantro, fried garlic, and a pungent dressing of lime and nuoc nam (fish sauce). Wash it all down with a tall glass of effervescent *soda chanh duong* (sweet lemonade) or a frosty bottle of Tsingtao beer. *$–$$; AE, MC, V; debit cards; lunch, dinner every day; beer and wine; reservations recommended; street parking; map:V4.* &

Pho Thai Hoa / ★★

1625 KINGSWAY, EAST VANCOUVER; 604/873-2348

Among the seemingly innumerable ethnic restaurants along the Kingsway corridor, Pho Thai Hoa stands apart from the rest. Albeit humble in both decor and price point, it certainly makes no compromise when it comes to flavour. Inexpensive menu options for Vietnamese meals in a bowl abound, and pho is the perfect place to start: clear, aromatic broth with your choice of meaty morsels. Beef lovers won't be disappointed with *pho dac biet,* a delectable hodgepodge of fatty brisket, tripe, meatballs, soft tendon, and rice noodles. Garnish to your liking from the accompanying condiment dish piled high with bean sprouts, basil, lime wedges, and chile peppers. Green papaya salad perks up your palate, tossed in tangy vinaigrette and topped with prawns and shredded pork. *Bot chien* rounds out the starch fix, toonie-sized rice cakes panfried to a crisp in sweet soya sauce with green onion and egg. *$; AE, MC, V; debit cards; lunch, dinner every day; no alcohol; no reservations; street parking; map:E3.* &

Pied-à-Terre / ★★★

3369 CAMBIE ST, WEST SIDE; 604/873-3131

You won't find any surprises here, and that's the way chef Andrey Durbach planned it. The menu adheres to well-executed classics at this tiny, crowded French-style neighbourhood bistro: coquilles St.-Jacques, steak tartare, coq au vin, mustard-crusted rabbit, steak frites. It's easy to linger over the unusually expert onion soup, and the crispy-skinned *poulet rôti* with a choice of peppercorn sauce or rosemary garlic (order both). Among desserts are textbook-perfect crème caramel and a not-too-sweet chocolate mousse paired with a shortbread cookie. The all-French wine list has good by-the-glass choices. It's French, so don't expect to order tea at the end of the meal. Servers all know their stuff. *$$; MC, V; debit cards; lunch Mon–Fri, dinner every day; full bar; reservations recommended; www.pied-a-terre-bistro. ca; street parking; map:D3.*

Pinkys Steakhouse / ★★

1265 HAMILTON ST, YALETOWN; 604/637-3135

Steak has returned with a glamourous vengeance, here in surroundings that go with your favourite pumps or your most tailored shirt. A lavish circular bar dominates in the centre, while luxury wallpaper accents and glittering chandeliers add to the "rock-star" appeal. The food takes a no-fuss approach to steak-house fare, from the chilled jumbo prawn cocktail with zesty cocktail sauce to the organic steak tartare with crisp melba toasts. Go for the millionaire's fillet cut (8 or 12 ounces) or the organic rib eye (12 ounces), along with a variety of sides that include fettuccine Alfredo and zippy horseradish bacon mashed potatoes. The wine listed is extensive, along with some select Pinkys treats for celebratory splurging. At press time a new location in Kitsilano had opened. *$$$; AE, MC, V; debit cards; lunch Fri, dinner every day; full bar; reservations recommended; www.pinkyssteakhouse.com; street and valet parking; map:S5.* &

Plan B Lounge and Eatery / ★

1144 HOMER ST, YALETOWN; 604/609-0901

No quickly thrown-together tapas here, but small plates of precisely executed and well-balanced cooking that eats like fine dining. Recent offerings include a roasted beet and goat cheese salad that pulled together sweet creaminess with the sharp tang of lemon and rounded bitterness of frisée. The meatiness of the cardamom and coffee lamb rack was brightened with little jewels of baby turnips and oyster mushrooms glossy with a lamb reduction. The satisfying chèvre and wildflower honey gelato ends the meal perfectly on a subtly floral note. The long, loungey space is, in true Yaletown fashion, anonymously sleek and comfortable, but the smart, friendly service is a cut above the neighbourhood's usual good-looking robots. *$$–$$$; AE, MC, V; no debit cards; dinner Mon– Sat; beer and wine; no reservations; www.planblounge. com; self-parking; map:S5.* &

Planet Veg / ★

1941 CORNWALL AVE, WEST SIDE; 604/734-1001

The first bite proves it all to those dubious carnivores: all veggie fare can indeed pack a tasty punch. Interiors of this small cafe may be basic, but the spicing and ingredient combos are heartily complex. Whole-wheat rotis, specialty pitas packed with *subjis* (spiced vegetable dishes), and baked samosas are all great eat-in or takeout fixes, especially with drizzlings of the sweet tamarind chutney. If you want your Indian flavours with a western twist, order the popular garden burger or grilled paneer sandwich and dip your bites in ketchup instead. And of course, wash it all down with a cup of chai or refreshing mango lassi. *$; MC, V; debit cards; lunch, dinner every day; no alcohol; no reservations; street parking; map:O6.* &

Pondok Indonesia / ★★

2781 COMMERCIAL DR, EAST VANCOUVER; 604/872-8718

A delicate tinkling of wooden chimes announces your arrival to this relaxed, unpretentious room where Catherine Tanurahardja shares family recipes passed down through many generations. Start with *tahu sayur isi*, tofu triangles stuffed with vegetables and deep-fried to a perfect crunch, served with a delicate peanut sauce. Sweet and piquant *ayam bumbu bali* is chicken simmered in a house-made red chile-pepper sauce that's also available for purchase if you'd like to dial up the heat in your own kitchen. Simmered in coconut milk and curry leaves, *gulai kambing* (lamb stew) offers a softer heat. Fill that last little bit of space with *pisang gulung manis*, fried crepe-wrapped bananas topped with vanilla ice cream and a drizzle of caramel sauce.

$$; MC, V; debit cards; lunch Mon–Fri, dinner every day; beer and wine; no reservations; www.pondokindonesia.com; street parking; map:E3. &

Provence Mediterranean Grill / ★★☆
Provence Marinaside / ★★☆

4473 W 10TH AVE, WEST SIDE; 604/222-1980
1177 MARINASIDE CRES, YALETOWN; 604/681-4144

The Mediterranean sun rules at the Mediterranean Grill, and seafood rules at Provence Marinaside, with the husband-wife team of Jean-Francis and Alessandra Quaglia. These restaurants rule the antipasti: Choose from various baked, grilled, stewed, or marinated items at $5 each—pissaladière, squid in vinaigrette, artichokes, and tomato with bocconcini. Appetizers include intense fish soup or warm goat cheese crusted with herbes de Provence on organic greens. Continue with bouillabaisse, served with a garlicky rouille and shards of Gruyère. Don't leave without a copy of the Quaglia's *New World Provence* cookbook. *$$$; AE, MC, V; debit cards; lunch Mon–Fri, dinner every day, brunch Sat–Sun; full bar; reservations recommended; www. provencevancouver.com; street parking; map:B2, S6.* &

Quattro on Fourth / ★★★
Gusto di Quattro / ★★

2611 W 4TH AVE, WEST SIDE; 604/734-4444
**1 LONSDALE AVE (ACROSS FROM LONSDALE QUAY MARKET),
NORTH VANCOUVER; 604/924-4444**

It's rare indeed to discover an Italian restaurant that neither clings too staidly to old-world ways nor veers too wildly toward innovation, yet manages to pay elegant homage to both. Warm, welcoming Quattro is that restaurant. It helps when the owner is the dynamic Patrick Corsi, descendant of one of Vancouver's well-known restaurant families, who has created a bright, airy room that avoids the typical Italianate clichés. It also helps when the chef is Bradford Ellis, who creates such deliciously decadent dishes as the *ravioli piemontese* stuffed with wild mushrooms, mascarpone, and just enough truffle oil, or the pistachio-crusted Alaskan black cod. This is the place to come for all the great Italian wines and for an impressive selection of grappa, best enjoyed on the secluded garden patio. *$$$; AE, DC, MC, V; debit cards; dinner every day; full bar; reservations recommended; www.quattrorestaurants.com; self-parking; map:C2, F1.* &

Raincity Grill / ★★☆

1193 DENMAN ST, WEST END; 604/685-7337

When the skies are clear over sparkling English Bay, the views from the picture windows and the patio of this elegantly polished West End space are jewel-like. However, even on a rainy day, there are few better places in the city for enjoying the natural splendour of Vancouver scenery and its indigenous ingredients. The food is all about the promotion of local, ethical sourcing, starting from the "spoons," small teasers of items such as Salt Spring Island mussels, scallops with mushrooms and hazelnuts, and albacore tuna with pickled carrot. Butternut squash and hazelnut soup with Dungeness crab salad is a series of silky, deeply flavourful spoonfuls. Meanwhile, pan-roasted BC sablefish with side-stripe shrimp, Salt Spring Island mussels, braised daikon, and North Arm Farms carrots, all in a mushroom broth, is a quintessential Vancouver mixing of local abundance with global Asian influences. Raincity is unfailingly exacting in all aspects of the dining experience, from the service to its award-winning wine list that features the best of the Pacific Northwest. *$$$–$$$$; AE, DC, MC, V; debit cards; lunch Mon–Fri, dinner every day, brunch Sat–Sun; full bar; reservations recommended; www.rain citygrill.com; valet and street parking; map:P3.* &

The Red Onion / ★

2028 W 41ST AVE, WEST SIDE; 604/263-0833
Forget drive-ins and head to Kerrisdale for the best double dogs in town. Two European-style wieners barely fit into the bun, with onions, grated cheddar cheese, and the Red Onion's special relish sauce to top it off. Grilled chicken burgers and hamburgers are delivered in foil pouches, piled high with all sorts of fixings. The french fries in a basket will easily feed two and are served with the best sour-cream-and-dill dip in town. Posters, hanging plants, and a Pabst Blue Ribbon neon beer sign complete the unpretentious atmosphere, enhanced by the aroma of grilling meats. *$; MC, V; debit cards; lunch, dinner every day; no alcohol; no reservations; street parking; map:C4.*

Rekados / ★★

4063 MAIN ST, EAST VANCOUVER; 604/873-3313
Together with wife Pinky and brother-in-law Larry Elima, chef/owner Charlie Dizon has taken Filipino cuisine upmarket. This chic, modern room is accented with dark wood and punches of red, a lounge music backbeat setting a cool vibe. Tables are at a premium on weekends, and the crowd ranges from those coming for a drink and a small-plates nosh to expat families celebrating special occasions. Creative cocktails are decidedly tropical with the addition of ingredients including mango juice and *kalamansi* juice to old-school favourites. Rekados means "ingredients" in Tagalog, and Dizon's artfully plated dishes smoothly articulate the Spanish, Chinese, and Malaysian influences on Filipino fare. Crispy *pata* is pure porcine goodness, a seasoned pork hock that's first slow-roasted, then flash-fried to a crackle. Indo-Malay-influenced adobo simmers grilled marinated chicken and tender braised pork in a velvety soy–coconut milk sauce. Most desserts put a playful spin on traditional sweets, but the strangely appealing corn and cheddar cheese *sorbetes* is the real deal. *$$; MC, V; debit cards; lunch, dinner Tues–Sun; full bar; reservations recommended; www.rekados.com; self-parking; map:E3.* &

BROOD FOOD: KID-FRIENDLY DINING

When you're out and about with a (not-so-) little one in tow and notice the clock ticking ever closer to meal time, fear not. You won't be stuck dining beneath the glow of the Golden Arches, as Vancouver has a wealth of restaurants that welcome young foodies in the making.

BURGOO (4434 W 10th Ave, West Side, and branches; 604/221-7839)
Rustic timbers and the flickering fireplace offer a homey backdrop for rib-sticking, soul-warming comfort food. Young ones can tuck into a kid-sized portion of white cheddar mac and cheese while Mom and Dad opt for a robustly flavoured bowl of *boeuf bourguignonne* or lamb tagine. Chocolate fondue for dessert is a surefire hit. *Lunch, dinner every day; www.burgoo.ca; map:B3.*

GO FISH! (1505 W 1st Ave, False Creek Fisherman's Wharf, West Side; 604/730-5040)
Arrive early to snag a picnic table and join the queue. Chef/owner Gord Martin's wharfside seafood shack is home to (arguably) Vancouver's finest fish-and-chips—and freshest, too, as locally caught fish is purchased directly from the boats moored just steps away. Served rain or shine, oyster po'boys and fish *tacones* are outrageously addictive. *Lunch every day; map:P6.*

GOLDEN SWAN (5380 Victoria Dr, East Side; 604/321-6621)
As more and more Chinese restaurants switch over to menus for dim sum, it's a treat to find one that still has old-school cart service where kids can choose their meals as the dishes roll past. Small portions make it easy to sample a wide variety of goodies without breaking the bank. Crunchy spring rolls and sweet, fluffy *ma lai goh* (steamed golden sponge cake) are sure to please the fussiest of eaters. Beat the inevitable lineup by calling ahead for reservations. *Lunch, dinner every day; map:F4.*

LITTLE NEST (1716 Charles St, East Vancouver; 604/251-9994)
With a well-stocked play area, including a custom-built toy kitchen for budding

Rinconcito Salvadoreño Restaurant / ★★☆

2062 COMMERCIAL DR, EAST VANCOUVER; 604/879-2600
This charming family-run restaurant—replete with a lively Latino playlist, and ice-cold *cervezas*—sees a steady stream of customers, both young and old, craving Ana Herrera's handmade pupusas. A signature El Salvadoran delicacy, these thick corn tortillas stuffed with chicharrón (chopped pork), frijoles (beans), queso (cheese), or a combination of the three (*revuelta*) are served with *chimol* (cooked salsa) and *curtido* (pickled cabbage salad); Herrera cranks out up to 300 of them on a busy night. Husband José is a cheerful

junior chefs, Little Nest is an ideal brunch destination for the Fisher-Price set, parents in tow. Chef/owner Mary MacIntyre, formerly of Lumière, offers an organic, locally focused menu that piques kids' interest with fun, healthy food such as Fruit Fries and "Alphabetty" Soup. A selection of sophisticated salads, all-day breakfasts, and fair-trade coffee caters to grown-up tastes. *Breakfast, lunch Tues–Sun; www.littlenest.ca; map:Z6.*

ROCKY MOUNTAIN FLATBREAD COMPANY (1876 W 1st Ave, West Side; 604/730-0321)

Wood-fired pizza is the order of the day, made with organic all-natural ingredients. Sunday and Monday evenings are Family Nights, and kids are invited into the kitchen to make their own pizzas while Mom and Dad relax with a glass of wine or a locally microbrewed beer. *Lunch, dinner every day; www.rockymountainflatbread.ca; map:O6.*

SECRET GARDEN TEA COMPANY (5559 W Boulevard, West Side; 604/261-3070)

High tea fit for a little princess (or prince) is served thrice daily. Kids' eyes invariably light up as an elegant three-tiered tray laden with tiny sandwiches, miniature pastries, and sweet scones with Devon cream and raspberry jam arrives at the table. When making reservations, ask for the Children's High Tea at a fraction of the regular price. *Breakfast, lunch every day; www.secretgardentea.com; map:C4.*

ZAKKUSHI CHARCOAL GRILL DINER (1833 W 4th Ave, West Side; 604/730-9844 and 823 Denman St, West End; 604/685-1136)

Both the young and the young-at-heart love a good barbecue, but here it's yakitori rather than burgers and hot dogs on the grill. Each kid-sized *kushi* stick costs less than a toonie—your pile of empty skewers is sure to grow at a remarkable rate. Little ones will be clamouring to try Pooh Bear's Afternoon Snack for dessert. *Dinner every day; www.zakkushi.com; map:O7, P2.*

—Joie Alvaro Kent

host, readily guiding newcomers through the menu of Salvadoran and Mexican fare. Notable dishes: *pollo encebollado*, chicken sautéed with onions in a bright tomato sauce, and Mar y Tierra, a hefty platter for two laden with grilled top sirloin steak and succulent prawns. *$–$$; cash only; lunch, dinner Wed–Mon; beer and wine; no reservations; street parking; map:F3.* &

Rocky Mountain Flatbread Company / ★

1876 W 1ST AVE, WEST SIDE; 604/730-0321
Expect a cosy environment where you can enjoy wood-fired pizzas that are made with all-natural, organic ingredients. While the food is a little more

expensive than at your average pizza joint, it amply makes up for it in quality. A salad with basil and blackberry dressing is a refreshing start before you dig into pizzas with toppings such as mesquite-barbecued organic chicken or sun-dried tomato and goat cheese. Kids will especially love family nights on Mondays and Sundays when they can make their own pizzas in the kitchen. Meanwhile, adults can choose from a variety of Californian and BC wines or a selection of local beers. *$$; AE, MC, V; debit cards; lunch, dinner every day; full bar; reservations recommended; www.rockymountainflatbread.ca; street parking; map:O6.* &

Rodney's Oyster House / ★★

405-1228 HAMILTON ST, YALETOWN; 604/609-0080

All oysters, all the time—that's the reason to visit this unpretentious fish house and bar. While the slogan here is "The lemon, the oyster, and your lips are all that's required," you can choose one of several sauces instead of taking your oysters straight. Also offered are a choice of creamy chowders, steamed mussels and clams, and local Dungeness crab. There are a few tables upstairs, but the main-floor bar is where the action is. Prices are moderate, especially given its location in trendy Yaletown. *$$–$$$; AE, E, MC, V; debit cards; lunch, dinner Mon–Sat; beer and wine; reservations recommended; street parking; map:S5.*

SalaThai Thai Restaurant / ★★☆

102-888 BURRARD ST, DOWNTOWN; 604/683-7999
3364 CAMBIE ST, WEST SIDE; 604/875-6999

A favourite of visiting celebrities, SalaThai serves authentic Thai cuisine in the heart of downtown. Well-priced lunch specials make it popular with the midday crowd, but the dinner menu fully showcases the range of traditional dishes. Lead in with *larb gai*, fresh mint adding brightness to the minced chicken salad's smoky spice. A healthy dose of Thai basil lifts *pad see-ew* above the pedestrian stir-fried rice noodles with your choice of meat. Tapioca pudding, served warm and sweet with coconut milk and morsels of banana and jackfruit, is a dessert that makes you happy. The Cambie Street location has been a neighbourhood favourite for more than 20 years. Decor would benefit from updating, but the food is spot-on. *$$; MC, V; debit cards; lunch, dinner every day (Burrard), lunch Mon–Fri, dinner every day (Cambie); full bar; no reservations; www.salathaidowntown.ca (Burrard), www.salathai.ca (Cambie); street parking; map:S4.* &

The Salmon House / ★★★

2229 FOLKESTONE WY, WEST VANCOUVER; 604/926-3212

After more than 30 years sitting (literally, if not culinarily) atop the local restaurant scene, this West Van institution has recently caught fire with a renewed focus on local, seasonal, and environmentally appropriate ingredients. It's still got the spectacular view and the West Coast Native artifacts that make it a must-visit for out-of-towners, but now it's become a dining destination for a whole new reason. The seafood is exceptional, especially the alder-grilled wild sockeye salmon or alder-smoked Fanny Bay oysters. But it's the "Uniquely BC" tasting menu that we love. Locals may bring visitors here for the unsurpassed view of the city, but they'll be back for the Nicola Valley braised short ribs with chanterelles, the grilled BC spot prawns, or the Vancouver Island Dungeness crab cakes—and the stellar local wines that go with them. *$$$; AE, DC, MC, V; debit cards; lunch Mon–Sat, dinner every day, brunch Sun; full bar; reservations recommended; www.salmonhouse.com; self-parking.* &

Saltlik / ★★

1032 ALBERNI ST, DOWNTOWN; 604/689-9749
Soaring interiors and an impressive backlit 1,200-bottle wine wall make this sleek downtown spot more than your average steak house. Attractive servers circulate in the dining room and adjoining lounge where equally pretty people mingle, cocktail in one hand and clutch purse in the other. Starters are consistent crowd pleasers, from pan-flashed shrimp in coconut cream with crunchy tortillas and avocado salsa to grilled chicken wings with sweet-chile-and-garlic dipping sauce. Make no apologies for indulging your carnivorous side with the skirt steak drizzled with black truffle oil or the veal strip loin with wild mushroom, veal, and cream reduction. The accessible wine list offers some solid, affordable choices. *$$–$$$; AE, MC, V; debit cards; lunch, dinner every day; full bar; reservations recommended; www.saltliksteakhouse. com; weekend valet and street parking; map:R3.* &

Salt Tasting Room / ★★★

45 BLOOD ALLEY, GASTOWN; 604/633-1912
Who says that you need a kitchen to run a successful restaurant? At this hugely popular wine and charcuterie bar, all the staff need are sharp knives, sharp wits, and even sharper palates. Salt—and the recent addition down-stairs, Salt Cellar—is the brainchild of local publican Sean Heather, whose mini-empire is helping revitalize an historic but long-neglected area of Van-couver. Tucked in a faintly alarming Gastown alley, Salt is a spare but inviting room with communal seating and a festive air. It's dominated by a chalkboard that lists international cheeses and cured meats, with a strong focus on such excellent local producers as Oyama Meats. Cheese and charcuterie are served in trios paired with lively condiments as well as an intriguing selection of wines by the glass. *$–$$; AE, MC, V; debit cards; lunch, dinner every day; beer and wine; reservations recommended for large parties; www.salttastingroom. com; self-parking; map:U3.*

Sanafir / ★★★

1026 GRANVILLE ST, DOWNTOWN; 604/678-1049
Inspired by the rich culture of the Silk Road and the aesthetics of the west-ern world, Sanafir (Arabic for "meeting place") is a sexy casbah oasis on Granville Street's seedy entertainment row. The upstairs lounge features high

ceilings offset by richly upholstered beds, and food is served on a tray so guests can eat while leaning forward, back, or against silk pillows. Trios of tapas, chosen by protein (beef, lamb, prawns, etc.) combine bold flavours and balanced textures, each offering a different take on an ingredient. The wild BC salmon is an inventive threesome including buttery seared coho over curry, crispy tea-smoked spring salmon, and intensely smooth sockeye tartare. The bar has an extensive collection of both Champagne vintages and fun picks to quaff in quantity. The kitchen is open late. *$$–$$$; AE, MC, V; debit cards; dinner every day; full bar; no reservations; www.sanafir.ca; valet parking Thur–Sat; map:S4.* &

Sandy's Cuisine / ★

4186 MAIN ST, EAST VANCOUVER; 604/677-4807

Weekdays may be quiet at this modest Filipino eatery-cum-*tindahan* ("grocery store"), but weekends see Filipino families crowding the tables, nostalgic for comforting tastes of home. Cooking-show host, restaurateur, and food writer Sandy Daza is a celebrity jack-of-all-foodie-trades in the expat community, and his *turo-turo* restaurant (translated as "point-point" to your items of choice) typifies the cafeteria-style dining so common in the Philippines. Daza takes a health-conscious approach to traditional recipes by choosing leaner cuts of meat but doesn't compromise when it comes to flavour in dishes such as *dinakdakan*, strips of lean pork cooked with ginger, onion, garlic, and coconut milk. Pandan chicken is a popular pick, first marinated for tenderness, then wrapped in pandanus leaves that infuse their delicate flavour during cooking. Adobo *kangkong* riffs on the meat-centric original with a sauté of water spinach, garlic, black beans, and soy sauce. *$; MC, V; debit cards; lunch, dinner Tues–Sun; no alcohol; no reservations; street parking; map:E3.* &

Sawasdee Thai Restaurant / ★★

4250 MAIN ST, EAST VANCOUVER; 604/876-4030

Vancouver's first Thai restaurant has seen a recent face-lift, lending understated warmth to this casual, upbeat room. Service is friendly and relaxed, welcoming newcomers and regulars alike. Spark up your taste buds with *larb gai*, a fiery salad of minced chicken seasoned with toasted rice, lime juice, cilantro, and a liberal helping of chiles. For a less spicy start, try the deep-fried chicken wings: deboned, then stuffed with bean-thread noodles, mushrooms, and julienned carrot and served with a piquant sweet chile dipping sauce. Crying Tiger Beef peaks the heat meter, balanced by the soft sweetness of roast duck red curry with pineapple, tomato, and bamboo shoots in coconut milk. Banana fritters with coconut ice cream are a tasty finish, but try the black rice pudding, comforting in its warm sweetness with chunks of taro and a coconut-milk topping. *$$; MC, V; debit cards; lunch Tues–Fri, dinner every day; full bar; reservations recommended; www.sawasdeethairestaurant.com; street parking; map:D3.* &

Sciué Italian Bakery Caffé / ★★

110-800 W PENDER ST, DOWNTOWN; 604/602-7263

Downtown crowds have fallen hard for this affordable, modern Italian cafe where gourmet meals arrive presto and the coffee aromas waft enticingly. Pronounced "SHOE-eh" (Naples slang for "good and fast"), this room and outdoor seating at the front are always buzzing with customers looking for a quick gelato, latte, or pastry fix. Devotees moan longingly over the thin-crusted flatbreads, *pane romano*, which come topped with fresh, authentic ingredients such as Roma tomatoes, sliced bocconcini cheese, and Italian sausage. The panini, named in homage to regions in Italy, also draw enthusiastic reviews. The Milano with pastrami, Brie, caramelized onion, and tomato will have you booking the next flight to Italy, if the gnocchi don't convince you first. At press time, a new Yaletown location opened at 126 Davie St (604/689-7263). *$; AE, MC, V; debit cards; breakfast, lunch Mon–Sat, dinner Mon–Fri; beer and wine; www.sciue.ca; street parking; map:S3.* &

Sea Harbour Seafood Restaurant / ★★★

3711 NO 3 RD, RICHMOND; 604/232-0816

The kitchen at Sea Harbour takes advantage of straight-from-the-market vegetables and local seafood to produce top-notch Cantonese-style cuisine. Live Dungeness crab is cooked with kabocha squash, fermented black beans, and garlic, the resulting sweet-salty sauce accentuating the briny, fresh flavours of the crab to dazzling effect. Hand-shredded free-range chicken is tossed with sand ginger (galangal, part of the ginger family) to add depth and savour. Gai lan (Chinese broccoli) stir-fried with cured meats highlights the famous local Chinese charcuterie. Other worthy offerings include chayote squash stir-fried with pork and Chinese olives, or the sweet-and-sour pork that is light years from the usual fast-food offering. Lunch is focused on dim sum, but dinner items can still be ordered. *$$–$$$; MC, V; debit cards; lunch, dinner every day; beer and wine; reservations recommended; self-parking; map:D5.* &

Shanghai Chinese Bistro / ★★

1124 ALBERNI ST, DOWNTOWN; 604/683-8222

Located just off the Robson Street shopping district, this bastion of Hong Kong–inflected northern Chinese cuisine has garnered a large and loyal following. Though the chile heat is dialed down somewhat, the flavours are fresh and clean. The shrimp and garlic spring rolls crackle with flavour, the crispy-bottomed Shanghainese pot stickers are full of juicy pork, and the vegetarian-friendly spicy eggplant and fried tofu hot pot bubbles with savoury heat. Traditional Cantonese dim sum is also top-notch: steamed shrimp dumplings, black bean pork spareribs, and wobbly egg tarts are standouts. The softly luscious chilled mango pudding is the best around. Weekday lunches are insanely popular with the downtown office crowd, so reservations are a must. Service is brightly efficient and friendly. *$–$$; AE, MC, V; no debit cards; lunch, dinner every day; full bar; reservations recommended; self-parking; map:R3.* &

The Shore Club / ★★☆

688 DUNSMUIR ST DOWNTOWN; 604/899-4400

The king of steak houses, David Aisenstat, has hatched a multimillion-dollar Vegas-like seafood house that offers a dining experience in a space that is every bit as alluring as its 36-foot-tall ceilings. And although seafood is the main course here—textbook-perfect lobster bisque, a refined wild salmon Wellington—you'll also find Aisenstat's Gotham Steakhouse (see review) favourites on the menu. Service is enthusiastic, and the approachable wine list has plenty of good wines by the glass. For sheer entertainment value, take a seat at the bar and engage in some prime people-watching. *$$$; AE, MC, V; debit cards; lunch Mon–Fri, dinner every day; full bar; reservations recommended; www.theshoreclub.ca; valet parking; map:T3.*

Simply Thai / ★★

1211 HAMILTON ST, YALETOWN; 604/642-0123

Established long before Yaletown fully embraced its inner glitz, this neighbourhood favourite continues to deliver authentic Thai flavours, much to the delight of longtime fans. The *som tum* ("papaya salad") is bright with lime and chiles against the crunch of green papayas, carrots, and peanuts. The intense *massaman* curry layers sweet palm sugar with the toastiness of crushed peanuts and the complex umami of fish sauce. At dinner, look for delicate steamed *cho muang* dumplings stuffed with spiced minced chicken; the *larb gai* salad fresh with mint, lemon, and crushed jasmine rice; and the richly flavoured roasted duck curry. A happy anomaly for an Asian restaurant, the wine list is well put together, with a large selection available by the glass. The well-meaning service staff can be a little absentminded when things get busy. *$–$$; MC, V; debit cards; lunch Mon–Fri (except holidays), dinner every day; wine only; reservations recommended; www.simplythairestaurant.com; self-parking; map:S5.* &

The Smoking Dog Bistro / ★★

1889 W 1ST AVE, WEST SIDE; 604/732-8811

Former customers Jean Séguin and Judith Andrews bought the Smoking Dog from the jovial Jean-Claude Ramond in 2005 and now run the bistro—and, happily, they're running it in the right direction. They've freshened up the place by introducing affordable neighbourhood dining. A new chef, Miguel Abella, is filled with good ideas of his own but is smart enough not to tamper with tradition. The large blackboards list the menu items—*pâté maison* served with five creamy slices, mixed greens, cornichons, and black olives; mimosa salad; French onion soup; signature steak frite; slow-braised lamb shank; cherry duck; and the grilled and roasted *côte de boeuf* offered at market price. The golden, lightly salted pommes frites have customers coming back the next day. Waitstaff in smart black shirts and long white aprons move expertly across the rustic wood floor and know many of their customers by name. This is, after all, a neighbourhood place, where one can sit at the curved bar and enjoy a glass of wine and the game or, on a warm summer evening, linger on the heated patio, entertained by the live jazz band (every Wednesday and Friday) and the stream of folk returning from the beach. *$$; AE, DC, MC, V; debit cards; lunch Mon–Fri, dinner Mon–Sat; full bar; reservations recommended; www.thesmokingdog.com; street parking; map:O6.*

So.Cial at Le Magasin / ★★☆

332 WATER ST, GASTOWN; 604/669-4488

Glittering Italian Murano chandeliers, original floor tiles, and a pressed tin ceiling—all in a charmingly restored 1911 heritage space—make for beautiful dining surroundings. The compact patio affords a view of the Gastown cobblestones. The chile-poached spot prawns are accompanied by smoked paprika yogurt and pickled carrot slaw. Mains are equally seductive, from the scallops with pulled-pork *nero ravioli* in tomato and olive oil sauce to the braised lamb shank with garlic confit and peas in a lamb consommé. The wine list has strong BC and California offerings. Downstairs is a cozy oyster and seafood bar, while next door is the very popular custom butcher shop and deli, where housemade charcuterie, terrines, and reasonably priced sandwiches are for sale. *$$$–$$$$; AE, MC, V; debit cards; breakfast Mon–Fri, lunch Mon–Fri, dinner every day, brunch Sat–Sun; full bar; reservations recommended; www.socialatlemagasin.com; valet and street parking; map:T3.* &

Sophie's Cosmic Cafe / ★

2095 W 4TH AVE, WEST SIDE; 604/732-6810

The walls of this funky Kitsilano diner are the flea market of a kitsch collector's dreams. On weekends, fans queue in the rain for big portions of stick-to-your-ribs breakfasts: pancakes; waffles; Mexican eggs with sausage, peppers, and onions spiced with hot-pepper sauce poured from a wine bottle (handle with caution: it's potent). There are plenty of vegetarian choices all day. Sophie's is a Kits institution, with the permanent mood of a mellow fiesta. *$–$$; MC, V; debit cards; breakfast, lunch, dinner every day, brunch Sat–Sun; full bar; reservations recommended; www.sophiescosmiccafe.com; street parking; map:N7.* &

Spice Alley Korean Restaurant & Bar / ★

1333 ROBSON ST, DOWNTOWN; 604/685-4468

After a day of black-belt shopping along Robson Street, stop in at Spice Alley, popular with the ESL student crowd, for some red-hot Korean fare. The playlist ranges from old-school pop to lounge music, and the vibe is a quirky mix of kitsch and cool. Fortify yourself with sips of *chamisul soju* (Korean rice and barley liquor) as you tuck into a bubbling hot pot of *bulgogi jeongol* that simmers away on a burner at your table: a mouth-flaming jumble of chile-laden broth, beef, mushrooms, onions, carrots, udon noodles, tofu, and zucchini. Beef bulgogi, thinly sliced beef in a sweet marinade, sautéed together with onions, zucchini, and carrots and served sizzling hot on a cast-iron plate, is a safe bet for those with more sensitive taste buds. Perhaps the best part is warm-weather dining out on the postage-stamp-sized patio, ringside seating for some of Vancouver's best people-watching as the Hite (Korean beer) flows late into the night. *$–$$; MC, V; debit cards; dinner every day; beer and wine; no reservations; street parking; map:R3.* &

Spice Islands Indonesian Restaurant / ★★★

3592 W 41ST AVE, WEST SIDE; 604/266-7355

A sense of calm envelops you the moment you step into this serene, intimate room. The soothing colour palette and understated decor set the scene for relaxed dining. Knowledgeable, attentive servers deftly guide you through chef Joseph Boon's menu reflecting the myriad ethnic influences on Indonesian cuisine. Start with *martabak*, a light and flaky take on a beef samosa, or *lemper*, white sticky-rice dumplings filled with kaffir-lime-scented chicken. Those with asbestos-lined taste buds should sample the *sambal babi*, tender braised pork shoulder in coriander sauce, and notch the heat quotient up to "Indonesian hot." In contrast, *opor ayam* is a rich, luxurious dish of chicken in a velvety nutmeg and coconut cream curry. Save room for dessert: *spekkoek* (or *lapis legit*) is an elegantly layered butter cake accompanied by a scoop of light, refreshing rambutan sorbet. The thoughtfully chosen wine list includes both international selections and BC favourites. *$–$$; DC, MC, V; debit cards; lunch Mon–Fri, dinner every day; full bar; reservations recommended; www.spiceislandsindonesian.com; street parking; map:B3.* &

Splitz Grill / ★★

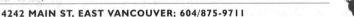

4242 MAIN ST, EAST VANCOUVER; 604/875-9711

This second outpost (the other is in Whistler) of Splitz Grill gives the burger (your choice of beef, lamb, chicken, salmon, sausage, or lentil) star treatment with fresh ingredients and a choice of toppings, which range from chili, garlic mayo, ketchup, tahini, sauerkraut, and hummus to fresh tomato, sprouts, salsa, and kosher pickles. The thick, house-cut fries still have their skins. Even including a soft drink, you haven't spent $10 and you're more than satisfied (although dessert does beckon in the form of ice cream sundaes, floats, shakes, cones, and a caramelized banana split). *$; MC, V; debit cards; lunch, dinner every day; no alcohol; no reservations; www.splitzgrill.com; street parking; map:E3.*

Steamworks Brewing Co. / ★
Steamworks TransContinental / ★

375 WATER ST, GASTOWN (AND BRANCHES); 604/689-2739
601 W CORDOVA ST, GASTOWN; 604/678-8000

Back before Vancouver became beer-vana for handcrafted ales and lagers, Gastown's funky Steamworks Brewing Co. was one of the city's first brew pubs. Now owner Eli Gershkovitch has taken his passion for vintage style across the parking lot to the historic Waterfront Station building (originally the Canadian Pacific Railway station), where he's opened Steamworks TransContinental. After a lengthy and expensive renovation of a sadly misused space, this has become one of the most beautiful rooms in Vancouver, all soaring ceilings, rich wood, plush banquettes, and high arched windows. Meanwhile, the original Steamworks appeals to a more casual crowd, especially with its urban patio. It's the perfect place for commuters to the North Shore and Fraser Valley to stop for a classic cocktail on the way home and stay for the better-than-average casual fare, including steaks, burgers, pizza, and shareables such as the barbecued duck spring rolls. *$$; AE, DIS, MC, V; no debit cards; lunch, dinner every day (Brewing), lunch Mon–Fri, dinner Mon–Sat (TransContinental); full bar; no reservations; www.steamworks.com; self-parking; map:U3.*

Stella's Tap and Tapas Bar / ★★

1191 COMMERCIAL DR, EAST VANCOUVER; 604/254-2437
Stella's hit upon a winning combination by pairing an impressive selection of Belgian beers and wines by the glass with a small-plates menu that takes diners on a global culinary jaunt. Sports fans line the sizable blond-wood bar on game nights, but it's more than just sports that brings them in: those serious about their ale angle for a front-row seat to eyeball the storied 10-step Belgian process of pulling a draught. The party often spills out onto the heated patio, a prime spot for watching the colourful Commercial Drive denizens. A lengthy list of sharing plates has something to whet every appetite, from eight varieties of moules frites (mussels and fries) to achiote-rubbed flatiron Yucatan steak tacos and local favourite sesame-crusted ahi tuna with wasabi aioli. Melting chocolate cake made with Belle Vue Kriek beer will sate any chocoholic's cravings. *$–$$; AE, MC, V; debit cards; lunch, dinner every day, brunch Sat–Sun; full bar; reservations recommended; www.stellasbeer.com; street parking; map:Z5.* &

Steveston Pizza Co. / ★

100-3400 MONCTON ST, RICHMOND; 604/204-0777
In 2006, after spending years on Holland America cruise ships creating menus, Nader Hatami sailed into the quaint fishing village of Steveston. He traded his life jacket for a white apron and decided to make the very best pizza. In the constricted quarters at the corner of Moncton and Third Avenue, customers line up for his takeout-only organic-crust pizzas and poetic attention to the menu. The Elements pizzas—Earth, Fire, Water, Air, Fifth Element—salute their namesakes. By design, Earth is heavy with Brie, Gouda, and Camembert, oven-dried tomatoes, roasted garlic, and enoki mushrooms. The Fifth Element caresses basil-kissed tomatoes, a love letter of mushrooms, and tender hearts of mozzarella with a taste of sesame and truffle oil. The Japanese pizza acknowledges the heritage of Steveston with wasabi-scented teriyaki chicken breast, enoki mushrooms, Hokkaido Camembert (imported directly from Japan), and sesame seaweed julienne. Hatami uses the techniques of his classical training and finishes each pizza with the flair of a high-end French restaurant. At press time, Hatami had added ravenously good veal and seafood lasagnas to his menu. *$; MC, V; debit cards;*

dinner Tues–Sun (take-out only); no alcohol; no reservations; www.steveston pizza.com; street parking; map:C7.

Subeez Cafe / ★

891 HOMER ST, YALETOWN; 604/687-6107

With a clientele so hip their fashion is dated before they leave the restaurant, Subeez is *the* spot for the alternative urban dweller. Almost everything has been recycled (the bathroom sinks are from Oakalla Prison) in this 225-seater. A mishmash of styles is reflected in the food as well as the decor. Chicken and Brie sandwiches, sun-dried tomato turkey burgers, and fries with a tantalizing garlic mayo dip will pop the piercings on any jaded slacker. A well-priced wine list and local microbrews are available to ease urban angst. Be prepared for casual service and the 30-speaker sound system that keeps urbanites on the edge. The kitchen's open till midnight (1am on weekends). *$; AE, MC, V; no debit cards; lunch, dinner every day, brunch Sat–Sun; full bar; reservations for parties of 8 and over; www.subeez.com; street parking; map:S4.*

Sun Sui Wah Seafood Restaurant / ★★★

3888 MAIN ST, EAST VANCOUVER; 604/872-8822
102-4940 NO 3 RD, RICHMOND; 604/273-8208

Twenty years ago, Sun Sui Wah's combination of fresh local seafood and exacting Cantonese techniques put Vancouver firmly on the Chinese culinary map. Today the competition is fierce for the high-end Cantonese dining dollar, but Sun Sui Wah continues to hold its own. The fresh house-made dim sum includes steamed prawn dumplings topped with the understated luxury of Dungeness crab meat. Chicken feet, steamed with black bean sauce, are an adventurous treat, and the baked tapioca pudding is Vancouver's best. The annual Alaskan king crab promotion is legendary, with crab legs split and steamed to sweet succulence under a blanket of chopped garlic. Chekiang vinegar–braised ribs perfectly balance savoury and sour notes. Service is smart and welcoming to non-Chinese customers. *$$–$$$; AE, MC, V; debit cards; lunch, dinner every day; beer and wine; reservations recommended; www. sunsuiwah.com; self-parking; map:E3.* &

Suvai Restaurant / ★★

2279 W 41ST AVE, WEST SIDE; 604/261-4900

This charming neighbourhood bistro offers a more upscale dining option among Kerrisdale's more casual cafes and sushi joints. What's most appreciated by devoted locals about Suvai, aside from its inviting Lilliputian room, are the reasonable prices. Start with seasonal Dungeness crab and shrimp cakes with chipotle aioli, or a bowl of full-bodied maple-roasted butternut squash soup with duck confit. The pan-roasted halibut with black olive tapenade and sautéed gnocchi and the roast rack of lamb with garlic mash, ratatouille, and rosemary jus are both noteworthy selections. The progressive wine list is very select, with a decent tour of the globe. *$$–$$$; AE, MC, V;*

debit cards; lunch Mon–Fri, dinner every day, brunch Sat–Sun; full bar; reservations recommended; street parking; map:C4. &

The Taco Shack / ★

1937 CORNWALL ST, WEST SIDE; 604/736-8226
3143 W BROADWAY ST, WEST SIDE; 604/737-8227

When ex–Canadian Football League linebacker Daved Benefield and fellow teammate Noah Cantor (of Vera's Burger Shack) opened their first location, locals rushed to taste their take on "authentic" CaliMex food. Word spread, and soon this "shack" became a popular destination for those seeking a quick, no-fuss taco fix. Unlike your regular fast-food joint, though, this operation relies on fresh, high-quality ingredients, even making their own corn tortillas daily. "Shack-style" tacos, three for $6.99, come with pico de gallo (chopped tomato, onion, and chiles), cilantro, salsa, and your choice of steak, chicken, or fish. Add quesadillas, a solid selection of zippy burritos, and Mexican Jarritos sodas, and you've got a winning combination. *$; MC, V; debit cards; lunch, dinner every day; no alcohol; no reservations; www. tacoshack.ca; street parking; map:O6, C3.* &

Tapastree Restaurant / ★★

1829 ROBSON ST, WEST END; 604/606-4680

After a few years, many neighbourhood restaurants get lazy, knowing that their regulars will always be there for them. Not Tapastree, a cozy little bistro just off busy Denman Street, where everyone from the chef to the busboy is as passionate about their locally inspired, globally flavoured small plates as they were when they opened a decade ago. Chef Mike Jeffs and partner Nicole Welsh offer an ever-changing menu with many delectable surprises— seared ahi tuna with ponzu sauce one day, fresh porcini mushrooms in cream another—but loyal fans keep coming back for the tender grilled lamb chops, the lively wine-by-the-glass list, the friendly service, and the entertaining view of the West End from the popular patio. *$$–$$$; AE, MC, V; debit cards; dinner every day; full bar; reservations recommended for large parties; www. tapastree.ca; self-parking; map:Q2.* &

Thomas Haas Patisserie and Café / ★★★

128-998 HARBOURSIDE DR,
NORTH VANCOUVER; 604/924-1847

Thomas Haas is, quite simply, one of the best pastry chefs in the world, as evidenced by the countless international awards he has won. Luckily for local sweet tooths, the German-born *Konditormeister* can't resist Vancouver's beauty—and Vancouverites can't resist his famous sparkle cookies, buttery croissants, and exquisite chocolates. They flock to his bright little jewel box of a pastry shop, near the North Shore Auto Mall, where his attentive staff serve pastries that masquerade as works of art, along with perfect espresso. But the best reason to brave the crowds—and there are always crowds—is for handcrafted chocolates such as the exotic ganache with passion fruit and

TEA PARTY: WHAT'S BREWING IN VANCOUVER?

Vancouver stays true to its British roots with establishments where the tea is always piping hot, the scones deliciously fresh, and the atmosphere as refined as the queen herself.

Tea shops are peaceful spaces, perfect for browsing for china cups or catching up over a pastry or two. The **SECRET GARDEN TEA COMPANY** in Kerrisdale (5559 W Boulevard, West Side; 604/261-3070; www.secretgardentea.com) is a neighbourhood darling that lovingly re-creates the coziness of an English tearoom. Visitors can stop in for the demi high tea or reserve ahead for the high tea with mini sandwiches, sweets, and scones (see "Brood Food: Kid-Friendly Dining"). Over at **MURCHIE'S** (825 W Pender St, Downtown; 604/669-0783; www.murchies.com), take a break from the downtown bustle and choose from a wide variety of teas, including mango black tea or oolong Min-Nan, all served on an elegant silver tray. Call in advance for afternoon tea service. At **T** (1568 W Broadway, West Side; 604/730-8390; www.tealeaves.com), the minimalist room exudes Zen-like calm. Choose from more than a hundred different teas—the masala black tea chai and the vanilla rooibos are especially good—and from fresh, homemade scones and cookies.

Consider a hotel option if you want an even grander experience. **FLEURI RESTAURANT** (845 Burrard St, Sutton Place Hotel, Downtown; 604/642-2900; www.vancouver.suttonplace.com) provides impeccably attentive service in a serene room. Book ahead for afternoon tea. Meanwhile, the luxurious **BACCHUS**

Tahitian vanilla. The exquisite paninis are also a must. Psst: The little ones will find a special surprise in the secret compartments on the bakery wall. *$; AE, MC, V; debit cards; breakfast, lunch 8am–5:30pm Tues–Sat; no alcohol; no reservations; www.thomashaas.com; self-parking; map:E1.* &

Tojo's / ★★★☆

1133 W BROADWAY, WEST SIDE; 604/872-8050

Hidekazu Tojo has developed a passionate following among food-obsessed sushi snobs. A loyal clientele fills his new location in an impressive, soaring room with a bustling yet relaxed atmosphere. Most want to sit at the 15-seat sushi bar, sip sake, and order *omakase*: "chef's choice." Tojo-san will create a parade of courses till you cry uncle. Although the *omakase* experience starts at $50 per person and goes up rapidly from there, it's worth putting yourself in Tojo-san's hands if your budget will bear it; he's endlessly innovative. He created the BC roll (barbecued salmon skin, green onions, cucumber, and daikon) now found in almost every Japanese restaurant in Vancouver. The wine list needs some work, and that may be why cold Masukagami sake is hot at Tojo's. *$$$$; AE, MC, V; debit cards; dinner Mon–Sat; full bar;*

RESTAURANT & LOUNGE (845 Hornby St, Wedgewood Hotel, Downtown; 604/608-5319; www.wedgewoodhotel.com) offers its afternoon tea on weekends only. A seat by the crackling fireplace is particularly idyllic, especially with tiers of gourmet finger sandwiches, English fruitcake, and lemon chiffon cake. Plus, you can make it a "royal" afternoon tea by adding a glass of Kir Royale or Sumac Ridge Brut. **900 WEST LOUNGE** (900 W Georgia St, Fairmont Hotel Vancouver, Downtown; 604/684-3131) celebrates the pomp of tradition with raisin scones, pastries, tea sandwiches, and fresh strawberries with Devonshire cream. The Champagne Tea comes with Moët & Chandon Nectar Imperial, while the Bubblegum version will turn the tots into tea converts.

Spectacular greenery is the backdrop for afternoon tea at the **FISH HOUSE IN STANLEY PARK** (8901 Stanley Park Dr, West End; 604/681-7275; www.fishhousestanleypark.com). Tea sandwiches—house-cured salmon on graham bread, ham salad on an asiago biscuit—tempt, as do the desserts, such as the chai-spiced butter balls and chocolate truffle squares. And at **PROVENCE MEDITERRANEAN GRILL** (4473 W 10th Ave, West Side; 604/222-1980; www.provencevancouver.com) and **PROVENCE MARINASIDE** (1177 Marinaside Cres, Yaletown; 604/681-4144), reserve for the *grand thé*, complete with Parisian chocolate macaroons, madeleines, and Provençal olive and cream cheese open-faced sandwiches. With such sumptuous afternoon tea, who needs dinner?

—Tara Lee

reservations recommended (required for omakase); *www.tojos.com; street parking; map:R7.* &

Tomahawk Restaurant / ★

1550 PHILIP AVE, NORTH VANCOUVER; 604/988-2612
Step inside Tomahawk and be greeted by garden gnomes, fake Native carvings, and paintings of the souvenir variety—it's the Louvre of tacky art. Legendary is the Yukon Breakfast—five rashers of bacon, two eggs, hash browns, and toast—served all day. For lunch, try the Big Chief Skookum Burger, if you can say it with a straight face, and chow down on a double beef-patty burger topped with a hot dog plus all the fixings, completed with a mountainous side order of fries, pickle, and slaw. Cap your feast with one of the baked-on-the-premises pies (lemon meringue, Dutch apple, banana cream). For more than 80 years, there's been no better experience at this Vancouver institution than having breakfast as the morning mist slides across the North Shore mountains, a telltale totem pole casting a long shadow in the golden light. *$; AE, MC, V; debit cards; breakfast, lunch, dinner every day; no alcohol; no reservations; www.tomahawkrestaurant.com; street parking; map:D1.* &

Tomato Fresh Food Café / ★★

2486 BAYSWATER ST, WEST SIDE; 604/874-6020
After moving from Cambie Street, this upscale diner has found a new Kitsilano home where loyal customers flock to enjoy fresh, seasonal cuisine. The room is airy and modern while still exuding disarming neighbourhood charm. Slide into one of its roomy booths, take in the cheery tomato-red walls, and try one of the many dishes that showcase the offerings of local organic producers. Favourites include the signature Westcoaster salad, the *bouillabaisse du pacifique*, and the pan-seared Pacific wild salmon with grilled asparagus and organic greens. The daily blue plate specials are a good way to sample the kitchen's inventive play with seasonal ingredients. The wine list, like the food itself, promotes local with a decent nod to the Old World. *$$; AE, MC, V; no debit cards; breakfast, lunch, dinner every day, brunch Sat–Sun; full bar; reservations recommended; www.tomatofreshfoodcafe.com; self-parking; map:C3.* &

Toshi Sushi / ★★½

181 E 16TH AVE, EAST VANCOUVER; 604/874-5173
Approaching this restaurant, you'll invariably be greeted by at least two of three things: a queue stretching out the door, a small crowded foyer, and a list of explicit instructions for the waiting-list policy. Add your name to the list on the wall and be prepared to cool your heels—unless you're there when the doors open. Decor is bright and simple, with a relatively pared-down, reasonably priced menu to match. Chef/owner Toshi Saito takes great pride in the freshness and quality of his food, and his skills shine in expertly prepared sashimi and generously portioned tuna *tataki*. Vegetarian options abound; choices include sweet-potato tempura rolls wrapped in delicate bean curd sheets and irresistible candied eggplant in miso and brown sugar. *$–$$; V; debit cards; dinner Tues–Sun; beer and wine; no reservations; street parking; map:D3.* &

Trafalgars Bistro / ★★

2603 W 16TH AVE, WEST SIDE; 604/739-0555
Every neighbourhood should have one of these: a cozy bistro where you can meet friends, romance a loved one, or celebrate the occasions of life with family. Partners Lorne Tyczenski and Stephen Greenham originally opened Sweet Obsession Cakes & Pastries (see Nightlife chapter) but eventually expanded to serve not only dessert and coffee but dinner and wine as well. The globally inspired menu is brief but complete as chef Chris Moran keeps the flavours fresh: poached eggs on potato latke for brunch, housemade lamb cheeseburger for lunch, seared veal liver batons with pancetta and white bean ragout or pan-roasted ling cod with lemon dumplings for dinner. The indulgent dessert menu suggests a dessert wine, liqueur, port, or brandy with each sweet treat. On a warm summer evening, ask for the table in the vineyard, and then decide on the chocolate hazelnut zuccotto, mango cheesecake, or warm toffee cake. *$$$; MC, V; debit cards; lunch every day,*

dinner Mon–Sat, brunch every day; full bar; reservations recommended; www. trafalgars.com; street parking; map:C3. &

Tramonto at the River Rock Casino Resort / ★★

8811 RIVER RD, RICHMOND; 604/247-8573

Bypass the slot machines and gaming tables and head upstairs to the third floor for the best bets in town: *primitivo*-marinated swordfish with arugula gnocchi, eggplant-filled tortellini, and cauliflower velouté with white truffle foam. Tramonto opened in 2005 and, under the direction of chef Sylvain Cuerrier, introduced northern Italian cuisine with a decided nod to the influence of surrounding Portuguese and Spanish cultures. The chef sources local products—Glorious Organics, BC spot prawns, Skeena River salmon—and follows the seasons by using copious kilos of berries in summer and squash in fall. For dessert you might try an assortment of Italian cheeses with fruits and nuts. There's a terrace for summer dining (portable heaters will keep you warm). Whether inside or out, diners transfix on the view as the softening day silhouettes the bridge traffic, the boats bobbing in the marina, the mountain ridges, and jumbo jets that descend into *il tramonto* ("the sunset"). The wine list is extensive, and service is knowledgeable and courteous. *$$$$; AE, MC, V; debit cards; dinner every day; full bar; reservations recommended; www. riverrock.com/dining/tramonto; self-parking; map:D5.* &

Trattoria Italian Kitchen / ★★★

1850 WEST 4TH AVE, WEST SIDE; 604/732-1441

Buonissimo! The Glowbal Group behind Italian Kitchen continues its streak with a cozy 100-seat trattoria in the upscale Kitsilano neighbourhood. This unpretentious Italian restaurant has a winning atmosphere and is an oasis of affordability with a kitchen that turns out adventurous trattoria-style cooking at comforting prices from $5 to $18. The Trat excels with hearty pastas and pizzas combining bold spices and flavours: *strozzapreti* (priest stranglers) with smoked chicken and caciocavallo cheese; thinly sliced veal with a tangy tuna aioli on crusty pizza; and an utterly delicious panzanella salad of Chianti vinegar–moistened Tuscan bread scattered with perfectly ripe heirloom tomatoes, grapes, arugula, and *burrata* cheese. Dessert beckons with *zeppole al cioccolato*—homemade fritters that have a wonderfully gooey chocolate interior that makes the vow of "I'll just have one" quickly forgotten. There's a good choice of over 50 wines from Tuscany, Piedmont, Veneto, and Sicily as well as a handful of boutique wines from BC and California. *$$–$$$; AE, JCB, MC, V; debit cards; lunch, dinner every day; full bar; reservations recommended; www.trattoriakitchen.ca; self-parking; map:O7.* &

Tropika / ★★

1128 ROBSON ST, DOWNTOWN (AND BRANCHES); 604/737-6002

A second-storey location and floor-to-ceiling windows afford an ideal vantage point for checking out the Robson Street antics below. This sleek, modern space boasts soaring ceilings, its slate and frosted glass offset by simple touches of Thai art. Colorful photographs help neophytes decipher the sizable menu of Malaysian and Thai dishes. Choice appetizers include chicken curry puffs, the Malaysian take on a samosa, and *roti canai*, lightly sweet and fluffy flatbread with a crispy exterior. Signature dish K. L. Crab (short for Kuala Lumpur) is finger-lickingly addictive, and *kari kambing* is tender chunks of stewed lamb in a deeply flavoured curry. Ice *kachang* is a refreshing finish to your meal: shaved ice with red beans, jelly, sweet corn, and evaporated milk. The original Cambie Street location is the homiest of the three, and Tropika at Richmond's Aberdeen Centre is the spot to sate your shopping-induced hunger. *$$; AE, MC, V; debit cards; lunch, dinner every day; full bar; reservations recommended; www.tropika-canada.com; street parking; map:R3.*

Uva Wine Bar / Cibo Trattoria / ★★☆

900 SEYMOUR ST, (NEAR MODA HOTEL), DOWNTOWN; 604/632-9560
Smart, sexy, and stylish, Uva is an oasis for those seeking a relaxed spot for a restorative drink with friends. The room, with its mix of gleaming marble, dark woods, and sleek white easy chairs, is overseen by Sebastien Le Goff, one of the friendliest and finest sommeliers in the city. Along with a sophisticated beer and cocktail selection, 20 wines are available by the glass, featuring a well-edited cross section of European, American, and local BC pours with curiosity-piquing samples from regions such as the Bekaa Valley in Lebanon. The drink-friendly foods, including briny mixed olives limned by lemon peel and chile, a wonderfully nuanced local pork coppa, and a devastating combination of *Gorgonzola dolce Ballarini* and golden honeycomb, are superb for civilized nibbling, perfect after a show at the nearby Orpheum Theatre or a late-night rendezvous. The well-informed service staff is genuinely warm and welcoming. At press time, the 52-seat Cibo (Italian slang for "food") impressed with clean, simple rustic dishes from Chef Neil Taylor, formerly of London's River Café. The wine list features esoteric Italian varietals including 30 different labels of Proscesso. *$–$$; MC, V; debit cards; dinner every day; full bar; no reservations; www.uvawinebar.ca; self-parking; map:S4.* &

Vij's / ★★★☆
Vij's Rangoli / ★★

1480 W 11TH AVE, WEST SIDE; 604/736-6664
1488 W 11TH AVE, WEST SIDE; 604/736-5711
Gregarious owner Vikram Vij serves imaginative Indian fare that's as far from run-of-the-mill curries as Vancouver is from his native Mumbai. His signature dish is the lamb "popsicles"—dainty racks of charbroiled lamb in a creamy fenugreek-scented curry. Other items on the seasonally changing menu might include BC spot prawns in coconut masala, ling cod in buttermilk and saffron broth, eggplant and papaya curry, or a ginger-infused seafood stew. Arrive early, or be prepared to wait an hour or more. The small wine list is excellent. If you can't stomach the lines, or if you're dining midday, stop into Rangoli next door, which serves more casual versions of Vij's food for

lunch, tea, and upscale takeout. On the way out, pick up a copy of his award-winning cookbook, *Vij's: Elegant and Inspired Indian Cuisine*. *$$–$$$; AE, MC, V; debit cards; dinner every day; beer and wine; no reservations; www.vijs. ca; www.vijsrangoli.ca; street parking; map:D3.* &

Vogue Chinese Cuisine / ★

1121-3779 SEXSMITH RD, RICHMOND; 604/224-8885

The first of a new crop of Taiwanese-style eateries to open in the Vancouver area, Vogue adds a level of modernity with an emphasis on restaurant design and accommodating service. The rustic food mixes the spice and punch of northern Chinese-style cuisine with Cantonese lightness. Chinese beef pancake wraps, with chilled marinated beef and flaky green onion pancake, make a terrific starter. Rich stews and hot pots are a Taiwanese favourite; the standout is their version of the "three cups chicken" dish: bone-in chicken pieces simmered with rice wine, toasted sesame oil, and soy sauce. The spicy shredded pork balances heat, garlic, and tang—perfect with a bowl of plain rice. *$–$$; cash or debit cards only; lunch, dinner every day; no alcohol; no reservations; self-parking; map:D5.* &

West / ★★★★

2881 GRANVILLE ST, WEST SIDE; 604/738-8938

West's new London-trained chef, Warren Geraghty, will have a huge influence on the way food is conceived and presented in Vancouver. He is a refined, painstaking chef whose plates are deceptively complex and masterfully executed. The menu boasts three eclectic five- and seven-course tasting menus with wine pairings. The seasonal tastes are focused around superlative ingredients. An ode to spring included courses of ceviched spot prawns tucked into a barely poached ravioli, and Queen Charlotte halibut with a watercress potato salad, clams, and mussels; the West is a seven-course iteration of classics prepared in astonishing ways (foie gras with bitter cocoa framed with a blueberry wine jelly, veal tenderloin with luscious sweetbreads); and the Vegetarian proves that vegetables in the hands of a skilled chef are superior to those served in the city's meatless restaurants. The regular menu might feature first courses of a quail duo—roasted breast and pastilla—and a tian of Dungeness crab and couscous, emphasizing a North African slant. Mains include inventive takes on spring salmon, sablefish, squab, partridge, and loins of rabbit and lamb. Rhonda Viani's hypercreative desserts and petits fours are impeccable, and we would happily bestow a fifth star on her chocolate praline mille-feuille and five-spice braised pineapple with a warmed Brie crepe. All the sophisticated touches are here: a beautifully designed room, clever cocktails, and canny wine matches from the 5,000-bottle, temperature-controlled wall of wine. The attentive maître d' Brian Hopkins and well-informed staff describe food with such assurance you'd think they were line cooks. If you reserve a table before 6:30pm, the $49 early prix-fixe meal is a steal. *$$$$; AE, DC, E, MC, V; debit cards; dinner every day; full bar; reservations recommended; www.westrestaurant.com; valet and street parking; map:D3.* &

White Spot / ★

1616 W GEORGIA ST, DOWNTOWN (AND BRANCHES); 604/681-8034

The first White Spot opened as a hamburger joint in 1928, went on to become the first drive-in restaurant in Canada, and now has more than 55 family/casual-style restaurants and Triple Os (express locations) in BC. It's as much a part of the city as is Stanley Park, and Vancouverites driving into town after months or years away have been known to stop first for a chocolate shake and a Legendary Burger Platter, which includes a Triple O Burger lavishly garnished with a "secret sauce." The clam chowder, the club sandwich, and the Pirate Pak for kids are also legendary. You'll find the ultimate in comfort foods, too: hot turkey sandwich, meat loaf, chicken potpie. Signature desserts include cheesecake and boysenberry pie. Service is slow at this location. *$; AE, MC, V; debit cards; breakfast, lunch, dinner every day; full bar; no reservations; www.whitespot.com; self-parking; map:Q2.*

Wild Rice / ★★

117 W PENDER ST, CHINATOWN; 604/642-2882

Located symbolically on the edge of Chinatown, this modern Chinese restaurant offers innovative cuisine that marries East and West. Sleek interiors convey the feng shui principles of balance, flow, and serenity. The food itself is equally refined: dishes use classic European techniques with Chinese flavour combinations. A moist salmon en papillote is accompanied by sweet-pea jasmine risotto with clams and scallops. The braised beef short ribs are nicely tender and come with a silky white-bean coriander purée. Stop in for a sharing plate and choose from one of the solid wine pairings or unique cocktails, such as the modern Caesar with cardamom-infused vodka, Clamato juice, tamarind, sambal, and fresh lime. *$$; MC, V; debit cards; lunch Mon–Fri, dinner every day; full bar; no reservations; www.wildricevancouver.com; street parking; map:U4.* &

The William Tell Restaurant / ★★★

765 BEATTY ST, DOWNTOWN; 604/688-3504

Following in his father's notable footsteps, Philippe Doebeli continues to offer guests the consummate fine-dining experience at this award-winning Vancouver landmark. This classic, elegant room with its old-school charm is a perfect spot for special-occasion dining and romantic tête-à-têtes. Professional black-vested servers are warm and gracious, serving classical French and Swiss-inspired dishes with a flourish. Traditional starters include carpaccio-style *Bündnerfleisch*, tissue-thin slices of air-dried beef tenderloin, and cheese fondue Vaudoise, a luxurious three-cheese blend with white wine and kirsch. Escalope of veal cosseted in a silky white-wine morel mushroom sauce is served with pan-crisped spätzle, a contrast to lighter West Coast–influenced dishes such as potato-crusted wild BC salmon. Desserts are rich and decadent: classic Grand Marnier soufflé, towering *meringue glacé au chocolat* and extravagant crepes suzette flambéed tableside. Close proximity to the entertainment district and the early-seating table d'hôte menu make the William Tell ideal for a preshow dinner and a nightcap to end the evening, perhaps with a choice from the much-lauded wine list or a flamboyant Café Diablo. Dining doesn't slow down on Sundays: both brunch and Swiss Farmers dinner buffets are veritable institutions. *$$$–$$$$; AE, MC, V; debit cards; dinner every day, brunch Sun; full bar; reservations recommended; www.the wmtell.com; valet parking; map:T4.* &

Won More Szechuan Cuisine / ★

201-1184 DENMAN ST, WEST END; 604/688-8856

Whether you eat in or take out, Sichuan is the fieriest of Chinese cuisines. Go for the three-alarm diced pork with peanuts and hot chile peppers or the spicy eggplant in black-bean sauce. For those looking to take a walk on the mild side, mu-shu shrimp or Singapore noodles, lightly curried and entwined with shrimp, barbecued pork, shredded omelet, and crispy bean sprouts, will turn your palate into a palace of wild flavour. The low-key Won More is just a few steps from English Bay, where you can walk the beach and work off the pork. *$; AE, MC, V; debit cards; dinner every day; beer and wine; no reservations; street parking; map:P3.*

YEW Restaurant + Bar / ★★★

791 W GEORGIA ST (FOUR SEASONS HOTEL), DOWNTOWN; 604/689-9333

The Garden Lounge closed for a radical makeover in fall 2007—it aspired to lofty heights, and it has reached them with YEW Restaurant + Bar. Named for the indigenous Pacific tree, this flashy newcomer with its soaring 20-foot ceilings, skylit glassed-in private dining room, and 14-seat communal table trumps any other room in the city. Executive chef Rafael Gonzalez's menu is worth exploring for the quality of all the ingredients, from the scallops ceviche in citrus and coriander to the mac and cheese for grown-ups—twisted tubes of pasta in a black truffle sauce—and the pre- and post-theatre Swiss fondue (with Oyama sausage). Dessert? A deadly Morello cherry cheesecake with cherry crumble is divine. Every wine is available by the glass from the mostly Pacific Northwest wine list, if you order two pours. Service is not quite yet up to Four Seasons standards. *$$–$$$$; AE, MC, V; debit cards; breakfast, lunch, dinner every day, brunch Sat–Sun; full bar; reservations recommended; www.fourseasons.com; valet parking; map:S3.* &

Yoshi Japanese Restaurant / ★★★

689 DENMAN ST, WEST END; 604/738-8226

A fanaticism for freshness and meticulous preparation has placed Yoshi firmly in the upper echelons of Vancouver Japanese restaurants. Recent starters include *swagani*, a crispy little still life of deep-fried river crabs. Beautifully cut sashimi is served over bowls of crushed ice to maintain sparkling freshness. Nigiri sushi blossoms with the sweet richness of coral-red wild sockeye salmon and ivory *o-toro* against gently warm rice. House-made buckwheat noodles are served chilled to accentuate buoyancy and subtle chew. A teapot of the noodle broth is mixed with the dipping sauce, creating a nutritious soup to be sipped contemplatively. The elegant cobalt room, busy with Japanese expats and sushi aficionados, opens to a gorgeous mountain view. The service is pleasingly polite and friendly. *$$$; AE, JCB, MC, V; debit cards; lunch Mon–Fri, dinner Mon–Sat; beer and wine; no reservations; www.yoshi japaneserestaurant.com; self-parking; map:Q2.* &

Yuji's Japanese Tapas / ★★☆

2059 W 4TH AVE, WEST SIDE; 604/734-4990

The spare, clean lines of this modern room offer an understated backdrop for chef/owner Yuji Otsuka's inventive, artfully plated dishes. Friendly, knowledgeable servers deftly guide you through the sizable menu marked by thoughtfully suggested wine and sake pairings. A creative array of original sushi rolls changes regularly, among them the *kamonegi*: an inside-out roll of grilled duck breast and green onion, encrusted with black sesame seeds and drizzled with a touch of teriyaki sauce. Perennial favourite sweet-potato tempura sticks are a menu mainstay, accompanied by a dipping duo of spicy ketchup and curry mayo. Beef *tataki* is perfectly executed, lightly seared and served in a tangy ponzu dressing with a liberal garnish of julienned apple, chopped scallions, and garlic chips. Finish off your meal with a dish of delicate, citrusy yuzu sorbet. *$$; MC, V; debit cards; dinner every day; full bar; reservations recommended; www.yujis.ca; street parking; map:O7.* &

Zakkushi Charcoal Grill Diner / ★★☆

1833 W 4TH AVE, WEST SIDE; 604/730-9844
823 DENMAN ST, WEST END; 604/685-1136

Cosy and intimate, Zakkushi envelops you in its charm. *Washi*-papered walls feature the work of noted Japanese artist Naoaki Sakamoto; distressed-wood floors and booths add rustic warmth. Traditional yakitori (grilled meat) is the order of the day—as little as $1.20 buys you a skewer of carnivorous goodness. Standouts include *ninniku memaki*, garlic chives wrapped in thinly sliced pork, and *ume shiso tsukune*, minced chicken topped with a shiso-leaf chiffonade and accompanied by a sour-plum sauce. Order *harumaki* for your seafood fix: a dainty rice crepe filled with minced tuna, avocado, pickled daikon, and carrot. Round out your meal with the strangely named but oddly comforting Pooh Bear's Afternoon Snack: vanilla ice cream drizzled with maple syrup served atop a square of toast. The original Zakkushi on Denman has a livelier vibe, bustling with a seemingly nonstop parade of locals, ESL students, and tourists. *$–$$; AE, MC, V; debit cards; lunch Fri–Sun, dinner every day; full bar; reservations recommended; www.zakkushi.com; street parking; map:O7, P2.*

Zen Fine Chinese Cuisine / ★☆

2015-8580 ALEXANDRA RD, RICHMOND; 604/233-0077

Though the recent proclamation by a New York food writer that Zen is the best Chinese restaurant in the world outside of China is an overstatement, chef Samuel Lau's goal to make authentic cuisine intelligently accessible is certainly praiseworthy. The multicourse menus are smartly edited to give individuals a full dining experience without the usual family-sized portions. The cooking holds true to the Cantonese ideals of clean flavours and top-notch ingredients, including using delicacies such as shark's fin and abalone. Double-boiled soup in tender young coconut is marvelously fragrant and full of natural sweetness. Lobster is carpeted with garlic and steamed to briny perfection. The service is charmingly earnest, the room relaxed and quiet. Let the restaurant know when making reservations if you are uncomfortable with controversial ingredients such as shark's fin. *$$$–$$$$; MC, V; no debit cards; dinner Mon–Sun; full bar; reservations recommended; self-parking; map:D6.* &

Zen Japanese Restaurant / ★★★

101-2232 MARINE DR, WEST VANCOUVER; 604/925-0667
The large, open kitchen piques your interest, but it's the vast expanse of glass that catches your eye, opening onto a sizable patio, beckoning alfresco diners on postcard-perfect summer nights. Chef Nobu Ochi takes an innovative approach to Japanese cuisine, drawing upon traditional flavours as his touchstone and infusing them with West Coast inspiration. His six-course *omakase* ("chef's choice") tasting menu allows diners to sample a variety of dishes at a leisurely pace. Tails Up! is a playful presentation of *kisu* (Japanese whitefish), first marinated, then stuffed with sweet spot-prawn pâté and lightly fried, served "tails up" in a pool of *saikyo miso* sauce. The list of artistic sushi rolls includes the Hamachi Peak (yellowtail, shiso leaf, and green onion wrapped in a tofu crepe and served tempura style) and the Speckled Scallop Roll (seasoned sweet scallops, avocado, and asparagus wrapped in a purple-shiso-infused soy wrap, drizzled with sweet soy). Don't be intimidated by the lengthy sake list: a tasting sampler offers three premium varieties. Finish off your meal with a palate-cleansing glass of ume (sweet plum) wine. (The newer Whistler location, situated at the base of the Creekside Gondola, is a chic, modern spot to unwind after a day on the slopes.) *$$$–$$$$; AE, DC, MC, V; debit cards; dinner every day; full bar; no reservations; www.zensushi. ca; street parking.* &

Zest Japanese Cuisine / ★★★

2775 W 16TH AVE, WEST SIDE; 604/731-9378
There's a hushed elegance to this sleek room, its clean lines and natural elements a seamless blend of eastern and western design sensibilities. Chef Yoshi Maniwa takes a similar approach in the kitchen, his dishes reflecting a modern take on traditional Japanese cuisine. The mixed mushroom sauté is a delectable jumble of shiitake, enoki, and shimeji mushrooms tossed in a subtly floral yuzu (Japanese citrus fruit) sauce and served atop a bed of organic greens. Crab and radish-sprout salad is a wealth of sweet, tender Dungeness and tobiko with a tart ponzu dressing. For the ultimate Japanese dining experience, call in advance to book a luxurious seven- or eight-course

LODGINGS

LODGINGS

Vancouver hotel accommodation ranges from luxurious to family-focused, from waterfront to community-oriented, but with three upscale boutique hotels slated to open in the heart of downtown after this book has gone to press, the city will offer a host of new places to stay. In early 2009 the **SHANGRI-LA** (1128 W Georgia St, Downtown; www.shangri-la.com), a luxury hotel, will offer 119 rooms on the first 15 floors of a 61-storey landmark building—the tallest in Vancouver—with cutting-edge architectural design. Across from the Shangri-La, affluent globe-trotters will be able to check into one of 127 rooms on the first 20 floors of the twisting 58-storey tower **RITZ-CARLTON** (1090 W Georgia St, Downtown; www. ritzcarlton.com) designed by Vancouver's Arthur Erickson. (Unfortunately, they'll have to wait until 2011.) Meanwhile, the **LODEN VANCOUVER** (1177 Melville St, Downtown; www.lodenvancouver.com), an urban waterfront hotel retreat inspired by the surrounding natural beauty, opens in late 2008 with 77 contemporary guest rooms.

Downtown/West End

Barclay House / ★★★

1351 BARCLAY ST, WEST END; 604/605-1351 OR 800/971-1351
Steps away from Stanley Park, the sophisticated Barclay House, located in a restored West End heritage building, distinguishes itself from other B&Bs with its attractive blend of traditional and modern design elements and custom furnishings. The six spacious suites (and no adjoining walls with your next-door neighbour) are based on different themes—the Beach and the Peak are especially light and airy. Expect chilled Henkell Trocken sparkling wine upon arrival, freshly baked cookies and bottled water delivered to your room daily, complimentary evening sherry, and free wi-fi and parking. $$$–$$$$; AE, MC, V; no debit cards; www.barclayhouse.com; free parking; map:Q3. &

English Bay Inn / ★★★

1968 COMOX ST, WEST END; 604/683-8002 OR 866/683-8002
Chances are good that once you settle in, you won't want to leave this English Tudor hotel located in the heart of Vancouver's West End. What really sets English Bay Inn apart from the crowd is its prime location, a mere block away from Stanley Park. Appealing touches include complimentary sherry and port, sumptuous Ralph Lauren linens, and a full breakfast that typically features eggs and wonderful homemade scones. The best suite is room number 5, a bilevel hideaway complete with its own fireplace, jetted tub, and skylight-lit loft bedroom. $$$–$$$$; AE, MC, V; no debit cards; www.englishbayinn.com; self-parking; map:P2. &

Fairmont Hotel Vancouver / ★★★

900 W GEORGIA ST, DOWNTOWN; 604/684-3131 OR 800/441-1414
One of the grand château-style hotels built by the Canadian Pacific Railway, this stately downtown hotel dates back to 1887. The spacious rooms retain their elegance with dark-wood furnishings and comfortable seating areas (ask for a room high above the street noise). There's a health club with a lap pool beneath skylights, and on the lower level, the Absolute Spa pampers (try the chocolate body wrap or the rose facial). Relax with afternoon tea or unwind over drinks in the 900 West Lounge, with live jazz every night. *$$$$; AE, MC, V; debit cards; www.fairmont.com; valet and self-parking; map:S3.* ⟨♿⟩

Fairmont Waterfront / ★★★

900 CANADA PLACE WY, DOWNTOWN;
604/691-1991 OR 800/441-1414
Located in an enviable position overlooking Vancouver Harbour, the Fairmont Waterfront has many rooms that boast a jaw-dropping view of Burrard Inlet, where floatplanes and cruise ships come and go, mountains looming large in the distance. The grand, light-filled lobby, accented in creams and whites with lavish flower arrangements, merely hints at the opulence found throughout. All rooms feature marble bathrooms, top-of-the-line beds, and original artwork. For the ultimate in pampering, splurge on a Fairmont Gold Club room, featuring a private concierge, complimentary breakfast, and late-afternoon hors d'oeuvres; you'll quickly grow accustomed to feeling like a member of a royal court. *$$$$; AE, MC, V; debit cards; www.fairmont.com/waterfront; self-parking; map:T2.* ⟨♿⟩

Four Seasons / ★★★★

791 W GEORGIA ST, DOWNTOWN;
604/689-9333 OR 800/332-3442
Although the hotel is a rather drab building when viewed from the bustling city street, once you enter the expansive lobby, you'll be transported into refined luxury and world-class service that is signature Four Seasons. After checking in to one of the guest rooms and snuggling into one of the world-famous down-dressed beds, you'll find it's easy to forget that you're in the heart of Vancouver with countless dining and entertainment options just steps away. Kids are welcomed not only with milk and cookies on arrival, but also with a teddy bear in each crib, a step stool in bathrooms, and their own plush bathrobes. For an escape from the big-city hustle, guests needn't travel farther than the fourth floor. An impressive sundeck surrounds Vancouver's only year-round part-indoor, part-outdoor pool, making it a surprising and irresistible spot to laze away a warm day. Plan dinner at YEW Restaurant + Bar (see the Restaurants chapter), one of the city's hippest restaurants and lounges. *$$$$; AE, MC, V; no debit cards; www.fourseasons.com/vancouver; valet and self-parking; map:T4.* ⟨♿⟩

HAVE PET, WILL TRAVEL

It's no wonder that Vancouver was ranked (by www.dogfriendly.com) as the best city in the United States and Canada to visit with your four-legged critter: the city offers plenty of pet-friendly lodging and terrific parks and beaches. (See Pet Owners in the Planning a Trip chapter for more information.)

VANIER PARK has a "doggy beach"; downtown, **"MOLE HILL"** at Thurlow; and Nelson has an off-leash area equipped with doggie water fountains. Some parks designate off-leash times—generally 6–10am and 5–10pm. For a list of parks, visit www.vancouver.ca/parks/info/dogparks. And wherever you stroll, remember to scoop.

You can also take in several attractions with your canine: historic Gastown (some stores allow dogs), Granville Island, the Capilano Bridge and Park, Minter Gardens, and Hell's Gate Airtram. Many ferries allow leashed dogs, perfect for a side trip to Victoria or the Gulf Islands. The city's public transportation allows small dogs in carriers. For more information, visit www.raincitydogs.com.

Pet-friendly Hotels

Many Vancouver hotels offer "pooch perks"—from special blankets and over-stuffed cushions to bottled water and house-made biscuits.

For $20 a night or $100 a week, the **CENTURY PLAZA HOTEL AND SPA** (1015 Burrard St, Downtown; 604/687-0575) will keep a finicky feline or pampered pooch happy with rooms equipped with food bowls, litter boxes and scoops, dog beds, and dog waste bags. And you don't have too far to go walkies; it's just around the corner from an off-leash dog park.

Yaletown's **OPUS HOTEL** (322 Davie St; 604/642-6787) doesn't charge extra for dogs, but they have a no-cat policy. The **PACIFIC PALISADES** (1277 Robson St, Downtown; 604/688-0461) welcomes pets of any species. Hannah, a rescue dog from the Society for the Prevention of Cruelty to Animals, can take four-legged guests for walks, and the concierge can arrange pet-walking services and provide maps to the nearest parks. No charges and no deposit.

Vancouver's **SUTTON PLACE HOTEL** (845 Burrard St, Downtown; 604/682-5511) has a VIP (Very Important Pet) programme, which includes in-room dining

Hotel le Soleil / ★★★

567 HORNBY ST, DOWNTOWN; 604/632-3000 OR 877/632-3030

Hotel le Soleil shines like a beacon amidst the high-rises and cookie-cutter monoliths nearby. The high-ceilinged lobby is a study in gilded opulence, while the 94 crimson and gold suites—although petite—are delightfully

for your pet with a menu that features an Alberta beef T-bone steak for dogs and a fish entrée for cats.

The **SYLVIA HOTEL** (1154 Gilford St, West End; 604/681-9321) welcomes all pets and has two books about the resident cat, Mr. Gottogo. With Stanley Park and English Bay at the doorstep, Sylvia boasts one of the best dog walks in the country. Treats and stay are on the house.

If you find yourself in Vancouver without your dog and really wish you had some doggy company, the **FAIRMONT WATERFRONT HOTEL** (900 Canada Pl Wy, Downtown; 604/691-1991) has a golden Labrador named Holly on staff that will accompany you on a walk around the seawall on Tuesdays and Fridays.

Services: From Shampoos to Sleepovers

Most hotels stipulate that your pet cannot be left in the room alone. If you have to leave your four-legged friend for any length of time, the **REX DOG HOTEL AND SPA** (760 Terminal Ave, East Vancouver; 604/696-5166) includes a water park (though it's not always needed) and minibar at check-in, private suites that sleep families of three (dogs, not humans), and a separate "small dogs only" area. Owners Karen and Barrie Balshaw suggest booking well in advance. Pickup and delivery service is available.

For $25 per hour, **CITYDOG PET CENTRE** (1250 Granville St, Downtown; 604/608-6959) will come to your hotel from 6:30pm until late, with one-day advance notice. They will room-sit (some owners don't want their pets to leave the hotel) and, of course, they walk.

Need pet day care? The **DOGHOUSE** has two locations: one for all-size dogs (2425 Manitoba, at W 8th, West Side; 604/708-6100), and another for small dogs only (105-1833 Anderson St, entrance to Granville Island; 604/737-7500).

Dirty dog? Skunked dog? Bad hair day? **IT'S STILL A DOG'S LIFE** (3428 W Broadway, West Side; 604/739-3647; www.itsstilladogslife.com) offers a self- or full-serve dog wash, grooming, and a 911 Skunk Kit.

Check out **DOGGY STYLE DELI** (985 Denman St, West End; 604/488-0388). Tables and chairs are scattered about the room to "eat in" or order from the take-out menu. It's OK to dine with your pooch; just bring your own human bag.

—Jane Mundy

decorated in the hotel's signature solar theme, featuring accents in silk brocade. If you grow weary of cocooning, you can use the state-of-the-art YWCA Fitness Centre next door at a discounted rate. Business centre; complimentary wi-fi in rooms. *$$$$; AE, MC, V; no debit cards; www.hotellesoleil.com; valet parking only; map:S3.* &

"O Canada" House / ★★★☆

1114 BARCLAY ST, WEST END; 604/688-0555 OR 877/688-1114

This lovingly maintained Victorian home, built in 1897, is where the national anthem "O Canada" was written in 1909. Set in a charming West End neighbourhood, the home exudes all the grace and comfort one would expect in such a refined and storied setting. Old-world details include the wraparound porch overlooking an English-style garden, plus a traditional front parlour. All seven of the guest suites are tastefully appointed, and for an incomparable stay, book either the Penthouse Suite or the Cottage, which has its own fireplace and private patio. Another draw is the well-stocked complimentary pantry, open 24 hours, should you crave a late-night snack such as muffins, scones, soda, or juice. *$$$–$$$$; MC, V; debit cards; www.ocanadahouse. com; free parking; map:R3.* ♿

Opus Hotel / ★★★★

322 DAVIE ST, YALETOWN; 604/642-6787 OR 866/642-6787

The hip, moneyed set forgo the staid, often unimaginative traditional Vancouver luxury hotels in favour of a stay at flamboyant, sexy Opus. Located in the heart of stylish Yaletown, the ultramodern hotel doesn't take itself too seriously. The bold design of each of the rooms takes as inspiration five fictitious personalities. Upon booking, guests choose which style best fits their mood. For example, red rooms are dubbed "Modern & Minimalist," with strong masculine lines throughout, while green rooms are "Artful & Eclectic," showcasing funky, irreverent decor. All guest rooms include flat-screen TVs, iHome radios with iPod docks, wi-fi, and superplush beds. Opus also shines thanks to its welcoming and competent staff. Like the hotel, the lobby bar and Elixir restaurant (see the Restaurants chapter) draw a well-put-together crowd in the evenings. *$$$$; AE, MC, V; debit cards; www.opushotel. com; valet parking only; map:S5.* ♿

Pacific Palisades Hotel / ★★

1277 ROBSON ST, DOWNTOWN; 604/688-0461 OR 800/663-1815

If you want to be right in the heart of the downtown shopping district, look at this contemporary boutique hotel in two former apartment towers just off busy Robson Street. Not for everyone, the Miami-style rooms are done in eye-popping greens and yellows (except for the suites, which mix cool teal with flaming orange). For the best views, request a room above the 10th floor. The large indoor pool and the nightly wine hour in the hotel art gallery are relaxing escapes. *$$$; AE, DC, MC, V; debit cards; www.pacificpalisadeshotel. com; valet and self-parking; map:R3.* ♿

Pan Pacific Hotel / ★★★☆

300-999 CANADA PL, DOWNTOWN; 604/662-8111 OR 800/937-1515 (U.S.), 800/663-1515 (CANADA)

No hotel in Vancouver has a more stunning location, a better health club, or a more remarkable architectural presence. Although everything one needs is close at hand at this gargantuan hotel, the atmosphere of this Pan Pacific feels better suited for businesspeople than couples splurging on a romantic getaway. But with its unbeatable location on Vancouver's waterfront, and just minutes from Robson Street, this central lodging option with well-appointed rooms may still appeal more to practical couples than anything off the beaten path. The most expensive rooms overlook the water and offer hypnotizing vistas of Stanley Park, the Lions Gate Bridge, and the North Shore mountains. With live jazz in the Cascades Lounge lobby, a heated outdoor pool, and two on-site restaurants, there's plenty to keep visitors entertained. *$$$$; AE, DC, MC, V; debit cards; www.panpacific.com/vancouver/overview.html; valet and self-parking; map:T2.* ঊ

Sheraton Vancouver Wall Centre Hotel / ★★☆

1088 BURRARD ST, DOWNTOWN; 604/331-1000 OR 800/663-9255
Just a few blocks from Robson Street, these stunning glass towers offer a stylish, avant-garde decor. Standard double rooms are small, although expansive views from the higher floors make them feel larger. Check in to a one-bedroom corner suite with a two-vista view; floor-to-ceiling windows face north up Burrard Street, with Grouse Mountain in the distance, and west to English Bay and the Coast Mountains beyond. The complex also features a full health club with a 15-metre (50-foot) lap pool. *$$$–$$$$; AE, DC, JCB, MC, V; debit cards; www.sheratonvancouver.com; valet and self-parking; map:R4.*

The Sutton Place Hotel / ★★★★

845 BURRARD ST, VANCOUVER; 604/682-5511 OR 800/961-7555
When Hollywood stars show up in Vancouver, this residential-style hotel is often where they stay. With its plush interior, Sutton Place would rank as a top hotel in any European capital. Each of the 397 soundproof rooms and suites has all the amenities one could want. The beds are king-sized; the furnishings, quality reproductions of European antiques. The bellhops snap to attention when you arrive. The Fleuri restaurant (604/642-2900) serves elegant meals (breakfast, lunch, and dinner), a civilized afternoon tea, and a decadent chocolate buffet—the richly paneled Gerard Lounge is one of the most popular watering holes in the Pacific Northwest. The city's best rental condominiums are located in a separate building (La Grande Résidence) connected to the hotel. *$$$$; AE, DC, JCB, MC, V; no debit cards; www.sutton place.com; valet and self-parking; map:S3.* ঊ

Sylvia Hotel / ★

1154 GILFORD ST, WEST END; 604/681-9321
In such an ideal location opposite English Bay Beach, it may not matter that the 120 rooms in this ivy-covered brick landmark are simple and unadorned. You might feel as though you're staying with a favourite aunt in her slightly shabby but comfortable apartment house; in fact, it was built as an apartment building in 1912. If you don't need anything elaborate, it's reasonably priced, so book well in advance. Legend has it that Vancouver's first cocktail

bar opened here in 1954, and you can still enjoy a predinner drink while watching the sun set. *$$; AE, MC, V; debit cards; www.sylviahotel.com; self-parking; map:O2.* &

Terminal City Tower Hotel / ★★★

837 HASTINGS ST, DOWNTOWN; 604/681-4121

This boutique property at the Terminal City Club (a private business club) gives the downtown hotels a run for their money, especially among business travellers. Each of the 60 guest rooms and suites is tastefully decorated, and many have outstanding views. The extensive club facilities available to guests include one of the city's best fitness centres, squash courts, a swimming pool, an historic billiards room, a library, and private restaurants. *$$$; AE, DC, MC, V; no debit cards; www.tctowerhotel.com; self-parking; map:T3.* &

Times Square Suites / ★★☆

200-1821 ROBSON ST, WEST END; 604/684-2223

Located at the bustling corner of Denman and Robson streets, Times Square offers apartment-style accommodations that are ideal for extended stays in the city's West End. The 42 one-bedroom suites are comfortably furnished with full-size kitchens and washer/dryer. A fireplace in each living room provides a cozy ambience on cold winter nights. Some upper-floor rooms have a partial park and mountain view. For warm summer nights, the rooftop barbecue is open for guests' use. There's also maid service twice a week. *$$$–$$$$; AE, MC, V; debit cards; www.timessquaresuites.com; self-parking; map:Q2.*

Victorian Hotel / ★

514 HOMER ST, DOWNTOWN; 604/681-6369 OR 877/681-6369

You get plenty of character for your money at this friendly 40-room inn in a restored 1898 building between Downtown and Gastown. It's not fancy, but all the rooms have wood floors, puffy duvets, and high ceilings. The best are the "deluxe" rooms on the second floor, which are furnished with a brass or sleigh bed and a handful of antiques; rooms 205, 206, and 207 have peekaboo mountain views. Even the 20 inexpensive shared-bath rooms are comfortable (ask for one with a bay window). A continental breakfast is served in the small but graceful lobby. *$$; AE, MC, V; debit cards; www.victorianhotel.ca; self-parking; map:T3.*

Wedgewood Hotel / ★★★★

845 HORNBY ST, DOWNTOWN; 604/689-7777

Offering old-world charm and scrupulous attention to detail, the Wedgewood is indisputably Vancouver's most esteemed boutique hotel. From the warm and personal service to the renowned Bacchus Restaurant (see the Restaurants chapter), this is everything a small luxury hotel should be—and then some. All of the finely appointed guest rooms feature balconies, genuine antiques, and Italian-marble bathrooms with separate showers and soaking tubs. Since this is an immensely popular spot for visiting honeymooners and celebrities, it's essential to book early. If money is no option, the opulent penthouse suites are truly breathtaking. *$$$$; AE, MC, V; debit cards; www. wedgewoodhotel.com; valet parking; map:S4.*

West End Guest House Bed & Breakfast / ★★

1362 HARO ST, WEST END; 604/681-2889 OR 888/546-3327
Don't be put off by the blazing-pink exterior of this 1906 Victorian home. Owner Evan Penner runs a fine eight-room B&B. Rooms are generally small but well furnished, all have feather beds, and there are antiques—as well as wireless Internet—throughout the house. Sherry or iced tea is offered on the deck overlooking the verdant garden or in the parlour, and breakfast is a three-course affair. Penner also rents a two-bedroom suite next door—a better choice for families with children. Free use of bicycles. *$$$; AE, MC, V; no debit cards; www.westendguesthouse.com; free parking; map:Q3.*

YWCA Hotel / ★★

733 BEATTY ST, DOWNTOWN; 604/895-5830 OR 800/663-1424
If you expect the Y to be a dreary rooming house, think again. Vancouver's modern YWCA is a comfortable, family-friendly downtown hotel, close to the theatres, sports arenas, and library. The no-frills rooms, while small, are functional, with minifridges and sinks; baths are private, semiprivate, or down the hall. While there are few amenities (no tissues, clocks, or coffeemakers here), there are kitchen and laundry facilities, and if your room feels cramped, you can stretch out in one of the communal lounges. Guests get free passes to the YWCA Fitness Centre, 10 blocks away (535 Hornby St). *$; AE, MC, V; debit cards; www.ywcahotel.com; self-parking; map:T5.* ♿

North Shore

Thistledown House / ★★★½

3910 CAPILANO RD, NORTH VANCOUVER; 604/986-7173
Set amidst a half-acre of lush lawns and gardens, yet only minutes from the fine dining and shopping of the city centre, this white 1920s Craftsman-style home is a vision of peace and tranquility. All of the guest rooms are worthy of a special getaway, but, if given the opportunity, book the "Under the Apple Tree" suite. With a king-size bed, fireplace, private patio, and jetted-air tub-for-two, there's little left for couples to desire. Breakfast is always a grand four-course affair, and afternoon tea includes European pastries, chocolates, fresh fruit flan, and sherry. *$$$–$$$$; MC, V; debit cards; www.thistle-down. com; self-parking.* ♿

Airport Area

Fairmont Vancouver Airport / ★★★

**3111 GRANT MCCONACHIE WY, VANCOUVER
INTERNATIONAL AIRPORT, RICHMOND; 604/207-5200 OR 800/676-8922**
While most airport hotels simply cater to harried business travellers, this technologically advanced lodging is an oasis of tranquility. A lobby waterfall and soundproof glass on all floors eliminate outside noise. The room heat turns on when you check in; lights turn on when you insert your key and turn off when you leave; illuminating the "do not disturb" sign routes calls to voice mail. Even if you're not a guest, you can while away preboarding time by the large fireplaces, at the bar, or in the workout facilities, or you can dine in the contemporary Globe@YVR (see the Restaurants chapter), which emphasizes regional ingredients. *$$$$; AE, DC, E, MC, V; debit cards; www.fairmont. com; valet parking; map:C5.*

EXPLORING

EXPLORING

Top 20 Attractions

1) GRANVILLE ISLAND AND FALSE CREEK
BENEATH GRANVILLE STREET BRIDGE
TO SCIENCE WORLD; 604/666-5784

Whether you're looking for a few organic avocados or 5,000 tonnes of foundation-ready cement, Granville Island (Granville Island Information Centre, 604/666-5784) is the place to go. Originally called "Industrial Island," this weekend shopping mecca was once an assortment of dusty factories and derelict warehouses. As Vancouver grew, most of the industries there left for cheaper and more spacious pastures, and the island became a grimy eyesore. That changed in the mid-1970s when two local visionaries decided the mud-flat had development potential (to wit, location, location, location). The federal government got on board, a little imagination was employed, and those warehouses haven't been the same since. Although more than 50 stores on the island still cater to the marine industry, out went bolts, anvils, and boilers, and in came art supplies, organic fruit, and flame-juggling buskers.

Taking over the tin sheds of a rope depot on the north corner of the island is the **PUBLIC MARKET**, the first new business venture to arrive. The **TRUCK FARMERS MARKET** is where BC farmers sell local veggies and flowers from the backs of their trucks. Nearby, the **NET LOFT** houses some of the most interesting shops. For the little ones, the **KIDS MARKET**, musicians, and tight-rope-walking buskers contribute to the lively atmosphere. For information on these markets, see the Shopping chapter.

In the summer, a visit to the **WATER PARK** (1540 Old Bridge St; 604/666-5784) and adventure playground off Cartwright is a must for parents with young children. *www.granvilleisland.bc.ca, www.granvilleisland.com; map:O6.*

As much as locals are loath to ever utter a bad word about Granville Island, we have to admit that parking here is a challenge. The problem is particularly tough on weekend mornings when the entire city seems to drop by. There's covered pay parking to supplement the free outside spaces, but if you're not having any luck finding a spot, try parking near the intersection of Fourth Avenue and Fir Street and walking a few blocks. The **AQUABUS** (south foot of Hornby St; 604/689-7781) provides regular shuttle service across False Creek from downtown to the island. There's also the **DOWNTOWN HISTORIC RAILWAY** (604/325-9990; Sat–Sun 1–5pm), which runs between Science World and Granville Island in the summer.

Once you've gotten to the island, relax and soak in the views. Most **RESTAURANTS** on Granville Island have capitalized on the waterfront setting, and there's no shortage of sights to take in as you relax over coffee or a meal (see the Restaurants chapter). There's also a pleasant **SEAWALL** (Kitsilano

TOP 20 ATTRACTIONS

1)	Granville Island and False Creek	11)	Kitsilano Beach
2)	Stanley Park	12)	Science World / Omnimax Theatre
3)	Vancouver's Botanical Gardens		
4)	Gastown	13)	Vancouver Aquarium
5)	Chinatown	14)	Robson Street
6)	Grouse Mountain and the Grouse Grind	15)	Vancouver Art Gallery
		16)	Golden Village
7)	The Bridges of Vancouver	17)	Steveston
8)	Museum of Anthropology	18)	Locarno and Jericho Beaches
9)	Lighthouse Park	19)	Wreck Beach
10)	SeaBus and Lonsdale Quay	20)	Casinos

Beach to Canada Place), a wide waterfront walkway paved in a mixture of surfaces—flagstone, wood, concrete—where you will find sheltered courtyards, inviting plazas, and grassy landscaped areas, as well as benches where you can sit and watch all the activity. Canada geese congregate on rocks rising from the large duck pond. Cormorants wait and watch for their dinners to swim by.

At the west end of the island is the **WATERSIDE WHARF**, edging Broker's Bay. Millions of dollars' worth of yachts are berthed here, and it's a good place to rent or charter a boat. If you already own a boat (or are in the market for one), check out the aquatic bonanza on Duranleau Street, where boat shops and repair stores cluster. Three marinas line the shores of False Creek, and sailboats, canoes, and kayaks abound.

Despite the presence of all the seafaring vessels, it should be noted that False Creek is not actually a creek. The name comes from the logbooks of a long-since-forgotten naval officer who, thinking the passage was a creek, guided his ship into it. Alas, it is simply an inlet. And now it is only half its original size, having been filled in during the Great Depression to create an industrial area.

False Creek may have shrunk, but it is still a popular paddling site. Each June, the **ALCAN DRAGON BOAT FESTIVAL** (110 Keefer St; 604/688-2382; www.adbf.com) takes place here. Slender, brilliantly coloured, exotically decorated boats come from around the world to take part in the races. Each one is paddled by 20 people, with rhythmic assistance from a drummer and a steersman. The best viewing is from the north shore of False Creek, near the Plaza of Nations, or near Leg-in-Boot Square on the south side. The festival also includes an international food fair and entertainment stage. *Map:U5.*

2) STANLEY PARK

Stanley Park's 404 hectares (1,000 acres), just west of the downtown core, survived severe winter storms in 2006. Several strong winds ripped thousands of trees from the ground and split many more. The seawall and trails through the park were closed for a time, and it will take years for the park to complete cleanup and restoration. The devastation of the most cherished acreage in British Columbia was felt by the whole country.

Described by one local writer as a thousand-acre therapeutic couch, this is still the park where Vancouverites come to unwind, from the Howe Street financial barons jogging off their adrenaline at lunch to the young kids who play in the sand on the weekends.

Thanks to the farsightedness of the city's founders, this sacred turf has remained parkland since it was permanently designated as such in 1886. The park is so beloved by locals that any change to the natural landscape, beyond trimming the hedges, is an issue of study and contention. A free-concert-in-the-park offer about 15 years ago by hometown hero Bryan Adams was turned down (no Central Park hucksterism here, thank you), as was an entreaty by Jaguar Motorcars to use the seawall as a backdrop for the unveiling of its new line of snazzy coupes.

So what's all the fuss about? Well, it's about natural woodlands—this is one of the last places in the Lower Mainland where you can stroll amidst old-growth forests. It's also about manicured gardens, quiet lagoons, ocean beaches, winding trails, summer theatre, a totem pole park, a great gift shop, an aquarium, and wildlife such as squirrels—lots of them. In 1909, the city of New York presented Vancouver with a gift of eight pairs of grey squirrels for the park. Now the place is riddled with the critters, and they almost outnumber the Canada geese. No worries; both the squirrels and geese are grateful for the place and are more than happy to pose for photos (the large, mainly nocturnal rat population is a little more circumspect). Park officials ask that you not feed any of the animals, as they easily become dependent on human food.

Like the squirrels, attractions are scattered throughout the park. The best place to start is the **SEAWALL**, along which you can walk, run, cycle, or in-line skate. (Bike rental outlets are at Georgia and Denman streets near the park entrance.) The seawall, the longest in Canada, is 10.5 kilometres (6.5 miles) long and features separate lanes for pedestrians and those on wheels (cyclists and skaters). Finally completed in 1980, it took 60 years to build. To allow undiminished views, no handrails border the wall. The paved path is nice and wide, so falling off is not a concern. Just don't go too fast if you're cycling.

The entire seawall can be walked in 2½ hours at a brisk pace. Or you can take a day to stroll around it, veering off to check out the surrounding attractions, stopping for coffee or lunch, or sitting in the sun and marvelling at the views, which are always incredible. Horse-drawn tours around the park are available March to October through **STANLEY PARK HORSE-DRAWN**

TOURS (just off Georgia St under overpass on the right; 604/681-5115). A free shuttle bus also runs daily between Stanley Park and most major hotels and landmarks downtown.

Near a statue of Lord Stanley are the formal **ROSE GARDENS**, surrounded by a mass of perennial plantings, just a few minutes' walk from the seawall. A popular place to start a walk around the seawall is **LOST LAGOON**, home to most of the park's geese, as well as turtles, a few fish, and some trumpeter swans. The fountain in the centre, built in 1936 to mark the park's Golden Jubilee, is illuminated at night. (A separate path runs around the lagoon.) Single sculls and eight-person sculls from the **VANCOUVER ROWING CLUB** (604/687-3400; www.vancouverrowingclub.ca) can often be seen skimming over the harbour waters. A statue of Scottish poet Robbie Burns is opposite the rowing club. A couple of minutes' walk inland from the seawall, in a country garden–like setting, is the **STANLEY PARK PAVILION CAFETERIA**, built in 1932 and now a heritage building. It looks out onto **MALKIN BOWL**, an outdoor theatre where revivals of classic Broadway plays are staged during July and August. Artists display their wares along a walkway in an informal, outdoor gallery atmosphere.

Spectacular totem poles carved by the Squamish people, the earliest inhabitants of this coast, stand near **BROCKTON POINT**. Featured on many a postcard, these totems have become symbols of Vancouver. Bring your camera, and in the evenings, maybe your earplugs; nearby is the **NINE O'CLOCK GUN**, an old English sea cannon placed in the park more than a hundred years ago. Once used to call fishermen home at night, the sound of the gun is now an evening ritual in the West End. Residents can check their watches by the boom at 9pm. Be warned: It is loud!

On summer weekends, watch an unhurried cricket match at **BROCKTON OVAL**. Just offshore, you can see Vancouver's nod to Copenhagen. *Girl in a Wet Suit*, a bronze statute created by Elek Imredy, is one of the few pieces of public art in this city that is recognizable on sight and appreciated by all. Enjoyed equally well is the slightly more mysterious "fire-breathing" dragon mounted on the seawall nearby. This wooden figurehead is a replica of the one that once fronted the SS *Empress of Japan*, an early passenger ship that used to visit Vancouver.

Another well-known feature is **LUMBERMAN'S ARCH**, made of Douglas fir and erected in 1952 to pay tribute to those in the logging industry. It sits in a meadow that is perfect for picnics or playing, with a delightful children's water park by the ocean and a busy concession stand nearby. Watch for the brave bunnies that hop in and out of the bushes. This lively area was once a Native village, and literally tonnes of shells from the village midden were used to surface the first road into the park in 1888.

The most developed area of the park is the **VANCOUVER AQUARIUM** (see no. 14 in this section). Nearby is the delightful **MINIATURE TRAIN**. Kids of all ages love the short but satisfying trip of 1.2 kilometres (0.75 mile), past forest and lake, weather permitting. While waiting to board the train, visit the **PETTING ZOO** with its resident peacock and other creatures.

BEAVER LAKE, speckled with water lilies, is a quiet place for contemplation or a gentle stroll. Numerous forest trails weave through hemlock, cedar, Douglas fir, maple, and spruce. The lake is situated inland, and although the trails are extremely popular with walkers and joggers, they're a bit isolated and should not be tackled solo.

As well as offering a panoramic view of the North Shore, **PROSPECT POINT** (north of Beaver Lake on the seawall) displays a cairn in memory of the Pacific Coast's pioneer steamship, the SS *Beaver*, which met its watery ruin in 1888. Nearby is the **PROSPECT POINT CAFE**, with an outdoor deck overlooking Lions Gate Bridge and the large, grassy Prospect Point picnic area, suitable for groups.

Along the northwest strip of the seawall is **SIWASH ROCK**, a rocky, offshore pinnacle that has withstood the harsh elements for centuries. Various Native legends have been spun around this bluff, which has one tiny tree clinging to its top. **THIRD BEACH**, a wide, sandy swimming area, is nearby. At Ferguson Point, locals take visitors to gaze at the views from the comfort of the **SEQUOIA GRILL RESTAURANT AT THE TEAHOUSE** (Ferguson Point, Stanley Park Dr; 604/669-3281; www.vancouverdine.com).

SECOND BEACH is one of the best places in town to watch the sunset, and children love the playground and picnic area. Several nights a week in summer, the paved area is awash with dancers—Scottish dancers, ballroom dancers, and square dancers all kick up their heels here. This is also a sports area, with shuffleboard, a lawn bowling green, and busy tennis courts. In addition, there's a pitch-and-putt golf course, bordered by a spring-blooming rhododendron garden. The excellent **FISH HOUSE IN STANLEY PARK** (see the Restaurants chapter) is a good place for either a casual lunch or a more formal dinner.

Numerous annual events are held in Stanley Park; call the **PARKS AND RECREATION BOARD** office (604/257-8400; www.city.vancouver.bc.ca/parks/parks/Stanley) for information and maps. *www.stanleypark.com; map:D1*.

3) VANCOUVER'S BOTANICAL GARDENS
VARIOUS LOCATIONS

When the Shaughnessy Golf Club moved a few kilometres south in 1960, the aim was to turn its 22.3-hectare (55.6-acre) course into a posh subdivision of sprawling mansions. The local gentry, unconvinced that their neighbourhood needed more homes, lobbied the city, the provincial government, and the Vancouver Foundation (led by Mr. W. J. VanDusen) to buy the grounds and turn them into a botanical garden. The result: a world-class bed of flowers and a ranking among North America's top 10 gardens. Set against the distant backdrop of the North Shore mountains, the **VANDUSEN BOTANICAL GARDEN** (5251 Oak St, Oakridge; 604/878-9274) offers a collection of small, specialized gardens within the framework of the main garden.

Among its famous flora are hundreds of variations of rhododendrons. In the springtime, the Rhododendron Walk blazes with colour. Nearby, the hexagonal Korean Pavilion is a focal point for the garden's Asian plant collection. Sculptures abound on the lawns, under trees, between shrubs, and in the Children's Garden, where a chubby cherub presides over a wishing fountain. A latticework of paths wanders through 40 theme gardens, skirting lakes and ponds, crossing bridges, and winding through stands of bamboo and giant redwoods. There is also a maze, walled by 1,000 pyramidal cedars. Planted in 1981, the maze is a children's delight and a favoured location for local TV and movie producers who need a spooky setting. Once you've seen all the flowers, kick back at **SHAUGHNESSY RESTAURANT** (5251 Oak St; 604/261-0011; www.vandusengarden.org; map:D4), a nice spot in a serene garden atmosphere.

Second only to VanDusen as an object of local devotion is the **UBC BOTANICAL GARDEN**, host of the annual fall Apple Festival (6804 SW Marine Dr, West Side; 604/822-9666). Spread over 44.52 rambling hectares (110 acres) overlooking the Strait of Georgia, the garden is ornamented with more than 10,000 different trees, shrubs, and flowers, including the largest collection of rhododendrons in the country. The grounds are divided into five distinct gardens, each with a different theme and character. The David C. Lam Asian Garden houses one of North America's leading collections of Asian plants. Surrounded by a second-growth coastal forest of firs, cedars, and hemlocks, the Asian Garden hosts maples, clematis, viburnums, and more than 400 varieties of rhododendrons. Climbing roses and flowering vines twine around the trees, and the rare blue Himalayan poppy and giant Himalayan lily bloom here.

The BC Native Garden displays more than 3,500 of the plants found throughout the province. A sinuous stone path through 3 hectares (8 acres) of biodiversity offers great views of the bog laurel, Labrador tea, cranberry, and sundew. The E. H. Lohbrunner Alpine Garden lives up to the challenge of growing high-elevation plants at sea level. This garden has one of the largest alpine collections in North America; its west-facing slopes, specially imported soil, and boulders and rocks protect low-growing mountain plants from Australia, South America, Europe, Asia, and Africa. Based on a Dutch engraving, the Physick Garden re-creates a 16th-century monastic herb garden. The traditional plants, which grow in raised brick beds, can all be used for medicinal purposes. England's Chelsea Physic Garden is the source for many of the plants here.

The Food Garden is an amazing example of efficient gardening. Tucked into 0.10 hectare (0.75 acre), it's a patchwork of a dozen raised beds and more than 180 fruit trees, and it successfully hosts a cornucopia of crops, including warm-season ones such as cantaloupes, as well as nearly lost heritage varieties of fruits and vegetables. All are harvested regularly and donated to the Salvation Army. Regular lectures, on everything from pruning to growing trees in containers, are available for gardeners. (See also Gardens in this chapter.) *Every day; mid-Mar–early Nov 10am–6pm, early Nov–mid-Mar 10am–4:30pm; www.ubcbotanicalgarden.org; map:A3.*

4) GASTOWN

HASTINGS AND WATER STS BETWEEN HOMER AND COLUMBIA STS

This is the edge of Vancouver, from which the city originally grew. Founded in 1867, the neighbourhood takes its name from its first notable inhabitant, Gassy Jack Deighton, a former river pilot famed for his verbal relentlessness (hence the nickname). After giving up the riverboat game, Gassy Jack started his own pub, the Globe Saloon. It was around this drinking hole that the community of Granville grew. In 1886, however, a Canadian Pacific Railway fire ripped out of control, destroying all but two of the original houses in less than an hour. After the blaze, the city shifted westward and was rechristened Vancouver. Eventually, the old neighbourhood disintegrated into a beer-soused skid-row area.

In the late 1960s, renovation and restoration of the district began. The streets were paved with cobblestones and red brick, decorative street lamps were installed, and trees were planted in front of the boutiques and restaurants that had just moved in. In 1971, Gastown was designated a heritage site. Urban historians and heritage planners from across North America have since flocked here to study the stunning revival of the neighbourhood.

In Gastown, all streets—Carrall, Powell, Water, Alexander—lead to Maple Tree Square. Nightclubs, art galleries, antique stores, coffee bars, jazz and rock music clubs, lounges, and restaurants all add to the attraction of this vibrant place. Since 2005, an **ECLECTIC MIX OF EATERIES** has opened: Salt Tasting Room, Le Marrakech Morrocan Bistro, the Latin American Cobre, Chill Winston, and So.Cial at le Magasin (see the Restaurants chapter).

Water Street's tourist traps have officially given way to the city's new **DESIGN CENTRE**, amidst the loft living, design studios, and face-lifted building facades. Inform Interiors has known what Vancouver wants for more than 30 years; recent renovations include a B&B Italia and Boffi showroom, as well as condo settings to showcase the best in international and Canadian design. Koolhaus moved into the area in 2007, relocating from its Kitsilano address. Another sleekly modern converted heritage space houses Obakki. See the Shopping chapter for more information on these and other Gastown stops.

The 2-tonne **GASTOWN STEAM CLOCK** on the corner of Cambie and Water streets was once powered by steam. The 5-metre-tall (16.4-foot-tall) clock whistles every 15 minutes and still sends forth clouds of steam every hour, but it's electricity that now turns this clock's crank. No favourite with locals trying to concentrate on work, the piping clock also rarely has the correct time! But with its big four-sided glass face, 20-kilogram (44-pound) gold-plated pendulum, and Gothic roof, the clock is a popular stop for photographers. Around the corner and beside the train tracks, Ray Saunders, who designed the clock, has a store filled with antique timepieces. Gassy Jack himself has not been forgotten—his statue stands proudly near the centre of Maple Tree Square.

Also nearby is **GAOLERS MEWS**. One of the few surviving legacies of the pre-1886 neighbourhood, this cobblestone, brick-strewn courtyard hosted the city's first ne'er-do-wells. Swept up in Gastown's revamping, the mews now resembles some of the finer nooks of Old Montreal (complete with Victorian streetlamps and potted plants). The cobblestone lanes continue out back to Blood Alley, without doubt the quaintest parking lot in the city. *www.gastown.org; map:U3–V4.*

5) CHINATOWN
BETWEEN ABBOTT AND HEATLEY STS, PRIOR AND POWELL STS

There are no rickshaw drivers or chickens being chopped on the sidewalks here, but it's as close as you'll get to Shanghai without a visa. Especially crowded between Carrall Street and Gore Avenue, Chinatown is the heart of a bustling bazaar of produce hawkers loudly promoting their wares. The market overflows with exotic vegetables, fruit, and seafood of various descriptions. It's easy to lose a few hours here, wandering through the tiny, incense-perfumed stores, examining the jade, ivory, rattan, brass, silk, and brocade. Navigate the busy sidewalks (dodging women laden with bulging shopping bags) and admire streetlights decorated with golden dragons, phone booths topped with pagoda-style roofs, and ornamental street signs, in both Chinese and English.

This neighbourhood dates back to the 1850s, when Chinese immigrants began arriving here to build the railways. By 1890, Vancouver's Chinese population exceeded 1,000, many of whom ran their own businesses. Now it is the second-largest Chinatown in North America, bustling with so many shops, restaurants, and cultural attractions that multilevel malls and parkades have been built to ease the congestion. Don't miss the **OPEN-AIR NIGHT MARKET** (Sat–Sun 6:30–11pm) at Main and Keefer streets during summer.

At the intersection of Pender and Carrall streets is a building famous for being the world's narrowest. The **SAM KEE BUILDING**, built in 1913, is only 1.8 metres (6 feet) wide and two storeys tall. Once a store that sold beautiful silks, it is now an insurance office. *www.findfamilyfun.com/chinatown.htm; map:U4–V4.*

6) GROUSE MOUNTAIN AND THE GROUSE GRIND
6400 NANCY GREENE WY, TOP OF CAPILANO RD,
NORTH VANCOUVER; 604/984-0661

Sailing 1,128 metres (3,700 feet) through the sky in an aerial tramway has to be one of the most breathtaking—and pleasurable—ways to ascend a mountain. Once at the summit of Grouse Mountain, you'll find the scenery amazing. Feathery firs stand just beneath you, the city spreads out at your feet, and Washington state's San Juan Islands—more than 160 kilometres (100 miles) to the south—are visible. Well known as a snowboarding and skiing haven, Grouse Mountain offers a different scene in summer. For hiking diehards as well as those who prefer relaxing strolls, Grouse has the answer.

The **SKYRIDE**, an enclosed gondola, glides up the mountain and drops you into the centre of the alpine activities. A chairlift will take you right to the peak for additional breathtaking views and enchanting sunsets. At the base of

---

SERIOUS ARCHITECTURE

As a city, Vancouver is still an infant on the global scale, but several buildings are testament to its transition from trading port to world-class city.

CANADA PLACE (999 Canada Pl, Downtown)

Not merely the most famous building in Vancouver, it's also the most versatile. What other local landmark could play host to 18 heads of state, 2,800 freighters and cruise ships, and Tchaikovsky's *Nutcracker*, all within the same year, and still be admired for its graceful looks? Its five stylized masts are a visual riff that has been copied around the world, although few recognise the design's home city. Built as the Canadian Pavilion for Expo '86, this $144.8 million leviathan encloses an all-star team of local tourism, tucking beneath its gleaming white sails a cruise terminal, a convention centre, an IMAX cinema, and the Pan Pacific Hotel (see the Lodgings chapter).

LIBRARY SQUARE (350 W Georgia St, Downtown)

Designed by Moshe Safdie, Library Square is one of those rare buildings that can turn heads and change traffic patterns. Long considered the poorer cousins of Robson Street, the eastern flanks of the downtown strip have been revived by this Roman Colosseum copycat. Although Safdie's square has given people a reason to wander east, not everybody appreciates the library's styling, least of all Safdie, who insists there's no connection between his $100 million design and the Italian version. While the design community fights it out, the public has

---

the mountain, a notice board outside the Skyride station has general information and a map of the trails. Once the lonely pursuit of the bushwhacking set, the **GROUSE GRIND** is the city's sweatiest see-and-be-seen hiking strip. Each year, approximately 100,000 enthusiasts scramble up the rocky 2.9-kilometre (1.8-mile) incline, from the foot of Grouse to the beer-and-nachos nirvana of **ALTITUDES BISTRO**. The Grouse Grind is a particularly popular evening hike. In the summer, the Skyride parking lot fills by 5:30pm, and within an hour 400-plus are normally on the trail. But don't join the flock if you're not ready for a workout: it's not called the Grind for nothing. Staff recommend sensible shoes and at least one water bottle. The average hiking time is 1½ hours, but those in a rush should know the record: 26 minutes, 19 seconds. It's free to hike, but if you don't want to schlep back down, spend $5 to ride the gondola.

For both young and not-so-young, an adventure playground awaits at the top of Grouse. Try snowshoeing, ice skating, or experience the thrill of the downhill in the Sno-Limo. Visit the two orphaned grizzly bears and captive-born grey wolf at the **REFUGE FOR ENDANGERED WILDLIFE**, a 2-hectare (5-acre) mountaintop enclosure. In summer, there's the modestly titled World

embraced the building's soaring atrium and comfortable piazza, not to mention the library's 1.2 million books.

MARINE BUILDING (355 Burrard St, Downtown)

Dressed in stunning terra-cotta finery, this 25-storey terminal soars above the darkened stoops of Hastings Street. Soon after it was built in 1929—the tallest building in the British Empire at the time—Guinness boss A. J. Taylor set up a lavish penthouse pied-à-terre (which his terrified-of-heights wife made him abandon) in the building. It's still there, peeking out above the classical lines and elegant swirls that have placed this building in the pantheon of Art Deco architecture. Awash in aqua-green and blue, the lobby is meant to resemble a huge, treasure-filled Mayan temple.

VANCOUVER LAW COURTS (800 Smithe St, Downtown)

Vancouver's Law Courts are unquestionably the coolest place in Canada in which to be handed a life sentence. This glass palace was designed to demystify the black-robed judiciary. Believing that justice should not only be done, but seen to be done, architects Arthur Erickson and Bing Thom wrapped the building behind a transparent facade. Finished in 1979, the final product is a radical departure from the original idea. Initially, the provincial government had visions of a 55-storey tower, but in 1973 Dave Barrett's New Democratic party won a surprise victory, fired the original architects, and knocked the plan on its side.

—Noel Hulsman

Famous Lumberjack show and the sculpture exhibit Tribute to the Forest. Helicopter tours are also available if you want to go higher. Round out the perfect day with a visit to the multimedia **THEATRE IN THE SKY** or attend one of a series of summer concerts. *www.grousemountain.com.*

7) THE BRIDGES OF VANCOUVER

VARIOUS LOCATIONS

Blessed with an elegant wire-and-iron design—and a fabulous location—**LIONS GATE BRIDGE** (Hwy 99, Stanley Park to West Vancouver) is unquestionably one of the most beautiful bridges in Canada. It takes its name from the two mountain peak "lions" on the North Shore. Connecting North Vancouver and downtown, this three-lane bridge is the stuff of countless postcards and endless intrigue, but now, nobody knows what to do with it. Lost souls periodically fling themselves off the 472-metre (1,548-foot) main span into the frosty, 13-kmh (24-mph) current of Burrard Inlet; miraculously, some survive to taunt death another day. Lions Gate is also a resilient enigma. Built in 1938 for $6 million, the big daddy of local bridges remains a conundrum: too narrow for the amount of traffic it supports, too breath-taking to dismantle. In 2000–01, the bridge underwent what seemed like a never-ending reconstruction; frequent closures wore tempers ragged and still didn't remedy the three-lane limitations of this landmark. Lions Gate sees more than 25 million vehicle trips per year—its future is a mystery waiting to be solved. *Map:D1.*

Neither as sleek nor as stylish as its colleague to the west, the **SECOND NARROWS BRIDGE** (Hwy 1, East Vancouver to North Vancouver) is wider and, unlike Lions Gate Bridge, able to handle heavy truck traffic; it receives most of the volume and is much safer during earthquakes. It wasn't always so secure. Midway through construction in June 1958, the north anchor arm buckled, killing 18 workers. It took $19 million, the lives of five more people, and two more years before the 3.2-kilometre (2-mile) span was finally finished. In 1994, the Second Narrows was renamed the **IRONWORKERS MEMORIAL BRIDGE**. *Map:F1.*

If not the most visually dramatic toll bridge ever invented, the **CAPILANO SUSPENSION BRIDGE** (3735 Capilano Rd, North Vancouver; 604/985-7474) is certainly the most popular. Swaying 70 metres (230 feet) above Capilano River Canyon, this wire cable skyway was originally built mainly of cedar and hemp. The bridge was inspired by an 1888 display at the Glasgow International Exhibition. A year later, Scottish engineer George Mackay moved to BC and began paving the Capilano Gorge. Stringing up the 137-metre (449-foot) span was his first step. It remains the longest and highest suspended footbridge in the world. Although always an enormous tourist attraction (about 800,000 visitors annually), this bridge gained further attention in 1999 when a 17-month-old infant fell from her mother's arms and miraculously survived a 47-metre (154-foot) plunge into the trees below. The newest addition to the rain-forest park is the award-winning Treetops Adventure, seven suspension bridges through the evergreens taking you up to 30 metres (100 feet) above the forest floor. *Every day; from 8:30–10am to 5–9pm year-round; www.capbridge.com; map:D0.*

Although shorter than its Capilano cousin a few kilometres away, the **LYNN CANYON SUSPENSION BRIDGE** (North Vancouver) is every bit as breathtaking. And even better, it's free of charge. Connecting Lynn Canyon Park with the fabulous hiking trails of Seymour Demonstration Forest (see Mount Seymour Provincial Park under Parks and Beaches in this chapter), this narrow wooden walkway is very near the parking lot at the entrance of the park. Swinging 82 metres (269 feet) above Lynn Creek, the bridge offers spectacular views of the steep cliffs and tree-lined edges of the canyon. The bridge, park, and creek are extremely popular sites, attracting both tourists and locals year-round. *Map:G0.*

Originally designed with two decks—an upper level for cars and a lower level for trains—the **BURRARD BRIDGE** (Burrard St, Downtown to West Side) was built in 1932 to better serve the West Side "suburbs" of Kitsilano, Shaughnessy, and neighbouring areas. This bridge is distinguished by the huge concrete portals at each end. In deference to the Art Deco style so popular at the time, the Vancouver Public Art Commission demanded that engineers build the portals to camouflage the bridge's steel structure and also insisted on a single deck. The bridge is now a major thoroughfare for downtown traffic. *Map:Q5.*

8) MUSEUM OF ANTHROPOLOGY

6393 NW MARINE DR, WEST SIDE; 604/822-3825

On the banks of Point Grey on the University of British Columbia's western edge, the ruins of three concrete gun emplacements point toward Burrard Inlet. When Arthur Erickson planned this building—on the site of a former Second World War military base—he aligned the position of the **GREAT HALL** with them. Inspired by coastal longhouses, Erickson integrated the landscape and natural light into all elements of the design, deferring to the environment far more than was the norm at the time. Completed in 1976, the museum immediately became one of Canada's finest examples of contemporary architecture. The museum is currently undergoing an extensive expansion, increasing its size by 50 percent. The new wing, slated to open in fall 2010, will provide unprecedented access to its collections.

From the moment you walk through the museum's carved wooden doors, it is hard to tell which is more awe-inspiring, the building or its contents. In the Great Hall, monumental totem poles, studded with carvings of ravens, bears, eagles, frogs, and beavers, gaze into the distance, seemingly imbued with the spirit of Northwest Coast Native artisans. Spotlit on a podium is *The Raven and the First Men* by late Haida artist Bill Reid, depicting how the mythic Raven tricked the First People into emerging from their clamshell. Reid's smaller works, in gold, silver, wood, and argillite, are also on display. The museum uses a visible storage system. Visitors are encouraged to open any of the dozens of drawers that contain one of the most comprehensive collections of Northwest Coast Native artifacts in the world, as well as objects from other cultures for comparison. The **KOERNER CERAMICS GALLERY** displays a collection of 600 European ceramics unique to North America, as well as specially commissioned ceramics and textiles by contemporary Vancouver artists. The **MASTERPIECE GALLERY** has carved works in silver, gold, stone, and wood. The gift shop is excellent.

Outside, between the museum and the Point Grey cliffs, is the **OUTDOOR SCULPTURE GARDEN**, which includes 10 **TOTEM POLES** towering over grassy knolls and two beautifully carved Haida houses that blend perfectly into the cliffside setting. The work is by some of the finest contemporary First Nations artists of the coast, including Bill Reid, Douglas Cranmer, Norman Tait, Walter Harris, Joe David, Jim Hart, and Mungo Martin. You can enjoy the totem poles and the breathtaking views from this little park whether the museum is open or not. At press time the museum was scheduled to be closed to the public until March 2009 for expansion. *Oct–mid-May Tues 11am–9pm, Wed–Sun 11am–5pm, mid-May–early Oct Wed–Mon 10am–5pm, Tues 11am–9pm; www.moa.ubc.ca; map:A2.*

9) LIGHTHOUSE PARK

MARINE DR TO BEACON LN, WEST VANCOUVER, 604/925-7000
Driving along West Vancouver's Marine Drive, where houses are perched atop cliffs, you might expect to find a beach park, but instead you'll find a dense forest edged with rock. No logging has been allowed here since the area was set aside as a reserve in 1881. Numerous trails, long and short, meander through the park and to the tidal pools. Allow at least a half day for exploring. There are maps and information boards in the large parking lot, which can fill up early on summer Sundays. The main trail to the ocean and the **POINT ATKINSON LIGHTHOUSE** (built in 1914) is well marked, a mere 10-minute downhill walk through gigantic Douglas firs, some 61 metres (200 feet) tall and 2 metres (6.5 feet) in diameter. Tours of the lighthouse are given daily in summer—just show up. Take a sweater, since it can be cool in the woods. Unspoiled wilderness only 30 minutes from downtown Vancouver, spectacular sunsets. *www.findfamilyfun.com/lighthouse.htm.*

10) SEABUS AND LONSDALE QUAY

BURRARD INLET AND NORTH VANCOUVER
Definitely the most affordable cruise in Vancouver, and one of the most scenic, the **SEABUS** (Cordova St at Granville, Downtown; 604/521-0400) sails back and forth between beautifully renovated **WATERFRONT STATION** in downtown Vancouver and Lonsdale Quay in North Vancouver. The station, a former Canadian Pacific Railway terminus, is now a destination in itself. Here, above small shops and coffee bars, a series of wonderful paintings depict the Rocky Mountains. The station is also the Vancouver terminus for the **SKYTRAIN**, automated light rapid-transit service, and the **WEST COAST EXPRESS**, commuter service to the Fraser Valley. It's a gorgeous heritage building. If you want to buy blueberries and other fresh produce, hop the SeaBus and cruise over to Lonsdale Quay.

The SS *Burrard Beaver* and the SS *Burrard Otter*—foot-passenger-only ferries—zip across the sheltered waters of Burrard Inlet in less than 15 minutes, much faster than their predecessors did at the turn of the last century. In 1900, years before any major bridges were built, a ferry chugged the same route. But the inlet wasn't as busy back then. Now the SeaBus must navigate through a thicket of freighters, cruise ships, sailboats, and even the occasional windsurfer. No need to worry—leave those distractions for the captain. Instead, simply enjoy the views. To the north tower the Coast Mountains; to the west lies Stanley Park, framed by Lions Gate Bridge. Southward, office towers and high-rises cluster behind the shining sails of Canada Place. Dramatic during the day, the SeaBus is equally enchanting in the evening, when the city lights are reflected on the water. *Every day; every 15 minutes during peak times; www.translink.bc.ca; map:U3.*

When the ride ends, you're at **LONSDALE QUAY MARKET** (123 Carrie Cates Ct, North Vancouver; 604/985-6261), a multilevel mall whose open-market concept contains a surprising number of intriguing shops: more than

90 boutiques and restaurants, including lots of food outlets, fashions for adults and kids, fresh and dried flowers, and specialty shops, such as Celtic Creations and the Games People. At ground level, the public market offers an array of fruits and vegetables, fish, breads, flowers, and meats. Have coffee outside in the sunshine and admire the stunning view. On the second floor are gift shops and boutiques, and on the third level is the entrance to the **LONSDALE QUAY HOTEL** (604/986-6111). Parking is abundant. *Every day; 9:30am–6:30pm; www.lonsdalequay.com; map:E3.*

Make a left turn at the North Van SeaBus terminal to get to **WATER-FRONT PARK**. There's plenty to see along the paved walkway that surrounds this small park. Along the seawall, plaques identify several outstanding downtown buildings, and a huge modern sculpture, *Cathedral*, by Douglas Senft, sits on the lawn. At **SAILOR'S POINT PLAZA**, dedicated to those who have lost their lives at sea, sits an elegant sundial by Tim Osborne, titled *Timelines*. A plaque also commemorates Captain George Vancouver, the first English explorer to reach Burrard Inlet. At the far end of the park, the **BCIT/PACIFIC MARINE TRAINING INSTITUTE** (265 W Esplanade, North Vancouver; 604/453-4100) is full of boats, ropes, and outboard engines for students working toward a marine career. During the summer this park is busy. Concerts are held on many Sunday afternoons, and numerous clubs hold festivals, exhibits, dances, and competitions here. *Map:E1.*

11) KITSILANO BEACH

CORNWALL AVE AND ARBUTUS ST, BORDERING ENGLISH BAY, WEST SIDE
Named after Chief Khahtsahlano of the Squamish First Nation, Kits Beach has become an institution, a year-round haven for joggers, dog walkers, and evening strollers, joined in the summer by swimmers and sun worshippers in search of warm rays and safe swimming. The beach has become a top beach-volleyball venue as well. Equally popular are the nearby tennis courts, basketball courts, and children's play area.

Open during the summer season, **KITSILANO POOL** (2305 Cornwall St; 604/731-0011) is one of the largest outdoor pools in the city, with lanes for serious swimmers and a separate section for young splashers. Replacing the high-tide "draw and fill" basin carved into the banks of English Bay, this 1979 Kits addition has tried to stay true to its original roots. The pool fills up in the spring with salt water, but now freshwater is pumped in to save the filters and foundation. Kits remains one of the last pools in North America to use the briny stuff. Its loyalty to swimmer-healthy seawater is appreciated; the pool averages more than 150,000 visitors during its three-month season. At 137 metres (436 feet) in length, it offers a swim of a mile in 11 laps.

On the south side of the pool is the **KITSILANO SHOWBOAT** (2300 Cornwall Ave), a favoured venue for beachside entertainment since 1935. Three evenings a week, amateur troupes can be seen singing and dancing here, weather permitting. Nearby is the shoreline path beloved of dogs and joggers. The route curves along the main beach area, past the **MARITIME MUSEUM** (1905 Ogden Ave; 604/257-8300; www.vancouvermaritimemuseum.com), the **VANCOUVER MUSEUM** (1100 Chestnut St; 604/736-4431; www.van museum.bc.ca), and the **PLANETARIUM** (1100 Chestnut St; 604/738-7827; www.hrmacmillanspacecentre.com), all the way to Granville Island. The whole route is a pleasant 30-minute walk. On the last Sunday in July, the annual **NANAIMO-TO-VANCOUVER BATHTUB RACE,** when dozens of hardy souls brave the Strait of Georgia in motorized bathtubs, finishes near Kitsilano Beach. *Map:N5–N6.*

12) SCIENCE WORLD/OMNIMAX THEATRE

1455 QUEBEC ST, EAST VANCOUVER; 604/443-7443

Beside a forest of construction cranes building the 2010 Winter Olympic Games Athletes' Village is a geodesic white bubble, shimmering on the eastern edges of False Creek. To children, the futuristic dome means **SCIENCE WORLD**, an interactive—and educational—playland of lights, sounds, and physics experiments.

Science World features permanent and travelling exhibits that dazzle the senses, offering hands-on experiences that involve everything from real tornadoes to exploding frozen zucchinis. Three main galleries explore the realms of biology, physics, and music; the fourth gallery is reserved for travelling exhibits. There is also a great gift shop with, suitably enough, a science-oriented theme.

Equipped with an enormous five-storey wraparound screen and a thunderous sound system, the **OMNIMAX THEATRE** presents IMAX films. Admission to Science World only is $16 adults, $13 youth 13–18 and seniors, $11 children 4–12. Admission to Omnimax only is $10, plus $5 for a second film. Admission to both Science World and Omnimax is $21 adults, $18 youth 13–18 and seniors, $16 children 4–12. *Every day; Mon–Fri 10am–5pm, Sat–Sun and holidays 10am–6pm; www.scienceworld.ca; map:V6.*

13) VANCOUVER AQUARIUM

STANLEY PARK, WEST END; 604/659-3474

The aquarium is in Stanley Park (see no. 2 in Top 20 Attractions), but it's such a favourite with locals and visitors that it deserves a ranking of its own. Many in the city have mixed feelings about the role of aquariums—do they preserve or imprison animals? Widespread opposition to killer whales in captivity led to the final lone orca, Bjossa, being given to San Diego SeaWorld in April 2001, although the aquarium directors deny that public pressure played a factor. While belugas and a dolphin remain, since 1992 the aquarium has had a self-imposed moratorium on taking more whales and dolphins from the wild.

Regardless of the debate, this aquarium consistently ranks among the best in North America. Setting the tone—and guarding the entrance—is Haida artist Bill Reid's magnificent 5.5-metre (18-foot) bronze killer whale sculpture, in its own reflecting pool. Inside, the Arctic, the Amazon, and places in between await you. With more than 8,000 species of aquatic life from the world's seas and oceans, the aquarium has received kudos as an important educational and research facility. It provides tours, talks, films, field trips, and a unique overnight programme that provides an opportunity to view animals during their 12 hours of nocturnal adventure.

The **PACIFIC NORTHWEST HABITAT** area offers a close look at inhabitants from local waters, including playful sea otters and gliding octopuses. Scuba divers feed the fish and harvest kelp fronds. The **AMAZON GALLERY**, 10 years in the making, is the only exhibition of its kind in Canada, re-creating part of the Amazon basin environment. Fish, reptiles, birds, insects, and plants thrive in the tropical humidity, created partly by computer-generated tropical rainstorms. The creatures in the gallery are amazing: four-eyed fish, scarlet ibises, anacondas, a suitably relaxed sloth, fluorescent fish. The **ARC-TIC CANADA** exhibition allows visitors to hear the languages of the whales, walruses, and seals of the cold blue world beneath the northern ice. Fascinating displays illustrate just how fragile this hostile northern environment is. You can go nose to nose with a smiling, curious beluga whale.

In 2005 the aquarium launched the concept of **OCEAN WISE**, a conservation programme to help restaurants and customers make environmentally friendly seafood choices. BC is known for its fresh, high-quality seafood, and more than 100 restaurant menus list seafood dishes with an Ocean Wise symbol, assuring you that the ingredients have been guaranteed sustainable by the Vancouver Aquarium. Admission is $19.95 adults, $14.95 youth 13–18 and seniors, $11.95 children 4–12, free for children 3 and under. Tickets are half-price an hour before closing. *Every day; winter 9:30am–5pm, summer 9:30am–7pm; www.vanaqua.org; map:D1.*

14) ROBSON STREET
BEATTY ST TO STANLEY PARK, DOWNTOWN TO WEST END

If Vancouver is Hollywood North, Robson Street is Vancouver's Rodeo Drive, a relentlessly trendy boulevard of prêt-à-porter boutiques and swank eateries. Longtime residents mourn the loss of the schnitzel houses and Bavarian bakeries that once graced "Robsonstrasse," but the street now thrives with the fresh styles of a fashion catalogue. Saddled with some of the steepest commercial rents in the country, Robson retailers are confronted with a simple challenge: Stay hip or find a cheaper strip. Success is rewarded—50,000 people stroll Robson's sidewalks on weekdays, 85,000 on weekends. Locals grit their teeth and plow through the masses expertly.

The street spans the city's central core, linking the entertainment district on downtown's eastern edge to Stanley Park in the West End. In between are shops, restaurants, and hotels. The street used to have a distinctly local, if slightly upscale, look. Over the years, the old wooden facades and two-storey stores and houses were bulldozed to make room for the glass-and-chrome cathedrals of international fashion. To stroll down Robson is to sample a series of walk-in billboards, sensory-enhanced environments designed to showcase merchandise (be it sneakers or swimsuits) and dazzle shoppers. The street has morphed into a funky retail playland, where moving the goods is second to making an eye-popping, surround-sound statement.

International name brands include Ferragamo, Armani, Club Monaco, Guess, bebe, Banana Republic, Swatch, Nike, Gap, Zara, French Connection, and Virgin Records, but if you want to shop Canadian, check out Roots, M.A.C., Boys' Co., LUSH, Lululemon, and Aritzia. Just a block north, you'll find Tiffany & Co., Chanel, Coach, Hermès, Louis Vuitton, and Lacoste.

In response, Vancouverites and tourists have voted with their feet. On weekend summer evenings, the crowds are so dense that the city posts cops at every corner just to keep the traffic moving. Some stores are flooded with up to 1,500 visitors a day. The two Starbucks outlets on the corner of Robson and Thurlow offer a perfect spot to have a java and do some people-watching. You might see Robin Williams stop to do a minimonologue or other celebrities enjoying the food and shopping on Robson. *Map:Q2–V5.*

15) VANCOUVER ART GALLERY
750 HORNBY ST, DOWNTOWN; 604/662-4719

Designed in 1907 by Victoria architect Francis Rattenbury—who also designed the Empress Hotel and the Parliament Buildings in Victoria—the former provincial courthouse, with its impressive stone lions and Greek columns, now houses the Vancouver Art Gallery. As part of the revamping of Robson Street, architect Arthur Erickson transformed the courthouse's cramped interior into four spacious floors, flooding them with light from the new glass-topped dome above the elegant rotunda.

The **EMILY CARR GALLERY** is filled with the work of British Columbia's most revered artist. A native of Vancouver Island, Emily Carr depicted the majesty of the coastal rain forests, towering totem poles, and the Natives who created them. Many of these works are from the turn of the last century. The other floors feature temporary exhibits. There is usually one big show each summer. Otherwise, on display are travelling exhibits of photography, video, or sculpture, or selections from the gallery's permanent collection, which focuses on contemporary local, Canadian, and North American art. Other works in the collection are by the Group of Seven (a group of Canadian landscape painters in the 1920s) and European masters. *Time* magazine described the art gallery as "an institution that moves at the same speed as the cyclotron that is Vancouver's art scene."

The **CHILDREN'S GALLERY** also has changing exhibits. Short talks are held several times a week. Children's and adult workshops are scheduled, as well as concerts, and one of the upper floors has a hands-on artists' studio in which children can create their own artworks.

The **GIFT SHOP**, off the main lobby, is an excellent place for unusual souvenirs, as well as postcards, posters, jewellery, books, and prints. Visit the **GALLERY CAFE** for coffee or lunch. Sit outside if weather permits and watch the crowds on Robson Street (see no. 14 in Top 20 Attractions). On the Georgia Street side of the art gallery are attractive, well-kept gardens and the **CENTENNIAL FOUNTAIN**. Surrounded by a blue, green, and white mosaic, the carvings on the rough-hewn rock in the centre depict Celtic legends. Designed in 1966 by R. H. Savery, the fountain commemorates the union of the Crown colonies of BC and Vancouver Island in 1866. Admission is $15.75 adult, $11.55 seniors, $10.50 students (with valid ID), $6.50 for children 5–12, free for children 4 and under, $42 for families (max 2 adults and 2 children). *Every day; Wed and Fri–Mon 10am–5:30pm, Tues and Thurs 10am–9pm; www.vanartgallery.bc.ca; map:S4.* &

16) GOLDEN VILLAGE
BETWEEN WESTMINSTER HWY AND CAPSTAN WY, NO 3 RD AND GARDEN CITY WY, RICHMOND

This is Vancouver's new postmodern Chinatown, the second-largest Asian community in North America. Here, Asian pop culture meets the western strip mall. No dragons, Ming designs, or decorative shops here—this swath of parking lots and big boxes is suburban planning at its bleakest. However, inside the several large shopping malls that form the core of so-called Asia West, you can find convincing iterations of suburban life in Tokyo (Yaohan Centre), Taipei (President Plaza), or Hong Kong (Aberdeen Centre, Parker Place, and Fairchild Square). From the rambutans of Johor to the calligraphies of Shanghai, the wares of Asia are on sale. The humble food courts provide the widest range of Asian street food to be found outside that continent.

Don't miss the **BUDDHIST TEMPLE** in the President Plaza (the only mall in the Western Hemisphere with one). The temple offers more than food for the soul. Buddhists and non-Buddhist visitors alike are offered free vegetarian lunch (with a view of the North Shore mountains) after the Sunday worship ceremonies (10am–12:30pm).

Select a fish from the tanks in the **T & T SUPERMARKET**, and staff will deep-fry it for you while you shop. Or try the street food in the **FOOD COURTS**: Singaporean curries, Vietnamese pho, northern Chinese dim sum, Chiu Chow stir-fries, Hong Kong coffee shop–style food, Japanese yakitori, or Taiwanese bubble pearl tea. Numerous bakeries and cafes, as well as karaoke bars, can be found throughout the area. Alexandra Road, unofficially known as **"FOOD STREET,"** offers more than 50 Asian restaurants within two blocks. Within the boundaries of the Golden Village, more than 400 restaurants serve authentic cuisine prepared by professional Asian chefs.

Celebrate **CHINESE NEW YEAR** for 15 days during January and February. Multicultural performances, including the Lion Dance and Chinese opera, are part of the exciting entertainment. *www.tourismrichmond.com; map:D6.*

17) STEVESTON
CHATHAM RD SOUTH TO FRASER RIVER

Once the biggest fishing port on the West Coast, with more than 50 canneries and 10,000 people crowding its boardwalks, Steveston is now bereft of active canneries. It remains a popular weekend destination for both tourists and locals, however, who buy prawns, crab, halibut, cod, and salmon fresh from the boats. Sitting at the mouth of the Fraser River, which still has the largest salmon run in North America, this community on the south side of Richmond is home to the largest fleet of commercial fishing vessels on Canada's west coast.

Parks Canada has reopened the former **GULF OF GEORGIA CANNERY** (4th Ave; 604/664-9009; www.richmond.ca/culture/sites/cannery.htm) as a national historic site. Along with the historical fishing village, the cannery is a must-see on the Steveston itinerary. You may catch old-timers repairing an old wooden seiner in the massive **BRITANNIA HERITAGE SHIPYARD**.

Japanese-Canadians helped build Steveston, and their heritage is still very much present in the community. They play an active role in the fishing industry, and nearby is the first **DOJO** (martial arts centre) to be built outside of Japan.

The **DYKES** that surround the southwestern edges of Steveston are ideal for a long stroll. Give yourself 2–3 hours to complete the walk. Great views of the waterfront can be found here, as well as glimpses of sea lions and blue herons. After your walk, stop for a coffee at one of the many cafes or pick up takeout at **DAVE'S FISH AND CHIPS** (3460 Moncton Rd; 604/271-7555) or at **PAJO'S** (see the Restaurants chapter), which floats on the water. Then perhaps join a whale-watching expedition or buy fresh sardines, shrimp, halibut, or salmon direct from the fishermen. *Map:C7.*

18) LOCARNO AND JERICHO BEACHES

NW MARINE DR BETWEEN TRIMBLE AND BLANCA STS, WEST SIDE

The oldest settlement in Point Grey is **LOCARNO**. The beach, one of the most spectacular in the city, has bones and shells, once part of a Native midden, dating back 3,000 years. At low tide it appears possible to walk to West Vancouver, across miles of tide-rippled sand speckled with shallow tidal pools. Warmed by the sun, these pools are perfect for children. Gulls stalk the water's edge, herons hunch in the shallows, and eagles sometimes circle overhead. A wide dirt path, well used by walkers and cyclists, runs along the top of the beach. Between the path and the road is a broad, grassy area with picnic tables and benches. A few trees bestow shade. All along this shoreline, you can see the green of Stanley Park, the wilderness of Lighthouse Park, and the gleaming fingers of the high-rises in the West End.

Locarno and Jericho beaches blend into each other. **JERICHO**—the name is a corruption of Jerry's Cove, named for Jerry Rogers, who cut timber on the slopes above the cove in the mid-19th century—offers the same beautiful views as Locarno. A Japanese-style bridge arches over a pond shaded by willows that stand in the middle of the park just back from the beach. Together with **SPANISH BANKS BEACH**, the seemingly limitless shoreline offers a paradise for beach lovers, windsurfers, and sailors. *Map:B2.*

19) WRECK BEACH

POINT GREY, MUSQUEAM RESERVE TO SPANISH BANKS WEST, WEST SIDE
Somewhere along the steep, muddy path that leads down the University
of British Columbia's western bluff, the social fabric loosens and the tight
stitches of inhibition tear open. By the time you're at the portable toilets
near the edge of Wreck Beach, it's off with the modesty and into the full
frontal—clothing is optional here. Aside from a few bundled-up rubberneck-
ers scoping the shoreline, most Wreckies take full advantage of Canada's only
Speedo-free beach. The 6-kilometre-long (3.6-mile-long) stretch of sand and
rock, washed by the currents of the **FRASER RIVER, STRAIT OF GEORGIA,** and
ENGLISH BAY, has become a mecca for an estimated 100,000 sun worshippers determined to avoid tan lines each summer.

Officially, the beach stretches from the Musqueam Reserve to Spanish
Banks West, but each section is subtly divided up among the habitués. On the
northern flank you tend to find a greater concentration of men, enjoying the
wilderness and each other's company. (Although naturalism is encouraged,
overt sexual activity runs counter to the Wreck way.) The central stretch,
removed from the water, is **VENDOR'S ROW,** an ad hoc food court of falafels,
"buffalo burgers," Peruvian empanadas, and cool drinks. BC's stringent
liquor laws aren't usually enforced here, so there's often a good supply of cold
beer and wine in any of the iceboxes that are toted up and down the shore.
(If you can flag down the Martini Lady, she'll make you a mean crantini.) On
Wreck's southern edge, a carnival-style atmosphere prevails. Volleyball nets,
boogie boards, Frisbees, and old hippies mix together happily. Body painting,
bocce ball, and beach casino are also favoured pursuits. There's gambling,
too, but this isn't Reno. The games are strictly "low stakes and no clothes."

Wreck Beach was named one of the world's great beaches by *Lifestyles of
the Rich and Famous.* This is surely one of the few spots in Canada where
you can lie on the beach and be served loose joints by a naked woman while
eagles float by lazily overhead. It's a fun and laid-back place to hang out on
a summer weekend, but don't expect complete anarchy. A strict code of con-
duct is upheld by the regulars who want to keep their stretch of sand peaceful
and hassle-free. In other words, don't come down just to gawk and giggle. Be
prepared to strip down at least partially to fit in.

Wreck Beach might be one of the world's best-known beaches, but when
Vancouver author Carellin Brooks published *Wreck Beach* (New Star Books,
2007), it was deemed too risqué for people sailing on BC Ferries, and the
book was soon banned. In the book, Brooks reveals everything you ever
wanted to know about the nude beach, uncovers the politics of acceptable
attire and behaviour, and explores the history and current threats to the
beach. *Map:B2.*

20) CASINOS

VARIOUS LOCATIONS

Come for the chips and stay for Dame Edna, Diana Ross, Wayne Newton, or Dana Carvey. The British Columbia Lottery Corporation provides an entertainment experience in the magnificent casinos scattered throughout Greater Vancouver. Each casino offers a unique atmosphere with live entertainment and restaurants. They advise you to know your limit and play within it.

Boulevard Casino

2080 UNITED BLVD, COQUITLAM; 604/523-6888

Located in the Boulevard Casino, the Red Robinson Show Theatre, named for one of British Columbia's broadcasting legends, is Canada's largest and most spectacular multipurpose gala theatre. With a capacity to seat over 1,000, the theatre boasts a star-studded lineup, with the likes of Tony Bennett, Huey Lewis & the News, Barenaked Ladies, April Wine, plus comedians Roseanne Barr, Craig Ferguson, and Canadian Brent Butt. The impressive lineup of A-list talent is entertainment you can bet on. *www.blvdcasino.com; map:K4.*

Edgewater Casino

750 PACIFIC BLVD, DOWNTOWN; 604/687-3343

Located at the Plaza of Nations and just steps from GM Place and BC Place, Edgewater Casino has over 500 slot machines, all the favourite table games, and Vancouver's largest poker room. Take a break at the VUE Bar & Lounge or Splash Bistro. *www.edgewatercasino.ca; map:U5.*

River Rock Casino Resort

8811 RIVER RD, RICHMOND; 604/247-8900

Just five minutes from the Vancouver Airport, this AAA four-diamond resort features stunning West Coast architecture. Amidst the ponds, waterfalls, 1,000 slot machines, and Racebook is a 950-seat show theatre where Lionel Ritchie, Boyz II Men, Liza Minelli, Jay Leno, Lisa Marie Presley, and Craig Ferguson (to name a few) have stepped onstage. With nine restaurants and bars, a spa, and a convention and meeting facility, as well as a 144-berth marina and hotel packages, the resort deals a winning hand. *www.riverrock.com; map:D5.*

Starlight Casino

350 GIFFORD ST, NEW WESTMINSTER; 604/777-2946

The newest casino to open is located in the Queensborough Landing area of New Westminster. The Redbar and Lounge entertains, with acts ranging from Vancouver's hottest cover bands to country music's rising stars. Schanks interactive sports bar has more than 120 video screens, an arcade, minigolf, and room enough for you and 1,000 fans to cheer on the home team. After sampling the 850 slot machines, 45 gaming tables, and electronic poker tables, fuel up at Shang Noodle House or Kirin Chinese restaurant and then watch some ballroom dancing. *www.starlightcasino.ca; map:H5.*

Neighbourhoods

No city is homogeneous, particularly Vancouver. It's actually an amalgamation of neighbourhoods, each with its own defined residential and shopping areas. And each has an interesting story to tell. Some background for the eight major neighbourhoods of Vancouver City follows.

AMBLESIDE

What Commercial Drive is to bohemian subculture, this West Vancouver neighbourhood (from Marine Dr to the water, from Taylor Wy to 22nd St, West Vancouver) is to baby strollers and the British high street. If Marks & Spencer were urban planners, Ambleside would be the result, a sensible-shoe shopping district where ladies' garments and pork pie shops sit side by side. In the spirit of genteel living, the neighbourhood also sports a well-stocked greenhouse and a string of private art galleries.

Nearby, Ambleside Park (see Parks and Beaches in this chapter) is an ideal place to mosey along the seawall while watching bulk freighters from China and Liberia float by, past Stanley Park, under Lions Gate Bridge, and toward the city's skyline. For the athletically inclined, the park offers playing fields, pitch-and-putt golf, and jogging trails. Picnic areas and a playground wait nearby. The sandy dunes are popular year-round. In the summer, impromptu volleyball games can be found most evenings.

Farther west, upscale **DUNDARAVE** is a busy shopping and restaurant district catering to Vancouver's wealthiest neighbourhood, located several hundred metres up the mountainside in a veritable rabbit warren of poshly appointed streets, lanes, and subdivisions. At the water's edge, the **BEACH HOUSE RESTAURANT** (see the Restaurants chapter) offers a beautiful view, outstanding seafood dishes, and a killer wine list.

COMMERCIAL DRIVE

In multicultural Vancouver, few areas are as ethnically and politically jumbled as this busy street in East Vancouver. The Drive (between Powell St and E Broadway, East Vancouver) has long been the home of local lesbians and sports some of the Good Vibrations look, with pink-triangle law firms and personal-appliance shops, such as the popular **WOMYN'S WARE INC.** (896 Commercial Dr, East Vancouver; 604/254-2543). Greying curmudgeons sip espressos, pierced vegans enjoy chatting over tea and clove ciggies, and grocers hawk cheap produce here—all within the same couple of blocks. Multiply that scene tenfold, toss in a repertory cinema, an alternative magazine joint, and some Nepali and hemp clothing boutiques, and you have a mix that would make Haight-Ashbury jealous. Whatever your ideology, there's a bumper sticker and a cafe here for you. *www.thedrive.ca; map:Z3–Z7.*

FALSE CREEK SOUTH

No neighbourhood has changed as dramatically as False Creek South, one of the largest urban redevelopment projects ever attempted in North America. Industrial land on both sides of False Creek disappeared in the 1970s and '80s, as Vancouverites reclaimed waterfront living. The first major phase of revamping the south shore was in the early 1970s, when the City Council began a concerted effort to clean up the smelly industrial wasteland, and the creek water turned from brown to green. Now, False Creek South is a park-like setting with live-aboard marinas and strata-council condominiums run by owner council cooperatives. On Fairview Slope, which forms the southern edge of the False Creek bowl, condos and townhouses have replaced crumbling old houses. The new dwellings display an astonishing range of architectural styles and colours—some reminiscent of Mediterranean waterfronts. Unfortunately, some of the architectural styles have severely backfired, as scores of shoddily constructed California-style condos (sans protective overhangs) have proven to be no match for Vancouver's famous rain. The result has been millions of dollars in "leaky condo" repairs and a multitude of tarp-covered buildings. However, most area residents are staying despite the costs. The population helps keep the core of the city alive and well, contributing to the success of Granville Island (see no. 1 in Top 20 Attractions).

KITSILANO

FOURTH AVENUE, the main street in Kitsilano, was Canada's Haight-Ashbury in the '60s. Now it offers designer boutiques such as Gravity Pope for hot footwear, the Comicshop, Candy Aisle, and organics-focused Capers Market, where you can provision for a picnic. Transient students and singles come and go, but a strong core of longtime residents still anchors in "Kits," one of the city's liveliest neighbourhoods, which overlooks the classic Vancouver view of sea, Stanley Park, and the North Shore mountains from Cornwall Street. **KITSILANO BEACH**, **VANIER PARK** (where the Vancouver Children's Festival is held each spring; see Parks and Beaches in this chapter), and Vancouver's largest **OUTDOOR SALTWATER POOL** with its wraparound view of the city and mountains are big summer draws.

Since its heyday on North America's counterculture map, Fourth Avenue has become yuppified as baby boomers, who now comprise 56 percent of Kits's population, moved in and hippies moved on. **BROADWAY**, with its own unique shops and a decidedly Greek flavour, runs parallel to Fourth Avenue near the area's southern edge. *www.kitsilano.net.*

PUNJABI MARKET

Home to many of the Lower Mainland's 250,000-strong Indo-Canadian community, the Punjabi Market is the place to go for great tandoori, a custom-fit *salwar kameez* (loose-fitting tunics and pants), or the latest blockbuster from Bollywood on videotape. In South Vancouver at 49th Avenue and Main Street, the market is a masala mix of all-you-can-eat *thali*—a meal consisting of a selection of Indian dishes served in small bowls on a round tray—houses, and sweet shops. This is the closest Vancouver gets to the authentic curries and cheap prices of northern India. South Indian chutneys and East African halal foods are also on hand. And there's more here than just food: sari boutiques, Rajasthani jewellery stores, and travel agents offering cut-rate flights to Delhi crowd the streets. Like the tightly packed bazaars of Bombay and Amritsar, the Punjabi Market is squeezed into a couple of blocks. A few hours of browsing here, and you'll be ready for the subcontinent.

SOUTH MAIN

What once was a shady street of antique stores, quirky cafes, hookers, and dilapidated hotels has become one of the fastest-changing neighbourhoods, now home to local designers of fashion and accessories, vintage clothing stores, casual fine-dining restaurants, and an endless supply of coffee shops. For years, the locals referred to the area from East Second Avenue to East 15th Avenue as SoMa (short for South Main), but the boundaries have lengthened as artist live-work lofts and a condo boom continue to spread southward toward 33rd Avenue. With young professionals and families moving into the area, so too have the European furniture and chic hardware stores. Expect to spend a couple of days exploring the small independent galleries, antique dealers, and creative boutiques (see "Neighbourhood Watch: South Main").

WEST END

This lively, vibrant neighbourhood in Vancouver's downtown core stretches from Coal Harbour to English Bay, with Stanley Park on one side and Burrard Street on the other. It's Canada's most densely populated area, an eclectic mix of graceful, tree-lined streets; restaurants and shops; skyscrapers and low-slung apartments; and a few remaining Edwardian-style houses that were once homes of the city's wealthy class.

The residents here are predominantly young adults and seniors, with few children. The West End also has western Canada's largest gay and lesbian population. This odd combination has made it one of Vancouver's most livable, tolerant, and safe neighbourhoods. Simply going for a walk can be fascinating, but tennis, in-line skating, sailboarding, summer band concerts, and pitch-and-putt golf also keep residents on their toes.

The three major streets are each seven blocks long: **DENMAN STREET**, a strip with a smorgasbord of restaurants; **DAVIE STREET**, with its busy shopping areas and nightlife; and **ROBSON STREET**, with lots of coffeehouses, pizza parlors, and traffic. The English Bay popcorn vendor, usually found near the intersection of Davie and Denman, pops and butters year-round. **BARCLAY HERITAGE SQUARE**, a unique, parklike site that includes nine historic working-class houses and period landscaping, has preserved some Victorian charmers.

The West End is also one of the two areas of Vancouver (the other is Yaletown; see description in this section) envied by city planners in other parts of North America, particularly those whose cities become dark, scary holes

THE RICHMOND OVAL

On one of a cluster of islands at the mouth of the Fraser River, Richmond, known as the Gateway to the Pacific Rim, is close to downtown Vancouver, Vancouver International Airport, the Tsawwassen BC Ferries terminal, and the Canada–U.S. border. With a population of more than 185,000, Richmond is an urban centre whose growth since 1990 has been made up of Asian immigrants; people of Chinese or South Asian ancestry now represent nearly 60 percent of its residents. Richmond, known as the "Island City, by Nature," has a vibrant, multi-cultural community that is infused with European, Japanese, Chinese, and Indian influences. Richmond (originally called Lulu Island) is one of the most fascinating islands on the West Coast, with six major shopping centres, international cuisine, and abundant recreational activities.

It is here where the 2010 Olympic and Paralympic Winter Games' speed-skating events will be held. The skating Oval was constructed in 2008. Set on the Fraser River waterfront overlooking the panoramic North Shore mountains, the Oval combines elements of the island's diverse cultures as well as the city's natural aspects through three main public spaces.

after the evening rush hour. Here, the core is alive and busy, relatively safe, and lighted 24 hours a day.

For more than two decades, Vancouver's Pride Society has held an **ANNUAL GAY PRIDE PARADE** in early August in the West End. Colourful floats and dancers in costumes pour down Denman, then Beach Avenue, before gathering for a mass celebration at Sunset Beach on English Bay.

Many gay and gay-friendly businesses are here, including **LITTLE SISTER'S BOOK & ART EMPORIUM** (1238 Davie St; 604/669-1753) and a funky array of shops, cafes, restaurants, and night nooks. Slightly smaller than San Francisco's Castro District, this neighbourhood remains "rainbow central," but an array of gay-centered hotels and dance bars have also begun to thrive in Gastown and on the border with Yaletown. *www.englishbay.com, www.seethewestend.com.*

YALETOWN

By the time you've finished reading this paragraph, Yaletown probably will have changed again. Another upscale restaurant will have opened, a skyscraping condo will have been added, or one more interior design firm will have decided that Yaletown is the only place for them. Unless you pine for the bruised and beaten warehouses of old, this heritage neighbourhood betwixt False Creek and downtown is a sterling case of gentrification gone right. Its narrow streets are living proof that the dilapidated can appear young again.

LEGACY PLAZA will welcome crowds and display public art. Two giant red lanterns created from translucent, durable fabric that responds to the changing wind and sky will be suspended over a large pond in the **WATERWORKS** space. The **RIVERSIDE** will be a festival space for up to 8,000, connecting the Oval to the river, where visitors can stroll along the Middle Arm Dyke Trail. The trail continues south to the fishing village of Steveston and beyond—in total, 77 kilometres (48 miles) of trails for walking or cycling.

Inside, the Oval will house a 400-metre (1,312-foot) oval speed-skating track roughly equalling the area of six international hockey rinks and will seat approximately 8,000 fans. The Oval will qualify for Silver certification on the Leadership in Energy and Environmental Design (LEED) scale; for example, storm water runoff will be recycled for the facility's many requirements, including the innovative water features.

Post-Games, the Oval will become a centre for sports and wellness, summer or winter, with the main floor offering ice, hardwood, and indoor tracks, as well as shopping, food services, and festival space.

—Arlene Kroeker

First settled in the 1890s by workers from the nearby Canadian Pacific Railway line, Yaletown evolved into the city's garment warehouse district before morphing into a yuppie hot spot with cafes, bars, billiard halls, boutiques, hair salons, art galleries, studios, and offices. Led by the massive Concord Pacific development project, Yaletown emerged in the late 1980s as an urbane model of hip, high-density living (and a welcome alternative to the West End's stodgy apartment blocks). Locals jumped at the prospect of living in cozy lofts and glass-walled homes high above the city. Designers and restaurateurs flocked to the cathedral ceilings and brick facades of the old warehouses. Even the luxurious **OPUS HOTEL** (see the Lodgings chapter) took up residence in 2002, winning numerous awards for being the best of the best in the world.

There's more to Yaletown than just munching and boozing and shopping, however. Behind the old brick facades is a high-tech cast of Vancouver start-ups that have resisted the Microsoft-style "glass campus in the suburb" approach to office space. Instead, they've gone for high-beam ceilings and character architecture. Many of them have survived the high-tech downturn to ensure that Yaletown remains a bijou, a lively neighbourhood for years to come. Plus, its waterfront views of False Creek and the grassy expanse of David Lam Park make this a great recreational escape.

Museums

BC Museum of Mining

**HWY 99 TO BRITANNIA BEACH ON HOWE SOUND,
SEA-TO-SKY HWY, BRITTANIA BEACH; 604/896-2233**

Take an hour-long drive along the scenic Sea-to-Sky Highway toward Squa-mish to this mine and museum, now a national historic site. The old Britannia Copper Mine, which in the 1920s was one of the largest copper mines in the British Commonwealth, once processed more than 6.4 million kilograms (14.1 million pounds) of ore daily. Guided underground tours on electric trains give a glimpse of what working life was like for miners, as do demon-strations of diamond drilling and copper mining. Exhibits include hundreds of old photographs, artifacts, and a slide show. You can pan for gold, "recov-ery guaranteed," meaning that you are sure to find traces of gold dust in your pan. It's cool in the underground mines, so bring a light jacket or sweater. Admission is $16.95 adults, $13.95 seniors and students, $11.95 youth to 18, free for children under 5, $55 for families. *Every day; first Sunday in May–Canadian Thanksgiving in Oct 9am–4:30pm; www.bcmuseumofmining.org.*

BC Sports Hall of Fame and Museum

**GATE A, BC PLACE STADIUM (EAST FOOT OF ROBSON ST),
777 PACIFIC BLVD S, DOWNTOWN; 604/687-5520**

This is the home of BC's most extensive collection of artifacts and archival materials on the province's professional and amateur sports and recreation history. Multimedia exhibits showcase BC's Olympic, Commonwealth, Stan-ley Cup, and Grey Cup champions. The heroic journeys of disabled BC athletes Terry Fox and Rick Hansen are commemorated in special galleries. Hands-on exhibits allow visitors to test their skills at climbing, throwing, or racing like the pros. Admission is $10 adults; $8 children, seniors, and students; free for children under 5; $25 for families. *Every day; 10am–5pm; www.bcsportshalloffame.com; map:T5.*

Burnaby Village Museum

**6501 DEER LAKE AVE (CANADA WY AT SPERLING AVE),
BURNABY; 604/293-6501**

If the kids ever bug you about what life was like way back before the dawn of time, this open-air museum provides painless answers to their questions. This delightful re-creation of a turn-of-the-19th-century town was built to honour BC's centennial in 1958. Step back through time and visit a blacksmith's shop, an 1890s dentist's office, a sawmill, and a print shop. In all, more than 30 buildings and outdoor displays depict daily life from 1890 to 1925. Authenti-cally costumed "residents" welcome you into their homes—which might be a pioneer log cabin—and workplaces. A church (available for weddings) and a schoolhouse have also been re-created, and the ice-cream parlour (available for birthday parties) is operational. A lovingly restored 1912 carousel, called

Carry-Us-All, was once an attraction at the Pacific National Exhibition from 1936 to 1989. Kids and adults alike will delight in a ride on this beautiful antique. The Interurban tram No. 1223 served Vancouver from 1913 to 1958, and after years of neglect, the car was refurbished by a team of volunteers and parked in the tram barn for all to enjoy. Admission is $11.22 adults, $5.66 children, $8.41 seniors and students, free for children under 5; Tues half-price. *Every day; May–Aug 11am–4:30pm, winter days and hours vary, call for information; www.burnabyvillagemuseum.ca; map:I3.*

The Canadian Museum of Flight

HANGAR 3, LANGLEY AIRPORT, 5333 216TH ST, LANGLEY; 604/532-0035
A fascination with vintage aircraft is evident at this mainly outdoor museum. The collection of more than 50 early aircraft includes a Tiger Moth, a Sopwith Camel, a Harvard, and an Avro Canuck. The transparent skin of a lumbering Second World War supply plane, the Lysander, reveals just how they do fly. Those interested in the technical side of things can browse in the library and the gift shop. The museum is an hour's drive south of downtown Vancouver. Admission is $7.55 adults, $5 seniors and youth, free for children under 6; $17 for families. *Every day; 10am–4pm; www.canadianflight.org.*

Fort Langley National Historic Site

MAVIS ST, LANGLEY; 604/513-4777
This former Hudson's Bay fur-trading post is the quickest route to the frontier days of 19th-century British Columbia. The 1839 storehouse is all that remains of the original compound, but Parks Canada has carefully reconstructed several nearby buildings. While interpreters in colonial garb will happily explain Fort Langley's historical significance as the place where in 1858 Britain first laid territorial claim to BC, your children will probably want to get their hands dirty by panning for gold or make like voyageurs by hoisting a few bales of (fake) fur. Vivid reenactments of life at the fort take place on holidays such as BC Day in August. Admission is $7.05 adults, $5.80 seniors, $3.40 children 6–16, free for children under 6; $17.60 for families. *Every day; June 30–Sept 3 9am–8pm, Sept 4–June 29 10am–5pm, closed Christmas to New Year's Day.*

The Herb Museum

343 E HASTINGS ST, EAST VANCOUVER; 604/842-7790
For those interested in psychoactive and nonpsychoactive medicines and herbal antiquity, a visit to Vancouver—or Vansterdam, as it is known in some circles—isn't complete without a stop at the grooviest museum in town: the Herb Museum. Opened in 2007, the roomy museum features 16 sections, which include such topics as live herbs, opium, marijuana, coca, cacti, stimulants, and synthetics, as well as a theatre/vapor lounge and retail outlet. There are displays of old medicine bottles dating back to the 1600s, dried herbs from the 1800s, bottles of sandalwood and wild yam approximately 100 years old, collections of kef and hashish pipes, cannabis medicine bottles,

and contemporary items like Marinol bottles. Besides the herbs and bottles, there are pulp-fiction novels, postcards, and illustrations of people smoking pipes from all over the world, photos of beautiful hallucinatory flowers, and a world-class bookcase and video library. Coca tea and chocolate aphrodisiacs are available in the retail area. Admission is $5–$50, depending on what you can afford. *Every day; Mon–Sat 1pm–7pm, Sun 3pm–7pm; www. herbmuseum.ca; map:*W4.

H. R. MacMillan Space Centre

1100 CHESTNUT ST, WEST SIDE; 604/738-7827

Sending your offspring into space (for the afternoon, at least) has never been so easy. Besides housing the H. R. MacMillan Planetarium and the Gordon Southam Observatory, the Space Centre lets visitors experience the reality of life amongst the stars. In the Cosmic Courtyard, exhibits include hands-on shuttle-docking simulations and a space suit from the *Apollo* launches, while Groundstation Canada offers daily live demonstrations and multimedia shows about space travel. Unflappable family members can take a ride off-planet, on the Virtual Voyages Motion Simulator. For anyone too cool for school, the Planetarium hosts 40-minute evening laser concerts, featuring music by a range of artists, such as Led Zeppelin and Radiohead. Admission is $15 adults; $10.75 seniors, youth, students, and children; $7 children under 5 with simulator, free for children under 5 without simulator; $45 for families. *Tues–Sun 10am–5pm; www.hrmacmillanspacecentre.com; map:*P5.

The Old Hastings Mill Store Museum

1575 ALMA ST, WEST SIDE; 604/734-1212

The wavy handmade glass distorts the beach scene visible through the windows, but this only adds to the charm of this cluttered museum inside Vancouver's oldest building, one of only a handful to survive the fire of 1886. Set in a little park beside the Royal Vancouver Yacht Club, this building started life as a company store for a lumber operation and, before Vancouver became a city, was the first post office in the fledgling town of Granville. Old muskets, Native baskets, satin clothing, chiming clocks, and a coach are only some of the items sheltered in the cool, dim interior. Admission by donation. *Every day; mid-June–mid-Sept Tues–Sun 11am–4pm, mid-Sept–mid-June Sat–Sun 1pm–4pm; map:*C2.

Pacific Museum of Earth

GEOLOGICAL SCIENCE CENTRE, UBC, 6339 STORES RD,
WEST SIDE; 604/822-6992

Pieces of glowing amber and 80-million-year-old *Lambeosaurus* dinosaur bones are just some of the treasures to be found in this fascinating place. Displays of glittering crystals and minerals, as well as fossils that are so beautiful they outshine gemstones, encompass about 4.5 billion years of mineral and fossil history. More than 9,000 specimens are exhibited.

Gift shop is open noon to 2pm. Admission by donation. *Mon–Fri 9am–5pm; www.eos.ubc.ca/resources/museum; map:A3.*

Vancouver Maritime Museum and St. Roch

1905 OGDEN ST, WEST SIDE; 604/257-8300

Vancouver's seagoing tradition is spectacularly documented in this museum, suitably perched on the southern shore of English Bay. A Kwakiutl totem pole stands near the entrance, a replica of the 30.5-metre (100-foot) pole presented to Queen Elizabeth II to mark BC's 1958 centennial. The museum is the home of a 1928 ketch, the *St. Roch*, now a national historical site. This Royal Canadian Mounted Police patrol boat was the first sailing vessel to navigate the Northwest Passage from west to east, a dangerous voyage of 28 months. The museum's permanent displays honour the city's growth as a port, the modern fishing industry, and 18th-century explorers. The museum also holds workshops, talks, and demonstrations—all with a nautical flavour.

At the Children's Maritime Discovery Centre, your little Ahabs can step aboard a full-scale tugboat, peer out at Vancouver Harbour through a powerful telescope, send a remote-controlled robot to the depths of the ocean—and those are just the beginning. Other permanent exhibits include the interactive Pirates' Cove, where choices run from digging up buried treasure to walking the plank. Stroll along the docks of the heritage harbour for an ever-changing view of vessels, both historic and modern. Behind the museum sits what looks like a large metal cocktail weenie, but it is in fact the *Ben Franklin*, a research submersible used in the 1960s in Florida to chart the Gulf Stream currents. It was partially funded by NASA, as it mimicked the conditions in space similar to those the *Apollo* astronauts would later undergo. Admission is $10 adults, $7.50 seniors and youth, free for children 5 and under; $25 for families. *Every day; Victoria Day–Labour Day 10am–5pm, rest of year Tues–Sat 10am–5pm, Sun noon–5pm; www. vancouvermaritimemuseum.com; map:O5.*

Vancouver Police Centennial Museum

240 E CORDOVA ST, EAST VANCOUVER; 604/665-3346

Even young people who weren't raised on a diet of *Cops* and *America's Most Wanted* will find this place fascinating, provided they have a strong stomach and a healthy sense of irony. "Mystery, History, and Intrigue" is the motto here. Cases full of seized weapons and counterfeit currency share this red-brick former coroner's building with police artifacts, archival photographs, and a rather grim forensic exhibit (don't worry, it's a mannequin). Meanwhile, several displays of real crime-scene evidence invite visitors to put their sleuthing skills to work. At the end of it all, take home a souvenir from—where else?—the Coppe Shop. *Mon–Sat 9am–5pm; www.vancouver policemuseum.ca; map:V4.*

Galleries

Inside, outside, upstairs, and downstairs, Vancouver has a wealth of public and private galleries. Many of the city's commercial galleries are located on South Granville, between the Granville Street Bridge and 16th Avenue; others are scattered throughout downtown, in Gastown, or on Granville Island, site of the Emily Carr Institute of Art & Design and the Charles H. Scott Gallery.

Native galleries present art by members of the Northwest Coast First Nations, as well as the Inuit of Canada's far north. Craft galleries offer an eclectic mix of colourful, creative, and even functional pieces. Artist-run spaces include the refreshingly irreverent **WESTERN FRONT** (303 E 8th Ave; 604/876-9343; www.front.bc.ca), now more than a quarter century old; **VIDEO IN/VIDEO OUT** (1965 Main St; 604/872-8337; www.vivomediaarts.com); **ARTS OFF MAIN** (216 E 28th Ave; 604/876-2785; www.artsoffmain.ca); and **ARTSPEAK** (233 Carrall St; 604/688-0051; www.artspeak.ca). The **CONTEMPORARY ART GALLERY** (555 Nelson St; 604/681-2700; www.contemporaryartgallery.ca) is an independent, publicly funded art gallery presenting a diverse programme of regional, national, and international art.

Art Beatus

108-888 NELSON ST, DOWNTOWN; 604/688-2633
Art Beatus seeks to present and promote contemporary international art. Its special focus is on artists of Asian origin, both local and offshore. The first Art Beatus opened in Hong Kong in 1992. *Mon–Fri; www.artbeatus.com; map:R4.*

Bau-Xi Gallery

3045 GRANVILLE ST, WEST SIDE; 604/733-7011
The Bau-Xi, established in 1965, is the oldest contemporary gallery in Vancouver and specializes in the works of Canadian artists such as Tom Burrows, Joe Plaskett, and the late Jack Shadbolt. Paintings are displayed in an uncrowded manner against a minimalist background, and open storage allows visitors access to a lot more than what's on display. *Mon–Sat; www.bau-xi.com; map:D3.*

Buschlen-Mowatt Gallery

1445 W GEORGIA ST, DOWNTOWN; 604/682-1234
This modern gallery on the edge of Stanley Park, overlooking Coal Harbour, focuses on international contemporary art, from the truly challenging avant-garde to huge, splashy, romantic works. Artists include Boaz Vaadia, Bernard Cathelin, Yehouda Chaki, Otto Rogers, and Mark Gaskin, to name a few. *Every day; www.buschlenmowatt.com; map:R3.*

Diane Farris Gallery

1590 W 7TH AVE, WEST SIDE; 604/737-2629

Enter the gallery through the Sculpture Garden and greet the wooden figures before experiencing Farris's many featured young artists. Enfant terrible Attila Richard Lukacs is just one of many gifted artists that this gallery shows, along with Chris Woods, Dale Chihuly, Angela Grossman, and Xue Mo. Farris's gallery is on the cutting edge of contemporary local and international art. *Tues–Sat; www.dianefarrisgallery.com; map:P3.*

Douglas Reynolds Gallery

2335 GRANVILLE ST, WEST SIDE; 604/731-9292

You'll find strictly Northwest Coast art here, including masks, totem poles, prints, and an exceptional selection of gold and silver jewellery. *Every day; www.douglasreynoldsgallery.com; map:P7.*

Equinox Gallery

2321 GRANVILLE ST, WEST SIDE; 604/736-2405

Another long-established, serious Vancouver gallery, the Equinox handles only the very best North American painters and graphic artists. Works are beautifully displayed in serene surroundings. *Tue–Sat; www.equinoxgallery. com; map:P7.*

Gallery of BC Ceramics

1359 CARTWRIGHT ST, GRANVILLE ISLAND; 604/669-3606

The teapot as a functional work of art is quite the norm in this Granville Island gallery, which showcases the sometimes amazing pottery of more than 60 BC artists. From funky to beautiful, useful to decorative, there isn't a clunky piece in sight. *Every day; map:Q7.*

Heffel Gallery

2247 GRANVILLE ST, WEST SIDE; 604/732-6505

Elegantly housed in an historic stone building, the Heffel Gallery specializes in international works by the august Group of Seven and many other respected Canadian landscape artists. Exhibits can be spread over its two floors, and there are lots of little spaces for quiet contemplation of a special work. *Mon–Sat; www.heffel.com; map:P7.*

Inuit Gallery

206 CAMBIE ST, GASTOWN; 604/688-7323 OR 888/615-8399

This longtime Gastown gallery has a well-deserved reputation as North America's leading Inuit art gallery. Collectors from around the globe buy here, and some of the beautifully produced exhibition catalogues are collectors' items. The Northwest Coast work here includes masks, wood carvings, and jewellery. Gallery employees know their subject and are usually delighted to share their knowledge. *Every day; www.inuit.com; map:T3.*

Marion Scott Gallery

308 WATER ST, DOWNTOWN; 604/685-1934

One of the oldest galleries in the city, the Marion Scott concentrates solely on Inuit art and always has some absolutely stunning works. *Every day; www. marionscottgallery.com; map:S3.*

Monte Clark Gallery

2339 GRANVILLE ST, WEST SIDE; 604/730-5000

One of the city's most influential gallery owners, Monte Clark has a great eye for emerging talent and has put Canada on the artistic map. He presents contemporary avant-garde artists, not only from Canada but also from the United States and Europe. *Tues–Sat; www.monteclarkgallery.com; map:P7.*

Morris and Helen Belkin Art Gallery

1825 MAIN MALL, UBC, WEST SIDE; 604/822-2759

The former UBC Fine Arts Gallery features ever-changing exhibitions of contemporary art and hosts lecture series and special events. *Tues–Sun; www. belkin-gallery.ubc.ca; map:B2.*

Or Gallery Society

103-480 SMITHE ST, DOWNTOWN; 604/683-7395

Conceptual, quirky, and cutting edge, the Or is a great showcase for local artists, and it's a must-see for the best in contemporary art. *Tues–Sat; www. orgallery.org; map:T4.*

Presentation House

333 CHESTERFIELD AVE, NORTH VANCOUVER; 604/986-1351

This is a long-standing venue for photographic art. From elegant black-and-white to contemporary full-colour photographs, Presentation House showcases exciting and beautiful exhibitions in this attractive older building. *Wed–Sun (closed Aug); www.presentationhousegall.com; map:E1.*

Robert Held Art Glass

2130 PINE ST, WEST SIDE; 604/737-0020 OR 800/665-0725

Watch how glass is blown in this cavernous workshop/studio, where the red-hot furnaces lend an unreal background to the exquisite works created by local artisans. Elegant vases, goblets, glasses, candlesticks, and decorative pieces are swirled through with colour, emphasizing their unique, fragile shapes. *Mon–Sat; www.robertheld.com; map:P7.*

Tracey Lawrence Gallery

1531 W 4TH AVE, WEST SIDE; 604/730-2875

Keep your eye on this young gallery, run by Tracey Lawrence. The focus is on early- to mid-career Canadian and American artists who are pushing the boundaries of art. *Tues–Sat; www.traceylawrencegallery.com; map:P7.*

Gardens

Vancouver's temperate climate and soft, plentiful rains encourage exuberant growth in limitless combinations of species. All over the city, gardens, parks, and green spaces are tucked into the corners of lots, squeezed between houses, stretched across a campus, or set in front of public buildings. High on a mountainside or beside the ocean are tiny private domains as well as sprawling hectares for public pleasure. The **DOGWOOD** is British Columbia's provincial flower, and in spring spreading trees are clothed in fragile, creamy blossoms. (See no. 3 in Top 20 Attractions for more outstanding garden examples.) Following are descriptions of some more of Vancouver's most wonderful gardens.

Dr. Sun Yat-Sen Classical Chinese Garden

578 CARRALL ST, CHINATOWN; 604/662-3207

This authentic Suzhou-style classical garden, which took six years to plan and two years to build, was the first of its kind outside China. Rocks, wood, plants, and water are used with deceptive simplicity, but gradually, contrasts are revealed—large and small, dark and light, hard and soft, straight and curved, artificial and natural. Windows frame courtyards, intricate carvings, or a rock whose heavily textured surface changes appearance with the play of light. Pavilions connected by covered walkways edge the milky jade waters of the pond, whose surface is speckled with water lilies. Most of the materials were imported from Suzhou, China's foremost garden city. Adjoining this serene, starkly elegant garden is Dr. Sun Yat-Sen Park, a simplified version of the main garden. *www.vancouverchinesegarden.com; map:V4.*

Nitobe Memorial Garden

UBC, WEST SIDE; 604/822-6038

This tranquil garden should be explored at leisure. As you stroll along the gently curving paths, note the care that went into the placement of every rock, tree, and shrub. Each element harmonizes with nature. Wander around, accompanied by the soothing sounds of the lake, waterfalls, and tiny streams; the gardens move from a beginning through growth and change to an ending. Native and imported plants and trees, azaleas, flowering cherries, irises, and maples provide colour year-round. In summer, visitors can witness the formal preparation of a tea ceremony—reservations are recommended. *www. nitobe.org; map:A3.*

Tilford Gardens

440-333 BROOKSBANK AVE, NORTH VANCOUVER; 604/984-8200

Created in 1968, these glorious gardens are a popular place for summer weddings, and it's easy to understand why. A choice of eight theme gardens provides the perfect setting—from a stunning display of roses to the cool formality of the White Garden. The Display Garden features colourful spring bulbs and spreading annuals. The Oriental Garden showcases traditional bonsai trees and a tranquil pond, and in the Native Garden, a footpath winds through a small, aromatic Pacific coast forest. The Herb Garden and the shady Colonnade Garden, with its soothing rock pool and numerous other botanical delights, are located with the others on the site of a former winery/distillery, whose buildings are now used as a shopping centre and movie studio complex. *www.parkandtilford.ca/pandtgardens.htm; map:F1.*

Parks and Beaches

Whether you're looking for a seaside stroll or a strenuous workout, dazzling views or deep aromatic forests, tennis courts or a shady picnic spot, one of Vancouver's more than 160 parks will deliver it. And, most likely, it'll have a beach nearby, for good measure.

Ambleside Park

**ALONG MARINE DR, TURNING SOUTH
AT 13TH ST, WEST VANCOUVER**

This aptly named West Vancouver park is an ideal place to amble along the seawall, enjoying the superb scenery that forms a backdrop for the marine traffic. For the energetic, there are playing fields, pitch-and-putt golf, a fitness circuit, and jogging trails, as well as picnic areas and a playground. The beach is popular with families on summer days. Impromptu volleyball games take place most evenings. Bird-watchers appreciate the bird sanctuary on an artificial island in the tidal slough. *www.findfamilyfun.com/amblesidebeach.htm.*

Barnet Beach Park

EAST ALONG INLET DR TO BARNET RD, BURNABY

Once the site of a busy mill town, this heritage park in north Burnaby is the perfect place to spend a day by the water. Traces of the old mill workings, which resemble a medieval castle, are a joy to youngsters. Safe, guarded swimming areas, a wharf for fishing and crabbing, picnic areas, barbecue pits, and a nonpowered boat launch area make this park a local favourite. On summer weekends the parking lot is often full, but there's plenty of parking on nearby side streets. *www.findfamilyfun.com/barnet.htm; map:I2.*

Belcarra Regional Park

**ALONG HASTINGS ST TO BARNET HWY, NORTH ON IOCO RD,
NORTH TO 1ST AVE (FOLLOW SIGNS), BURNABY/PORT MOODY;
604/432-6352 FOR GROUP PICNIC RESERVATIONS**

It's well worth the hour's drive from downtown Vancouver to this park, which is really two parks in one—Belcarra and White Pine Beach. The huge, grassy sweep of the Belcarra picnic area sloping gently down to Indian Arm on Burrard Inlet is ideal for individual and group picnics. Sasamat Lake has one of the warmest beaches on the Lower Mainland. Well-marked trails follow the ocean edge at White Pine Beach, and the sheltered caves make perfect picnic and sunning spots. Tidal pools with their varied marine life are an endless source of entertainment. Crabbers and fishers bask in the sunshine on the dock, waiting for a bite (permits required). Kids love the imaginative adventure playground. Mudflats on the southern tip of Bedwell Bay provide interesting beachcombing. Busy on weekends; signs along Ioco Road tell you if the park is full. *www.gvrd.bc.ca/parks/Belcarra.htm; map:I1–J2*.

Capilano River Regional Park

ALONG CAPILANO RD N BETWEEN EDGEMONT AND MONTROYAL BLVDS, NORTH VANCOUVER

This park spanning North Vancouver and West Vancouver ranges from the urban to the wild. The immense Cleveland Dam, named after Vancouver's first water commissioner, Ernest Cleveland, harnesses the Capilano River and supplies Vancouver's water. Clearings beside the dam provide great viewpoints of the spillway. Pleasant picnic areas abound near the colourful flower gardens. Follow signs through the woods to the **FISH HATCHERY** (604/666-1790), where a glass-fronted observation area shows the fishways that assist salmon battling their way upriver to return to their birthplace. Displays chronicle the life cycle of the Pacific salmon, and breeding tanks hold minute salmon and trout fry. Below the hatchery is wilderness, with long and short hikes beside the rushing river as well as inland. The **CAPILANO SUSPENSION BRIDGE** (604/985-7474) is a swinging, 137-metre (450-foot) bridge that spans the Capilano River Canyon and is the area's oldest tourist attraction (see no. 7 in Top 20 Attractions). Fishing in the river can be rewarding. *www. gvrd.bc.ca/parks/CapilanoRiver.htm; map:D0*.

Central Park

BETWEEN BOUNDARY RD AND PATTERSON AVE, KINGSWAY AND IMPERIAL ST, BURNABY

One of the oldest parks in the city, straddling the boundary between Vancouver and Burnaby, this lovely park was named after its New York counterpart. Once a military reserve for the defence of New Westminster, the park has an award-winning playground specially designed to include children with disabilities. Longer trails for joggers and cyclists meander through the park. Horseshoe pitches, pitch-and-putt golf, tennis courts, a swimming pool, and lawn bowling greens ensure this park has something for everyone. Vancouver's professional soccer team, the Whitecaps, play their home games at Swangard Stadium during spring and summer. *www. city.burnaby.bc.ca/visitors/attractions/prkstr.html; map:G4*.

Cypress Provincial Park

TAKE EXIT 8 OFF HWY 1, TO TOP OF CYPRESS BOWL RD, WEST VANCOUVER

This West Vancouver park is perfect for those who like their wilderness manageable. Trails are steep and can be muddy and rough, but they are well marked. Huge old trees have thick, textured bark. Swirling mist in the tree-tops adds to the feeling that you are a long way from civilization when, in fact, the parking lot is a short walk away. Cypress Creek has carved a deep, narrow canyon, and the roar of the water foaming through the steep walls echoes around the park. From the canyon, the creek plunges in a spectacular cascade to the wide creek bed and its smooth, water-worn boulders. The main trail, which can be muddy and slippery, climbs steadily upward through heavy forest and underbrush, occasionally opening to natural viewpoints. Downhill and cross-country skiing and tobogganing are popular activities at the Cypress Bowl Ski Area in winter. *www.out-there.com/cypress.htm.*

David Lam Park

PACIFIC BLVD, SOUTH FOOT OF HOMER ST
AND DRAKE ST, YALETOWN
Named for a Chinese-Canadian philanthropist and former lieutenant governor of BC, this park is one of the biggest green spaces in the mammoth Concord Pacific redevelopment of the north shore of False Creek. *Map:S6.*

English Bay Beach

BEACH AVE, BETWEEN DENMAN AND BURRARD STS, WEST END
In the 1920s and '30s, throngs of Vancouverites would gather on this wide, sandy beach and along the pier. A Jamaican seaman, Joe Fortes, lived in a little cottage on the beach and for 25 years was a self-appointed lifeguard, teaching many youngsters to swim. A bronze drinking fountain in tiny Alexandra Park, across Beach Avenue, stands in tribute to Fortes. A delightful gingerbread-embellished bandstand is also found here, and a band plays on warm Sunday afternoons. The pier is gone, but crowds still come to swim and sunbathe. In July and August, English Bay is the setting for the **CELE-BRATION OF LIGHT** (604/641-1193), an international fireworks competition that takes place over four nights. Every New Year's Day, Vancouver's traditional Polar Bear Swim takes place near the bathhouse off Beach Avenue. The number of onlookers is always larger than the number of brave swimmers who begin the year with a chilly dip. *www.englishbay.com/eb/walk1. htm; map:O2–P3.*

Garry Point Park

7TH AVE AT CHATHAM ST, RICHMOND
This park on the extreme southwestern tip of Richmond is rich with the history of boatbuilding and the lore of fish canneries. At the turn of the 19th century, more than 2,000 fishing boats waited at the mouth of the Fraser River to set out into the Strait of Georgia. The nearby town of Steveston (see no. 17 in Top 20 Attractions) is preserved much as it was a century ago, when the first cannery went into operation. It is still an important fishing area. You can buy fish fresh off the boat from Steveston quay or enjoy a meal nearby in one of the many excellent fish-and-chips restaurants. This is also the perfect place to watch freighter traffic heading up the main arm of the Fraser. Equally popular is picnicking in one of the many sandy bays that edge this park (beach fires permitted). A small Japanese garden is evidence

of the strong Japanese presence in Steveston. Kite fliers flock to the open, grassy field where steady breezes from the strait provide a challenge. North of the park are scenic riverside trails that run along Richmond's dykes, which are well used by walkers and cyclists. *www.findfamilyfun.com/garrypoint. htm; map:B7.*

George C. Reifel Migratory Bird Sanctuary

WESTHAM ISLAND TO ROBERTSON RD, LADNER; 604/946-6980
A bird-watcher's paradise, these 330 hectares (850 acres) of former tidal flats were reclaimed through diking and were eventually transformed from a hunting ground to a rest stop for hundreds of species of migrating waterfowl and other winged creatures. (See also Nature and Animal Observation in the Recreation chapter.) *www.ducks.ca/reifel/index.html.*

Iona Beach Park

**ALONG FERGUSON RD NEAR SOUTH TERMINAL
OF VANCOUVER INTERNATIONAL AIRPORT, TO
IONA ISLAND CAUSEWAY, RICHMOND**
Based on the premise "If you can't hide it, flaunt it," one of Vancouver's major sewage outfall pipes has been transformed into a unique walking and cycling path that extends 4 kilometres (2.5 miles) into the Strait of Georgia. A surprisingly romantic stroll, considering its primary purpose, the pathway on top of the pipe evokes the sensation of being at sea on an ocean liner. At the end of the walkway, a viewing tower gives a bird's-eye view of the strait and, on clear days, distant glimpses of Vancouver Island and the mountains of the Olympic Peninsula in Washington state. Beaches are sandy and flat, ideal for kite flying, swimming, and sunning. The waters are sheltered, good for canoeing and kayaking. Driftwood rims the shore, and the Fraser River marsh on the island's south side is a haven for migrating birds on their way to and from Arctic breeding grounds; ducks, songbirds, and sandpipers congregate here in vast numbers. *www.gvrd.bc.ca/parks/ionabeach.htm; map:B4.*

Lynn Headwaters Regional Park

PARK RD, PAST LYNN VALLEY RD, NORTH VANCOUVER
The Lynn Canyon Suspension Bridge (see no. 7 in Top 20 Attractions) and Ecology Centre (604/981-3103) are near the entrance to the 250-hectare (617-acre) Lynn Headwaters Regional Park. The ecology centre, an educational resource and interpretive facility, is considered the ideal location to begin a hike. Guided walks are available. *www.findfamilyfun.com/lynncanyon.htm.*

Mount Seymour Provincial Park

**MT SEYMOUR PKWY, NORTH ON MT SEYMOUR RD,
NORTH VANCOUVER; 604/986-2261**
At Mount Seymour Provincial Park, downhill and cross-country skiing are popular in the winter. When the snow melts, it's a prime location for hiking. On a clear day, BC's Gulf Islands and Washington State's San Juan Islands can

---

THE GREEN PARTY: FARMERS MARKETS

Locavores support local growers who deliver fresh, seasonal food to the community through a variety of marketplaces, but visitors can also delight in the tastes and artisan treasures that abound year-round.

GRANVILLE ISLAND TRUCK FARMERS MARKET (1584 Johnston St)
Every Thursday, 9am–3pm from June to October, the Truck Market offers first-class, farm-fresh produce—and a chance to connect with the farmers who grew it. *www.granvilleisland.com.*

KITSILANO FARMERS MARKET (W 10th Ave and Larch St)
Every Sunday, 10am–2pm, June through October, farmers and local artisans gather under white tents. *www.eatlocal.org.*

LADNER VILLAGE MARKET (48th Ave in Ladner Village, Ladner)
This open-air market features more than 100 vendors on three blocks of the village centre. The vendors vary each of the second and fourth Sundays in June, July, and August, 10am–4pm, offering sweets, savouries, and exquisite craftsmanship. *www.bcfarmersmarket.org/directory/ladner.htm.*

RILEY PARK FARMERS MARKET (30th Ave and Ontario St)
Wednesday afternoons, 1–6:30pm, June through October, in the parking lot of the Nat Bailey Stadium, find fresh pickings for dinner. *www.eatlocal.org.*

SUMMER NIGHT MARKET (12631 Vulcan Wy, Richmond)
Authentic Asian street food and designer knockoffs can be found at this popular spot, where thousands of people mingle among the many booths. Open all summer from 7pm to midnight on Fridays and Saturdays, 7pm–11pm Sunday. *www. summernightmarket.com.*

---

be seen in the distance from several lookouts. Farther down the mountain, in the 5,600-hectare (14,000-acre) **SEYMOUR DEMONSTRATION FOREST** (604/432-6286), you will find some of Vancouver's most popular routes for in-line skating and world-famous technical mountain biking. *Map:G1–H1.*

Pacific Spirit Regional Park

BETWEEN NW MARINE AND SW MARINE DRS, CAMOSUN ST AND UBC, WEST SIDE
Pacific Spirit is one of the Greater Vancouver Regional District's newest parks, offering more than 800 hectares (2,000 acres) of wilderness. Adjacent to the University of British Columbia, some 55 kilometres (34 miles) of trails designated for walkers, cyclists, and horseback riders plunge through thick second-growth forest, edge deep ravines, and wind along cliff tops that overlook beaches with spectacular views of English Bay, Howe Sound, and

TROUT LAKE FARMERS MARKET (E 15th and Victoria Dr)

Food doesn't get fresher than at this festive farmers market open every Saturday from 9am–2pm mid-May until Thanksgiving. Entertainment, crafts, and coffee. *www.eatlocal.org.*

UBC FARM MARKET (6182 S Campus Rd)

A 2001 class project grew into a market garden that produces almost 250 varieties of organic vegetables, herbs, flowers, and small fruits. All market proceeds are used in its operation. Open Saturdays, June to October, 9am–1pm. *www.landfood.ubc.ca/ubcfarm.*

WEST END FARMERS MARKET (Nelson Park, 1100 block of Comox St)

Just behind St. Paul's Hospital, downtown locals and visitors find fresh produce and artisan crafts on Saturdays, 9am–2pm, from June to October. *www.eatlocal.org.*

WINTER FARMERS MARKET (Wise Hall, 1882 Adanac St at
Victoria Dr)

On the second and fourth Sunday of the month, November to April, 10am–2pm, vendors fill the Wise Hall and spill out onto Adanac Street with their root vegetables, apples, honey, eggs, artisan cheese, baked goods, pickles, and wild seafood. *www.eatlocal.org.*

YALETOWN FARMERS MARKET (Mainland and Davie sts)

From noon to 5pm, every Saturday from June to October, find vegetables, fruits, funky fashions, baked goods, and cool crafts. *www.yaletowninfo.com/events/farmersmarket.aspx*

—Arlene Kroeker

the north arm of the Fraser River. There's plenty of small wildlife here, and early in the morning you may even catch a glimpse of a coyote. Just above the Locarno Beach cliffs on the Spanish Trail is an open area covered with wild roses, fireweed, and salmonberry bushes. It's called the Plains of Abraham, and a dairy farm operated here at the turn of the 19th century (traces of the brick foundation remain on the south edge). A serene forest on the edge of the city, Pacific Spirit Regional Park is well named. *Map:B3.*

Vanier Park

**WEST OF BURRARD BRIDGE, NORTH OF CORNWALL AVE
AT CHESTNUT ST, WEST SIDE**

The ocean breezes that blow over this wide, grassy space on English Bay make it one of the best places in town to fly a kite. It's also home to the **H. R. MAC-MILLAN SPACE CENTRE** (see Museums in this chapter), considered one of the best planetariums in North America. The planetarium and the **VANCOUVER MUSEUM** (604/736-4431), which has displays chronicling the history of Vancouver and the Lower Mainland, offer frequently changing shows. Both are in the building with the conical roof, which was designed to resemble the shape of a traditional, Native cedar-bark hat, a fitting tribute to the coastal people who originally lived on this tip of land. Outside the building is the wishing pool guarded by George Norris's stainless steel fountain, *Crab*.

On the west side of the museum parking lot is the **VANCOUVER MARITIME MUSEUM** (see Museums in this chapter), which shelters the historic Royal Canadian Mounted Police vessel the *St. Roch*, as well as offering fascinating information about Vancouver's seagoing heritage. Nearby is Heritage Harbour, where a unique mix of ordinary and unusual vessels are moored. At the end of May, families flock to the red-and-white-striped tents of the **VANCOUVER INTERNATIONAL CHILDREN'S FESTIVAL** (604/708-5655), where performers from around the world entertain multitudes of children with an amazing variety of theatre, music, dance, circus, storytelling, and multimedia productions. During the summer, Shakespearean plays are presented by the **BARD ON THE BEACH** troupe (604/739-0559). *www.findfamilyfun. com/vanierpark.htm; map:P5*.

Organized Tours

The ideal way to explore Vancouver is on foot, but sometimes it's worth checking out more comfortable options. Choices range from a carriage ride through Stanley Park to a wild helicopter ride across the glaciers of the Coast Mountains. Some local companies offer tours of their operations, letting you in on some of the behind-the-scenes workings of the city. The **PORT OF VANCOUVER** (1300 Stewart St, Downtown; 604/665-9000; www.portvancouver.com), for example, during regular business hours has tours for groups of 10 or more, and self-guided tours for individuals. Both are free. And for something different from the usual city tour that's ideal for wine aficionados, **DOMAINE DE CHABERTON** (1064 216th St, Langley; 604/530-1736 or 888/332-9463; www.domainedechaberton. com; Feb–Nov Mon–Fri 2pm and 4pm, Dec–Jan Mon–Fri 3pm) offers tours of its winery, which is a 45-minute drive south of downtown. After a tour, indulge in the highly regarded, on-site **BACCHUS BISTRO** (604/530-9694 for reservations) is open for lunch and dinner.

AIR TOURS

Glacier Air

46001 GOVERNMENT RD, SQUAMISH; 604/898-9016 OR 800/265-0088
This company provides helicopter and airplane excursions and it specializes in icy explorations. Packages include flights around the Tantalus mountain range, followed by a quick landing and a walk on the Serratus Glacier. Tours feature views of volcanic rock formations, hanging glaciers, and high-elevation waterfalls. Prices range from $199 for the Tantalus Moutain

Rumbling Glacier tour to $259 for the Serratus Glacier Picnic. *Every day; www.glacierair.com.*

Harbour Air Seaplanes

COAL HARBOUR RD, 2 BLOCKS WEST OF CANADA PLACE, DOWNTOWN; 604/274-1277 OR 800/665-0212
You can cover a lot of ground in an airplane and avoid traffic problems to boot. Harbour Air offers eight tours around the Vancouver area and beyond. The Vancouver Panorama tour runs 30 minutes ($99 per person); an aerial tour of glaciers north of the city is 75 minutes ($269 per person); a 3-hour Orca whale–watching expedition in the Haro Strait is $299 per person. *Every day; www.harbour-air.com; map:T2.*

BOAT TOURS

Aquabus

SOUTH FOOT OF HORNBY ST, DOWNTOWN; 604/689-7781
This is Vancouver's cutest way to get around, rain or shine, since 1983. The fleet of rainbow-lettered 12-passenger ferries serves a network of stations along the False Creek shoreline, including Granville Island, Stamps Landing, Science World, Plaza of Nations, and Yaletown. The ferries leave every 5 to 15 minutes between 6:40am and 9:30pm daily. Fares $2.50–$3.50 adults, $1.25–$1.75 children and seniors; bikes acceptable for extra 50 cents; leashed dogs welcome. Sightseeing 25-minute minicruises of False Creek on the 22-seat ferry are offered year-round from the landing point outside the public market on Granville Island. Excursions $6 adults, $4 kids. *Every day; www.theaquabus.com; map:Q6.*

False Creek Ferries

SUNSET BEACH BEHIND VANCOUVER AQUATIC CENTRE, WEST END; 604/684-7781
For more than 25 years, these little blue ferries have carried passengers between Granville Island and the aquatic centre. Seasonally, they expand their service between the Vancouver Maritime Museum, Vancouver Museum, H. R. MacMillan Space Centre, Stamps Landing, and Science World. With 10 vessels, including four 20-passenger "super-mini-ferries," they continue to be a fun way to travel around False Creek. Fares $2.50–$5 adults; discounts for children under 12 and seniors over 65; day passes and books of 10 prepaid discount tickets available onboard. *Every day; www.granvilleislandferries. bc.ca; map:O5.*

Harbour Cruises

NORTH FOOT OF DENMAN ST, WEST END; 604/688-7246 OR 800/663-1500
Take to the water in another way—Harbour Ferries offers a 75-minute tour of the city three times daily aboard the MPV *Constitution*, a delightful paddle

wheeler that churns through Burrard Inlet. Tours $25 adults, $21 youth and seniors, $10 children 5–11. The company also offers brunch cruises between May and October. Boarding takes place at the north foot of Denman Street at 9am, and the yacht leaves at 9:30am, tracing a route around Stanley Park toward West Vancouver's Ambleside Park, then back to English Bay. It returns at about noon. Brunch is continental. Tours are $45 adults and seniors, $35 for children 2–12. *www.boatcruises.com; map:Q1.*

CYCLING TOURS

City by Cycle

VARIOUS LOCATIONS; 604/730-1032

A four-hour tour begins at Coal Harbour and goes around the Stanley Park seawall, through Chinatown and Yaletown, onto the Aquabus (see review in this section), and over to Granville Island and back downtown. The terrain is relatively flat and the ride easy enough for novice riders. The hosted tour provides historical information, as well as current events info and points of interest. Pickup and drop-off available at downtown hotels. Tours $69 adult, $49 youth; includes bike and helmet rental. *Every day; Apr1–Oct 15; www. citybycycle.com.*

FOOD TOURS

Edible British Columbia

GRANVILLE ISLAND PUBLIC MARKET, GRANVILLE ISLAND; 604/812-9660

From a gourmet kayaking adventure to a culinary exploration of Granville Island or a journey to the Okanagan for personalized wine tastings and food pairings, Edible BC takes foodie visitors to Vancouver's best food neighbourhoods. Tours include whiskey tastings, wine dinners at a farmhouse or vineyard, a cooking class with a top Vancouver chef, or a guided excursion through Chinatown, Commercial Drive, or the East Indian spice markets on Main Street. Choose from a one-day walking tour or a multiweek culinary adventure. *www.edible-britishcolumbia.com; map:Q6.*

HORSE-DRAWN TOURS

Stanley Park Horse-Drawn Tours

STANLEY PARK, WEST END; 604/681-5115

The easiest way to enjoy the serenity of Stanley Park is by horse-drawn carriage. Carriages leave the lower parking lot at regular intervals and meander through the 404-hectare (1,000-acre) park. A professional guide narrates each trip, which visits all main points of interest. Tours $24.99 adults, $23.58 students and seniors, $14.99 kids 3–12; $55.95 for families of two adults and two kids or students. *Every day Mar–Oct; www.stanleypark.com; map:Q1.*

MOTOR TOURS

West Coast City and Nature Sightseeing

STANLEY PARK, WEST END; 604/451-1600
Tour the city by minibus, stopping at museums and other attractions. The four-hour tour visits the totem poles in Stanley Park, Granville Island, and the Lookout at Downtown Harbour Centre Tower. As well, you experience Chinatown, the West End, Robson Street, and Gastown. Tours $61 adults, $41 children. *Every day at 10:30am; www.vancouversightseeing.com; map:Q1.*

TROLLEY TOURS

Vancouver Trolley Company

875 TERMINAL AVE, EAST SIDE; 604/801-5515 OR 888/451-5581
Take a jolly ride upon a trolley. It's an ideal way to familiarize yourself with the myriad charms of Vancouver. At any one of 23 stops, you can jump off and explore some of Vancouver's favourite attractions, catching the next trolley 30 minutes or even three hours later—and you pay only once. The bright red-and-gold vehicles—reproductions of the trolleys that were common on Vancouver's streets around 1890—trundle you unhurriedly through the city. A relaxing, fun way to explore. Fares $35 adults, $32 seniors and students, $18 kids 4–12. *Every day; www.vancouvertrolley.com; map:V6.*

WALKING TOURS

Architectural Institute of BC

100-440 CAMBIE ST, DOWNTOWN; 604/683-8588
Free walking tours of downtown Vancouver neighbourhoods are offered in the summer. *Tues–Sat 1pm; www.aibc.ca; map:U3.*

Walkabout Historic Vancouver

VARIOUS LOCATIONS; 604/720-0006
Guides dressed in period attire will lead you on this two-hour adventure through downtown Vancouver. The itinerary features buildings and streets of historical and architectural interest in Gastown, Chinatown, and Granville Island. Hear tales and the folklore of the city's early pioneers while walking by their local haunts. $25 per person. *Every day; 10am and 2pm; www.walkabouthistoricvancouver.com; map:S3.*

WILDERNESS TOURS

Rockwood Adventures

6578 ACORN RD, SECHELT; 888/236-6606
An opportunity for visitors to get out of the city without going very far at all, year-round Rockwood offers Rainforest Walks: tours led by knowledgeable guides through Stanley Park, Capilano River Canyon, Lighthouse Park, Lynn Canyon and Cypress Falls, and Bowen Island in nearby Howe Sound. Hiking

experience is not necessary, as Rockwood allows participants to savour the stunning temperate rain forest at a leisurely pace. The last old-growth forest in the area is home to towering cedars, Douglas firs, and hemlocks, some of which are 600 years old and taller than many of the downtown buildings seen in the distance from the rocky shoreline. Any of the Rainforest Walks are the ideal way to cap a visit to the Lower Mainland. The walks are $85 for adults, $78 for seniors and students 12–25, $60 for children 4–11, and free for children under 3. Urban Tours, Float Plane Excursions, or West Coast Food and BC Wine Explorations are also on the menu. Tours from a half day to five days. *www.rockwoodadventures.com.*

Vancouver All-Terrain Adventures

652-1755 ROBSON ST, DOWNTOWN; 778-371-7830

This outdoor outfit specializes in wilderness explorations for city slickers wishing to travel in style. Tours are made in luxury Suburban SUVs with leather interiors and custom fittings; these recreational limos whisk you up the Sea-to-Sky Highway: you can play golf at the par-72 Furry Creek Golf and Country Club, or travel beyond Whistler for trout fishing. Options to the SUV mode of travelling include helicopter, floatplane, snowmobile, and Zodiac raft. Tours from a few hours to overnight trips. Prices are not cheap, varying by package. *www.all-terrain.com; map:Q2.*

SHOPPING

SHOPPING

Shopping Areas and Malls

DOWNTOWN VANCOUVER

The downtown area of Vancouver (map:N1–V5) has experienced a lot of growth and seen many changes in the past few years. Many international luxury-goods companies have opened flagships recently, including Tiffany and Co., Cartier, Hermès, Gucci, Wolford, and London's Agent Provocateur. Granville Street's entertainment district has also seen a retail renaissance, with a Nike Women's flagship and quirkier entries such as Preloved up-cycled clothing.

ROBSON STREET is the meeting place of cultures and couture, with thousands of locals and tourists strolling amongst its many shops every day. Weekends are very crowded, but there's lots to see, since the street runs from Granville Mall in the east to Denman Street in the west (map:Q2–U4). You'll find art books, jewellery, and gifts by local artists at the Gallery Shop in the **VANCOUVER ART GALLERY** and a string of flagship stores for international fashion companies, local fashion chains, and a plethora of casual shoe stores (see also no. 15 in Top 20 Attractions in the Exploring chapter). For groceries, there's a **MARKETPLACE IGA** (909 Burrard St) and a new **WINE STORE** in the Sutton Place Hotel (845 Burrard St). On Robson and Burrard streets you'll find a **CHAPTERS** megabookstore, and entering Yaletown at Robson and Homer streets, you'll find the splendid **VANCOUVER PUBLIC LIBRARY** with its store, Bookmark, which has gifts for literary folk.

Once just a cluster of dilapidated warehouses across the tracks from False Creek's mills and factories, **YALETOWN** (map:S5–T6) is now a highly desirable piece of history-crammed real estate. Though the area was originally slow to attract a retail market (like most garment districts, don't expect much action before noon), it now houses a number of ultrahip clothing stores (Global Atomic Designs, Atomic Model, Vasanji) and a high concentration of high-end home furnishings (Chintz and Company, the Cross, and North America's first Marimekko store) amidst a thriving restaurant and bar scene at night (see also Neighbourhoods in the Exploring chapter). **URBAN FARE**, a gourmet grocery store and cafe, helps yuppie loft dwellers make better use of their stainless steel kitchen appliances.

PACIFIC CENTRE (700 W Georgia St to 777 Dunsmuir St, Downtown; 604/688-7236; map:T3) is downtown's biggest and busiest mall, connecting department stores Hudson's Bay Company and **SEARS** (701 Granville St, Downtown; 604/685-7112). The mall includes Vancouver's first H&M fashion store and other bargain-priced chains and links to the much smaller **VANCOUVER CENTRE** mall. With a 200-name list of outlets, Pacific Centre is, not surprisingly, crowded year-round. There is mall access on Granville, Howe, Dunsmuir, and Seymour streets.

Connected to Pacific Centre is **HUDSON'S BAY COMPANY** (674 Granville St, Downtown; 604/681-6211; www.hbc.com; map:T3), which has been serving Canadians in one capacity or another for more than 300 years. The Bay is the only store in town that carries authentic Hudson's Bay blankets, with their distinctive coloured stripes on a cream background, as well as jackets made from the same material. The official outfitter for the 2010 Olympics, the Bay has recently reissued classics as souvenir items in its Olympics shop, and it houses a new outlet for ultrachic espresso company Nespresso. Also downtown are **ARMY & NAVY** (27 W Hastings St; 604/682-6644; map: V3), offering work pants, plaid shirts, and steel-toed boots, as well as great bargains on fishing gear, shoes, and bed linens—in a less proletarian environment, courtesy of a swish new marketing campaign. At the other end of the fashion spectrum, Vancouver's newly built **HOLT RENFREW** designer department store (737 Dunsmuir St, Downtown; 604/681-3121; www.holtrenfrew. com; map:T3) houses boutiques for Prada, Tiffany, Louis Vuitton, Gucci, and a great denim department for men. Its concierge desk near the escalator can help you find your way around the city, make dinner plans, or even direct you to other shopping areas.

SINCLAIR CENTRE (757 W Hastings St, Downtown; 604/659-1009; map: T3) is not a large shopping centre, but it merits a look for two very good reasons. First, it is a striking example of the reclaimed-heritage school of architecture, where fine old buildings are put to alternative use without destroying their charm. Second, it contains the high-end designer department store Leone (and its downstairs less-expensive sister store L2), as well as Plaza Escada.

HISTORIC DISTRICTS

Downtown Vancouver also encompasses historic **GASTOWN** (map:T3–V3), once a quaint and cobbled tourist destination that has recently experienced a revival. The old warehouses and office buildings have been restored and refurbished, and summer and weekends find the streets bursting with both visitors and the local Web firms and design agencies that love the large, lofty offices (see also no. 4 in Top 20 Attractions in the Exploring chapter). Drop by **LE MAGASIN** (337 Water St), just east of Waterfront station, to see a particularly handsome refit of an antique structure housing So.Cial (see the Restaurants chapter), and visit its take-out butcher and deli, popular for hefty sandwiches at lunchtime. A wander down historic Blood Alley (also called Trounce Alley) off Carrall Street will take you to Salt Tasting Room (see the Restaurants chapter), housed, with the glorious new **INFORM INTERIORS** (97 Water St; 604/682-3868) furniture store, in a LEEDS-certified green building. Across the street, Inform opened a second location (50 Water St), where they feature the latest in timeless contemporary furniture, lighting, and accessories; for more than 30 years, they've had an eye on form, function, and value.

Cobbler John Fluevog (65 Water St; 604/875-9004) has a massive new studio and store to showcase his funky shoes in a museumlike environment. **KOOLHAUS** (1 Water St; 604/875-9004) offers household items from beds, sheets, and lighting to home office and garden accessories for the condo crowd. **OBAKKI**'s new flagship store (44 Water St; 604/669-9727) showcases primarily fashion collections by Canadian designers, but take note of Brent Comber's gorgeous benches, crafted from reclaimed wood. **PEKING LOUNGE** (83 E Pender St; 604/844-1559) pays tribute to Chinese history, art, and culture by offering a mix of Vancouver contemporary style with Asian aesthetics. You'll also find quirky little fashion gems such as **HUNT & GATHER** (225 Carrall St; 604/633-9559) and **NOUVELLE NOUVELLE** (209 Abbott St; 604/602-2234) and fashion-forward menswear at Roden Gray (231 Cambie St; 604/689-7302).

Although the Chinese-Canadian population of Vancouver is now concentrated in Richmond, the old **CHINATOWN** is still a vital and interesting area to visit and shop. You'll find it a few blocks east and west of Main Street on Pender and Keefer streets (map:U4–V4). The Chinese groceries and apothecaries have been there for generations, and many display remnants of Vancouver's days as a neon mecca. Many buildings in this area were built by Chinese artisans in a style not usually found outside China. Stores to check out include the original **MING WO** cookware shop (23 E Pender St), **CATHAY IMPORTERS** (104 E Pender St), and **CHINESE JADE AND CRAFTS** (44 E Pender St). Nearby you'll find local designer **ERIN TEMPLETON**'s studio-store (511 Carrall St, at Pender) of high-fashion handmade shoes and bags. Try **T&T SUPERMARKET** (179 Keefer Pl) for a vast variety of Asian foods, from mango sponge cake to live seafood, and the **TEN REN TEA & GINSENG CO.** (550 Main St) for teas and natural soothers. Various Chinese apothecaries have herbalists who can be consulted without an appointment—try **TUNG FONG HUNG MEDICINE CO.** (536 Main St). In summer, there's a night market around Main and Keefer on Friday, Saturday, and Sunday from 6:30pm to 11:30pm. The merchandise is mostly cheap Hong Kong imports and fake luxury goods, but the bustling atmosphere, neon lights, Asian languages and food, and steamy, wet streets are like a scene from the classic 1982 sci-fi film *Blade Runner*. (See also no. 5 in Top 20 Attractions in the Exploring chapter.)

NEIGHBOURHOODS

Under the Granville Street bridge on **GRANVILLE ISLAND** (Granville Island Information Centre, 604/666-5784; www.granvilleisland.bc.ca, www.granvilleisland.com; map:Q6–Q7), warehouses and factories have been transformed into the **PUBLIC MARKET** (1689 Johnston St; 604/666-5784; every day 9am–7pm), with more than 50 shops and stalls hawking fresh radishes, dolmades, freshly baked bread, fudge, salmon, pottery, art, crafts, and everything in between. Locals and tourists flock to this lively place for a tremendous selection of fresh food and gourmet items, musicians and street theatre. The **TRUCK FARMERS MARKET** (1585 Johnston St; Thurs late May–Oct) in the Arts Club Theatre parking lot is where BC farmers sell local veggies and flowers from the backs of their trucks. A walk off the beaten path through the corrugated-steel warehouses will furnish a glimpse of glass-blowers, metalworkers, weavers, and other artisans at work; many of them have storefronts. The **NET LOFT** (1666 Johnston St; every day 10am–7pm) building contains small shops and craft displays, with everything under one roof, from beads to Northwest Coast carvings. All around are aromatic bakeries, bookshops, glass galleries, and pottery studios. The **KIDS MARKET** (1496 Cartwright St; 604/689-8447; every day 10am–7pm) is chockablock with games, gifts, hobbies, art and craft supplies, toys, and video games. Canada's first sake winery, **ARTISAN SAKEMAKER STUDIO** (1339 Railspur Alley; 604/685-7253; Wed–Sun noon–6pm; www.artisansakemaker.com), can be found between a goldsmith and a potter and offers samples of the three handcrafted sakes.

SOUTH GRANVILLE, from Granville Bridge toward 16th Avenue (map: D3), borders on the prestigious Shaughnessy neighbourhood and has traditionally catered to the carriage trade. It is sometimes referred to as Gallery Row, but while the art galleries represent internationally renowned painters and photographers, equally impressive is a new crop of Occidental antique stores—to supplement the existing British ones—that import treasures from Japan, Indonesia, and India. Top **EATERIES** (Chow, Vij's, Vij's Rangoli, and West; see the Restaurants chapter), the newly refurbished Stanley Theatre, the elegant **MEINHARDT FINE FOODS** (3002 Granville St; 604/732-4405), the new **18 KARAT** (3039 Granville St; 604/742-1880) Asian design emporium, and cookware from a recently opened **WILLIAMS SONOMA** (2903 Granville St; 778/330-2581) can be found here today. Top international designer clothing at **BACCI'S** (2788 Granville St; 604/733-4933) and **MISCH** (2960 Granville St; 604/731-1017) makes for excellent window shopping.

A visit to the malls—Aberdeen Centre (4151 Hazelbridge Wy; 604/273-1234), Yaohan Centre (3700 No 3 Rd; 604/231-0601), President Plaza (3320-8181 Cambie Rd; 604/270-8677), Parker Place (4380 No 3 Rd; 604/273-0276), and Fairchild Square (4400 Hazelbridge Wy; 604/273-1234)—that make up Richmond's **ASIA WEST** district (map:D5) is an experience unique in North America (see no. 16 in Top 20 Attractions in the Exploring chapter). The malls sprang up along a stretch of No. 3 Road between Capstan and Alderbridge ways in the mid-1990s to service a newly settled community of mostly Hong Kong expatriates. The malls house Chinese herbalists, huge all-Asian supermarkets, inexpensive Japanese housewares, toys and candy, designer luggage, and lots of fashion-forward clothes and shoes for petite women. Don't let the marked prices dissuade you—a simple inquiry will often bring them down substantially. Do be persuaded to stay for lunch—the food courts offer a tempting variety of Asian street foods at bargain prices. Yoahan Centre is the most interesting, with its Japanese **DAISO** store where everything is $2 and North America's first **BEARD PAPA**, the cream puff chain that took Japan by storm.

For information on **NORTH VANCOUVER**'s top shopping attraction, **LONSDALE QUAY MARKET** (123 Carrie Cates Ct, North Vancouver; 604/985-6261; www.lonsdalequay.com; map:E1), see no. 10 in Top 20 Attractions in the Exploring chapter.

Apart from the massive Park Royal Shopping Centre, the shops along Marine Drive in **WEST VANCOUVER** (map:C1–D1) reflect the British heritage of the area's original European settlers. Some stores try a little hard to be quaint, but in general they carry a good stock of quality merchandise. West Vancouver is one of the more prestigious neighbourhoods in the Lower Mainland, so expect prices that reflect this.

PARK ROYAL SHOPPING CENTRE (2002 Park Royal S, West Vancouver; 604/925-9576; www.shopparkroyal.com; map:C1–D1) has the distinction of being Canada's first shopping mall, as well as the North Shore's largest and most prestigious shopping centre. It straddles Marine Drive in West Vancouver, just across Lions Gate Bridge. (Out-of-town visitors, note: It's too far to walk, so take the bus or drive.) Parking is free and plentiful, and there's an open-air food market in summer. Be thankful for the numerous spots to buy comfort shoes here (Rockport, Ingledew's, Dudek); you may be covering acres of shops. Its new open-air mall called the **VILLAGE AT PARK ROYAL** has been extremely successful even during rainy weather (an honour-system umbrella programme operates in winter) and keeps expanding. Yogawear, eco-chic housewares, beauty boutiques, Whole Foods, and crowded cafes and restaurants make it a unique (if highly packaged) shopping experience.

Shops from A to Z

ANTIQUES

French Country Antiques

125 E 4TH AVE, EAST SIDE; 604/730-7124
Fancy a candelabra from an ancient Gallic church? Or salt-worn oyster baskets from Brittany? Perhaps your taste runs more to grape baskets from Champagne, a rustic *bibliothèque*, or a bust from the last dukedom in France. Whatever your whimsy, you are likely to find it (or something even better) at this warehouse off Main Street. *By appointment only; www. frenchcountryantiques.org; map:V7.*

R. H. V. Tee & Son (England)

7963 GRANVILLE ST, WEST SIDE; 604/263-2791
The provenance of this stately shop goes back almost as far as some of the antiques. The current Mr. Tee is the fourth generation of his family in the business, and he personally selects the pieces for the shop on his many trips to England. *Tues–Sat; www.teeantiques.com; map:D4.*

Uno Langmann Ltd

2117 GRANVILLE ST, WEST SIDE; 604/736-8825
This long-established, internationally recognized gallery specializes in European and North American paintings from the 18th, 19th, and early 20th centuries. Langmann also features furniture, porcelain, and silver. *Tues–Sat; www.langmann.com; map:P7.*

APPAREL

Aritzia

1110 ROBSON ST, DOWNTOWN (AND BRANCHES); 604/684-3251
Six locations feature high-end, high-tech fashions for women. Hot, in, definite fashion statements for the very brave or the very young. Brands change seasonally, but look for the exclusive Talula and Wilfred labels. Next door, the new Aritzia Base caters to a slightly more sophisticated customer, with Anna Sui and Ella Moss. *Every day; www.aritzia.com; map:C4.*

Bacci's

2788 GRANVILLE ST, WEST SIDE; 604/733-4933
Avant-garde designers who appeal to the city's fashion-conscious are a specialty—UK handbag designer Anya Hindmarch, Jean-Paul Gaultier, Martin Margiela, Dries Van Noten, and Chloé are just a few. The adjoining Bacci's at Home boutique holds exquisite gift items, such as Japanese ceramics, Designers Guild linens, and Kiehl's New York skin care line. *Mon–Sat; www.baccis.ca; map:D3.*

bebe

1000 ROBSON ST, DOWNTOWN; 604/681-1819 OR 877/232-3777
Founded in San Francisco in 1976, bebe is a hit with Japanese tourists; the look is body-conscious with an emphasis on trendy separates. This is the highly successful women's clothing company's first Canadian store. *Every day; www.bebe.com; map:R3.*

Betsey Johnson

1033 ALBERNI ST, DOWNTOWN; 604/488-0314
The designer is known for her irreverent New York style, ruffly dresses, and signature hot pink shopping bags. Her clothing is flirty and very feminine. *Every day; www.betseyjohnson.com; map:S4.*

The Block

350 W CORDOVA ST, DOWNTOWN, 604/685-8885
A Vancouver institution, the Block has supported indie designers since they were making floral baby-doll dresses back in the early '90s. Loeffler Randal, Ella Moss, and Surface to Air are some of the names they get behind now. Men, there's a department for you, too. *Every day, www.theblock.ca; map:U3.*

Boboli

2776 GRANVILLE ST, WEST SIDE; 604/736-3458
The stone archway gracing the entrance to this high-end designer store is fabled to have come from a ruined Mexican cathedral. Inside, exclusive fashions and footwear await discriminating shoppers. The adventurous gentleman will find many imports, including Issey Miyake, Pal Zileri, and Dai Fujiwara. Ladies can rub fashionably clad elbows with such names as

NEIGHBOURHOOD WATCH: SOUTH MAIN

Known as SoMa to the local hipsters, Main Street from Eighth Avenue to 24th Avenue houses the best selection of local designers and one-off boutiques in the city (plus fun bars such as the Cascade Room for liquid refreshment).

EUGENE CHOO (3683 Main St; 604/873-8874)

Eugene Choo features mod clothing selected by rakish owner Kildare, as well as women's carved wood jewellery and Erin Templeton leather purses; in summer, there's a plant market in the back alley. *Every day; www.eugenechoo.com; map:D3.*

HUM (3623 Main St; 604/708-5486)

One of the newer kids on the block, Hum is completely dedicated to Vancouver designers: you'll find pale metallic leathers, chic takes on the fanny pack, and the must-have clutch purse by local Sienna Ray. *Every day; www.humclothing.com; map:D3.*

JONATHAN + OLIVIA (2570 Main St; 604/637-6224)

On the "Olivia" side: edgy jeans by Cheap Monday, knits by Paris's Vanessa Bruno, Isabella Fiore, and Chloë Sevigny's line for Opening Ceremony. On the "Jonathan" side: Rag & Bone trousers, a black Filippa K wool peacoat. *Every day; www.jonathanandolivia.com; map:D3.*

Blumarine, Missoni, and Alberta Ferretti; there are also shoes by Sergio Rossi and accessories by Kenzo. *Mon–Sat; map:D3.*

Boys' Co.

1044 ROBSON ST, DOWNTOWN (AND BRANCHES); 604/684-5656

Murray Goldman, the venerable king of men's ready-to-wear in Vancouver, spawned this upmarket, youth-oriented store, run by son David. Denim, clubwear, and suits imported from Germany, England, and Italy, as well as a top-quality house sportswear label. *Every day; www.boysco.com; map:S4.*

Brooklyn

418 DAVIE ST, DOWNTOWN; 604/683-2929

A massive denim section, great oversized watches, leather satchels and duffel bags, casual-yet-cool brands like Morphine Generation for guys who like fashion and are sick of the ubiquitous Lacoste, Fred Perry, and Penguin. Shop here, and people will swear you're in some band from L.A. *Every day; www. brooklynclothing.com; map:S5.*

LARK (2315 Main St; 604/879-5275)

A big, gallery-like space with well-selected items: men's handmade shoes from Italy, Jorg & Olif Dutch city bikes, Japanese sunglasses, women's clothing and accessories from local lines and Los Angeles. *Every day; www.lark8thave.com; map:D3.*

MAYA (2442 Main St; 604/708-3911)

Textile treasures from Rajasthan, including handmade and block-printed table-cloths in sun-bleached florals and French liberty prints, are a steal starting at just $40. *Every day; map:D3.*

REGIONAL ASSEMBLY OF TEXT (3934 Main St; 604/877-2247)

A one-stop shop for gifts under $20: modern glassware etched with letters, old-fashioned stationery sets, the most precious selection of greeting cards, handmade wrapping paper, chalkboards. *Every day; www.assemblyoftext.com; map:D3.*

SCOUT (152 E 8th Ave; 604/879-7903)

Cool, original dresses in Vancouver for less than $150—as long as you don't mind that Lindsay Lohan and Cameron Diaz are wearing them too. This little store is many a fashion stylist's little secret. *Every day; map:D3.*

—Sarah Bancroft

DKNY

2625 GRANVILLE ST, WEST SIDE; 604/733-2000

The ever-expanding Donna Karan empire's Vancouver address features men's and women's DKNY, plus the Pure, Jeans, and Active collections; shoes; and accessories. DKNY lingerie and children's shoes (infant to 13 years) are also available. *Every day; www.dkny.com; map:D3.*

El Kartel

121-A, 1025 ROBSON ST, DOWNTOWN; 604/683-2171

Owned by Mexican hipsters, this high-energy shop sells funky sneakers, hats, and edgy Mexican sportswear, and the Artful Dodger, from London. *Every day, www.elkartel.com, map:S4.*

Enda B

4346 W 10TH AVE, WEST SIDE; 604/228-1214

A warning to casual browsers: this store combines a large selection of designer fashions for men and women with the savviest wardrobe consultants in town. Don't enter unless you're fully prepared to walk out with something you love. You'll also find accessories and jewellery, a good shoe section, and EB Kids. *Every day; www.enda-b.com; map:B3.*

Ermenegildo Zegna

PACIFIC CENTRE (TOP FLOOR), DOWNTOWN; 604/681-7988
The first Canadian store for this Italian textiles-and-clothing manufacturer houses upscale menswear collections and has retained its traditional cachet by resisting putting its name on colognes or underwear. Cashmere cloth is a specialty. *Every day; www.zegna.com; map:T3.*

Hill's of Kerrisdale

2125 W 41ST AVE, WEST SIDE; 604/266-9177
A hallowed institution in the area since 1919, this mini–department store stocks men's, women's, and children's designer clothing, plus private-school uniforms. Quality labels include Kenneth Cole, Diesel, and Teenflo; shoes include Nine West. Local jewellery bedecks a vintage counter display. *Every day; www.hillsofkerrisdale.com; map:C4.*

Holt Renfrew

737 DUNSMUIR ST, DOWNTOWN; 604/681-3121
The new three-level flagship for Canada's designer-department store has become more crowd friendly with its Designer Contemporary department for ladies upstairs, a great hair salon and spa, shu uemura's first Canadian cosmetics and eyelash bar, and, in fall 2008, a rooftop restaurant. The central atrium lets you spy the perfect YSL handbag from one floor up, and if you're here in August or January, the infamous "Now or Never" sales offer up to 80 percent off designer items. *Every day; www.holtrenfrew.com; map:T3.*

Jacob

PACIFIC CENTRE, DOWNTOWN (AND BRANCHES); 604/683-4110
What began 30 years ago as a menswear shop in a small Quebec town has grown to a small empire of locations across Canada. This massive new store carries the Jacob line for women as well as their popular lingerie. *Every day; www.jacob.ca; map:T3.*

Komakino

109 W CORDOVA ST, DOWNTOWN; 604/618-1344
The store's brands (Raf Simmons, Rick Owens) are artfully graffitied on the front windows, but check the Web site—this guerrilla store is always on the move. Slim, tailored, black, edgy Japanese men's fashions. *Every day; www. komakino.ca; map:U3.*

Leone

SINCLAIR CENTRE, DOWNTOWN; 604/683-1133
Definitely worth a visit—and not just for the sheer architectural splendour of it all. Set like a jewel in the exquisite Sinclair Centre, this store showcases international men's and women's designers in separate galleries—Versace, Miu Miu, Prada, Dolce & Gabbana, Hugo Boss, Jil Sander, and many more. Shoes and accessories round out the main floor, while Versace housewares

are on the top floor. The basement houses L2, a contemporary designer and jeans department, and their own busy little Italian cafe. *Every day; www. leone.ca; map:T3.*

Margareta Signature Collection
1512 MARINE DR, WEST VANCOUVER; 604/926-9066
Design classics, designed and manufactured for the store's own label. Styles range from the elegant to the casual. Custom-made and custom-fitted fashions are a specialty. *Every day; www.margaretadesign.com; map:D1.*

Mark James
2941 W BROADWAY, WEST SIDE; 604/734-2381
His name is synonymous with men's fashion-forward dressing. Inside, find suits from Armani, Ermenegildo Zegna, Dolce & Gabbana, and Hugo Boss alongside sportswear from Diesel. *Every day; www.markjamesclothing.com; map:C3.*

Misch
2960 GRANVILLE ST, SOUTH GRANVILLE; 604/731-1017
The girl who likes to find the next big designer just before Anna Wintour does will love the well-culled choices here from L.A., New York, and Paris: Vanessa Bruno, Sonya Rykiel, Phillip Lim, and their ilk. *Every day; www. misch.ca; map:D3.*

Obakki
44 WATER ST, GASTOWN; 604/669-9727
A gallery-like store from this local label owned by the wife of one of the Nickelback rockers. Architectural, natural fibers and pleasing neutral tones abound. Do check out the massive cash desk installation by woodworker Brent Comer. *Every day; www.obakki.com; map:U3.*

Salvatore Ferragamo
918 ROBSON ST, DOWNTOWN; 604/669-4495
Extraordinary fashions in an exclusive international boutique. This was once the only Canadian operation of this company, which can be found in major cities around the world. *Every day; www.ferragamo.com; map:S3.*

Wear Else?
2360 W 4TH AVE, WEST SIDE (AND BRANCHES); 604/732-3521
The dependable fashion consultants here can outfit you with an entire wardrobe—or the classic pieces that will be its foundation. Both international and Canadian designers are represented, and there is a large selection of shoes and accessories. *Every day; www.wearelse.com; map:N7.*

Zonda Nellis

2203 GRANVILLE ST, WEST SIDE; 604/736-5668

Unique loomed fabrics are used to create simple yet distinctive fashions. Nellis is a local designer with an international clientele. *Mon–Sat; www.zondanellis. com; map:Q7.*

BAKERIES

Cupcakes

1116 DENMAN ST, WEST END (AND BRANCHES); 604/974-1300

The window displays are enough to get you off your low-carb diet, and the cupcakes are fun, but the lopsided Dr. Seuss cakes are the hit of the modern baby showers. Look for specialty Canuck cakes during the hockey playoffs and pride cupcakes during the gay pride parade. *Every day; www.cupcakesonline. com; map:Q2.*

La Baguette et L'Echalote

1680 JOHNSTON ST, GRANVILLE ISLAND; 604/684-1351

Owners Mario Armitano and Louise Turgeon create classic French baked goods, such as their *pain de campagne*, a country-style baguette; decadent chocolate truffles; and seasonal fruit flans. For those on special diets, they bake organic loaves with no yeast, no sugar, and no salt. Their takeaway sandwiches are also good for picnics. *Every day; www.labaguette.ca; map:Q6.*

Le Patisserie Lebeau

1728 W 2ND AVE, WEST SIDE; 604/731-3528

For fine Belgian waffles, jewel-like pastries, excellent coffee, and standards such as croissants and *pain au chocolat*, residents of Kitsilano and beyond seek out this patisserie-for-purists on the route to Granville Island. Their famous chicken baguette sandwiches sell out every day, so get there early. *Wed–Sun; map:P7.*

Mix the Bakery

4430 W 10TH AVE, WEST SIDE; 604/221-4145

The Point Grey hot spot supplies its authentic French baguettes to the city's top restaurants, including Elixir at the Opus Hotel. Try the classic Jamon Jamon sandwich on a rustic baguette or the Chimayo Grilled Chicken on sourdough. There are usually lineups for crispy breakfast scones such as triple ginger and citrus-cranberry. *Every day; www.mixthetbakery.com; map:B3.*

The Savary Island Pie Company

1533 MARINE DR, WEST VANCOUVER; 604/926-4021

More than a dozen varieties of retro-style fruit and cream pies to choose from, or drop off your fresh fruit and they'll bake you a pie. Savary makes the best soda bread outside of Ireland, as well as delicious paninis and salads. Their high standards of homey meals and a beer and wine license make this one of the coolest hangouts on the North Shore. *Every day; map:D1.*

Siegel's Bagels

1883 CORNWALL AVE, WEST SIDE (AND BRANCHES); 604/737-8151

For bagel bingers who love a chewy Montreal-style bagel with a handmade look. Siegel's bagels come in pumpernickel, cinnamon-raisin, caraway, multigrain, onion, sesame, orange poppyseed, and more varieties. Also find knishes stuffed with potato or spinach, vegetable rolls, and a selection of hearty breads, including classic challah. Try the Montreal smoked meat or lox and cream cheese. Eat in or take out 24 hours at this location. *Every day; www. siegelsbagels.com; map:O6.*

Terra Breads

2380 W 4TH AVE, WEST SIDE (AND BRANCHES); 604/736-1838

Terra Breads has a clientele avid for its crusty hearth-baked breads, which are baked fresh every morning in a stone-deck oven and naturally leavened by a slow process using natural yeast starters. Terra's French baguettes are made in the authentic French tradition—the bakers use only unbleached flour without additives, fillers, or preservatives. Among the exceptional breads are white or *levain* rounds, fabulous black olive or rosemary-and-olive oil loaves, Italian cheese bread, raisin rye, fig with anise, a very fine focaccia, and grape and pine nut loaves. Their cafe (53 W 5th Ave) is busy at lunch with healthy salads, real lemonade, and good coffee. Try the lamb and pear panini. *Every day; www.terrabreads.com; map:Q6.*

BOOKS, MAGAZINES, AND MAPS

Albion Books

523 RICHARDS ST, DOWNTOWN; 604/662-3113

A very personal place for people who love old books and jazz and like to talk about them with kindred souls. The big difference between this used bookstore and others is its selection of sheet music, jazz on vinyl, and CDs, which Albion employees will cheerfully play for you. *Every day; map:T3.*

Aviation World

105-6080 RUSS BAKER WY, RICHMOND; 604/718-7400

Appropriately located at the airport's south terminal, this store has really taken off. It has increased its sections on the technical aspects of aviation, which should thrill engineers, designers, and mechanics. Also, shelf loads of handbooks, regulation books, and maintenance manuals. *Mon–Sat; map:D7.*

Banyen Books & Sound

3508 W 4TH AVE, WEST SIDE; 604/732-7912 OR 800/663-8442

Along with its extensive stock of New Age and self-help books, Banyen also has a great selection of vegetarian cookbooks, religious texts, and tarot cards, plus New Age and world music recordings and spoken-text cassette tapes. *Every day; www.banyen.com; map:Q6.*

Barbara-Jo's Books to Cooks

1740 W 2ND AVE, WEST SIDE; 604/688-6755
NET LOFT, GRANVILLE ISLAND; 604/684-6788
Find an excellent selection of culinary titles by local and celebrity chefs. Bonus: Wine tastings and cooking demonstrations in the test kitchen often accompany book signings. A second location is in Granville Island's Net Loft. *Every day; www.bookstocooks.com; map:P7.*

Blackberry Books

UNIT 3–1666 JOHNSTON ST, NET LOFT, GRANVILLE ISLAND; 604/685-6188
A cute little Granville Island location provides a perfect backdrop for an extensive selection of popular fiction and nonfiction. There are satisfying classic and craft sections as well at this family bookstore. *Every day; www. bbooks.ca; map:P7.*

Book Warehouse

632 W BROADWAY, WEST SIDE (AND BRANCHES); 604/872-5711
Known for minimal merchandising (hence lower prices); expect to pay at least 20 percent less than at other stores for best-selling hardcovers and paperbacks. *Every day; www.bookwarehouse.ca; map:D2.*

Chapters

788 ROBSON ST, DOWNTOWN (AND BRANCHES); 604/682-4066
This overexpanded chain of superstores purchased by Indigo in 2001 spelled the demise of many small, neighbourhood magazine stores and bookshops, but if you like your best sellers attractively merchandised, this is where to find them. Each big, rather bland store also contains a Starbucks coffee outlet. *Every day; www.chapters.indigo.ca; map:R3.*

The Comicshop

2089 W 4TH AVE, WEST SIDE; 604/738-8122
For 25 years this unique little spot has served Vancouver's comic connoisseurs with new issues and collector's items. *Every day; www.thecomicshop. ca; map:O7.*

Duthie Books

2239 W 4TH AVE, WEST SIDE; 604/732-5344
The true bibliophile must make a pilgrimage to Duthie's last existing location. Since 1957, Duthie Books has been serving the literati and hoi polloi alike with its comprehensive selection of the popular and the obscure; in 1999 it was forced to close all but this location due to increased competition in the marketplace. Helpful, knowledgeable staff. *Every day; www.duthiebooks. com; map:S4.*

International Travel Maps and Books

530 W BROADWAY, WEST SIDE; 604/879-3621

Wherever you're going, this store can help you find your way. It has one of the largest map and guidebook selections in Canada. *Every day; www.itmb. com; map:T4.*

Kidsbooks

3083 W BROADWAY, WEST SIDE (AND BRANCHES); 604/738-5335

To say this store is dedicated to children's literature is to make a terrible understatement. There are books and book talks, book readings and book launchings. And did we mention the books? The staff are especially helpful in choosing gifts for out-of-town children, and gift wrapping is free. *Every day; www.kidsbooks.ca; map:C3.*

MacLeod's Books

455 W PENDER ST, DOWNTOWN; 604/681-7654

Walking into MacLeod's is like walking into a Dickens novel: layers and mazes of books are piled to the ceiling. Each area of antiquarian books and collectibles is meticulously classified, and the store is heavily into history: British Columbian, Asian, military, marine, Native (Plains, Northeast, etc.). Ninety percent of the stock is used and/or out of print. *Every day; map:T4.*

Mayfair News

1535 W BROADWAY, WEST SIDE; 604/738-8951

Can't find your hometown newspaper? Need a copy of an obscure magazine? Try the Mayfair News collection of more than 5,000 periodicals. *Every day; map:S3.*

32 Books

3185 EDGEMONT BLVD, NORTH VANCOUVER; 604/980-9032

How this little bookstore, a relative newcomer, manages to nab readings by some of the world's hottest authors is testament to the dedication of its feisty owner. Do check the events calendar online. *Mon–Sat; www.32books.com; map:E1.*

The Travel Bug

3065 W BROADWAY, WEST SIDE; 604/737-1122

Off to the Serengeti? The Outback? The Bronx? Owner Dwight Elliot can find you just the right travel guide and foreign-language phrase book from his stock of more than 6,000 titles. Then he'll equip you with the essential travel accessories, from money belts (security holster, sock safe) to tele-plug-ins for computers to travellers' sleep sacks (an essential item for the hosteller). Elliot can even provide the carry-on luggage in which to stow it all. *Every day; www. travelbugbooks.ca; map:C2.*

UBC Bookstore

6200 UNIVERSITY BLVD, WEST SIDE; 604/822-2665

For an independent bookstore, the one at UBC is huge—one of the biggest in western Canada, though most of the floor space is devoted to university logowear and student supplies rather than books. If you can muster the strength, peruse the more than 100,000 titles, from anatomy to zoology. Veer off into another section and you'll find BC pottery, varsity jackets, art supplies, cameras, fax machines, and a major computer department. Don't let the fact that it sounds like a mall put you off. The staff is dedicated to books, and you can sit and read in the comfy chairs. *Mon–Sat; www.bookstore.ubc. ca; map:B2.*

Wanderlust

1929 W 4TH AVE, WEST SIDE; 604/739-2182

When it's time for those boot heels to go wandering, Tony McCurdy and his helpful staff can make sure you're prepared. They carry thousands of books about foreign lands, with entire bookcases devoted to some countries. Travel accessories include water purifiers, mosquito nets, safety whistles, convertible packs, and language tapes. *Every day; www.wanderlust.com; map:O7.*

CANDY AND CHOCOLATE

Candy Aisle

2083 W 4TH AVE, WEST SIDE (AND BRANCHES); 604/739-3330

This sweetshop carries British, Australian, American, and Canadian candies (remember Nerds?) and lures customers in with sidewalk sandwich boards that read, "Don't just stand there, buy candy." Subtle. *Every day; www.candyaisle. com; map:O7.*

Chocolate Arts

2037 W 4TH AVE, WEST SIDE; 604/739-0475

Greg Hook collaborated with Native artist Robert Davidson to open this sweetshop and has created fabulous-tasting chocolates that look like fine art. Chocolate medallions with Haida designs are the perfect gift to impress out-of-towners, and the liqueur-laced truffles are incredible. *Every day; www. chocolatearts.com; map:N7.*

Daniel le Chocolat Belge

1105 ROBSON ST, DOWNTOWN (AND BRANCHES); 604/688-9624

Back in 1987, Daniel supplied his secret-formula chocolates to heads of state who were attending Vancouver's Commonwealth Conference, testimony to his highly developed sense of presentation, packaging, and decoration—not to mention his exquisite array of hazelnut paste, creamy caramel, delicious ganache creams, and liqueur truffles, sleekly enrobed in pure, rich chocolate. *Every day; www.danielchocolates.com; map:S6.*

Mink

863 W HASTINGS ST, DOWNTOWN; 604/633-2451

Retro bonbons are the order of the day at Mink Chocolates at the base of the Terminal City building. Try the burnt-caramel chocolate bars that taste like crème brûlée or the superpopular PB & J bars. In the cafe, order chocolate fondues with a baby hibachi for roasting marshmallows. *Every day; www. minkchocolates.com; map:T3.*

Purdy's

PACIFIC CENTRE, DOWNTOWN (AND BRANCHES); 604/681-7814

A Vancouver institution, and the place to fill up a stocking or Easter basket. The factory store (2777 Kingsway St) has prepackaged seconds in big bags on weekdays. *Every day; www.purdys.com; map:T4.*

Thomas Haas Patisserie and Café

128-998 HARBOURSIDE DR, NORTH VANCOUVER; 604/924-1847

Like something out of Charlie's wildest fantasy, the ceiling of this always bustling cafe is designed like an unfolded chocolate box, and the candy-drop glass lamps are imported from Germany. In the salon, sample cakes and pastries, espressos and paninis, while watching the chocolates being made (using real fruits, spices, liqueurs, Tahitian vanilla, and walnuts from Grenoble) in the demonstration kitchen. Don't miss the lemon-drop powder room. (See review in Restaurants chapter.) *Tues–Sun; www.thomashaas.com; map:E1.*

CHILDREN'S CLOTHING

Dandelion Kids

1206 COMMERCIAL DR, EAST VANCOUVER, 604/676-1862

An emphasis on organic clothes and fair-trade toys makes this a destination for eco-chic parents. Also find blond-wood toddler kitchens from France and a small consignment section. *Every day; www.dandelionkids.ca; map:Z6.*

Isola Bella

5692 YEW ST, WEST SIDE; 604/266-8808

Exclusive designer togs for tots—much of the stock is imported from France and Italy—of European quality. You'll also find footwear for fashionable little feet and beautiful gift items for children. From newborn to size 16. *Mon–Sat; www.isolabella.ca; map:C4.*

Lilikiks

2305 W 41ST AVE, WESTSIDE; 604/263-5459

Aimed at girls ages 7 to 14, this local label makes top-quality fashions for today's high-achieving, highly active, highly discerning teens and preteens. *Every day; www.lilikiks.com; map:C4.*

Modern Kid

45 WATER ST, GASTOWN; 604/662-3181
Modernist blond-wood dollhouses, Like-a-Bike wood scooters, and brightly coloured toys and clothes for tiny design-o-philes. Prices are high, but so is the quality. Great gift wrapping and online store, too. *Every day; www.modernkid. com; map:U3.*

CONSIGNMENT

Front and Co.

3772 MAIN ST, EAST VANCOUVER; 604/879-8431
Now comprised of three storefronts taking up the better part of the block, this group of stores offers new housewares, men's and women's consignment (think fashion-forward and funky), new accessories, and high-end vintage dresses. The window displays, which range from bacchanalian banquet scenes to elaborate masquerade balls, are the handiwork of the female artist who runs the shops. *Every day; map:D2.*

Happy Three

3629 W 4TH AVE, WEST SIDE (AND BRANCHES); 604/730-9638
Not only can you find great designer bargains here (Chanel, Jean-Paul Gaultier, Prada, Gucci), but there are plenty of new samples of designer knockoff accessories from Hong Kong factories. Little sweater sets and sling bags are a bargain. Sizes are mostly on the small side. *Every day; map:C3.*

Kisa's of Kerrisdale

2352 W 41ST AVE, WEST SIDE; 604/266-2885
Down the stairs through the ivy-bedecked entrance, you'll find a very nice selection of designer consignment fashion, jewellery, shoes, handbags, and accessories. Owner Barbara McDonald has an eye for the unique and offers new or gently worn clothing with well-known labels, many from Europe. Merchandise is also offered on eBay. *Mon–Sat; map:C4.*

MacGillycuddy's for Little People

4881 MACKENZIE ST, WEST SIDE; 604/263-5313
A consignment store for children's wear, selling clothing, footwear, and some hand-knit pieces, as well as furniture. *Mon–Sat; map:C4.*

Second Suit

2036 W 4TH AVE, WEST SIDE; 604/732-0338
Although the quality of the consignment goods here is good and styles are no more than one season old, the real draw is the samples for men and women for the upcoming season. As a bonus, clothes are organized by colour rather than style so you can steer completely clear of canary yellow if you wish. Also find designer sunglasses and jewellery. *Every day; www.secondsuit.com; map:O7.*

Turnabout Collections Ltd.

3060 W BROADWAY, WEST SIDE (AND BRANCHES); 604/731-7762
High-quality consignment, carrying some designers. The West Broadway store is casual, fun, and funky for men and women (jeans, sportswear, bathing suits). The South Granville store carries prestige labels for women, such as Donna Karan, Issey Miyake, and Armani, with an emphasis on evening wear. *Every day; www.turnaboutclothing.com; map:D3.*

COOKWARE

Basic Stock Cookware

2294 W 4TH AVE, WEST SIDE (AND BRANCHES); 604/736-1412
Rack after rack of shining pots and pans of every size and description, and every gadget you could ever want to clutter your kitchen drawers. A selection of coffee beans, and everything you need to use them, is also offered. *Every day; www.basicstock.ca; map:N7.*

Cookworks

1548 W BROADWAY, WEST SIDE (AND BRANCHES); 604/731-1148
Find high-end kitchen tools, such as retro-style chrome spa juicers and ice crushers from New York, professional cookware lines Henckel and Calphalon, a whole wall of brightly coloured silicone cooking tools, as well as Mario Batali's fantastic grill pans and pasta pots. *Every day; www.cookworks.ca; map:C3.*

Ming Wo

23 E PENDER ST, CHINATOWN (AND BRANCHES); 604/683-7268
Since 1917, Ming Wo has maintained the highest standards of quality in the cookware and kitchenware it carries. A large stock of hard-to-find items and a reputation for value have kept Vancouverites (especially university students) loyal to the store. You'll find Ming Wo in suburban shopping centres and several Vancouver locations; the shop in Chinatown is the original. *Every day; www.mingwo.com; map:U4.*

Williams-Sonoma

2903 GRANVILLE ST, WEST SIDE; 778/330-2581
You've got to wonder if the crowds piling into Vancouver's first outlet for this upscale American chain are there for the high-end cookware, packaged-food court, and French stoves, or the free coffee and minimuffins from the central test kitchen. *Every day; www.williams-sonoma.ca; map:D3.*

FLORISTS AND GARDEN SHOPS

The Avant Gardener

1460 MARINE DR, WEST VANCOUVER (AND BRANCHES); 604/926-8784
This is a great store for the serious gardener or the confirmed browser. (And what gardener isn't both?) Gardening stock and patio furniture sit alongside

decorator accents and designer T-shirts. *Every day; www.avantgardener. com; map:C1.*

Get Fresh Flowers

1332 DAVIE ST, WEST END; 604/685-3500

Modern arrangements in low glass vases, such as their signature tightly packed roses or tulips, grace the city's most fashionable desks and cocktail rounds. *Every day; www.getfreshflowers.ca; map:Q4.*

Hilary Miles Flowers

1-1854 W 1ST AVE, WEST SIDE; 604/737-2782 OR 877/737-2786

Talented bouquet impresario Hilary Miles has been collaborating with fashion designers for more than 25 years, creating floral chefs d'oeuvre for movie sets, weddings, special events, and, if you're lucky, maybe even your living room. *Mon–Sat; www.hilarymiles.com; map:O6.*

Southlands Nursery

6550 BALACLAVA ST, WEST SIDE; 604/261-6411

Under the skilful guidance of renowned local gardener, florist, and TV personality Thomas Hobbs, this nursery offers indoor and outdoor plants—plus the perfect containers in which to display them. Hobbs is known for his expertise with (and fondness for) orchids, so expect a good selection. *Every day; map:C4.*

Thomas Hobbs Florist by Maureen Sullivan

2127 W 41ST AVE, WEST SIDE; 604/263-2601 OR 800/663-2601

Though now under the ownership of Maureen and Jim Sullivan, this remains one of the finest florists—and certainly the best-known one—in the Vancouver area. Tasteful and creative arrangements are presented in handsome containers. *Every day; www.thomashobbsflorist.com; map:C4.*

GIFTS AND JEWELLERY

Atkinson's

1501 W 6TH AVE, WEST SIDE; 604/736-3378

Originally an executive gift service, the family-owned store holds two floors of European crystal, silver, china, and even a children's gift boutique. Splurge on Lalique, Baccarat, Ercuis, and Limoges, or treat yourself to bed, table, and bath linens imported from Pratesi of Italy and double-damask Irish table linens. *Tues–Sat; www.atkinsonsofvancouver.com; map:P7.*

Birks

698 HASTINGS ST, DOWNTOWN (AND BRANCHES); 604/669-3333

When Henry Birks opened his doors in the beginning of the 19th century, he could hardly have known that one day his empire would stretch from sea to sea: today, Birks stores are found in every major Canadian city. For generations, brides have received their engagement rings from here (especially since Birks teamed up with renowned local jeweller Toni Cavelti), have registered here, and have received their subsequent anniversary presents from this store—all items coming in that distinctive blue box. Don't miss the special case of estate jewellery. *Every day; www.birks.com; map:T3.*

Chachkas

2423 GRANVILLE ST, WEST SIDE; 604/688-6417

Whether you're looking for the perfect little gift for a friend or a selfish little treat for yourself, you'll find plenty to choose from at this shop, which carries a large selection of jewellery, decorative items, prints, and imports. *Every day; www.chachkas.ca; map:R3.*

Hammered and Pickled

1494 OLD BRIDGE ST, GRANVILLE ISLAND; 604/689-0615

Two young female jewellery designers have teamed up in this Granville Island studio, where you can watch them make and polish pieces by hand before putting them into the display cases. Working mainly with silver and semiprecious stones, each designer has a distinctive style, and many of the pieces are one of a kind. *Every day; map:Q6.*

Karl Stittgen and Goldsmiths

2203 GRANVILLE ST, WEST SIDE; 604/737-0029

A local favourite with a far-reaching reputation, designer Karl Stittgen creates fabulous handmade jewellery of gold and gems. Singularly handsome pieces. *Mon–Sat; map:P7.*

Martha Sturdy

16 W 5TH AVE, WEST SIDE; 604/872-5205

A local star with international appeal (London, Hong Kong, and New York are her biggest markets), Sturdy made the bold metal and cast-resin jewellery that was a staple gift for retiring *Vogue* editors in the 1980s and has appeared in Marc Jacobs's runway shows. Now her sculptural housewares and furniture, also mostly made of metal and cast resin, are design items coveted the world over. Her local factory facilities now house both a store and art gallery. *By appointment only; www.marthasturdy.com; map:D3.*

HOME FURNISHINGS

Bernstein & Gold

1168 HAMILTON ST, YALETOWN; 604/687-1535

Everything in this lifestyle store is keyed to the cream-and-gold decor—for a luxe appeal. Overstuffed and slip-covered furniture is made in BC, accessories are imported from Europe, and linens and bedding are of very high quality. *Every day; www.bernstein-gold.com; map:T5.*

THE SILK ROAD

Proximity to Asian silk has made Vancouver the lingerie capital of Canada, with local designers selling as far away as Saks Fifth Avenue, Dubai. Example: Oprah is such a fan of the silk pajamas by Christine Vancouver that she wore them on the cover of her magazine.

AGENT PROVOCATEUR (1026 Alberni St, Downtown; 604/258-7943)
Canada's first Agent Provocateur store features a pair of birdcages large enough to hold lingerie models for special living window displays. An amazing 3D black lacquer forest upstairs—a first for any AP store worldwide—houses naughty toys; famous vintage-inspired lingerie sets from London grace mirrored walls. *Every day; www.agentprovocateur.com; map:S4.*

DIANE'S LINGERIE AND LOUNGEWEAR (2950 Granville St, West Side; 604/738-5121)
Receive kid-glove treatment from helpful staff when choosing a gift. Underpinnings in all sizes, from well-known manufacturers; sleepwear ranging from prosaic jammies to sexy negligees; the largest selection of brassieres in BC. *Mon–Sat; www.dianeslingerie.com; map:D3.*

Country Furniture

3097 GRANVILLE ST, WEST SIDE; 604/738-6411

If anything is going to convince you of the beauty and simplicity of pioneer life, it's a visit to this store. Faux-finished reproduction tables, decorative folk art, painted cabinets, and French accessories are the things you'll find in this laid-back, somewhat crowded store. *Every day; www.countryfurniture. net; map:D3.*

The Cross

1198 HOMER ST, YALETOWN; 604/689-2900

A 5,000-square-foot heritage building now houses the Cross, a decorator's delight of bespoke linens, design books, grosgrain ribbons, delicate sugar bowls, massive white candles, a baby gift section, and a new home-decorating service. Imagine the girl who wears only the finest French lingerie to bed—and then imagine her living room. *Every day; www.thecross design.com; map:S5.*

Inform Interiors

50 WATER ST, GASTOWN; 604/682-3868

Canada's most famous furniture designer, local Niels Bendtsen, founded this sleek store that stocks both his own line and dozens of carefully chosen

GATEAU LINGERIE (115-1058 Mainland St, Yaletown; 604/688-8322)

The most adorable little lingerie store is full of frothy confections (lace, ribbons, dusty pink satin) from Elle MacPherson Intimates, Anna Sui, Betsey Johnson, and edgy Ed Hardy Intimates. *Every day; www.gateaulingerie.com; map:S6.*

LA JOLIE MADAME (Pacific Centre, Downtown; 604/669-1831)

Ultrafeminine lingerie in a wide range of sizes; much of the stock is imported. Friendly, knowledgeable staff. *Every day; map:T4.*

SCARLET (460 Granville St, Downtown; 604/605-1607)

Beautiful lingerie from a tasteful boudoir shop full of sensual European imports like La Perla as well as local Canadian talent. Also a good selection of Elle "the body" MacPherson's covetable undies; a great online store for gift giving. *Every day; www.scarletshop.com; map:T4.*

STAPLES (1447 Clyde Ave, West Vancouver; 604/921-7763)

Staples's fancy silk long johns are what they're wearing under their Descente ski suits up on Cypress Mountain; travellers stock up on wash-and-wear basics in every shade imaginable, all with coordinating camisoles. *Mon–Sat or by appointment; www.staplesonline.com; map:D1.*

—Sarah Bancroft

others—all contemporary, some with a modernist influence. Now housed in a new green building complete with a lawn on the roof (to better display patio furniture) the trilevel store is an architectural marvel. It's the kind of place where your purchase is signed by the designer and comes with a numbered authentication certificate. Find Philippe Starck, Mies van der Rohe, Alias, Agape, and the like. Stock is mostly from Italy, with pieces from England, Scandinavia, and New York. Every single item in the store is akin to art (several pieces are in fact in the permanent collection of New York's Museum of Modern Art), and celebrities—such as Bryan Adams—ship purchases as far away as London. *Every day; www.informinteriors.com; map:U3.*

Koolhaus

1 WATER ST, GASTOWN; 604/875-9004

The latest modern furniture store to decamp to Gastown offers stunning modular column lights, classics such as Le Corbusier glass dining tables, and beautiful black marble tables with white veining. Most items come in various sizes, so they can furnish your condo as well as your ski chalet. *Every day; www.koolhausdesign.com; map:U3.*

Liberty

1635 W BROADWAY, WEST SIDE
(AND BRANCHES); 604/682-7499 OR 800/599-9289
Everything is dramatic and oversized at this locally owned chain. A Gothic theme prevails with overstuffed couches covered in damask pillows, chandeliers and signature candelabras, and stuffed crows in the rafters. Downstairs are iron beds, luscious linens, a children's furniture section, and shelves of decorative items such as Japanese lanterns. *Every day; www.libertyinside.com; map:C2.*

Montauk

1062 HOMER ST, YALETOWN; 604/331-2363
The all-white Yaletown store is a West Coast first for the Montreal-based furniture manufacturer that was inspired by the American beach village of Montauk. Understated and contemporary, the slip-covered sofas', chairs', and ottomans' hardwood, coil supports, and goose-down elements are guaranteed for 24 years. *Tues–Sun; www.montauksofa.com; map:S5.*

MUSIC (RECORDINGS, CDS, TAPES, AND INSTRUMENTS)

A & B Sound

556 SEYMOUR ST, DOWNTOWN (AND BRANCHES); 604/687-5837
You can't always get what you want, but chances are you'll leave satisfied. These stores boast a large stock of records, tapes, and CDs at great prices, as well as a good selection of electronics and even a small bookstore with good discounts. Their biannual sales draw lineups several blocks long. *Every day; www.absound.ca; map:T3.*

Highlife Records and Music

1317 COMMERCIAL DR, EAST VANCOUVER; 604/251-6964
For 20 years, this shop has been carrying music from around the world—specializing in Latin, African, and Caribbean sounds—as well as a selection of vintage instruments. *Every day; www.highlifeworld.com; map:Z6.*

Neptoon Records

3561 MAIN ST, SOUTH MAIN; 604/324-1229
An eclectic mix of just about everything, especially rare and out-of-print vinyl. You'll find lots of music-related memorabilia, including some hard-to-find concert posters from as far back as the 1960s. *Every day; www.neptoon. com; map:E4.*

Tom Lee Music

929 GRANVILLE ST, DOWNTOWN (AND BRANCHES);
604/685-8471 OR 888/886-6533
Tom Lee Music has the largest selection of musical instruments in the Lower Mainland and several floors from which to choose. Find Yamaha, Petrof, Steinway, and others. *Every day; www.tomleemusic.ca; map:S4.*

Zulu Records

1972 W 4TH AVE, WEST SIDE; 604/738-3232
New wave, punk, electronic, techno, hip-hop, rap, and other modern sounds. Zulu carries its own label of independent recordings and doubles as a ticket venue for concerts. *Every day; www.zulurecords.com; map:O7.*

NATIVE ART AND CRAFTS

Hill's Native Art

165 WATER ST, GASTOWN; 604/685-4249
Hill's is famous for its wide selection of aboriginal art and handiwork, spread over three floors. It's somewhat infamous too, given that Bill Clinton picked up a carving here to give Monica Lewinsky when he was in town for the Asia-Pacific Economic Conference. Art ranges from original paintings and limited editions to gold and silver jewellery (the designs are carved, not cast). Each piece is signed. Hill's is also the best-known source for beautiful, durable Cowichan sweaters and real moccasins. *Every day; www.hillsnativeart.com; map:U3.*

Lattimer Gallery

1590 W 2ND AVE, WEST SIDE; 604/732-4556
This small gallery features aboriginal art of an extremely high calibre. Many items are purchased for collections. You'll find carvings, jewellery, prints, ceremonial masks, drums, and totems—all created by Native artists in the traditional motifs of the Northwest Coast peoples. *Every day; www.lattimergallery. com; map:P7.*

Museum of Anthropology

6393 NW MARINE DR, UBC, WEST SIDE; 604/822-3825 OR 604/822-5087
In addition to a fine selection of Northwest Coast art and books, the museum shop features Inuit prints, soapstone sculpture, and other handmade craftwork. It also happens to be situated in one of the most beautiful examples of modern architecture in the city. *Every day; www.moa.ubc.ca; map:A2.*

ONE-OF-A-KIND SHOPS

The Bright Side

3036 W BROADWAY, WEST SIDE; 604/734-3036
An optimistic store dedicated to the good life carries things such as fair-trade toys, supercomfy socks, and casual clothing with inspiring, spread-the-love messages. The coffee cups sold here are presumably half full, not half empty. *Every day; www.lifeisgoodvancouver.com; map:C3.*

Buddha Supplies Centre

4158 MAIN ST, CHINATOWN; 604/873-8169
At Chinese funerals, people burn joss—paper replicas of earthly belongings—to make the deceased more comfortable in the afterlife. At this tiny store,

VINTAGE CHIC

The movie industry's demand for midcentury props and wardrobe, plus the general run on anything that resembles modernist design, equals dozens of vintage stores opening up every year. The following spots (some of which have been around since the '70s) are owned by people who do their research, stock quality items, and provide unique services.

BURCU'S ANGELS (2535 Main St, West Side; 604/874-9773)

A staff-described "organic entity," with 24-hour "free box," large sizes in service to bigger women and transvestites, and the owner's penchant for magic tricks. *Every day; map:D3.*

CABBAGES & KINX (315 W Hastings St, Downtown; 604/669-4238)

A little bit of everything: T-shirts with subverted corporate logos, used military wear, jewellery, wigs, vintage clothes, (um) smoking paraphernalia, fetish wear in PVC and custom leather. Staff are exceptionally friendly and pierced. *Every day; map:U4.*

DELUXE JUNK (310 W Cordova St, Gastown; 604/685-4871)

Suppliers in far-flung areas of the province scour rural thrift shops and jumble sales for pristine vintage finds. The store stays au courant by forecasting fashion trends into the next season, then filling up with a huge selection just in time for the trend to hit. *Every day; www.deluxejunk.com; map:U3.*

you'll find combustible cell phones, fax machines, and even a miniature cardboard penthouse apartment with a Mercedes in the driveway. *Every day; map:V7.*

The Flag Shop

1755 W 4TH AVE, WEST SIDE; 604/736-8161
This is where you'll find flags for the country, the province, and the city—as well as a number of nonflag items such as pins, crests, decals, and wind socks. *Every day; www.flagshop.com; map:P7.*

Golden Age Collectables

852 GRANVILLE ST, DOWNTOWN; 604/683-2819
It's hard to say which age these folks consider golden, but they do have a fine selection of movie posters, baseball and other sport cards (some bearing autographs), and other flotsam of youth. There are also lots of comic books, posters, and T-shirts, with comic—and comical—designs. *Every day; map:S4.*

THE FABULOUS FIND (1853 Main St, South Main; 778/836-0480)
Vintage Marimekko children's curtains from Finland, midcentury light fixtures and chandeliers, sleek melamine dishware and carafes from Denmark and Holland in an array of pop-art colours. Look for Rosti, Heller, and Dansk. *Every day; map:D3.*

METROPOLITAN HOME (217 W Hastings St, Downtown; 604/681-2313)
This 18-year-old store specialized in midcentury modern furniture well before it was all the rage. The focus has shifted from '50s-style kitchenware to the best of slick modernism. *Every day; map:S3.*

MINTAGE (320 W Cordova St, Gastown; 604/646-8243 and
1714 Commercial Dr, East Vancouver; 604/871-0022)
Find high-quality vintage gear and several in-house lines of reworked vintage clothes at this relative newcomer. Look on walls for the most valuable items; don't miss shoes and bags. *Every day; www.mintagevintage.com; map:U3.*

TRUE VALUE VINTAGE (710 Robson St, Downtown; 604/685-5403)
Underground emporium of vintage stuff for guys and girls, emphasizing the '60s, '70s, and '80s: beaded shell tops, leather blazers, real Cowichan sweaters, rare Levi's, authentic motorcycle jackets. Movie wardrobers load up here. *Every day; map:R4.*

— Sherry McGarvie

Grand Prix Hobbies, Crafts & Gifts Ltd.

3038 W BROADWAY, WEST SIDE; 604/733-7114
Grand Prix is a 40-year-old institution on West Broadway that specializes in model sets, including exquisitely detailed train sets for nostalgia buffs, models of fighter planes and battleships, Star Trek figures, and miniature worlds. It's all here. In the summer, a popular item is the build-it-yourself rocket, which can actually be launched (outside, please!). There's also a good selection of arts and crafts supplies, such as paints, beads, and ribbons. *Every day; www. grandprixhobbies.ca; map:D3.*

The Umbrella Shop

1106 W BROADWAY, WEST SIDE (AND BRANCHES);
604/669-9444 OR 877/427-6559
Given Vancouver weather, it's easy to believe that this store has been around for more than 70 years. You'll find a veritable deluge of bumbershoots in all sizes, shapes, and fabrics. Many of the umbrellas are constructed on the premises, will last for years, and can be repaired at the shop. *Mon–Sat; www. theumbrellashop.com; map:T3.*

SHOES

Bentall Centre Shoe Renew

BENTALL CENTRE (LOWER LEVEL), DOWNTOWN; 604/688-0538
If your sole needs a little TLC, this little shop can help you out in its downtown location and make repairs while you wait. *Mon–Fri; map:T3.*

Dayton Shoe Co.

2250 E HASTINGS ST, EAST VANCOUVER; 604/253-6671 OR 800/342-8934
These boots were made for loggers, but they're now a staple for rock stars and fashion mavens all over the world and are regularly spotted in movies shot in Hollywood North. Not bad for a little shop on the East Side. Johnny Depp has been wearing his since his *21 Jump Street* days: Dayton puts a lifetime guarantee on its products. *Mon–Sat; www.daytonboots.com; map:E2.*

Gum Drops

2029 W 4TH AVE, WEST SIDE; 604/733-1037
Now that Chanel, Marc Jacobs, and Coach make gum boots, here's a store that sells nothing but superstylish puddle jumpers for kids and adults alike. *Every day; www.gumdrops.ca; map:O7.*

John Fluevog

65 WATER ST, DOWNTOWN; 604/688-6228
837 GRANVILLE ST, DOWNTOWN; 604/688-2828
The undisputed leader in footwear innovation in the country. Fluevog still lives and works here, even though his sculptural creations are just as famous in New York and London. Find the classic Angel boots and shoes, or go for the new lines of 1940s-style heels in patent leather. This new flagship store boasts an upstairs design studio and is housed in a glassed-in gap between two historic buildings. *Every day; www.fluevog.com; map:U3.*

Quick Cobbler

430 W 2ND AVE, WEST SIDE; 604/682-6354
This place managed to save a pair of black leather Chloé boots that went through the ringer during a Toronto snowstorm. It's a big and airy space (the antithesis of cobblers of yore) that's both efficient and thrifty. *Every day; www.quickcobbler.com; map:U7.*

SKIN AND HAIR CARE

LifeSpa

ROYAL CENTRE, 102-1055 W GEORGIA ST, DOWNTOWN; 604/683-5433
Weekday lunchtime treatments at this pretty new spa near the entrance to the Hyatt Regency come with a free gourmet salad and sandwich. Light therapy, Botox, and men's services are also popular. *Every day; www.lifespa. ca; map:T4.*

L'Occitane

3051 GRANVILLE ST, WEST SIDE; 604/734-4441
101-755 BURRARD ST, DOWNTOWN; 604/688-1198
A longtime favourite of *Vogue* editors in New York, this French chain has developed a strong following addicted to its luxurious *eau de linge* (scented ironing water) and verbena-infused candles. It's the Provençal equivalent of the Body Shop, but the company practised nonexploitative trade well before eco-marketing was all the rage. Known for its use of traditional Provençal soap-making techniques, as well as natural ingredients such as African shea butter and French lavender, the company also prints all its labels in Braille. The men's line of skin-care products is exceptional too. *Every day; www. loccitane.ca; map:D3.*

LUSH

1020 ROBSON ST, DOWNTOWN (AND BRANCHES); 604/687-5874
LUSH carries skin-care and bath products that pamper and please, and all are made locally. Their bread and butter is the Bath Bomb, a richly scented concoction that makes the most mundane ablution a wickedly wonderful experience. *Every day; www.lush.ca; map:D3.*

Masc

433 DAVIE ST, DOWNTOWN; 604/688-4555
Men's grooming products include Mojito-scented cologne (one part lime, one part rum) and remedies for everything from razor burn to under-eye bags. Super-helpful staff. *Every day, www.mascformen.com, map:S5.*

Optaderm

340-2184 W BROADWAY, WEST SIDE; 604/737-2026
This skin-care shop, and the skin-care products and cosmetics of the same name, have garnered a fanatical following. Drop by for one of the shop's luxurious European facials and pick up some fabulous lotions and potions; staff are happy to supply samples. All products are made locally. *Tues–Sat; www.optaderm.com; map:N7.*

Pure Studio Hair & Esthetics

2355 SPRUCE ST, WEST SIDE; 604/730-7873
Pure hospitality with warm, team-oriented service and personalized hair care and aesthetics. Make-up artist Luc Lacroix is one of the best in the business. *Tues–Sat; map:R7.*

Suki's

3157 GRANVILLE ST, WEST SIDE (AND BRANCHES); 604/738-7713
Suki's has long been an established name in Vancouver for exceptional haircuts and care. Here you are assured the best cut and the best head massage (called a shampoo) at any one of its locations. The state-of-the-art South Granville shop was designed by noted local architect Arthur Erickson. The

salons are open seven days a week (and some evenings) for busy clients. *Every day; www.sukis.com; map:D3.*

Tech 1 Hair Design

1057 CAMBIE ST, YALETOWN; 604/689-1202
Highlights, lowlights, single-process treatments: quality colour using L'Oreal products are this salon's calling card. The aesthetic services offered in three treatment rooms upstairs are outstanding. If Remee is available for a cut and blow-dry, book it. At press time the salon was moving to a new location. *Tues–Sat; www.tech1hairdesign.com; map:T5.*

Vida Wellness Spa

SUTTON PLACE HOTEL, 845 BURRARD ST, DOWNTOWN (AND BRANCHES); 604/682-8410
BC has more spas per capita than anywhere else in Canada, which means stiff competition. This spa group, owned by the founder of the matchmaking service Lavalife, has it nailed. Treatments, based on the ancient Indian practise of Ayurveda, can be very transformative—especially to the uninitiated. This location in particular is beautifully designed and very quiet. *Every day; www. vidawellness.com; map:T4.*

SPECIALTY FOODS

Bosa Foods

1465 KOOTENAY ST AND 562 VICTORIA DR, EAST VANCOUVER; 604/253-5578
Victoria Drive favourite Bosa Foods has opened a massive new warehouse store filled with discount Italian groceries and deli items, perfect for stocking the pantry. Don't miss the fresh pasta bar with a view into the wooden aging room stuffed with massive wheels of Parmigiano-Reggiano. Fresh almonds and walnuts, Star-brand tinned Mediterranean tuna, frozen *sacchetini* pasta, frozen pizza dough from Calabria Bakery, and Raincity Crisps are all kitchen staples for busy people like you. *Mon–Sat, www.bosafoods.com; map:Z6.*

The First Ravioli Store

1900 COMMERCIAL DR, EAST VANCOUVER; 604/255-8844
Vancouver's oldest and most popular Italian supermarket presents an impressive array of fresh pastas and sauces. People crowd the aisles on weekends in pursuit of unusual canned items, olive oils, imported pasta, marinated vegetables, and deli meats. *Every day; map:Z7.*

Fujiya

912 CLARK DR, EAST VANCOUVER (AND BRANCHES); 604/251-3711
Fujiya stores are the best source for Japanese foods and pearl rice in town. They also have weekly specials and carry a wide variety of inexpensive kitchenware, including steamers, woks, and kitchen tools. You'll find some of the

best buys in sushi supplies here, such as bamboo mats for rolling rice in nori. Take-out sashimi available. *Every day; www.fujiya.ca; map:Z4.*

Gourmet Warehouse

1340 E HASTINGS ST, EAST VANCOUVER; 604-253-3022

Make up a gift basket of fancy pastas, such as porcini or squid ink, for the goth foodie in the family. Buy that elusive *macha* tea whisk you've always wanted, and vow to drink the wretched stuff. Collect stocking stuffers of edible gold flakes, nutmeg graters, and handy silicone basting brushes for the Martha Stewart wannabe in your group. Pick up C's fig and black pepper crackers and a wheel of Camembert for the lunch guests who are still sticking around at cocktail hour. Surprise your pyromaniac brother with a crème brûlée set, including blowtorch. You can also book private cooking classes for groups. *Every day; www.gourmetwarehouse.ca; map:F3.*

J, N & Z Deli

1729 COMMERCIAL DR, EAST VANCOUVER; 604/251-4144

This place smells wonderful, with its smoky hams, bacon, and sausages hanging neatly from a rack over the counter. The Polish kielbasas, Berliner ham, and smoked pork chops are legendary, and the locals' secret love is the incomparable red pepper and eggplant spread. The lineups start early on weekend mornings, and it supplies some of the best charcuterie boards in town, including those at Salt Tasting Room (see the Restaurants chapter). *Tues–Sat; map:Z7.*

Les Amis du Fromage

1752 W 2ND AVE, WEST SIDE; 604/732-4218
518 PARK ROYAL S, WEST VANCOUVER; 604/925-4218

Say "cheese" at this hot spot owned by mother-daughter team Alice and Allison Spurrell. It's a favourite among Vancouver's top chefs because of the selection, quick turnover, and affordable prices of their 500 cheeses. The freezer is stocked with take-out soups and entrées, all made from scratch. Buy their cheese, and you can have free use of their raclette machines and cheese fondue setups. The Spurrells will also guide you to a great wine to partner with your cheese selection. A second location can be found on the North Shore at Park Royal. *Every day; www.buycheese.com; map:P7.*

The Lobster Man

1807 MAST TOWER RD, GRANVILLE ISLAND; 604/687-4531

Buy your lobsters on Granville Island while they're still kicking. In addition to live lobsters, the Lobster Man sells a wide variety of seafood-related gift items (utensils, accessories, and spices, among other things) for hard-to-please friends. Staff will even pack your crustaceans, at no extra charge, for travel or shipping. *Every day; www.lobsterman.com; map:Q6.*

ASIAN PURVEYORS

Even before world-class Asian restaurants came to the forefront of Vancouver's dining consciousness, there has always been a strong food culture among the city's immigrant communities. Blessed with outstanding local products and one of the busiest seaports in the world, Asian food purveyors have supplied fussy consumers, hungry for familiar flavours, for decades.

H-MART (200-550 Robson St, Downtown, and branches; 604/609-4567)

Known for its organic and high-end products, H-Mart has a selection of Korean foods that is astounding both in range and quality, at great prices. Bump shopping carts with foreign-language students stocking up on spicy instant noodles and Korean families shopping for kimchee, live seafood, and richly marbled beef. *Every day; map:S4.*

IZUMI-YA JAPANESE MARKETPLACE (160-7971 Alderbridge Wy, Richmond; 604/303-1171 and 909 Denman St, West End; 604/683-1174)

The real treat of great Japanese food stores is putting together a delicious takeaway meal from the deli and scouring the snack aisle for new finds. Izumi-Ya scores big-time on both counts. House-made chicken kara age, sushi rolls, and bento boxes are fresh and a great value. Add a Pocari sports drink and a box of Pocky for the quintessential Japanese picnic. *Every day; www.izumiya.ca; map:D6, Q2.*

KEI'S BAKERY (2351 Burrard St, West Side; 604/714-5385)

Indulge in a starch-laden slice of Japan at this charming family-run *pan-ya-san*, or Japanese bakery. Traditional fillings and flavours include Mount Matcha, with its sweet green-tea topping, and strawberry–red bean *pan*; savoury offerings feature the unquestionably Japanese *yakisoba sand. Thurs–Tues; map:O7.*

Longliner Sea Foods

1689 JOHNSTON ST, GRANVILLE ISLAND; 604/681-9016

The Longliner is one of the best fish markets on Granville Island. Expect to find Vancouver's professional cooks eyeing the goods alongside you. Pristine scallops, giant prawns, squid, and whole fish shine alongside less common piscine fare. The staff is generous with cooking advice. *Every day (closed Mon in winter); map:Q6.*

Meinhardt Fine Foods

3002 GRANVILLE ST, WEST SIDE; 604/732-4405

There's a good selection of gourmet and imported goodies, as well as upscale takeout, in this South Granville supermarket. A new location has opened

MICHÉLE CAKE SHOP (6033 W Boulevard, West Side; 604/261-3284 and 140-6211 Buswell St, Richmond; 604/207-6975)

From display cases laden with delectable baked treats, the Portuguese egg tarts beckon to you with their rich, buttery siren song. Mango cakes are a jewel-like tropical delight when in season, and thickly sliced white bread makes buttered toast seem like a guilty pleasure. *Every day; map:C4.*

SOUTH CHINA SEAS TRADING CO. LTD. (125-1689 Johnston St, Granville Island; 604/681-5402 and 1904 Grant St, East Vancouver; 604/254-5403)

From handcrafted, small-batch Mexican cheese to maitake mushrooms, kaffir lime leaves, and calamondin, South China Seas Trading Co. stocks Vancouver's most comprehensive supply of exotic ingredients. Also find unique cookbooks, rare spices, fragrant teas, and an impressive array of chiles—everything you'll need for an international adventure in your own kitchen. *Every day; www.south chinaseas.ca; map:Q6, E2.*

T&T SUPERMARKET (179 Keefer Pl, Chinatown and branches; 604/899-8836)

Forget soup to nuts: try Chinese roasted duck to frozen dumplings. Clean, bright, and astoundingly well stocked, the supermarket's offerings reflect the Asian cook's uncompromising demand for freshness at rock-bottom prices. The live seafood in giant tanks, butchers cutting meat to order, lunch ladies serving cooked foods, and jostling hordes of shoppers all add up to a huge sensory treat. *Every day; www.tnt-supermarket.com; map:U4.*

TINLAND COOKWARE (244 E Pender St, East Vancouver; 604/608-2890)

Frequented by Chinese chefs, this is a no-nonsense cache of gleaming cleavers, giant pots, and professional tools. Look for traditional ironwood chopping blocks—dark as walnut, dense, and increasingly rare. *Every day; map:V4.*

—Joie Alvaro Kent and Lee Man

next to the Ridge Theatre at 3151 Arbutus Street (604/732-7900). *Every day; www.meinhardt.com; map:D3.*

Oyama Sausage Company

17-1689 JOHNSTON PL, GRANVILLE ISLAND; 604/327-7407

The name in town that has become synonymous with all things cured, salted, and smoked—it's a veritable charcuterie-lover's paradise. Owner John van der Lieck, a fifth-generation sausage maker, has garnered such a loyal and enthusiastic following because of his perfectionist obsession with his craft. Natural spices arrive direct, sourced meat must adhere to exacting feed requirements (even insisting on hazelnuts to improve hog fat flavour), and only the highest quality liquor is used to flavour his premium sausages. Devotees queue to stock up on the more than 300 types of chorizos, prosciuttos, terrines, pâtés, bacon, fresh links, and salamis. It's all there, from a traditional Hungarian bratwurst to a more exotic but equally flavourful venison with chocolate and cherries. Let the salivating begin. *Every day; www.oyamasausage.ca; map:Q6.*

Parthenon Wholesale & Retail Food

3080 W BROADWAY, WEST SIDE; 604/733-4191

It's not a Greek island, but on a rainy day it's great to pretend while nibbling such delicacies as taramasalata, baklava, dolmades, Greek olives, shockingly good feta, and their famous "God's Dip." Mediterranean expats travel from all over the city for Parthenon's inexpensive soaps made from olive oil and basil. *Every day; map:C3.*

Que Pasa Mexican Foods

12031 NO 5 RD, RICHMOND; 604/737-7659

Que Pasa is Vancouver's best source for the elusive spices and ingredients needed for Mexican cooking. This small shop carries a variety of Mexican deli items and fresh vegetables: tomatillos, chiles, cactus, and jicama. There are many brands of salsa, including the store's own chunky style (in hot, medium, and mild), as well as its superior tortilla chips. In addition, we've discovered piñatas, Mexican candles, and margarita glasses. Que Pasa also sells a practical *molcajete*—a kind of mortar and pestle for grinding rice into flour—and has a good stock of Mexican cookbooks. *Every day; www. quepasafoods.com; map:P3.*

Quince

1780 W 3RD AVE, WEST SIDE; 604/731-4645

Looking to sharpen your knife skills? There's a class for that. Need to learn curry in a hurry? There's a class for that, too. The gorgeous new Quince Cooking Studio near Granville Island features a state-of-the-art kitchen, lemon sorbet–coloured chairs, and live herb boxes where you can snip and bag exotic greens. Classes, led by notable pastry chefs and instructors, range from an evening session followed by dinner and wine at the harvest table (from $80) to nine-day intensive technique courses ($750). And if you decide the culinary life is just not your gig, the bright and modern studio is stocked with vacuum-sealed Quince meals that slip nicely into your purse, thanks. *Every day; www.quince.ca; map:Q6.*

The Stock Market

1689 JOHNSTON ST, GRANVILLE ISLAND; 604/687-2433

Owners Georges and Joanne LeFebvre used to delight guests with their culinary expertise at their restaurant, Le Chef et Sa Femme. Now they help you delight your guests with the complete selection of stocks, sauces, dressings, and marinades available at their Granville Island shop. Everything is fresh and made with no preservatives, so selection depends on the season. If you're lucky, they'll be serving their fish chowder or lentil soup. *Every day; map:Q6.*

Urban Fare

177 DAVIE ST, YALETOWN; 604/975-7550
305 BUTE ST, DOWNTOWN; 604/669-5831

Located in Yaletown, Urban Fare is the only supermarket in the city where you can sip a glass of wine with your crab cakes. In addition to grocery items, there's organic produce (including Asian), a pasta bar, an olive bar, and lots of ethnic foods and spices. It's a hip, attractive source for prepared food selections for an inspired breakfast, lunch, or dinner—to go or to eat in the Urban Fare cafe. While the store bakes its own breads, it also brings in sourdough rye from Poilâne—one of France's best bakeries. Yes, they deliver. *Every day; www.urbanfare.com; map:S6.*

Vista d'Oro

20856 4TH AVE, LANGLEY; 604/514-3539

If you're running out of places to take the kids, and the prospect of another hair-raising trip to Science World just won't get anyone in the car, consider a trip to Vista d'Oro farms, situated on 10 acres (4 hectares) with 400 fruit trees in Langley. The Farmgate Shop, located in a carriage house next to the professional kitchen, sells preserves, pastries, cheese, and chocolates, as well as heirloom fruits and vegetables. There are more than 40 varieties of heirloom tomato plants and herbs on offer (impress your dinner guests with exotics such as Green Zebra striped tomatoes, fragrant French thyme, or pineapple sage), and the first release from the new winery is slated for November 2008. *Thurs–Sat, seasonal; www.vistadoro.com.*

SPORTS EQUIPMENT AND SPORTSWEAR

Coast Mountain Sports

2201 W 4TH AVE, WEST SIDE (AND BRANCHES); 604/731-6181

Affordable camping, hiking, climbing, and travel gear. Boots, sleeping bags, water purifiers, and high-tech items such as freeze-dried food and satellite tracking systems. Kind, knowledgeable staff. *Every day; www.coastmountain. com; map:O7.*

Cyclone Taylor Sporting Goods

6575 OAK ST, WEST SIDE (AND BRANCHES); 604/266-3316 OR 800/665-2188

This shop is known as the place for skating gear. You can suit up a hockey team (ice or in-line), get your figure skates sharpened, or find safety equipment for a whole family of skaters. The second location is the pro shop in the Richmond Ice Centre. *Every day; www.cyclonetaylor.com; map:F7.*

The Diving Locker

2745 W 4TH AVE, WEST SIDE; 604/736-2681 OR 800/348-3398

Equipment sales, rentals, and instructions. The Diving Locker has been in business more than 40 years. *Every day; www.vancouverdivinglocker.com; map:C2.*

Lululemon Athletica

2113 W 4TH AVE, WEST SIDE (AND BRANCHES); 604/732-6111

Now with stores in New York and Asia, this local yogawear outfitter had one of the most dramatic IPOs in Canadian history. Using fabrics made from soy, bamboo, and seaweed, its highly functional garments are also highly fashionable. At its original store, located on a strip of West Fourth dubbed "Kits-afornia" for its New Agey vibe, staff members are encouraged to write slogans on the windows and post the company manifesto in the changing rooms. *Every day; www.lululemon.com; map:O7.*

Mountain Equipment Co-op

130 W BROADWAY, WEST SIDE; 604/872-7858

Join for five bucks, then shop to your heart's content amidst racks of all the gear you'll need to enjoy the great outdoors. The store is huge, reflecting the enormous popularity of adventure sports and their trappings, whether your idea of an adventure is battling the current in a kayak or taking the bus to UBC. *Every day; www.mec.ca; map:U7.*

3 Vets

2200 YUKON ST, WEST SIDE; 604/872-5475

One of the oldest and most respected outfitters in the area, 3 Vets is famous for its low prices. You'll find good-quality, basic equipment for entry-level campers and hikers, plus stainless steel coolers, dehydrated food, and cheap snowshoe rentals. *Every day; www.3vets.com; map:T7.*

Westbeach

370-328 WATER ST, GASTOWN; 604/731-6449

'Boarders chill out by the in-store half pipe and oil their wheels while young Japanese exchange students buy up a storm in the front. Phat pants, hoodies, bikinis, and Hawaiian shirts, as well as excellent technical snowboarding clothes and hardware. *Every day; www.westbeach.com; map:P7.*

STATIONERY AND ART SUPPLIES

Opus Framing and Art Supplies

1360 JOHNSTON ST, GRANVILLE ISLAND
(AND BRANCHES); 604/736-7028

Opus is ideally situated on Granville Island across the street from the Emily Carr Institute of Art & Design. A discount art-supply and do-it-yourself framing shop, Opus offers the lowest prices in the city and is an unparalleled source for art and framing supplies—more than 8,000 in-stock items. Most of the knowledgeable staff have art or design degrees. *Every day; www.opusframing. com; map:Q6.*

Paper-Ya

1666 JOHNSTON ST, GRANVILLE ISLAND; 604/684-2531
Here you'll find a terrific selection of Japanese rice paper and paper-related gifts from around the world, as well as papermaking kits for fledgling artists. *Every day; www.paper-ya.com; map:Q6.*

The Vancouver Pen Shop

512 W HASTINGS ST, DOWNTOWN; 604/681-1612
The giant pen in the window is your first clue to the giant selection offered here: Caran d'Ache, Faber-Castell, Montblanc, Cross, Waterman, and Parker pens as well as inks and cartridges. The shop also stocks calligraphy accessories, lower-priced pens, and high-end notepads. *Mon–Sat; map:T3.*

Winton's Social Stationery

2529 W BROADWAY, WEST SIDE; 604/731-3949
The helpful staff can supply your personal invitations in a matter of days, or you can choose from an extensive in-store selection. They also sell blank greeting cards that are extremely laser printer–friendly. Guest books, picture frames, and other related gifts. *Every day; www.wintons.ca; map:C3.*

Zing Paperie & Design

60-323 JERVIS ST, DOWNTOWN; 604/630-1885
At this new shop located on the Coal Harbour seawall, design-o-philes and greeting card addicts will be in a papery heaven. The clean, modern card selection includes lots of local talent (PaperLuxe, Flaunt, Paperqueen) as well as iconic names such as Style Press. Custom work is a specialty. *Mon–Sat; www.zingdesign.ca; map:R1.*

TOYS

Kaboodles

4449 W 10TH AVE, WEST SIDE (AND BRANCHES); 604/224-5311
This is the perfect store for stocking goody bags for kids' parties, but there's much, much more than a great selection of low-cost crowd pleasers. Check out the umbrellas, the backpacks, and the colourful stuffed toys. Cards and gift wrap, too. *Every day; www.kaboodlestoystore.com; map:B3.*

Kids Market

1496 CARTWRIGHT ST, GRANVILLE ISLAND; 604/689-8447
Not just toys, of course. The market features more than 20 specialty shops and services, including clothing, art supplies, and a hair salon for kids. It's where you'll find the best kite shop in the city, and kids just love to visit. See also Neighbourhoods under Shopping Areas and Malls in this chapter. *Every day; www.kidsmarket.ca; map:Q6.*

The Toybox

3002 W BROADWAY, WEST SIDE; 604/738-4322
High-quality toys, and lots of them (except toy guns, which on principle they
don't stock). Some of the merchandise is upmarket, but lots of lower-priced
items will please. Games galore. *Every day; map:C3.*

WINE, BEER, AND SPIRITS

Visitors used to purchasing their wine at a corner store may be perplexed by
the peculiarities of BC liquor laws. The distribution and sale of wine, beer, or
spirits are under control of the **BRITISH COLUMBIA LIQUOR DISTRIBUTION
BRANCH** (BCLDB; www.bcliquorstores.com). You can buy wines at several
private wine shops and at 20 Vintners Quality Alliance (VQA) stores (www.
winebc.com) across the province. You can purchase beer and wine in stores
attached to neighbourhood pubs, but the only place you can buy spirits is at a
BCLDB outlet. For store locations and product information, go to the Web site.
BC law prohibits the sale of alcohol to persons under the age of 19.

BC Liquor Stores
Signature BC Liquor Stores

5555 CAMBIE ST, WEST SIDE (AND BRANCHES); 604/266-1321
The Cambie Street liquor store, the flagship government-operated retail outlet, is a 15-minute drive from the downtown core. Located at the corner of
39th Avenue, it contains thousands of products, including wine, beer, cider,
coolers, and spirits. Wine enthusiasts will be impressed by the variety of
vintages for sale from all over the world. Often, labels that have long since
disappeared in London, New York, and San Francisco await the keen wine
buff here. For a complete list of signature stores in the province, visit the Web
site. *Every day; www.bcliquorstores.com; map:T7.*

Dundarave Wine Cellars

2448 MARINE DR, WEST VANCOUVER; 604/921-1814
At this upscale store in the West Vancouver village of Dundarave, you'll find
a bit of everything, although West Coast wines from BC to Chile dominate.
Every day; map:D1.

Edgemont Village Wines

**3050 EDGEMONT BLVD, NORTH VANCOUVER
(AND BRANCHES); 604/985-9463
1811 W 1ST AVE, WEST SIDE; 604/732-8827
3536 W 41ST AVE, WEST SIDE; 604/269-9433**
If you are looking for homegrown British Columbia Vintners Quality Alliance (VQA) wines, this is the place to head. You'll find just about everything
produced in the province, including an extensive array of ice wine. *Every day;
www.villagevqawines.com.*

Everything Wine

998 MARINE DR, NORTH VANCOUVER; 604/929-7277
The biggest and best selection—nearly 3,000 labels in 12,000 square feet—at competitive prices, plus expertise and enthusiasm when you want help. This is where to go for the ultimate wine-buying experience in the city. *Every day; www.everythingwine.ca; map:D1.*

Firefly Fine Wines and Ales

2857 CAMBIE ST, WEST SIDE; 604/875-3325
Take the mystery out of wine shopping at this new retailer, where bottles are categorized from "aromatic" to "black teeth" rather than by varietal. But the pièce de résistance is a stainless steel wine-sampling machine like they have in France: just place your glass under a bottle, press a button, and voilà, a little taste—perhaps the amazing Venturi-Schulze pinot noir from Vancouver Island. *Every day; www.fireflyfinewinesandales.com; map:D3.*

Liberty Wine Merchants

4583 W 10TH AVE, WEST SIDE (AND BRANCHES); 604/224-8050
Robert Simpson is the man behind the wines at Liberty, now with eight branches. Hip, savvy, and blessed with a fine palate, he encourages his store managers to do their own thing—and they do. There's a fine core selection of Champagne, Burgundy, and Bordeaux wines, as well as a strong California/Northwest section. The rest varies to reflect the manager's taste. *Every day; www.libertywinemerchants.com; map:B2.*

Marquis Wine Cellars

1034 DAVIE ST, WEST END; 604/684-0445
John Clerides has an eclectic mix of hard-to-find international wines at his West End private wine shop, with strong representation from the Pacific Northwest, Santa Barbara, and Australia. Top-of-the-line stemware and very knowledgeable staff. *Every day; www.marquis-wines.com; map:P3.*

Sutton Place Wine Merchant

SUTTON PLACE HOTEL, 855 BURRARD ST, DOWNTOWN; 604/642-2947
This downtown hotel's La Residence tower is where actors live during extended shoots. And now they have fine wine vintages right at their doorstep, thanks to this new shop specializing in rare wines. *Every day; www. suttonplacewinemerchant.com; map:R3.*

Taylorwood Wines

1185 MAINLAND ST, YALETOWN; 604/408-9463
Free wine tastings on Thursday and Sunday afternoons attract the single minglers from the surrounding lofts. New releases, reserve wines, all VQA wines from BC. *Every day; www.taylorwoodwines.com; map:S5.*

PERFORMING ARTS

PERFORMING ARTS

With the 2010 Winter Olympics fast approaching, the Vancouver performing arts community is proving to be a world-class competitor. From large-scale, mainstage productions to the most innovative independent shows, there is something for every culture vulture.

Local daily and weekly newspapers provide listings for a broad spectrum of happenings, but the **ARTS HOTLINE** (604/684-ARTS) is probably the best source of up-to-date information. The 24-hour hotline is staffed by the **ALLIANCE FOR ARTS AND CULTURE** (938 Howe St, Downtown; www.allianceforarts.com; map: S4), an umbrella organization serving hundreds of members across all disciplines. For tickets to many of the events described in this chapter, contact **TICKETMASTER** (604/280-4444; www.ticketmaster.ca). Many local companies use Vancouver's exclusive half-price day of show ticket outlet, **TICKETS TONIGHT** (200 Burrard St, plaza level, Downtown; 604/684-2787; www.ticketstonight.ca; map:T2), which also sells regular advance tickets.

Theatre

Vancouver's theatre scene offers a mosaic of live performances that range from glorious period pieces to site-specific performance art to practically everything in between. Two large-scale companies and many small, innovative groups keep theatregoers entertained year-round. The city's colleges and universities mount excellent theatre productions, dance recitals, and jazz concerts while classes are in session. **UNIVERSITY OF BRITISH COLUMBIA**'s (www.theatre.ubc.ca) theatre season runs September through April at the **FREDERIC WOOD THEATRE, TELUS STUDIO THEATRE,** and **DOROTHY SOMERSET STUDIO THEATRE.** During the same months, quality performances take place at the **SIMON FRASER UNIVERSITY THEATRE** (www.sfu.ca/sca), **LANGARA COLLEGE'S STUDIO 58** (www.langara. bc.ca/studio58), and the **CAPILANO COLLEGE PERFORMING ARTS THEATRE** (www.capcollege.bc.ca/news-events/performing-arts.html).

Other companies performing in Vancouver and on tour include **AXIS THEATRE COMPANY** (604/669-0631; www.axistheatre.com), **BOCA DEL LUPO** (604/684-2622; www.bocadellupo.com), **FULL CIRCLE PERFORMANCE** (604/683-0497; www.fullcircleperformance.ca), **HEADLINES THEATRE COMPANY** (604/871-0508; www.headlinestheatre.com), **PI (PINK INK) THEATRE** (604/872-1861; www. pitheatre.com), **RUBY SLIPPERS THEATRE** (604/602-0585; www.rubyslippers.ca), **RUMBLE PRODUCTIONS** (604/662-3395; www.rumble.org), **TOUCHSTONE THEATRE** (604/709-9973; www.touchstonetheatre.com), **URBAN INK PRODUCTIONS** (604/692-0885; www.urbanink.ca), **VAGABOND PLAYERS** (604/521-3055; www. vagabondplayers.ca), and many, many more.

Listed below are some of Vancouver's main venues and festivals featuring live theatre. (The **FIREHALL ARTS CENTRE** is listed under Dance later in this chapter. For information on the **VANCOUVER INTERNATIONAL CHILDREN'S FESTIVAL,** see Vanier Park under Parks and Beaches in the Exploring chapter.)

Arts Club Theatre Company

1585 JOHNSTON ST, GRANVILLE ISLAND; 604/687-1644

The Granville Island Stage and neighbouring Arts Club Revue Stage, run since 1972 by artistic managing director Bill Millerd, are located in the heart of lively Granville Island; the theatre company is the largest nonprofit theatre in western Canada. Millerd's third stage at the Stanley Industrial Alliance Stage (2750 Granville St, near 13th Ave; 604/687-1644) runs productions from contemporary drama to Shakespeare to big-budget musicals. The year-long offerings on the main Granville Island stage include a cornucopia of drama, comedy, and musical classics, with a focus on 20th-century works. For those who enjoy a drink during the show, the cabaret-style Revue Stage is the perfect spot for light theatre and musical comedy; it's also the home of the Vancouver TheatreSports League. Intermission on the False Creek dock or at the bustling Backstage Bar & Grill is an added attraction. The bar, which supports the theatre, has its own entertainment and is a popular destination for actors, artists, and musicians. *www.artsclub.com; map:Q6.* &

Bard on the Beach

VANIER PARK, WEST SIDE; 604/739-0559

Since 1990, the play's the thing all summer long at Vanier Park on Vancouver's waterfront. Open-ended tents provide the stage for the three Shakespearean works offered in repertory against a spectacular backdrop of city, sea, and mountains. Dress in comfortable layers; the evening cools down quickly after each breathtaking sunset. Seating is by general admission, so arrive early to "select and sticker" your seat; cushions recommended. Equally entertaining is the variety of festival spin-offs, from wine tastings and salmon barbecues to auctions and opera recitals. *June–Sept; www.bardonthebeach.org; map:O5–P5.* &

Chutzpah! Festival

VARIOUS LOCATIONS; 604/257-5145

Chutzpah! the Lisa Nemetz International Showcase of Jewish Performing Arts, stimulates with spectacular music, drama, dance, and comedy for 10 days each year. Performances take place at the Norman Rothstein Theatre, Wosk 2nd Stage, and the Chan Centre for the Performing Arts. Chutzpah! is a not-to-be-missed lineup of more than 25 performances and workshops with over 100 international, Canadian, and local artists of the highest calibre. *www.chutzpahfestival.com.* &

PuSh International Performing Arts Festival

VARIOUS LOCATIONS; 604/605-8284

Produced over 19 days each winter, the annual PuSh festival presents ground-breaking work in theatre, dance, music, and various hybrid forms of performance. It attracts acclaimed local, national, and international artists and their work. In a short time, PuSh has become one of Vancouver's signature events, presenting work that is visionary, genre-bending, multidisciplined, startling, and original. *Jan; www.pushfestival.ca.* &

Queen Elizabeth Theatre

HAMILTON ST AT W GEORGIA ST, DOWNTOWN; 604/665-3050

On the Queen E's spacious stage, theatre's grand traditions are at home. This elegant, 2,900-plus-seat theatre is one of Vancouver's main venues for lavish touring musicals each spring and summer, hosting dance, rock, and pop concerts and many multicultural shows the rest of the year. It's also home to Vancouver Opera and Ballet British Columbia (see Classical Music and Opera and Dance in this chapter). The Vancouver Playhouse (see review in this section) is next door. *www.city.vancouver.bc.ca/theatres; map:T4.* &

Shadbolt Centre for the Arts

6450 DEER LAKE AVE, BURNABY; 604/291-6864

Named in honor of the late BC painter Jack Shadbolt and his writer/curator wife Doris, the Shadbolt Centre, a performance and teaching centre in Burnaby's Deer Lake Park, houses two theatres, banquet facilities, and multi-use studios. Host to theatre performances, concerts, literary events, and an annual summer arts festival, the Shadbolt's main focus is teaching. Classes include dance, acting, music, and the visual arts. *www.shadboltcentre.com; map:H4.* &

Theatre Under the Stars

MALKIN BOWL, STANLEY PARK, WEST END; 604/687-0174

A summer tradition, Theatre Under the Stars is Canada's only truly open-air theatre. Two Broadway musicals are offered in repertory each summer, and casts feature a combination of professional and amateur performers, lending the event an enthusiasm that makes for perfect family entertainment. Festival seating accommodates some 1,500 people, with space for another 400 to bring a blanket and cozy up on the grass. With a spectacular backdrop of forest, stars, and moon, who could ask for anything more? *Mid-July–mid-Aug; www.tuts.bc.ca; map:Q1.* &

Vancouver East Cultural Centre

1895 VENABLES ST, EAST VANCOUVER; 604/254-9578

Beautifully restored in 1973, this 1914 church began its second face-lift in 2007, maintaining all its heritage attributes while creating a new studio, theatre, and box office. The centre, known to locals as the "Cultch," continues year-round programming throughout renovations, which will be complete in 2009, and remains one of Vancouver's most intriguing performance venues, where the tried-and-true shares the stage with the brand-new and where diversity is the key ingredient in programming. A supportive rental facility for local theatre, dance, and music presenters, the facility has hosted more than 8,000 performances and welcomed nearly two million visitors in its 35-year history. Daring dance, alternative theatre, and performance art, as well as music to keep your toes tapping or your heart swelling, all come alive in this cultural landmark. *www.vecc.bc.ca; map:E2.* &

CREATIVE COLLABORATIONS: SEE SEVEN

Artist-driven and collaborative in spirit, **SEE SEVEN** (www.seeseven.bc.ca) was inaugurated in 1997 as a joint initiative for Vancouver's independent theatre community to raise awareness, build audiences, and share resources. See Seven is known for provocative, relevant, and challenging work, reaching out to the performing arts community at large for productions in which art and risk are at the forefront.

See Seven uses membership fees and other resources to promote its member theatres throughout the season, and the power of collective marketing attracts an ever-growing and diversified audience. Attendees purchase a season pass, which, as the name suggests, allows them to "see seven" professional theatre performances at an impressively discounted rate.

Member participants include Sea Theatre, Theatre Conspiracy, the Firehall Arts Centre, Ruby Slippers Theatre, urban ink productions, Pi Theatre, Theatre Replacement, Solo Collective, Touchstone Theatre, and Rumble Productions, to name just a few from the past 10 years.

—Sherry McGarvie

Vancouver International Fringe Festival

VARIOUS LOCATIONS, GRANVILLE ISLAND; 604/257-0350
Voted Vancouver's Best Arts Festival five years in a row, the Vancouver International Fringe Festival delivers an eclectic mix of theatrical offerings from the ridiculous to the sublime. Featuring all ages and levels of experience and accepted on a nonjuried basis, 100-odd companies present at least 500 performances, over 11 days in 10 indoor theatres (some are wheelchair-accessible) on and around Granville Island. Admission is extremely reasonable and varies from event to event. *www.vancouverfringe.com; map:Q6.*

Vancouver New Play Festival

1398 CARTWRIGHT ST, GRANVILLE ISLAND; 604/685-6228
Put yourself at the centre of what's new in Canadian theatre! For a week each spring, the Vancouver New Play Festival on Granville Island is your chance to see, hear, and experience the newest works from some of Canada's hottest playwrights. Actors take the stage, script in hand, in these preview presentations of eight new plays, giving an insider's look at the future of Canadian theatre. Admission to all events is by donation; reservations are highly recommended. *May; www.playwrightstheatre.com; mapQ6.* &

Vancouver Playhouse

HAMILTON ST AT DUNSMUIR ST, DOWNTOWN; 604/873-3311
The Vancouver Playhouse Theatre Company produces six shows during its
fall-through-spring season. The largest regional theatre company in western
Canada, it blends the classic and the modern in its repertoire, including Canadian premieres and Broadway plays. The 670-seat theatre is home to many
of Canada's finest actors, and productions are invariably top quality, with
spectacular sets, luscious costumes, and terrific soundscapes. The Playhouse
is also home to the Friends of Chamber Music, the Vancouver Recital Society
(see Classical Music and Opera in this chapter), and many dance companies.
Oct–May; www.vancouverplayhouse.com; map:T4. &

Vancouver TheatreSports League

1585 JOHNSTON ST, GRANVILLE ISLAND; 604/738-7013
Vancouver TheatreSports League is an international phenomenon, producing
and staging some of the most daring and innovative improv in the world, performing to more than 200,000 enthusiasts yearly, four nights a week. Boasting six International Improv Comedy Awards, TheatreSports offers hilarious,
affordable entertainment at Granville Island's Arts Club New Revue Stage.
On any given night, various members of the 30-plus, very odd troupe might
improvise on a specific theme, satirize the hottest TV shows, or stage competitions in which teams vie for approval as they create vignettes based on audience suggestions. Performances are for mature audiences; under 19 must be
accompanied by an adult. *Year-round; Wed–Sat; www.vtsl.com; map:Q6.* &

Classical Music and Opera

Vancouver's classical music community continues to produce and present world-
class works from the international repertoire. Institutions such as the Vancouver
Symphony and Vancouver Opera (the second-largest company in Canada) attract
ever more diverse audiences, and smaller choral and chamber music groups are
flourishing. Both amateur and professional groups—including Chor Leoni Men's
Choir, the Elektra Women's Choir, Musica Intima, the Vancouver Bach Choir, the
Vancouver Cantata Singers, the Vancouver Chamber Choir, and Vetta Chamber
Music—perform at theatres, hotels, churches, and community centres throughout
the city. Several groups regularly tour Europe and North America and have won
prestigious international awards. For classical, opera, and choral events listings, call
the **ARTS HOTLINE** (604/684-ARTS) or visit **ALLIANCE FOR ARTS** (www.alliance
forarts.com) for links to their member Web sites. Listed below are some of the main
venues, series, and organizations that enliven Vancouver's classical music scene.

Chan Centre for the Performing Arts

6265 CRESCENT RD, UBC, WEST SIDE; 604/822-2697
The Chan Centre for the Performing Arts at the University of British Columbia campus has earned an international reputation for its striking design and

stellar acoustics. Hosting year-round performances by local, national, and international orchestras, chamber groups, choirs, and festivals, its 1,400-seat Chan Shun Concert Hall is regarded as one of the continent's finest concert spaces. During a typical season, the programme might include a visit from Le Mystère des Voix Bulgares (the Bulgarian State Female Vocal Choir), a series of summer concerts by the Vancouver Symphony Orchestra (see review in this section), and several distinguished soloists presented by the Vancouver Recital Society (see review in this section). The Chan Centre also hosts concerts by the UBC School of Music, and its 300-capacity TELUS Studio Theatre hosts plays by Theatre at UBC. *Year-round; www.chancentre.com; map:A2.* &

Chinese Cultural Centre

50 E PENDER ST, CHINATOWN; 604/658-8850
With events from violin recitals to Chinese opera to a French film festival, the Chinese Cultural Centre is truly multicultural. Local and international groups from the worldwide Chinese community also use the centre as a venue for fascinating exhibitions of paintings and photography, as well as book launchings and dance programmes. The centre also offers classes in language, and arts and crafts. *www.cccvan.shawbiz.ca; map:V4.* &

Early Music Vancouver

VARIOUS LOCATIONS; 604/732-1610
More and more converts are discovering the sublime sounds of Early Music Vancouver, which presents a series of performances from fall through spring, including various chamber orchestras, choirs, and other recitals in concert halls and churches throughout the city. Music from the Middle Ages to the 18th century is performed on original instruments by some of the finest early-music specialists. As an extension of the organization's main season, the Early Music Summer Festival (mid-July–mid-Aug) presents the sounds of harpsichords, lutes, and violas da gamba on the UBC campus. Local and international proponents of early music share the stage and classrooms, providing a cornucopia of musical pleasures for everyone from the novice listener to the advanced music scholar. *Oct–May; www.earlymusic.bc.ca.* &

Enchanted Evenings

DR. SUN YAT-SEN CLASSICAL CHINESE GARDEN, CHINATOWN; 604/662-3207
During summer, the Dr. Sun Yat-Sen Classical Chinese Garden (see Gardens in the Exploring chapter) presents a Friday-night concert series. It includes recitals of Asian classical music performed on traditional instruments by groups such as Silk Road and the Vancouver Chinese Music Ensemble. Illuminated by lanterns, the grounds provide a soft background for music and a chance to wander through the garden. *Fri July–Sept; www.vancouverchinese garden.com; map:V4.* &

PERFORMING ARTS

Friends of Chamber Music

**VANCOUVER PLAYHOUSE, HAMILTON ST AT DUNSMUIR ST,
DOWNTOWN; 604/437-5747**
Celebrating its 60th season, the Friends of Chamber Music presents the
world's premier chamber music ensembles during this 10-concert series that
takes place fall through spring. Since 1954, the company has also helped build
the careers of emerging ensembles, hosting the annual Young Musicians competition. Devotees of chamber music may feel they have discovered manna
with this 10-concert festival that features such groups as the Emerson String
Quartet. The group has received accolades in the past for its special presentation of the complete Beethoven quartets, featuring the renowned Bartók
String Quartet. *Tues Oct–Apr; www.friendsofchambermusic.ca; map:T4.* &

Music in the Morning

**VANCOUVER ACADEMY OF MUSIC, 1270 CHESTNUT ST,
VANIER PARK, WEST SIDE; 604/873-4612**
Music in the Morning is a distinctive morning concert series that inspires its
audiences with masterpieces of the past, while challenging them with music
of our time performed by the finest local, national, and international talent.
Born in the living room of artistic director June Goldsmith over two decades
ago, Music in the Morning fills a unique niche in the city of Vancouver,
appealing to people who prefer their cultural events with their coffee. So
successful in its programming, Music in the Morning has expanded its mandate to include a Composers and Coffee education series, Rush Hour for the
downtown crowd, Family Musik for the whole family, outreach programmes
in the community and school system, and special events in larger venues.
Sept–Apr; www.musicinthemorning.org; map:P5. &

Vancouver New Music

VARIOUS LOCATIONS; 604/633-0861
From indie to abstract, acoustic to outlandish, to minimalism at its most
sublime, Vancouver New Music has earned a reputation for presenting the
world's hottest composers of contemporary music. At any time during its fall-
to-spring season, you may witness music history in the making. Vancouver
New Music commissions and premieres new works by Canadian composers,
such as Hildegard Westerkamp, Jocelyn Morlock, Stefan Smulovitz, and Stefan Udell. The society also presents the annual Vancouver New Music Festival, an international conglomerate of some of the most innovative voices in
music today. *Oct–Mar; www.newmusic.org.* &

Vancouver Opera

**QUEEN ELIZABETH THEATRE, HAMILTON ST AT W GEORGIA ST,
DOWNTOWN; 604/683-0222**
Opera is now one of the hippest tickets in town, and audiences flock to
Vancouver Opera, the result of clever marketing, ongoing reevaluation of
the organization's artistic vision, and the influence of megamusicals. The

company presents four or five productions each season (a mix of contemporary and traditional works), as well as a fund-raising gala concert and recitals by distinguished soloists such as Richard Margison and Bryn Terfel. The sets are spectacular, and the artists—including some of North America's brightest singing talents—are of international calibre. If you present a current transit stub or a monthly pass, you receive 10 percent off your next ticket to a performance. *Nov–May; www.vancouveropera.ca; map:T4.* &

Vancouver Recital Society

VARIOUS LOCATIONS; 604/602-0363

As one of the few recital series in North America dedicated to presenting international artists, both emerging and established, the Vancouver Recital Society has built an international reputation for innovation and excellence in programming. The society, guided by founder and artistic director Leila Getz, has presented such luminaries—long before they became household names—as Cecilia Bartoli, Maxim Vengerov, Yo-Yo Ma, András Schiff, and Bryn Terfel and championed such Canadian musicians as Angela Cheng, Richard Raymond, and Jon Kimura Parker. *Oct–May; www.vanrecital.com.* &

Vancouver Symphony Orchestra

ORPHEUM THEATRE, GRANVILLE ST AT SMITHE ST, DOWNTOWN; 604/876-3434

This doyen of the classical music scene has its home in the magnificent 1927 Orpheum Theatre, where thick red carpets, ornate rococo gilding, and sweeping staircases transport you to an earlier, more gracious era. Under the leadership of music director Bramwell Tovey, the 74-member orchestra continues to pursue new artistic heights. More than 10 subscription series offer music lovers a wide variety of aural delicacies, from traditional symphonic fare to a more adventurous repertoire to pops concerts featuring Dixieland, Celtic fiddling, and Latin jazz. A focus on Canadian artists and compositions has added a new dimension to the VSO's offerings, although a number of illustrious soloists, such as Yo-Yo Ma and Dame Evelyn Glennie, continue to grace the Orpheum stage. The popular Kids' Koncerts and Tiny Tots Series provide opportunity for children to experience symphonic music in a fun, relaxed atmosphere. In addition to its main-stage concerts and special events, the VSO performs in the parks of the Lower Mainland during summer. The orchestra also plays series throughout the Lower Mainland surrounding Vancouver, regularly tours the province, and is heard cross-country 18 times a year on CBC radio. *Sept–June; www.vancouversymphony.ca; map:S4.* &

Dance

Vancouver has established a reputation as a world centre of contemporary dance, attracting performers and independent choreographers from all over Canada, the United States, and abroad, who offer lively and original performances to

CITY ARTS AND LECTURES

Nothing whets the appetite more than an evening of brain stimulation. Lectures, workshops, and lively debates not only take participants to the heart of what Vancouver is, they help define Vancouver's place in the world of ideas and culture.

The **VANCOUVER ART GALLERY** (750 Hornby St, Downtown; 604/662-4719; www.vanartgallery.bc.ca) regularly hosts curator's lectures and artist's talks in conjunction with their major exhibitions. Also at the VAG, during spring and summer seasons, tours are offered of selected current exhibitions as they premiere. Several other galleries throughout the city host panel discussions and artist's lectures, among them the **CHARLES H. SCOTT GALLERY** (www.chscott.eciad.ca), the **MORRIS AND HELEN BELKIN GALLERY** (www.belkin.ubc.ca), **PRESENTATION HOUSE GALLERY** (www.presentationhousegall.com), and the **WESTERN FRONT** (www.front.bc.ca). For updates on art gallery lectures, contact the **ALLIANCE FOR ARTS AND CULTURE** (604/681-3535; www.allianceforarts.com).

During the academic year, **SIMON FRASER UNIVERSITY**'s downtown Harbour Centre campus (515 W Hastings St, Downtown; 778/782-5100; www.sfu.ca/city) sponsors a wide variety of free public lectures as part of the **CITY PROGRAM**'s attempts to foster a better understanding of Vancouver and its future. While lectures on city planning and regional economic development might sound a little dry, there are also short-term, inexpensive courses in urban photography, urban landscape drawing, and Vancouver architecture.

Light Resource Lectures on Architecture & Design is a long-running and popular series of free lectures between October and April sponsored by the **ARCHITECTURAL INSTITUTE OF BRITISH COLUMBIA** (100-440 Cambie St, Downtown; 604/683-8588; www.aibc.ca; map:U4) as part of its aim to increase public awareness of the practise of architecture. The series, which brings in prestigious guest speakers from as far away as Helsinki and Tokyo, encourages public debate about Vancouver's triumphs and tragedies in contemporary architecture and design.

appreciative audiences. Look for regular programmes by Vancouver-based choreographers **KAREN JAMIESON** (www.kjdance.ca), **JUDITH MARCUSE** (www.jmprojects.ca), and **JENNIFER MASCALL** (www.mascalldance.ca), as well as companies such as **EDAM DANCE** (www.edamdance.org), the **HOLY BODY TATTOO** (www.holybodytattoo.org), **KOKORO DANCE** (www.kokoro.ca), and many more. For the most comprehensive information on upcoming dance events, contact the umbrella organization, **DANCE CENTRE** (604/606-6400; www.thedancecentre.ca). The following are the main dance venues, companies, festivals, and series in Vancouver.

A similar series is the Builders of Vancouver panel discussions on a wide range of topics, from art in public space to street-level architecture. Lectures are held at UBC at Robson Square (800 Robson St, Downtown; 604/683-8588; www. lecturesonarchitecture.net; map:S4).

If you're game for a night at the opera, why not an afternoon? Installments of the **WESTERN CANADIAN OPERA SOCIETY**'s (www.operaclub.net; 604/942-6646) Sunday series—held monthly starting at 2pm from September to June—could include historical talks, audiovisual presentations, and an aria or two from a top-flight soprano. For its annual Western Canadian Opera Lecture, the society hosts a luminary from the international opera world. The club also organizes group opera tours. Meetings are held at SFU's Harbour Centre campus (515 W Hastings St; 604/291-5000; map:T3).

PHILOSOPHERS' CAFÉ (www.sfu.ca/philosopherscafe) holds public discussions year-round in restaurants, coffee shops, and bookstores throughout Vancouver—even at the beach in summer, proving that philosophy needn't be boring or stuffy. An invited guest is introduced and briefly presents the evening's issue. Topics can cover a wide range, from the proverbial quest for God to reality TV. A moderator then opens the floor for some lively debate. There's no need for any formal training, as long as you can eat, drink, and carry on conversation.

UNIQUE LIVES & EXPERIENCES (www.uniquelives.com) brings high-calibre guests such as Adrienne Clarkson, Lily Tomlin, Rita Moreno, and Caroline Kennedy to the Vancouver chapter of North America's foremost women's lecture series. Each formidable speaker shares stories from her life experiences, then takes questions from the audience. The monthly evenings typically run September through June at the **ORPHEUM THEATRE** (Granville St at Smithe St, Downtown; map:S4). Tickets are available from the **EVENTS UNLIMITED BOX OFFICE** (877/973-8124 toll free) or on the Web site.

—Nick Rockel, Anya MacLeod, and Sherry McGarvie

Ballet British Columbia

**QUEEN ELIZABETH THEATRE, HAMILTON ST AT
W GEORGIA ST, DOWNTOWN; 604/732-5003**

Since 1986, BC's premier contemporary ballet company has earned a glowing reputation for its bold, exciting performances. Under the artistic directorship of noted choreographer John Alleyne, Ballet BC offers dance enthusiasts a potpourri of modern and classical dance each fall through spring as part of its popular danceAlive! series. Guests range from the Royal Winnipeg Ballet to the Moscow Classical Ballet, and the company has performed works from such masters as George Balanchine, Martha Graham, and Twyla Tharp. The company itself performs two programmes each season, including Canadian and world premieres of innovative works. Alleyne's choreography has raised the company's national and international profile through such celebrated works as the *Don Juan Variations*, *The Faerie Queen*, *Orpheus*, *Scheherazade*, *Carmina Burana*, *The Rite of Spring*, and *A Streetcar Named Desire*. *Sept–May; www.balletbc.com; map:T4.* &

Dancing on the Edge Festival

VARIOUS LOCATIONS; 604/689-0926

Celebrating its 20th anniversary in 2008, this two-week celebration of new dance, held each summer, attracts first-rate talent from around the globe. Always fresh and daring, its 60 to 70 shows are offered from early afternoon to the wee hours of the morning. In addition, guest choreographers offer scheduled classes throughout the festival, as well as preshow chats and dance talks. Venues can be as adventurous as dance itself—from Vancouver's breathtaking beaches to city street corners. Most performances, however, take place on the traditional stages of the Firehall Arts Centre (280 E Cordova St, East Side; 604/689-0926; www.firehall.org; map:V4) and the Scotiabank Dance Centre (677 Davie St, Downtown; 604/606-6400; www.thedance centre.ca; map:R5). *July; www.dancingontheedge.org.* &

Vancouver East Cultural Centre

1895 VENABLES ST, EAST VANCOUVER; 604/254-9578

The Vancouver East Cultural Centre presents the finest Canada has to offer in contemporary dance each fall to spring. If it's on the cutting edge, you'll find it at the "Cultch." Past programmes have included innovative dance and theatre artists, including La La La Human Steps, Big Bang, Paul-André Fortier, and Peggy Baker, as well as the cream of Vancouver's rich dance scene and some international artists. See also Theatre in this chapter. *Sept–June; www.vecc.bc.ca; map:E2.* &

Vancouver International Dance Festival

VARIOUS LOCATIONS; 604/662-7441

Since 2000, the Vancouver International Dance Festival has put Vancouver on the international map of dance through the presentation of performances and workshops by local, national, and international dance artists. Provocative, inspirational, and jaw-dropping performances and workshops take place in studios and on stages throughout the city each spring. From belly dancing to tap, butoh to ballet, flamenco to free-form, there is something to keep everyone on their feet. *Late Feb–1st week of Apr; www.vidf.ca.* &

Film

Once called Hollywood North, Vancouver has grown up in the movie industry and is now known as simply one of the best places to make movies—anywhere. It has also developed its own infrastructure of talented and award-winning producers, editors, directors, writers, and actors working on their own projects from development through production.

As far back as 1935, when Louis B. Mayer of MGM Studios sent crews to shoot the Mountie scenes for the classic film *Rose Marie*, Vancouver has provided great locations that appear on the screen as the streets of New York, the mountains of Montana, and, yes, even Hollywood itself.

Locals have gotten used to seeing the stars that come with all these productions, but celebrity spotting is still a popular pastime. The list of stars who have both worked and played in the area recently continues to be impressive: Jessica Alba, Jennifer Aniston, David Arquette, Halle Berry, Anna Faris, Hugh Jackman, Ashley Judd, Ben Kingsley, Ashton Kutcher, and Michelle Pfeiffer, to name but a few.

Vancouver has served as the centre for such recent films as *I, Robot*, *Spy Game*, the *X-Men* series, the *Scary Movie* series, *Black Christmas*, *The Exorcism of Emily Rose*, *Unforgettable*, *Catwoman*, *Fantastic Four*, *The Core*, *The Invisible*, *Mission to Mars*, and *Juno*. Vancouver has also become home to a growing number of TV series and movies of the week, and while *Stargate SG-1* may have ended, *Stargate Atlantis* is still in production in Vancouver. *Battlestar Galactica*, *Men in Trees*, *Eureka*, *Intelligence*, *Smallville*, *4400*, *The L Word*, *Reaper*, and *Supernatural* are just a few shows in production now. Because it offers quick and central access to a wide variety of stunning landscapes, Vancouver has also developed a reputation for its downtown scenes and alleyway locations. Some of the most frequently filmed locations are the steps of the Vancouver Art Gallery on Robson Street, Gastown, and the alley south of Hastings Street between Cambie and Abbott streets. Anytime you see the long white trailers and people with headsets keeping a watchful eye, or a line of cars with foreign license plates, you know there is some filming in progress. For a listing of what's filming now in BC, contact the **BC FILM COMMISSION HOT LINE** (604/660-3569; www.bcfilmcommission.com). Another news source is industry magazine **REEL WEST DIGEST** (www.reelwest.com).

If you want to be a film extra, Vancouver is the place to be. While you'll spend many long, tedious hours waiting for your scene, what better way to watch the making of a movie close-up? It's not only an educational experience; you'll be fed well while making a decent day's wages. Who knows? You might make it past the cutting room floor and see yourself on the big screen. Several agencies handle extra casting in Vancouver, including **LOCAL COLOR** (604/685-0315) and **KEYSTONE EXTRAS** (604/685-2218). Head shots are a must, and there is usually a onetime fee of around $25 to register. For more than just extra work, check out several talent agencies in town, including **CHARACTERS** (604/733-9800), **LUCAS TALENT** (604/685-0345), **TWENTY-FIRST CENTURY ARTISTS INC** (604/251-6070), and **HODGSON MANAGEMENT GROUP** (604/687-7676).

Film aficionados frequent the **DUNBAR THEATRE** (4555 Dunbar St, West Side; 604/228-9912; map:B3), the **PARK THEATRE** (3440 Cambie St, South Vancouver;

604/290-0500; map:D3), the **VARSITY THEATRE** (4375 W 10th Ave, West Side; 604/222-2235; map:B3), and **FIFTH AVENUE CINEMAS** (2110 Burrard St, West Side; 604/734-7469; map:P7), all of which screen an eclectic selection of first-run and repertory independent movies. For $12, patrons of the Fifth Avenue and Park cinemas can purchase an Alliance Cinemas one-year membership at the box office of either theatre. The membership includes reduced admission prices at both theatres, plus concession stand discounts. The **RIDGE THEATRE** (3131 Arbutus St, West Side; 604/738-6311; www.ridgetheatre.com; map:C3), the **HOLLYWOOD THEATRE** (3123 W Broadway, West Side; 604/738-3211; www.hollywoodtheatre.com; map: C3), and **DENMAN PLACE DISCOUNT CINEMA** (1737 Comox St, West End; 604/683-2201; map:P2) are home to the popular, inexpensive, second-run double bill. The **PACIFIC CINÉMATHÈQUE** (1131 Howe St, Downtown; 604/688-FILM; www.cinematheque.bc.ca; map:R4) is touted as a year-round film festival offering retrospectives of important directors, lecture series, classic foreign films, and a variety of independent and experimental Canadian films. The cinema gathers together work from countries such as Canada, France, Germany, Israel, and the UK. Screenings are evenings only, six days a week, excluding Tuesdays, when the mainstream theatres drop their prices. For a **COMPLETE LISTING OF FILMS** showing throughout the Vancouver area and theatre websites, visit www.cinemaclock.com.

Local film festivals and events, in addition to the two reviewed, include the **VANCOUVER JEWISH FILM FESTIVAL** (604/266-0245; www.vjff.org), held in May at the **NORMAN ROTHSTEIN THEATRE** (950 W 41st Ave, West Side; 604/257-5111; map:D4). In February there is the **REEL 2 REAL INTERNATIONAL FILM FESTIVAL FOR YOUTH** (604/224-6162; www.r2rfestival.org), and in early August, the **VANCOUVER QUEER FILM + VIDEO FESTIVAL** (604/844-1615; www.out onscreen.com) offers screenings of international films and videos at various venues. A popular indie-film night—and a chance for film-biz hipsters to socialize—is the **CELLULOID SOCIAL CLUB** (604/730-8090), held once a month at the **ANZA CLUB** (3 W 8th Ave, South Main; 604/876-7128; www.anzaclub.org; map:V7). In addition to being a venue for exhibitions, installations, and festival screenings, film co-op **VIDEO IN STUDIOS** (1965 Main St, South Main; 604/872-8337; www. videoinstudios.com; map:V6) hosts quarterly producer nights.

Vancouver International Film Festival (VIFF)

VARIOUS LOCATIONS; 604/683-3546

The VIFF is the third-largest film festival in North America, with more than 150,000 attendees each fall at approximately 575 screenings of 350 films from more than 50 countries. At seven centrally located theatres (some with wheelchair access), viewers can catch dramatic features, documentaries (the VIFF has the biggest documentary section of all North American festivals), comedies, and animated shorts. These are theatrically grouped under categories such as Dragons and Tigers: The Cinemas of East Asia, Climate for Change, and Canadian Images, showcasing the best of Canadian cinema. The festival also features a three-day trade forum. *Late Sept–early Oct; www. viff.org.* &

Whistler Film Festival

VARIOUS LOCATIONS IN WHISTLER; 604/935-8035

Since its inception in 2001, the Whistler Film Festival has evolved from being perceived as a regional event to being a noteworthy addition to the global film festival circuit. With more than 90 films from around the globe over five days each winter, this is becoming the event of the season. *Dec; www. whistlerfilmfestival.com.* &

Literature

Finally, the rest of the world has caught on that Vancouver is a hotbed of writing talent: authors such as Mary Novik, David Chariandy, Jen Sookfong Lee, and Timothy Taylor add their voices to the strong tradition of writing in Vancouver. Locally, the literary scene stays healthy thanks largely to the efforts of regional book and magazine publishers, a growing community of writers, and widespread enthusiasm for readings and other public events celebrating literacy. For the scoop on Vancouver writers, pick up a copy of Alan Twigg's quarterly **BC BOOKWORLD** (604/736-4011; www.bcbookworld.com), which contains profiles, interviews, gossip, literary polemics, and reviews of the latest BC books.

Complementing Vancouver's strong poetry and spoken-word venues, the city has enough reading series to satisfy even the most voracious literary appetite. **CHAPTERS BOOKSTORES** (www.chapters.ca) regularly host in-store readings and book signings (see also the Shopping chapter), as does indie favourite **PULP FICTION** (604/876-4311; www.pulpfictionbooksvancouver.com). The **VANCOUVER PUBLIC LIBRARY** (350 W Georgia St, Downtown; 604/331-3603; www. vpl.vancouver.bc.ca) is also a busy venue for local, national, and international authors.

On the first and third Monday of each month, enjoy open poetry slams at **CAFE DEUX SOLEILS** (2096 Commercial Dr, East Vancouver; 604/254-1195; www.cafe deuxsoleils.com; map:Z7), where audience members are selected to be the judges. **CAFE MONTMARTRE** (4362 Main St, South Main; 604/879-8111; map:Z7) hosts **THUNDERING WORD HEARD** each Sunday, and **PANDORA'S COLLECTIVE** (www. pandorascollective.com) hosts year-round open mics, workshops, and readings at various locations around the city.

If screenwriting is your game, the **VANCOUVER SCREENWRITERS GROUP** (www.vancouverscreenwriters.com) runs regular events, from script critiques to meet and greets. Event locations vary from the historic and often filmed **BARCLAY MANOR** (1447 Barclay St, West End) to local bars. The Web site also boasts active forums for the latest news. The **PRAXIS CENTRE FOR SCREENWRITERS** (515 W Hastings St, Ste 3120, Downtown; 778/782-7880; www.praxisfilm.com; map:T3) sponsors a range of courses and workshops on topics related to screenwriting and filmmaking, from seminars on pitching and script development through advanced screenwriting courses. Guest writers and directors have included Noel Baker, Peter Behrens, Atom Egoyan, Stuart Kaminsky, Hanif Kureishi, Sally Potter, and Tom

Rickman. Its script library of 2,000 feature films, TV series, and documentaries is an excellent resource, and access to the library is free of charge.

The events and festivals described below are major celebrations of the written word in Vancouver.

Kootenay School of Writing (KSW)

309-207 W HASTINGS ST, DOWNTOWN; 604/313-6903
This is the place to go for the extreme in experimental poetry and fiction. Obscure, obtuse, and mind-bending in its approach to writing, KSW is one of the pulses of the literary fringe. Check out the Web site for workshop and lecture information. *www.kswnet.org; map:U4.*

Sunshine Coast Festival of the Written Arts

ROCKWOOD CENTRE, SECHELT; 800/565-9631
Every summer, highly regarded Canadian authors and their fans gather at Sechelt's picturesque Rockwood Centre, on the Sunshine Coast (about 90 minutes north of Vancouver by car and ferry), for a long weekend of readings, book signings, and lively discussions over drinks. Nightly author receptions make this an excellent opportunity to mingle with the writers in an intimate setting. Canada's longest-running summer gathering of Canadian writers and readers ends with a barbecue dinner. *Aug; www.writersfestival.ca.* &

Vancouver International Writers (& Readers) Festival

GRANVILLE ISLAND; 604/681-6330
Canada's second-largest literary event, this annual six-day Granville Island festival features poets, playwrights, and novelists from across Canada and around the world each fall. Highlights include the Alma Lee Opening Night Event, the Sunday Brunch, and the Duthie Lecture, held in honour of late Vancouver bookseller Bill Duthie. In its 20-year history, the festival has presented such literary luminaries as Martin Amis, Margaret Atwood, Roddy Doyle, Timothy Findley, Tomson Highway, John Irving, Frank McCourt, Rohinton Mistry, Alice Munro, Michael Ondaatje, J. K. Rowling, Salman Rushdie, and Carol Shields, as well as innumerable regional favourites. *End of Oct; www.writersfest.bc.ca; map:Q7.* &

Word on the Street

LIBRARY SQ, 350 W GEORGIA ST, DOWNTOWN; 604/684-8266
Every fall, the downtown Vancouver Public Library and adjacent CBC Plaza host this one-day book and magazine fair, which coincides with collaborative events across Canada. Alongside more than 130 exhibitors from the West Coast publishing community, participants include literacy organizations, booksellers, comic book creators, and roving performers who bring words to life in this festival of literacy. *Last Sun in Sept; www.thewordonthestreet. ca; map:T4.* &

NIGHTLIFE

NIGHTLIFE

Nightlife by Neighbourhood

BURNABY
Mountain Shadow Pub

COQUITLAM
Boone County Country
   Cabaret

DOWNTOWN
Atlantic Trap & Gill, The
AuBar
Bacchus Piano Lounge
Caprice
Cecil Exotic Show Lounge
Ceili's Irish Pub
Century Restaurant /
   Heist Lounge
Commodore Ballroom
Crush Champagne Lounge
Doolin's Irish Pub
El Furniture Warehouse
Ginger 62
Gotham Steakhouse
   & Cocktail Bar
Granville Room
Joe Fortes Seafood
   & Chop House
Library Square
Murchie's Tea & Coffee
900 West Lounge
Plaza Club
Railway Club, The
Republic
Roxy, The
Royal, The
Sanafir
Shark Club Bar and Grill
Sip Resto Lounge

Tonic
Waves Coffee
Yale, The
Yuk Yuk's

EAST SIDE
Brickhouse Late Night
   Bistro & Bar
Cascade Room, The
Joe's Café
La Casa Gelato
No. 5 Orange
Ten Ren's Tea & Ginseng
Whip Restaurant &
   Gallery, The

GASTOWN
Alibi Room
Blarney Stone, The
Canvas Lounge
Chill Winston
Lotus Sound Lounge /
   Honey Lounge
Met, The
Modern, The
Shine
Steamworks Brewing Co.

GRANVILLE ISLAND
Backstage Lounge
Dockside Brewing
   Company

**NEW
WESTMINSTER**
Met Bar & Grill, The

**NORTH
VANCOUVER**
Sailor Hagar's Brew Pub

WEST END
Calling, The
Celebrities
Cloud 9 Piano Lounge
1181
49th Parallel Coffee
   Roasters
Gerard Lounge
Numbers
Oasis
Odyssey, The
PumpJack Pub
True Confections

WEST SIDE
Bean Around the World
Cellar Restaurant &
   Jazz Club, The
Fairview Pub
Notte's Bon Ton Pastry
   & Confectionery
Steamworks Brewing Co.
Sweet Obsession
   Cakes & Pastries
Tearoom T

YALETOWN
AFTERglow
Bar None
Dix Barbecue and Brewery
George Ultra Lounge
Richard's on Richards
Yaletown Brewing
   Company

Nightlife by Feature

BAR GAMES/ BILLIARDS

Blarney Stone, The
Brickhouse Late Night
   Bistro & Bar
Library Square
Mountain Shadow Pub
Numbers
PumpJack Pub
Sailor Hagar's Brew Pub
Shark Club Bar and Grill
Steamworks Brewing Co.

BLUES

Commodore Ballroom
Fairview Pub
Railway Club, The
Yale, The

CABARET

Commodore Ballroom

COCKTAILS/ MARTINIS

AFTERglow
Alibi Room
Brickhouse Late Night
   Bistro & Bar
Canvas Lounge
Cascade Room, The
Century Restaurant /
   Heist Lounge
Chill Winston
1181
George Ultra Lounge
Georgia Street Bar and Grill
Ginger 62
Gotham Steakhouse
   & Cocktail Bar
Granville Room
Joe Fortes Seafood
   & Chop House

Modern, The
900 West Lounge
Republic
Sanafir
Sip Resto Lounge

COFFEE, TEA, AND DESSERT

Bean Around the World
49th Parallel Coffee
   Roasters
Joe's Café
La Casa Gelato
Murchie's Tea & Coffee
Notte's Bon Ton Pastry
   & Confectionery
Sweet Obsession
   Cakes & Pastries
Tearoom T
Ten Ren's Tea & Ginseng
True Confections
Waves Coffee

COMEDY

Oasis
Yuk Yuk's

COUNTRY/FOLK

Boone County Country
   Cabaret
Railway Club, The
Roxy, The

DJ/DANCE

AuBar
Bar None
Caprice
Ceili's Irish Pub
Celebrities
Century Restaurant /
   Heist Lounge

Crush Champagne Lounge
Doolin's Irish Pub
1181
Library Square
Lotus Sound Lounge /
   Honey Lounge
Met, The
Modern, The
Numbers
Oasis
Odyssey, The
Plaza Club
Republic
Richard's on Richards
Royal, The
Shark Club Bar and Grill
Shine
Tonic

EDITORS' CHOICE

Alibi Room
Caprice
Celebrities
Dockside Brewing
   Company
1181
49th Parallel Coffee
   Roasters
George Ultra Lounge
Ginger 62
La Casa Gelato
Modern, The
Notte's Bon Ton Pastry
   & Confectionery
Republic
Sanafir
Sweet Obsession
   Cakes & Pastries
True Confections

GAY/LESBIAN
Celebrities
1181
Numbers
Oasis
Odyssey, The
PumpJack Pub

GOOD VALUE
Atlantic Trap & Gill, The
El Furniture Warehouse
Mountain Shadow Pub
Odyssey, The
Sailor Hagar's Brew Pub

HOUSE
Crush Champagne Lounge
Republic
Richard's on Richards
Sip Resto Lounge

IRISH
Blarney Stone, The
Ceili's Irish Pub
Doolin's Irish Pub

JAZZ
Bar None
Cellar Restaurant &
   Jazz Club, The
Commodore Ballroom
Fairview Pub
Georgia Street Bar and Grill
Oasis

KARAOKE
Met, The
Numbers

LATE-NIGHT EATS
AFTERglow
Alibi Room
Atlantic Trap & Gill, The
Backstage Lounge

Brickhouse Late Night
   Bistro & Bar
Calling, The
Canvas Lounge
Cascade Room, The
Cecil Exotic Show Lounge
Century Restaurant /
   Heist Lounge
Chill Winston
Cloud 9 Piano Lounge
Dix Barbecue and Brewery
Dockside Brewing
   Company
El Furniture Warehouse
Exotic Showroom
Fairview Pub
George Ultra Lounge
Gerard Lounge
Ginger 62
Gotham Steakhouse
   & Cocktail Bar
Granville Room
Joe Fortes Seafood
   & Chop House
900 West Lounge
Sailor Hagar's Brew Pub
Sanafir
Sip Resto Lounge
Steamworks Brewing Co.
Whip Restaurant &
   Gallery, The
Yaletown Brewing
   Company

LIVE MUSIC
Atlantic Trap & Gill, The
Backstage Lounge
Bar None
Blarney Stone, The
Ceili's Irish Pub
Cellar Restaurant &
   Jazz Club, The
Cloud 9 Piano Lounge

Commodore Ballroom
Doolin's Irish Pub
Fairview Pub
Georgia Street Bar and Grill
Gerard Lounge
Library Square
Met Bar & Grill, The
Mountain Shadow Pub
Oasis
Railway Club, The
Richard's on Richards
Roxy, The
Yale, The

OUTDOOR PATIOS
Backstage Lounge
Caprice
Ceili's Irish Pub
Dockside Brewing
   Company
Gotham Steakhouse
   & Cocktail Bar
Met Bar & Grill, The
Sailor Hagar's Brew Pub
Steamworks Brewing Co.
Whip Restaurant &
   Gallery, The

PEELER BARS
Cecil Exotic Show Lounge
No. 5 Orange

PIANO BARS
Bacchus Piano Lounge
Cloud 9 Piano Lounge
Georgia Street Bar and Grill
Gerard Lounge
900 West Lounge

REGGAE/
WORLD BEAT
Fairview Pub
Shine

ROCK

Commodore Ballroom
Railway Club, The
Republic
Shark Club Bar and Grill

ROMANTIC

AFTERglow
Bacchus Piano Lounge
Crush Champagne Lounge

SPORTS BARS

Library Square
Met, The
Met Bar & Grill, The
Mountain Shadow Pub
Sailor Hagar's Brew Pub
Shark Club Bar and Grill

VIEW

Backstage Lounge
Calling, The

Cloud 9 Piano Lounge
Dockside Brewing
  Company
Steamworks Brewing Co.

WINE BARS

Chill Winston
Crush Champagne Lounge
900 West Lounge

NIGHTLIFE

Change is in the air for Vancouver's nightlife scene as owners of new clubs, lounges, and bars attempt to trump each other with impressive renovations, sound systems, small-plates menus, and drink creations. Innovation is the key to success in this city, where nightclubbers are addicted to novelty. Consequently, many bar owners look to hot spots around the globe for inspiration and strive to create rooms that are reminiscent of New York, Miami, London, or even Egypt—anything to make club crawlers feel like they're experiencing something out of the ordinary.

The diversity of nightlife in a city rich with options ensures that everyone will be able to find a scene that suits their style—if you know where to look. By day, Vancouver's many distinct neighbourhoods define where you shop, eat, and sightsee: Downtown for designer clothing, Yaletown for trendy meals, the West End for ocean views from English Bay. At night, these same neighbourhoods define where you party. After dark, Yaletown is where professional urbanites move from tasteful restaurants to posh lounges for Champagne cocktails and enlightened conversation. The West End is home to a number of gay bars that range from flashy, over-the-top venues featuring drag shows to casual pubs. In Gastown, hundred-year-old buildings house cutting-edge underground dance clubs, making for an eclectic mix of old and new, while the East Side is all about down-to-earth bars and chill crowds.

The heart of the entertainment district is undoubtedly Granville Mall. Located in the centre of downtown Vancouver, this seven-block section of Granville Street has undergone a massive overhaul in the last few years as the city has experimented with closing the area to traffic in a bid to make it more pedestrian-friendly. Although the traffic-free area never quite worked, late-night venues popped up everywhere, completely taking over most of this neon strip. The 30- and 40-something jet-setters flock to the tasteful lounges, while those in their 20s cram into the dance clubs that make up this entertainment zone.

Given their notoriously fickle patrons, Vancouver nightclubs, pubs, bars, and lounges sometimes can assume a new identity—or simply disappear—almost overnight. Before visiting any of the establishments mentioned in this chapter, you might want to call ahead to make sure the circus hasn't picked up and left town. Otherwise, the best print sources for up-to-date listings are the *Georgia Straight* (www.straight.com) and the entertainment sections of the *Vancouver Sun* (www.canada.com/vancouversun), the *Province* (www.canada.com/theprovince), and 24 *Hours Vancouver* (www.vancouver.24hrs.ca). Online, **TELUS** (www.my telus.com), **CLUBVIBES** (www.clubvibes.com), and **CLUBZONE** (www.clubzone. com) all carry nightlife information for Vancouver. For daily updates of concert announcements, check out **TICKETMASTER** (www.ticketmaster.ca).

A word of caution to smokers: Provincial bylaws forbid smoking inside all commercial buildings and within a 6-metre (approximately 20-foot) radius of all doors, windows, and air intakes. With the density of buildings in Vancouver, you'll be hard-pressed to find somewhere to light up without breaking the law, so it's best to leave the cigarettes (and temptation) at home; otherwise, expect a lengthy walk to the outskirts of the core.

Music and Clubs

AuBar

674 SEYMOUR ST, DOWNTOWN; 604/648-2227

Be one of the beautiful people in this brick-walled, upscale nightclub catering to the haves and the wannabes. Once you get by the scores of bouncers doing their best Secret Service impressions, breathe a sigh of relief, grab a drink at one of three bars, and check out the crowded dance floor. It's not cheap, and the dress code is strict, but it's that air of exclusivity that draws people in. Music is hip-hop, R&B, and top 40, and the well-toned clientele are mid-20s and up. *AE, MC, V; every day; full bar; www.aubarnightclub.com; map:T4.*

Bar None

1222 HAMILTON ST, YALETOWN; 604/684-3044

A brick-and-beam Yaletown gathering place from the mists of the early '90s, this lamplit living room still has members of the well-dressed, well-coiffed, and well-toned under-40 set queuing up to arrange themselves along its lengthy bar. The stage (really a part of the floor) is occupied by a house jazz-funk band Mondays and Tuesdays; other nights it stands conspicuously empty until patrons are emboldened by the DJ's thoughtful offerings of soul, house, top 40, and other danceable grooves. Try to hang loose, but do keep your stomach sucked in. *AE, MC, V; Mon–Sat; full bar; www.donnellynightclubs.ca; map:S6.*

The Blarney Stone

216 CARRALL ST, GASTOWN; 604/687-4322

Four nights a week, the Riverdance phenomenon isn't lost on the hundreds of attractive 19- to 30-year-olds who pour into this rollicking Gastown club. The Olde Irish pub decor makes for a mead-hall atmosphere, complete with a sturdy house band eager to turn every weekend into a St. Paddy's Day celebration and every patron into an honorary native of the Emerald Isle. The crowd may be on the young side, but don't be surprised to see entire families party-ing together. *AE, MC, V; Wed–Sat; full bar; www.blarneystone.ca; map:V4.*

Boone County Country Cabaret

801 BRUNETTE AVE, COQUITLAM; 604/525-3144

Why do cowboy hats turn up at the sides? So four people can fit into a pickup—and 300 into Boone County on weekends. This place is raucous, with a cramped layout that makes it seem busier than it really is. A large square bar fills much of the back half of the place, and raised tables and a decent-size dance floor take up the rest. Depending on your skill (or your liq-uid courage), you may want to join in on some country line dancing. Week-ends are so busy you'll have to grease your chaps to slide into a standing-room spot, so mosey in early to grab a seat. *AE, MC, V; Wed–Sat; full bar; map:J3.*

Caprice

967 GRANVILLE ST, DOWNTOWN; 604/681-2114

If you're itching to try out the latest cocktail fad (Jäger Bomb, anyone?) and top 40s are your thing, then join the hordes of college coeds lining up down the block to get into Caprice. But beware: Although this place caters to stu-dents, a flannel-wearing campus bar crowd it isn't. This recently renovated nightclub has two storeys (each with its own bar), a high-energy dance floor, and a swanky VIP area that attracts more bronzed, plucked, and perfectly coiffed 19- to 25-year-olds than *Canada's Next Top Model.* Wednesday nights and weekends are busy, so submit a guest list for you and your friends through Caprice's Web site to ensure you get in. 21 and over on Saturday. *MC, V; every day; full bar; www.capricenightclub.com; map:S4.*

Ceili's Irish Pub

670 SMITHE ST, DOWNTOWN; 604/697-9199

You'd think that with Doolin's and the Blarney Stone, Vancouver wouldn't need another Irish bar—but Ceili's, which opened in early 2007, proves that just isn't so. Catering to late-20- and 30-somethings with cash to spend, its three levels consist of a restaurant, a nightclub, and a heated rooftop patio with a retractable ceiling that opens up to a stunning view of the sky on sum-mer nights. Live music throughout the week, but on Wednesday DJ Johnny Infamous spins top 40 and dance, drawing a younger crowd who arrive in complimentary limos available through prebookings on the club's Web site. *MC, V; every day; full bar; www.ceilis.com; map:S4.*

Celebrities

1022 DAVIE ST, WEST END; 604/681-6180

Outgoing bartenders, a vibrant mix of partygoers, and music that you just can't help but dance to make this one of Vancouver's most popular bars for attractive, young gay men—and their straight girlfriends. Women love this place and come in droves on Tuesday night when drinks are on special and Celebrities opens its doors for people of all sexualities. The rest of the week is just as much fun, but it's reserved for the gay male crew only. *AE, MC, V; Tues–Sun; full bar; www.celebritiesnightclub.com; map:R4.*

The Cellar Restaurant & Jazz Club

3611 W BROADWAY, WEST SIDE; 604/738-1959

Kitsilano residents flock to neighbourhood spots like the Cellar, which shakes up a residential stretch of West Broadway with live jazz six nights a week and a spicy Cajun-Louisiana menu. The raging red walls of this tiny basement club are usually covered with someone's art exhibition, while carefully placed mirrors give the welcome illusion of a second room next door. A sometimes boisterous crowd—which may be dominated by older hipsters or younger bebop aficionados, depending on the night's entertainment—pack the black booths and low-slung tables, sipping martinis that come in a color for every week of the year. Cover charge $5–$25, depending on the players, which can range from local up-and-comers to international stars. *AE, MC, V; every day; full bar; www.cellarjazz.com; map:C3.*

Commodore Ballroom

868 GRANVILLE ST, DOWNTOWN; 604/739-SHOW

This legendary live venue with a 900-person capacity brings in some of the world's best rock, pop, blues, and jazz artists. The club is also a coveted stage for up-and-coming and established local acts. While the room has been restored to an opulent version of its 1930s Art Deco glory (with an updated lighting and sound system, of course), the fabulously springy dance floor remains the same. *AE, MC, V; 5–7 nights a week (call for concert dates); full bar; www.livenation.com; map:S4.*

Crush Champagne Lounge

1180 GRANVILLE ST, DOWNTOWN; 604/684-0355

A sexy Miami vibe and an extensive—and pricey—Champagne list draws an older crowd to Crush, where most people are 25 and up. Draped chiffon and flickering candles set a sleek lounge area apart from the white-hot dance floor where patrons groove to house and hip-hop. Saturday nights feature live percussionists performing with popular DJs, and there is no cover is if you present a bill from Sip (down the street) at the door. *MC, V; Wed–Sat; full bar; www. crushlounge.ca; map:S5.*

Doolin's Irish Pub

654 NELSON ST, DOWNTOWN; 604/605-4343

Amidst the sea of upscale lounges and trendy nightclubs at Granville Mall, Doolin's stands out as the place to kick back and enjoy a pint. The unpretentious decor and offbeat mix of Celtic and rock music make for a fun, friendly crowd and, more often than not, a good old-fashioned Irish singalong. Live music and no cover Sunday to Thursday; DJs on Friday and Saturday nights with cover in effect. *AE, MC, V; every day; full bar; www. doolins.ca; map:S5.*

AFTER HOURS

Vancouver's after-hours scene was hugely popular in the '90s, but over the past 10 years it has slowly faded into the background of the city's nightlife. But in a city where mountains, forests, and beaches are right at your doorstep and exercise is practically a religion, you shouldn't be too shocked to learn that most Vancouver-ites prefer to skip the late-night parties in favour of early-morning yoga classes.

That said, some hard-core clubgoers do choose to stay up until the wee hours, dancing the night away at various locations across the city. The vast majority of this partying goes on at illegal raves, where drug use runs rampant and shady characters dominate the scene. However, there's still fun to be had for law-abiding partyers after the clubs close down around 2am to 3am—that is, if you have money to spend. At the two legal after-hours bars, the cover charge can be up to $30, because they aren't licensed to sell alcohol after 3am. Expect to pay around five bucks a pop for energy drinks.

GORG-O-MISH (695 Smithe St, Downtown; 604/694-9007)

About as upscale as after hours gets in Vancouver; a modern room with plush white leather couches and racy red walls draped in white chiffon. Often compared to European nightclubs, Gorg-o-Mish is known for its amazing sound system that pumps music (spun by some of the city's top DJs) through the bar until well after dawn breaks for a crowd that just won't quit. After 3am, the line gets bigger and the cover charge does too, so come early. *2:30am–10am Fri–Sat; map:S4.*

WORLD/CLUB 816 (816 Granville St, Downtown)

Conveniently located right in the heat of the action on Granville Mall. A grungy basement bar, it's not the swankiest place to go, but the gay crowd that fills it on weekends doesn't seem to mind. House, trance, and hard dance are played by DJs that rotate weekly, keeping the music selection fresh. *12am–6am Fri–Sat; map:S4.*

—Tara Schmidt

1181

1181 DAVIE ST, WEST END; 604/687-3991

Although many of Vancouver's gay bars focus solely on what it means to be a *gay* bar, 1181 focuses on what it means to be a *great* bar—and as a result, it stands out from the rest. The stylish interior designed by local firm Battersby Howat is inviting and comfortable, the cocktails are expertly mixed, and the music is a mix of house, disco, and funk. And the gay thing? It happened all on its own. *AE, MC, V; every day; full bar; www.tightlounge.com; map:Q4.*

Fairview Pub

898 W BROADWAY (RAMADA INN), WEST SIDE; 604/872-1262

A Ramada may seem like an unusual location for a live music club, but this is one bar that is dedicated to showcasing some of the city's best jazz, rock 'n' roll, R&B, blues, funk, and reggae bands. Although not comfy enough to be considered intimate, the room is just the right size, and there's hardly a bad seat in the house. A small dance floor sits in front of the tiny stage, and when the band gets cooking, so does the crowd. The atmosphere is casual, so come as you are. Live music on Wednesday through Saturday as well as Monday nights. *AE, DC, DIS, V; every day; full bar; www.fairviewpub.ca; map:S8.*

Library Square

300 W GEORGIA ST, DOWNTOWN; 604/633-9644

Although it's located at Vancouver's landmark Central Library, the Library Square pub couldn't be less like its quiet and subdued namesake. Instead of bookshelves lining the walls in this sleek room, flat-screen TVs broadcast a variety of sports while foosball and pool tables take the place of study carrels. In a surprising twist for a sports bar, local artists are featured each month, so while the crowd might be boisterous hockey fans one night, it can be artsy folk conversing over cocktails the next. On weekends, it turns into a nightclub when live DJs and bands play to a decently busy dance floor. *AE, MC, V; every day; full bar; www.librarysquare.ca; map:T4.*

Lotus Sound Lounge / Honey Lounge

455 ABBOTT ST (HERITAGE HOUSE HOTEL), GASTOWN; 604/685-7777

Perched where Chinatown, skid row, and downtown converge, the anti-quated Lotus Hotel is a bright spot in a blighted part of town. Down a flight of marble stairs is the Lotus Sound Lounge, a small, pillared room where the ceiling is low, the decor plush, and the attitude high. A mixed crowd dances to drum 'n' bass, deep house, old-school break beats, and funk on the small-ish dance floor Mondays through Saturdays. Upstairs is the more low-key Honey Lounge, where you can sink into an armchair and reminisce about your misspent youth. *MC, V; every day; full bar; www.markjamesgroup.com/lotus_hotel.html; map:U4.*

The Met

320 ABBOTT ST, GASTOWN; 604/915-5336

There's something refreshing about an unpretentious neighbourhood bar that stakes its reputation on nothing more than good music, good beer, and good times. Enjoy the game on one of their 14 screens during the week, then party with DJ My!Gay!Husband! on the weekend. Or rustle up some liquid courage and take your turn at karaoke on Wednesday night. *MC, V; every day; full bar; map:U4.*

The Modern

7 ALEXANDER ST, GASTOWN; 604/647-0121

When your bar is located in a heritage building, you can pay homage to the days of old with stately decor and pleasant background music that encourages polite conversation (been there, done that). Or you can do what legendary hospitality management company Donnelly has done with the recently opened Modern, and revitalize the space into a contemporary nightclub complete with smoked glass, mirrors, LEDs, and a state-of-the-art sound system. With its edgy design, discriminating taste in music, and DJs and bartenders that number among the city's best, this has rapidly become one of the crown jewels of Vancouver nightlife. *AE, MC, V; Thurs–Sat; full bar; www.donnellynightclubs. ca; map:V3.*

Numbers

1042 DAVIE ST, WEST END; 604/685-4077

Regulars of all ages squeeze into denim and leather and cram into a room that's as intriguing as the gay clientele. Corridors connect five levels and three bars. Grab a stool down below in the Kok-Pit, or head up top and take a shot on one of the pool tables. The tunes are cranked up at 10pm nightly, and the midlevel dance floor fills until closing with swaying bodies. Cover varies depending on the day and time of night. *AE, MC, V; every day; full bar; www. numbers.ca; map:R5.*

Oasis

1240 THURLOW ST, WEST END; 604/685-1724

Oasis is a funky club that refuses to label itself—instead, choosing to be everything to everybody: a self-proclaimed "dirty party" spot for gays, lesbians, and adventurous straight folk on Tuesday; a live jazz venue for a mixed crowd on Wednesday; a comedy lounge with the occasional drag show on Thursday; a dance haven with topless bartenders on Friday. Pick a night according to your personal preference, or try them all out: we guarantee you won't get bored. *AE, MC, V; every day; full bar; www.oasisvancouver.com; map:Q4.*

The Odyssey

1251 HOWE ST, WEST END; 604/689-5256

At the Odyssey, a large contingent of bisexuals mingle with gays and a growing number of straight patrons, which sometimes motivates management to pluck gay people from the ever-present lineup and usher them through the door. Work up a sweat on the dance floor and then cool off by stepping outside to the rear garden. Or, if you've put in your time at the gym, strip naked and lather yourself in an elevated shower, starting at midnight on Thursdays. Also features drag shows and $3 "anything from the bar" drinks on Monday night. *AE, MC, V; every day; full bar; map:R5.*

Plaza Club

881 GRANVILLE ST (GRANVILLE MALL), DOWNTOWN; 604/646-0064

One of the city's larger venues, Plaza is a refreshing break from the many cramped clubs that pack you in like sardines. With a soaring ceiling and an open floor plan that orients everything, from the second-floor balcony to the first-floor booths and stage, toward the circular bar in the centre of the room, it gives you much-needed breathing space for enjoying the crowds without having them practically sitting in your lap. Weekends are lively when a youthful crew dances up a storm until the wee hours. *MC, V; every day; full bar; www.plazaclub.net.*

The Railway Club

579 DUNSMUIR ST, DOWNTOWN; 604/681-1625

This casual, second-storey spot is long and narrow, with a large, long bar cutting the room in two. The caboose shape makes it an intimate setting for innovative live entertainment, which over the years has included dozens of up-and-coming rock, pop, folk, and blues artists. Try to arrive early enough to grab a seat in the front section next to the stage; chances are, you'll be glad you did. Although the Railway is a club, nonmembers are welcome, at a slightly higher cover charge. *AE, MC, V; every day; full bar; www.therailwayclub.com; map:T4.*

Republic

958 GRANVILLE ST (GRANVILLE MALL), DOWNTOWN; 604/669-3266

Breaking out of the Vancouver mold where "British" means indie music in dark, dreary underground haunts, Republic shows an upscale side of London chic that's found nowhere else in the city. At street level, the well-heeled crowd dances beneath chandeliers and sips martinis at a bar that runs the length of the room; the second floor boasts another bar, a VIP lounge with table service, and an enclosed patio overlooking the bustling street below. One of the only clubs guaranteed to be busy every night of the week. *AE, MC, V; every day; full bar; www.donnellynightclubs.ca; map:S4.*

Richard's on Richards

1036 RICHARDS ST, YALETOWN; 604/687-6794

Better known as Dick's on Dicks, this is Vancouver's quintessential "meet market," a place where young folks who drive expensive cars come to boogie down to house DJs and add some zest to their social lives. Richard's is also a popular and intimate live venue, with the accent on local groups and some hot touring artists. The second level offers a bird's-eye view of the dance floor, so if you're wearing something flimsy and skintight, count on being ogled from above. Special events throughout the week; regular dance nights on weekends only, so expect long lines. *AE, MC, V; Fri–Sat; full bar; www. richardsonrichards.com; map:S5.*

The Roxy

932 GRANVILLE ST, DOWNTOWN; 604/331-7999

After the young suburbanites have hit the mall and the college crowd has hit the books, they all hit the Roxy for classic rock. This place has been drawing massive lineups since forever, and its owners aren't about to mess with a simple but successful formula. Behind four bars, the gin slingers do their *Cocktail*-era Tom Cruise imitations, juggling joy juice, catching bottles behind their backs, and clanging a hanging bell whenever a generous donation makes its way into their tip jar. A pair of fiendishly competent cover bands split the week. Casual dress, with the latest Robson Street looks in abundance. *AE, MC, V; every day; full bar; www.roxyvan.com; map:S4.*

The Royal

1029 GRANVILLE ST, DOWNTOWN; 604/685-7527

Join college students and backpackers from the hostel above the Royal in the club's seemingly endless and slow-moving line. Once you're inside (assuming you eventually get in, that is), the vibe is casual but the young crowd keeps the party alive by dancing anywhere and everywhere: on the stage, on the pole, in the cage, and sometimes atop the bar. The decor is lacking and the restrooms can be scary, but brave it in the name of having a good time. *MC, V; every day; full bar; www.theroyal.ca; map:S4*

Shark Club Bar and Grill

180 W GEORGIA ST, DOWNTOWN; 604/687-4275

Frantically busy when the Canucks play home games at nearby GM Place, the Shark Club is an upscale, tiered sports bar offering soothing decor of oak and brass, punctuated by an array of sports memorabilia. In addition to the usual assortment of interpersonal games being played among the crowd, you'll find 36 TV screens showing games of other kinds, along with the requisite pool tables. After 10, live DJs fire up top 40 and classic rock, and the dance floor fills fast. All 225 seats are occupied and a lineup is in place Thursday through Saturday. *AE, DC, MC, V; every day; full bar; www.sharkclubs.com; map:T4.*

Shine

364 WATER ST, GASTOWN; 604/408-4321

This silver-white club in the heart of Gastown shimmers with a relaxed, electronic lounge vibe. The minimalist decor and plush round couches add up to a sophisticated feel, as does the sound of some of the best DJs Vancouver has to offer. Those with eclectic tastes will enjoy Shine's ever-changing musical offerings: everything from '50s and '60s hits on Mondays to reggae on Wednesdays and funk on Saturdays. Or forget about the music and go for the drink specials and $3 cover on Laser Dance Tuesdays. *AE, MC, V; every day; full bar; www.shineclub.ca; map:T3.*

Tonic

919 GRANVILLE ST, DOWNTOWN; 604/669-0469

On Thursday night Tonic's good for drink specials, but the rest of the week it can be hit or miss. Although the staff are friendly and the music isn't bad, some nights feature prerecorded rather than live DJs, and the narrow space can feel like a closet even when the crowd is moderately sized. But if you're not up to waiting in line for 30 minutes at more popular Granville clubs, it's not a bad option. *MC, V; every day; full bar; www.thetonicclub.com; map:S4.*

The Yale

1300 GRANVILLE ST, DOWNTOWN; 604/681-9253

To fully appreciate the blues, they should be enjoyed in the same atmosphere in which they were created: a tattered old place in a tough part of town. Welcome to the Yale. The building, which has been around for more than 100 years, has hosted both iconic and up-and-coming R&B artists for the last 20. The room is long and narrow, with a teeny stage that's hard to see from the back, but you can always squeeze yourself onto the stage-front dance floor for a closer peek. Cover varies, and jam sessions take place on the weekends. *AE, MC, V; every day; full bar; www.theyale.ca.*

Yuk Yuk's

1015 BURRARD ST (CENTURY PLAZA HOTEL), DOWNTOWN; 604/696-9857

This venue originated as the Flying Club during Expo '86 and is still going strong as a member of the world's largest comedy club chain. It's the perfect place for comedy: a theatre-style setting ensures a perfect vantage point from any of 225 seats in the house. Hilarious (or at least here's hoping) touring acts from across the continent appear Wednesday through Saturday. Reservations recommended. *AE, MC, V; Tue–Sat; full bar; www.yukyuks.com; map:R4.*

Bars, Pubs, and Taverns

Alibi Room

157 ALEXANDER ST, GASTOWN; 604/623-3383

Located in a heritage building, the sleek, modern Alibi Room is a restaurant where real film people can be seen enjoying a real meal. But beyond its Hollywood cachet, this is an excellent place to meet a group of friends for drinks or to try out the new English bistro menu that came with a recent ownership change. After you finish in the bustling dining room, move downstairs to the cool lounge, which in a strange role reversal is often more subdued than the restaurant. *MC, V; every day; full bar; www.alibi.ca; map:V3.*

The Atlantic Trap & Gill

612 DAVIE ST, DOWNTOWN; 604/806-6393

A refreshingly down-to-earth oasis of a pub, the Trap & Gill is a second home to transplanted Maritimers and Newfoundlanders. East Coasters have a well-deserved reputation as being some of the friendliest folks in Canada, so don't be surprised if someone sitting next to you at one of the rough-hewn tables strikes up a conversation. Alpine and Schooner beer is shipped in especially from Nova Scotia, as are the fresh lobsters and mussels. Live Celtic-influenced music plays in the back room Thursdays and Saturdays. No cover charge, ever, and daily seafood specials. *AE, MC, V; every day; full bar; www. trapandgill.com; map:R5.*

Brickhouse Late Night Bistro & Bar

730 MAIN ST, EAST SIDE; 604/689-8645
Until the Brickhouse came along, there was nowhere on this gritty stretch of Main Street to enjoy a quiet drink—let alone a safe one. The thoughtful owners have created a welcoming atmosphere in the small, narrow room that's homey but not dowdy. Down-to-earth locals enjoy good old-fashioned conversation or try their hand at darts and pool. Upstairs is another find: the candlelit bistro, serving great West Coast food until 2am most nights. *MC, V; every day; full bar; map:V4.*

The Calling

1780 DAVIE ST, WEST END; 604/801-6681
Tourists and West Enders alike stop by this beachfront pub in the late evening to watch the sun set over English Bay. As a classic neighbourhood pub, the menu doesn't hold a lot of surprises, but with a number of good beers on tap and solid cocktails, it's worth the view. *MC, V; every day; full bar; www. donnellypubs.ca; map:P3.*

The Cascade Room

2616 MAIN ST, EAST SIDE; 604/709-8650
Back in the day, Vancouver's first brewery made a signature beer called Cascade, which would eventually become the name for this trendy bar that now stands on the very same spot where the beer was once brewed. Owned and operated by the same people who run the popular Habit Lounge next door, Cascade (see the Restaurants chapter) serves standard pub fare but wows with its pure fresh-fruit cocktails, expertly shaken by award-winning bartender Nick Devine. *MC, V; every day; full bar; www.thecascade.ca; map:E3.*

Cecil Exotic Show Lounge

1336 GRANVILLE ST, DOWNTOWN; 604/683-5029
As strip joints go, the Cecil is a palace: well-lit and friendly, with good pub grub and eye-poppingly attractive performers. And since Canadian laws allow exotic dancers to take it all off, the place is often packed with American tourists pinching themselves under the table to make sure they're not dreaming. If you're here for the entertainment (and who isn't?), there's a good view of the stage—outfitted with a shower and a hot tub—from just about anywhere in the room. *AE, DC, MC, V; every day; full bar; www.cecil.ca; map:R5.*

Century Restaurant / Heist Lounge

432 RICHARDS ST, DOWNTOWN; 604/633-2700

This two-storey former bank is half restaurant, half bar. Century, on the first floor, serves up a Latin-themed menu and cocktail list in a well-appointed room that showcases turn-of-the-20th-century architecture with exposed pillars and restored wood finishings. Upstairs, Heist Lounge offers drinks in darker quarters where DJs preside over a small dance floor. *MC, V; every day; full bar; www.centuryhouse.ca; map:T3.*

Dix Barbecue and Brewery

871 BEATTY ST, YALETOWN; 604/682-2739

On a good night, you'll find the tables and bar stools of this handsome, brick-lined Yaletown gathering spot filled with everyone from fashionable 20-somethings to recalcitrant boomers. Many of them are here for the barbecue—slow-smoked ribs, pork shoulder, and brisket straight from the Southern Pride cooker, along with the obligatory sides of collard greens and creamed corn. Of course, the food cries out for one of the brewed-on-the-premises lagers, or perhaps a shot or two of Kentucky bourbon. *AE, MC, V; every day; full bar; www.markjamesgroup.com/dix.html; map:T5.*

Dockside Brewing Company

1253 JOHNSTON ST (GRANVILLE ISLAND HOTEL), GRANVILLE ISLAND; 604/685-7070

This woody meeting spot for up-and-coming (i.e., just turned 30) stockbrokers, lawyers, and entrepreneurs has great views onto False Creek and a decent selection of brewed-on-the-premises lagers and ales. In summer, there's a smashing outdoor patio; in fall and winter, the combination of funk and house music and crackling fireplace make for a kind of Gen X drawing room. And all year-round, you'll meet (or at least hear) people who bear absolutely no resemblance to the laid-back Vancouverites of legend. *AE, MC, V; every day; full bar; www.docksidebrewing.com; map:R7.*

El Furniture Warehouse

989 GRANVILLE ST (GRANVILLE MALL), DOWNTOWN; 604/677-8080

Olé! El Furniture is a wildly popular Mexican-style restaurant and bar that just happens to be *the* place to grab a bite to eat and a drink (or two or three) before hitting the clubs. Over-the-top Mexican decor and rambunctious patrons shelling (and often tossing around) the signature complimentary peanuts make for a fun and boisterous atmosphere that's perfect for kicking off a night of fun. Wings are 15 cents on Wednesday, so come early or expect a wait. *MC, V; every day; full bar; www.elfurniturewarehouse.com; map:S4.*

The Met Bar & Grill

411 COLUMBIA ST, NEW WESTMINSTER; 604/520-1967

New Westminster isn't exactly famous for its snazzy drinking establishments, but the Met has raised the stakes considerably. A 150-seat pub with a back patio and a wraparound oak bar, it shows off the renovated 119-year-old hotel once owned by the family of late actor Raymond Burr. At lunch and dinner, you'll find judges and city councillors mixing with students and construction workers, all feasting on standard pub fare while glued to one of the TVs broadcasting satellite sports events. Drink specials every day, plus wings on Tuesdays and live entertainment on weekends. *AE, MC, V; every day; full bar; map:I5.*

Mountain Shadow Pub

7174 BARNET RD, BURNABY; 604/291-9322
Clad in weathered wood and stained glass, this Tudor-style inn is as good looking as the 20- to 35-year-olds who fill it to the rafters. There's an upper level that overlooks an open centre section, allowing you to either hide away upstairs for a long view of the frivolities or mix it up in the action on the main floor, where there's a pool table. Live music occasionally. Weekends are jam packed. Drink and food specials every day of the week. *AE, MC, V; every day; full bar; www.shadowpub.com; map:H2.*

No. 5 Orange

205 MAIN ST, EAST SIDE; 604/687-3483
Vancouver peeler bars: where women shower for men who don't. This hallowed hall of hedonism has been fuelling fantasies for more than 25 years—meaning that it's older than most of the ladies who dance here. The decor and food are okay, but the location is on the grotty side. *AE, DC, MC, V; every day; full bar; map:V3.*

PumpJack Pub

1167 DAVIE ST, WEST END; 604/685-3417
Much of the city's gay nightlife draws a mixed crowd, but the PumpJack, with its emphasis on leather and fetish attire, is not one of them. Strictly gay, it's a casual place to shoot pool or play a game of pinball, but it gets wild when the week is capped off with a Sunday kegger. Every second Saturday features a leather contest—check the Web site or call for dates. *MC, V; every day; full bar; www.pumpjackpub.com; map:Q4.*

Sailor Hagar's Brew Pub

86 SEMISCH AVE, NORTH VANCOUVER; 604/984-3087
Sailor Hagar's exclusive, handcrafted brews are pushed through temperature-controlled lines to a set of original British beer engines and taps. Just a two-block stroll from Lonsdale Quay and the SeaBus, this brewpub offers inviting decor featuring a carved solid oak fireplace and bar, an excellent menu of pub fare, satellite TV sports, a pool table, and a heated patio with an outstanding view of Vancouver. Thursday night is the hot time to hoist a few and play a few rounds of darts, but Tuesday and Wednesday are the times to go for cheap eats, with $5 steaks and $4 pastas, respectively. *AE, DC, MC, V; every day; full bar; map:E1.*

Steamworks Brewing Co.

375 WATER ST, GASTOWN; 604/689-2739
IC-900 MAIN ST, THE VILLAGE AT PARK ROYAL MALL,
WEST SIDE; 604/922-8882

For years, the Steamworks Brewing Co. (see the Restaurants chapter) stood guard at the entrance to Gastown, and now a second location has opened up across the water. At the original pub, a bank of windows offers a semicircular vista of railway yards, Burrard Inlet, and the North Shore. If you venture down the set of spiral mahogany stairs, you'll find an even cozier lounge. Shoot some stick at a pair of pool tables, or shoot the breeze around the oyster bar with one of the 25- to 45-year-old suits who make this place hop. The West Vancouver location is much of the same, and although it's smaller inside, the large, heated outdoor patio more than makes up for it. *AE, DC, DIS, JCB, MC, V; every day; full bar; www.steamworks.com; map:U3, D1.*

Yaletown Brewing Company

IIII MAINLAND ST, YALETOWN; 604/681-2739

The other half of a busy Yaletown restaurant, the YBC's pub has stuck with the same exposed brick and polished wood decor it had when it opened in the early '90s—which is apparently just fine with its loyal patrons. The real attractions are the friendly service, the beer-friendly grub (try the thin-crust pizzas), and the half dozen or so tasty lagers and ales dispensed from copper kegs on display at the back. By early evening the place fills up with the suits, shoppers, and software workers who keep the Yaletown business district humming. *AE, MC, V; every day; full bar; www.markjamesgroup.com/ yaletown.html; map:S5.*

Lounges

AFTERglow

1079 MAINLAND ST, YALETOWN; 604/604-0835

Attached to the übertrendy Glowbal Grill & Satay Bar (see the Restaurants chapter), AFTERglow is a sexy after-dinner lounge where fashionable scenesters come to flirt with one another in the dim lighting. Sultry music and a small-plates menu meant to be shared make this intimate, 50-seat lounge a seductive alternative to the commotion of Granville Mall. *AE, MC, V; every day; full bar; www.glowbalgrill.com; map:S5.*

Bacchus Piano Lounge

845 HORNBY ST (WEDGEWOOD HOTEL),
DOWNTOWN; 604/689-7777

Nestled in one of the city's best hotels, this elegant retreat is a 60-seat sensation. From 5pm to midnight, a piano player serenades imbibers with everything from soft rock to old lounge standards. Attire is usually dressy, with wall-to-wall suits in attendance Friday and Saturday nights. Call ahead for a reservation. *AE, DC, DIS, E, MC, V; every day; full bar; www.wedgewood hotel.com; map:S4.*

Backstage Lounge

1585 JOHNSTON ST, GRANVILLE ISLAND; 604/687-1354

Originally designed as a spot where theatre patrons could exit a play and then embark on a little play of their own, the Backstage Lounge has succeeded almost too well. So many young and old West Siders pop by this haunt on weekends to listen to live music that the theatregoers can barely squeeze in. The room is simple, the crowd is well mannered and jubilant, and the grub's not bad, either. Wednesdays find students from the nearby Emily Carr Institute of Art & Design hoisting cheap pints and spilling out onto one of the best waterfront patios in town. *AE, MC, V; every day; full bar; www.theback stagelounge.com; map:Q6.*

Canvas Lounge

99 POWELL ST, GASTOWN; 604/609-9939

Combining art and the art of drinking in a gorgeous space in Gastown, Canvas is an art gallery by day and an upscale lounge by night. A stylish and affluent crowd enjoys tapas and cocktails as they muse over the work of local painters that adorns the walls. It's the best time you'll ever have in an art gallery. *MC, V; Thurs–Sat; full bar; www.canvaslounge.ca; map:V3.*

Chill Winston

3 ALEXANDER ST, GASTOWN; 604/288-9575

In a city gone cocktail crazy, Chill Winston complements its cocktail menu with an adventurous wine list that offers good value with by-the-glass selections. In this warm and inviting candlelit room, expect upbeat diners noshing on smoked salmon and pizza from the small-plates menu (see the Restaurants chapter) while arguing over the merits of old- versus new-world wine. *MC, V; every day; full bar; www.chillwinston.ca.*

Cloud 9 Piano Lounge

1400 ROBSON ST, WEST END; 604/687-0511

Every city should have one: a revolving lounge, 40 storeys or so above street level, with an easygoing atmosphere and a view that goes on for miles. Cloud 9 treats tourists and locals to a 90-minute round-trip that encompasses English Bay, the North Shore mountains, and downtown by day; after dark, the ride continues, with the added bonus of live music later in the week. Seen the city lights go by too many times? Order a refill, kick back in your armchair, and gaze into the twinkling constellations on the ceiling. *AE, DC, JCB, MC, V; every day; full bar; www.cloud9restaurant.ca; map:R3.*

WHERE TO EAT IF YOU'RE A NIGHT CRAWLER

Late-night dining in Vancouver isn't gourmet, but it's more than decent. The city offers a wealth of options for hungry clubgoers, insomniacs, and people who didn't eat enough at dinner. So if you're not willing to settle for a fast-food joint on the Granville Mall, look here. All of the restaurants on it serve good food in comfortable surroundings, and at least one of them is sure to suit your taste and budget.

BENNY'S BAGELS (2503 W Broadway, West Side; 604/731-9730)
A mellow, many-cornered place to work on your novel or fill up on dough after the clubs close. *Until 1am Sun–Thurs, all night Fri–Sat; map:C3.*

BRICKHOUSE BISTRO (730 Main St, East Side; 604/689-8645)
The candlelit upstairs dining room offers entrées, appetizers, and desserts almost too good for a place open this late. Great specials and prices. *Until 2am Tues–Sat, midnight Sun–Mon; map:V4.*

ELWOOD'S (3145 W Broadway, West Side; 604/736-4301)
A little like dining in someone's converted garage. Wings, burgers, nachos, and other hangover fighters share the menu with surprisingly sophisticated tapas. *Until about 2:30am every day; map:C3.*

George Ultra Lounge

1137 HAMILTON ST, YALETOWN; 604/628-5555

Bright red leather booths line the brick walls of this tony room where a fiery glass chandelier hangs front and centre, calling attention to the well-stocked bar. The menu is small, but George's specialty is cocktails, and their inspired list of liquid offerings doesn't disappoint. A six-seat room with private table service called "the G Spot" is available for small-group bookings. *AE, MC, V; Mon–Sat; full bar; www.georgelounge.com; map:S6.*

Gerard Lounge

845 BURRARD ST (SUTTON PLACE HOTEL), WEST END; 604/682-5511

How does the other half live? Very well, thank you, if this lounge is any indication. The decor is posh, with an understated elegance—about what you'd expect from western Canada's best place for celebrity-watching. After a hard day on the set, the movie crews and stars repair to Gerard to let their famous butts sink into the comfy couches around the fireplace. There are only 50 seats, but a promenade with 25 more awaits, and you'll still hear the piano from there. *AE, DC, DIS, MC, V; every day; full bar; www.vancouver.suttonplace. com/restaurant_bar.htm; map:S4.*

GYOZA KING (1508 Robson St, Downtown)

Gyoza of every description, plus sushi, noodle soups, and a big serving of stylish young Japanese folks. Lots of options for vegetarians. *Until 1am Mon–Sat, 11:30pm Sun; map:Q3.*

MARTINI'S (151 W Broadway, West Side; 604/873-0021)

Cozy neighbourhood eatery known for good whole-wheat pizzas, but pasta, sandwiches, and appies are tasty too. Bonus: reasonably priced drinks. *Until 1am Mon–Thurs, 2am Fri–Sat, midnight Sun; map:U8.*

TRUFFLES BISTRO (1943 Cornwall Ave, East Vancouver; 604/733-0162)

Enjoy soothing samba and jazz until 2am, alongside generous Mediterranean-inspired plates and truly sinful homemade desserts. The wine and beer is affordable and the hot chocolate approaches divinity. *Until 2am every day; map:O6.*

WAAZUBEE CAFE (1622 Commercial Dr, East Vancouver; 604/253-5299)

Always lively neighbourhood gathering place with a wide-ranging menu featuring lots of vegetarian options. *Until 1am Mon–Sat, midnight Sun, map:Z6.*

—Tara Schmidt

Ginger 62

1219 GRANVILLE ST, DOWNTOWN; 604/682-0409

If Stanley Kubrick had designed a lounge in Malaysia, this is what it might have looked like. A large room, gorgeously done up in hues of red and gold, and a sweeping bar attract the faithful night after night. The food, meant for sharing on retro TV trays, is fusion tapas and small plates at their casual finest. The custom-designed couches and ottomans are the perfect place to have an exotic cocktail and check out the beautiful people. No cover charge, but take note: A strict dress code is in effect at all times. *AE, MC, V; every day; full bar; www.ginger62.com; map:R5.* &

Gotham Steakhouse & Cocktail Bar

615 SEYMOUR ST, DOWNTOWN; 604/605-8282

Next door to a proletarian SkyTrain entrance, the upmarket Gotham Steakhouse (see the Restaurants chapter) targets people who can actually afford to pay $60 for a porterhouse with the trimmings—namely, American tourists and high-rolling locals. Its dramatic, slender bar—affectionately known as the G Spot—is often jammed with the latter, in particular that fastidious variety of 30- to 50-year-old male. *AE, MC, V; every day; full bar; www.gotham steakhouse.com; map:T3.* &

Granville Room

957 GRANVILLE ST, DOWNTOWN; 604/633-0056
An impeccable blend of old-school supper club and cosmopolitan cocktail lounge, this dark, brick-walled room is a sophisticated spot to enjoy small plates while imbibing from a 14-page bar menu. The effortlessly chic come for a casual drink before the clubs open, but Granville Room's seductive vibe lures more than a few to stay for the night. *AE, MC, V; every day; full bar; www.granvilleroom.ca; map:S4.*

Joe Fortes Seafood & Chop House

777 THURLOW ST, DOWNTOWN; 604/669-1940 OR 877/669-JOES
Lawyers, stockbrokers, and even non-stuffy folks start their weekend festivities with a visit to the lounge area of Joe's, named after a turn-of-the-20th-century Vancouver lifeguard. Friday afternoon, it's packed with well-heeled movers and shakers clad in suits and well-cut business attire. The mood is jubilant, and the decor resembles that of a U.S. chophouse. *AE, DC, DIS, E, MC, V; every day; full bar; www.joefortes.ca; map:R3.*

900 West Lounge

900 W GEORGIA ST (HOTEL VANCOUVER), DOWNTOWN; 604/669-9378
In many ways, downtown Vancouver hotel lounges are ideal places for a quiet drink. The chairs are comfortable, the service is gracious, and you get those little plates of salty nibblies with your beverage. In ideal circumstances, they also feature a top-notch wine list and exceptional food. Such is the case with Hotel Vancouver's 900 West. On weekends, both the lounge and the wine bar are prime spots for people-watching amidst the lavish heritage surroundings of Hotel Vancouver, which helps make up for the somewhat expensive drink prices. *AE, JCB, MC, V; Mon–Sat; full bar; map:S3.*

Sanafir

1026 GRANVILLE ST, DOWNTOWN; 604/678-1049
A blend of Moroccan and Egyptian design influences everything—from the papyrus menus to the rich tapestries and handcrafted urns—in this opulently styled room. Affluent movers and shakers balance atop ultrahip cube seats on the lower level or rub elbows with visiting celebs from the comfort of luxurious leather beds upstairs. A unique tapas menu and an inventive selection of cocktails (hint: the Marrakech Mint is out of this world) completes the A-list experience. *AE, DC, MC, V; every day; full bar; www.sanafir.ca; map:S4.*

Sip Resto Lounge

1117 GRANVILLE ST, DOWNTOWN; 604/687-7474
You can have your drink and eat it too at this innovative lounge where every menu item is made with a splash of liquor, beer, or wine. The edgy cuisine is complemented by an inventive cocktail list, and both are served up in an ultrasexy New York–style room with a mature, sophisticated clientele. The

music is mainly house, and there's no cover charge, but reservations are recommended. *MC; V; every day; full bar; www.siplounge.com; map:S5.*

The Whip Restaurant & Gallery

209 E 6TH AVE, EAST SIDE; 604/874-4687
The artists, designers, and photographers who live and work in the Main and Broadway area have made the Whip their communal living room. Don't be intimidated, though; chances are, nobody is going to shun you for not knowing who Le Corbusier or treat you to a public display of his or her rattled artistic nerves. In fact, the congenial 30-something patrons are here to get away from all that: to sink into a comfy chair, down a pint or two of microbrew, and (a little later on, perhaps) order the right appetizer to help soak up the alcohol. In keeping with the communal living room theme, you'll find vintage furnishings that look as if they've been borrowed from a dozen different apartments. If you come during warm weather, you'll also find open French doors and streetside tables. *MC, V; every day; beer and wine; www. thewhiprestaurant.com; map:V7.*

Coffee, Tea, and Dessert

Bean Around the World

4456 W 10TH AVE, WEST SIDE (AND BRANCHES); 604/222-1400
With its sister stores around the Lower Mainland, this retail roasting shop helps supply Vancouver's addiction to fresh roasted beans. It's an inviting, cosy-sweater kind of place that serves a mix of sippers: early-bird exercisers, retired folk, students, parents with kids in tow. This coffeehouse gives its beans a slightly lighter roast than many other beaneries. Not only does this preserve varietal distinctions, it also provides more caffeine kick in the cup. Curl up by the roaster and warm your cheeks over a latte served in a filling, consoling bowl. *Every day; www.cowboycoffee.ca; map:B3.*

49th Parallel Coffee Roasters

2152 W 4TH AVE, WEST END; 604/420-4900
The Piccolo brothers' Italian coffee chain, Caffe Artigiano, has had Vancouverites swooning over their smooth, aromatic espressos since the first store opened in 2000. In late 2007, after selling this successful chain, they opened up 49th Parallel, and the accolades (including a Krups Kup of Excellence) immediately started rolling in. The unparalleled java is matched only by the shop's beautiful design: it's a modern space accented in shades of turquoise and chocolate brown. A must-visit for coffee lovers. *Every day; www.49thparallelroasters.com; map:N7.*

Joe's Café

1150 COMMERCIAL DR, EAST SIDE; 604/255-1046

Intellectuals, bohemian philosophers, poets, feminists, and political agitators mix with cue-hustling locals at this vigorous pool hall and cafe. Joe's doesn't glamorize espresso or otherwise try to be popular; it just is. All Joe needs to do is serve up his comely drinks with the famed foam. Despite the seedy decor and Laundromat lighting, this place is a well-worn neighbourhood hangout. Knowing, deliberate hands prepare espresso standards, along with hybrids such as espresso bica and butterscotch milk. The Carioca lait coffee is a dwarf-size latte that can be ordered with a refreshing slice of lemon. *Every day; www.joescafebar.com; map:Z5.*

La Casa Gelato

1033 VENABLES ST, EAST SIDE (AND BRANCHES); 604/251-3211

If you are seeking a slightly different taste, be sure to visit this ice cream emporium. It has more than 500 flavours of ice cream, many of which (we guarantee) you have never tried. How about dill pickle? Or blue cheese, balsamic vinegar, wasabi, or beer sorbetto? Luckily, they'll let you taste as many as you want before you buy, and traditional flavours are on standby. *Every day; www.lacasagelato.com; map:Y5.*

Murchie's Tea & Coffee

825 W PENDER ST, DOWNTOWN (AND BRANCHES); 604/669-0783

This coffee purveyor with British roots has chosen a lighter roast to bring out and preserve varietal nuance, and beans are always fresh (they get dumped after seven days). Choose from more than 40 blends and varietals, including the house blend (Murchie's Best). Some 50 varieties and blends of tea, loose or bagged, are also available. John Murchie's no. 10 blend is literally world renowned—it's sold by mail to more than 40 countries. This longtime merchant has assembled an engaging collection of brewing paraphernalia and gifts, from clay teapots and English bone china to samplers, gift boxes, and traditional chocolate-coated ginger. *Mon–Fri (downtown), varies by location; www.murchies.com; map:X4.*

Notte's Bon Ton Pastry & Confectionery

3150 W BROADWAY ST, WEST SIDE; 604/681-3058

Mr. Notte came from Italy, Mrs. Notte came from France, and sometime in the early 1930s they opened a tea shop. Second-generation Nottes still labour away behind the scenes, creating the kind of picture-perfect pastries you remember from your childhood. Unless you're heavily into plastic geraniums, the backroom tearoom is unassuming at best. But here, motherly waitresses serve up some of the most wickedly delicious pastries in the city: mocha filbert meringues, chocolate eclairs, cream puffs, napoleons, diplomat cake. A selection, under a plastic dome, gets left on your table. Only the most ascetic person can stop at one. This place is a Vancouver tradition, and around teatime you can have your tea leaves or tarot cards read by itinerant fortune-tellers. *Tues–Sat; www.nottesbontonpastryconfec.supersites.ca; map:C3.*

Sweet Obsession Cakes & Pastries

2603 W 16TH AVE, WEST SIDE; 604/739-0555

Lorne Williams and Stephen Greenham turn out some of the best-tasting, most addictive desserts in town from this bakery. Try their triple chocolate mousse and creamy fruit cheesecakes, and you'll understand why they supply the finest Vancouver restaurants with finales. Sweet Obsession is also known for home-made lemon curd, biscotti, and hazelnut sponge with Frangelico and chocolate hazelnut cream. Everything is made from scratch with the finest ingredients, including items on the tasty menu at partner Trafalgars Bistro (see the Res-taurants chapter), where you can dine on a nice prelude or just skip right to dessert—we understand. *Every day; www.sweetobsession.ca; map:C3.*

Tearoom T

1568 W BROADWAY, WEST SIDE; 604/878-3000

It's nice to find people who take an interest in their work, but these folks are obsessed—in a sedate, polite way, of course. This tea shop offers 250 differ-ent kinds of tea leaves and blends, including noncaffeinated, fruit tisanes, and herbals. Drop by for a tasting on the third Monday of the month, or take a tea tour. If you're just coming in for an afternoon cuppa, they'll do their best to do it the traditional way: either English, with locally made scones and Devonshire cream, or in a special Chinese tea service that gets the most from each infusion. They carry an extensive selection of teaware, cups, pots, and kettles from Alessi, Kotobuki, and Jenaer Glass. Expert staff are happy to make up gift boxes or put together a mail order. *Every day; www.tealeaves. com; map:P8.*

Ten Ren's Tea & Ginseng

550 MAIN ST, EAST SIDE; 604/684-1566

Bordered by the sensory pleasures of Chinatown and the squalor of Vancou-ver's skid row is Ten Ren, where a visit is a unique, vigorous experience. You'll find no tea cozies or chrome tea balls. One of 78 shops worldwide, Ten Ren offers many varieties and grades of Chinese tea: loose or in bags, green, baked, or fermented. Popular are Ti Kwan, jasmine, and King's Tea (the Ten Ren blend). As you browse, fortify yourself with a ginger or ginseng tea on tap. To the newcomer, the shop's staff can seem anxious for you to buy—it's really just enthusiastic to share its delicious teas. The north wall showcases many types and grades of ginseng, most of it not from the Far East but from the ideal cli-mate and soil of Wisconsin. *Every day; www.tenrenstea.com; map:V4.*

True Confections

866 DENMAN ST, WEST END (AND BRANCHES); 604/682-1292

These dessert outlets sell 40 kinds of grand cheesecakes, mile-high chocolate cakes, Belgian mousse tortes, pies, and more than 70 other desserts. They also happen to be the only dessert restaurants in the city with a liquor license, so indulge in a postdinner apertif with your postdinner bite. *Every day; www. trueconfections.ca; map:P2.*

Waves Coffee

492 W HASTINGS ST, DOWNTOWN; 604/915-WAVE
This new franchise breathes fresh life into Vancouver's caffeine scene—no small feat, considering they're up against a certain corporate coffee giant that dominates every city corner. Of course, serving up organic, free-trade roasts in a pleasant setting isn't the only reason they're suddenly so popular: it's the fact that their stores are open 24 hours a day with free wireless Internet access. Expect lots of student cramming for exams in the dead of night. *Every day; www.wavescoffee.ca; map:T3.*

RECREATION

RECREATION

Outdoor Activities

To use a high-tech analogy, if Vancouver's stupendous mountain and oceanside scenery is the city's "hard drive," then activities such as mountain biking, hiking, sea kayaking, running, and boardsailing are the "software." While some visitors are content to merely gaze at the landscape from a waterfront bistro or the seat of a convertible, most people want to go forth and viscerally experience that beauty firsthand.

Vancouver has been featured in virtually every major outdoor adventure publication in North America during the past decade, and it's likely no other city in North America offers such diverse activities—from mild to extreme. To find out about events going on and places to go, get a copy of the free publication *Coast*, an outdoor recreation magazine available at retail stores, libraries, and community centres in the city.

BICYCLING

Vancouver's superb recreational cycling trails offer expansive views of the sea and mountains as they wind through stands of fir, cedar, and hemlock, following the shoreline of numerous bays and inlets. Not all of the treasures are 100 percent natural: you'll find neighbourhoods to explore and places to stop for cappuccino, pizza by the slice, fish-and-chips, or frozen yogurt. Cyclists with more time can explore the Sunshine Coast and Gulf Islands, with the help of the largest ferry system in the world.

All bicyclists are required by provincial law to wear a helmet—failure to don one may result in a fine. It's against the law to cycle while wearing a headset, so keep it in your day pack. Both a headlight and taillight are legally required for cycling near dawn and dusk—and at night, of course. Also, bring a shackle-style U-lock if you plan to stop and shop or walk around—unfortunately, bike theft is rampant.

The best one-stop source for bicycling information is **CYCLING BRITISH COLUMBIA** (332-1367 W Broadway, West Side; 604/737-3034; www.cyclingbc.ne; map:C3). Its small library has maps, bike routes, guidebooks, and a calendar for both road and mountain bike races. Racers should note that **CRITERIUMS** (www.escapevelocity.bc.ca), short lap-style races, are held each Tuesday throughout the summer at the University of British Columbia; check the Web site for details on upcoming races. For off-road cycling, see Mountain Biking in this chapter.

Perhaps befitting its "Left Coast" locale and social mores, Vancouver has *Momentum: The Magazine for Self-Propelled People*, a politically charged and vastly entertaining monthly journal dedicated to bicycle advocates, commuters, and Critical Mass rabble-rousers. It's available for free at all Lower Mainland bike shops, as well as suitably sympathetic cafes. Another worthwhile organization fighting on behalf of cyclists' rights is **BETTER ENVIRONMENTALLY SOUND TRANSPORTATION** (BEST; www.best.bc.ca), which publishes handy, helpful pamphlets outlining great reasons to "go green" and ride your two-wheeler.

The city of Vancouver produces *Cycling in Vancouver*, a good map of bike routes printed on tear-resistant paper. It's distributed free at most bike shops. In recent years, there's been a major push by the city's planning department to reduce accidents between cars and bikes by pairing high-volume streets with bike routes a few blocks away. Off-Broadway, which takes riders along Seventh and Eighth avenues, and Midtown/Ridgeway, which goes along 37th Avenue, are the best east-west routes; the Ontario, Cypress, and Sunrise routes cover the city from north to south. The Midtown route even features several unique urban art sculptures featuring a velo theme. Although you will encounter some cars on these quiet streets, through traffic is deterred by concrete barriers that force cars back onto the main thoroughfares. Here are our picks for the best rides in Vancouver:

Gulf Islands

From March to October, cyclists use the BC Ferries dock in the community of Tsawwassen (pronounced "se-WAH-sehn"), at the south tip of Delta, as a departure point for exploring the southern Gulf Islands; Salt Spring, Galiano, Mayne, North Pender, South Pender, and Saturna islands are the most popular. All of these islands are havens of transcendent splendour and solitude. Accommodations range from provincial park campgrounds to a variety of bed-and-breakfasts. Swimming coves, pubs, and shady arbutus trees give welcome relief from the occasional hill. You can also take BC Ferries from Horseshoe Bay at the western tip of West Vancouver. Bear in mind that schedules change seasonally. If you're travelling in a motor vehicle, be prepared for lengthy lineups during the summer months and for an extra charge for an overheight vehicle if you have a vehicle with bikes mounted on a roof rack. Check with **BC FERRIES** (888/223-3779, reservations 888/724-5223 in BC, 604/444-2890 outside BC; www.bcferries.bc.ca) for sailing times or to make vehicle reservations for major routes between Vancouver and Vancouver Island.

River Road to Steveston

Families often do just a portion of this fun, flat, 36-kilometre (22.5-mile) loop in the suburb of Richmond. Park your car on the west side of the Dinsmore Bridge. Cycle along the gravel path on the dyke to the fishing village of **STEVESTON** (map:C7). Once there, buy an ice cream or sample fish-and-chips. The finely pebbled route is level but twisty in spots. There is no finer place to watch the sun go down than **GARRY POINT PARK** (map:C8), just west of Steveston. **STEVESTON BICYCLE** (3731 Chatham St; 604/271-5544; map:C8) rents bikes in the summer.

THE GREAT INDOORS

When the sun disappears behind ominous grey clouds in Vancouver, the choices of activities range from gym rock-wall climbing to indoor swimming, from bowling to driving out golf balls. But if you want to make your heart beat faster, play laser tag or try go-kart racing, two popular indoor activities that are a hit with adventure types of all ages.

Blow off steam and play tag at **PLANET LAZER**'s four Lower Mainland locations (Richmond, Burnaby, New Westminster, and Langley; 604/448-9999; www. planetlazer.com); its facilities are the largest in North America. Games take place in a high-tech, three-level, 4,200-square-metre (14,000-square-foot) arena, complete with theatrical smoke, wild lighting, fluorescent paint, ramps, catwalks, obstacles, mazes, graphics, and futuristic music. Players don a power-pack vest that energizes the laser weapon, provides lit targets for the opposition to aim at, and routes scoring information to the control room. The phaser weapon shoots out a harmless laser beam that travels more than 300,000 kilometres per second (186,000 miles per second), is as thick as a pen, and travels in a straight line. The object is to "tag" your foes with laser fire, but the trick—and the real adrenaline rush—is to find them and

Seaside Bicycle Route

This terrific 20-kilometre (12.4-mile) route links the **STANLEY PARK SEAWALL** (map:D1) with other waterfront pathways around **FALSE CREEK** (map:D2), **VANIER PARK** (map:D2), **KITSILANO BEACH** (map:C2), and **JERICHO BEACH** (map:B2), ending below the University of British Columbia at **SPANISH BANKS** (map:A2). A less crowded alternative to Stanley Park's seawall, this route offers more rest-stop options: a cappuccino on Cornwall Avenue, swimming at Kitsilano Pool, strolling at Jericho Beach, or kite flying in Vanier Park. Parts of this route follow city streets; look for the green-and-white bike-route signs. Maps can be picked up at several information kiosks along the way. **RECKLESS BIKE STORES** (1810 Fir St, West Side; 604/731-2420; www.rektek.com; map:P7), the nearest rental shop, will deliver rentals to your hotel for a small fee.

Stanley Park Seawall

No cycle visit to Vancouver is complete without a spin around this 8.8-kilometre (5.5-mile) **SEAWALL** (map:D1). Watch seaplanes taking off and landing in Burrard Inlet, stop and smell the rose gardens, brace yourself for the Nine O'Clock Gun, shout out at Hallelujah Point, and gulp great breaths of cedar-scented air while trying not to disturb nesting Canada geese around **LOST LAGOON** (map:P1). To escape the crowds, venture off the pavement onto packed-dirt trails inside the park's core. Many bike-rental shops

avoid being tagged yourself amidst the orchestrated chaos around you. When you do get tagged—and you will—your vest hums and vibrates unmistakably. Physical ability, mental dexterity, problem solving, and planning are integral to the game, creating a challenging environment for adults and fun for children and youths.

If it's the need for speed you're after, **TBC INDOOR KART RACING** (2100 Viceroy Pl, Richmond; 604/232-9196; www.tbcir.ca) has the solution for all Mario Andretti and Jacques Villeneuve wannabes, with head-to-head racing excitement in every event. TBC's state-of-the-art timing system and clean-air exhaust system ensure drivers are getting close to the real racing experience without the bad fumes. Female racers get a break on the race price every Friday. Air hockey, pool, and other activities are available for those waiting for their turn. You must arrive at the facility at least an hour before closing to complete the waiver form and view the safety-briefing video. It's wise to call ahead for track availability. Drivers must be at least 145 centimetres (4 feet 7 inches) tall and 11 years old to drive the karts at TBC. *Mon–Fri 11am–11pm, Sat–Sun 11am–midnight; last race is 30 minutes prior to closing.*

—Ian Walker

are found near the Georgia/Denman Street entrance to Stanley Park. One of the best is **BAYSHORE BIKE RENTALS** (745 Denman St, West End; 604/688-2543; www.bayshorebikerentals.ca; map:Q2), who also rent in-line skates.

CANOEING AND KAYAKING

British Columbia doesn't have a kayak or canoe on its coat of arms, but it could. More than 50,000 residents of the province go kayaking or canoeing, and paddlers can take their pick of thousands of lakes and rivers, as well as offshore islands—many uninhabited.

On any day of the year, marine enthusiasts carry on the Northwest Coast Native tradition by paddling modern versions of the *baidarka*, or sea kayak. The sea kayak is longer and sleeker than its white-water cousin, and some boats are specially constructed for tandem paddlers. Most of the bays and inlets around Vancouver are perfect for even novice paddlers, but taking an introductory course is a good idea. All kayak rental shops close to Vancouver offer such lessons. Learn the basic paddle strokes and self-rescue techniques, then rent single- or two-person kayaks at **JERICHO BEACH** (map:B2), **GRANVILLE ISLAND** (map:Q6), or **DEEP COVE** (map:H1).

Author Betty Pratt-Johnson is the grande dame of white-water trips in the province. A number of her books cover flatwater kayaking and canoeing across British Columbia. *Kayak Routes of the Pacific Northwest Coast* by Peter McGee and *Sea Kayaking Canada's West Coast* by John Ince and Hedi

Köttner are indispensable guides to exploring the province's 27,000 kilometres (16,875 miles) of coastline. Marine charts and tide tables are available from most Vancouver marine stores.

The **WHITEWATER KAYAKING ASSOCIATION** (www.whitewater.org) and the **SEA KAYAKING ASSOCIATION OF BRITISH COLUMBIA** (www.skabc.org) are useful sources of information about paddle sports in the province. They can be contacted through the **OUTDOOR RECREATION COUNCIL OF BRITISH COLUMBIA** (47 W Broadway, West Side; 604/737-3058; map:C2).

Bowen Island

Bowen Island is a short ferry hop from Horseshoe Bay, at the west end of West Vancouver. Located right beside the dock, **BOWEN ISLAND SEA KAYAKING** (604/947-9266; www.bowenislandkayaking.com) rents kayaks for short tours from one of its three bases around the island. Tides, winds, and boat wakes can be tricky, but the views in Howe Sound, a major fjord north of Vancouver, are tremendous.

False Creek and English Bay

The waters of **ENGLISH BAY** (map:C2) toward Stanley Park, and by Kitsilano Beach and west toward Spanish Banks, offer a mix of benign and moderately challenging conditions. Watch for unpredictable winds and tides around **SPANISH BANKS** (map:A2), on the south side of English Bay, and at Lighthouse Park in West Vancouver on the north side. Sea kayakers are prohibited from using the busy **FREIGHTER AND CRUISE-SHIP LANES** (map:E1) between the Lions Gate and Second Narrows bridges. For absolute beginners, the pondlike surface of **FALSE CREEK** (map:R7) offers reassurance but little natural ambience. Many other paddle-driven watercraft share these waters. You can rent boats at **ECOMARINE OCEAN KAYAKING CENTRE** (1668 Duranleau St, Granville Island; 604/689-7575; www.ecomarine.com).

Flatwater Lakes and Rivers

Several small bodies of water that are suitable for easy canoeing or sea kayaking are within a two-hour drive of Vancouver. East of the city, on the north side of the Fraser River, you'll find Alouette Lake, Pitt Lake, Widgeon Slough, and the Harrison River. Canoe rentals are available at Alouette Lake, with camping in adjacent **GOLDEN EARS PROVINCIAL PARK** (604/924-2200; www.discovercamping.ca); reservations recommended through the Web site.

Gulf Islands

A large black fishing bird of the West Coast, the cormorant, flies only a few inches off the water. Sea kayaking is the best way of getting a cormorant's-eye view of the Gulf Islands, a long archipelago between Vancouver Island and the mainland. The paddling here is done in safe, scenic waters. Pocket-size, pebble-beach coves shaded by rust-barked arbutus trees beckon the weary paddler. If you have your own boat, get on the ferry and follow your instincts. Beware: Although this area is one of the sunniest and most temperate in the province, the water is frigid, even in summer, and the tide can move water unpredictably as it sweeps through the twists and turns of the little straits between the islands. Less experienced kayakers should stay close to shore, where an easy swim leads to safety in case of a spill. These days, it seems as though each of the islands has at least one kayak rental shop. Suggestions include **GULF ISLANDS KAYAKING** (250/539-2442; www.seakayak.ca) on Galiano Island, **SEA OTTER KAYAKING** (250/537-5678 or 877/537-5678; www.saltspring.com/kayaking) on Salt Spring Island, **MOUAT POINT KAYAKS** (250/629-6767) on Pender Island, and **MAYNE ISLAND KAYAK AND CANOE RENTALS** (250/539-2463 or 877/535-2424; www.kayakmayneisland.com).

Indian Arm

This finger-shaped fjord bends northward from Burrard Inlet for 30 kilometres (18.8 miles), deep into the heart of the Coast Mountains. Travel **INDIAN ARM** (map:I1), and you will see impenetrable forests growing on impossibly steep hillsides, rising from the shoreline for hundreds of vertical metres. You can rent boats at the **DEEP COVE CANOE AND KAYAK CENTRE** (2156 Banbury Rd, North Vancouver; 604/929-2268; www.deepcovekayak.com) and paddle across Indian Arm—about 1.5 kilometres (1 mile)—to Jug Island Beach or **BELCARRA PARK** (map:I1). A paddle to the south leads to **CATES PARK** (map:H1), where Malcolm Lowry wrote *Under the Volcano*. It takes about four hours to reach the head of this glorious fjord. Inexperienced paddlers should beware of swells from the wakes of passing yachts, speedboats, and sailboats. **BELCARRA PADDLING COMPANY** (604/936-0236; map:J2), on the other side of Deep Cove (reached via a circuitous route through Port Moody), offers essentially the same paddling experience as starting from Deep Cove does. Custom tours of Indian Arm are provided by **LOTUS LAND ADVENTURES** (800/528-3531; www.lotuslandtours.com). Geared specifically for tourists staying at Vancouver-area hotels, Lotus Land picks you up at your hotel, looks after all of the guiding and equipment rental, and throws in a great salmon barbecue. No paddling experience necessary.

Powell River Forest Canoe Route

The Powell River Forest Canoe Route, located on the Sunshine Coast north of Vancouver, takes in more than 57 kilometres (35.6 miles) of canoeing and 8 kilometres (5 miles) of portages. Eight lakes are on the loop, but easy access to various parts of the route via logging roads makes day trips popular. The entire circuit takes a week to complete, rewarding paddlers with good views of coastal rain forest and glimpses of inaccessible, seldom-visited mountain peaks and a great deal of peace and quiet. This route is best paddled April through November, since the higher lakes are frozen during the winter and roads become inaccessible. Call **SUNSHINE COAST FOREST DISTRICT OFFICE** (604/485-0700) in Powell River for maps and directions.

Sunshine Coast

Less visited than the southern Gulf Islands or Vancouver
Island, the Sunshine Coast, north of Vancouver and Howe Sound, offers tremendous paddling opportunities for everyone, from white-water rodeo cowboys to families looking for calm lakes to explore. Sechelt Inlet is a 35-kilometre-long (22-mile-long) combination freshwater and saltwater indentation in the Coast Mountains. Eight marine park campsites are found en route. At the head of the inlet is where you'll find Skookumchuck Narrows—a white-water paradise, especially around the full moon, when the tides conspire to turn this usually benign stretch of water into a boiling froth. (The word *skookumchuck* is Chinook jargon—a West Coast Native patois—for "powerful.") Sea kayaks are available for rent in the communities of Sechelt, Egmont, and Powell River.

CLIMBING AND MOUNTAINEERING

The Coast Mountains stretch northward from the 49th parallel, the largest portion of a massive cordillera that extends from the Mexican border to Alaska. Within that huge geographical territory, hundreds of unclimbed summits and cross-country traverses remain to be tackled. Virtually every kind of mountaineering challenge can be found within a day's drive of downtown Vancouver, from frozen-waterfall climbing in the town of Lillooet, northeast of Vancouver, to rock climbing the sunbaked granite of the Smoke Bluffs near Squamish, a town north of Vancouver on the way to Whistler. Spectacular glacier ascents can be made in Garibaldi Provincial Park and on the peaks surrounding the Joffre Lakes Recreation Area east of Pemberton (also north of Vancouver, near Whistler).

Some of the best views of Vancouver can be seen from the summit of several prominent peaks that dwarf the city skyline. Most of these are accessible via well-maintained hiking trails. A word to the wise: Fog, rain, wind, and freezing temperatures can turn even the least-technical climb into an ordeal, so always carry extra food and clothing, even for a day trip, and let people know where you're going and when you expect to return.

There are so many hiking and mountaineering organizations in the province that they have their own umbrella group, the **FEDERATION OF MOUNTAIN CLUBS OF BRITISH COLUMBIA** (130 W Broadway, West Side; 604/873-6096; www.mountainclubs.org; map:C2). Trail building, safety and education, wilderness preservation, and public awareness of mountain recreation issues are all part of the organization's mandate. Courses run by the federation's **CANADA WEST MOUNTAIN SCHOOL** (47 W Broadway, West Side; 604/878-7007; www.themountainschool.com; map:C2) include mountaineering, glacier travel, rock climbing, and trekking in the summer; avalanche training, ski touring, snow camping, and waterfall ice climbing in the winter. Highly experienced and certified instructors teach the courses; the school has never had a fatality or serious accident during its three decades of operation.

Cypress Provincial Park

NORTH OF WEST VANCOUVER; 604/924-2200
BLACK MOUNTAIN in Cypress Provincial Park can be climbed on foot or reached by chairlift. Nearby Cabin Lake, on the **BADEN-POWELL TRAIL**, is a good spot for a refreshing midsummer dip. The two-hour **BLACK MOUNTAIN LOOP TRAIL** is perfect for introducing the family to the joys of hiking in the mountains. *www.elp.gov.bc.ca.*

Garibaldi Provincial Park

NORTH-NORTHWEST OF VANCOUVER VIA HWY 99;
604/689-9025 BC PARKS
Garibaldi Provincial Park is accessible from several points along Highway 99 en route to the resort city of Whistler. Diamond Head, Black Tusk Meadows, Singing Pass, and Wedgemount Lake provide varying degrees of challenge and are suitable for day trips or overnight expeditions. Perhaps the most outstanding landmark is **BLACK TUSK**, a volcanic plug that is 2,315 metres (7,595 feet) tall. The trail to its base starts at Taylor Campground. Because of crumbling rock and high exposure, climbing the tusk itself is only for experienced mountaineers; check trail and weather reports. *www.elp.gov.bc.ca.*

Mount Seymour Provincial Park

NORTH OF DOWNTOWN VANCOUVER; 604/986-2261
This mountainous park is a 30-minute drive north from downtown Vancouver. Hiking to the top of the three rounded summits, each slightly higher than the last, provides a surprisingly authentic wilderness experience if you go there midweek or on snowshoes in winter. Your reward is an unparalleled view: north into the heart of the Coast Mountains, south beyond the urban sprawl to the Gulf Islands and San Juan Islands, east to the sleeping volcano of Mount Baker in northern Washington state and western Washington's Cascade Range, and west toward Vancouver Island. The mountainous 8-kilometre (5-mile) return trip takes about four hours. *www. elp.gov.bc.ca;map:Eo.*

Tantalus Range

North of Vancouver and halfway along the Sea-to-Sky Highway, which runs from Squamish to Whistler, a vehicle pullout provides a panoramic view of the most spectacular subrange of mountains in southwestern BC. The Tantalus Range is a series of jagged, heavily glaciated summits clustered on the west side of the Squamish River. There are two access points to the Tantalus: the Lake Lovely Water Trail (a canoe is needed to ferry climbers and gear across the swiftly flowing river) and via Sigurd Creek. For detailed information, contact the **BC FOREST SERVICE, SQUAMISH DISTRICT OFFICE** (604/898-2100; www.for.gov.bc.ca/dsq). Climbing in the Tantalus is a rugged wilderness experience, on par with just about anything in the Rockies or Alaska, and your group should be well prepared. **BLACKCOMB HELICOPTERS** (604/938-1700; www.blackcombhelicopters.com) will fly you in to Lake Lovely Water; most

---

THE PERFECT FIT

You need only see the plethora of competitions—and the titles such as Knee Knacker trail or the Test of Metal race—taking place around Vancouver to know how seriously locals strive to make mountain trails steeper, routes tougher, and themselves even fitter.

Like many of their West Coast cousins, Vancouverites play hard at achieving that body beautiful—and it's easy to see why. Enveloped by mountains and ocean which are reached within minutes, city folk enjoy embracing the great outdoors all year round.

Most of the city is designed with the rollerblader, biker, runner, or walker in mind. The renowned Seawall—the 8.8-kilometre (5.5-mile) waterfront surrounding Stanley Park—has paths specifically for your favoured activity (the route reopened after the hurricane winds of 2006 devastated 3,000 trees). Forgot to pack your inline skates? Plenty of stores rent them, including **BAYSHORE RENTALS** (745 Denman St; 604/688-BIKE; www.bayshorebikerentals.com) which also offers bicycles; or try **SPOKES** (1798 West Georgia St; 604/688-5141; www.vancouverbikerental.com).

Labouring on the Grouse Grind on the North Shore—a must-do for visitors— might have you wishing you had taken the local mountain's adjacent (and effortless) **SKYRIDE GONDOLA** (www.grousemountain.com). Yet many run up this steep vertical climb to 1,100 metres (covering around 3 kilometres) and down again every day during the summer.

If the indoor workout appeals more, there are many sports clubs around the city. For easy drop-ins, head to **SWEAT CO.** (736 Richards St 604/683-7938;

---

climbers stay at a sturdy cabin operated by the **ALPINE CLUB OF CANADA** (403/678-3200; www.alpineclubofcanada.ca).

CLIMBING INDOORS

Many local rock climbers learn their craft indoors at the **EDGE CLIMB-ING CENTRE** (2-1485 Welch St, North Vancouver; 604/984-9080; www.edgeclimbing.com; map:D1). This rock climber's version of an indoor jungle gym is western Canada's most comprehensive climbing facility, with more than 15,000 square feet of climbing surface. The carved holds and textured surfaces present a reasonable simulation of routes and situational problems found on the real crags. All of the routes are rated, with varying degrees of difficulty. Even if you get vertigo standing too close to a guardrail, it's fun to watch the human spiders in action. You can take courses, rent shoes and harnesses, and play until 11pm, seven days a week. **CLIFFHANGER** (670 Industrial Avenue, Downtown; 604/874-2400; www.cliffhangervancouver.com; map:V5) offers two popular climbing gyms, the second in Coquitlam

www.sweatcostudios.com). The ambience of this converted brothel with its bare-brick walls and intimate rooms will help you forget how that muscle burn might feel in the morning. Nearby at **GROUNDWORK ATHLETICS** (10-736 Granville St; 604/685-7576; www.groundworkathletics.ca), the larger, more industrial space is home to some of the city's most-acclaimed personal trainers and is where elite athletes often work out while in the city. For a swimming pool added to the mix of fitness equipment and group classes, check out the swish **YWCA** (535 Hornby St; 604/895-5777; www.ywcavan.org).

Yoga has a sizeable and extremely loyal following in Vancouver. There is an **ANNUAL YOGATHON**—it's quite the experience seeing 2,000 people downward dogging at the same time—held every July (www.campmoombayogathon.com). For great classes, check out the **PRANA YOGA AND ZEN CENTRE** (1083 Cambie Street; 604/682-2121; www.pranayoga.com).

Nearly 200 free-to-use tennis courts pockmark the city, the most well known of which are the Stanley Park facilities. Etiquette dictates that if you sit by a court currently in use, the players should allow you on after no more than 30 minutes.

And playing on the water is a national summer pastime here, and the places to rent equipment are well established. Sailing, kayaking, windsurfing, rowing, windsurfing . . . Phew. If you're not exhausted by these endless fitness possibilities, you'll soon understand why thousands from all over the world relocate here every year for the lifestyle alone.

—Lucy Hyslop

(98 Brigantine Dr; 604/526-2402; www.cliffhangercoquitlam.com;). All offer drop-in sessions.

CLIMBING ON ROCK FACES

For a taste of the real thing, drive 60 kilometres (37 miles) north on Highway 99 to Squamish. The **STAWAMUS CHIEF** (www.stawamuschiefpark.ca) is a striking 700-metre (2,297-foot) granite monolith that towers above the waters of Howe Sound. At this writing, more than 1,200 climbing routes track its various walls, faces, and slabs. A vehicle pullout north of Shannon Falls provides an excellent vantage point for seeing climbers in action. Less dramatic but equally challenging climbs can be found in Murrin Provincial Park and on the Smoke Bluffs—Canada's first rock-climbing park. Novice climbers will like the grippy granite and easy moves on Banana Peel, Diedre, Cat Crack, and Sugarloaf. Lessons and guiding are available through **SQUAMISH ROCK GUIDES** (604/815-1750; www.squamishrockguides.com).

DIVING

The clean, cold, clear waters between Vancouver Island and the Lower Mainland are home to more than 450 fish species, 600 plant species, 4,000 species of invertebrates—and the ghosts of countless sunken vessels. The best time to dive is in winter, since plankton growth in summer often obscures visibility. Both charter and do-it-yourself diving are popular here.

Betty Pratt-Johnson's *101 Dives from the Mainland of Washington and British Columbia* is essential reading for divers. Wreck divers interested in some nautical history should pick up a copy of Fred Rogers's *Shipwrecks of British Columbia*. Get air, tanks, and the latest news on what's hot from **INTERNATIONAL DIVING CENTRE** (2572 Arbutus St, West Side; 604/736-2541; www.diveidc.com; map:C2). For local knowledge, pick up a copy of *Diver* magazine at dive shops throughout the Lower Mainland and Sunshine Coast.

The federal **DEPARTMENT OF FISHERIES AND OCEANS, FISHING INFORMATION** (401 Burrard St, Downtown; 604/666-2828; www.pac.dfo-mpo.gc.ca; map:S2) is a good place to start your planning; the department's listings in the Blue Pages at the back of the Vancouver phone book provide numbers for openings and closures for numerous species of fish and shellfish. As well, local fishing shops provide lots of information and free copies of government regulations, which sometimes change seasonally. **SHELLFISH RED TIDE UPDATES** (604/666-2828) can provide you with the latest information on this naturally occurring toxic plankton that can affect shellfish during various periods of the year.

Sunshine Coast

With more than 100 dives mapped by local enthusiasts, Powell River, a town north of Vancouver at the north end of the Malaspina Peninsula on the Sunshine Coast, is officially the scuba-diving capital of Canada. Charters, rentals, compressed air, and guides are all available through **BEACH GARDENS RESORT & MARINA** (604/485-6267; www.beachgardens.com). Wreck diving is the attraction here. Look for the remains of the *Shamrock* off Vivian Island and the HMCS *Chaudiere*, a World War II frigate—and now an artificial reef for divers—intentionally sunk a few years ago off Kunechin Point in Sechelt Inlet. Rare red coral thrives in these waters, along with octopus and wolf eels. Many divers seek out the sunken statue of a mermaid that resides near the BC Ferries dock at Saltery Bay.

Whytecliff Marine Park

This fine undersea park in West Vancouver contains a variety of marine life in its protected cove and nearby waters. Copper Cove, Telegraph Cove, and Cates Park in **DEEP COVE** (map:H1), all in the same general area, are also local favourites. Be sure to check local regulations before harvesting edibles such as crabs or sea cucumbers.

FISHING IN SALT WATER AND FRESHWATER

BC's scenic coastline and unspoiled wilderness make a magnificent backdrop for fishing, which compensates for the rare occasion when anglers get skunked. Freshwater anglers can catch salmon and trout—including char, the legendary steelhead. Saltwater anglers can try for five species of salmon, plus rockfish, lingcod, and halibut.

Two government agencies administer sport fishing. The federal **DEPARTMENT OF FISHERIES AND OCEANS** (604/666-2828; www.dfo-mpo.gc.ca) regulates saltwater fishing, and the provincial **MINISTRY OF ENVIRONMENT, LANDS, AND PARKS** (604/582-5200; www.gov.bc.ca/env) regulates freshwater fishing. Licenses are required for either type of fishing. You can purchase them at tackle shops, which are also great sources of information about where the fish are biting, throughout the Lower Mainland. These shops, as well as tourist information centres, also have free copies of provincial and federal sport-fishing regulations. The section on catch-and-release in streams and lakes is particularly important for the freshwater angler. Fly fishermen and women would do well to pick up a copy of Art Lingren's *Irresistible Waters: Fly Fishing in B.C. Throughout the Year.*

Fraser River

The Fraser is one of the largest untamed rivers left in the West; its watershed extends almost to the provincial border with Alberta and includes a great hairpin swath of British Columbia. All five species of West Coast salmon (coho, chinook, chum, sockeye, and pink) make a pilgrimage up the Fraser annually to their spawning grounds, some of which are hundreds of kilometres upstream. Though the salmon fishery has been degraded by overfishing, unseasonably warm water, and loss of habitat as a result of logging and development, make no mistake—the Fraser is still a thriving, abundant ecosystem and one of the most productive salmon rivers in the world. It's also one of the most regulated, so ensure you are up-to-date by picking up a free copy of the sport-fishing rules when you get your license.

Because the Fraser empties into the ocean after traversing a wide urban delta, its water level is subject to tidal influx. **DEAS ISLAND REGIONAL PARK** (604/224-5739; map:E8) in the Vancouver suburb of Richmond, south of the city, and **MCDONALD BEACH** (604/231-0740; map:C4) at Sea Island (where Vancouver International Airport is located) are the most popular places to wet a line close to where the Fraser reaches its terminus. These are also the places on the Fraser where you're most likely to find the rare white sturgeon, a gigantic bottom feeder that often lives to be a century old.

Salmon enhancement programmes are at work on several of the Fraser's tributary creeks, with spawning channels and fish hatcheries constructed to improve productivity. Literally hundreds of mountain creeks feed major Fraser tributaries, including the Pitt, Harrison, Stave, Chilliwack, and Vedder (and those are just the main feeders in the Fraser's delta area). Though some of the more popular spots are standing-room-only on weekends, the fishing here can be truly world-class. On the north side of the Fraser, as you move east of

Vancouver, the best bets include Rolley Lake, Kanaka Creek, the Ruskin Recreation Area, and the Harrison River. On the south bank, also going east, Glen Valley, Derby Reach, and Matsqui Trail Regional Park are the action places. The Chilliwack River has a tremendous coho salmon run in the fall.

Horseshoe Bay and Hole in the Wall

Howe Sound, a 40-kilometre (25-mile) inlet that starts at Horseshoe Bay northwest of Vancouver, is perfect for saltwater fishing. Whether you're out to hook the fish of your dreams or just want a few relaxing hours on the ocean within sight of land (an area of water the locals call the "saltchuck"), **SEWELL'S MARINA** (West Vancouver; 604/921-3474; www.sewellsmarina.com) offers a fleet of 60 rental boats, as well as regularly scheduled group fishing tours. Salmon can be caught at the legendary Hole in the Wall, a what-you-mightexpect geographical feature, several kilometres north of the marina.

Rice Lake

This lake is in the **LOWER SEYMOUR CONSERVATION RESERVE** (604/432-6286; www.gvrd.bc.ca/water/lscr.htm) north of Vancouver. To get there, take the Mount Seymour Parkway exit from Highway 1 and follow Lillooet Road past Capilano College to the road's end. The lake is wheelchair accessible. The Seymour River provides excellent angling opportunities as well.

GOLFING

The popular lotus-land image of going skiing in the morning and golfing in the afternoon in Vancouver is not as far-fetched as you might think. Although golf courses aren't in prime condition in December or January, by the time April rolls around, many of the Lower Mainland links are in midsummer shape. The **CITY OF VANCOUVER** (www.city.vancouver.bc.ca/parks/golf/teetips.htm) operates several municipal golf courses, and some privately owned courses are open to the public as well. A sampling of the best follows. Tee times can be booked online, but note that times for weekends go quickly, and you need a credit card to reserve a space.

Fraserview Golf Course

7800 VIVIAN DR AT E 54TH AVE, EAST VANCOUVER; 604/257-6923
The Thomas McBroom–designed course overlooks the Fraser River from the southeast slope of the city. The award-winning course measures 6,126 metres (6,700 yards) and offers a variety of challenges for golfers of all skill levels. The popular course also has received designation as a certified Audubon sanctuary; it is a significant habitat for birds in an urban setting. *Open year-round; map:F4.*

Mayfair Lakes Golf Course

5460 NO 7 RD, RICHMOND; 604/276-0585
"Water, water, everywhere" might be the unofficial motto of this attractive course in the Vancouver suburb of Richmond. It's not as tree-lined as some

of the more established tracks but definitely a must-play in terms of challenge and design. Par 71, 6,073 metres (6,641 yards). Watch for salmon jumping in some of the water hazards—it's guaranteed to distract your swing. *Every day; map:F6.*

Peace Portal Golf Course

16900 4TH AVE, SURREY; 604/538-4818
Glance to the right on Highway 99 as you enter Canada from Interstate 5 where it leaves Washington state, and you'll see one of the Lower Mainland's oldest courses. Named after the international boundary monument that straddles the border south of Vancouver, the local favourite was established in 1928. *Every day.*

Queen Elizabeth Pitch and Putt

CAMBIE ST NEAR 33RD AVE, SOUTH VANCOUVER; 604/874-8336
Serious golfers might scoff at the inclusion of a lowly pitch and putt in this type of listing, but this course offers some of the most breathtaking views of the city from its vantage point atop Little Mountain, a former rock quarry and now a spectacular park in the centre of uptown Vancouver. The P&P is great fun and well used. Nongolfers can stroll the adjacent grounds of Queen Elizabeth Park or visit the Bloedel Conservatory while playing through on the third hole. *Every day; map:E3.*

University Golf Club

5185 UNIVERSITY BLVD, WEST SIDE; 604/224-1818
This gorgeous, well-maintained course is a treat to play no matter what the season. You don't need any connection with the nearby University of British Columbia to play here, and many people attend classes under the tutelage of several certified Canadian Professional Golfers Association pros. *Every day; map:B3.*

HIKING

A telltale sign of the popularity of hiking in Vancouver is that the "bible"— *103 Hikes in Southwestern British Columbia*—is into its sixth edition. A companion volume, *109 Walks in the Lower Mainland*, is almost as popular. Originally authored by David and Mary Macaree, and now taken over by Jack Bryceland and volunteers from the British Columbia Mountaineering Club, the latter book is indispensable. Several of the most popular hikes are listed in the Climbing and Mountaineering section of this chapter; what follows is a more diverse selection.

Garibaldi Provincial Park

NORTH OF VANCOUVER; 604/924-2200
The jewel of West Coast mountain parks has more than 90 kilometres (56 miles) of developed hiking trails. The beautiful Singing Pass can be reached by taking the Whistler Village Gondola (see the Whistler chapter) and following

GLAMPING

You've set your sights on the raw wilderness. How wild do you want it? Wild, but not that wild? Exotic, remote, but cushioned with down-filled creature comforts? Try "glamping," where glamour meets camping, under a starry sky marked only by a chandelier. Instead of "boggy pup tent," think "spacious safari canopy with Persian carpets on the polished wood floors." Meals from a Coleman stove? Not a chance. The chef's a pro, the silver is polished, the linen crisp.

Rough it, resort-style, in a temperate rain forest on the west coast of Vancouver Island at the **CLAYOQUOT WILDERNESS RESORT** (www.wildretreat.com). Leave the comfort of a wood-floored safari tent with Oriental carpets, antique furnishings, and remote-controlled propane woodstoves for hiking, horseback riding, fly-fishing, kayaking, and wildlife-watching. Or just play snooker, have a massage, and lounge in chef Timothy May's open-kitchen bar.

—Kasey Wilson

a well-defined trail over the intriguingly named Musical Bumps. The pass is particularly beautiful in August, when the meadows are filled with blooming lupine, Indian paintbrush, and saxifrage. Cheakamus Lake, Diamond Head, and Black Tusk Meadows are all worthwhile day trips. If you're going to Black Tusk, a huge granite surge, avoid the crowds and boredom of the infamous Barrier Switchbacks by using the alternative Helm Creek Trail (use the same access as the Cheakamus Lake turnoff). *www.env.gov.bc.ca/bcparks*.

Golden Ears Provincial Park

EAST OF VANCOUVER VIA HWY 7; 604/924-2200

Although many hikers like the rugged trails of Garibaldi Park and the North Shore, Golden Ears, east of Vancouver, provides some spectacular views of seldom-visited glaciers and mountains. The best part about climbing Golden Ears is that, although it looks incredibly steep from its precipitous west face, the route up the east side is little more than an exerting hike, although it sometimes calls for the use of hands. Fit hikers can tackle the 1,706-metre (5,597-foot) North Ear, but an early start is necessary as the trailhead is almost at sea level. Once on top, you can marvel at the spectacular view of two nearby large freshwater bodies: Pitt Lake and Alouette Lake. Alouette is suitable for swimming. This is not a short day trip, and it should be attempted only after the upper meadows are free of snow. *www.env.gov.bc.ca/bcparks*.

Grouse Mountain

With its gondola towers and lighted ski runs visible from many parts of the Lower Mainland, Grouse Mountain (1,128 metres/3,700 feet), north of Vancouver, is one of the city's best-known natural landmarks. In winter, this is a popular ski resort during the day; night skiing (until 11pm) is romantic, with a swooshing descent toward the carpet of city lights spread out below. In warmer seasons, purists can traipse up the Grouse Grind trail, adjacent to the gondola-style Skyride track, to the Observatory Restaurant at the base of the ski runs, then follow a ski run to the top; the less energetic can take the Skyride tram up and save their energy for the alpine trails. Either way, the views are utterly breathtaking. Maps are available at the guest services booth at the **GROUSE MOUNTAIN SKYRIDE TICKET OFFICE** (Grouse Mountain Resorts; 604/980-9311; www.grousemountain.com).

Howe Sound Crest Trail

NORTH OF VANCOUVER; 604/924-2200
Strong day hikers may want to tackle the Howe Sound Crest Trail. It's a 30-kilometre (18.8-mile) trek—and that's just one way—across several summits north of Vancouver, including Black Mountain, Mount Harvey, Mount Brunswick, and Deeks Peak, ending in picturesque Porteau Cove. Portions of this trail can be reached at various points along Highway 99 north of Horseshoe Bay, but to do the whole trip, you need to have somebody drop you off at Cypress Bowl and meet you at Deeks Creek. Stiff hills and slippery descents are encountered en route, and weather can change quickly. Still, this trail has some awesome views of Howe Sound and the Georgia Strait. *www.env.gov.bc.ca.*

Lighthouse Park

WEST VANCOUVER; 604/925-7200
In less than 30 minutes from Vancouver, you can find unspoiled wilderness on the bluffs above West Vancouver's Point Atkinson. Lighthouse Park features one of the few remaining stands of old-growth Douglas fir trees. The Douglas fir is the second-tallest tree species found in North America, bested only by the California redwood. This park is fun to walk through, regardless of the weather. There are no crowds during the misty, moody winter months. The smooth igneous rock surrounding the lighthouse provides an ideal spot to rest and enjoy a picnic. Eagle nests, rust-red arbutus trees, and the red-and-white lighthouse, casting its beam across the water, complete this beautiful West Coast postcard. *www.westvancouver.net.*

Manning Provincial Park

EAST OF VANCOUVER; 604/924-2200
A three-hour drive east on the Trans-Canada Highway and a relatively short jaunt along Highway 3—take the Hope-Princeton route at the Hope interchange—Manning Provincial Park is spectacular when in bloom. In June, stop at the Rhododendron Flats pullout near the highway; in August, see the brilliant carpet of alpine wildflowers at higher elevations. Trained park naturalists are on duty during periods of peak bloom, and the trail to the alpine meadows is ideal for children as well. If the kids are restless, have them smell the fragrant Sitka valerian, a white wildflower known for its mildly calming effect. *www.env.gov.bc.ca/bcparks.*

Pitt River Dykes

**PITT MEADOWS AT SOUTHWEST CORNER OF
MAPLE RIDGE; 604/530-4983**

The Pitt is a major tributary of the Fraser, and a walk along its dykes can be enjoyed at any time of year. You can drive directly to Pitt Lake and take in the breathtaking view of the Coast Mountains to the north, then work your way south along the river's edge, past Chatham Reach, and on toward the Pitt's confluence with the Fraser. If you visit and find the water is gone, your eyes will not have deceived you: the Pitt is subject to changing river levels as a result of tidal activity. During spring and fall, the polder is a haven for ducks, geese, herons, sandhill cranes, and a variety of songbirds. *www.gvrd.bc.ca.*

HORSEBACK RIDING

Cowboys roam the ranges on the Ponderosa-size ranches of the Cariboo and Chilcotin of central BC, but city slickers need only don hats and boots (and pants!) for horseback riding in the Fraser Valley.

Campbell Valley Regional Park

This nature park features equestrian trails, cross-country jumps, picnicking, and nature-study areas. Hop off your horse and pick a handful of blackberries at summer's end. From Highway 1 going east from Vancouver, take the Langley 200th Street exit southbound. Travel 14.5 kilometres (9 miles), then turn east on 16th Avenue for the North Valley entrance. Horses can be rented at **LANGLEY 204 RIDING STABLES** (543 204th St, Langley; 604/533-7978; www.corporate-living.com/langley204).

Golden Ears Provincial Park

A great place for both urban cowboys and the saddle-savvy to trail-ride. Commercial stables in Maple Ridge organize summer day rides to Alouette Lake. Hitch your horses, swim in the lake, then head 'em home. **J. P.'S GOLDEN EARS RIDING STABLE** (13175 232nd Ave, Maple Ridge; 604/463-8761) is 48 kilometres (30 miles) east of Vancouver on Highway 7.

Manning Provincial Park

This park, less than three hours' drive east of Vancouver in the Cascade Range, is a spectacular place to ride horseback. Several hundred kilometres of horse trails crisscross the park. Bring your own horse or rent one at the **MANNING PARK CORRAL** (Manning Park Resort; 250/840-8822; www.manningparkresort.com).

HOT-AIR BALLOONING

Fraser Valley

Langley Airport serves as the base for several companies specializing in hot-air balloon tours. **FANTASY BALLOON CHARTERS** (Langley Airport, Unit 209, 5333 216th St, Langley; 604/530-1974; www.fantasyballoon.com)

specializes in dawn or dusk Champagne flights, taking wing once the air is cooler and less susceptible to turbulent currents. It's the most relaxing way to get an eagle's-eye view of Mount Baker, Golden Ears, and the patchwork quilt of rich farmland bordering the Fraser River.

ICE SKATING

Unlike Canadian cities with below-zero temperatures, Vancouver has a mild winter climate that isn't generally conducive to traditional winter recreational activities such as tobogganing and ice skating. Nevertheless, several recreation facilities are open to skaters, and some outdoor ponds are suitable for a quick pirouette or double axel when an infrequent cold snap hits.

When Arctic air comes pouring out of the north, many of the ponds in **VANCOUVER PARKS** (604/257-8400; www.city.vancouver.bc.ca/parks) freeze over. The Parks Board cordons off part of **LOST LAGOON** (map:P1) in Stanley Park for free public skating until rising temperatures and precipitation make ice levels unsafe. Other ponds are located in **QUEEN ELIZABETH PARK** (map:D3) in uptown Vancouver near 33rd Avenue and Cambie Street, along the south shore of **FALSE CREEK** (map:S6) near the downtown core, and on **COMO LAKE** (map:K3) in Coquitlam.

Karen Magnussen Recreation Centre

2300 KIRKSTONE RD, NORTH VANCOUVER; 604/983-6555
Named after an Olympic medallist who grew up in the neighbourhood, this North Vancouver facility is the premier skating rink on the North Shore. *Every day; map:E1.*

Kerrisdale Cyclone Taylor Arena

5670 EAST BLVD, WEST SIDE; 604/257-8121
This arena on the west side of Vancouver holds special parties to commemorate events such as St. Patrick's Day. *Open fall and winter (call for public skating schedule); map:C4.*

Kitsilano Community Centre

2690 LARCH ST, WEST SIDE; 604/257-6976
Year-round public skating is available at one of Vancouver's oldest and most popular recreation centers. *Every day; map:C3.*

Riley Park Community Centre

50 E 30TH AVE, SOUTH VANCOUVER; 604/257-8545
If the ponds on Queen Elizabeth Park aren't quite frozen over, this nearby recreation centre in uptown Vancouver can provide an artificial alternative during the winter. *Map:E3.*

IN-LINE SKATING

Vancouver was named one of North America's top 10 in-line cities by Condé Nast's (now defunct) *Women's Sports and Fitness* magazine. Still, the city's rather hilly geography means that you should have your braking techniques honed, especially if you're going to be out among pedestrians on city streets.

Kerrisdale Cyclone Taylor Arena

5670 EAST BLVD, WEST SIDE; 604/257-8121
Like many other Vancouver ice-skating arenas, Kerrisdale becomes a popular in-line skating centre when the ice is taken out in the spring, and it even has an energetic street hockey league for boys and girls. *Map:C4.*

Lower Seymour Conservation Reserve

NORTH VANCOUVER; 604/987-1273
Only in North Vancouver could you go in-line skating through a wilderness environment that has scenery to rival a national park. The $3 million, 10-kilometre (6-mile) road paved specifically for bikers and bladers makes it a must-do for in-line fanatics. Take the Capilano Road exit from Second Narrows Bridge, part of the Trans-Canada Highway, and follow the signs to Lower Seymour Conservation Reserve. *Map:Fo.*

Stanley Park Seawall

Bladers can travel on parts of the 8.8-kilometre (5.5-mile) seawall that circles Stanley Park near the downtown core, taking in the spectacular viewpoints. This is a busy pedestrian and cycling area, and each group takes their rights seriously. Follow the route's rules of etiquette. Stanley Park has an in-line skating patrol, organized by local blading guru/activist Lorne Milne, that offers Band-Aids to those who fall on padless knees and elbows and advice to those new to in-lining. *Map:D1.*

University of British Columbia

On the far west side of Vancouver, skaters can share an undulating cycle path that loops along 16th Avenue through Pacific Spirit Regional Park and back along Chancellor Boulevard into **UNIVERSITY VILLAGE** (map:B3). The paved shoulder of **MARINE DRIVE**, from West 16th Avenue to West 49th Avenue (map:B3), is also prime skating territory.

KITE FLYING

When the winds blow whitecaps on the waters of English Bay, it's time to unravel the kite strings and join other fliers at one of the seaside parks.

Garry Point Park

The windswept meadows at the mouth of the Fraser River in Steveston, south of Vancouver, are flat and exposed to south and westerly winds. This park isn't visited often by Vancouverites, but it's well worth the trip. If the wind dies, you can always enjoy a beach bonfire. Drive south out of Vancouver across the Oak Street Bridge, continue along Highway 99 to the Steveston Highway turnoff, just before the George Massey Tunnel, then go west (to your right) along the Steveston Highway as far as you can go. Turn south (to your left) to the park. *Map:B7.*

Vanier Park

This park on Kitsilano Point is a frequent-flyer spot, where many enthusiasts fly high-performance combat kites that engage in exciting dogfights. *Map:P5.*

MOUNTAIN BIKING

Although many recreation-oriented towns claim to be a mountain-biking mecca, there is a good case for making the Vancouver-Pemberton corridor the fat-tire capital of North America. Every possible accessory and kind of bike is available in the area's specialty stores, and some of the finest frames and components are built in Vancouver. Designers test their prototypes on some of the most technically difficult trails to be found anywhere. See also the Whistler chapter.

The North Shore

The North Shore mountains of Vancouver have become the proving ground for riders from all over the continent. The shore's vertiginous terrain and fecund overgrowth provide only half the challenge—the other half is the work of a crew of dedicated trail builders, who have created a fun house of dizzyingly challenging descents on the flanks of Mount Seymour, Mount Fromme, and Cypress Mountain. Some of these trails are almost entirely "elevated" above the forest canopy, and riders must negotiate log-ladders, teeter-totters, and skinny bridges barely a tire-tread wide. General areas in which you can pick up the trails include below Cypress Mountain in West Vancouver, behind Grouse Mountain, and in the Lower Seymour Conservation Reserve. **DEEP COVE BIKE SHOP** (4310 Gallant Ave, North Vancouver; 604/929-1918; www.covebike.com; map:H1) can provide details. **BICYCLE SPORTS PACIFIC** (3026 Mountain Hwy, North Vancouver; 604/988-1800; map:G1) is the closest shop to the North Shore trails.

This terrain is not suitable for novice riders and should never be cycled alone. Frequent riders are asked to help maintain the trails and obey proper etiquette when encountering other users. The **NORTH SHORE MOUNTAIN BIKING ASSOCIATION** (www.nsmba.bc.ca) works hard to keep these trails maintained and open. To get a taste of what it's like to "ride the Shore," check out the most excellent **NSMB E-ZINE** (www.nsmb.com).

Pacific Spirit Regional Park

This large tract of land near UBC was one of the earliest places to be discovered by mountain bikers, and it remains popular despite trail closures in some areas. Wardens patrol the park and have the authority to fine those who stray. Trails are especially muddy—and uncrowded—after a few days of rain. A great place to get your first single-track fix. Some of the most challenging riding is in the obscure northeast sector of the park. *Map:B3.*

THE BALD EAGLE—THAT GREAT BC SYMBOL

The bald eagle is the only eagle unique to North America and is found from Alaska and Canada to northern Mexico. At one time, the word bald meant "white," not "hairless." About 70,000 eagles live in Alaska. With another 20,000 in British Columbia, the northwest coast of North America is their greatest stronghold.

The largest gathering of bald eagles in southwestern British Columbia occurs along the banks of the Squamish River as it flows past Brackendale. Each year, November through mid-Feb, thousands of these majestic avian specimens come from points north and east to feast on a late-fall coho salmon run. Biologists aren't quite sure why the Squamish (and its tributary, the Mamquam River) is so popular—one theory holds that the depletion of salmon runs in other parts of the province is to blame—but there's no denying the vast number of birds that roost along these rivers during the winter.

It's a bit surprising to find such abundance of a bird that's just been taken off the endangered species list. Indeed, if you walk the trails or riverbanks at this area in the predawn darkness and wait for the first rays of sunlight, you'll be rewarded by the sight of 70 to 80 eagles in a single tree! (As crowds of bird-watchers and sightseers gather later in the day, the eagles start roosting farther away.) Additionally, a flock of trumpeter swans can often be seen near the mouth of the Squamish River.

The **SUNWOLF OUTDOOR CENTRE** (604/898-1537; 877/806-8046; www. sunwolf.net) offers naturalist-guided raft tours of the Squamish River during the winter. The **BRACKENDALE ART GALLERY** (604/898-3333; www.brackendale artgallery.com) pays homage to the eagles by hosting an official eagle count in January each year (dates vary each year). In 1994 a record number of 3,769 eagles were counted.

—Steven Threndyle

Squamish and Whistler

Once the snow melts and Vancouverites have retired their skis and snow-boards for the season, the toys of summer are pulled out. The Sea-to-Sky Country, the local nickname for the area between the towns of Squamish and Whistler, offers as much variety for mountain bikers as it does for skiers: wide-open cross-country ski trails, old logging roads leading to magnificent stands of old-growth red cedar, and some of the gnarliest and most techni-cally difficult riding imaginable. Not all of the trails are easy to find, so pick up the *Squamish-Whistler Mountainbike Trail Guide* (produced by Elaho) or *Mountain Bike Adventures in Southwest British Columbia: 50 Rides* (Moun-taineers Books). The two can't-miss races are the Test of Metal (Squamish) held each June and the Cheakamus Challenge (Whistler) in September. The Cheakamus's 58-kilometre (36-mile) course features gear-grinding ascents, white-knuckle descents, and a great postrace party.

Novices will enjoy the Lost Lake Loop. Stop for a refreshing dip either at the public beach on the south side of the lake or at a clothing-optional dock on the east side. For a greater challenge and a bit more solitude, Brandywine Falls and Cheakamus Lake (both Whistler) are ideal trips, often scheduled by one of the local guiding companies, such as Epic (604/932-3742; www.epicride.com) and Backroads Whistler (604/932-3111; www.backroads whistler.com). Hard-core riders will head straight for legendary trails like the Emerald Forest, A River Runs Through It, Northwest Passage, and the Rebob Trail. Bike rentals are available throughout the valley. Whistler-Blackcomb (604/938-9511; www.whistlerbike.com) also has a world-class mountain-biking park that's open once the snow melts; technical stunts as well as scenic single-track are the rewards here. (Note: There is a charge.) Lessons, guided descents, and a variety of rentals are all available.

NATURE AND ANIMAL OBSERVATION

Although the intrusion of civilization has pushed aside the habitat of indigenous flora and fauna, in Greater Vancouver many areas still exist where one can observe the rhythms and life cycles of the natural world. Birds, fish, whales, and other animals are constantly foraging for food in the same places where Native people hunted them centuries ago. The Fraser River Delta is a favourite stopping point for migrating flocks of snow geese, brants, and terns.

Many clubs and associations provide detailed information on nature observation in the province. The **VANCOUVER NATURAL HISTORY SOCIETY** (604/737-3074; www.naturevancouver.ca) holds field trips and has a birders' hotline that tells where rare birds have been spotted. The umbrella organization for the province is the **FEDERATION OF BC NATURALISTS** (604/737-3057; www.bcnature.ca), which can provide details on area clubs.

George C. Reifel Migratory Bird Sanctuary

ON WESTHAM ISLAND; 604/946-6980

Naturalists come from all over the world to this bird sanctuary at the mouth of the Fraser River, 10 kilometres (6 miles) west of Ladner. More than 250 species of birds can be sighted; peak viewing season is October through April. This wetlands environment is especially attractive to shorebirds such as herons, geese, and ducks. Occasionally, migratory birds from Asian countries lose their way and end up here, drawing crowds of ornithologists seeking to cross another exotic bird off their life lists. Kids love to feed seeds to the quacking hordes of ducks that are looking for a free handout. Take a picnic, sneak into a bird blind, or climb up a viewing tower—particularly in November during the Snow Goose Festival. Admission is $4 for adults; $2 for children and seniors 60+. *Every day; www.reifelbirdsanctuary.com.*

Greater Vancouver Zoo

ALDERGROVE; 604/856-6825

The Greater Vancouver Zoo—in a town east of Vancouver near Abbotsford—has 48 well-treed, parklike hectares (120 acres) that are home to more than 100 species of animals, including tigers, wolves, zebras, rhinoceroses, bears, parrots, flamingos, ostriches, bison, and many others—all roaming freely. You can walk, cycle, or drive through the farm, a favourite with kids. Drive 48 kilometres (30 miles) east of Vancouver, along the Trans-Canada Highway; take the 264th Street exit. *Open year-round; www.gvzoo.com.*

Maplewood Farm

405 SEYMOUR RIVER PL, NORTH VANCOUVER; 604/929-5610

Teeming with domestic animals, North Vancouver's municipal park farm is a great hit with kids. Its Rabbitat and Goathill areas are particularly popular for petting farm animals. Visitors to the 2-hectare (5-acre) farm can also take part in daily milking-by-hand demonstrations. Watch for special family events such as the Sheep Fair in May, the Farm Fair in September, and Christmas caroling in December. From Vancouver via the Second Narrows Bridge, exit 23-B (Deep Cove/Mount Seymour exit), turn left at the second traffic light. *Open year-round; www.maplewoodfarm.bc.ca; map:G1.*

Richmond Nature

11851 WESTMINSTER HWY, RICHMOND; 604/718-6188

This park offers everything you always wanted to know about bogs—and there are a lot of interesting things to know! Interpretive trails and a Nature House, complete with salamanders and snakes, make this a hidden gem in the suburban sprawl. Free admission. *Open year-round; www.richmond.ca/parksrec/ptc/naturepark/about.htm.*

Salmon Spawning

The **CAPILANO SALMON HATCHERY** (604/666-1790; map:E0), a federal government fish hatchery set on the Capilano River amongst majestic red cedars and lush huckleberry bushes, is a family favourite. Meander through the self-guided facility, where information panels describe the life cycle of Pacific salmon, then watch juvenile fish in the ponds or see returning salmon from the ocean jumping up a series of chutes (July through December). This park also boasts some of the tallest trees still standing on the Lower Mainland—the Giant Fir is more than 500 years old and 61 metres (200 feet) tall. Drive up Capilano Road in North Vancouver, take the first left past the suspension bridge onto Capilano Park Road, then proceed about 1.5 kilometres (1 mile) to the hatchery. Free admission. *Open every day.*

Every four years (2010, 2014, 2018 . . .) it's worth taking the six-hour drive (one way) to the **ADAMS RIVER** for the fall sockeye run. Fish return every year, of course, but these are the peak years, and that's when seeing them come back is truly spectacular. This is one of the great life-cycle stories in nature, in which salmon that have spent almost their entire lives in the

Pacific Ocean return up the Fraser River and Thompson River to spawn and die. Head west from Salmon Arm on Highway 1 to Squilax, then northeast on the paved highway for 3.8 kilometres (2.4 miles) to the junction just after the Adams River Bridge. The **ADAMS RIVER SALMON SOCIETY** (www. salmonsociety.com) is in the process of constructing an interpretive facility to help visitors appreciate and understand the ecology of the salmon and the environment. The centre is expected to be completed by 2010.

Whale-Watching

The best lookout locations for spotting grey whales are on the west coast of **VANCOUVER ISLAND**, a five-hour drive from Vancouver (including the ferry ride from Horseshoe Bay in West Vancouver to Nanaimo). Migrating grey whales can be seen beginning in late November but are more often seen in March and April, as they travel between their Mexican calving lagoons and Arctic feeding grounds. Many whale-watching **BOAT CHARTERS** operate out of the west coast communities of Tofino, Bamfield, and Ucluelet. There are good land viewpoints in the **LONG BEACH** area. Bring your binoculars if you plan just to watch from the beach. The Wickaninnish Centre at **WICKA-NINNISH BEACH** is a prime viewing spot. Contact **PACIFIC RIM NATIONAL PARK** (250/726-7721; www.pc.gc.ca/pn-np/bc/pacificrim/index_e.asp) for more information.

BC's second-largest city, Victoria, is one of the best places in the province for spotting killer whales, also known as orcas. In fact, on your ferry ride over to Vancouver Island, you may see a pod from the deck. **SEACOAST EXPEDITIONS** (250/383-2254 or 800/386-1525; www.seacoastexpeditions. com), Victoria's founding whale-watching company, advertises a "100 percent success rate" on its three-hour trips during peak months of June through September. Listen on the hydrophone (a type of water microphone) to orcas chatting. An on-board naturalist educates visitors about the flora and fauna encountered en route. Seacoast also makes two-hour excursions to **RACE ROCKS ECOLOGICAL RESERVE AND LIGHTHOUSE** to view California sea lions and Steller's sea lions, along with harbour seals, porpoises, colonies of cormorants, and bald eagle nests.

RIVER RAFTING

For a sheer adrenaline rush, it's hard to beat a day's rafting on one of the province's many stretches of white water, interspersed with a lazy drift through calm patches. Watch for deer nibbling on shoots and leaves near the water's edge, bald eagles whirling on air currents overhead, or even grizzled prospectors panning for gold. River rafting is regulated (for safety reasons) by the provincial government under the Commercial River Rafting Safety Act.

Chilliwack River

Located 96 kilometres (60 miles) east of Vancouver, this river is popular just after spring runoff, which occurs about early May–mid-July, for one-day rafting trips. The Chilliwack River is also popular with white-water kayakers.

Contact **HYAK WILDERNESS ADVENTURES** (604/734-8622 or 800/663-7238; www.hyak.com) for information.

Fraser River

Most one-day Fraser River excursions are offered May through August. Customers travel in motorized rafts downriver to communities along the Fraser Canyon from Boston Bar to Yale, about four hours' drive east of Vancouver. Raft Scuzzy Rock, China Bar, and Hell's Gate with experienced operators such as Lytton's **KUMSHEEN RAFT ADVENTURES** (250/455-2296 or 800/663-6667; www.kumsheen.com).

Nahatlatch River

The Nahatlatch River, a four-hour drive north of Vancouver, seethes with boiling chutes of white water May through mid-August. Join the Nahatlatch experts, **REO RAFTING ADVENTURES** (604/461-7238 or 800/736-7238; www.reorafting.com) for a wild ride through rapids with ominous-sounding names like the Meat Grinder, Lose Your Lunch, and the Big Chill. Free overnight camping is available at REO's private campsite.

Thompson River

The emerald-green waters of the Thompson River provide a pleasant mix of casual floating and stomach-churning white water. Rafters follow the Thompson southward from Spences Bridge (about a four-hour drive from Vancouver, east and then north along Hwy 1) to the takeout point at Lytton, where the clear Thompson joins the murky, silt-laden Fraser. The trip includes thrilling rapids such as the Devil's Kitchen and the Jaws of Death. Contact **HYAK WILDERNESS ADVENTURES** (604/734-8622 or 800/663-7238; www.hyak.com) for information.

RUNNING AND WALKING

Especially during peak periods, such as lunch hour and after work, there are so many runners on the municipal pathways that visitors to Vancouver might be forgiven for asking, "Is there some kind of race happening today?" Once you include in-line skaters, mountain bikers, triathletes, and race walkers, it seems as though the entire city is clad in Lycra tights and carrying water bottles. Exposure to fitness starts early, with jogging moms pushing their infants in specially constructed strollers, and continues into the golden years, with local Masters (competitors 40 and over) routinely running faster than men and women half their age. The **SUN RUN** (www.vancouversun.com/sunrun) is Canada's largest 10-kilometre (6.2-mile) road race, with its more than 50,000 participants made up of elite athletes, recreational joggers, and walkers alike.

Ambleside Park

As the name implies, this West Vancouver park is a great place for a beachside amble or jog. Watch cruise ships, freighters, barges, and even the odd battleship passing underneath Lions Gate Bridge into Burrard Inlet. Start at the east end of the park, where the Capilano River enters the ocean, and follow the seawall west. Great views across the First Narrows, Lions Gate Bridge, and Stanley Park. *Map:Co.*

Central Park

The wooded trails of Central Park, near the suburb of Burnaby, begin at the boundary between Burnaby and Vancouver, just off Kingsway. Track athletes regularly use Swangard Stadium for interval workouts. For runners who wish for more diversity, a fitness circuit featuring a variety of exercise options is available nearby. *Map:F4.*

Kitsilano Beach and Vanier Park

A 5-kilometre (3-mile) network of flat asphalt and dirt paths skirts Vanier Park on the Kitsilano side of Burrard Street Bridge. The paths follow the water around Kitsilano Point and past the Vancouver Museum, the Pacific Space Centre, the Maritime Museum, and Kitsilano Beach. In the summer, Kitsilano Beach is the Vancouver home of the bronzed and muscle-bound, and there's always a game of beach volleyball or street basketball happening. *Map:N5.*

Lost Lagoon, Stanley Park

The 1.6-kilometre (1-mile) trail that encircles Lost Lagoon is an easy stroll and a great spot for watching nesting Canada geese in spring. At intervals, the fountain in the centre of the lagoon emits a fine spray in a pattern that you have to watch for a few minutes to figure out. *Map:P1.*

Pacific Spirit Regional Park

Surrounding the University of British Columbia, this park contains 50 kilometres (31.1 miles) of walking and jogging trails through deciduous and coniferous forests, including Camosun Bog. Trails vary in length; you can enjoy a short stroll or take a more vigorous walk all the way from the Fraser River Estuary to Spanish Banks. The Visitor Centre is located on the north side of 16th Avenue, just west of Cleveland Trail. *Map:B3.*

Stanley Park Seawall

The longest seawall in Canada, at 8.8 kilometres (5.5 miles), is a great place to jog or walk. Plaques set in the wall at 0.5-kilometre intervals detail the wall's history. Runners and walkers can also detour into the park. The seawall is a brisk, nonstop, two-hour walk. *Map:P1.*

SAILING

Perhaps no sport quite defines the West Coast lifestyle like sailing. From two-person, high-speed catamarans to double-masted schooners, virtually every kind of sailboat can be found in the waters around Vancouver. Some of the best cruising is in Georgia Strait, where the landmass of Vancouver Island shelters many tiny bays and inlets that make perfect anchorages. **MACSAILING**, located in the Jericho Sailing Centre (1300 Discovery St, West

Side; 604/224-7245; www.macsailing.com; map:B2) offers instruction for the novice to the expert racer and complete rental facilities for qualified sailers. **COOPER BOATING CENTRE** (1620 Duranleau St, Granville Island; 604/687-4110 or 888/999/6419; www.cooperboating.com; map:U5) offers combination learn-to-sail cruises and classroom lectures to develop navigation and other nautical skills.

English Bay

During the summer, **COOPER BOATING CENTRE** (1620 Duranleau St, Granville Island; 604/687-4110 or 888/999-6419; www.cooperboating.com; map: Q6) will take you on three-hour cruises in English Bay on 6- to 12-metre (20- to 40-foot) yachts. Cruising in English Bay can also consist of a leisurely sail into spectacular Howe Sound, where salmon, killer whales, and dolphins are often seen.

Gulf Islands

Several sailing schools offer five-day cruise-and-learn trips around the Gulf Islands, including **LAND'S END SAILING SCHOOL** (604/818-8984 or 877/818-7245; www.landsend.vc.ca) and **ISLAND CRUISING** (No 1-C 9851 Seaport Pl, Sidney; 250/656-7070 or 800/663-5311; www.islandcruising.com). Or you can rent a yacht, with or without a skipper, and cruise the islands to discover the solitude of arbutus-lined coves, the charm of neighbourhood pubs and restaurants, and the thrill of watching marine life, such as harbour seals, whales, porpoises, and sea otters.

Princess Louisa Inlet

This saltwater bay is carved deep into the Coast Mountains wilderness. Located on the Sunshine Coast north of Sechelt, its calm waters and cascading waterfalls make it an ideal sailing destination. Farther north, **DESOLATION SOUND MARINE PARK** (North of Powell River and Lund on the Sunshine Coast; 90 miles north of Vancouver) is also a favourite summertime objective.

SKIING: CROSS-COUNTRY

The moist, mild climate of the south coast means that skiers take their chances on conditions when skiing locally. In Vancouver, cross-country skiing can be either as casual as a trip around a golf course or city park during one of the city's infrequent snowfalls or as extreme as a multiday expedition into the heart of the Coast Mountains. Cross-country skiers generally divide into two groups: aerobic-sports enthusiasts, who prefer striding or skating along specially manicured, machine-grooved tracks, and backcountry skiers, who blaze their own trails into the wilderness. The former can take classes in skate skiing, waxing, and racing strategy, while the latter will be interested in telemarking, backcountry navigation, avalanche awareness, and winter camping. Near Whistler is where you'll find the **SPEARHEAD TRAVERSE**, a multiday high-mountain trip, where the skiing is almost entirely on glaciers. Local weather conditions can change rapidly, and extra food and clothing should always be brought in a day pack. Winter backcountry ski courses are taught through the **FEDERATION OF MOUNTAIN CLUBS OF BRITISH COLUMBIA'S CANADA WEST MOUNTAIN SCHOOL** (47 W Broadway, West Side; 604/878-7007; www.themountainschool.com; map:V8). See also the Whistler chapter.

Cypress Mountain

NORTH VANCOUVER; 604/922-0825 OR 604/419-7669 (FOR CONDITIONS)

The groomed trails closest to Vancouver are at Cypress Mountain on the North Shore. You'll find 19 kilometres (11.8 miles) of groomed, track-set trails radiating from historic **HOLLYBURN LODGE**. A backcountry trail to the top of Hollyburn Mountain is also navigable, but it is quite steep in places and not suitable for children or inexperienced skiers. Nevertheless, the view over the city and into the Coast Mountains is unforgettable. Because Cypress is the closest place for Vancouver parents to take their kids for an authentic winter experience, it's not really a place to get away from it all. Rentals and lessons are available through the mountain. *www.cypressmountain.com; map:Co.*

Garibaldi Provincial Park

NORTH-NORTHWEST OF VANCOUVER VIA HWY 99; 604/924-2200

The alpine meadows of Singing Pass, Black Tusk, and Diamond Head, which yield an awesome profusion of wildflowers in summer, are blanketed with several metres of snow each winter. These three areas are prime backcountry skiing territory, with conveniently located small huts for protection from the elements. Backcountry skiers travelling in any areas within Garibaldi Park should be entirely self-sufficient, and everyone should be trained in avalanche safety. *www.env.gov.bc.ca/bcparks.*

Manning Park Resort

EAST OF VANCOUVER; 250/840-8822

Three hours east of Vancouver, Manning Park Resort offers skiers everything they could ask for: cross-country trails especially designed for skating and classic techniques, hundreds of square kilometres of rugged Coast Mountains ski touring, and even a challenging little downhill area for perfecting telemark turns. **SIGGE'S SPORT VILLA** (2077 W 4th, West Side; 604/731-8818 or 877/731-8818) in Kitsilano organizes bus trips from Vancouver that can include transportation, rentals, and lessons. Manning is a good place to take kids, and the ticket prices won't break the bank, either. Overnight accommodation is available in wonderful log cabins or at the main lodge. Also check with **MANNING PROVINCIAL PARK** (604/924-2200; www.env.gov.bc.ca/bcparks) for more information. *www.manningpark.com.*

SQUAMISH: GOING TO THE EXTREMES

Forget team spirit. Carve your own path and find out where your limits lie in **SQUAMISH**, British Columbia.

Conveniently located only 45 minutes north of Vancouver, Squamish is a small city surrounded by the dramatic Coast Range Mountains and Pacific Ocean, where there's an abundance of world-class recreational opportunities. Rock climbing, windsports, and mountain biking are just some of more than 25 activities available in the region. Discover hiking, river rafting, kayaking, sailing and boating, fishing, diving, golfing, snowmobiling, and horseback riding in and around the five provincial parks that surround the area.

Sir Richard Branson, the British entrepreneur known for his success in the recording and airline industries, used "Canada's Recreation Capital" as a setting for a major business announcement in 2005. Helicopters circled overhead as the 58-year-old enjoyed a 40-minute kite-surfing session in the strong winds off the **SQUAMISH SPIT**—considered by windsurfing aficionados to be one of the top 10 windsport locations in the world—and against the backdrop of the monolithic rock-climbing playground of the **STAWAMUS CHIEF**.

In 1960 Jim Baldwin and Ed Cooper made the first ascent of the Grand Wall on the Chief, and since then climbers from around the globe have made Squamish the country's premier rock-climbing mecca. The Chief satisfies any climber's sense of adventure with easy slabs, 18-pitch gear routes, a massive boulder field

---

Mount Seymour Provincial Park

**NORTH VANCOUVER; 604/986-2261 OR
604/718-7771 (FOR CONDITIONS)**

Mount Seymour on the North Shore is another local favourite, especially for those with backcountry skiing aspirations. The skiing between First (Pump) Peak and Second Peak can be excellent, especially after a big snowfall. Outside the downhill-ski-area boundary, skiers must stay close to the marked trail, especially in foggy weather. It's common for skiers or snowshoers to become lost in this bluff-filled, confusing terrain. The back bowls beyond the ski area are popular with snowboarders. *www.mountseymour.com; map:G1–H1.*

SNOWBOARDING AND DOWNHILL SKIING

With the possible exception of Salt Lake City, no city in North America boasts such excellent skiing facilities within a two-hour drive from downtown as does Vancouver. The closest areas are on the North Shore. Cypress Mountain, Grouse Mountain, and Mount Seymour all have respectable vertical drops and are ideal places to learn the sport. The crown jewel, though, lies 90 minutes

at its base, and all manner of aid routes.

Mountain Bike Magazine rated Squamish as one of the top 25 wildest and most exotic places to ride in the world. More than 100 trails offer everything from easy riding for the whole family to intense white-knuckle single-track riding.

Just 15 kilometres (9 miles) south of Squamish on Highway 99 is **PORTEAU COVE PROVINCIAL MARINE PARK** in the magnificently scenic Howe Sound. As the first underwater park in BC, it is home to a cliff dive, a human-made reef, three sunken ships, and various other wrecks.

SHANNON FALLS PROVINCIAL PARK, 2 kilometres (1.25 miles) south of Squamish on Highway 99, boasts BC's third-largest waterfall, as well as a number of hiking trails. The area also offers great historical and geological attractions such as the West Coast Railway Museum and BC Museum of Mining in Britannia Beach.

Community events include the Mountain Bike Festival in June, with the grueling 67-kilometre (41.5-mile) Test of Metal mountain bike race, the Bob MacIntosh Triathlon in July, and the Squamish Days Loggers Sports with international logging competitions in August.

For more information, the **VISITOR CENTRE** is located beside Highway 99 in the ultracool **SQUAMISH ADVENTURE CENTRE** (102-38551 Loggers Ln; 604/815-4994 or 866/333-2010; www.squamishchamber.com).

—Ian Walker

north of Vancouver, at the resort city of Whistler, North America's largest ski destination (see the Whistler chapter).

Cypress Mountain

NORTH VANCOUVER; 604/922-0825 OR 604/419-7669 (FOR CONDITIONS)
Cypress, the largest downhill facility on the North Shore, can be a fantastic place to ski after a big snowstorm. For the advanced skier, it boasts some excellent mogul skiing, especially the Top Gun run underneath the Sky Chair. The half pipe draws lots of local boarders, too. Cars driving the Cypress Mountain road should be equipped with tire chains or good winter-tread tires. *www.cypressmountain.com; map:Co.*

Grouse Mountain

NORTH VANCOUVER; 604/980-9311 OR 604/986-6262 (FOR CONDITIONS)
Closer to Vancouver, Grouse's ski runs and lit trails are visible from most parts of the Lower Mainland. You can take the bus from downtown right to the base of the mountain, where you're shuttled to the top on the Skyride,

an aerial tram that gives a spectacular view of the city and all the way across Georgia Strait to Vancouver Island. Although Grouse's slopes are a fraction of the length of those found at Whistler, it's still a great place to go for a quick ski fix. *www.grousemountain.com.*

Hemlock Valley

Tucked in a side-valley tributary of the Fraser River, Hemlock is one of the least-conspicuous ski areas in the province. Its quaint day lodge and older, slower lifts make it a throwback to the days when even downhill skiing was an adventure sport. But that's a good thing, since powder skiing here often lasts longer than it does at more-crowded destination resorts. Some slopeside accommodation is available through privately rented cabins and **HEMLOCK RESORT** (604/797-4411 or 866/567-6866; www.hemlockvalleyresort.com).

Mount Seymour

NORTH OF DOWNTOWN VANCOUVER; 604/986-2261 OR 604/718-7771 (FOR CONDITIONS)

This ski area within the provincial park of the same name is where many Vancouverites are exposed to skiing or snowboarding for the first time. The inexpensive learn-to-ski programmes are often operated in conjunction with the local schools. There's a great tobogganing area at the south end of the parking lot. Seymour's somewhat irregular terrain also makes it popular with snowboarders looking to ollie off buried stumps and logs. All-season tires or chains are recommended for the road to Seymour. *www.mountseymour.com; map:G1–H1.*

SNOWSHOEING

Snowshoeing is a tried-and-true way of getting off into the snowy backwoods terrain that is often too uneven for cross-country skiers.

Grouse Mountain

NORTH VANCOUVER; 604/980-9311

Known as the Peak of Vancouver, Grouse is a popular destination for snowshoeing. The **MUNDY ALPINE SNOWSHOE PARK** offers four groomed and marked trails ranging from 1 kilometre (0.6 mile) to 3.5 kilometres (2.2 miles). Seminars and lessons, along with friendly competitions, are held regularly. *www.grousemountain.com.*

Manning Provincial Park

EAST OF VANCOUVER; 604/924-2200

Three hours east of Vancouver, Manning has extensive snowshoeing terrain in its vast backcountry. As with any winter backcountry activity, snowshoeing entails being wary of avalanches and changing weather conditions, as well as having mountain navigation skills. **MANNING PARK RESORT** (250/840-8822; www.manningparkresort.com) offers rentals and guided excursions. *www. env.gov.bc.ca/bcparks.*

Mount Seymour Provincial Park

**NORTH VANCOUVER; 604/986-2261 OR
604/718-7771 (FOR CONDITIONS)**
Over the Second Narrows Bridge, 16 kilometres (10 miles) north of Vancouver, Mount Seymour offers snowshoe rentals and instruction. Snowshoers of all ages can skirt some of the winter cross-country trails, including Goldie Lake Loop, Flower Lake Loop, and Hidden Lake Loop. Guided snowshoeing tours, drop-in nights, and rentals are operated through the hill. *www. mountseymour.com; map:G1–H1.*

SWIMMING

Vancouver's 11 sandy beaches are fine for swimming, even in slightly brisk temperatures. Lifeguards patrol in June, July, and August. Favourite swimming beaches include English Bay (site of the annual New Year's Day Polar Bear Swim), Sunset Beach, Kitsilano Beach (especially after a strenuous session of beach volleyball), Jericho Beach, Locarno Beach, and Spanish Banks. Jericho, Locarno, and Spanish Banks are also popular with cycling and windsurfing crowds.

Kitsilano Pool

2305 CORNWALL AVE, WEST SIDE; 604/731-0011
Kits Beach has a gigantic outdoor saltwater pool adjacent to English Bay. It is heated to 26 degrees Celsius (79 degrees Fahrenheit) and has a graduated depth, making it ideal for both children and strong swimmers. *Every day (Victoria Day–Labour Day); www.city.vancouver.bc.ca/parks/rec/pools; map:N6.*

Newton Wave Pool

13730 72ND AVE, SURREY; 604/501-5540
Because the waters of Vancouver are protected from the ocean swells of the Pacific coast, surfing is not part of the city's aquatic culture. But in the suburb of Surrey, south of Vancouver, a wave-action leisure pool generates 1-metre (3-foot) waves for bodysurfing. There are also two giant waterslides, a wading pool, a steam room, a whirlpool, a weight room, and even a licensed lounge. *Every day; www.surrey.ca; map:L7.*

Second Beach Outdoor Pool

STANLEY PARK, WEST END; 604/257-8371
Along the Stanley Park seawall, this outdoor pool is popular with locals and visitors alike during the summer months. *Every day (late June–Labour Day); www.city.vancouver.bc.ca/parks/rec/pools; mapO1.*

Splashdown Waterpark

4799 NULELUM WY, TSAWWASSEN; 604/943-2251
The owners of Splashdown Water Park have taken advantage of Tsawwassen's sunny location—half the annual rainfall of downtown Vancouver—to construct a giant 3-hectare (7-acre) park, featuring 11 waterslides. There's a

full range of summertime fun to be enjoyed here, including volleyball, basketball, and minigolf. It's a great place to pack a picnic and perhaps the most reliable spot in the Lower Mainland for getting a suntan. *Every day (Victoria Day–Labour Day); www.splashdownpark.ca.*

University of British Columbia Aquatic Centre

6121 UNIVERSITY BLVD, WEST SIDE; 604/822-4522
UBC has Olympic-size indoor and outdoor pools with a sauna, steam room, whirlpool, exercise gym, and toddler pool. Open late into the evening for public swimming. *Every day; www.aquatics.ubc.ca; map:A3.*

Vancouver Aquatic Centre

1050 BEACH AVE, WEST END; 604/665-3424
Overlooking Sunset Beach, the Vancouver Aquatic Centre features an Olympic-size indoor pool, sauna, whirlpool, and toddler pool. *Every day; www.city.vancouver.bc.ca/parks/rec/pools; map:Q5.*

TENNIS

Keen tennis players can perfect their topspin lob or two-fisted backhand year-round on Vancouver's 183 public courts, even though the outdoor season officially runs March through October. Most public courts are free and operate on a first-come, first-served basis.

STANLEY PARK has 21 courts (the wait can be lengthy during peak periods), 17 by the **BEACH AVENUE ENTRANCE** (map:O1) and four by **LOST LAGOON** (map:Q1) at the foot of Robson Street. April through September, you can book a Beach Avenue court for a small fee. **QUEEN ELIZABETH PARK** courts (33rd Ave at Cambie St, South Vancouver; map:D3) are centrally located in the city but can be quite hot when there's no breeze. **KITSILANO BEACH PARK** (West Side; map:N5) has 10 courts near the ocean, with a concession stand nearby for a cool drink or french fries. **JERICHO BEACH PARK** (West Side; map:B2), behind the Jericho Sailing Center, offers great rugby viewing on the pitch south of the courts while you wait your turn.

WINDSURFING

Although Vancouver is practically surrounded by water and exposed to breezes from every direction, capricious conditions can test the patience of high-speed sailors looking for waves to jump and steady, consistent winds. But the light winds often found on the beaches of the city's West Side are ideal for learning to windsurf.

WINDSURE WINDSURFING SCHOOL (1300 Discovery St, West Side; 604/224-0615; www.windsure.com; map:B2) operates out of the Jericho Sailing Centre. Its specialty is an intensive six-hour course that guarantees results. **PACIFIC BOARDER** (1793 W 4th Ave, West Side; 604/734-7245; www.pacificboarder.com; map:O7) in Kitsilano sells boardsailing equipment and wet suits, along with surfboards and body boards.

For some of the most consistent wind conditions in North America, drive an hour north from Vancouver to the town of Squamish—the name comes from a Native word meaning "place where the wind blows." The **SQUAMISH SPIT** is a human-made dyke that separates the saltwater bay of Howe Sound from the frigid waters of the Squamish River. Skim out on your board within view of the Stawamus Chief, Shannon Falls, and Howe Sound. Conditions are best May through August, when afternoon thermals generated by warm air create steady, consistent conditions. The water is cold, so a thick wet suit or dry suit is mandatory, especially if you are still developing your jibing and water-start skills. **SQUAMISH WINDSPORTS SOCIETY** (604/588-4161; www.squamishwindsurfing.org) administers the park, charging a daily fee to pay for rescue boats, washroom maintenance, and liability insurance. To get to the spit, follow Highway 99 north to Squamish and turn left at the Cleveland Avenue intersection. Turn right on Buckley Avenue as it turns into Government Road. Follow Government Road as it loops back past the Railway Museum and the BC Rail yards (on the left). A sign on the right directs you to the 4-kilometre-long (2.5-mile-long) gravel road. The **WIND REPORT** (604/892-2235) is updated several times each day.

Spectator Sports

While Vancouver boasts a significant population that would rather be playing sports than watching them, there's a multitude of options for all seasons when it's time to watch somebody else sweat it out. Vancouver boasts professional hockey, football, and soccer teams, plus a minor league baseball club and a major junior hockey franchise. The National Hockey League's Vancouver Canucks and Canadian Football League's BC Lions have enjoyed a resurgence of late, and they're playing in front of the largest crowds in decades.

BC Lions Football

BC PLACE STADIUM, 765 PACIFIC BLVD, DOWNTOWN; 604/589-7627
The Lions play in the Canadian Football League. A longer, wider field and only three downs to make 10 yards means that a passing game predominates, making it a far more exciting sport than its American counterpart. Action is the name of the game in this league, which is decades older than the American National Football League. Avid fans enjoy home games downtown June through late October; the season culminates in Grey Cup championship. Tickets available through Ticketmaster (604/280-4444; www.ticketmaster.com) and at the gate. *www.bclions.com; map:T5.*

Hastings Park Horse Racing

NEAR HASTINGS AND RENFREW STREETS,
EAST VANCOUVER; 604/254-1631
From spring through fall, the thoroughbreds race at the Hastings Park racecourse, on the grounds of the Pacific National Exhibition. It's easy to get

2010 WINTER OLYMPICS IN VANCOUVER

In Vancouver February 12–28, 2010, the 2010 Olympic Winter Games will be a sight to see—and a lot of people will be doing just that. About 1.4 million tickets to events ranging from hockey to skiing, curling to ice skating, went on sale in October 2007 to a demand so large, the seating at many of the events had to be determined by lottery.

The Olympics will start with a huge opening ceremony in downtown Vancouver at the 59,000-seat BC Place Stadium. It will be the first time in Winter Olympics history that so many people will be able to see the Opening Ceremony from the stands and the first time ever that such a ceremony has been held under a covered roof, which gives ceremony producers a lot of options for putting on the big show, knowing the elements won't be a factor.

During the Olympics, the stadium is expected to be filled every night to the brim with people going to the Victory Celebrations. A lot of high-profile entertainment and cultural events will be held there (and throughout the city) leading up to the gold, silver, and bronze medal awards amidst Olympic pomp and ceremony highlighting that day's winners.

As the Opening Ceremonies get under way, so too will the two Olympic Live Sites in downtown Vancouver. One is a block away from the stadium on what is now a city-block-size gravel parking lot at Cambie and West Georgia streets; the other is a kilometre away at David Lam Park at Pacific Boulevard and Drake Street, on the northern waterfront of False Creek, across from Granville Island (the island is to be another hotbed of entertainment). The Live Sites will be host to thousands of people visiting and shopping at innovative pavilions from the companies and governments that are supporting the Games. That audience will also be watching entertainment live (and replays) on huge TV screens of the day's sporting events in Vancouver and from nearby Richmond, West Vancouver, and Whistler.

caught up in the excitement of an afternoon's racing. General admission is free. *Post time 6:15pm Wed–Fri, 1:15pm Sat–Sun and holidays mid-April–Nov; www.hastingspark.com; map:F2.*

Vancouver Canadians Baseball

4601 ONTARIO ST, EAST VANCOUVER; 604/872-5232

Historic Nat Bailey Stadium (known affectionately as the "Nat") is home to Canada's last remaining Major League Baseball affiliate (Oakland Athletics). The Canadians play in the eight-team single-A Northwest League June through September and are Vancouver's best team for your sporting buck.

The Live Site nearest the stadium, which is expected to hold up to 10,000 people, will operate free 10am–10pm; the one at the park, with a capacity of 11,000, will operate 10am–11pm, with a nightly finale. During the day, a major pavilion at Robson Square will focus on business-to-business celebrations, but there'll be fun for the kids there too, as the newly renovated General Electric Ice Plaza will be in operation.

Another major venue area for the Games in 2010 will be on the famous Pacific National Exhibition Grounds in East Vancouver, near Hastings and Renfrew streets. The huge Forum building will house the sprawling Olympic accreditation centre, which will issue tickets and permission tags that allow hundreds of thousands of people to get into specific areas of the Games' venues. At the nearby Coliseum, whose NHL-sized ice sheet has been expanded to Olympic size and whose seats have all been replaced by the Vancouver Organizing Committee (VANOC) for the 2010 Olympic and Paralympic Winter Games, the Olympic short-track speed skating and world-famous figure-skating competitions will be held.

Near Little Mountain, in uptown Vancouver, the world's finest curling rink, Hillcrest, has just opened so that Canadian teams can start practising two seasons in advance of the Games on the actual ice they'll be using during the Games. In East Vancouver, two new permanent ice rinks are rising from the remains of the Trout Lake arena and the Killarney Arena. They'll be used by the Olympics for practise rinks for hockey players.

At the University of Vancouver, Olympic hockey games will be played during the round-robin tournaments that will feed teams to the playoffs at GM Place. The feeder tournaments will play in the new ice arenas VANOC built to replace the ancient Thunderbird rink, but they'll be used for generations of hockey players, amateur and professional, to come.

For more information on these and other venues, check out the **OFFICIAL WEB SITE** for the Games (www.vancouver2010.com).

—Peter Morgan

Located on the eastern side of scenic Queen Elizabeth Park, Nat Bailey is regarded by many as the best little ballpark in the world, and you'll be hard-pressed to get a ticket for its popular "nooners." Tickets available through the club or online. *www.canadiansbaseball.com; map:D3.*

Vancouver Canucks Hockey

GM PLACE, 800 GRIFFITHS WY, DOWNTOWN; 604/899-7400
Although the National Hockey League has been diluted by the addition of too many teams and a punishing regular-season schedule, a well-played hockey game is still the coolest game on earth. The hometown Canucks have had a

few bright, shining moments during their 30-year history, but their inconsistent ways and failure to live up to potential have bred a certain degree of cynicism amongst locals. Still, the faithful stick with the team through good times and bad, and the large number of expats from other parts of Canada makes getting tickets a challenge—especially when the Montreal Canadiens or Toronto Maple Leafs are in town. The regular hockey season begins in October and finishes in April. Tickets available through Ticketmaster (604/280-4444; www.ticketmaster.com) and at the gate. *www.canucks.nhl.com; map:V5.*

Vancouver Giants Hockey

100 N RENFREW ST, EAST VANCOUVER; 604/444-2687

Want a low-cost alternative to the bigs? The Giants are the second-largest market in the 22-team Western Hockey League and the 2007 Memorial Cup champions. Playing out of the Pacific Coliseum, the former home of the Canucks, the Giants offer all the heart, all the passion, but none of the egos associated with their major league cousins. The season runs September through April and tickets are available from Ticketmaster (604/280-4444; www.ticketmaster.com) and at the gate. *www.vancouvergiants.com; map:F2.*

Vancouver Whitecaps Soccer

SWANGARD STADIUM, BOUNDARY RD
AND KINGSWAY, EAST VANCOUVER; 604/899-9823

Vancouver's diverse ethnicity has created a ready-made audience for soccer, especially amongst homesick Brits, Portuguese, and Italians. The Vancouver Whitecaps (once known as the '86ers) played their first season during the year of Expo '86 and promptly won four straight Canadian soccer league titles before switching to the United Soccer Leagues First Division, an 11-team international circuit. The season runs early May through September. Tickets available through Ticketmaster (604/280-4444; www.ticketmaster.com) and at the gate. *www.whitecapsfc.com; map:F4.*

VICTORIA AND BEYOND

VICTORIA AND BEYOND

How to Get Here

BY FERRY

BC FERRIES (604/444-2890, from Victoria 250/386-3431 or 888/223-3779; www.bcferries.com) departs the mainland from **TSAWWASSEN**, 38 kilometres (24 miles) south of Vancouver (follow Hwy 99 to the Hwy 17 turnoff and continue southwest to the Tsawwassen ferry terminal), to **SWARTZ BAY**, 32 kilometres (20 miles) north of Victoria, eight or more times a day; schedules vary seasonally. The scenic trip takes 90 minutes, but allow about three hours each way to include the drive between downtown and the ferry terminal at both ends, as well as some waiting time at the docks. Loading begins about 20 minutes before departure, so be sure to arrive ahead of time. Ferries are equipped with many conveniences: indoor lounge seating, Internet access, outdoor benches, cafeteria, gift shop, children's play area, and a video arcade. Year-round fares are $47.15 one way per car, $14.25 for the driver and each additional passenger, $7.75 for children under 11, free for children under 5; BC seniors travel free Mon–Thurs; for an extra $15 one-way reservations can be made via phone or online, a welcome option for sheer convenience.

An alternative ferry route to Victoria is via the **HORSESHOE BAY–NANAIMO FERRY**, which passes by Bowen and Gabriola islands during its 95-minute voyage. The waterfront village of Horseshoe Bay in West Vancouver (follow BC Hwy 99 north to Vancouver, turn west onto Georgia Street, go through Stanley Park, cross the Lions Gate Bridge and follow Hwy 1 to Horseshoe Bay ferry terminal) merits a visit while you wait to board the ferry. If your destination is Victoria, or if you are starting from Victoria and want to end up in downtown Vancouver, allow about five hours each way. The 113-kilometre (70-mile) drive between Nanaimo and downtown Victoria is along the picturesque Trans-Canada Highway (Hwy 1). It winds through the pastoral Cowichan Valley, up to the Malahat Summit with breathtaking views of the Saanich inlet, and down through the lush rain forest of **GOLD-STREAM PROVINCIAL PARK**.

BY BUS

PACIFIC COACH LINES (604/662-8074, from Victoria 250/385-4411; www.pacificcoach.com) offers frequent, reliable service via the Tsawwassen–Swartz Bay BC Ferries route. Buses depart from the Vancouver bus terminal (Pacific Central Stn, 1150 Station St, East Vancouver—check the schedule—and the trip takes approximately four hours, arriving at the downtown Victoria bus depot (700 Douglas St) behind the Empress Hotel; fare is $43.00 one-way, including ferry fare; free for BC seniors Monday through Thursday.

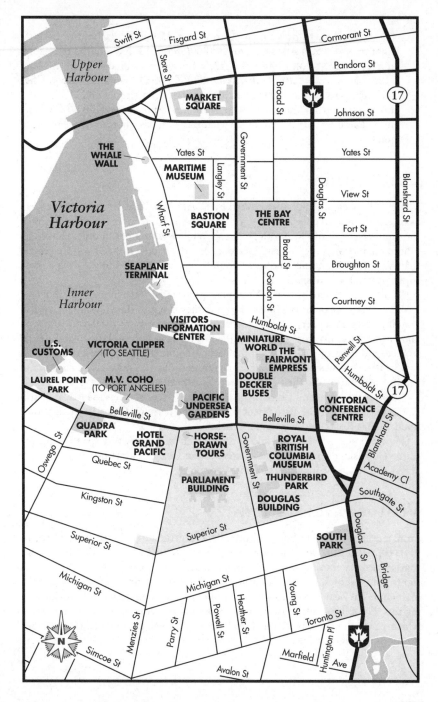

BY AIR

The fastest link to downtown Victoria is a 35-minute harbour-to-harbour flight by **HARBOUR AIR SEAPLANES** (800/665-0212; www.harbour-air.com) or **WEST COAST AIR** (800/347-2222; www.westcoastair.com); fare is about $135 one way. **HELIJET AIRWAYS** (800/665-4354; www.helijet.com) has helicopter service starting from $229 one way. Both airlines and Helijet offer direct service from Vancouver Airport's south terminal (see How to Get Here in the Planning a Trip chapter) to Victoria, with free shuttle service to many hotels.

Orientation

Victoria, BC's capital city, was ranked by *Condé Nast Traveler* magazine readers as one of the top 10 cities in the world to visit, and Vancouver Island was ranked the number-one island in North America. While Victoria hasn't quite shaken its "more English than the English" persona, and the pace is decidedly more genteel than Vancouver's, the city and its surrounds are growing up and showing a more sophisticated and exciting side.

While tourists can still stroll sculpted gardens, sip afternoon tea, shop for Irish linens, or meander the Inner Harbour, they can also dine lavishly in award-winning restaurants serving local organic ingredients; taste local wines, ciders, and craft brews; or shop at some of the hottest new fashion houses and design stores—and most of it's located in the very walkable **DOWNTOWN CORE**.

The **INNER HARBOUR**, in front of the Empress Hotel, can be viewed as ground zero for orientation. To the right, or north, is **GOVERNMENT STREET**, which leads to historic Old Town and Chinatown, and to the left, or south is the Royal British Columbia Museum, the Parliament building, the heritage James Bay neighbourhood, Dallas Road, and Beacon Hill Park.

However you arrive, you'll find gorgeous scenery at every turn: picturesque firs of the Gulf Islands; the Olympic, Cascade, and Coast mountains south and east across the Straits of Juan de Fuca and Georgia.

Visitor Information

From a central Inner Harbour location, the energetic staff at **TOURISM VICTORIA VISITOR INFO CENTRE** (812 Wharf St; 250/953-2033 or 800/663-3883; www. tourismvictoria.com) dispense free maps and useful information on the various sights, tours, shows, and special events in the city, the island, Gulf Islands, and the mainland. They can also help with last-minute accommodations and provide dining tips. For a list of local happenings, pick up a free copy of *Monday Magazine*, which offers the city's best weekly calendar of events. It is available at various locations throughout the city.

Getting Around

Most attractions, shops, restaurants, hotels, banks, and other services are within a 12-square-block radius. If you plan to stray beyond the main downtown core, alternative forms of transportation will save your soles.

The **VICTORIA REGIONAL TRANSIT SYSTEM** operated by **BC TRANSIT** (250/382-6161; www.bctransit.com) has more than 40 bus routes through Greater Victoria. Fares are calculated on a per-zone basis: $2.25 one way, single zone; $3 one way, two zones; discounts for children, students, and seniors with proper identification; transfers good for travel in one direction only with no stopovers; a $7 day pass (also available at Visitor Info Centre and ticket outlets displaying Fare Dealer symbol) covers unlimited travel throughout the day. *Every day 6am–midnight.*

VICTORIA HARBOUR FERRY COMPANY (250/708-0201; www.victoriaharbour ferry.com) squires passengers (maximum 12) to and from 12 shore points all along the Inner Harbour and the Gorge Waterway; hotel docking ports include the Empress, Coast Harbourside, and Ocean Pointe Resort. You can get on at any stop and take a round-trip, 45-minute cruise. Fare $20 per person, $18 for students and seniors, $10 for children under 12; $5 to cross the Inner Harbour. *Sailings every 15 minutes 9am–9pm; Nov–Feb 11am–4pm Sat–Sun, weather permitting.*

It's best to call for a cab; drivers don't always stop on city streets for flag-downs. Try **YELLOW CABS** (250/383-7111) or **BLUE BIRD CABS** (250/382-8294). A horse-drawn carriage ride with **VICTORIA CARRIAGE TOURS** (corner of Belleville and Menzies sts; 250/383-2207 or 877/663-2207) is a romantic and eco-friendly way to introduce yourself to Beacon Hill Park and the city's architecture; the larger **TALLY-HO** carriages (corner of Belleville and Menzies sts; 250/383-5067 or 866/383-5067) offer rides at a family rate.

For **BIKES AND SCOOTERS**, Victoria has many bike lanes that run through the city, as well as paved paths along parks and beaches. The **GALLOPING GOOSE TRAIL** (www.gallopinggoosetrail.com) is the most popular, with 60 kilometres (37 miles) of trails that go from Victoria to Sooke, via asphalt to rain forest to canyon. Helmets are mandatory, and it's illegal to cycle on sidewalks. You can rent bikes for around $7 an hour ($24 a day) at **CYCLE BC** (250/380-2453; www.cyclebc. ca) or motorized scooters for $16 an hour ($59 a day), helmets included. Baby strollers are also available at $5 an hour ($20 per day).

Traffic is often heavy and **PARKING IS SCARCE** in downtown Victoria. It helps if there's parking at your lodgings. If not, be prepared to circle around awhile for metered, on-street parking. Parking lots are located on View Street between Douglas and Blanshard, on Johnson Street near Blanshard, and on Yates Street near Bastion Square. Note that metered parking is free after 6pm during the week and free all day Sundays and holidays.

Most major **RENTAL CAR AGENCIES** have downtown pickup/drop-off locations, including **AVIS** (800/879-2847), **BUDGET RENT-A-CAR** (800/268-8900), **HERTZ CANADA** (800/263-0600), and **NATIONAL CAR RENTAL** (800/387-4747). If you are a CAA or AAA member, ask the reservations agent for a member discount.

Tours of Victoria and the Region

Vintage double-decker buses offer various narrated tours of the city, including Chinatown, Antique Row, a sunset tour, scenic views of Mount Baker, homes and gardens of tweedy Oak Bay, and the estates of the Uplands. Modern motor coaches drive out to the famed Butchart Gardens and Butterfly World. The **GRAY LINE WEST** (250/388-6539 or 800/667-0882; www.graylinewest.com) kiosk for tickets and tours is always set up on the sidewalk in front of the Empress Hotel and inside the hotel.

The vast surrounding ocean is home to exquisite wildlife and sea mammals, including spectacular pods of killer whales. **OCEAN EXPLORATIONS** (602 Broughton St; 250/383-6722 or 888/442-6742; www.oceanexplorations.com) commands a fleet of large Zodiac boats that take passengers (12 max) on three-hour tours through the San Juan Islands or west around the rugged tip of Vancouver Island. Whale sightings and close encounters are common April to October as migrating salmon return. Up to eight expeditions leave daily from the Inner Harbour, led by experienced guides/naturalists, knowledgeable about the marine environment and its inhabitants. Many photo opportunities exist when the boat slows or stops to observe wildlife and points of interest during the tour. In the off-season, participants can experience an up close and personal look at dolphins, seals, porpoises, sea lions, eagles, and sea birds.

Thrill seekers can hook up with **ADRENA LINE ZIPLINE ADVENTURE TOURS** (250/642-1933 or 866/947-9145; www.adrenalinezip.com) and harness themselves in for a two-hour circuit through the majestic forests of Sooke Hills. Participants zip over 3,200 feet at a maximum speed of 60 kmh (37 mph), with the highest vantage points at 150 feet. The Zip West van picks up participants daily in the parking lot below the Tourism Victoria Visitor Info Centre.

TRAVEL WITH TASTE (250/385-1527; www.travelwithtaste.com) conducts various tours through the wine-growing and farming regions of the Saanich Peninsula, Cowichan Valley, Salt Spring Island, and a meadery-honey farm in Sooke. Most tours include a lunch, and host Kathy McAree can arrange custom tours for groups, including real estate tours. For those with limited time, her four-hour urban foraging tour of downtown Victoria offers an informative taste of the city's best purveyors, including tea masters, artisan bakers, a chocolatier, a charcuterie, and, of course, wine sellers.

BLUE PLANET KAYAKING (866/595-7865; www.blueplanetkayaking.com) offers outdoor enthusiasts gourmet food with a taste of the outdoors. Tour operator and chef James Bray leads tours through the Gulf Islands, to the wilds of Clayoquot Sound, or for orca-watching in Johnson Strait. You'll be sustained with meals of brioche French toast in the morning with homemade jam, free-range bacon, and locally roasted coffee; dinners might include organic chicken confit and other regional ingredients paired with a local pinot noir. And all this on a Coleman stove! His popular Gulf Island Gourmet Weekend tours must be booked well in advance.

Seaweed expert Diane Bernard of **OUTER COAST SEAWEED** (877/713-7464; www.outercoastseaweeds.com) leads seasonal two-hour hands-on tours on the

GHOSTLY VICTORIA

GHOSTLY WALKS (250/384-6698; www.discoverthepast.com) is a 90-minute spine-tingling journey through the haunted alleyways and courtyards of Chinatown and Old Town Victoria. Historian and captivating storyteller John Adams leads tours throughout the year that commence at 7:30pm at the Tourism Victoria Visitor Info Centre at the Inner Harbour (see Visitor Information in this chapter). You can't miss him; he'll be waiting at the door dressed in black! Tickets $12 for adults, $10 for students and seniors, $30 for families; cash only; reservations not required. *Every day May 1–Oct 31; winter Sat–Sun.*

The **OLD CEMETERIES SOCIETY** (250/598-8870; www.oldcem.bc.ca) conducts walking tours of many of Victoria's cemeteries, but the majority of tours—with good cause—go to Ross Bay Cemetery. Tours commence from Starbucks at the **FAIRFIELD PLAZA** (1516 Fairfield Rd), across from the cemetery. The theme of the tours changes every week and is a veritable who's who of Victoria, including coal magnate Robert Dunsmuir; Billy Barker, who struck it rich in the gold rush and died a pauper; and Victoria-born artist Emily Carr. Other themes include Gossip in the Graveyard, Murder Most Foul, and, close to Halloween, a ghost walk. Tours $5; cash only. *Every Sun at 2pm.*

—Shelora Sheldan

shores of Whiffen Spit in Sooke. Bernard, dubbed the Seaweed Lady, teaches participants about the different varieties of seaweeds, their nutritional benefits, and different methods of preparing them. Gum boots and walking sticks are included, and a seaweed lunch at nearby Sooke Harbour House can be arranged for an additional charge. Bernard also hand-harvests seaweed products for chefs and has created a seaweed-based skin-care line that's carried at many spas throughout Vancouver Island.

For self-directed tours of the best wineries, cideries, and meaderies on Vancouver Island and the Gulf Islands, pick up a free copy of the **WINE ISLANDS MAP** (www.wineislands.ca). Extensive and well written, the book-format map also alerts foodies to the best restaurants along your journey that serve regional fare and farms that make and sell artisanal cheeses or organic produce.

Restaurants

Brasserie l'Ecole / ★★

1715 GOVERNMENT ST, VICTORIA; 250/475-6260
Small and lively with a neighbourhood feel, Brass—as the locals call it—serves hearty French country fare utilizing West Coast ingredients. Chef Sean

311

Brennan's comfort plates run the gamut from *boeuf bourguignonne* to Sooke trout with brown butter or cider-braised duck legs. Enjoy classic cocktails, or choose from an outstanding Belgian and French beer selection or the wine list that holds many French and international gems. *$$–$$$; AE, MC, V; debit cards; dinner Tues–Sat; full bar; reservations recommended; www.lecole. ca; street parking.* ঌ

Cafe Brio / ★★★

944 FORT ST, VICTORIA; 250/383-0009 OR 866/270-5461

From the vine-covered patio evoking a Tuscan landscape to a room awash in rich colours, with wall-to-wall art, Cafe Brio warmly embraces you. Chef Laurence Munn cooks up a contemporary West Coast menu with Italian flavours, mirroring the seasons with local ingredients. Begin with the latest accomplishments from the on-site curing room, which segues nicely to entrées that are a balance of land- and sea-based fare. Consummate hosts and owners Greg Hays and Silvia Marcollini keep the spirit lively with a smart wine card of West Coast and worldly picks. *$$$–$$$$; AE, MC, V; debit cards; dinner every day; full bar; reservations recommended; www.cafe-brio.com; street parking.* ঌ

Empress Room / ★★☆

721 GOVERNMENT ST (FAIRMONT EMPRESS HOTEL), VICTORIA; 250/389-2727

This grand 100-year-old space boasts tapestried walls and 20-foot ceilings with original carved mahogany beams, all of which transports you to an earlier, gentler time and place. Chef Ken Nakano couples international cooking styles with fresh local ingredients. Dinner entrées include wild salmon with wild rice croquettes and roasted garlic velouté, free-range chicken with wild mushroom duxelles and truffled demi-glace. An excellent selection of local handcrafted cheeses offers a perfect way to round out a meal. Service is impeccable. The wine list is a finely tuned ode to Pacific Northwest gems, with excellent German and French rarities. *$$$$; AE, DC, MC, V; debit cards; dinner every day; full bar; reservations recommended; www.fairmont.com; self-parking.* ঌ

Il Terrazzo Ristorante / ★

555 JOHNSON ST, VICTORIA; 250/361-0028

The big, bold northern Italian flavours in this beautiful restaurant, tucked away in Waddington Alley across from Market Square, are a favourite with cruise ship passengers. Surrounded by six outdoor fireplaces, lots of brick, and an abundance of plants and flowers, Il Terrazzo offers a haven of privacy. (Alfresco dining on the covered heated terrace is possible nearly year-round.) The diverse menu—classic minestrone soup, smoked tuna carpaccio, wood-oven pizzas, pastas, exquisite big meat dishes—is a little repetitive on the ingredient list but delicious nonetheless. An extensive wine list showcases an excellent range of fine Italian wines, big on Tuscany. *$$$–$$$$; AE, DC, MC, V; debit cards; lunch Mon–Fri, dinner every day May–Sept; full bar; reservations recommended; www.ilterrazzo.com; street parking.* ঌ

J & J Wonton Noodle House / ★★

1012 FORT ST, VICTORIA; 250/383-0680

You might easily walk past this popular Chinese restaurant with its unassuming facade, but when the door opens and tantalizing aromas of ginger, garlic, and black beans embrace your senses, you'll be drawn in. This busy, modest, spotless restaurant treats you to the flavours of Hong Kong, Singapore, Sichuan, and northern China. A large kitchen window lets you watch the chefs busily preparing such dishes as wonton soup, imperial prawns with spicy garlic wine sauce, spicy ginger fried chicken, half a barbecued duck, and Sichuan braised beef hot pot. Noodles, made fresh daily on the premises, are a specialty; attention is paid to serving only local seafood. Service is friendly, efficient, and knowledgeable. Surprise island wines are on offer. $–$$; AE, MC, V; debit cards; lunch, dinner Tues–Sat; beer and wine; no reservations; www.jjnoodlehouse.com; between Vancouver and Cook sts; street parking. &

Niche Modern Dining / UNRATED

225 QUEBEC ST, VICTORIA; 250/388-4255

Inside this Victorian exterior in James Bay lies a sleek, contemporary room. Chef Jason Leizert crafts an innovative, terse menu that speaks volumes. Briny oysters served with seaweed ice cream are a refreshing segue to crispy sweetbreads with capers and lemon. Entrées—perhaps veal cheeks with roasted sunchokes, beets, and blue cheese butter, or pan-seared scallops over spiced beet purée with fennel powder and sage oil—are innovative. Desserts surprise: a tobacco-infused chocolate cake, amaretto truffles with salt. A prix-fixe lunch menu provides excellent value, and the cozy side bar area is perfect for a bite and cocktail after work. The wine list offers many hard-to-source BC picks, peppered throughout with old-world choices; also a well-chosen craft brew list. $$$; AE, MC, V; debit cards; lunch Wed–Sun, dinner every day; full bar; reservations recommended; www.nichedining.com; self-parking.

Paprika Bistro / ★★★

2524 ESTEVAN AVE, OAK BAY; 250/592-7424

George Szasz's elevated cuisine draws from modern and European influences, beginning with essentials from his homegrown produce and house-made charcuterie, which changes weekly. Pork merguez and rabbit sausage with black beans are two delicious examples. All meats are sourced from local organic farms, and seafood is sustainably sought. The wine list, headed up by Linda Szasz, is well chosen to complement the food served, with great island picks. The restaurant is situated a block and a half from Willows Beach in Oak Bay, a great place for a walk after dinner. $$$; AE, MC, V; debit cards; dinner Mon–Sat; full bar; reservations recommended; www.paprika-bistro.com; at Beach Dr; street parking. &

Re-Bar Modern Foods / ★

50 BASTION SQ, VICTORIA; 250/361-9223

Located in Bastion Square, Rebar serves healthy vegetarian fare with an innovative, global touch. Get your mojo working with one of their healthy made-to-order juices: the Super Conductor is a blend of apple, lemon, and banana with a hit of spirulina, said to promote mental clarity. Continue the healing with Oriental salads festooned with nuts and seeds, the daily quesadilla, healthy soups, hearty curries, and stir-fries. The almond burger is legendary, and they offer small portions for kids. Breads and desserts are all homemade with lots of whole grains. Brunch and lunch lineups are guaranteed, so get there early, but you can reserve for the dinner hour, where the vibe is chill and local wines are smartly paired with dishes such as Salt Spring Island mussels in a coconut curry with Asian vegetables and fresh basil over jasmine rice. And don't forget to pick up a copy of their award-winning cookbook. *$$–$$$; AE, DC, MC, V; debit cards; breakfast, lunch, dinner Mon–Sat, brunch Sat–Sun; beer and wine; reservations recommended for dinner; www. rebarmodernfoods.com; at Langley St; street parking.*

Spinnakers Gastro Brewpub and Guesthouse / ★★

308 CATHERINE ST, VICTORIA; 250/384-6613

With pride of place, overlooking the Inner Harbour, Canada's oldest brewpub offers 12 serious brews, including three Belgian-style fruit ales made with local fruit. The kitchen shakes up the tired concept of pub food by utilizing local purveyors, organic produce, and, of course, beer. Don't miss the mile-high apple pie for dessert, or purchase miniversions in their Provisions store on the way out, along with beer breads, Spinnakers brews, and vinegars in decorative bottles. Rooms and suites, delightfully appointed with art and antiques, are available in three nearby guesthouses. *$$–$$$; AE, MC, V; debit cards; lunch, dinner every day; full bar; reservations recommended; www.spinnakers.com; across Blue Bridge, or take harbour ferry; self-parking.*

Stage / ★★

1307 GLADSTONE AVE, VICTORIA; 250/388-4222

Presented by George and Linda Szasz of Paprika Bistro, Stage is its casual sister for small plates, wines, and cocktails. Nestled in a heritage brick building with high ceilings and a semi-open kitchen, Stage offers spirited service—especially when patrons from nearby Belfry Theatre pop in after curtain call. Tender octopus competes for star billing along with heirloom tomato salad with *haloumi* cheese. Don't miss the *lángos*, a Hungarian fry bread served with garlic and *fleur de sel* or slathered with artichoke hearts, tomatoes, and goat cheese. Follow with hearty pork belly over white beans or chicken with pancetta and spätzle. Inviting price points and 17 wines by the glass—including smart 3-ounce tasters—encourage repeat visits. *$$; AE, MC, V; debit cards; dinner every day; full bar; reservations for 8 or more; at Fernwood; self-parking.* ﾑ

Zambri's / ★★½

110-911 YATES ST, VICTORIA; 250/360-1171

Set in the Harris Green neighbourhood, Zambri's offers a refreshing take on Italian cuisine. Lunch is a casual affair, with the daily specials written on a blackboard and ordered at the counter in front of the open kitchen: hearty meatball sandwiches, pastas, soups, local snapper with pancetta and roasted potatoes, pork ribs on polenta, a stunning antipasti selection of locally sourced greens and vegetables. Return for dinner, when, along with candlelight and table service, chef Peter Zambri ups the ante with seductively rich vitello tonnato; cannelloni with ricotta, veal, spinach, and pecorino cheese; or strip loin with Gorgonzola fonduta and truffle oil. Espresso-laced tiramisu paired with grappa or *limoncello* is a spectacular finish. The tidy wine list shows strength with rare Italian varietals and a few island winners too. *$$–$$$; MC, V; debit cards; lunch, dinner Tues–Sat; beer and wine; reservations for large parties only; www.zambris.ca; self-parking.*

Lodgings

Abigail's Hotel / ★★★

906 MCCLURE ST, VICTORIA; 250/388-5363 OR 800/561-6565

Abigail's is all 1920s Tudoresque gables, gardens, and crystal chandeliers. There are 17 odd-shaped rooms in the original three-storey building; the adjacent four-storey building contains six additional spacious rooms. The Honeymoon Suites on the third floor of the old building are grandly appointed with king beds, down duvets, wood-burning fireplaces, and fresh flowers. The Coach House Suites marry dark wood wainscotting with contemporary wallpaper and fabrics, as well as Arts and Crafts stained-glass lamps, king-size canopied beds, two-person Jacuzzis, wet bars, armoires, and leather loveseats. Wine, beer, and sherry accompany afternoon appetizers in the library. Spa treatments are offered at their small on-site spa Pearl, popular with wedding parties. Breakfast—homemade granola or eggs Benedict with grilled bacon and sweet potato cakes—can be enjoyed on the adjoining patio. *$$$–$$$$; AE, MC, V; debit cards; www.abigailshotel.com; at Vancouver St; self-parking.*

Delta Victoria Ocean Pointe Resort and Spa / ★★

45 SONGHEES RD, VICTORIA; 250/360-2999 OR 800/667-4677

The Delta Ocean Pointe Resort commands presence on the Inner Harbour. The massive 239-room, seven-suite waterfront resort stands as a modern counterpoint to the classic Empress and the provincial government's Parliament Buildings on the other side. The gracious lobby features lots of marble and dramatic flower arrangements. The understated guest rooms are done in pale earth tones and light furnishings; the ones facing the harbour command great views. Lure, the hotel's restaurant on the main floor, is the spot to reserve for summer fireworks viewing over dinner. Facilities include a 24-hour business centre, pool, tennis court, gym, and luxurious European spa. Walk the seawall over to Spinnakers for lunch or over the Johnson Street Bridge into downtown. The Harbour Ferry also docks at the hotel. *$$–$$$$; AE, DC, JCB, MC, V; debit cards; www.deltahotels.com; at Vic West across Johnson St Bridge; self-parking.* &

Fairholme Manor / ★★★

**638 ROCKLAND PL, VICTORIA; 250/598-3240
OR 877/511-3322**

On expansive grounds adjacent to Government House, this stately and secluded B&B built in 1885 is sheer elegance. Proprietor Sylvia Main has opted for an expansive contemporary feel, offset with period antiques, fresh flowers, and tasteful carpeting, instead of the usual fuss, lace, and chintz. The six suites with fireplaces and 14-foot ceilings are graciously appointed with overstuffed chairs and couches, king sleigh beds, and luxurious bedding. Spa-quality amenities include oversized Jacuzzi tubs, minifridges, TV, phone, high-speed Internet access, and great magazines. The Olympic Room, with a double walk-in shower, overlooks the garden and offers unobstructed mountain views; enjoy breakfast on the room's sunny patio or in the dining room. Breakfasts are sumptuous affairs—and their best-selling cookbook attests to that—using organic ingredients from the manor's garden; the sticky buns are legendary. *$$$–$$$$; AE, MC, V; debit cards; www.fairholmemanor.com; at Charles St; self-parking.*

Fairmont Empress Hotel / ★★★

721 GOVERNMENT ST, VICTORIA; 250/384-8111 OR 800/441-1414

With its commanding views of the Inner Harbour, the Empress stands like a grande dame before an admiring audience. The ivy-covered landmark, once owned by the Canadian Pacific Railway, has enjoyed a richly layered past involving royals and celebrities. The opulent marble lobby and grand staircase sweep visitors up to the Tea Lobby, the Bengal Lounge, or one of 477 rooms. Suites are furnished with Victorian antiques and stately furnishings, deluxe king beds with feather duvets, and green marble sinks in the bathroom. Treasure hunts with prizes are arranged for children. A separate elevator whisks guests to the Romantic Attic on the seventh floor, featuring a turreted room with round bed; the Fairmont Gold rooms command the best views and include private check-in, concierge service, and a separate lounge to enjoy continental breakfast or afternoon appetizers with a tipple from the honor bar. *$$$–$$$$; AE, DC, MC, V; debit cards; www.fairmont. com; self-parking.* &

Hotel Grand Pacific / ★★

463 BELLEVILLE ST, VICTORIA; 250/386-0450 OR 800/663-7550

Overlooking the Inner Harbour, the Grand Pacific is the second-largest hotel in Victoria and the only one built according to feng shui principles. All 308 rooms exude an understated elegance and have balconies—many with more than one—with city, mountain, and harbour views. The state-of-the-art athletic club boasts a 25-metre (82-foot) ozonated pool, kid's pool, steam and dry saunas, gym, Jacuzzi, and separate spa with a hair salon. A wonderful kid's programme brings them cookies-and-milk vouchers and introduces them to the ducks that swim in a pond in front of the hotel. The Pacific restaurant serves a buffet breakfast every morning; the Mark is the on-site fine dining option. Fourteen of the hotel's rooms are specifically designed for persons with disabilities, featuring automatic doors, roll-in showers, angled mirrors, and low-rise beds. *$$$–$$$$; AE, DC, DIS, JCB, MC, V; debit cards; www.hotelgrandpacific.com; self-parking.* &

Laurel Point Inn / ★★★

680 MONTREAL ST, VICTORIA; 250/386-8721 OR 800/663-7667

A favourite with the celebrity and film industry set, Laurel Point Inn, with its modern, angular architecture, rests on a promontory offering views of the Inner Harbour or the ship channel from each of its 200 rooms and suites. Check out the studio suites in the Erickson Wing, recently renovated, which are beautifully appointed with graceful, modern decor, leather chairs, wireless Internet access, flat-screen TVs, original artwork, and marble throughout, including spacious bathrooms with soaker tubs, peekaboo showers, and thick, cuddly robes. Luxurious amenities include body sugar, mouthwash, and lip balm. Spectacular Asian artifacts are displayed throughout the hotel, along with a restful sculpted Japanese garden at the water's edge. Facilities include a heated indoor pool, sauna, fitness center, and in-room spa service. The gift shop sells local artisan foodstuffs; the newly built restaurant Aura complements the hotel's modernity. *$$$–$$$$; AE, DC, DIS, MC, V; debit cards; www.laurel point.com; at Belleville St; self-parking.* &

Magnolia Hotel / ★★★

623 COURTENAY ST, VICTORIA;
250/381-0999 OR 877/624-6654

Steps away from the Inner Harbour, the Magnolia exudes contemporary elegance, attracting both corporate clientele and couples in search of romance. Rooms with dark wood and soothing shades of blue throughout have feather pillows and bedding, Aveda amenities, wi-fi, Roger's Chocolates pillow-side, and fresh fruit, candy, and bottled water on arrival. The Diamond Level rooms provide a bit more space with the addition of harbour views and a fireplace, and a few rooms are wheelchair accessible. Find an Aveda spa on the second floor, with a small fitness area. The hotel has an Asian-inspired restaurant and lounge, Sanuk, on one side, and Hugo's, a brewpub, on the other. Because of its emphasis on personal service, the hotel was named one of the Three Top Hotels in Canada in a recent *Condé Nast Traveler* magazine poll. Small-pet friendly. *$$$–$$$$; AE, DC, DIS, E, JCB, MC; V; debit cards; www.magnoliahotel.com; at Gordon St; valet parking.* &

Oswego / UNRATED

500 OSWEGO ST, VICTORIA; 250/294-7500 OR 877/767-9346

This new modern brick-and-slate hotel tucked away a few blocks from the Inner Harbour exudes sophisticated, laid-back chic. The 80-suite hotel offers one or two bedrooms or studios with Murphy beds. All suites have kitchen facilities, and those on the top floor enjoy spacious living rooms with over-sized leather furniture, flat-screen TVs, and expansive balconies offering spectacular water, city, and mountain views. Bathrooms are well-appointed with luxe amenities, plush towels, and robes. The cucumber-infused water and fresh fruit in the lobby is a refreshing touch, and so is the freshly ground coffee for your pod coffeemaker, along with the daily paper. The hotel is small-dog-friendly, furnishing pets with a personalized doggie bowl and treats. The staff is exceedingly professional; the daily buffet breakfast included with the price of the room is substantial. Lovely bar and dining area on the main floor, with comfy couches and fireplace. *$$$–$$$$; AE, MC, V; debit cards; www. oswegovictoria.com; at Kingston St; street and self-parking.* &

Prior House Bed & Breakfast / ★★★

620 ST CHARLES, VICTORIA; 250/592-8847 OR 877/924-3300

This grand B&B occupies an English mansion built during the Edwardian period for the king's representative in British Columbia. It's in the quiet Rockland neighbourhood, about 1.6 kilometres (1 mile) from downtown and just steps away from the public gardens at Government House. Many of the rooms have fireplaces and views of water; the Governor's Celebration Suite has an extravagant bath with a whirlpool tub, mirrored ceiling, gold fixtures, king bed, and crystal chandeliers. Those with small pets can stay in one of the spacious lower-level Hobbit Garden Studios, with private entrances, full kitchens, and direct access to the gorgeous Victorian garden. A full breakfast may be taken in the dining room or in the privacy of your room. Afternoon tea is served 3–5pm. *$$$–$$$$; MC, V; no debit cards; www.priorhouse.com; at Rockland Ave; self-parking.*

Top 10 Attractions

1) VICTORIA'S HISTORIC BUILDINGS

FROM POINT ELLICE TO VIEW ROYAL AND DOWNTOWN

The 19th-century Scottish and British immigrants who settled Vancouver Island left their physical mark on this city, building everything from humble thatched cottages to magnificent mansions and opulent public buildings. You can start a tour of these heritage buildings by boarding the little **VICTORIA HARBOUR FERRY** (250/708-0201) at the Inner Harbour for the 10-minute cruise up the Gorge (a long, narrow saltwater inlet).

The first stop is the **POINT ELLICE HOUSE** (2616 Pleasant St; 250/387-4697; www.pointellicehouse.ca), where you step up onto the landing dock and back into the 19th century. (Tip: Arrive by water, not by land; neighbouring auto repair garages could spoil the mood.) Until 1977, Point Ellice was the home of the gardening-besotted O'Reilly family, whose slip into genteel poverty meant subsequent generations never replaced the original Victorian furnishings. Sir John A. Macdonald, Canada's first prime minister, once dined at this spot. June is when the thick scent of the garden's old-fashioned damask roses permeates the air. Afternoon tea consists of lavender shortbread, scones and Devon cream, and other sweet treats served on the croquet lawn, along with a tea specially created for the house by the tea masters at Victoria's Silk Road Teas. Afternoon tea is $23 plus tax for adults, free for children under 6, including tour of the house; reservations suggested. *May–Oct 15 11am–4pm every day.*

Take the ferry back to the **FAIRMONT EMPRESS HOTEL** (721 Government St; 250/384-8111). It was designed by architect Francis Mawson Rattenbury. A story unto himself, Rattenbury obtained his first commission, after his arrival from England at age 25, for the provincial government's **LEGISLATIVE BUILDINGS** (501 Belleville St; 250/387-3046 for tours) in 1897. The beautiful Empress Hotel, which has marked 100 years, allows you to take a peek back into earlier times with its heritage architecture and flourishes (see Lodgings in this chapter). Check the hotel's archives on the lower level to learn about the days when a suite cost $15, when the King of Siam and Rudyard Kipling stayed in this opulent edifice. For a more lively and informative tour, Mandy Kray from **WALKABOUTS TOURS** (250/592-9255; www.walkabouts.ca) conducts hourlong tours of the hotel; meet in front of the clock at the Fairmont Store to be regaled with tales, history, trivia, and maybe even a ghost story or two. Tour is $10. *Tours every day at 10am May–Oct.*

Afternoon tea is served in, of course, the **TEA LOBBY**, which had its creaky but beautiful floor replaced, replicating the original. In high season (May–Oct), the six-course and traditional menus are more than a meal. The hotel's signature tea blend, a robust mix of African, Chinese, Assam, green, and Kenyan teas, is followed by fruit compote and a three-tiered tray bearing both savoury and sweet delights. Raisin scones are served with clotted cream and strawberry preserves; tea sandwiches range from cucumber, chicken curry, and mango to mushroom pâté with truffle oil. The Royal Tea offers a glass of Steller's Jay Brut at an extra charge. Service is gracious and efficient, and the waitstaff are a font of tea and hotel trivia. Afternoon tea $39–$60 in summer, including a tin of the Empress blend; reservations required. *Afternoon tea every day; low season noon–3:15pm, May–Oct noon–5:15pm.*

The **BENGAL LOUNGE** offers a popular curry buffet at lunch and dinner, featuring an assortment of curries, including vegetarian options, with lots of condiments, naan bread, and pappadam. A dress code at the Empress calls for "smart casual" attire, including jeans but not running shoes, short shorts, or tank tops. Lunch is $25 per person, reservations essential; dinner is $29 per person. *Lunch, dinner every day 11:30am–2:30pm and 5:45–9:30pm; lounge open till midnight.*

The 19th-century painter and notorious eccentric Emily Carr was born in **CARR HOUSE** (207 Government St; 250/383-5843). This is where her father's gardening habits inspired her to comment that he "was more British than Britain." (She's often wrongly credited with making this observation about Victoria.) When she wasn't creating one of her magnificent paintings later in life, she ran a James Bay boardinghouse. Terrorizing the guests with her menagerie—which included a monkey, a white rat, stray cats, and bobtailed sheepdogs—Carr once turned a garden hose on a boarder who refused to bring in his washing. Admission is $6 for a self-guided tour. *Tours every day May 1–Sept 30.*

The residence of a pioneer doctor who settled here during the 1850s can be viewed at **HELMCKEN HOUSE** (675 Belleville St, behind Thunderbird Park), which still contains the original imported British furnishings and the good doctor's medicine chest. Admission is by donation, free if you purchase Royal BC museum tickets. *Every day noon–4pm July–Sept.*

Head east to the four-storey **CRAIGDARROCH CASTLE** (1050 Joan Cres; 250/592-5323; www.craigdarrochcastle.com), which was built during the 1880s to serve as Robert Dunsmuir's home. This Scottish coal-mining magnate had the 39-room Highland-style castle decorated like the interior of a Gothic novel to induce his wife, Joan, to stay in the "Wild West." It worked: she stayed until her death in 1908. Detailed woodwork, Persian carpets, stained-glass windows, paintings, and sculptures fill every regal corner of this monument to one man's matrimonial devotion. Admission $11.75, free for children 5 and under; on-site parking. *Every day 10am–4:30pm.*

Children both young and old should not miss the **VICTORIA BUG ZOO** (631 Courtney St; 250/384-2847; www.bugzoo.bc.ca), which among its many features has a surprisingly cute miniature apartment scaled to its cockroach denizens. Admission $8 for adults, $5 for children 6–12 years. *Open 11–6 pm every day.*

2) ROYAL BRITISH COLUMBIA MUSEUM

675 BELLEVILLE ST; 250/356-7226 OR 888/447-7977

The Royal British Columbia Museum is one of the finest of its kind in the country. Outside the entrance to this contemporary concrete-and-glass museum is a glass-enclosed display of Native totem poles and large sculptural works. Displaying dramatic dioramas of BC's temperate rain forest, seacoast, and ocean floor, as well as a full-scale reconstruction of Victorian-era downtown and Chinatown inside, it's definitely a must-see. Of particular interest is the Northwest Coast First Nations exhibit, which is rich with spiritual and cultural artifacts. There's also an IMAX theatre and Thunderbird Park, where the Mungo Martin Longhouse and a handful of totem poles remind visitors of the city's original heritage. Admission tickets are good for 24 hours, so if you go in after noon, you can go back the next morning. Admission $14 for adults, free for children 5 and under. *Every day (except Christmas and New Year's Day) 9am–5pm; www.royalbcmuseum.bc.ca.*

3) BUTCHART GARDENS

800 BENVENUTO AVE, BRENTWOOD BAY; 250/652-5256 OR 888/824-7313

Butchart Gardens is a mecca for gardening enthusiasts from every corner of the globe. At the turn of the 20th century, cement manufacturer Robert Butchart exhausted the limestone quarry near his home. Rather than leaving the land to waste, his wife, Jenny, relandscaped the quarry into what was named the Sunken Garden, which opened to the public in 1904. Jenny's gardening prowess was widely acclaimed, inspiring her to add an English rose garden. Eventually the Butcharts realized they'd gotten carried away and opened their home and gardens as an attraction. Their great-great-granddaughter now owns and manages this year-round floral spectacle with a million-plus plants, recently designated a National Historic Site of Canada. Consider visiting in the evening, when the gardens are illuminated with thousands of coloured lights, crowds are thinner, and entertainers give free performances. On Saturday nights in July and August, fireworks displays, set to music, add further sparkle.

Lunch, dinner, and afternoon tea are offered in the **DINING ROOM RESTAURANT** (250/652-8222 for reservations) located in the historic residence. A more casual menu is served in the **BLUE POPPY RESTAURANT** (250/652-8222 for reservations); you can get a quick snack in the **COFFEE SHOP**. At the **SEED AND GIFT STORE**, you'll find a fine selection of plant seeds, gardening books, cards, calendars, and other collectibles. The gardens are 20 minutes from downtown Victoria: take Blanchard Street (Hwy 17) north toward the ferry terminal, then turn left at Keating Crossroads. Depending on the season, admission ranges from $5.50 to $26.50 for adults, free for children 4 and under; admission good all day—for $3.50, you may return the next day. *Every day from 9am (closing times vary by season); www.butchartgardens.com.*

4) CHINATOWN

STORE TO DOUGLAS STS, JOHNSON TO FISGARD STS

Canada's oldest Chinatown was established in Victoria in 1858. Although Chinatown covers only about six blocks, centering on Fisgard and Government streets, this area still speaks of its rich heritage. Newly arrived mainland Chinese got their first break, in the form of spiritual and physical aid, in the balconied **CHINESE SETTLEMENT HOUSE** (1715 Government St). A Buddhist temple was on the ground floor; temporary quarters and social services were offered until a job was secured and living quarters were arranged. The original temple has since been moved to the second floor.

A half block along is another historic building, the pagoda-style **CHINESE IMPERIAL SCHOOL** (Zhongua Xuetang, 36 Fisgard St) constructed by the Chinese Benevolent Society in 1908, the year after the Victoria School Board banned non-Canadian-born Chinese children from attending public school. Today it offers standard classes, as well as Chinese language instruction, for all ages on weekends.

Arching the entry to Chinatown is the dragon-headed **GATE OF HARMONI-OUS INTEREST** (Fisgard St at corner of Government St), completed in 1882 and restored in 1997 by the Chinese Benevolent Society to commemorate the visit of Princess Carolina Louise Alberta. The two stone lions that guard the foot of the gate were imported from Suzhou, China.

About halfway down the block is **FAN TAN ALLEY** (between Fisgard St and Pandora Ave), Canada's narrowest thoroughfare, about a half block west of Government Street. It measures just 1.2 metres (4 feet) across at both ends, although it widens to 1.8 metres (6 feet) in the centre. Its doorways still bear their original Chinese signage and lead to a labyrinth of small courtyards that were once home to a factory that legally produced opium and ran gambling parlours and bachelor rooming houses. Those enterprises have been replaced by craft shops and clothing stores, such as **HEART'S CONTENT** (18 Fan Tan Alley; 250/380-1234), which purveys hip apparel such as Doc Martens shoes and funky clothing. The alley's exotic allure has all but vanished, although **TURTLE EXPRESS** (3 Fan Tan Alley; 250/384-2227) offers southern Asian imports such as jewellery, fabric, and decorative items, and the **NEW TOWN BARBERSHOP** (10 Fan Tan Alley; 250/382-3813) still offers a $10 haircut.

All sorts of imported Chinese items can be purchased on Fisgard Street, ranging from fresh produce, honey buns, and medicinal herbs to dishware and furniture. **FAN TAN GALLERY** (541 Fisgard St; 250/382-4424) offers an eclectic and contemporary mix of home accents, giftware, and ephemera. Also check out **DRAGON ALLEY** (532½ Fisgard St), another long and narrow space, home to live-work condos offering handmade furniture, clothing designs, acupuncture treatments, and a restaurant.

5) MARITIME MUSEUM OF BRITISH COLUMBIA

28 BASTION SQ; 250/385-4222

In less than an hour, you can walk across downtown or stroll along most of the waterfront, past the sailboats and floatplanes to Bastion Square and the former provincial courthouse. That's where one of Victoria's lesser known but fascinating attractions is: the Maritime Museum. It houses more than 5,000 artifacts, including the *Trekka*—the 6-metre (20-foot) ketch that sailed solo around the world during the 1950s, and *Tilikum*—the converted 11.5-metre (38-foot) Native dugout canoe that made an equally impressive two-year passage to England at the turn of the 20th century. Admission $10 for adults, free for children 5 and under. *Every day 9:30am–4:30pm (closed Christmas Day); www.mmbc.bc.ca.*

6) BEACON HILL PARK

SOUTHGATE ST TO DALLAS RD,
BETWEEN DOUGLAS AND COOK STS

It's a short walk from downtown and the Royal British Columbia Museum to 75-hectare (186-acre) Beacon Hill Park, which has splendid ocean views, as well as impressive stands of indigenous Garry oak trees. These distinctive

VANCOUVER ISLAND THREE-DAY TOUR

DAY ONE: From Victoria, get a healthful breakfast at **RE-BAR MODERN FOODS,** then head north and hop aboard one of the Swartz Bay ferries to Salt Spring Island. Browse the **SATURDAY FARMERS MARKET** in the heart of Ganges and pick up some organic bread and artisanal cheeses for a picnic, or have lunch at **MOBY'S MARINE PUB** (124 Upper Ganges Rd; 250/537-5559), then drive up Cranberry Road to the top of **MOUNT MAXWELL** for a panoramic view. Taste the terroir at both the **SALT SPRING VINEYARDS** (1700 block of Fulford-Ganges and Lee rds; 250/653-9463; saltspringvineyards.com) and **GARRY OAKS WINERY** (1880 Fulford-Ganges Rd; 250/653-4687; www.garryoakswine.com), and check in to the **SKY VALLEY INN** (421 Sky Valley Rd; 250/537-9800 or 866/537-1028; www.skyvalleyinn.com) before dinner at **RESTAURANT HOUSE PICCOLO** (108 Hereford Ave; 250/537-1844; www.housepiccolo.com).

DAY TWO: After breakfast at Sky Valley, zip out to Vesuvius Bay on the island's western side and catch the ferry to Crofton, on Vancouver Island just south of Chemainus. From there, drive north on the Trans-Canada Highway (Hwy 1). Just past Ladysmith, take a side trip to Cedar to lunch at the **CROW AND GATE PUB** (2313 Yellow Point Rd, Cedar; 250/722-3731). At Nanaimo, continue north on the inland Highway 19 to Parksville, then take Highway 4A west to visit Coombs and browse the **OLD COUNTRY MARKET** (250/248-6272; www.oldcountry market.com), where goats graze on the grass rooftop. Continue west, joining Highway 4, and pause on the road to Port Alberni to admire the old-growth trees of Cathedral Grove in **MACMILLAN PROVINCIAL PARK** (www.cathedralgrove. com). Keep on driving to the wild west coast, then turn north to Tofino. Check in to a room at the **MIDDLE BEACH LODGE** (250/725-2900; www.middlebeach. com) and dine by the surf at the **POINTE RESTAURANT** in the **WICKANINNISH INN** (500 Osprey Ln, Tolfino; 250/725-3100; www.wickinn.com).

DAY THREE: After coffee and a muffin at Middle Beach Lodge, head out for a morning of surf lessons, whale-watching, or kayaking. Have lunch at **SOBO** in downtown Tofino, then drive to the inimitable Long Beach. Spend the afternoon exploring the beach, then check in for the night at **TAUCA LEA RESORT AND SPA** (1971 Harbour Dr; 250/726-4625; www.taucalearesort.com) in Ucluelet and dine at its **BOAT BASIN** restaurant.

looking—and protected—trees are found in Canada only on Vancouver Island and two of the Gulf Islands (Salt Spring and Hornby). Donated to the city in 1882 by the Hudson's Bay Company, the park also features manicured lawns, ponds, colourful floral gardens, picnic tables, and a 100-year-old cricket field.

323

It's a lovely spot to escape from the downtown shopping mania. The **BEACON HILL CHILDREN'S FARM** (Circle Dr; 250/381-2532) offers a petting zoo filled with friendly barnyard animals. Zoo admission $3 for adults, $2 for children. *Every day Feb–Sept 10am–5pm.*

7) ABKHAZI GARDENS

1964 FAIRFIELD RD; 250/598-8096

Located just a short distance from downtown is this exquisite heritage home and garden built in 1946 by Prince and Princess Abkhazi. They worked with the natural landscape, producing a garden with gorgeous vistas that is a stunning example of West Coast design. The garden flows around glaciated rocky slopes, with magnificent native Garry oaks, 50-year-old Japanese maples, carpets of naturalized bulbs, and heirloom rhododendrons. After the couple's death, the property changed hands and was threatened with redevelopment. The BC Land Conservancy stepped in and saved the garden and home, which is impeccably maintained by volunteers. Wonderful spot for afternoon tea. Admission $10 for adults; free for children 12 and under. *Every day 11am–5pm Mar–Sept 30; www.conservancy.bc.ca.*

8) ART GALLERY OF GREATER VICTORIA

1040 MOSS ST; 250/384-4101

This gallery features one of the world's finest collections of Oriental art and the only Shinto shrine in North America. Housed in a contemporary structure that extends into the Edwardian-style Spencer Mansion (donated to the city in the 1950s), the gallery showcases nearly 10,000 works of art, including paintings and drawings by European painters, premier BC artist Emily Carr, and contemporary Canadian artists. Check the Web site for upcoming exhibits. The museum store is a wonderful place to shop. Admission $10 for adults Tues–Sun, free for children 12 and under; by donation first Tues every month. *Every day (closed Christmas Day); Fri–Wed 10am–5pm, Thurs 10am–9pm; www.aggv.bc.ca.*

9) ROYAL LONDON WAX MUSEUM

470 BELLEVILLE ST; 250/388-4461

This wax museum is worth a visit—and a chuckle—even if you've seen the original Madame Tussaud's in London. The 300 handcrafted wax figures were imported from the famed waxworks, including a few gory favourites from her infamous Chamber of Horrors. *Every day 9:30am–5pm; extended hours in summer; www.waxmuseum.bc.ca.*

10) FISGARD LIGHTHOUSE NATIONAL HISTORIC SITE & FORT RODD HILL

603 FORT RODD HILL RD, OFF OCEAN BLVD; 250/478-5849

The Fisgard Lighthouse, perched on a point of volcanic rock, has guided ships toward Victoria's sheltered harbour since 1873. It is Canada's oldest beacon on the Pacific. Displayed on two floors of the lightkeeper's house are the stories of the lighthouse, its caretakers, and the terrible shipwrecks (more than 2,000) that gave the Vancouver Island coastline the ominous name "the graveyard of the Pacific."

FORT RODD HILL is so close to the lighthouse that the concussion from its artillery guns once blew out the lighthouse windows. The exciting history of this 1890s coastal artillery garrison can be seen in its original guns, camouflaged searchlights, and underground magazines. Multimedia presentations, room re-creations, and artifact displays inform and entertain. Bring a lunch so you can picnic on the grounds, where military concerts are held on summer Sunday afternoons. Admission $4 for adults, free for children 5 and under. *Every day 10am–5:30pm Feb 15–Oct 31; call for off-season hours (closed Christmas Day); www.fortroddhill.com.*

Shopping

A few of the retail shops along Government Street take you back to Queen Victoria's era. You'll pass heritage buildings with gleaming brass, mahogany, and stained-glass interiors. One of these, the **OLD MORRIS TOBACCONIST** (1116 Government St; 250/382-4811; www.oldmorris.com), has been around since 1892. It ships custom-blended tobaccos throughout the world, offers both Cuban and non-Cuban cigars, and stocks nifty shaving gear, smoking accessories, seltzer bottles, and walking sticks. **MUNRO'S BOOK STORE** (1108 Government St; 250/382-2464; www.munrobooks.com), which *Macleans* columnist Allan Fotheringham once called "Canada's best bookstore," is a real book lovers' haunt with its great selection of literature and children's books. **ROGERS' CHOCOLATES** (913 Government St; 250/384-7021; www.rogerschocolates.com) purveys chocolate-covered Victoria creams in many flavours, such as raspberry, mint, and coffee.

Modern and classic Irish linens can be found at the **IRISH LINEN SHOP** (1019 Government St; 250/383-6812; www.irishlinenvictoria.com). **OUT OF IRELAND** (1000 Government St; 250/389-0886) carries a fine selection of Aran hand-knit fishermen's sweaters, Magee hand-woven blazers and shirts, kilts, women's sweaters, throws, capes, Celtic wedding jewellery, and official Guinness merchandise.

The **BAY CENTRE** (Government St between Fort and View sts) is home to the Bay department store, along with four floors of well-known chain stores.

Serious antique hunters should head for **ANTIQUE ROW** (800–1100 blocks of Fort St). **VANITY FAIR ANTIQUES AND COLLECTIBLES MALL** (1044 Fort St; 250/380-7274) is always worth a perusal. Try your luck at the weekly auction houses, Tuesdays, at **LUND'S** (926 Fort St; 250/386-3308; www.lunds.com) or Thursdays at **KILSHAW'S** (1115 Fort St; 250/384-6441; www.kilshaws.com).

If your shopping tastes lean toward indigenous crafts, head to **OUT OF THE MIST** gallery (716 View St; 250/480-4930 or 800/337-1107), where owner T. J. Starke carries museum-quality Northwest Coast and North American Indian art, carvings, weavings, and sculpture. For traditional Cowichan sweaters and newly crafted items, try the **COWICHAN TRADING COMPANY** (1328 Government St;

250/383-0321; www.cowichantrading.com), which stocks some of the finest, warmest Cowichan sweaters with traditional animal and geometric motifs. All are knitted by local First Nations women. Find also Native carvings, animal pelts, moccasins, and jewellery, plus popular maple-sugar candy and smoked salmon.

Johnson, Pandora, and Store streets define historic **MARKET SQUARE** (560 Johnson St; 250/386-2441), built in the 1800s when gold prospectors and sailors were on the prowl and needed a hotel room or outfitting for the Klondike. It has been lovingly restored and is home to many eclectic shops, including **DIG THIS** (250/385-3212; www.digthis.com), a gardener's paradise, and **MUFFET & LOUISA** (250/382-3201; www.muffetandlouisa.com), a high-end kitchen and bedding store.

The 500-block Johnson Street side of the square also shares space with the **LOJO** (lower Johnson) area, reknowned for its concentration of hip fashion boutiques. Deck yourself out with the latest chic threads, including in-house La Poeme designs, at **REBEL REBEL** (585 Johnson St; 250/380-0906; www.rebelrebel fashion.com). **SMOKING LILY** (569 Johnson St; 250/382-5459; www.smokinglily. com) is the city's tiniest shop, with original hand-silkscreened skirts, scarves, and handbags. Find vintage polyester at **FLAVOUR** (581 Johnson St; 250/380-3528), Canadian designer threads complemented by Italian shoes at **SUASION** (562 Johnson St; 250/995-0133), and yoga outfits at **LULULEMON** (584 Johnson St; 250/383-1313; www.lululemon.com).

The newly established **DESIGN DISTRICT** (Store, Herald, Pandora, Fisgard, Government, and Chatham sts) encompasses everything from warehouse-style design stores to intimate ateliers, with a focus on home decor; going from one to another shop is a wonderful way to spend an afternoon. **BESPOKE** (517 Johnson St; 250/298-1105; www.bespokeinteriors.com) offers down-filled sectionals and heirloom-quality furniture pieces; **CHINTZ & CO** (1720 Store St; 250/381-2404; www.chintz.com) is an expansive and breathtaking two-floored warehouse of exquisite fabrics, draperies, furniture, and home accents. **LIBERTY** (1630 Store St; 250/385-6003; www.libertyinside.com), in a heritage brick and fir-beamed building, sparkles with chandeliers, custom slip-covered furniture, beds, bedding, and fun objets d'art. Tiny **ONLYHUMAN GALLERY** (8 Dragon Alley, 532½ Fisgard St; 250/592-9712; www.onlyhuman.ca) is home to local furniture designer Chris Rothery's designs and eco-chic pieces from Vancouver and San Francisco designers.

Victorians love a good bargain and can be found scouring the city's thrift stores for the latest treasures. In the downtown core, find **VALUE VILLAGE** (1810 Store St; 250/380-9422), **SALVATION ARMY** (525 Johnson St; 250/384-3755), the **WIN STORE** (785 Pandora St; 250/361-9303), and the **ST. VINCENT DE PAUL** (833 Yates St; 250/382-3213).

Performing Arts

Built at the turn of the 20th century and renovated during the 1970s and 1990s, the **ROYAL THEATRE** (805 Broughton St; 250/386-6121or 888/717-6121; www. rmts.bc.ca) presents concerts by the Victoria Symphony, dance recitals, and international music acts. It's also home to the **PACIFIC OPERA VICTORIA** (1815 Blanshard St, Ste 500; 250/385-0222; www.pov.bc.ca). The opera has five performances each of three different productions during the fall, winter, and spring, ranging from Mozart and Tchaikovsky to Puccini classics. The **VICTORIA SYMPHONY ORCHESTRA** (846 Broughton St; 250/385-6515; www.victoriasymphony. ca) performs frequent concert programmes throughout the year. Every summer, the orchestra performs the internationally acclaimed Symphony Splash on a barge on the Inner Harbour. The symphony culminates with fireworks and the 1812 Overture. Suggested donation is $5, and most folks bring their own chairs early in the day to stake their spot.

Another performing arts venue, the **MCPHERSON PLAYHOUSE** (3 Centennial Sq; 250/386-6121), offers music, comedy, and theatre. This garishly ornate Edwardian edifice, built in 1914 as North America's first Pantages Vaudeville Theatre, is home to productions by the **VICTORIA OPERATIC SOCIETY** (10-744 Fairview Rd; 250/381-1021; www.vos.bc.ca), whose performances include Broadway musicals such as *Evita* or *Into the Woods*.

The **SAVE-ON-FOODS MEMORIAL CENTRE** (1925 Blanshard St; 250/220-2600; www.saveonfoodsmemorialcentre.com) is not a grocery store but a new world-class venue for bigger musical and theatrical events such as Cirque du Soleil, trade shows, and sports competitions. Boasting superior acoustics and a 7,000-seat capacity, it is also home to the **SALMON KINGS** hockey team (250/220-7889; www.salmonkings.com).

For live theatre, head to the **BELFRY THEATRE** (1219 Gladstone Ave; 250/385-6815; www.belfry.bc.ca) in the Fernwood neighbourhood. It's a converted heritage church, where nationally acclaimed productions of drama and comedy draw Vancouverites across the Strait of Georgia September through May. Tickets $21–$36; slight discount for afternoon matinees, seniors, and students. For tickets, call or visit the box office (every day 9am–5pm) or purchase them at **TOURISM VICTORIA'S INFO CENTRE** (812 Wharf St).

Festivals

Victoria prides itself on its festivals, and there's usually something exciting to take in, contrary to the city's quiet nighttime reputation. Every spring the **VICTORIA TEA FESTIVAL** (www.victoriateafestival.com) is a one-day event celebrating teas from around the world with informative lectures and tea tastings. It's followed by **CHOCOLATE FEST** 250/475-1117; www.chocolatefest.ca), an important fundraiser for Big Brothers, Big Sisters. Enjoy exquisite chocolate, including workshops and wine tastings.

The annual **VICTORIA FRINGE FESTIVAL** takes place from late August to mid-September. Hosted by the **INTREPID THEATRE COMPANY** and **METRO STUDIO** (1014 Government St; 250/383-2663; www.intrepidtheatre.com), the festival has events scheduled from noon until midnight for one week, including the work of 50 international alternative-performance companies. One of the most anticipated summer performances is the **SUNSET VICTORIA SYMPHONY SPLASH**

(250/385-9771; www.victoriasymphony.ca), an inner-harbour concert held on a floating barge the first Sunday in August.

JAZZFEST INTERNATIONAL (250/388-4423; www.jazzvictoria.ca) sets the musical tune every June with swing, bebop, fusion, and improv, presented at noon-hour and evening performances at Centennial Square and other venues around the city. **BLUES BASH** happens at the end of the summer, with R&B and blues performed outdoors at Ship's Point on the Inner Harbour. The **VICTORIA SUMMER MUSIC FESTIVAL** (250/727-3229; www.vsmf.org/vsmf) brings chamber music to the city from the end of July to the beginning of August. All concerts take place in the Phillip T. Young Recital Hall, School of Music, University of Victoria campus.

Beyond Victoria

Sooke

From Victoria, drive north on Trans-Canada Hwy (Hwy 1) to Colwood Sooke exit; drive west on Sooke Rd (Hwy 14) for about 45 minutes.

Sooke sits on Vancouver Island's wild and rugged west coast, but it's less than an hour away from downtown Victoria. Thanks to the protective (and scenic) curve of Washington's mountainous Olympic Peninsula, which looms only 24 kilometres (15 miles) across the water, much of Sooke is sheltered from the heavy surf, rain, and strong winds associated with the coast at Tofino, farther north. Excellent parks and trails can be accessed at Sooke. **ALL SOOKE DAY,** held the third Saturday in July, is the longest-running logger sports event in Canada, attracting about 10,000 visitors annually. The annual **STINKING FISH STUDIO TOUR** (250/391-3973; www.stinkingfishstudiotour.com) invites locals and visitors into more than 20 artists' studios throughout the Sooke-Metchosin area for a week in summer.

EAST SOOKE REGIONAL PARK (East Sooke Rd off Gillespie Rd; www.eastsookepark.com), with 1,422 hectares (3,512 acres) of natural and protected coastal landscape, is a popular hiking spot. In fact, the East Sooke Park Coast Trail is one of Canada's premier day hikes. The 10-kilometre (6-mile) trip is challenging for even experienced hikers. Aylard Farm is the starting point for easy, brief excursions out to a series of ancient **NATIVE PETROGLYPHS**.

The **SOOKE REGION MUSEUM** (2205 Otter Point Rd; 250/642-6351; www.sookeregionmuseum.com) is well worth a stop for history buffs. Step over the threshold at the Moss Cottage and enter the year 1902. The museum displays Native artifacts as well as logging equipment and sponsors BC's largest **JURIED FINE-ARTS SHOW** (www.sookefinearts.com) every August. Ask at the **SOOKE INFOCENTRE**, housed in the museum, for directions to French Beach Provincial Park, Sandcut Beach (it's easy to miss the sign), China Beach Provincial Park (which has a 15-minute trail that takes you to a secluded sandy beach, with a hidden waterfall), and Mystic Beach (a rugged 20-minute trail). Beware of the incoming tide at Mystic; it has trapped unwary people on rocks and sandbars.

French Beach, 11 kilometres (7 miles) east of Jordan River, is the start of the rigorous **JUAN DE FUCA MARINE TRAIL** (250/391-2300; www.juandefucamarine trail.com), the more accessible younger sister to the West Coast Trail. Zip down to the beach for a picnic or spend a few days hiking the length of the coastal park to Sombrio Beach 34 kilometres (21 miles) east of Jordan River, popular with local surfers in fall and spring. **BOTANICAL BEACH** (follow signs at end of paved road just west of Port Renfrew) has exceptionally low tides in early summer that expose miles of sea life in sheltering pools.

The **GALLOPING GOOSE TRAIL**, a scenic, 60-kilometre (35-mile) unpaved path, was formerly the rail line between Victoria and Leechtown, just north of Sooke. You can, as they say, "walk the Goose, cycle the Goose, or ride the Goose on horseback." The easternmost access to the trail is located across from Six-Mile House on Sooke Road. The stretch that heads east along Sooke Basin is the only section of the trail with a waterfront view. You can rent a bike from **SOOKE CYCLE** (6707 West Coast Rd; 250/642-3123; www.sookebikes.com); a Sooke Cycle employee will escort you to the trail.

Take a break at the **TUGWELL CREEK HONEY FARM & MEADERY** (8750 West Coast Rd; 250/642-1956; www.tugwellcreekfarm.com), BC's first licensed meadery. From May to September, stop in to taste Melomel, a delicate, sweet blend of the farm's berries and honey.

Indulge your sweet tooth with Viennese delicacies at **LITTLE VIENNA BAKERY** (6-6726 West Coast Rd; 250/642-6833). A solid fan base from Sidney to Victoria orders the ethereal, multilayered apple strudel, while locals arrive early for pastry chef Michele Ruttkiewicz's croissants and cinnamon schnecken. The lunch crowd indulges in the Austrian mushroom cheese soup and a fresh baguette with the European cheeses.

You'll find tasty and reasonably priced meals, as well as colourful locals, at the **17-MILE PUB AND LIQUOR SHOPPE** (5126 Sooke Rd; 250/642-5942). This former stage stop also served as a school and a jail before its current incarnation as a pub. The piano is more than 150 years old (it was shipped around the Horn of Africa), and the tiles are circa 1940. The menu is the usual burgers, fries, wings, and calamari concept, but you can go West Coast with the bouillabaisse for under $20. Grab a pint and play a round of darts, pool, or backgammon.

Climb aboard **SUSHI ON THE SEA** (6669 Horne Rd, wharf; 250/642-6669; www.sushionthesea.com), a restaurant aboard Captain Ralph Hull's 80-foot boat *Rolano*, for the most unusual dining experience Sooke has to offer. Ralph, a colourful character who produced the Wolfman Jack radio show, officiates as waiter and storyteller, while partner Kari Osselton rolls out sushi's greatest hits. The communal table for eight must be booked ahead, especially in summer. Begin with sake-steamed mussels before moving on to the popular spicy tuna, the Captain's roll with eight types of seafood, or fresh crab rolls.

If it's all too beautiful to leave behind at the end of the day, some places to stay and dine in Sooke are destinations themselves. The **SOOKE HARBOUR HOUSE** (1528 Whiffen Spit Rd; 250/642-3421 or 800/889-9688; www.sookeharbour house.com) has set the standard for fresh, local, organic West Coast cuisine and is considered one of North America's finest inns. Owners Frederique and Sinclair

Phillip have gained a culinary reputation locally and internationally. The grounds, lobby, hallways, and themed rooms double as an art gallery for an array of Native and local artwork. All rooms have views, a private balcony, soaker tub, wood-burning fireplace, lush robes, and seaweed-based bath products, all graciously appointed with fresh flowers, decanters of port, and fresh-baked cookies. Chef Edward Tuson adheres to Slow Food principles, incorporating ingredients from the on-site garden along with organic, indigenous, and sustainable ocean- and land-based fare. The menu changes daily, with entrées ranging from seared scallops in a trumpet mushroom broth with grand fir oil and wild rice to cumin-dusted grilled pork tenderloin in a red wine reduction with local hazelnut and Montana cheese mashed potatos. The inn proudly pairs food with selections from their award-winning collection of more than 600 wines. A newly built patio nestled amongst the pines provides a romantic setting on balmy summer evenings. You can stroll along adjacent Whiffen Spit—rain gear is provided—or just curl up in a chair and read a book from the library. A lavish breakfast, such as hazelnut–maple syrup waffles with loganberry purée or garden vegetable quiche with scones and preserves, is delivered to your room in the morning, and an outstanding lunch box is prepared upon request. The inn offers daily tours of the gardens, featuring more than 200 edible plants, flowers, and herbs.

At **COOPER'S COVE** (5301 Sooke Rd; 250/642-5727 or 877/642-5727; www. cooperscove.com), chef/owner Angelo Prosperi-Porta combines a restful European-style bed-and-breakfast with a cooking school. Four bright and airy guest rooms overlook the sloping flower and vegetable gardens with views of Sooke Harbour. King beds, robes, slippers, fresh flowers, and house-made chocolate truffles all go nicely with a glass of sherry or port. A buffet breakfast includes house-smoked chicken or smoked salmon omelet. Interactive dinners with the chef are available upon request, or reserve a space in the afternoon cooking class. Culinary aficionados may prefer the chef's three-day intensive cooking class.

Nestled in the wooded hills with distant views of the water, **HARTMANN HOUSE B&B** (5262 Sooke Rd; 250/642-3761; www.hartmannhouse.bc.ca) offers a welcome respite for adults only. The storybook stone house is enveloped by a 210-metre (700-foot) trellised garden of flowers, herbs, and vegetables. Breakfast, prepared with fruits and herbs from the Hartmanns' garden, is a gourmet affair, from spiced rhubarb parfait to shrimp omelets with artichokes. Two luxurious, self-contained suites feature a private entrance, king-sized bed, whirlpool tub, fireplace, kitchenette, sitting room, and wide-plank fir floors. Upon arrival, a bottle of champagne, chocolates, and a fruit-and-cheese platter awaits.

Guests stay at the **MARKHAM HOUSE** (1853 Connie Rd; 250/642-7542 or 888/256-6888; www.markhamhouse.com) for its gentle pleasures: tea on the patio, country hospitality, feather beds, fireside sherry. The immaculately groomed grounds of the Tudor-style B&B feature a small river, a trout pond, a putting green, a croquet lawn, and more than 100 species of irises. Each of the four guest rooms, one with a double Jacuzzi overlooking the pond, is filled with antiques, as well as the modern amenities of wi-fi and telephones.

The Soderberg family owns 1.6 kilometres (1 mile) of beachfront and 16 hectares (40 acres) of wild, undeveloped, wooded coastline. Perched among the trees near the cliff side is their **POINT-NO-POINT RESORT** (10829 West Coast Rd; 250/646-2020; www.pointnopoint.com). The 20-plus cottages and cabins offer kitchens and fireplaces; some boast a hot tub on the deck. Four of the cabins accommodate families, but there's no Internet access or TVs; the only distractions you'll hear are the crashing of the waves and the crackle of the fireplace.

Sidney and the Saanich Peninsula

From Victoria, drive 15 minutes north on Hwy 17 to West Saanich Rd (Hwy 17A), or continue to the city of Sidney.

Although urban development encroaches on this rural area, there are still bucolic corners, wineries, and farms to be found, particularly off West Saanich Road, en route to the floral splendour of **BUTCHART GARDENS** (see no. 3 in Top 10 Attractions in this chapter).

Taste a variety of white wines amidst fruit trees and peacocks at **STARLING LANE WINERY** (5271 Old West Saanich Rd; 250/881-7422; www.starlinglane winery.com). **MARLEY FARM WINERY** (1831-D Mt Newtown Rd; 250/652-8667; www.marleyfarm.ca) makes grape and fruit wines in a farm setting, while **WINCHESTER CELLARS** (6170 Old West Saanich Rd; 250/544-8217; www. winchestercellars.com) produces certified organic award-winning whites and reds and a herbal gin. Small lots of whites and reds, including a stellar Ortega, can be found at **CHALET ESTATE WINERY** (11195 Chalet Rd; 250/656-2552; www. chaletestatevineyard.ca).

After browsing through Sidney's bookstores, stay a while at the **SIDNEY PIER HOTEL & SPA** (9805 Seaport Pl; 250/655-9700 or 866/659-9445; www.sidneypier. com). The contemporary glass-and-slate building is a departure for the retirement community of Sidney. Found at the edge of the Sidney Pier, the 55-room hotel provides a parklike setting with unobstructed views over the ocean to the Gulf and San Juan islands. Chef Gordon O'Neill provides unfussy local fare in **HARO'S WATERFRONT** restaurant. Cowichan Bay chicken served with fingerling potatoes, or fava beans over a wild mushroom ragout, represent forest and farm.

Malahat

From Victoria, drive north on Trans-Canada Hwy (Hwy 1) toward Cormorant St.

"The Malahat," a section of the Trans-Canada Highway from Victoria to Mill Bay, is an ominous word among local drivers: it signals steep roads up Malahat Mountain; on the positive side, spectacular views from the summit overlook the Saanich Inlet and surrounding mountains. Lush Douglas firs overhang the narrow highway through **GOLDSTREAM PROVINCIAL PARK** (3400 Trans-Canada Hwy/Hwy 1; 250/478-9414; www.goldstreampark.com), about 13 kilometres (8 miles) northwest of Victoria, where hundreds of bald eagles gather to feed on salmon December to February.

The **AERIE RESORT AND SPA** (600 Ebedora Ln; 250/743-7115 or 800/518-1933; www.aerie.bc.ca) is perched atop Malahat Mountain, in a forest of arbutus and fir trees. The architecture draws on faux-Mediterranean and Empire decadence, with breathtaking views of Finlayson Arm. The Aerie offers 28 spacious guest rooms and suites in three buildings, including the loftier Villa Cielo with penthouse suites and butler service. Furnished with Persian carpets, European king-sized poster beds, and luxurious bedding, the hotel also offers a fitness centre, an outdoor tennis court, and spa services. In the intimate contemporary dining room, chef Castro Boateng creates imaginative regional cuisine from area purveyors. Entrées range from house-made boudin blanc with white bean cassoulet to seared scallops over crab cakes with basil-cauliflower purée and butternut squash. Private cooking classes or seasonal mushroom foraging tours with a local monk are also offered. The wine list boasts 600 approachable and international gems, with emphasis on BC products.

Cowichan Valley

To travel directly to the valley from Sidney or the Swartz Bay ferry terminal, bypass Victoria by boarding the Brentwood Bay–Mill Bay Ferry (250/386-3431 or 888/223-3779; www.bcferries.com).

The fertile farmland and forest of the Cowichan Valley stretches from the town of Shawnigan Lake north to Duncan, then west to Cowichan Lake; the microclimate lends itself to viticulture, making it Vancouver Island's best-known wine-growing region. Try a pinot noir at **BLUE GROUSE VINEYARDS** (4365 Blue Grouse Rd, off Lakeside Rd; 250/743-3834; www.bluegrousevineyard.com). **VENTURI-SCHULZE VINEYARDS** (4235 Trans-Canada Hwy/Hwy 1; 250/743-5630; www.venturischulze.com) makes sought-after estate wines and internationally acclaimed balsamic vinegar. At **ZANATTA WINERY** (5039 Marshall Rd; 250/748-2338; www.zanatta.com) enjoy lunch in a 1903 farmhouse, or dine overlooking the orchard at **MERRIDALE CIDERWORKS** (1230 Merridale Rd; 250/743-4293 or 800/998-9908; www.merridalecider.com).

The charming seaside village of Cowichan Bay, just off Highway 1, is built on pilings over the water. The Wooden Boat Society shares space with a Native artisans' studio at the **COWICHAN BAY MARITIME CENTRE AND MUSEUM** (1761 Cowichan Bay Rd; 250/746-4955; www.classicboats.org). The **UDDER GUYS ICE CREAM PARLOUR** (1759 Cowichan Bay Rd; 250/746-4300; www.udderguys icecream.com) can fulfill cravings for fish, chips, and ice cream.

The picturesque **COWICHAN BAY FARM** (1560 Cowichan Bay Rd; 250/746-7884; www.cowichanbayfarm.com) supplies pasture-raised duck and chicken to the island's best restaurants. You can purchase duck confit and chicken sausages at the self-serve farm stand at the end of the driveway.

HILARY'S CHEESE AND DELI (1737 Cowichan Bay Rd; 250/748-5992; www. hilaryscheese.com) offers more than 100 artisanal cheeses, including the owners' own farm specialties. Pair chèvre with a fresh baguette from next door at **TRUE GRAIN BREAD** (1725 Cowichan Bay Rd; 250/746-7664; www.truegrain. ca), where owner Jonathan Knight stone-grinds heritage red fife wheat on-site.

The **MASTHEAD** (1705 Cowichan Bay Rd; 250/748-3714; www.themasthead restaurant.com), located in an historic former hotel overlooking the bay, features oysters on the half shell and a fantastic selection of Vancouver Island wines.

Duncan

Forty-five minutes north of Victoria on Trans-Canada Hwy (Hwy 1).

Duncan, the City of Totems, features intriguing totem poles. In old downtown, espresso-based drinks and sandwiches can be had at **COFFEE ON THE MOON** (5849 Kinch Ave; 250/715-1540), or pub food and microbrews at **CRAIG STREET BREWING COMPANY** (25 Craig St; 250/737-2337). The **QUW'UTSUN' CULTURAL AND CONFERENCE CENTRE** (200 Cowichan Wy; 250/746-8119 or 877/746-8119) on Duncan's southern edge features authentic Native cuisine in the **RIVER-WALK CAFÉ**, plus a chance to watch knitters at work on the region's renowned Cowichan sweaters and carvers crafting totem poles.

Local chef and author Bill Jones offers cooking classes and serves dinner in the kitchen of his 1918 farmhouse, **DEERHOLME FARM** (4830 Stelfox Rd; 250/748-7450). In town, **BISTRO ONE SIXTY ONE** (161 Kenneth St; 250/746-6466), hidden behind grapevines, features roasted Cowichan Bay Farm duck complemented with a vanilla and blood-orange reduction. A restored 1894 manor house overlooks the breathtaking 130-acre **FAIRBURN FARM** (3310 Jackson Rd; 250/746-4637; www.fairburnfarm.bc.ca), a water-buffalo dairy farm, inn, restaurant, and culinary school.

Salt Spring Island

From Victoria, ferries leave from Swartz Bay and arrive 35 minutes later at Salt Spring's Fulford Harbour, a small artists' village. Ganges, the main hub of the island, is a further 20-minute drive.

Salt Spring is the largest and most populated of the southern Gulf Islands. The mild climate invites visitors to enjoy eight lakes, ocean swimming, numerous parks, wineries, organic farms, and myriad arts and crafts. Nonnative settlement dates back to the mid-19th century; early settlers included African Americans from San Francisco after the Civil War and Kanakas, workers from the Pacific Islands. The **SALT SPRING ISLAND VISITOR INFORMATION CENTRE** (121 Lower Ganges Rd; 250/537-4223 or 866/216-2936; www.saltspringtoday.com) offers maps and information, including the handy **SALT SPRING STUDIO TOUR MAP** (www.saltspringstudiotour.com), which lists potters, weavers, jewellers, carvers, bakers, and cheesemakers.

MOUNT MAXWELL PROVINCIAL PARK, 11 kilometres (7 miles) southwest of Ganges on the west side of the island, rises 610 metres (2,000 feet) above sea level, offering peaceful walks and spectacular views. For walk-in camping and seaside walks, try **RUCKLE PROVINCIAL PARK** (10 minutes from Fulford Harbour ferry dock, turn right onto Beaver Rd; 250/539-2115 or 877/559-2115;

www.env.gov.bc.ca/bcparks), on the east side of the island. St. Mary Lake and Cusheon Lake are great spots for a dip.

Locals hangout at **BARB'S BUNS** (1-121 McPhillips Ave; 250/537-4491) for pastry and coffee and at **MOBY'S MARINE PUB** (124 Upper Ganges Rd; 250/537-5559) for microbrews and hearty soups. The popular rain-or-shine **SATUR-DAY FARMERS MARKET** (www.saltspringmarket.com) runs March to October in Ganges' Centennial Park. The **SALT SPRING APPLE FESTIVAL** (250/653-2007) in September highlights more than 350 organic and heirloom varieties of apples grown on the island.

Cheese-and-wine picnic plans? **MOONSTRUCK CHEESE** (1306 Beddis Rd; 250/537-4987; www.moonstruckcheese.com) makes nine varieties of organic cheese from their herd of Jersey cows, and **SALT SPRING ISLAND CHEESE** (285 Reynolds Rd; 250/653-2300) makes award-winning goat and sheep cheeses that visitors can sample in the tasting room. You'll need wine to go with the cheese: **GARRY OAKS WINERY** (1880 Fulford-Ganges Rd; 250/653-4687; www.garry oakswine.com) provides a Gewürztraminer, Zweigelt, and pinot gris. **SALT SPRING VINEYARDS AND B&B** (151 Lee Rd; 250/653-9463; www.saltspringvineyards. com) produces 12 wines, including a blackberry port made from the vineyard's organic berries.

Located on 22 acres on the Ganges waterfront, **HASTINGS HOUSE** (160 Upper Ganges Rd; 250/537-2362 or 800/661-9255; www.hastingshouse.com) caters to discriminating guests. The 19th-century Sussex-styled manor is listed in *1,000 Places to See Before You Die*, and its regionally inspired restaurant is rated one of the best in BC. The 18 guest suites are situated in seven lovingly restored and constructed buildings; amenities include porches and balconies, English country antiques, luxury bedding, and the work of local artists. Enjoy Sunday brunch overlooking the garden and harbour views, breakfast baskets delivered every morning, afternoon tea, cocktails in front of the foyer's enormous fireplace, or a famous Salt Spring Island lamb dinner. Explore BC's natural beauty with a stroll through the sculpture garden and along the shoreline, and then succumb to a spa pampering.

Tofino and Long Beach

From Vancouver, take ferry from Horseshoe Bay to Nanaimo. Drive north on Island Hwy (Hwy 19) to Parksville bypass. Turn west, onto Hwy 4, across the island (approximately 2½ hours). Continue past Ucluelet junction, north to Tofino. Tofino Air (800/665-2359; www.tofinoair.ca) flies in about 60 minutes from Vancouver International Airport to the Tofino/Long Beach airport.

Winter gusts often reach 100 kph (60 mph) on Vancouver Island's wild west coast, where the next stop across the vast Pacific Ocean is Japan. The ocean waves come directly from the Antarctic or, after mid-October, from Alaska. It's the long Antarctic swells—15 seconds apart—that have made this coast famous for its thousands of shipwrecks and has turned Tofino into Canada's surfing capital. Local entrepreneurs have made this area the winter storm-watching capital of the Pacific Northwest, and the storms are definitely worth seeing.

However, most of the tourists who find their way to Vancouver Island's **PACIFIC RIM NATIONAL PARK** arrive between April and October. The park is segmented into three parts: the Broken Group Islands in Barkley Sound, Long Beach, and the West Coast Trail. The small towns of Ucluelet (pronounced "yoo-CLUE-let") and Tofino bracket Pacific Rim National Park, and both towns celebrate the **PACIFIC RIM WHALE FESTIVAL** (www.pacificrimwhalefestival.com) mid-March to mid-April. That's when 20,000 Pacific grey whales pass by on their annual migration from Baja, Mexico, to the Arctic Ocean. Ucluelet, at the park's south end, is closer to Highway 4 and claims to be the world's whale-watching capital. Spring is best for whale watching, but some companies—and there are many—guarantee sightings into October. Check with the **TOFINO VISITORS CENTRE** (1426 Pacific Rim Hwy; 250/725-3414; www.tourismtofino.com). Anyone parking in the park must purchase a day pass, available at parking machines with a major credit card.

TOFINO, a charming, walkable town with fewer than 2,000 residents, is also the gateway to Clayoquot (pronounced "KLY-kwot") Sound, home to Vancouver Island's largest intact, ancient, temperate rain forest. To see local indigenous plants, visit the 12-acre **TOFINO BOTANICAL GARDENS** (1084 Pacific Rim Hwy; 250/725-1220; www.tbjf.org).

Don't miss the self-guided, 0.75-kilometre-long (0.5-mile-long) boardwalk loop through the weirdly shaped woods on **SHOREPINE BOG TRAIL**, where stubby stands of hemlock, yellow cedar, and red cedar are centuries old. Outside the park, **HALF MOON BAY TRAIL** winds through twisted stands of cedar and hemlock to reach a stairway that descends to a sandy beach.

LONG BEACH is the park's defining stretch of beach. The 19 sandy kilometres (11 miles) of surf-swept sand is best explored by hiking the beach, its headlands, and the woodland trails. Cox and Chesterman beaches are famous for booming breakers; MacKenzie Beach for relative warmth; Templar Beach for secluded peace. Florencia Bay (also known as Wreck Bay), former home to hippie squatters, is a local favourite—no crowds, and the tidal pools teem with marine life.

Numerous tour and whale-watching companies explore the coast. **TLA-OOK CULTURAL ADVENTURES** (250/725-2656; www.tlaook.com) offers guided trips in traditional Nuu-chah-nulth dugout canoes to Meares Island, a sunset paddle, or full-day adventures that include a traditional wild salmon barbecue. Climb in a Zodiac at **OCEAN OUTFITTERS** (250/725-2866 or 877/906-2326; www.ocean outfitters.bc.ca) and be swept away to watch whales and wildlife or explore Hot Springs Cove. You can also overnight at **HOT SPRINGS COVE LODGE** (250/670-1106 or 866/670-1106; www.hotspringcove.com). **BROWNING PASS CHARTERS** (250/725-7742; www.browningpass.com) offers knowledgeable, low-impact wildlife-watching tours in Clayoquot Sound. Surfers, beginners or experienced, hit the waves with the **PACIFIC SURF SCHOOL** (101-430 Campbell St; 250/725-2155 or 888/777-9961; www.pacificsurfschool.com).

Gift shops and galleries are sprinkled throughout Tofino. The longhouse of **EAGLE AERIE GALLERY** (350 Campbell St; 250/725-3235 or 800/663-0669) sells art by renowned Tsimshian artist Roy Henry Vickers. **HOUSE OF HIMWITSA** (300 Main St; 250/725-2017 or 800/899-1947; www.himwitsa.com) features First Nations masks and jewellery. Fill up on organic coffee, baked treats, and counterculture news at the **COMMON LOAF BAKE SHOP** (180 1st St; 250/725-3915), fresh sushi at the **INN AT TOUGH CITY** (350 Main St; 250/725-2021), and seafood plates at the **SCHOONER ON SECOND** (331 Campbell St; 250/725-3444; www.schoonerrestaurant.com). For seductive handmade chocolates and ice cream, visit **CHOCOLATE TOFINO** (1180 Pacific Rim Hwy; 250/725-2526; www.chocolatetofino.com).

Except for the camping available at **GREEN POINT CAMPGROUND** (877/737-3783; www.pc.gc.ca) located at the park's midway point, all accommodation lies outside the park boundaries. If you can't bear to leave, book into the acclaimed **WICKANINNISH INN** (500 Osprey Ln, at Chesterman Beach; 250/725-3100 or 800/333-4604; www.wickinn.com). Just 5 kilometres (3 miles) south of Tofino, this splendid, multimillion-dollar oceanfront structure offers a roaring fire in the tranquil lobby when it's howling outside plus 46 comfy guest rooms each with a view, gas fireplace, and soaker tub. Shake off the rain slicker and boots (provided by the inn) and settle in at On-the-Rocks bar or indulge at the Ancient Cedars Spa before dining at the **POINTE**. The restaurant serves up Pacific Northwest cuisine with lofty panoramic views of crashing waves. Book ahead to enjoy simple steamed crab with garlic butter, a prawn tasting of three locally caught varieties, or cedar-glazed wild salmon accompanied by an impressive wine list.

The inn with the best guest lounge is the delightful oceanfront Ralph Lauren–inspired **MIDDLE BEACH LODGE** (400 Mackenzie Beach Rd; 250/725-2900 or 866/725-2900; www.middlebeach.com), where guests disappear into down-filled easy chairs by the great rock fireplace or snooze in Adirondack chairs on the deck. The 25 guest rooms are adult-only, but the family-oriented Lodge at the Headlands has 20 guest rooms.

At the edge of Tofino's town centre, **CABLE COVE INN** (201 Main St; 250/725-4236 or 800/663-6449; www.cablecoveinn.com) has seven guest rooms that overlook their private beach and the ocean beyond. An on-site Ashram spa features Ayurvedic treatments that begin with a relaxing outdoor cedar sauna.

Forage the local restaurants for a taste of the island's west coast. Try Tofino spot prawns sautéed with plum wine and ginger or Thai hot and sour seafood soup at the **RAINCOAST CAFÉ** (1-120 4th St; 250/725-2215; www.raincoastcafe.com). **SHELTER RESTAURANT** (601 Campbell St; 250/725-3353; www.shelterrestaurant.com) serves stout-steamed mussels amidst sunset views, and **SOBO** (311 Neill St; 250/725-2341; www.sobo.ca) dishes up wild salmon–stuffed *inari* pockets and cornmeal-crusted oysters.

WHISTLER

WHISTLER

How to Get Here

BY CAR

From Vancouver, it is usually a 90-minute drive up the scenic, and romantically named, **SEA-TO-SKY HIGHWAY** (Hwy 99; 604/815-4010 or 877/4SAFE99; www.seatoskyimprovements.ca) from West Vancouver through Squamish to North America's top-ranked ski resort. As a main thoroughfare for the 2010 Winter Olympics, however, the road is undergoing a long-overdue $600 million upgrade, so check for any possible delays via the hotline or online. The 125-kilometre (75-mile) route winds through the lush forests that rim Howe Sound and the perennially snowcapped Coast Mountains. Whether you travel by car, bus, or train, you'll find the route to Whistler is a visually awe-inspiring overture to the majestic beauty you'll find at journey's end. If you're driving, don't get distracted by the breathtaking views—the curves of the road demand constant attention.

Along the way, you pass the quiet residential communities that surround Howe Sound, such as Horseshoe Bay, Lion's Bay, Porteau Cove, and Furry Creek. Britannia Beach, about a half hour north of Horseshoe Bay, was once the largest processor of copper in the British Empire. It has the revamped **BC MUSEUM OF MINING** (Britannia Beach; 604/896-2233 or 800/896-4044; www.bcmuseumofmining.org), a few precious-stone outlets including **CASSIAR MOUNTAIN JADE STORE** (604/896-0077; www.jadecity.ca), and a few places to grab a snack: look for the blue bus of **MOUNTAIN WOMAN** (Copper Beach Ests; 604/896-2468) for great burgers and fries and **GALILEO COFFEE COMPANY** (Britannia Beach; 604/896-0272; www.galileocoffee.com) for freshly roasted coffee and scrumptious treats. If you want serious food in a seriously casual setting, drive about 15 minutes farther and stop at the **KLAHANIE RESTAURANT** (Darrell Bay Rd; 604/892-3435; open 7am–9pm) overlooking Shannon Falls. Kids of all ages love the hundreds of rabbits that inhabit the surroundings. Afterward, visit **SHANNON FALLS** (east side of Hwy 99, just south of Stawamus Chief Mtn) and take a stroll along the base of this beautiful waterfall. Six times the vertical drop of Niagara Falls, it's the fifth-largest waterfall in the world, plummeting 335 metres (1,100 feet).

Drive up Highway 99 a bit farther to watch rock climbers from around the world scale Smoke Bluffs or the imposing 650-metre (2,133-foot) granite mass that is Stawamus Chief—reputedly the second-largest granite monolith in the world after the Rock of Gibraltar. You can also view the climbers while having lunch at the **HOWE SOUND INN AND BREWING COMPANY** (37801 Cleveland Ave, Squamish; 604/892-2603; www.howesound.com), where wonderful handcrafted ales are served in both a charming brewpub and the Northbeach Lounge and Grill, which has an inventive menu specializing in

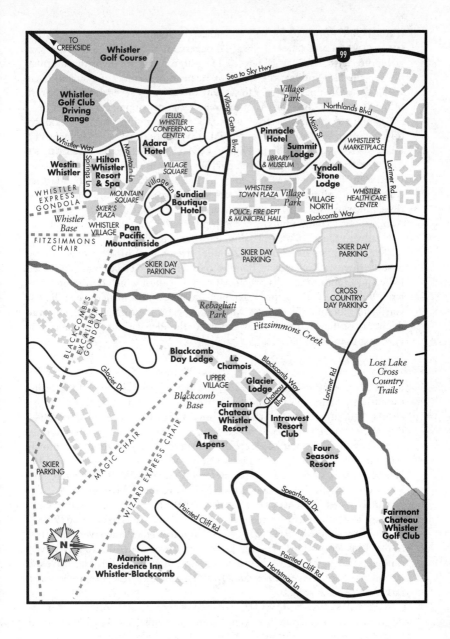

regional fare—or head for myriad choices in Squamish. Stop at the **SQUA-MISH ADVENTURE CENTRE** (38551 Loggers Ln SS1; 604/815-4994; www.adventurecentre.ca), a swish new building housing plenty of visitor information on the area dubbed the Outdoor Recreation Capital of Canada. Even without the Olympics, it's easy to see why this town—as well much of the rest of the Sea-to-Sky corridor—is undergoing rapid development.

If you're a train spotter from way back or want to introduce your kids to this tradition, turn west on Centennial Way, approximately 3 kilometres (2 miles) north of McDonald's on Highway 99 in Squamish, to the **WEST COAST RAILWAY HERITAGE PARK** (Centennial Wy, Squamish; 604/898-9336; www.wcra.org). This 5-hectare (12-acre) park houses Canada's second-largest collection of rolling railway stock. Its 95 vintage railway cars and locomotives, in various stages of restoration, are set in a beautiful natural landscape. Admission is $10 for adults, $32 for families; $2.50 surcharge to ride miniature railway. Open 10am–5pm summer, 10am–4pm winter.

The remaining 40-kilometre (24-mile) stretch to Whistler winds its way past the town of Brackendale, home of the annual bald eagle count, and Alice Lake and Brandywine Falls provincial parks, both of which border on Garibaldi Provincial Park, before reaching Alta Lake and Whistler's town limits. Garibaldi's looming Black Tusk Mountain, according to Native legend, was the home of the Thunderbird, which made thunder with its wings and shot lightning bolts from its eyes.

BY BUS

If you don't want to miss a single second of spectacular scenery on this beautiful drive, take the bus to Whistler. A two-hour, 45-minute trip is offered by **PERIMETER TRANSPORTATION** (604/266-5386 in Vancouver, 604/905-0041 in Whistler), which shuttles passengers daily between Vancouver International Airport and the Whistler bus loop. (It also runs from a number of downtown Vancouver hotels to Whistler ones.) The bus is a popular form of travel for Whistler locals, so reservations are preferable year-round. One-way fares are $57.75 for adults, $31.50 for children 5–12, free for children under 5.

GREYHOUND CANADA TRANSPORTATION CORPORATION (Pacific Central Stn, 1150 Station St, Vancouver; 800/661-8747 in Vancouver; 2029 London Ln, Whistler; 604/932-5031) whisks you from the Vancouver bus depot to the Whistler bus loop. The trip takes about three hours. Buses leave seven times daily from Vancouver between 5:30am and 7pm. Return trips leave the Whistler bus loop seven times daily between 5:30am and 7:15pm. One-way fare is $19.95 for adults.

SNOWBUS (866/SNOWBUS; www.snowbus.ca) also offers a service between Richmond, Burnaby, Vancouver, and Whistler Creekside and taxi loop. One-way fares start at $18.87.

BY TRAIN

For a romantic alternative, take the **WHISTLER MOUNTAINEER** (604/606-8460 or 888/687-7245; www.whistlermountaineer.com), which departs the North Vancouver train terminal (1311 W 1st St, Vancouver) daily at 8.30am, wending its way up the Howe Sound coastline through the Cheakamus River Valley and Garibaldi Provincial Park. The trip includes a leisurely breakfast, reaching the Whistler train station on Lake Placid Road at 11:30am, April through October. The return trip leaves Whistler at 3pm and includes afternoon tea, returning to North Vancouver at 6pm. Tickets (including meal) are $110 for adults one way, $199 for adults round-trip; discounts available for seniors and children.

BY PLANE

WHISTLER AIR (604/932-6615) offers a 30-minute floatplane service between Vancouver and Whistler twice daily May 1 to October 14. One-way ticket is $159.

Orientation

Way back in 1914, Alex and Myrtle Philip bought 4 hectares (10 acres) of land on Alta Lake for $700. They spent the summer building a ski resort and named it Rainbow Lodge. It attracted an enthusiastic audience of Europeans, Americans, and Canadians who had taken up skiing—a hot new sports craze at the time. There weren't many groomed trails on nearby London Mountain (now called Whistler Mountain) when the Philips first opened, but that changed pretty quickly when skiing became a popular winter pastime after the Second World War. In 1964 a group of investors began developing the valley, and in 1965 it was officially renamed Whistler after the indigenous hoary marmot, which is known for its shrill, whistling call.

The area's reputation soared during the 1980s when nearby Blackcomb Mountain opened, doubling the overall skiing acreage and boasting a mile-high vertical drop: North America's highest. For several years, the twin glacial peaks of Whistler and Blackcomb mountains have been rated North America's number-one ski resort by numerous ski and travel magazines, and it's also gained a reputation as a world-class year-round resort. Its reputation is soaring further with the newly opened Peak to Peak gondola that links Blackcomb and Whistler with an 11-minute, 7.5-metre-per-second (25-foot-per-second) journey. The long-discussed dream comes with a number of global firsts: the highest lift of its kind and the longest unsupported lift span in the world (almost three and a half times the length of the Golden Gate Bridge and eight times as high as Niagara Falls), the Peak to Peak is branded "one of the technical wonders of the world" and a rival to the Grand Canyon.

In ski season, you'll hear plenty of foreign accents in the chairlift lines, along with those of the many Aussie liftees. The Horstman Glacier on Blackcomb Mountain is open for skiing and snowboarding as late as mid-August. If you're seeking

THE LURE OF THE RINGS

In October 2007, 1.6 million tickets for the 2010 Olympic Winter Games—half of which were priced under $100—went on sale in a bidding frenzy. (The 250,000 Paralympic Winter Games tickets are available in 2009.) Whistler will also have free-of-charge Live Sites with a mix of medal ceremonies, entertainment, and other cultural events.

Fancy standing on a podium complete with mock medals, seeing the Olympic equipment up close and learning more about the Olympics in Whistler? Stop by the **OLYMPIC VISITORS CENTRE** (near Brewhouse, end of Main St, Village North), open every day. It's run by effervescent volunteers whose knowledge and enthusiasm will fire up even those who thought they couldn't care less about the games.

The annual **CELEBRATE 2010: CULTURAL FESTIVAL** (www.tourismwhistler. com or www.vancouver2010.com) is a monthlong free and ticketed event in February that leads to the Olympics. The festival aims to tap into the rich heritage and cultural seam along the Sea-to-Sky corridor from Vancouver to Whistler.

If you're wondering what the meaning is behind **ILANAAQ**, the Vancouver Organizing Committee's (VANOC) multicolored giant-with-open-arms logo, it's exactly what it looks like: a gesture of friendship welcoming the world. Modeled on the traditional *Inukshuk* created by the Inuits as a directional pointer, it

mountain air, Whistler is an ideal getaway for nonskiing visitors who want to hike, fish, mountain bike, paddle, raft, or simply experience the incredible beauty of the Coast Mountains during the spring, summer, and fall.

Surrounded by the 10,000-foot peaks of Garibaldi Provincial Park, Canada's first resort municipality is actually four cheek-by-jowl communities: Whistler Village, the main hub; Upper Village, at the base of Blackcomb Mountain; Creekside, the southernmost community, at the original gondola base of Whistler Mountain; and Village North, the northernmost development, which consists of the Marketplace and Town Plaza. Although the areas have grown exponentially with the construction of a number of multimillion-dollar condos, retail stores, and restaurants, walking in the pedestrian-only villages still evokes the intimate feel of a European resort. Sociable plazas are accessed via broad pedestrian-only boulevards, unexpected byways, and pathways that connect the various communities. Both mountains can be accessed from any of the four villages, thanks to a well-organized series of interconnecting high-speed lifts and gondolas. Free shuttle buses link each village, and local buses connect outlying residential areas to each village. The result of all this careful planning is a place where individual transportation is not needed to get to food, lifts, or nightlife: everything is a pleasant 2- to 10-minute stroll from your hotel or condo.

can also be seen in the flesh outside the Roundhouse Restaurant at the top of the Whistler Gondola. Furry Olympic mascots to watch out for are **QUATCHI**, **SUMI**, and **MIGA** (sometimes caught wandering in the village to the amusement of children—and adults with cameras). You'll see these characters—inspired by Aboriginal mythological creatures—on a selection of merchandise from plush animals to Olympic pins.

Competition for **HOTEL ACCOMMODATION** (www.vancouver2010.com) in the Whistler area is likely to be as tough as the Games themselves. VANOC estimates it will need 20,000 of the 30,000 hotel rooms available for the Games in order to house groups for which it is responsible. However, VANOC is working with tourism associations and hotels to plan accommodation for spectators—and, with stories emerging of normal nightly rates elevating from $289 to $1,400, also to encourage rates to be kept reasonable. Private rentals are another major option, with some residents deciding to rent out their homes rather than stay; Web sites such as www.rent2010.net quickly followed the Games announcement.

Citius, Altius, Fortius (faster, higher, stronger): With Whistler's meteoric rise in just four decades from small mountain community to international behemoth hosting the 21st Olympic Winter Games, you would be hard pressed to find another village that strove as doggedly to live up to the Olympic ideal.

—Lucy Hyslop

Visitor Information

The **WHISTLER VISITOR INFO CENTRE** (201-4230 Gateway Dr, Whistler; 604/935-3357 or 800/991-9988; www.whistlerchamber.com) provides information about accommodations, restaurants, outfitters, and special events year-round. It's open daily 9am–6pm in the summer and 9am–5pm the rest of the year.

Three information kiosks are open in the summer. **VILLAGE BOOTH** (at Greyhound Bus Loop) is open 10am–8pm daily. The **VILLAGE KIOSK** (in Village Sq) is open noon–6pm daily. The **NORTH KIOSK** (by gazebo) is open 10am–6pm daily.

Call **WHISTLER RESORT** (800/WHISTLER or 800/944-7853 official reservation service) for accommodation reservations, upcoming events, and general information on Whistler. It's advisable to make accommodation arrangements before your arrival at Whistler.

Getting Around

The walk between Whistler Village and the Upper Village takes about five minutes. Similarly, Village North can be reached on foot from either Whistler Village or the Upper Village in about five to seven minutes. Free shuttle buses link each village.

343

If you're staying in any of the outlying neighbourhoods, such as Nester's Village, Alpine Meadows, Emerald Estates, White Gold Estates, or Tamarisk, consider using the year-round public transit service. The **WHISTLER TRANSIT SYSTEM** or **WHISTLER AND VALLEY EXPRESS (WAVE) BUS LINE** (604/932-4020) buses operate daily, with frequent stops right at the gondolas, providing an efficient and economical alternative to hunting down a parking space. One-day fares are $5 for adults, $3 for seniors and students; discounted TripCards available for 10 or 20 rides and 7 or 30 days.

Whistler's taxis operate around the clock. Not only can **AIRPORT LIMOUSINE SERVICE** (604/273-1331), **SEA TO SKY TAXI** (604/932-3333), and **WHISTLER STAR EXPRESS** (866/874-1311 or 604/874-4896) shuttle you between destinations, these companies also offer taxi tours, golf course transfers, and transport to Vancouver International Airport.

Trips to outlying Pemberton, Mount Currie, or Lillooet require a car. **AVIS** (at Cascade Lodge, 4315 Northland Blvd, Upper Village; 604/932-1236) has reservation agents to book rental cars or SUVs for side trips.

Restaurants

Araxi Restaurant & Bar / ★★★★

4222 WHISTLER VILLAGE SQ, WHISTLER VILLAGE; 604/932-4540

A cousin to Vancouver's highly rated CinCin, Blue Water Cafe, and West restaurants (see reviews in Restaurants chapter), the perennially trendy Araxi not only attracts a young, beautiful, and well-heeled crowd, it's also one of Whistler's long-standing culinary cornerstones. It can be jam-packed and hectic some nights, but be patient, or grab a seat at the bar; the patio is popular in summer. With the village's first 100-mile menu, Araxi embraces the locavore movement. Executive chef James Walt showcases such ingredients sourced within this radius as Qualicum Beach scallops with North Arm Farm peaches or creamed corn with braised leeks and beurre rouge. Dessert? Go for the pear-and-almond tart (frangipane and caramel-poached pears). Even Heston Blumenthal—owner of the U.K.'s three-Michelin-star Fat Duck, heralded as the "best restaurant in the world"—gave Araxi his seal of approval during a recent visit. Three sommeliers ensure Araxi's big, changeable, and impressive wine cellar is yours to explore every night. *$$$$; AE, MC, V; debit cards; lunch, dinner every day May–Oct, dinner only Dec–Apr (closed first two weeks in May); full bar; reservations recommended; www.araxi.com.* &

Bearfoot Bistro / ★★★★

4121 VILLAGE GREEN (LISTEL WHISTLER HOTEL), WHISTLER VILLAGE; 604/932-3433

Irrepressible proprietor André St. Jacques goes to great lengths to provide luxe wining and dining at luxe prices. Be prepared to give your credit card number when you reserve, with a $50 per person fee in case you forget to cancel. Three tasting menus start at $98; we highly recommend putting your palate in the hands of wunderkind Melissa Craig—crowned Canada's Best Chef during the 2008 Canadian Culinary Championships—for a chef's five-course tasting menu ($135), along with sommelier Daniel Robitaille's spot-on and informative wine pairings ($125 supplement). Main courses range from an explosive yellowfin tuna (*kinpachi* sashimi, fresh wasabi, and soy Pop Rocks) to an inventive Quebec foie gras (parfait, plum port jelly terrine, toasted brioche, and gingerbread) to Kobe beef cooked to perfection. The dessert menu changes daily at the whim of talented pastry chef Dominic Fortin (try the ice-wine-poached pear, pine-nut strudel, and olive oil ice cream). The newly revamped wine cellar is a small museum for oenophiles, with collections such as the Château Mouton Rothschild back to 1945 and Moët et Chandon back to 1914. *$$$$; AE, DC, MC, V; debit cards; dinner every day; full bar; reservations recommended; www.bearfootbistro.com; at Whistler Wy.* &

The Beet Root Café / ★

129-4340 LORIMER RD, VILLAGE NORTH; 604/932-1163
No one is quite as perky at 7:30am as Dublin transplant and owner Paula Ryan. Beet Root—on the old site of Auntie Em's—is recommended by locals for tasty homemade food. From the full works—eggs, bacon, tomatoes, beans, roasted potatoes, and toast—to granola muesli with yogurt, wild berries, apricot, and organic bananas to breakfast burritos, both meat lovers and vegetarians will be set for the day. Voted the Best New Restaurant by readers of the *Pique*, the local newspaper, the café also serves a hearty, traditional Irish stew in the evening that's quite unlike anything else available in Whistler. *$; MC, V; debit cards; breakfast, lunch, dinner every day; no alcohol; no reservations.* &

Caramba! / ★★

12-4314 MAIN ST, VILLAGE NORTH; 604/938-1879
This fun, boisterous, Mediterranean-influenced restaurant reflects owner Mario Enero's ability to wow even those who are on a modest budget. He's combined high-energy service with big, soul-satisfying portions of down-home pasta, pizza, and roasts. Start with savoury baked goat cheese served with a tomato coulis and garlic toast points. Then delve into fettuccine Natasha, accented with chunks of fresh salmon and a peppery vodka-and-tomato cream sauce. Munch on a melanzane pizza heaped with roasted eggplant, Roma tomatoes, and goat cheese. Or try the mouthwatering grilled bay trout with bacon-and-onion mashed potatoes. They'll also whip up a takeout meal. Kids and adults both love the platter of three-cheese macaroni after a strenuous day on the slopes. *$$; AE, MC, V; no debit cards; lunch every day (summer), Fri–Sun (winter), dinner every day; full bar; no reservations; www.caramba-restaurante.com.* &

345

Ciao-Thyme / ★★

1-4573 CHATEAU BLVD, UPPER VILLAGE; 604/932-7051

The old Chef Bernard's now has a new name and is run by Ryan Liebrecht, sous-chef under Bernard Casavant, who left to join Burrowing Owl Winery (see the Okanagan Valley chapter). Following Casavant's reputation for fresh local ingredients, Liebrecht's food is a flawless fusion of classic French and Pacific Northwest cuisines. Start with the Brie-and-carrot soup, and then try the pan-seared wild salmon fillet. Locals keep coming back for the free-range fried egg sandwich with aged cheddar and bacon on a toasted granola bun. Fresh-baked pies are a treat. BC wines and beers dominate. *$; AE, MC, V; debit cards; breakfast, lunch, dinner every day; beer and wine; no reservations; www.chefbernards.ca.* &

Dubh Linn Gate / ★★

4320 SUNDIAL CRES (PAN PACIFIC LODGE),
WHISTLER VILLAGE; 604/905-4047

Homesick denizens of the Emerald Isle find a wealth of good cheer, fine "slow-pour" draughts, and heaping mounds of finely prepared pub fare in this transplanted bit of olde Ireland. The pub's entire interior, including the unfinished-wood floors and lots of stained glass, was built back in the old country and imported to its prime base-of-the-mountain location. The patio is right at the bottom of the slopes. Live Celtic music serenades après-skiers indoors during the evening while they consume generous portions of steak-and-ale pie, "fat of the land" Irish stew, and ale-battered cod-and-chips. *$$; AE, MC, V; no debit cards; breakfast, lunch, dinner every day; full bar; no reservations; www.dubhlinngate.com.* &

Edgewater Lodge Restaurant / ★★★

8020 ALPINE WY (EDGEWATER LODGE), WHISTLER; 604/932-0688

This is one of the few spots with a good view of both Whistler and Blackcomb. Wallowing in the solitude of its own undeveloped 45-acre Green Lake estate, this intimate restaurant (plus seasonal lakeside garden seating) is the perfect spot for a private, relaxed, romantic sunset tête-à-tête. The menu is traditional but remarkably appealing and includes starters such as pan-seared Camembert and mains like schnitzel with hunter's mushroom sauce and rich mashed potatoes, or sweet, tender venison raised on the lodge's own ranch in northern BC. Finish with a slice of the luscious signature dessert: Black Tusk Chocolate Cake. *$$; AE, MC, V; debit cards; dinner Wed–Sun Sept–June, every day Jul–Aug; full bar; reservations recommended; www.edgewater-lodge.com; 4 km (2.5 mi) north of Whistler Village, across from Meadow Park Sports Centre.* &

Elements / ★★★

4359 MAIN ST (SUMMIT LODGE), VILLAGE NORTH; 604/932-5569

Accolades adorn this trendy "urban tapas parlour," which has lost none of the buzz it first received at its opening in 2005, especially on "Crazy Monday" lunchtimes, when the bistro (part of the Wild Wood Restaurants' family) heaves with locals on their day off after the weekend rush. Its cutting-edge red and brown decor, copper accents, and contemporary low seating and suede banquettes make it an intimate, secret den. Tapas, remember, is all about sharing. Start with to-die-for ahi carpaccio with sesame soy dressing, avocado salsa, and wonton chips, followed by the refreshing iceberg lettuce cup served with ragùlike hoisin pork and papaya along with condiments such as soy-roasted cashews, and add the signature potato tartlet and baked frittata. With food this divine, you'll want to keep the dishes all to yourself. *$$; AE, MC, V; debit cards; breakfast, lunch, dinner every day; full bar; no reservations; www.wildwoodrestaurants.ca/htm/pbistro.html.* &

Fifty Two 80 Bistro / ★★★

4591 BLACKCOMB WY (FOUR SEASONS), UPPER VILLAGE; 604/935-3400
The well-orchestrated menu is not so large that it leaves you racked with indecision, though the wine menu is exhaustive. It caters to children, but some of executive chef Scott Thomas Dolbee's choices are happily grown-up: starters include ahi carpaccio, avocado, asparagus, and Champagne vinaigrette; entrées range from venison loin, braised cabbage, cauliflower marzipan, and Romanesco to generously portioned baked wild salmon, fingerling potatos, and braised butter lettuce and black truffle. A range of three to five courses (starting at $60) is a perfect reward after perhaps carving the number of feet on Blackcomb Mountain's vertical mile—the origin of the restaurant's name. End with the bittersweet chocolate "pudding" with honeycomb. *$$$; AE, DC, MC, V; no debit cards; breakfast, lunch, dinner every day; full bar; reservations recommended; www.fourseasons.com/whistler/dining.* &

Hy's Steakhouse / ★★☆

4308 MAIN ST (DELTA WHISTLER VILLAGE SUITES), VILLAGE NORTH; 604/905-5555
Hy's delivers beef better than some of the finest traditional Manhattan and Midwestern establishments that specialize in the same tender subject. This spot, with white linens, warm cherry wood, and supple leather chairs, serves up steaks that range in size from not-so-petite filet mignon and New York strip (with cracked black peppercorns and a smooth green-peppercorn sauce) to we-couldn't-finish-it chateaubriand. It's one of the few places left in North America where you can order a steak "blue" and not end up with medium rare. Nonsteak types find that the kitchen also knows its way around seafood. The crisp Caesar salad is a garlic lover's delight that doesn't skimp on shaved Parmesan and croutons. The prawn cocktail and starter portion of blackened ahi tuna are similarly generous and delectable. Hy's also offers an excellent variety of Pacific Northwest wines. *$$$; AE, DC, MC, V; debit cards; dinner every day; full bar; reservations recommended; www.hyssteakhouse.com.* &

Il Caminetto di Umberto / ★★★

4242 VILLAGE STROLL, WHISTLER VILLAGE; 604/932-4442

This slice of the Tuscan countryside is the ubiquitous Umberto Menghi's answer to fine dining in Whistler (he also owns the casual Trattoria di Umberto reviewed in this chapter, as well as some famous Vancouver spots reviewed in the Restaurants chapter). Not surprisingly, few things can top an après-ski meal here of fresh pasta and a bottle of Umberto's own Bambolo wine, even though this perennial favourite packed the tables together too tightly, and the bar and cabaret are noisy. Tuscan-style specials besides pasta include roasted rack of lamb with rosemary-and-garlic crust. Milanese-style osso buco is served with sautéed vegetables and a saffron-tinted risotto. Leave room for the mascarpone cheesecake. *$$$–$$$$; AE, DC, MC, V; debit cards; dinner every day; full bar; reservations recommended; www.umberto.com/village; Whistler Village Sq.* &

La Rua / ★★★

4557 BLACKCOMB WY (LE CHAMOIS), UPPER VILLAGE; 604/932-5011

Mario Enero runs a stylish but comfortable restaurant that prides itself on snap-of-the-finger service and a great wine list. Chef R. D. Stewart has devised some superb dishes served in portions that will satisfy the most ravenous skier or mountain biker. Start with the crab-and-lobster cake with *Espelette* pepper aioli. No one makes better lamb—marinated rack with roast garlic mash and brandy sauce—or toothsome pastas, such as the pappardelle and beef tenderloin. Save room for homemade sorbets and biscotti. *$$$$; AE, DC, MC, V; debit cards; dinner every day; full bar; reservations recommended; www.larua-restaurante.com.* &

The Mix by Ric's / ★★

4154 VILLAGE GREEN, VILLAGE NORTH; 604/932-6499

The tapas menu allows for as short—or long—a bite as you desire, which is a good thing, since you cannot make reservations in this popular hangout. The pine-nut-crusted wheel of Brie with homemade compote is a classic, while the Mixed Up foie gras poutine—fries with caramelized Vidalia onions, crunchy bacon bits, and foie gras gravy—is a rather sophisticated twist on a Canadian favourite and a perfect pairing with a Mixtini or Mixballs (the Mix pun runs deep around here). If you don't think you can wait the 15 minutes or so it takes to create the molten chocolate cake, order it first. *$$$; AE, MC, V; debit cards; breakfast, lunch, dinner every day; full bar; no reservations; www. ricsgrill.com/bc.* &

Mountain Club / ★★

4314 MAIN ST, VILLAGE NORTH; 604/932-6009

There's no doubt that the Mountain Club, twinned with the Ocean Club in Vancouver and branded as "Aspen meets New York in the heart of Whistler," is at the vanguard of a recent influx of sexy, hip urban restaurants in Whistler. British executive chef Paul Roberts's menu is a simple split between "ocean"—try the divine crab cakes with sea asparagus—and "earth": mac and cheese, molasses-braised beef short ribs, or organic beef tenderloin to silence the most hardened meat aficionado. Even so, you would be forgiven for heading straight to the dessert menu: Vancouver's unsurpassable pastry maestro Thomas Haas presents his lemon tart or Stilton cheesecake or chocolate fondant. The wine list and cocktails are extensive. *$$; AE, MC, V; debit cards; lunch every day in summer, dinner every day; full bar; reservations recommended; www.themountainclub.ca.* &

Quattro at Whistler / ★★★

4319 MAIN ST (PINNACLE INTERNATIONAL HOTEL),
VILLAGE NORTH; 604/905-4844
Right from the start, carbo-loading skiers loved to slide into Antonio Corsi's restaurant at the Pinnacle International Hotel. Quattro at Whistler is upbeat, vibrant, and innovative. *La cucina leggera,* or "the healthy kitchen," is the motto, a concept that fits the West Coast sensibility like a good set of ski boots. Fungi fanciers love the carpaccio featuring sliced portobello mushrooms topped with flavourful white truffle oil and shaved Asiago. Kudos also for the grilled scallops and prawns, served with a painstakingly prepared Dungeness crab risotto inside a phyllo roll. Corsi's pasta dishes are equally inspired; try the gnocchi with Gorgonzola topped with roasted pecans. Entrées of crispy deboned Cornish game hen or roasted lean duck breast, accompanied by sun-dried blueberry and port wine sauce, are irresistible. The portions are generous, and the *l'abbuffata* sampler menu for four or more very hungry people will not disappoint. The mainly Italian wine list is stellar. Desserts (which change daily) are stunning. *$$$; MC, V; no debit cards; dinner every day (closed mid-Oct–mid-Nov); full bar; reservations recommended; www.quattrorestaurants.com; Town Plaza.* &

Rim Rock Cafe / ★★★

2117 WHISTLER RD (HIGHLAND LODGE),
CREEKSIDE; 604/932-5565
Filled to the rafters with a hip local crowd, this cozy cafe with a stone fireplace has been dishing out great food for years. Split into two levels (smokers in the downstairs bistro), Bob Dawson and Rolf Gunther's restaurant is remarkable proof that fresh seafood and wondrous cuisine are not anomalies in the mountains. The fresh sheet features starters such as the Rasputin—award-winning Fanny Bay raw oysters topped with vodka, crème fraîche, and caviar. Main events range from herb-infused salmon to a mouthwatering grilled wild caribou. The Death by Chocolate dessert can make grown men cry. During the summer, book a table on the cozy back patio and dine amidst the fresh herbs in the chef's garden. The well-chosen 300-label wine list is largely affordable. *$$$$; AE, MC, V; debit cards; dinner every day (closed Oct 20–Nov 20); full bar; reservations recommended; www.rimrockwhistler.com.*

Splitz Grill / ★★

4369 MAIN ST (ALPENGLOW), VILLAGE NORTH; 604/938-9300

It's been a long time since a hamburger (or any of its '90s-style chicken, wild salmon, spicy lentil, or Italian sausage cousins) has been this thick, juicy, and utterly tantalizing. Splitz struck the right chord in the hearts of locals and visitors by offering a not-so-humble grilled sandwich on a crusty bun with your choice of toppings ranging from chili, garlic mayo, tahini, sauerkraut, and hummus to fresh tomato, sprouts, salsa, and kosher pickles. The thick, house-cut fries still have their skins. Even including a soft drink, you haven't spent $10, and you're more than satisfied—although dessert does beckon in the form of ice cream sundaes, floats, shakes, cones, and a caramelized banana split. *$; V; debit cards; lunch, dinner every day; beer and wine; no reservations; Town Plaza.* &

Sushi Village / ★★

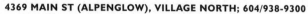

4272 MOUNTAIN SQ (WESTBROOK HOTEL),
WHISTLER VILLAGE; 604/932-3330

Where do the locals go to satisfy their appetites for healthy portions of "down-home" Japanese cuisine? Sushi Village. You can't miss it, even though it's perched on the second floor of the Westbrook Hotel. You'll see ravenous young skiers and snowboarders patiently waiting alongside upscale sophisticates to get a table. It's worth the wait. Consistently delicious and extremely fresh sushi, sashimi, and *maki* platters, as well as abundant combinations served in wooden sushi boats, are prepared at the counter by animated experts. Tempura, gyoza, yakitori, teriyaki, and satisfying meal-size noodle soups are just a few of the home-style hot dishes offered. The food is straightforward, dependable, and a truly good deal. Semiprivate tatami rooms and takeout are both available. *$$; AE, DC, MC, V; debit cards; lunch Wed–Sun, dinner every day (Sat–Sun only, off-season); full bar; reservations recommended; www.sushivillage.com.* &

Trattoria di Umberto / ★★★½

4417 SUNDIAL CRES (MOUNTAINSIDE LODGE),
WHISTLER VILLAGE; 604/932-5858

Two large, romantically lit dining rooms separated by a massive open kitchen welcome you to this busy, lively, very northern Italian establishment. Animated conversation is as much a part of the atmosphere as the poolside view and rustic Italian decor. Classic Tuscan starters such as antipasto Toscano or hearty Tuscan bean soup warm both heart and soul. But it's entrées like tiger prawns and scallops that will leave you singing the kitchen's praises. No trattoria can exist without pasta and risotto dishes: Umberto's Italian comfort food ranges from chicken tortellini with Alfredo sauce to penne and Italian sausage ragù. A respectable wine list, along with the requisite cappuccino and espresso; desserts (don't miss the tiramisu) are large enough to share. *$$$–$$$$; AE, DC, MC, V; debit cards; lunch, dinner every day; full bar; reservations recommended; www.umberto.com/truck.htm.* &

Lodgings

Adara / ★★★

4122 VILLAGE GREEN, WHISTLER VILLAGE; 604/905-4009 OR 866/502-3272
"Boutique" may have become overused in the hotel business, but this relatively new kid on the Whistler block reflects the word's true meaning: instant personal service from the get-go. Greetings at your car, skis put away for you in the locker room, friendly reactions to your every whim—all amidst achingly chic decor that is also wonderfully functional: floating fireplaces, TV/DVD in sitting room and bedroom, Bodum French press coffeemakers. The tiled entrance inside each suite allows skiers and snowboarders to wear their boots up to their rooms. Luxuriate in Frette robes and fake fur throws on your bed, while you puff on your own personal oxygen and listen to the iPod iHome system. There's even a white-noise generator to soothe you to sleep. *$$$; AE, MC, V; debit cards; www.adarahotel.com; valet parking.* &

Durlacher Hof / ★★★

7055 NESTERS RD, NESTER'S VILLAGE; 604/932-1924
Shoes off, Haflinger on. Hospitality at Durlacher Hof begins in the traditional Austrian fashion with the donning of these hand-knit pure wool slippers, which gain guests (including bad boy Sean Penn) entrance into Erika and Peter Durlacher's immaculate alpine country inn a short ride from Whistler Village. Eight guest rooms (some are suites) invoke the original 1970s spirit of Whistler with hand-carved pine furniture and comfortable beds with goose-down duvets. In addition to the hot tub and sauna on-site, some guest rooms have soaker tubs. Part Mother Teresa who just can't do enough for her guests and part sergeant-major with a relentless drive for perfection, Erika never stops. Her lavish breakfasts are a new reason to smile when the sun comes up: a groaning sideboard holds special dishes she prepares for each guest, perhaps *Kaiserschmarrn* (pancakes with stewed plums), freshly baked breads, and lean *Schinkenspeck* (ham). An honour bar and a warm fire welcome guests home at night. *$$$–$$$$; MC, V; no debit cards; www.durlacherhof. com; free parking.* &

Edgewater Lodge / ★★

8020 ALPINE WY, WHISTLER; 604/932-0688
The 12-room Edgewater Lodge sits in the privacy of its 19-hectare (45-acre) estate beside Green Lake. It's a low-key resort, eschewing the highly competitive atmosphere of the village proper. Each guest room has its own private outside entrance and a lakefront view (although there aren't any fireplaces to complete the picture). Each room has a television, but the unobstructed view of the lake, the snowcapped mountain, and the wildlife that visit the grounds daily are far more entertaining. The outdoor Jacuzzi provides a serene place to commune with nature. The Edgewater's restaurant (see Restaurants in this chapter) offers memorable cuisine, a limited wine list, and outstanding

service. *$$$–$$$$; AE, MC, V; debit cards; www.edgewater-lodge.com; 4 km (2.5 mi) north of Whistler Village, across from Meadow Park Sports Centre; free parking.* &

Fairmont Chateau Whistler Resort / ★★★☆

4599 CHATEAU BLVD, UPPER VILLAGE; 604/938-8000 OR 800/606-8244

This is the place to see and be seen in Whistler—where a valet parks not only your car but also your ski gear or mountain bike. The hotel's 550 rooms are steps away from the base of Blackcomb Mountain, with a dozen or so exclusive shops on-site. The spa is especially swank, offering various facials, body wraps, and herbal and aesthetic treatments, as well as massage and shiatsu. The health club has a heated pool flowing both indoors and out, where swimmers can splash away under the chairlifts or soak in the Jacuzzi under the stars. Outside, an 18-metre-long (58-foot-long) lap pool has underwater music. Guest rooms are well-lit and reasonably sized. The elegantly appointed suites offer comfortable sitting rooms (some have fireplaces) and bedrooms, as well as spacious European-style bathrooms. The duplex suites on the top floor are grand in size and comfort. The Entree Gold Floors—fully stocked honour bar and hors d'oeuvres in the evening, continental breakfast in the morning—offer a wood-paneled lounge with a fireplace. The resort has three tennis courts and its own 18-hole golf course (designed by Robert Trent Jones Jr.). On-site restaurants include the Wildflower, Mallard Bar & Lounge (Robin Leach proclaimed this "the premier address at Whistler"), and the popular deli, Portobello. Locals from the Lower Mainland can book a BC residents rate, depending on availability. *$$$–$$$$; AE, DC, MC, V; debit cards; www.fairmont.com/whistler; valet parking $30, self-parking $25.* &

Four Seasons Whistler Resort / ★★★★

**4591 BLACKCOMB WY, UPPER VILLAGE; 604/935-3400
OR 800/819-5053**

Canada's signature four-star hotel chain is ably represented in Whistler by this massive complex with 273 luxuriously rustic rooms, a separate building of 37 private residences, and a 15-room spa. The entry is quintessential Four Seasons: a sweeping driveway that leads to a discreetly elegant hallway with exquisite West Coast art and a hushed, professional atmosphere. Each room has a stellar view of surrounding mountains and some balconies are totally secluded. Upon arrival, your ski equipment is sent to the ski concierge at the bottom of Blackcomb Mountain, and at the end of the day a staff member is stationed at the hill to help with your skis and boots. Bask in the outdoor pool or the three Jacuzzi tubs; plus, just to make sure you're warm enough, hot chocolate shots are delivered every half hour. *$$$$; AE, DC, MC, V; no debit cards; www.fourseasons.com/whistler; valet parking $32.* &

Le Chamois / ★★

4557 BLACKCOMB WY, UPPER VILLAGE; 604/932-8700 OR 800/777-0185

This six-storey condo hotel is dwarfed by its gargantuan neighbour, the Chateau Whistler. Light, airy, and reasonably sized, the 62 studio, one-bedroom, and two-bedroom suites feature simple Euro-style furnishings. Single-bedroom suites accommodate four: the living area has either a sofa bed or a Murphy bed. Every room has a view, though views of the mountain cost more. During high season, the hotel requires a minimum stay of five to seven nights, depending on room type. During summer, a two-night minimum stay is required for all rooms. All guest rooms are privately owned condos. Some incorporate personal touches: one three-bedroom corner suite is furnished with a piano, and another displays photos of the owner posing on the slopes. The compact Pullman-style kitchens feature all the things you need for preparing quick meals, including a microwave, a refrigerator, and all utensils. But don't miss the two restaurants downstairs: the elegant La Rua (see Restaurants in this chapter) and Thai One On's more casual dining. Other amenities include a small conference area, a very small fitness room with an outdoor pool, and a Jacuzzi. Children under 12 stay free. *$$$–$$$$; AE, DC; DIS, MC, V; debit cards; www.lechamoishotel.com; self-parking $12, $8 off-season.* &

Pan Pacific Whistler Mountainside / ★★★

4320 SUNDIAL CRES, WHISTLER VILLAGE; 604/905-2999 OR 800/327-8585

The Pan Pacific's first resort lodge nabbed one of the most desirable locations in Whistler, just a few paces from both the Blackcomb and Whistler gondolas in Whistler Village. Each of the 121 studio, one-bedroom, and two-bedroom suites has massive double-paned windows, a fireplace, fully equipped kitchen, and dishwasher; some rooms have a balcony. The maple-hued wood furnishings evoke the sturdy yet comfortable mission style. Guests have access to a small but adequate fitness centre, steam room, two outdoor Jacuzzis, swimming pool, laundry room, ski and bike lockers, and the Dubh Linn Gate (see Restaurants in this chapter), which serves hearty, well-prepared Irish pub food. Ask about special romance and activity packages. *$$$–$$$$; AE, MC, V; debit cards; www.panpac.com; valet parking $25 per night.* &

The Summit / ★★

4359 MAIN ST, VILLAGE NORTH; 604/932-2778 OR 888/913-8811

Situated right on Main Street, the Summit's understated facade and lobby conceal a welcome surprise. The 81 one-bedroom, executive studio, and studio suites in this full-service hotel are beautifully designed, featuring soft earth tones, rich wood furnishings, fireplaces, fully equipped kitchenettes, and comfy marble bathrooms. Unlike its immediate neighbours, the Summit delivers all the comforts of home in each suite: kimonos, hair dryers, an iron and ironing board, TV and VCR, balcony, in-room coffee and tea service, voice mail, and phones with dataports. Amenities include a concierge, bell service, ski or bike storage, laundry facilities, sauna, heated outdoor pool, hot

---

THE 2010 WINTER OLYMPICS

Come February 12–28, 2010, alpine skiing, which also includes super-G, giant slalom, and super combined, will be just part of a whole range of other activities Whistler Mountain will be hosting at the **WINTER OLYMPICS** (www.vancouver 2010.com)—and later at the **PARALYMPICS**, March 12–21, 2010.

Even if a Pineapple Express front storms in (bringing rain instead of snow) just as it did during an International Olympic Committee visit in 2005, organizers say the 269 snowmaking machines at this premier North American resort will ensure that the snow will go on (from bare to race conditions in five days—plus 13 million gallons of water) on this part of Whistler, known as Creekside, a perennial favourite face of Whistler Mountain, especially for families. Creekside's Olympic action will be watched live by a 7,600-strong crowd.

You could also join the throng of 12,000 people at the new **WHISTLER SLIDING CENTRE** on Blackcomb Mountain, within easy reach of the village. The 1,700-metre-long (5,577-foot-long) concrete sliding track, completed to the tune of $104.5 million in December 2007, will capture the dynamic sports of luge, skeleton (you know, hurtling head first on a sliver of metal half the size of the athlete's

---

tub, valet service, playpens, and a free ski shuttle. A continental breakfast is included, and the award-winning, unmissable Elements tapas restaurant (see Restaurants in this chapter) is at ground level. *$$$–$$$$; AE, DC, DIS, JCB, MC, V; debit cards; www.summitlodge.com; Town Plaza; self-parking $15 per night, $10 off-season.* ⅃

The Westin Resort and Spa / ★★★☆

4090 WHISTLER WY, WHISTLER VILLAGE; 604/905-5000 OR 800/937-8461
Whistler's luxury all-suite hotel is perfectly positioned just steps from the gondola that takes you to the top of Whistler. Every suite—refurbished in 2008–09—has upscale kitchen appliances, soaker tubs, custom-designed sumptuous beds, high-speed Internet access, and video games. Amenities are corporate-minded: business centre, convention facilities, multilingual staff. There's also babysitting services, an indoor/outdoor pool, and a health and fitness facility—but if it's privacy you're after, you can also order WestinWorkout rooms with your own treadmill, stationary cycle, and other features. The food is excellent at the hotel's Aubergine Grille (the free-flowing chocolate fountain is a real hit), a soaring room with a mountain-view terrace. The overall interior finishing and custom furniture throughout the Westin was masterminded by Canadian design guru Robert Ledingham. Nonsmoking. *$$$–$$$$; AE, DC, MC, V; no debit cards; www.westin.com/whistler; valet parking $28 per night, self-parking $24.* ⅃

body), and bobsled—with speeds of up to 153 kph (95 mph), it's easy to see why it's dubbed "Formula 1 on ice." (The track's first international competition is February 2009's Tobogganing World Cup.) Long after the 80-plus countries have battled it out at these Games, this track will continue to showcase the sports to the general public and provide a legacy for the resort.

WHISTLER OLYMPIC PARK (604/698-4004; www.whistlerolympicpark.com), situated 18 kilometres (11 miles) southwest of Whistler in the majestic Callaghan Valley, a longtime favourite of backcountry skiers, will have three temporary stadiums each holding 12,000 people to view biathlon, cross-country skiing, Nordic combined, and ski jumping, of which both the normal and the large hill will be seen by all visitors as they enter the venue. (You won't see women jumping; despite repeated hullabaloo from Canadians and Americans to have females included in the only Olympic sport not open to both sexes, the International Olympic Committee ruled their development in the sport is still in the early stages.) Before and after the games, these trails will provide much recreational opportunity for residents and visitors; day tickets $16 for adults.

—Lucy Hyslop

The Whistler Pinnacle / ★★★

4319 MAIN ST, VILLAGE NORTH; 604/938-3218 OR 888/999-8986

The Pinnacle's name and logo have little to do with the size or shape of this centrally located, four-storey hotel. However, they properly represent the level of comfort you'll find in all 84 studios. Each guest room has a gas fireplace, a fully equipped kitchenette, a TV and DVD player, voice mail and wireless Internet connection, deluxe amenities, in-room coffee and tea service, and a double Jacuzzi soaker tub. The heated outdoor pool, hot tub, and guest laundry facilities are welcome touches, as is the evening room service offered by the house restaurant, Quattro at Whistler (see Restaurants in this chapter). Even though it's a 20-minute walk to the Whistler Village base, this is an outstanding getaway for skiers. $$$–$$$$; AE, MC, V; debit cards; www.whistlerpinnacle.com; Town Plaza; self-parking $15 per night. &

Exploring

Cradled amongst mountains that rise majestically above the tree line to permanently snowcapped peaks, Whistler is a mecca for skiers, snowboarders, ice skaters, and other snow enthusiasts. In recent years, however, this winter resort has also attracted thousands of year-round visitors who aspire to less frosty pursuits, such as sightseeing, shopping, dining and dancing, hiking, running, kayaking and canoeing, fly-fishing, in-line skating, horseback riding, tennis, and bicycling.

It's impossible not to be drawn outdoors into this merry blend of natural serenity and hedonistic bustle. Unlike most ski resorts, Whistler can easily be strolled from end to end. Pedestrian-only thoroughfares meander past endless shops and cafes. Here you can also find many outfitters offering guided excursions of all kinds, from helicopter skiing (and picnicking) to fly-fishing via snowmobile to paragliding above the slopes to zip-trekking above the canyon. You can arrange a white-water rafting or jet-boat trip, dogsledding, or even a snowshoeing tour. You can rent mountain bikes or in-line skates (the village is crisscrossed with terrific trails, which lead out to longer, more challenging rides), skis, snowboards, and just about any other piece of outdoor sports equipment. If just reading this leaves you exhausted, you can find a table at a sun-drenched slopeside cafe, order a latte, and simply watch the world go by.

Can't—or won't—ski or board? Hop on a **SNO-LIMO** (888/568-5466; www. sno-limo.com) on Whistler and Blackcomb, and let someone else have sore muscles at the end of the day while they chauffeur you in a gliding seat down mountain runs as you sit back and take in the vista, starting from $90. Straightforward **SIGHTSEEING ON BOTH MOUNTAINS** (604/932-3141 or 800/766-0449; www.whistlerblackcomb.com) costs less than skiing: $29.95 for adults during the day; discounts available for seniors and children. The **WHISTLER ACTIVITY AND INFORMATION CENTRE** (4010 Whistler Wy; 604/932-3928) can supply you with info on guided hiking and cycling tours offered by outfitters on both mountains.

Feeling flush? Helicopter tours of the surrounding mountains are provided by **BLACKCOMB HELICOPTERS** (604/938-1700) or **PEMBERTON HELICOPTERS** (604/932-3512). Glacier tours, heli-picnics, heli-hiking, and snowshoeing are all available.

To find out what Whistler was like before the skiers arrived, visit the **WHISTLER MUSEUM & ARCHIVES SOCIETY** (4329 Main St, Village North; 604/932-2019; www.whistlermuseum.org). Established in 1986, the museum presents the culture of the Native people who have lived in both the Whistler and Pemberton valleys for thousands of years. The village's turn-of-the-19th-century settlement by Scottish and British workers who were lured by railway and logging companies is re-created in its exhibits. Through pictures, artifacts, and an interactive Web site exhibit, learn how the Philips changed the face of Whistler when they built their Rainbow Lodge. A video viewing area features the history and development of Whistler as a ski resort. Admission is $5 for adults. Open every day 10am to 4pm in summer, Thursday through Sunday 10am to 4pm rest of the year.

For epicureans and oenophiles, there's **CORNUCOPIA** (604/932-3928; www. whistlercornucopia.com), Whistler's festival of food and wine. Held in November, this delicious escape offers Whistler visitors five days of BC's finest food and wine, plus a gala reception, seminars, tasting workshops, and cooking demonstrations by local chefs and food personalities.

Shopping

The Whistler villages are brimming with apparel, jewellery, crafts, specialty gifts, cosmetics, and sports equipment shops. **AFFINITY SPORTS** (Le Chamois Hotel, 4557 Blackcomb Wy, Upper Village; 604/938-1743) has a good selection of ski apparel and accessories (plus rentals). **AMOS & ANDES** (4321 Village Gate Blvd, Village North; 604/932-7202) has a notable collection of hand-knit sweaters for both men and women, plus cool cotton summer dresses.

In the same building, you'll find **KEIR FINE JEWELLERY** (4321 Village Gate Blvd, Whistler Village; 604/932-2944), with its selection of designer pieces created by Canadian artisans, as well as Italian gold and Swiss watches. **PATH GALLERY** (4338 Main St, Town Plaza, Village North; 604/932-7570; www.pathgallery.com) presents a large collection of Native paintings and carvings. Natural cosmetics and body treatments from **LUSH** (Delta Whistler Village Suites, Town Plaza, Village North; 604/932-5445) and the **BODY SHOP** (Blackcomb Lodge, Whistler Village; 604/932-2639) may have originated back in England but have caught on like wildfire here and in Vancouver.

KATMANDU (4368 Main St, the Marketplace, Village North; 604/932-6381) supplies outdoor and camping gear, and rents, repairs, and sells mountain bikes, snowboards, skis, and snowshoes. Check out the selection of local books, national bestsellers, magazines, and newspapers at **ARMCHAIR BOOKS** (5205 Village Sq, Whistler Village; 604/932-5557). Try a Cuban cigar from the **WHISTLER CIGAR COMPANY** (4314 Main St, Town Plaza, Village North; 604/905-2423), where you'll find everything from Montecristos and Macanudos to cigar trimmers and cases.

One of Whistler's coolest (and most overlooked) nooks of commerce is **FUNCTION JUNCTION** (at traffic lights as you enter Whistler from the south), a rustic local shopping area south of Creekside. From hi-fis and clothes to snowboards and skis placed wittily next to crutches, the thrift stock at the **RE-USE-IT CENTRE** (1003 Lynham Rd, first right after turning into Function Junction; 604/932-1121; open 10am–5:30pm every day) can be a veritable gold mine; not surprisingly, locals don't like the RUIC too widely advertised.

Nightlife

Start your evening at **CITTA'S BISTRO** (4271 Village Stroll, Whistler Village; 604/932-4177), the nighttime gathering place for locals. Sip a cocktail or have a quick meal before heading around the corner to the **SAVAGE BEAGLE BAR** (4222 Village Sq, Whistler Village; 604/938-3337), a theme-based nightclub that features DJs and occasional live bands and attracts the young-and-beautiful snowboarding crowd. The **WINE BAR** at the Bearfoot Bistro (see Restaurants in this chapter) draws a lively crowd. This dimly lit and very comfortable piano bar offers jazz combined with a very congenial bar staff.

If you're looking for a pub atmosphere, there's no better place than the **DUBH LINN GATE** (see Restaurants in this chapter), which offers an authentic Irish-pub interior, a fine menu of brews and single malts, and live Celtic music nightly. **TOMMY AFRICA'S BAR** (Blackcomb Lodge, Whistler Village; 604/932-6090) was voted as the "best place to dance" by locals. **MAXX FISH** (4228 Village Stroll, Whistler Village; 604/932-1904; www.maxxfish.com) offers a mix of everything from live blues to DJs, and the **MIX BY RIC'S** (see Restaurants in this chapter) is a magnet for its Sunday night DJ sessions. For après-ski, the **LONGHORN SALOON AND GRILL** (604/932-5999) or the **GARIBALDI LIFT CO.** (604/905-2220)—GLC, for those in the know—near the Whistler and Blackcomb gondolas and **DUSTY'S BAR AND BARBECUE** (604/905-2171) at the Creekside base of Whistler Mountain are favourite rendezvous that have been around for years.

MERLIN BAR AND GRILL (604/938-7700) at the base of Blackcomb is reputed to have the sun on its patio for a longer period than any other spot in Whistler, while the **AMSTERDAM CAFÉ PUB** (604/932-8334) in the Village Square caters to 20-somethings and ranks right up there for people watching.

BUFFALO BILL'S BAR AND GRILL (4122 Village Green, Whistler Village; 604/932-6613), across from the Whistler Conference Centre, plays top 40 tunes and is one of the few places that attracts an older crowd. The **MAURICE YOUNG MILLENNIUM PLACE** (4335 Blackcomb Wy, Whistler Village; 604/935-8410) is Whistler's gathering spot for concerts, theatrical performances, and lectures. It also has a day-care facility and a fully supervised teen centre open to all youths, as well as a video-editing school and a recording studio.

Recreation

Whistler has developed year-round recreation and is as busy in the summer as it is during the ski season. During the summer, skiing and sightseeing lift tickets are available, with discounts for seniors, students, and children. Saturday nights during the summer are a special treat, when Whistler Mountain is open until 8pm.

DOWNHILL SKIING AND SNOWBOARDING

Whistler offers every type of snow enthusiast a great place to play. Owned and operated by Intrawest, **WHISTLER MOUNTAIN** (866/218-9690, snow report 604/687-7507 in Vancouver, 604/932-4211 in Whistler; www. whistlerblackcomb.com) has a 1,530-metre (5,020-foot) vertical and more than 100 marked runs for downhill and telemark skiing, as well as a huge half pipe, a terrain park, and a mini park and pipe for snowboarders. The mountain is serviced by high-speed gondolas, high-speed quads, chairs, and T-bars. Helicopter service provides access to another 100-plus runs on nearby glaciers. At lower elevations, outfitters can be booked and equipment rented for snowshoe excursions.

Near the top, the **ROUNDHOUSE LODGE** offers everything from lattes and cookies to barbecued chicken, Chinese stir-fries, sushi, deli sandwiches, burgers, and a licensed dining room, plus a gift shop and nearly 360 degrees of both indoor and outdoor seating with excellent views of the surrounding mountains. (Surprisingly, prices are on par with venues down at the base.)

FRESH TRACKS

The closest way for an amateur skier or boarder to experience the thrills of going for gold in a race is to buy a **FRESH TRACKS TICKET** ($17.62 for adults, $12.81 for children 7–12, free for children 6 and under, plus a day ticket—from $71 per adult—to ski or board) and be ready to board the Whistler Village Gondola from around 7am.

That entitles you to an all-you-can-eat buffet-style breakfast at the Roundhouse Lodge at the top of the Whistler Mountain Gondola, but that's not the point. When the giant cowbell in the restaurant is rung and the words "runs are open" declared, you and a maximum of only 650 others have the mountain to yourselves for a glorious hour. That's the time to stand atop the 3-kilometre-long (1.9-mile-long) **DAVE MURRAY** men's or **FRANZ'S RUN** women's downhill courses and have the uncrowded run of your life.

With 33 turns, steep pitches (the Weasel), and narrow sections (Coaches Corner), you might even enjoy a little hot air toward the imaginary finishing line on the Dave Murray run—named after one of the Crazy Canucks who took the ski world by storm in the '70s and '80s. Franz's Run—a nod to Franz Wilhelmson, a driving force in seeing Whistler Mountain open in February 1966—offers 29 turns over a similar 28 percent slope gradient.

Just remember the Alpine Responsibility Code: Staff can revoke your pass for unsafe skiing or boarding—and besides, there is none of the 30 kilometres (18.5 miles) of safety netting usually wrapped around the courses. Be aware, also, that Fresh Tracks allows you one ride up in the gondola, so keep up top unless you're happy to wait for the normal lift opening times.

—Lucy Hyslop

Below the lodge is **CHIC PEA**, and above is the **HARMONY HUT** (at Harmony Express chair), **RAVEN'S NEST** (at top of Creekside gondola), and **DUSTY'S** (at base of Creekside gondola), all of which serve food on the mountain, as does the **GARIBALDI LIFT COMPANY BAR & GRILL** (at Whistler Village gondola base).

Also owned by Intrawest, **BLACKCOMB MOUNTAIN** (866/218-9690, snow report 604/687-7507 in Vancouver, 604/932-4211 in Whistler; www.whistler blackcomb.com) has a 1,609-metre (5,280-foot) vertical and another 100-plus marked runs, as well as two half pipes and a park that are serviced by a high-speed gondola, high-speed quads, chairs, and T-bars. There's a connector gondola situated at the base of Whistler Village that also transports you to Blackcomb, so you don't have to shoulder your skis and hike to the Upper Village. Nine restaurants serve visitors, including the **WIZARD GRILL** and

MERLINS at the base. Toward the top, eating establishments include **GLACIER CREEK LODGE**, the Rendezvous Lodge's **CHRISTINE'S**, and the **HORSTMAN** and **CRYSTAL HUTS**.

Blackcomb Mountain's **HORSTMAN GLACIER** is open from May to early August for snowboarders and skiers. Free guided ski tours are available daily to show intermediate and expert skiers and boarders how to maximize their ski time and get the most out of the mountains (truly worth doing!). These ski-tour ambassadors can also direct you to the hottest ski day routes with names like the Grand Tour, the Weather Chaser, and Expedition Extreme. Winter lift tickets $71 per day for adult dual-mountain pass; discounts available for seniors, students, and children; season passes and express-card discounts for multitrip visitors also offered. Gondolas for both mountains open every day 8:30amto 3pm late November through late Jan, 8:30am to 3:30pm late January through late February. One mountain closes mid-April; the other remains open to first week of June (in 2009, Blackcomb will remain open and Whistler closes April 20). Horstman Glacier on Blackcomb Mountain is accessible for skiers and boarders noon–3pm early June–late July.

CROSS-COUNTRY SKIING AND SNOWSHOEING

Cross-country skiers appreciate the 32 kilometres (19 miles) of well-marked seasonal trails groomed for both Nordic and skate skiing that run throughout the Whistler municipality, as well as the 35 kilometres (21 miles) of trails at the **MAD RIVER NORDIC CENTRE**. A superpopular route in town is the 15-kilometre (9-mile) Lost Lake circuit of easy to very difficult marked trails, which you can enter across the street from the Blackcomb Mountain parking lot. A 4-kilometre (2.5-mile) portion of this trail is illuminated for night skiing as well. Passes are $8 per day; one-hour Nordic or skate lesson costs about $35. The village's **VALLEY TRAIL** system connects the municipality's various communities, from Alta Lake to Green Lake; in winter it's transformed into a trail groomed for both Nordic and skate skiing that can be accessed at no charge.

GARIBALDI PROVINCIAL PARK (604/898-3678) maintains 7 kilometres (4.2 miles) of marked, groomed trails at Singing Pass and another 10 kilometres (6 miles) at Cheakamus Lake Trail. On Highway 99 north of Mount Currie, **JOFFRE LAKES PROVINCIAL PARK** is a tranquil forested area with a few short trails that wind deep into the forest and circle the glacial lakes.

Snowshoers who want to hike Whistler Mountain must book a hike with **OUTDOOR ADVENTURES@WHISTLER** (Whistler Mountain; 604/932-0647; www.adventureswhistler.com). Otherwise, you're free to trek in designated areas at Mad River Nordic Centre and the Lost Lake circuit.

OTHER WINTER SPORTS

Call the **WHISTLER ACTIVITY AND INFORMATION CENTRE** (604/932-3928) for information on paragliding lessons (with or without skis), dogsled trips, snowshoe hikes, snowmobile tours, and sleigh rides. **COUGAR MOUNTAIN**

ADVENTURE LTD (36-4314 Main St, Town Plaza, Village North; 604/932-4086 or 888/297-2222; www.cougarmountain.ca) is a reputable outfitter that books dogsled and snowshoe tours to nearby glaciers. Located 4 kilometres (2.5 miles) from the village, the **MEADOW PARK SPORTS CENTRE** (604/935-8350) is Whistler's outstanding aquatic, ice, and fitness facility, offering ice skaters a place to lace up their skates and stretch their legs.

HIKING

Hike through the lush alpine meadows if you prefer to stop and smell the wildflowers. Besides hikes in the immediate vicinity, the two- to three-hour hike up into the glorious **ANCIENT CEDARS GROVE** on Cougar Mountain (off Hwy 99, up a gravel road off north shore of Green Lake) is well worth it; you can smell the grove before you see it. For a much flatter stroll, take the pleasant half-hour walk to the dramatic waterfalls at **NAIRN FALLS PROVINCIAL PARK**, 32 kilometres (20 miles) north of Whistler. Access is on the right-hand side of Highway 99 as you drive from Whistler toward Pemberton.

MOUNTAIN BIKING

Diehards can ski Horstman Glacier until mid-August, but come summer, do what the locals do. Turn your back on Whistler Village Square and head for either mountain, the Valley Trail, or the road to Pemberton on your mountain bike. In the summer, mountain-bike rentals are available at Whistler ski shops, at the base of the Whistler gondola, and on Blackcomb at **CANSKI** (604/938-7744).

The **WHISTLER MOUNTAIN BIKE PARK** (866/218-9690; www.whistler bike.com) is accessible via the Whistler Village gondola for $40 and features more than 200 kilometres (62 miles) of single-track trail, as well as an unusual skills-development course. Exhilarating descents back to the village are possible on both single- and double-track trails. Camps and instructional programmes are available as well.

RIVER RAFTING

The stunning Coast Mountains provide the scenic backdrop for rafting on several rivers in the Whistler area. Trips range from white-knuckle excitement on the Green, Birkenhead, or Elaho rivers to placid float trips down the Squamish and Lillooet rivers. **WHISTLER RIVER ADVENTURES** (604/932-3532; www.whistlerriver.com) and **WEDGE RAFTING** (604/932-7171; www. wedgerafting.com) operate daily trips from late spring to the end of September. During the summer, guided river-rafting trips down the Squamish are operated through **SUNWOLF OUTDOOR CENTRE** (877/806-8046; www. sunwolf.net). During the winter, guided eagle-viewing float trips down the Cheakamus River are operated through **CANADIAN OUTBACK ADVENTURES** (604/921-7250) and Sunwolf Outdoor Centre.

OTHER OUTDOOR ACTIVITIES

One of the most exciting activities to take off in recent years is "zipping" 60 metres (200 feet) above Fitzsimmons Creek in Whistler. Strapped into a harness and attached to cables, you can go backward, forward, or upside down all year-round. **ZIPTREK ECOTOURS** (604/935-0001 or 866/935-0001; www.ziptrek.com) even tells you about the old-growth forest that surrounds you.

Take your sailboard to Alta Lake (where windsurfing started in Canada), just west of Whistler Village, on the other side of Blueberry Hill. Dip your raft, canoe, or kayak into the River of Golden Dreams, north of Whistler Village; it connects Alta Lake to Green Lake. Pull out your fly rod and try for a few trout at Birkenhead Lake, a 40-minute drive north of Whistler. **WHISTLER OUTDOOR EXPERIENCE COMPANY** (604/932-3389) is a broker for guided hikes, mountain horseback riding, river rafting, kayaking, and fly-in fishing trips.

If you want a real thrill, try paragliding off Blackcomb Mountain with **ALPINE AIRSPORTS** (604/935-9247), or go to the kiosk at the base of Blackcomb at the Adventure Zone. With a qualified pilot, the two of you jump off the mountain's face and drift peacefully down to the base. The close-up view of the terrain as you pass over at an altitude of 50 metres (164 feet) is terrific. The **BLACKCOMB ADVENTURE ZONE** (604/932-2394 ext 2) at the base of Blackcomb is open during the summer and has everything from horseback riding, mountain biking, and paragliding to a trapeze school.

OKANAGAN VALLEY

OKANAGAN VALLEY

How to Get Here

BY CAR

Most visitors travel to the region by car. From the Trans-Canada Highway (Hwy 1), you can enter the Okanagan Valley from the east via Highway 97 at Sicamous or from the west via Highway 5 (the Coquihalla Connector). Kelowna is located on Highway 97.

BY AIR

If you plan to fly to the Okanagan, the **KELOWNA INTERNATIONAL AIRPORT** (www.kelownaairport.com) is served by **AIR CANADA** (888/247-2262; www.aircanada.com), **CENTRAL MOUNTAIN AIR** (888/865-8585; www.flycma.com), **HORIZON AIR** (800/252-7522; www.alaskaair.com), and **WESTJET** (800/538-5695; www.westjet.com).

The **PENTICTON REGIONAL AIRPORT** (www.cyyf.org) has daily flights from Vancouver with Air Canada and **PACIFIC COASTAL AIRLINES** (800/663-2872; www.pacific-coastal.com).

Orientation

For first-time visitors to British Columbia, the cosmopolitan pleasures of Vancouver, a city set on the edge of the rain forest, can be all-captivating. But for those with a nose in search of New World vineyards and blue-green lakes, a distinctly different experience awaits less than an hour by air or a four-hour drive east from Vancouver.

The Okanagan has something to offer in any season. The valley is laden with orchards, making it especially appealing in springtime when the apple, cherry, peach, pear, and plum trees are in full bloom. Golfing in the Okanagan is good news for duffers and scratch players alike; more than 50 courses range from par 3 to 9 with 18 or 27 holes. In the summer, it's hot enough for prickly pear cacti to flourish down by the U.S. border, and it's frosty enough in fall for the production of Canada's renowned ice wine. Grapes are left on the vine well after October's harvest, often into November and December—and occasionally into January or February. Fall brings the **OKANAGAN WINE FESTIVAL** (www.owfs.com), with its 150-plus events throughout the valley. Winter powders the ski slopes at Big White, boasting one of the highest elevations (1,756 m/5,760 ft) of any ski resort in BC.

The Okanagan is divided into three main regions: the north is centred around Kelowna (population approximately 150,000), the Penticton-based central region is around Naramata, and the south is centred at Oliver, with Osoyoos to the south. Quieter times are in June or September, when the weather—and tourist traffic—is more moderate.

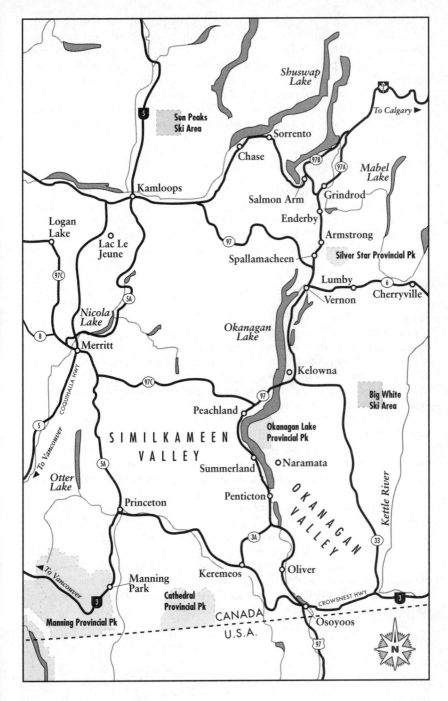

Okanagan Lake, the crown jewel in a necklace of lakes extending north to south from Vernon to Osoyoos, is an 80-mile narrow fjord lake, carved by Pleistocene-era glaciers. Its depth prevents it from freezing in most winters, and its moderating influence and expanse have made the Okanagan Valley a mecca for agriculture, tourism, and residential development. Most valley towns are on the lake, making a visit to the beach and a cool dip a mandatory (and refreshing) part of the Okanagan summer experience. The valley is in transition, from its old seasonal tree-fruit-based economy to one now firmly rooted in the vineyards.

Visitor Information

A leisurely pace will get you from one end of the Okanagan Valley to the other—Vernon to Osoyoos—in less than three hours, not including time spent touring. Count on at least a one-hour drive between Penticton and Kelowna or between Penticton and Osoyoos. Major roads such as Highway 97 are well marked, but finding your way on some of the back roads can be tricky.

Kelowna and Beyond

The location of Kelowna, the largest and liveliest of the Okanagan cities, makes it a convenient base to explore the valley. Don't be fooled by the strip malls and big-box retailers on the outskirts: Kelowna's old downtown, abutting the shore of Okanagan Lake, remains vibrant and diverse. The Cultural District (www.kelownaculturaldistrict.com), once the hub to the Okanagan fruit-packing industry, is home to artists and performers with art galleries, a museum, a community theatre, and a centre for the arts.

The **WINE MUSEUM** (1304 Ellis St; 250/763-0433; www.kelownamuseum.com), located in the historic Laurel Packinghouse, has an extensive wine boutique that stocks BC labels, including rare vintages. It's also home to the equally fascinating **ORCHARD MUSEUM**. The Wine Museum provides some background on the Okanagan's winemaking history, and it also has plenty of brochures on things to do in the valley.

Kelowna even has its own version of the Loch Ness monster: Ogopogo. Although Indian legends support a creature living in Okanagan Lake long before white settlers arrived in this area, Ogopogo is very much a present-day phenomenon. Each year, sightings are reported of a "lake demon" some 6 to 15 metres (20 to 50 feet) long, with a horse- or sheep-shaped head and an undulating, serpent-like body. An official spotting site has been designated at the Gray Monk Estate Winery, and there's a million-dollar reward offered for a sighting. It's just another reason to visit this valley known as BC's Riviera.

Penticton and Naramata

Farther south on Highway 97, you'll encounter Penticton (population 33,000), the city of "Peaches and Beaches," which might just as easily be called Festival City. There's always some serious fun going on in this town that's spread between Okanagan and Skaha lakes, including weeklong **WINE FESTIVALS** (www.the winefestivals.com) in May, August, and October; **PACIFIC NORTHWEST ELVIS FESTIVAL** (www.pentictonelvisfestival.com) in June; a campy **BEACH BLANKET FILM FESTIVAL** (www.beachblanketfilmfest.com), with movies projected on a screen floating 7.5 metres (25 feet) offshore on Okanagan Lake in July; the **AUGUST PEACH FESTIVAL** (www.peachfest.com), now in its sixth decade; and a jazz festival in September. The **PENTICTON & WINE COUNTRY TOURISM INFO CENTRE** (553 Railway St, Penticton; 250/493-4055 or 800/663-5052; www. tourismpenticton.com) has details on the area as well as wine tasting, wine touring, and purchasing wines.

Penticton is also home to the August swim-bike-run **IRONMAN CANADA TRIATHALON** (www.ironman.ca) every year, for which tonnes of ironmen and -women turn out. Some of the best rock climbing in BC occurs at the Skaha Bluffs on Penticton's southeastern outskirts. **SKAHA ROCK ADVENTURES** (www.skaha rockclimbing.com) guides climbers on many of the bluff's 120 cliffs.

North of Penticton off Highway 97, the picturesque village of **NARAMATA** (population 2,000) is surrounded by wineries. Rugged Naramata Road leads you through slopes and headlands that jut into Okanagan Lake. The Naramata Bench on the eastern lakeshore is a narrow strip of land that drops down to the shore bluffs. This is one of the Okanagan's best vineyard locations, thanks to the tempering lake effect and the sandy loam. Several wineries offer small plates and bistro-style dining. Fabulous baskets from the Bench can be found in the tasting room at **ELEPHANT ISLAND ORCHARD WINES** (2730 Atkins Loop, Naramata; 250/496-5522; www.elephantislandwine.com).

Oliver and Osoyoos

Farther south on Highway 97, you'll encounter the towns of **OKANAGAN FALLS**, **OLIVER**, and **OSOYOOS**. Approaching Oliver, you'll see a long, sloping benchland the locals refer to as the "Golden Mile." It is home to so many vineyards and wineries that the town of Oliver has declared itself the "Wine Capital of Canada." In addition, the South Okanagan is a wondrous produce basket. Travellers on the stretch of Highway 97 between Oliver (population 4,300) and Osoyoos (population 4,500) pass the most beautiful agricultural land in the entire Okanagan Valley. Since the 1990s, vineyards have been planted, and many of the award-winning Okanagan wines have come from this region. Leading red varieties are cabernet franc, cabernet sauvignon, merlot, pinot noir, Syrah, and zinfandel; whites include chardonnay, sauvignon blanc, and Viognier. Contact the **OLIVER VISITOR CENTRE** (36205 93rd Ave, Oliver; 250/498-6321 or 866/498-6321;

ROMANCING THE DESERT

Every summer when the yellow moon is full over Canada's only desert (just north of Osoyoos), it's time for a night owl's-eye view of wine country. Here's a taste of the annual **ROMANCING THE DESERT** event: it's a hot August night, with the fragrance of antelope brush and sage in the air. You've got a primo Okanagan wine in your glass, locally inspired appetizers in hand. Meander along the 1.5-kilometre (1-mile) boardwalk in the desert, home to a host of fragile flora and fauna.

Along the boardwalk, volunteers from the Osoyoos Desert Society deliver a two-hour tour of one of North America's most endangered ecosystems, part of the Great Basin Desert that runs through the western United States. Later, take in the full moon rising over the mountains, along with views of the Okanagan Valley, from the deck of the **DESERT CENTRE** (www.desert.org). Add more wine, plus local cheeses and dessert, to cap one of Okanagan's most unusual experiences.

—Kasey Wilson

www.oliverchamber.bc.ca) and the **OSOYOOS VISTOR INFO CENTRE** (Hwys 3 and 97, Osoyoos; 888/676-9667; www.destinationosoyoos.com) for details.

The **OSOYOOS DESERT CENTRE** (250/495-2470 or 877/899-0897; www. desert.org) protects Canada's only desert, where less than 12 inches of precipitation fall annually and cacti, prickly pear, sagebrush, and western rattlesnakes survive in the dry, sandy environment. Close by, the Osoyoos Indian Band owns and operates the **NK'MIP** (pronounced "IN-ka-meep") **DESERT CULTURAL CENTRE** (1000 Rancher Creek Rd; 250/495-2985 or 800/665-2667; www.nkmipdesert. com) and **NK'MIP CELLARS** (1400 Rancher Creek Rd; 250/495-2985; www. nkmipcellars.com), the only aboriginal winery in North America.

Okanagan Valley Wine Country

Just being discovered by wine lovers, British Columbia's Okanagan Valley and the neighbouring Similkameen Valley located just west of the Okanagan provide unforgettable wine tasting and dining overlooking pristine lakes. These valleys, with about 165 wineries and more on the way, rank among the most scenic wine regions in the world.

The north Okanagan is on the same latitude that runs through Germany's Rhine wine region. But the Okanagan's unique geography packs in the terroir to grow everything from full-bodied Syrah and silky pinot noir to bracing Rieslings. Summers are hot and dry (vines are all irrigated). Because of the valley's northern location, the very long growing days provide as many heat units, if not more, than in California.

Smaller wineries are open by appointment only, largely because their new releases sell out so quickly. Many, but not all, wineries charge modest fees for tastings or tours, especially for reserve wines or ice wines. Generally, fees are refundable against wine purchases. Larger wineries are open all year, but the primary touring season coincides with the Okanagan's best weather, from mid-April through mid-October.

The wine regions are four and a half to five hours by road east of Vancouver—longer if one stops to enjoy the mountain landscapes. Highway 3, British Columbia's southernmost highway, passes through the Similkameen on the way to the south Okanagan. The Similkameen is an organic farming hotbed, with the fruits and vegetables sold at fruit stands in Keremeos and nearby Cawston. Good highway signs direct tourists to the valley's 10 small wineries, a full day of touring. The stars are **HERDER WINERY & VINEYARDS** (2582 Upper Bench Rd, Keremeos; 250/499-5595; www.herder.ca), operated by California-born and -trained Lawrence Herder; **OROFINO VINEYARDS** (2152 Barcelo Rd, Cawston; 250/499-0068; www.orofinovineyards.com), built with straw bales; **SEVEN STONES WINERY** (1143 Hwy 3, Cawston; 250/499-2144; www.sevenstones.ca) and **FORBIDDEN FRUIT WINERY** (620 Sumac Rd, Cawston; 250/499-2649; www.forbiddenfruit wines.com). Be sure to stop for a hearty Bavarian lunch and a loaf of fresh-baked bread at **CROWSNEST VINEYARDS** (2036 Surprise Dr, Cawston; 250/499-5129; www.crowsnestvineyards.com).

Highway 3 forks at Keremeos, with nearly all wineries on the south fork, which continues on through the low Richter Pass to Osoyoos at the very south end of the Okanagan wine region, a quaint village with Santa Fe–style architecture and plenty of motels. Nk'Mip Cellars welcomes visitors with excellent merlot, pinot noir and chardonnay; the best buy is a crisp pinot blanc.

Head north on Highway 97. The wineries on the west side of the valley occupy what is called the Golden Mile (from the mines that operated there a century ago). There is outstanding chardonnay at **GOLDEN MILE CELLARS** (13140 316A Ave, Rd 13, Oliver; 250/498-8330; www.goldenmilecellars.com), a winery curiously built like a small castle. Continuing north, stop at **INNISKILLIN OKANAGAN** (Rd 11 West, Oliver; 250/498-6663; www.inniskillin.com) for malbec and zinfandel. **HESTER CREEK** (13163 326 Ave, Oliver; 250/498-4435; www.hestercreek. com) and **GEHRINGER BROTHERS** (Rd 8, Oliver, 250/498-3537) are across from each other at the top of Road 8 with differing but complementary wine styles. A little farther north, **TINHORN CREEK**'s (32830 Tinhorn Creek Rd, Oliver; 250/498-3743; www.tinhorn.com) tasting room has the best view in the valley and good pinot gris. Hester Creek's seven luxury villas offer similar views for those staying overnight.

A short drive across the valley takes you to Black Sage Road, where rows and rows of vines reach toward the mountains on the Okanagan's east flank. **BURROW-ING OWL ESTATE WINERY** (first-rate reds, renowned pinot gris) at the south end of Black Sage Road (100 Burrowing Owl Pl, Oliver; 250/498-0620; www.bovwine. com) is a destination with a fine restaurant and luxury inn. Continuing north, stop at **DESERT HILLS** (30480 71st St at Black Sage Rd, Oliver; 250/498-1040; www. deserthills.ca) for Syrah; at **LE VIEUX PIN** (34070 73rd St, Oliver; 250/498-8388;

THREE ONE-DAY OKANAGAN WINE-TASTING TOURS

It takes a week to visit all the Okanagan wineries with public tasting rooms, but if time is short, one-day tours provide a snapshot of this beautiful wine region. The tours can easily be linked. Be sure to check the British Columbia Wine Institute Web site (www.winebc.com) for wine tour itineraries and maps. If you prefer a guided tour, contact **OKANAGAN WINE COUNTRY TOURS** (1310 Water St, Kelowna; 250/868-9463 or 866/689-9462; www.okwinetours.com). Half-day, full-day, and overnight tours can be booked with or without vineyard lunches or dinners. If you do multiday tours, stay near the winery clusters so that the drive back to your hotel doesn't eat into touring. The Okanagan is a long, narrow wine region with lots of traffic in peak summer season.

DAY ONE: NORTH OKANAGAN TOUR—Starting in Kelowna, head on Lakeshore Road to **CEDARCREEK** (5445 Lakeshore Rd; 250/764-8866; www.cedarcreek.bc.ca), where the tasting room opens at 10am. Retracing your route, call at **ST. HUBERTUS** (5225 Lakeshore Rd; 250/764-7888; www.st-hubertus.bc.ca). Make a 1pm lunch reservation at nearby **SUMMERHILL PYRAMID WINERY** (4870 Chute Lake Rd; 250/764-8000; www.summerhill.bc.ca). After lunch, take the new W. R. Bennett Bridge over Okanagan Lake for the short drive toward Mount Boucherie and a tour of the spectacular **MISSION HILL** winery (1730 Mission Hill Rd, Westbank; 250/768-7611; www.missionhillwinery.com). Finish the afternoon in the nearby **QUAILS' GATE** tasting room (3303 Boucherie Rd, Kelowna; 250/769-4451; www.quailsgate.com), and consider relaxing there for dinner before heading back to your hotel.

DAY TWO: NARAMATA ROAD TOUR—Starting in Penticton, head northeast to **LA FRENZ** (740 Naramata Rd; 250/492-6690; www.lafrenzwinery.com), where the Australian-inspired tasting room opens at 10am. Then drop in at nearby **RED ROOSTER** (891 Naramata Rd; 250/492-2424; www.redroosterwinery.com), and

---

www.levieuxpin.ca) for show-stopping merlot; and at **QUINTA FERREIRA** (34664 71st St at Black Sage Rd, Oliver; 250/498-4756; www.quintaferreira.com), where the Portuguese family who owns it has fine malbec. North of Oliver, the self-proclaimed wine capital of Canada, the sprawling **JACKSON-TRIGGS WINERY** (38691 Hwy 97 N, Oliver; 250/498-4981; www.jacksontriggswinery.com) doesn't give tours but offers wines in an elegant new tasting room.

Just north of McIntyre Bluff, the cliff towering over the highway to the west, is the Okanagan Falls wine region, where the appointment-only **BLUE MOUNTAIN VINEYARD & CELLARS** (Allendale Rd, Okanagan Falls, 250/497-8244; www.bluemountainwinery.com) is known for its pinot noir and its photogenic vineyard.

besides tasting the wines, take time for the art gallery. If the weather is grand, make a 1pm lunch reservation at the shaded patio at **LAKE BREEZE** (930 Sammet Rd; 250/496-5659; www.lakebreeze.ca). Then head to nearby **ELEPHANT ISLAND** (2730 Aikins Lp; 250/496-5522; www.elephantislandwine.com) for remarkable fruit wines. Continue to **THERAPY VINEYARDS** (940 Debeck Rd; 250/496-5217; www.therapyvineyards.com) for the winery's Freud series wines, including SuperEgo. Many of the small wineries along Naramata Road open tasting rooms only when they have wine to sell. Don't miss **LAUGHING STOCK** (1548 Naramata Rd; 250/493-8466; www.laughingstock.ca) or **BLACK WIDOW** (1630 Naramata Rd; 250/487-2347; www.blackwidowwinery.com), if open. On the way back to your hotel, stop for dinner at **HILLSIDE'S BARREL ROOM BISTRO** (1350 Naramata Rd; 250/493-6274; www.hillsideestate.com).

DAY THREE: SOUTH OKANAGAN TOUR—Starting in Oliver (B&B accommodations are the best option here), drive south on vine-bordered Black Sage Road on the east side of the valley. Just south of town, the family-owned **QUINTA FERREIRA** (34664 71st St at Black Sage Rd; 250/498-4756; www.quintaferreira.com) opens at 10am with a warm Portuguese welcome. If it's open, visit neighbouring **LE VIEUX PIN** (34070 73rd St; 250/498-8388; www.levieuxpin.ca). Then head to **DESERT HILLS** (30480 71 St at Black Sage Rd; 250/498-1040; www.deserthills.ca) for a low-key visit and Syrah with the twins who run this winery, Randy and Jesse Toor. Book lunch at **BURROWING OWL** (100 Burrowing Owl Pl; 250/498-0620; www.bovwine.ca). Get directions to the road across the valley and head north on Highway 97. Stop at **GOLDEN MILE** (13140 316A Ave; 250/498-8330; www.goldenmilecellars.com) where the tasting room is in a small castle. Continue north to **TINHORN CREEK** (32830 Tinhorn Creek Rd; 250/498-3743; www.tinhorn.com), where you can view the entire valley from the tasting room. Return to Oliver for dinner at The **TOASTED OAK WINE BAR AND GRILL** (34881 97th St; 250/498-4867).

There's a nearby family-owned winery cluster within walking distance of each other: Gewürztraminer champion **WILD GOOSE** (2145 Sun Valley Wy, Okanagan Falls; 250/497-8919; www.wildgoosewinery.com); merlot specialist **STAG'S HOLLOW** (2237 Sun Valley Wy, Okanagan Falls, 250/497-6162; www.stags hollowwinery.com) and **TANGLED VINES** (2140 Sun Valley Wy, Okanagan Falls; 250/497-6416; www.tangledvineswinery.com). Close by is **NOBLE RIDGE VINE-YARD** (2320 Oliver Ranch Rd, Okanagan Falls, 250/497-7945; www.nobleridge. com), with good meritage.

After stopping for ice cream at **TICKLEBERRY'S** (Main St; 800/667-8002; www.tickleberrys.com) in Okanagan Falls, you are faced with a choice. Take the winding road up Hawthorne Mountain just west of town to **SEE YA LATER RANCH** (Green Lake Rd, Okanagan Falls; 250/497-8267; www.hmvineyard.com), the only winery with a dog cemetery. Or take winding Eastside Road (on the eastern shore of Skaha Lake) to **BLASTED CHURCH** (378 Parsons Rd, Okanagan Falls; 250/497-1125; www.blastedchurch.com), a winery that celebrates the community's rich history with caricature labels on its fine wines.

With many hotels and B&Bs, Penticton is a base for exploring the 22 wineries along the meandering Naramata Road on the east side of Okanagan Lake. Award-winning Jeff Martin offers **LA FRENZ** wines in a tasting room that looks like farm buildings from his native Australia (740 Naramata Rd, Penticton; 250/492-6690; www.lafrenzwinery.com). The added appeal at **RED ROOSTER** (891 Naramata Rd, Penticton; 250/492-2424; www.redroosterwinery.com) is its second-floor gallery featuring local art. **HILLSIDE** (1350 Naramata Rd, Penticton; 250/493-6274; www.hillsideestate.com) and **LAKE BREEZE** (930 Sammet Rd, Naramata; 250/496-5659; www.lakebreeze.ca) show off their wines at their popular winery bistros. **ELEPHANT ISLAND** (2730 Aikins Loop, Naramata; 250/496-5522; www.elephantislandwine.com) offers a refreshing change with the Okanagan's best fruit wines. **LANG VINEYARDS** (2493 Gammon Rd, Naramata; 250/496-5987; www.langvineyards.com) is a longtime favourite of Riesling lovers.

There is another winery node across the lake at Summerland, about 10 minutes north of Penticton on Highway 97, beginning with **SILKSCARF** (4917 Gartrell Rd, Summerland, 250/494-7455; www.silkw.net), so named because owner Roie Manoff once flew F-4 Phantoms in the Israeli Air Force. Further along this road, **THORNHAVEN** (6816 Andrew Ave, Summerland; 250/494-7778; www.thornhaven.com) encourages picnics on the winery's shaded patio overlooking vineyards. The nearby Gewürztraminer specialist **DIRTY LAUNDRY WINERY** (7311 Fiske St, Summerland; 250/494-8815; www.dirtylaundry.ca) has labels inspired by a long-closed local laundry that fronted for a bordello. The leading Summerland winery is sparkling wine specialist **SUMAC RIDGE** (17403 Hwy 97, Summerland; 250/494-0451; www.sumacridge.com), with the oldest winery restaurant and top-flight VIP tastings.

Continuing north on Highway 97 through Westbank, the bell tower at the **MISSION HILL** winery (1730 Mission Hill Rd, Westbank; 250/768-7611; www.missionhillwinery.com) pierces the sky on Mount Boucherie. The stunning architecture is matched by the wines, educational tours, and a superb open-air restaurant. There is an equally fine restaurant close by at pinot noir specialist **QUAILS' GATE** (3303 Boucherie Rd, Kelowna, 250/769-4451; www.quailsgate.com), where the tasting room boasts high-tech spittoons. More informal winery visits are offered at **LITTLE STRAW** (2815 Ourtoland Rd, Kelowna, 250/769-0404; www.littlestraw.bc.ca), **MT. BOUCHERIE** (829 Douglas Rd, Kelowna; 250/769-8803; www.mtboucherie.bc.ca), and organic **ROLLINGDALE** (2306 Hayman Rd, Kelowna, 250/769-9224; www.rollingdale.ca).

Busy Kelowna, with its hotels, restaurants, and international airport, can be either the start or the end of your wine tour. Close to downtown, historic **CALONA VINEYARDS** (1125 Richter St, Kelowna; 250/762-3332; www.calonavineyards.ca) is British Columbia's oldest continuing winery, having opened in 1932. The winery is the exclusive producer of sovereign opal, a spicy white from the only wine grape developed in the Okanagan.

To find the other wineries, head east from downtown on Pandosy Street, named for the missionary who planted Kelowna's first vineyard about 1860. Pandosy becomes Lakeshore Road, with good winery signage. **TANTALUS VINEYARDS** (1670 Dehart Rd, Kelowna, 877/764-0078; www.tantalus.ca), an outstanding Riesling producer, is building a showpiece winery with a panoramic city view. Further along Lakeshore, **SUMMERHILL** (4870 Chute Lake Rd, Kelowna; 250/764-8000; www.summerhill.bc.ca), another organic producer, offers tours of the Okanagan's most unusual aging cellar, a scale model of the Great Pyramid.

Nearby **ST. HUBERTUS** (5225 Lakeshore Rd, Kelowna; 250/764-7888; www.st.-hubertus.bc.ca), run by two Swiss families, came back stronger than ever after a 2003 forest fire tore through the vineyard and destroyed the original winery. Neighbouring pinot noir champion **CEDARCREEK** (5445 Lakeshore Rd, Kelowna; 250/764-8866; www.cedarcreek.bc.ca), spared major fire damage, perches amid its vines like a pristine white temple. Both CedarCreek and Summerhill have acclaimed restaurants.

A casual restaurant operates at the **GRAY MONK WINERY** (1055 Camp Rd, Okanagan Centre; 250/766-3168; www.graymonk.com), near Lake Country, a community on Highway 97 about 15 minutes north of Kelowna's airport. This family-owned winery—now into the fourth generation—imported French vines in 1976 to plant the Okanagan's first pinot gris, now BC's hottest white variety. On the way to Gray Monk, stop also at **ARROWLEAF** (1574 Camp Rd, Lake Country; 250/766-2992; www.arrowleafcellars.com), another family-owned winery with notable pinot gris and Gewürztraminer. If it fits your schedule, watch a spectacular Okanagan sunset from Gray Monk's restaurant deck.

Restaurants

Barrel Bistro Room / ★

1350 NARAMATA RD (HILLSIDE ESTATE WINERY), NARAMATA; 250/493-6274
Plan to stop for lunch or dinner on the Naramata Bench at the casual Barrel Bistro Room at Hillside, a pristine hilltop winery with stunning views from the post-and-beam restaurant or the dining terrace upstairs. Choose the Okanagan Cold Plate with house-made baguette, artisanal cheeses, wild boar terrine, cured salmon, tapenade, and condiments paired with a rosé or cabernet franc. At dinner, get right to the meat of the matter: roasted rack of New Zealand lamb caramelized to a crunch and tempered by a Dijon rosemary glaze matches well with a bottle of Mosaic, their award-winning Bordeaux blend. The friendly staff will invite you on a winery tour and even open the wine shop after hours. *$$–$$$; AE, MC, V; debit cards; lunch every day, dinner Sat–Sun May–mid-June, every day mid-June–mid-Oct; wine only; reservations recommended; www.hillsideestate.com; self-parking.* &

The Bench Artisan Food Market / ★

368 VANCOUVER AVE, PENTICTON; 250/492-2222

Located at the entrance to the Naramata Bench winery route, the Bench Artisan Food Market is brimming with local artisanal specialty products. An extensive deli offers Poplar Grove cheeses, olives, cold cuts, and sandwich fixings as well as prepared foods to go. With tables inside and seven tables on the patio, you can eat in or take out. The store also offers decadent desserts, including a frozen apricot mousse cake made with Elephant Island apricot wine and freshly baked Okanagan fruit pies. In the small but well-stocked grocery section, they carry the best in sauces, spreads, organic oils, vinegars, local dressings, marinades, and other condiments. *$; MC, V; debit cards; breakfast, lunch Mon–Sat; market open every day July–Aug; no alcohol; no reservations; www.thebenchmarket.com; street parking.* &

Bouchons Bistro / ★★★½

1180 SUNSET DR, STE 105, KELOWNA; 250/763-6595

Bouchons is all about Gallic charm, authentic bistro cuisine, and a truly hedonistic wine cellar. The menu unabashedly features pâté and foie gras, as well as duck, cassoulet, rabbit, steak tartare, and tenderloin. As lovers of French cuisine would expect, the sauces are divine. The bowl of pommes frites is regionally famous. The three-course table d'hôte is consistently excellent. For dessert, choose from pastries, soufflés, crème brûlée, or a classic cheese plate. Looking for something truly special to top an evening? Try the Grand Marnier tasting flight. *$$$; MC, V; no debit cards; dinner every day (closed Feb 15–Mar 15); full bar; reservations recommended; www.bouchonsbistro. com; street parking.* &

Bus Depot Cafe / ★

307 ELLIS ST, PENTICTON

Early-morning bus stations can be depressing places, but not in the cheerful two-level cafeteria at the Penticton Greyhound bus depot, known as the Hound by locals. The place exudes a '50s-era travelling-salesman charm: yellow plastic trays, brown Formica tables, and a steady flow of just-woke-up types that include hungover duos, Naramata winemakers, and beeper-belted delivery men. Breakfast is available 7am–2pm, when the cafe closes. Fortify yourself with the house special: two eggs, bacon, sausages, and fluffy pancakes for $5.50, or two eggs, bacon, crispy fried hash browns riddled with green onions, and toast for $4.57. As it should be in any self-respecting cafe, service is fast despite the number of people. *$; cash only; breakfast, lunch Tues–Sun; no alcohol; reservations not accepted; street parking.*

Cellar Door Bistro / ★★★

17403 HWY 97 (SUMAC RIDGE ESTATE WINERY), SUMMERLAND; 250/494-0451

A perfect interlude in a day of wine tasting is a meal at the Cellar Door Bistro, located inside Sumac Ridge Estate Winery along the highway between

Penticton and Kelowna. After tasting the award-winning wines of Sumac Ridge, take in a meal that defines Okanagan Valley cuisine: fresh regional ingredients that often are downright inspiring. Executive chef Roger Planiden took the Fairmont's Globe@YVR restaurant to a higher plane at the Vancouver Airport, and he's on a similar track here: tender braised-beef short ribs served aside Tiger blue cheese–potato purée and house-made stone fruit relish; pan-seared wild salmon with pearl couscous with sun-dried Okanagan tomato tapanade and a bright sautéed kale with lemon cream. The wine list includes those from Sumac Ridge and its sister wineries (Hawthorne, Jackson-Triggs, Inniskillin, and Nk'Mip), as well as dozens of other wineries in the valley. The ambience is never stuffy yet always elegant. *$$; AE, DIS, MC, V; debit cards; lunch, dinner every day (closed Jan–Feb); beer and wine; reservations recommended; www.sumacridge.com; self-parking.* &

Fresco Restaurant / ★★★★

1560 WATER ST, KELOWNA; 250/868-8805

Co-owners Audrey Surrao and chef Rodney Butters have created an elegant space and a menu that captures the contemporary West Coast bounty, focusing largely on organics. Chef Butters's style is simple yet sophisticated, regional yet refined. His signature menu includes a creamy offering of roasted Dungeness crab, oat-crusted buttery Arctic char, savoury double-smoked bacon and spinach flan, grilled Pontiac spuds with maple butter, and the famous double chocolate–mashed potato brioche dessert served with sorbet of Second Wind Farm raspberries and warm bitter chocolate sauce. The wine list, which merits capacious, high-end stemware, touts an impressive array of local and imported bottles, including some rare finds. Impeccable service and attention to detail. *$$$; AE, MC, V; debit cards; dinner Tues–Sat (closed Jan); full bar; reservations recommended; www.frescorestaurant.net; street parking.* &

Harvest Dining Room / ★★★

2725 KLO RD (HARVEST GOLF CLUB),
KELOWNA; 250/862-3177 OR 800/257-8577

Good news for golfers and nongolfers: this is not your typical 19th hole. Yes, you can get a pitcher of beer and Kelowna's best burger at the Harvest Grille, but for a serious dining experience, try the Harvest Dining Room at this award-winning golf course in east Kelowna. The menu tends toward seasonal ingredients that help shape the distinctly local cuisine. Seafood from the BC coast shares the table with Okanagan cheeses and the club's orchard fruit. The maple-brined Kurobuta pork loin (named for the fabled black hogs of Japan) paired with a comforting Parmesan polenta and sunchokes is outstanding, as are all of the organic duck dishes. Service is attentive, and the wine list has an extensive collection of local and imported wines, including some hard-to-find selections. *$$$; AE, DC, MC, V; debit cards; lunch, dinner every day; full bar; reservations recommended; www.harvestgolf.com/dining. html; self-parking.* &

VINEYARD DINING: YOUR GUIDE TO THE BEST WINERY RESTAURANTS

It wasn't so long ago that a visit to an Okanagan winery was for a wine tasting only, and you'd be lucky to find a cheese platter on offer. Today, many vintners hire winery chefs to promote their brands. This breed of chef has the task of matching food with wines rather than the reverse, resulting in some of the finest food in the region found on-site at wineries. Here are the must-visit restaurants where food and wine are perfectly paired.

BARREL BISTRO ROOM (see Restaurants in this chapter)

CELLAR DOOR BISTRO (see Restaurants in this chapter)

THE GRAPEVINE RESTAURANT (Gray Monk Estate Winery, 1055 Camp Rd, Okanagan Centre; 250/766-3168 or 800/663-4205) Open for lunch March to mid-Oct and dinner May to September. *www.grapevinerestaurant.ca.*

OLD VINES PATIO & RESTAURANT (see Restaurants in this chapter)

THE PATIO AT LAKE BREEZE (Lake Breeze Vineyards, 930 Sammet Rd, Naramata; 250/496-5619)

Hooded Merganser Bar and Grill / ★★★

21 LAKESHORE DR W, PENTICTON; 250/487-4663

Named after a rare and reclusive diving duck that landed during the restaurant's name selection process, the Hooded Merganser is built on a pier that straddles Lake Okanagan at the Penticton Lakeside Resort. Wall-to-wall wraparound windows provide panoramic views of the lake and mountains outside. Inside the woodsy dining room, chef Chris Remington's menu features traditional dishes and fresh local delicacies. Despite its duck moniker, the kitchen turns out only one version—a five-spiced, crisp-skinned pan-seared breast. Echoes of Korean barbecue grace the grilled sticky short-ribs appetizer. The signature dish is an eight-hour lasagne alternating layers of braised beef brisket and delicate pasta. The wine list admirably represents the best local wineries. *$$$; AE, MC, V; debit cards; lunch, dinner every day; full bar; reservations recommended; www.hoodedmerganser.ca; self-parking.*

Old Vines Patio & Restaurant / ★★★

3303 BOUCHERIE RD (QUAILS' GATE ESTATE WINERY), KELOWNA; 250/769-4451 OR 800/420-9463

Restaurants are opening in wineries throughout the Okanagan Valley, a trend not seen at this level elsewhere on the West Coast (not even in Napa!). A great example is the Old Vines Patio at Quails' Gate Estate Winery. Located on the west side of Lake Okanagan (don't be fooled by the Kelowna address—this

Open for lunch every day May to September, brunch Sunday during Okanagan Wine Festival. *www.lakebreeze.ca*.

THE SONORA ROOM (Burrowing Owl Estate Winery, 100 Burrowing Owl Pl, Oliver; 250/498-0620 or 877/498-0620) Open year-round serving dinner Thursday through Monday, plus lunch during Okanagan Wine Festival. *www.bovwine.ca*.

SUMMERHILL SUNSET BISTRO (Summerhill Pyramid Winery, 4870 Chute Lake Rd, Kelowna; 250/764-8000 or 800/667-3538) Open for lunch and dinner every day. *www.summerhill.bc.ca*.

THE TERRACE (Mission Hill Family Estate, 1730 Mission Hill Rd, Westbank; 250/768-6467) Open (weather permitting) for lunch May to mid-October and dinner mid-June to August. *www.missionhillwinery.com*.

THE VINEYARD TERRACE (CedarCreek Estate Winery, 5445 Lakeshore Rd, Kelowna; 250/764-8866 or 800/730-9463) Open every day for lunch mid-June to mid-September. *www.cedarcreek.bc.ca*.

—Kasey Wilson

isn't anywhere near downtown), the restaurant is quintessentially Northwest and fiercely regional. Choose Dungeness crab cakes with Okanagan apples or grilled Fraser Valley quail for starters, then move on to halibut from the Queen Charlotte Islands or even wild arctic caribou for a main course. The views of the vineyard and lake are as divine as the food. Winemaker Grant Stanley is one of the Okanagan's innovators, so you'll want to do tasting flights of Quails' Gate wines, especially their pinot noirs. Service is friendly. *$$$; AE, MC, V; debit cards; lunch, dinner every day, brunch Sun; beer and wine; reservations recommended; www.quailsgate.com; self-parking.* &

Theo's / ★★★

687 MAIN ST, PENTICTON; 250/492-4019
The hospitality of the Theodosakis family has made this restaurant a local institution for more than 25 years. The seats around the fireplace are in big demand, but in any season you'll enjoy an intimate courtyard ambience filled with beautiful art, antique tapestries, and vintage family photographs. The traditional rustic Greek dishes are chock-full of feta cheese and spices. You can make a meal from the appetizers alone: the tangy tzatziki, garlicky hummus, and taramasalata (mullet fish roe) dips are creamy and filling. Theo's platter for two provides a cornucopia of traditional Hellenic favourites, including Greek salad, moussaka, spinach pie, dolmades avgolemono (tender grape leaves filled with herb-laced rice and ground beef baked with a

traditional Greek lemon sauce), beef souvlaki, and *paithakia skaras* (broiled rack of lamb chops). For dessert, order the *bougatsa*, a Greek street food of creamy custard wrapped in phyllo. The impressive list of local wines reflects the owners' passionate support of the booming regional wine scene. *$$; AE, MC, V; debit cards; lunch, dinner every day; full bar; reservations recommended; www.eatsquid.com; street parking.* &

Toasted Oak Wine Bar & Grill / ★★★

34881 97TH ST, OLIVER; 250/498-4867 OR 888/880-9463

Located in Oliver's historic original firehall, with an imposing hose tower, the Toasted Oak—under the direction of chef Jeffrey Brandt and sommelier Jay Drysdale—offers food and wine that practically come from its backyard. Wild morel risotto, local duck breast with Similkameen prunes, and artisan cheeses are outstanding. An astounding number of more than 350 nouveau and vintage BC wines are available by the glass or in flights. There's also a wine shop on the premises. *$$–$$$; AE, MC, V; debit cards; lunch, dinner every day; full bar; reservations recommended; www.winecountry-canada. com; self-parking.* &

Waterfront Wines / ★★★

103-1180 SUNSET DR, KELOWNA; 250/979-1222

If you like funky chic, Waterfront Wines in Kelowna is for you. This establishment is a combination wine shop, restaurant, and bar. Stop in for a bottle of wine to take with you, and maybe slow down long enough to sample the cheese plate or a bowl of olives. If you decide to linger awhile, order several small plates, including scallops, prawns, and calamari, or dive right into the big plates of beef, chicken, pork, lamb, or seafood. And the wine list? It's loaded with regional favourites and international discoveries classified as Blondes (white wines), Red Heads (red wines), and Airheads (sparkling). Additionally, the single-malt whiskey list is nothing short of impressive. *$$–$$$; AE, MC, V; debit cards; dinner every day; full bar; reservations recommended; www.waterfrontwines.com; self-parking.* &

Lodgings

Burrowing Owl Estate Winery Guesthouse / ★★★

100 BURROWING OWL PL, OLIVER; 250/498-0620 OR 877/498-0620

The latest and one of the most spectacular spots to stay in the Okanagan Valley is the intimate 10-room guesthouse at Burrowing Owl Estate Winery. The spacious, air-conditioned rooms have private balconies, and on the grounds are a 25-metre (82-foot) swimming pool and a hot tub. In addition to Burrowing Owl's award-winning wines, a dozen other wineries are a few minutes away. The popular Sonora Room, Burrowing Owl's on-site restaurant, is open for lunch and dinner with both indoor and outdoor dining. *$$$; AE, MC, V; no debit cards; www.bovwine.ca; self-parking.* &

Cove Lakeside Resort / ★★★

4205 GELLATLY RD, WESTBANK; 877/762-2683
For sheer luxury, it's tough to beat the Cove Lakeside Resort, located 20 minutes south of Kelowna. Dock your boat at the marina and check in to a one-, two-, or three-bedroom waterside suite overlooking Okanagan Lake. Each includes a fully equipped kitchen (with a wine fridge), fireplace, entertainment centre, and floor-to-ceiling windows. The Cove Couples package includes a one-bedroom suite with French doors that open onto an expansive balcony, deep soaking tubs, and hour-long massages. There are pools, hot tubs, tennis courts, a putting green, and a waterslide. For beachside picnics, there are fire pits and a barbecue area. *$$$; AE, MC, V; no debit cards; www. covelakesideresort.com; self-parking.*

Hotel Eldorado / ★★★

500 COOK RD, KELOWNA; 250/861-4779
The Eldorado has been a mainstay in Kelowna since it was built in 1926 by an Austrian countess. The property provides a unique combination of history, setting, and boutique-style attention to detail. In addition to the original hotel, the newer, more luxurious hotel has 30 guest rooms and six spacious luxury suites with jetted tubs, kitchenettes, plasma TVs, and views of Okanagan Lake. Full spa treatments are a few steps away, as is the popular lakeside dining room. *$$$; AE, DC, MC, V; debit cards; www.eldoradokelowna.com; self-parking.* &

Manteo Resort / ★★★

3762 LAKESHORE, KELOWNA; 250/860-1031
Water is the key to life at the Manteo Resort, located within steps of the shores of Okanagan Lake. Exceptional suites and two-storey villas feature incredible views and outdoor patios with barbecues. In the main hotel, the contemporary one-bedroom lakeview suite is your best bet, with separate kitchen and living area. The boating centre allows guests to partake in an outstanding choice of water sports, and the more serious-minded can take advantage of trained instructors and video analysis of their performance. *$$$$; AE, DC, MC, V; debit cards; www.manteo.com; self-parking.* &

Naramata Heritage Inn & Spa / ★★★

3625 IST ST, NARAMATA; 250/496-6808
At the 100-year-old Naramata Heritage Inn & Spa, each of the 12 guest rooms has been lovingly restored and named after a world-class wine region. Rooms feature private balconies, high ceilings, antique furnishings, and clawfoot tubs. The low-key wine bar, open to travellers who are not staying at the inn, turns out perfect flatbreads and pizzas from its wood-fired stone oven. *$$$; MC, V; debit cards; www.naramatainn.com; self-parking.* &

Observatory Bed and Breakfast / ★★

1270 HWY 3 E, NO 3 OBSERVATORY RD, OSOYOOS; 250/495-6745

For an out-of-this-world experience, stay at Jack and Alice Newton's Observatory B&B—an astronomy-themed bed-and-breakfast perched 488 metres (1,600 feet) above the floor of the Okanagan Valley. The Eclipse suite is a bargain—it has two bedrooms with king-size beds, a living room, and a kitchen. But you won't want to cook when you taste Alice's generous hot breakfast fare. Your stay includes Jack's introductory tour of the night skies through a 40-centimetre (16-inch) computer-controlled telescope in the rooftop observatory. *$$; M, V; debit cards; www.jacknewton.com; self-parking.*

Penticton Lakeside Resort, Convention Centre & Casino / ★★

21 LAKESHORE DR W, PENTICTON; 250/493-8221 OR 800/663-9400

In the central Okanagan Valley, the Penticton Lakeside Resort is a destination all its own. This is an especially good option if you are travelling the wine country as a family. The rooms are fairly basic, but the waterside location is the best in Penticton. Activities available down at the expansive dock include boating, waterskiing, sailing, parasailing, windsurfing, and jet-skiing. VIP guests are greeted with freshly baked chocolate chip cookies, a Penticton Lakeside tradition—but you can also buy them in the casino. *$$–$$$; AE, M, V; debit cards; www.pentictonlakesideresort.com; self-parking.*

SameSun Backpacker Lodge / ★

245 HARVEY AVE, KELOWNA; 250/763-9814

For the cash-conscious, SameSun Backpacker Lodge in Kelowna has private rooms starting at $49. Technically a hostel, the lodge is clean and bright, located right in the downtown heart of the city. *$; MC, V; debit cards; www. samesun.com; self-parking.*

Spirit Ridge Vineyard Resort & Spa / ★★

1200 RANCHER CREEK RD, OSOYOOS; 250/495-5445 OR 877/313-9463

At the eastern edge of Osoyoos, on a spectacular bench overlooking the shores of Osoyoos Lake, you'll find the Spirit Ridge Vineyard Resort & Spa, created in partnership with the Osoyoos Indian Band. It has 94 desert-themed villas and suites, a wine-country inspired restaurant—Passa Tempo—a spa and an outdoor pool, a waterslide, a hot tub, and a fitness centre. *$$$–$$$$; AE, M, V; debit cards; www.spiritridge.ca; self-parking.*

Index

A

A & B Sound, 208
Abigail's Hotel, 315
Abkhazi Gardens, 324
Absolute Spa, 33
Adams River, 290–91
Adara, 351
Adrena Line Zipline Adventure
    Tours, 310
Aerie Resort and Spa, 331–32
Affinity Sports, 357
AFTERglow, 258
Agent Provocateur, 206
Aijsai Sushi Bar, 51
Air Canada, 3, 364
Air tours, 180–81
Airport Limousine Service, 344
Airports, 2, 364
Akbar's Own Dining Lounge, 52
Albion Books, 197
Alcan Dragon Boat Festival, 141
Alibi Room, 254
Alliance, 27
Alliance for Arts and Culture, 226,
    234
Alpine Airsports, 362
Alpine Club of Canada, 276
Ambleside, 161
Ambleside Park, 174, 292–93
American Grille, The, 52
Amos & Andes, 357
Amsterdam Café Pub, 358
Amtrak, 8
Animal Clinic, 31
Animal observation, 289–91
Annapurna, 52
Antique Row, 325
Antiques, 190
Anza Club, 238
Apparel, 191–96
Aqua Riva, 53
Aquabus, 181
Araxis Restaurant & Bar, 344
Architectural Institute of BC, 183,
    234
Aritzia, 191
Armchair Books, 357
Army & Navy, 187
Arrowleaf, 373
Art Beatus, 170
Art Gallery of Greater Victoria, 324
Art supplies, 220–21
Artisan Sakemaker Studio, 189
Arts Club Theatre Company, 227
Arts Hotline, 226
Arts Off Main, 170
Artspeak, 170

Ashiana Tandoori Restaurant, 53
Atkinson's, 204
Atlantic Trap & Grill, The, 254–55
Au Petit Café, 53
AuBar, 246
August Peach Festival, 367
Aurora Bistro, 54
Avant Gardener, The, 203–4
Aviation World, 197
Axis Theatre Company, 226

B

Bacchus Piano Lounge, 258–59
Bacchus Restaurant & Lounge, 54,
    118–19
Bacci's, 189, 191
Backstage Lounge, 259
Bakeries, 196–97
Bald eagles, 288
Ballet British Columbia, 235–36
Banana Leaf Malaysian Cuisine, 54
Banks, 31
Banyen Books & Sound, 197–98
Bar None, 246
Barbara-Jo's Books to Cook, 198
Barb's Buns, 334
Barclay Heritage Square, 163
Barclay House, 130
Barclay Manor, 239
Bard on the Beach, 227
Barnet Beach Park, 174
Barrel Room Bistro, 371, 373
Bars, 254–58
Baseball, 302–3
Basic Stock Cookware, 203
Bau-Xi Gallery, 170
Bay, 28
Bayshore Bike Rentals, 271
Bayshore Rentals, 276
BC Automobile Association, 24
BC Bookworld, 239
BC Children's Hospital, 13
BC Ferries, 5, 7, 306
BC Institute of Technology, 36
BC Lions Football, 301
BC Liquor Stores, 222
BC Mobility Opportunity Society,
    13
BC Museum of Mining, 166, 338
BC Paraplegic Association, 13
BC SPCA Groom Shop, 31
BC Sports Hall of Fame and
    Museum, 166
BC Transit, 309
BCIT/Pacific Marine Training
    Institute, 153
Beach Blanket Film Festival, 367

Beach House, The, 55, 161
Beacon Hill Children's Farm, 324
Beacon Hill Park, 322–23
Bean Around the World, 263
Bearfoot Bistro, 344–45
Beaver Lake, 144
bebe, 191
Beer, 222–24
Beet Root Café, The, 345
Belcarra Paddling Company, 273
Belcarra Park, 174–75, 273
Belfrey Theatre, 327
Bench Artisan Food Market, The,
    374
Bengal Lounge, 319
Benkei Ramen Noodle Shop, 55
Benny's Bagels, 260
Bentall Centre, 32
Bentall Centre Shoe Renew, 212
Bernstein & Gold, 205
Bespoke, 326
Beth Israel, 28
Betsey Johnson, 191
Beyond Restaurant and Lounge, 55
Bicycle Sports Pacific, 287
Bicycles, 25–26, 182, 268–71
Bikes 'N' Blades, 26
Bikram's Yoga, 33
Billiards, 243
Bin 941/942 Tapas Parlour, 56
Birks, 204–5
Bishop's, 56
Bistro One Sixty One, 333
Bistro Pastis, 56–57
Bistrot Bistro, 57
Black Widow, 371
Blackberry Books, 198
Blackcomb Adventure Zone, 362
Blackcomb Helicopters, 275–76,
    356
Blackcomb Mountain, 359
Blarney Stone, The, 246–47
Blasted Church, 372
Block, The, 191
Blue Bird Cabs, 309
Blue Grouse Vineyards, 332
Blue Mountain Vineyard & Cellars,
    370
Blue Planet Kayaking, 310
Blue Poppy Restaurant, 321
Blue Water Cafe + Raw Bar,
    57–58
Boat tours, 181
Boboli, 191–92
Boca Del Lupo, 226
Body Shop, 357
Boneta, 57–58, 58–59
Book Warehouse, 198

Bookstores, 14, 197–200, 239
Boone County Country Cabaret, 247
Bosa Foods, 214
Botanical gardens, 144–45
Bouchons Bistro, 374
Boulevard Casino, 160
Bowen Island, 272
Boys' Co., 192
Brasserie L'Ecole, 311–12
Breakfast restaurants, 45
Brickhouse Late Night Bistro & Bar, 255, 260
Bridges, 149–51
Bridges Seafood Restaurant, 58
Bright Side, The, 209
Brix Restaurant, 59
Brockton Point, 143
Brooklyn, 192
Browning Pass Charters, 335
Bubble King, 75
Bubble tea, 74–75
Bubble World, 74
Buddha Supplies Centre, 209–10
Buddhist Temple, 29
Buffalo Bill's Bar and Grill, 358
Burcu's Angels, 210
Burgoo, 106
Burnaby, 20, 42, 242
Burnaby Village Museum, 166–67
Burrard, 20
Burrard Bridge, 150–51
Burrowing Owl Estate Winery, 369, 371
Burrowing Owl Estate Winery Guesthouse, 378
Bus Depot Cafe, 374
Buschlen-Mowatt Gallery, 170
Buses, 5, 22, 306, 340
Business services, 27
Butchart Gardens, 321

C

C Restaurant, 60
Cabbages & Kinx, 210
Cable Cove Inn, 336
Cactus Club Cafe, 60
Cafe Brio, 312
Café de Paris, 60–61
Cafe Deux Soleils, 239
Café Kathmandu, 61
Cafe Montmartre, 239
Calabria, 15
Calling, The, 255
Calona Vineyards, 372–73
Cambie Street Bridge, 25
Campbell Valley Regional Park, 284
Canada Customs, 4
Canada Line, 3
Canada Place, 148
Canada Safeway, 29

Canada West Mountain School, 274
Canadian Museum of Flight, The, 167
Canadian National Institute for the Blind, 13
Canadian Outback Adventures, 361
Candy, 200–1
Candy Aisle, 200
Cannery Seafood House, The, 61
Canoeing, 271–74
Canski, 361
Canvas Lounge, 259
Capers, 29
Capilano College, 36, 226
Capilano River Regional Park, 175
Capilano Salmon Hatchery, 290
Capilano Suspension Bridge, 150
Caprice, 247
Car(s), 8–9, 23–24
Car rentals, 2, 24
Caramba!, 345
Cardero's, 61–62
Carepoint Medical Centres, 30
Carr House, 320
Cascade Room, The, 59, 62, 255
Casinos, 160
Cassiar Mountain Jade Store, 338
Cates Park, 273
Cathay Importers, 188
CDs, 208–9
Cecil Exotic Show Lounge, 255
Cedarcreek, 370, 373
Ceili's Irish Pub, 247
Celebrate 2010: Cultural Festival, 342
Celebrities, 247–48
Cellar Door Bistro, 374–75
Cellar Restaurant & Jazz Club, The, 248
Celluloid Social Club, 238
Central Computer, 28
Central Mountain Air, 364
Central Park, 175, 293
Centre, 15
Century, 33
Century Plaza Hotel and Spa, 132
Century Restaurant/Heist Lounge, 256
Chachkas, 205
Chalet Estate Winery, 331
Chambar Belgian Restaurant, 59, 62
Chan Centre for the Performing Arts, 230–31
Chao Phraya Thai Restaurant, 62–63
Chapters Bookstores, 198, 239
Charles H. Scott Gallery, 234
Chen's Shanghai Restaurant, 63, 94
Children, 13, 106–7

Children's clothing, 201–2
Chill Winston, 259
Chill Winston Restaurant & Lounge, 63
Chilliwack River, 291–92
Chinatown, 21
    description of, 147
    restaurants, 42
    shopping, 188
    in Victoria, 321–22
Chinese Cultural Centre, 231
Chinese food, 45–46
Chinese Imperial School, 321
Chinese Jade and Crafts, 188
Chinese Settlement House, 321
Chintz & Co, 326
Chocolate, 200–1
Chocolate Arts, 200
Chocolate Fest, 327
Chocolate Tofino, 336
Choices, 30
Chow, 64
Christ Church Anglican Cathedral, 28
Churches, 28–29
Chutney Villa, 64
Chutzpah! Festival, 227
Ciao-Thyme, 346
Cibo Trattoria, 122
CinCin Ristorante & Bar, 64–65
Cioppino's Mediterranean Grill & Enoteca, 65
Citta's Bistro, 357
City Animal Control Home, 31
City by Cycle, 182
Citydog Pet Centre, 133
Classical music, 230–33
Clayoquot Wilderness Resort, 282
Cliffhanger, 276–77
Climbing, 274–77
Clothing, 201–2
Cloud 9 Piano Lounge, 259
Coal Harbour, 29
Coal Harbour Dental, 30
Coast Mountain Sports, 219
Coast Restaurant, 65
Cobre, 65–66
Cocktails, 58–59, 243
Coffee, 243, 263–66
Coffee on the Moon, 333
College of Physicians and Surgeons, 16, 30
Comicshop, The, 198
Commercial Drive, 161
Commodore Ballroom, 248
Common Loaf Bake Shop, 336
Compukits, 27
Computer repairs and rentals, 27–28
Congee Noodle House, 66
Consignment, 202–3

Contemporary Art Gallery, 170
Cookware, 203
Cookworks, 203
Cooper Boating Centre, 294
Cooper's Cove, 330
Copy services, 27
Cornucopia, 356
Costs, 10–11
Cougar Mountain Adventure Ltd, 360–61
Country Furniture, 206
Couriers, 27
Cove Lakeside Resort, 379
Cowichan Bay Farm, 332
Cowichan Bay Maritime Centre and Museum, 332
Cowichan Trading Company, 325–26
Cowichan Valley, 332–33
Craig Street Brewing Company, 333
Craigdarroch Castle, 320
Crave, 66
Crema Productions, 15
Criteriums, 268
Cross, The, 206
Cross-country skiing, 294–96, 360
Crow and Gate Pub, 323
Crowsnest Vineyards, 369
Cru, 66–67
Crush Champagne Lounge, 248
CSC Computer Service Centre, 27
Cupcakes, 196
Currency, 11
Cycling BC, 268, 309
Cycling tours, 182
Cyclone Taylor Sporting Goods, 219
Cypress Mountain, 295, 297
Cypress Provincial Park, 175–76, 275

D

Dai Tung Chinese Restaurant, 67
Dan Japanese Restaurant, 67
Dance, 233–36
Dance Centre, 234
Dancing, 243
Dancing on the Edge Festival, 236
Dandelion Kids, 201
Daniel le Chocolat Belge, 200
Dave's Fish and Chips, 158
David Lam Park, 176
Davie Laundromat, 29
Dayton Shoe Co., 212
DB Bistro Moderne, 67–68
Deas Island Regional Park, 279
Deep Cove Bike Shop, 287
Deep Cove Canoe and Kayak Centre, 273
Deerholme Farm, 333

Delany's on Denman, 15
Delilah's Restaurant and Bar, 68
Delta Victoria Ocean Pointe Resort and Spa, 315–16
Deluxe Junk, 210
Denman Fitness, 30
Denman Place Discount Cinema, 238
Dental Clinic @ Robson, 30
Dental services, 30
Department of Fisheries and Oceans, 278–79
Desert, 368
Desert Hills, 369, 371
Desolation Sound Marine Park, 294
Dessert, 243, 263–66
Diane Farris Gallery, 171
Diane's Lingerie and Loungewear, 206
Dig This, 326
Dim sum, 46, 94–95
Dining Room Restaurant, 321
Dirty Laundry Winery, 372
Disabilities, 13–14
Diva at the Met, 68
Diving, 278
Diving Locker, The, 219
Dix Barbecue and Brewery, 256
DKNY, 193
Dockside Brewing Company, 256
Doggy Style Deli, 133
Doghouse, 17, 133
Doña Cata Mexican Foods, 68–69
Doolin's Irish Pub, 248
Douglas College, 36
Douglas Reynolds Gallery, 171
Downhill skiing, 296–98, 358–60
Downtown
    lodgings, 130–37
    nightlife, 242
    restaurants, 42
    shopping, 186–87
Dr. Sun Yat-Sen Classical Chinese Garden, 173
Dragon Alley, 322
Dragon Ball Tea House, 75
Dry cleaners, 28–29
Dubh Linn Gate, 346, 357–58
Dunbar Theatre, 237
Duncan, 333
Dundarave, 161
Dundarave Wine Cellars, 222
Dunne and Rundle, 32
Durlacher Hof, 351
Dusty's Bar and Barbecue, 358
Duthie Books, 198

E

Eagle Aerie Gallery, 335
Earls, 69
Early Music Vancouver, 231

East Is East/Chai Gallery, 69
East Sooke Regional Park, 328
East Vancouver, 43, 242
Ecomarine Ocean Kayaking Centre, 272
Edam Dance, 234
Edge Climbing Centre, 276
Edgemont Village Wines, 222
Edgewater Casino, 160
Edgewater Lodge, 351–52
Edgewater Lodge Restaurant, 346
Edible British Columbia, 182
18 Karat, 189
El Furniture Warehouse, 256
El Kartel, 193
Elements, 346–47
Elephant Island, 371–72
Elephant Island Orchard Wines, 367
1181, 249
Elixir, 70
Ellie Tropical Cuisine, 70
Elwood's, 260
Emily Carr Gallery, 156
Emily Carr Institute of Art and Design, 36
Empress Room, 312
Enchanted Evenings, 231
Enda B, 193
English Bay, 272, 294
English Bay Beach, 176
English Bay Inn, 130
Equinox Gallery, 171
Ermenegildo Zegna, 194
Eugene Choo, 192
Everything Wine, 223
Exchange rates, 11, 16
Ezogiku Noodle Cafe, 70–71

F

Fabulous Find, The, 211
Fairburn Farm, 333
Fairfield Plaza, 311
Fairholme Manor, 316
Fairmont Chateau Whistler Resort, 352
Fairmont Empress Hotel, 316, 319
Fairmont Hotel Vancouver, 33, 131
Fairmont Vancouver Airport, 17, 138
Fairmont Vancouver Hotel, 17
Fairmont Waterfront, 131
Fairmont Waterfront Hotel, 133
Fairview Pub, 250
False Creek, 272
False Creek Ferries, 181
False Creek South, 162
Families, 13
Fan Tan Alley, 322
Fantasy Balloon Charters, 284–85
Farmers markets, 178–79

Federation of Mountain Clubs of British Columbia, 274, 295
Fedex Kinko's, 27
Ferries, 5, 8, 306, 309, 318
Festivals, 327–28
Fiddlehead Joe's Eatery & Bar, 71
Fifth Avenue Cinemas, 238
Fifty Two 80 Bistro, 347
Film, 237–39
Firefly Fine Wines and Ales, 223
First Ravioli Store, The, 214
Fisgard Lighthouse National Historic Site, 324–25
Fish House in Stanley Park, 71–72, 119
Fisherman's Terrace Seafood Restaurant, 71
Fishing, 279–80
Five Sails Restaurant, 72
Flag Shop, The, 210
Flash Courier, 27
Flatwater Lakes, 272
Flavour, 326
Fleuri Restaurant, 118
Floata Seafood Restaurant, 72
Florists, 203–4
Flow Yoga, 34
Flygirl, 15
Flying Beaver, 72–73
Food tours, 182
Forbidden Fruit Winery, 369
Foreign visitors, 16
Fort Langley National Historic Site, 167
Fort Rodd Hill, 324–25
49th Parallel Coffee Roasters, 263
Four Seasons, 131
Four Seasons Hotel
   in Vancouver, 17
   in Whistler, 17, 352
Fraîche, 73
Fraser River, 20, 279–80, 292
Fraser Valley, 284–85
Fraserview Golf Course, 280
French Country Antiques, 190
Fresco Restaurant, 375
Friends of Chamber Music, 232
Fritz European Fry House, 73
Front and Co., 202
Fuel Restaurant, 73–74
Fujiya, 214–15
Full Circle Performance, 226

G
Galileo Coffee Company, 338
Galleries, 170–72
Gallery of BC Ceramics, 171
Galloping Goose Trail, 309, 329
Gaolers Mews, 146–47
Garden shops, 203–4
Gardens, 173–74

Garibaldi Lift Co., 358–59
Garibaldi Provincial Park, 275, 281–82, 295, 360
Garry Oaks Winery, 323, 334
Garry Point Park, 176–77, 269, 286–87
Gastown, 43, 146–47, 187
Gastropod, 74–75
Gate of Harmonious Interest, 322
Gateau Lingerie, 207
Gateway Valet and Concierge, 3
Gays, 15–16, 244
Gehringer Brothers, 369
Geological Survey of Canada, 24
George C. Reifel Migratory Bird Sanctuary, 177, 289
George Ultra Lounge, 260
Gerard Lounge, 260
Get Fresh Flowers, 204
Ghostly Walks, 311
Gifts, 204–5
Ginger 62, 261
Gingeri Chinese Cuisine, 94
Glacier Air, 180–81
Globe@YVR, 75
Glowbal Grill & Satay Bar, 76
Go Fish!, 76, 106
Gogo Tea Cafe, 75
Gold Coin Laundry, 29
Golden Age Collectables, 210
Golden Ears Provincial Park, 282, 284
Golden Mile, 371
Golden Mile Cellars, 369
Golden Swan, 106
Golden Swan Restaurant, 95
Golden Village, 157
Goldfish Pacific Kitchen, 76
Goldstream Provincial Park, 306, 331
Golfing, 280–81
Gorg-O-Mish, 249
Gotham Steakhouse & Cocktail Bar, 76–77, 261
Gourmet Warehouse, 215
Gramery Grill, 77
Grand Prix Hobbies, Crafts & Gifts Ltd., 211
Grand View Szechuan Restaurant, 77
Granville Island, 43, 140–41, 188, 242
Granville Island Truck Farmers Market, 178
Granville Room, 262
Grapevine Restaurant, The, 376
Gratuities, 12
Gray Line West, 310
Gray Monk Winery, 373
Greater Vancouver Zoo, 290
Green Basil Thai Restaurant, 77–78

Green Point Campground, 336
Greyhound Canada Transportation Corporation, 340
Griffins, 78
Grocery stores, 29–30
Groundwork Athletics, 277
Grouse Grind, 147–49
Grouse Mountain, 147–49, 282–83, 297–98
Gulf Islands, 269, 272–73, 294
Gulf Islands Kayaking, 273
Gulf of Georgia Cannery, 158
Gum Drops, 212
Gusto di Quattro, 104
Gyms, 30
Gyoza King, 78, 261

H
Habit Lounge, 78–79
Hair care, 212–14
Hal Mae Jang Mo Jib, 79
Hammered and Pickled, 205
Handydart, 14
Hanwoori Korean Restaurant, 79
Hapa Izakaya, 79–80
Happy Three, 202
Harbour Air Seaplanes, 4, 181, 308
Harbour Centre, 36
Harbour Cruises, 181–82
Hare Krishna Temple, 29
Hart House Restaurant, 80
Hartmann House B&B, 330
Harvest Dining Room, 375
Hastings House, 334
Hastings Park horse racing, 301–2
Headlines Theatre Company, 226
Heart's Content, 322
Heffel Gallery, 171
Helijet Airways, 4, 308
Helmcken House, 320
Hemlock Valley, 298
Herb Museum, The, 167–68
Herder Winery & Vineyards, 369
Hermitage, The, 80
Herons Restaurant, 80–81
Hester Creek, 369
Highlife Records and Music, 208
Hiking, 281–84, 361
Hilary Miles Flowers, 204
Hilary's Cheese and Deli, 332
Hill's Native Art, 209
Hill's of Kerrisdale, 194
History, 6–7
H-Mart, 216
Ho Yuen Kee, 81–82
Hockey, 303–4
Hole in the Wall, 280
Hollyburn Lodge, 295
Hollywood Theatre, 238
Holt Renfrew, 187, 194
Holy Body Tattoo, 234

Home furnishings, 205–8
Honey Lounge, 250
Hon's Wun-Tun House, 81
Hooded Merganser Bar and Grill, 376
Horizon Air, 364
Horizons Restaurant, 81
Horse racing, 301–2
Horseback riding, 284
Horse-drawn tours, 182–83
Horseshoe Bay, 280, 306
Horseshoe Bay–Nanaimo Ferry, 306
Horstman Glacier, 360
Hospitals, 30
Hot Springs Cove Lodge, 335
Hot-air ballooning, 284–85
Hotel Eldorado, 379
Hotel Grand Pacific, 316–17
Hotel le Soleil, 132–33
House of Himwitsa, 335
Howe Sound Crest Trail, 283
Howe Sound Inn and Brewing Company, 338
H.R. MacMillan Space Centre, 168
Hudson's Bay Company, 187
Hum, 192
Hyak Wilderness Adventures, 292
Hy's Encore, 82
Hy's Steakhouse, 347

I
Ice skating, 285
IGA Marketplace, 29
Il Caminetto di Umberto, 348
Il Giardino di Umberto, 82
Il Terrazzo Ristorante, 312–13
Ilanaaq, 342
Imperial Chinese Seafood Restaurant, 82–83, 95
Incendio, 83
Incendio West, 83
Indian Arm, 273
Indoor climbing, 276–77
Inform Interiors, 187, 206–7
In-line skating, 285–86
Inn at Tough City, 336
Inniskillin Okanagan, 369
Insignia International, 27
Inter Currency Exchange Corporation, 16
International Buddhist Society Temple, 29
International Diving Centre, 278
International Securities Exchange, 16
International Travel Maps and Books, 24, 199
Internet, 17–18, 36
Intrepid Theatre Company, 327
Inuit Gallery, 171

Iona Beach Park, 177
Irish Heather, The, 83
Irish Linen Shop, 325
Island Cruising, 294
Isola Bella, 201
ISTS, 27
Italian Kitchen, 83–84
It's Still a Dog's Life, 17, 133
Izakayas, 87
Izumi-Ya Japanese Marketplace, 216

J
J & J Wonton Noodle House, 313
J, N & Z Deli, 215
Jackson-Triggs Winery, 370
Jacob, 194
Jamia Masjid, 28
Jazz, 244
Jazzfest International, 328
Jericho Beach, 158
Jericho Beach Park, 300
Jewellery, 204–5
Joe Fortes Seafood & Chop House, 84, 262
Joe's Café, 264
Joffre Lakes Provincial Park, 360
John Fluevog, 212
Jonathan + Olivia, 192
Josephine's Restaurant and Catering, 84
Juan de Fuca Marine Trail, 329
Judith Marcuse, 234
Jules Bistro, 85

K
Kaboodles, 221
Kamei Royale Japanese Restaurant, 85
Karaoke, 244
Karen Jamieson, 234
Karen Magnussen Recreation Centre, 285
Karl Stittgen and Goldsmiths, 205
Katmandu, 357
Kat's Tea Hut, 75
Kayaking, 271–74, 310
Kei's Bakery, 216
Kelowna, 366
Kelowna International Airport, 364
Kerrisdale, 21
Kerrisdale Cyclone Taylor Arena, 285, 286
Keystone Extras, 237
Khalsa Diwan Society's Gurdwara Sahib, 29
Kids Market, 189, 221
Kidsbooks, 199
Kilshaw's, 325
Kim Phung Vietnamese Restaurant, 85

Kingyo, 86
Kintaro Handmade Tonkotsu Ramen, 86
Kirin Mandarin Restaurant, 87–88, 95
Kisa's of Kerrisdale, 202
Kiss Store, The, 15
Kitanoya Guu, 88
Kite flying, 286–87
Kitsilano, 21, 162
Kitsilano Beach, 153–54, 293, 300
Kitsilano Community Centre, 285
Kitsilano Farmers Market, 178
Kitsilano Pool, 153, 299
Kitsilano Showboat, 153
Klahanie Restaurant, 338
Kokoro Dance, 234
Komakino, 194
Koolhaus, 187–88, 207
Kootenay School of Writing, 240

L
La Baguette et L'Echalote, 196
La Belle Auberge, 88
La Bretagne Crêperie, 88
La Buca, 89
La Casa Gelato, 264
La Cucina Italiana, 89
La Frenz, 370
La Jolie Madame, 207
La Piazza Dario Ristorante Italiano, 89
La Régalade French Bistro, 90
La Rua, 348
La Terrazza, 90
Ladner, 43
Lake Breeze, 371, 372
Lander Village Market, 178
Landmark Hot Pot House, 89
Land's End Sailing School, 294
Lang Vineyards, 372
Langara College, 36
Lark, 193
Lattimer Gallery, 209
Laughing Stock, 371
Launderdog Daycare, 17
Laundromats, 28–29
Laurel Point Inn, 317
Le Chamois, 353
Le Crocodile, 90–91
Le Gavroche, 91
Le Magasin, 187
Le Marrakech Moroccan Bistro, 91
Le Patisserie Lebeau, 196
Le Vieux Pin, 369, 371
Legal services, 30–31
Legendary Noodles, 91–92
Lens & Shutter, 32
Leone, 194–95
Les Amis du Fromage, 215
Lesbians, 15–16, 244

Liberty, 208, 326
Liberty Wine Merchants, 223
Libraries, 34
Library Square, 148–49, 250
LifeSpa, 212
Lift, 92
Lighthouse Park, 152, 283
Lilikiks, 201
Lime Japanese Cuisine, 92
Limousines, 25
Lions Gate Bridge, 149–50
Literature, 239–40
Little Nest, 106–7
Little Sister's Book & Art
    Emporium, 15, 164
Little Straw, 372
Little Vienna Bakery, 329
Live music, 244
Lobster Man, The, 215
Local Color, 237
Locarno Beach, 158
L'Occitane, 213
Loden Vancouver, 130
Lodgings
    Okanagan Valley, 378–80
    Vancouver, 130–38
    Victoria, 315–18
Lolita's South of the Border
    Cantina, 92–93
London Drugs, 31
Long Beach, 334–36
Longhorn Saloon and Grill, 358
Longliner Sea Foods, 216
Lonsdale Quay Hotel, 153
Lonsdale Quay Market, 152–53,
    189
Lost Lagoon, 293
Lotus Island Adventures, 273
Lotus Sound Lounge, 250
Lounges, 258–62
Lower Seymour Conservation
    Reserve, 280, 286
Lululemon, 326
Lululemon Athletica, 220
Lumberman's Arch, 143
Lumière with Daniel Boulud, 93
Lund's, 325
LUSH, 213
Lush, 357
Lynn Canyon Suspension Bridge,
    150
Lynn Headwaters Regional Park,
    177

M

MacGillycuddy's for Little People,
    202
MacLeod's Books, 199
MacMillan Provincial Park, 323
Magazines, 34, 197–200
Magnolia Hotel, 317

Malahat, 331–32
Mangia e Bevi Ristorante, 93
Manning Park Resort, 295
Manning Provincial Park, 283–84,
    295, 298
Manteo Resort, 379
Maple Medical Clinic, 30
Maplewood Farm, 290
Maps, 197–200
Marcello Pizzeria & Ristorante,
    94–95
Margareta Signature Collection, 195
Marine Building, 149
Marion Scott Gallery, 172
Maritime Museum, 153–54, 322
Mark James, 195
Market Square, 326
Marketplace IGA, 186
Markham House, 330
Marley Farm Winery, 331
Marquis Wine Cellars, 223
Martha Sturdy, 205
Martini's, 261
Masc, 213
Masjid At-Taqwa, 28
Masthead, 332–33
Maurice Young Millennium Place,
    358
Max Dental, 30
Maxx Fish, 358
Maya, 193
Mayfair Lakes Golf Course, 280–81
Mayfair News, 199
Mayne Island Kayak and Canoe
    Rentals, 273
McDonald Beach, 279
McPherson Playhouses, 327
Me & Julio, 92–93
Meadow Park Sports Centre, 361
Medical services, 30
Medicentre, 30
Meinhardt Fine Foods, 189,
    216–17
Melriches, 15
Memphis Blues Barbeque House,
    95–96
Merlin Bar and Grill, 358
Merridale Ciderworks, 332
Messenger services, 27
Met, The, 250
Met Bar & Grill, The, 256
Metropolitan Home, 211
Michéle Cake Shop, 217
Middle Beach Lodge, 323, 336
Ming Wo, 203
Mink, 201
Mintage, 211
Misch, 189, 195
Mission Hill Winery, 370, 372
Mistral French Bistro, 96
Mix by Ric's, The, 348, 358

Mix the Bakery, 196
Moby's Marine Pub, 323, 334
Modern, The, 251
Modern Kid, 202
Montauk, 208
Monte Clark Gallery, 172
Montri's Thai Restaurant, 96
Moonstruck Cheese, 334
Morris and Helen Belkin Art
    Gallery, 172, 234
Morton's the Steakhouse, 96–97
Motomachi Shokudo, 86
Motor tours, 183
Mouat Point Kayaks, 273
Mount Maxwell, 323
Mount Maxwell Provincial Park, 333
Mount Seymour, 298
Mount Seymour Provincial Park,
    177–78, 275, 296, 299
Mountain biking, 287–89, 361
Mountain Club, 348–49
Mountain Equipment Co-op, 220
Mountain Shadow Pub, 257
Mountain Woman, 338
Mountaineering, 274–77
Moustache Café, 97
Mt. Boucherie, 372
Muffet & Louisa, 326
Munro's Book Store, 325
Murchie's, 118
Murchie's Tea & Coffee, 264
Museum of Anthropology, 151, 209
Museums, 166–69. See also specific
    museum
Music
    classical, 230–33
    live, 244
    nightlife, 246–54
    recorded, 208–9
Music in the Morning, 232

N

Nahatlatch River, 292
Nairn Falls Provincial Park, 361
Naramata, 367
Naramata Heritage Inn & Spa, 379
Native art and crafts, 209
Nat's New York Pizzeria, 97
Nature observation, 289–91
Neighbourhoods. See also specific
    neighbourhood
    description of, 161
    nightlife by, 242–45
    restaurants by, 42–44
    shopping by, 188–90
Neptoon Records, 208
Net Loft, 189
New Town Barbershop, 322
New West, 43
New Westminster, 20
Newspapers, 34

Newton Wave Pool, 299
Niche Modern Dining, 313
Night Owl Bird Hospital, 31
Nightlife, 242–66
900 West Lounge, 119, 262
Ningtu Restaurant, 97–98
Nitobe Memorial Garden, 173
Nk'mip Cellars, 368
No. 5 Orange, 257
Noble Ridge Vineyard, 371
Noodle Box, The, 98
Norman Rothstein Theatre, 238
North Shore, 287
North Vancouver, 43, 137, 189
Northern Delicacy, 98
Notte's Bon Ton Pastry &
    Confectionery, 264–65
Nouvelle Nouvelle, 188
Novex Courier, 27
Nu, 98–99
Numbers, 251
Nyala African Cuisine, 99

O
"O Canada" House, 134
Oasis, 251
Oasis Bubble Tea, 75
Obakki, 188, 195
Observatory Bed and Breakfast,
    380
Ocean Explorations, 310
Ocean Outfitters, 335
Octopus Garden Restaurant, 99
Odyssey, The, 251
Okada Sushi Japanese Restaurant,
    99–100
Okanagan Valley
    Kelowna, 366
    lodgings, 378–80
    map of, 365
    Naramata, 367
    Oliver, 367–68
    orientation, 364, 366
    Osoyoos, 367–68
    Penticton, 367
    restaurants, 373–78
    transportation to, 364
    visitor information, 366
    Wine Country, 368–73
Okanagan Wine Festival, 365
Old Cemeteries Society, 311
Old Country Market, 323
Old Hastings Mill Store Museum,
    The, 168
Old Morris Tobacconist, 325
Old Vines Patio & Restaurant,
    376–77
Oliver, 367–68
Oliver Visitor Centre, 367
Olympic Visitors Centre, 342

Olympic Winter Games, 302–3,
    354
Omnimax Theatre, 154
Onlyhuman Gallery, 326
Opera, 230–33
Optaderm, 213
Opus Framing and Art Supplies, 220
Opus Hotel, 132, 134, 165
Or Gallery Society, 172
Orchard Museum, 366
Organized tours, 180–84
Orientation, 20–21
Original Tandoori Kitchen, 100
Orofino Vineyards, 369
Orpheum Theatre, 235
Osoyoos, 367–68
Osoyoos Desert Centre, 368
Osoyoos Visitor Info Centre, 368
Osteria Napoli Ristoranté, 100
Oswego, 318
Out of Ireland, 325
Out of the Mist, 325
Outdoor Adventures@Whistler,
    360
Outdoor Recreation Council of
    British Columbia, 272
Outer Coast Seaweed, 310–11
Oyama Sausage Company, 217–18
Oysters, 49

P
Pacific Boarder, 300
Pacific Central Station, 5
Pacific Centre, 186
Pacific Centre Dental, 30
Pacific Cinémathèque, 238
Pacific Coach Lines, 5, 8, 306
Pacific Coastal Airlines, 364
Pacific Museum of Earth, 168–69
Pacific Northwest Elvis Festival, 367
Pacific Opera Victoria, 327
Pacific Palisades Hotel, 132, 134
Pacific Rim National Park, 291
Pacific Rim Whale Festival, 335
Pacific Spirit Regional Park, 178–79,
    287, 293
Pacific Surf School, 335
Pajo's, 100–101, 158
Pan Pacific Hotel, 134–35
Pan Pacific Whistler Mountainside,
    353
Pandora's Collective, 239
Paper-Ya, 221
Paprika Bistro, 313
Paralympics, 354
Park(s), 174–80. See also specific
    park
Park 'N Fly, 3
Park Royal Shopping Centre, 190
Park Theatre, 237–38
Parking, 24

Parkside, 101
Parthenon Wholesale & Retail
    Food, 218
Path Gallery, 357
Patio at Lake Breeze, The, 376
PDX Courier, 27
Peace Portal Golf Course, 281
Pear Tree, The, 101
Pearl Castle, 75
Peking Lounge, 188
Pemberton Helicopters, 356
Penticton, 367
Penticton & Wine Country Tourism
    Info Centre, 367
Penticton Lakeside Resort,
    Convention Centre & Casino,
    380
Penticton Regional Airport, 364
Performing arts
    classical music, 230–33
    dance, 233–36
    opera, 230–33
    theatre, 226–30
    Victoria, 326–27
Perimeter Transportation, 340
Pets, 16–17, 31, 132–33
Pharmacies, 31
Philosophers' Café, 235
Phnom Penh, 101–2
Pho Thai Hoa, 102
Photography equipment and
    services, 32
PI Theatre, 226
Piano bars, 244
Pied-à-Terre, 102
Pinkys Steakhouse, 102–3
Pitt River Dykes, 284
Pizza, 49
Plan B Lounge and Eatery, 103
Planet Lazer, 270
Planet Veg, 103
Planetarium, 154
Plaza Club, 252
Point Atkinson Lighthouse, 152
Point Ellice House, 318–19
Point-No-Point Resort, 331
Poison Control Centre, 13
Police, 32
Pondok Indonesia, 103–4
Port Coquitlam, 43
Porteau Cove Provincial Marine
    Park, 297
Post offices, 32–33
Powell River, 273
Prana Yoga and Zen Centre, 277
Praxis Centre for Screenwriters,
    239
Presentation House, 172
Presentation House Gallery, 234
Princess Louisa Inlet, 294
Prior House Bed & Breakfast, 318

Prospect Point, 144
Prospect Point Cafe, 144
Provence Marinaside, 104, 119
Provence Mediterranean Grill,
   104, 119
Public libraries, 34
Public restrooms, 33
Pubs, 254–58
Pulp Fiction, 239
PumpJack Pub, 257
Punjabi Market, 162–63
Purdy's, 201
Pure Studio Hair & Esthetics, 213
PuSh International Performing Arts
   Festival, 227

Q
Quails' Gate, 370, 372
Quattro at Whistler, 349
Quattro on Fourth, 104
Que Pasa Mexican Foods, 218
Queen Elizabeth Park, 285, 300
Queen Elizabeth Pitch and Putt,
   281
Queen Elizabeth Theatre, 228
Queer Film Festival, 16
Quick Cobbler, 212
Quince, 218
Quinta Ferreira, 370–71
Quw'utsun' Cultural and
   Conference Centre, 333

R
R. H. V. Tee & Son (England), 190
Radio stations, 35
Railway Club, The, 252
Raincity Grill, 104–5
Raincoast Café, 336
Re-Bar Modern Foods, 314, 323
Rebel Rebel, 326
Reckless Bike Stores, 26, 270
Recordings, 208–9
Recreation, 268–318
   animal observation, 289–91
   bicycling, 25–26, 182,
      268–71
   canoeing, 271–74
   climbing, 274–77
   cross-country skiing, 294–96,
      360
   diving, 278
   downhill skiing, 296–98,
      358–60
   fishing, 279–80
   golfing, 280–81
   hiking, 281–84, 361
   horseback riding, 284
   hot-air ballooning, 284–85
   ice skating, 285
   in-line skating, 285–86
   kayaking, 271–74

kite flying, 286–87
mountain biking, 287–89,
   361
mountaineering, 274–77
nature observation, 289–91
river rafting, 291–92, 361
running, 292–93
sailing, 293–94
skiing, 294–98
snowboarding, 296–98,
   358–60
snowshoeing, 298–99
spectator sports, 301–4
swimming, 299–300
tennis, 300
walking, 292–93
Whistler, 358–62
windsurfing, 300–1
Red Onion, The, 105
Red Rooster, 370, 372
Reel 2 Real International Film
   Festival for Youth, 238
Regent College, 36
Reggae, 244
Regional Assembly of Text, 193
Rekados, 105
Rental cars, 2, 24, 309
Republic, 252
Restaurant House Piccolo, 323
Restaurants, 54–142
   by food, 45–51
   by neighbourhood, 42–44
   Okanagan Valley, 373–78
   by star rating, 40–42
   Victoria, 311–15
Restrooms, 33
Re-Use-It Centre, 357
Rex Dog Hotel and Spa, 133
Rice Lake, 280
Richard's on Richards, 252
Richmond, 43, 164–65
Richmond Nature, 290
Ridge Theatre, 238
Riley Park Community Centre, 285
Riley Park Farmers Market, 178
Rim Rock Cafe, 349
Rinconcito Salvadoreño Restaurant,
   106–7
Ritz-Carlton, 130
River rafting, 291–92, 361
River Rock Casino Resort, 33, 160
Riverwalk Café, 333
Robert Held Art Glass, 172
Robson Street, 155–56, 163, 186
Rock climbing, 277
Rockwood Adventures, 183–84
Rocky Mountain Flatbread
   Company, 107–8
Rocky Mountaineer, 8
Rodney's Oyster House, 108
Rogers' Chocolates, 325
Rollingdale, 372

Romantic restaurants, 49
Roxy, The, 253
Royal, The, 253
Royal British Columbia Museum,
   320
Royal Centre Medical, 30
Royal London Wax Museum, 324
Royal Theatre, 326–27
Ruby Slippers Theatre, 226
Ruckle Provincial Park, 333–34
Rumble Productions, 226
Running, 292–93

S
Saanich Peninsula, 331
Sailing, 293–94
Sailor Hagar's Brew Pub, 257
SalaThai Thai Restaurant, 108
Salmon House, The, 108–9
Salmon spawning, 290–91
Salons, 33
Salt Spring Apple Festival, 334
Salt Spring Island, 333–34
Salt Spring Island Cheese, 334
Salt Spring Vineyards, 323
Salt Springs Vineyard and B&B, 334
Salt Tasting Room, 109
Saltlik, 109
Salty Tongue Urban Deli, 83
Salvation Army, 326
Salvatore Ferragamo, 195
Sam Kee Building, 147
SameSun Backpacker Lodge, 380
Sanafir, 109–10, 262
Sandy's Cuisine, 110
Savage Beagle Bar, 357
Savary Island Pie Company, The,
   196–97
Save-on-Foods Memorial Centre,
   327
Sawasdee Thai Restaurant, 110
Scarlet, 207
Schara Tzedeck, 28
Schooner on Second, 336
Science World, 21, 154
Sciué Italian Bakery Caffé, 111
Scotty's One Hour Cleaners, 28
Scout, 193
Sea Harbour Seafood Restaurant,
   111
Sea Kayaking Association of British
   Columbia, 272
Sea Otter Kayaking, 273
Seabus, 23, 152–53
Seafood, 49–50
Seaplanes, 4–5, 308
Sears, 186
Seawall, 140, 142, 270–71, 286,
   293
Second Beach Outdoor Pool, 299
Second Narrows Bridge, 150

Second Suit, 202
Secret Garden Tea Company, 107, 118
See Seven, 229
See Ya Later Ranch, 372
Semperviva, 34
Seniors, 13
Sequoia Grill Restaurant at the Teahouse, 144
Seven Stones Winery, 369
17-Mile Pub and Liquor Shoppe, 329
Sewell's Marina, 280
Shadbolt Centre for the Arts, 228
Shanghai Chinese Bistro, 111
Shangri-La, 130
Shannon Falls, 338
Shannon Falls Provincial Park, 297
Shark Club Bar and Grill, 253
Shaughnessy Restaurant, 145
Shebeen Whisk(e)y House, 83
Shelter Restaurant, 336
Sheraton Vancouver Wall Centre Hotel, 135
Shine, 253
Shoes, 212
Shopping, 186–223
Shore Club, The, 112
Sidney, 331
Sidney Pier Hotel & Spa, 331
Siegel's Bagels, 197
Sigge's Sport Villa, 295
Signature BC Liquor Stores, 222
Silk, 206–7
Silkscarf, 372
Simon Fraser University, 36, 234
Simon Fraser University Theatre, 226
Simply Thai, 112
Sinclair Centre, 187
Sip Resto Lounge, 262–63
Siwash Rock, 144
Skating, 285–86
Skiing
    cross-country, 294–96, 360
    downhill, 296–98, 358–60
Skin care, 212–14
Sky Valley Inn, 323
Skyride Gondola, 276
Skytrain, 22–23
Smoking Dog Bistro, The, 112–13
Smoking Lily, 326
Sno-Limo, 356
Snowboarding, 296–98, 358–60
Snowbus, 4, 340
Snowshoeing, 298–99
Sobo, 323, 336
Soccer, 304
So.Cial at Le Magasin, 113
Society of Translators and Interpreters of BC, 16

Sonora Room, The, 377
Sooke, 328–31
Sooke Cycle, 329
Sooke Harbour House, 329–30
Sooke Infocentre, 328
Sooke Region Museum, 328
Sophie's Cosmic Cafe, 113
South China Seas Trading Co. Ltd., 217
South Granville, 189
South Main, 163, 192–93
Southlands Nursery, 204
Spa Utopia, 33
Spas, 33
Specialty foods, 214–19
Spectator sports, 301–4
Spice Alley Korean Restaurant & Bar, 114–15
Spice Islands Indonesian Restaurant, 114
Spinnakers Gastro Brewpub and Guesthouse, 314
Spirit Ridge Vineyard Resort & Spa, 380
Spirits, 222–24
Splashdown Waterpark, 299–300
Splitz Grill, 114, 350
Spokes, 276
Spokes Bicycle Rental & Espresso Bar, 26
Sports, 301–4
Sports bars, 245
Sports equipment/sportswear, 219–20
Squamish, 288–89, 296–97
Squamish Adventure Centre, 340
Squamish Rock Guides, 277
Squamish Spit, 296, 301
St. Hubertus, 370, 373
St. Paul's Hospital, 30
St. Vincent De Paul, 326
Stage, 314
Stag's Hollow, 371
Stanley Park, 21, 142–44, 270, 300
Stanley Park Horse-Drawn Tours, 182
Stanley Park Seawall, 140, 142, 270–71, 286, 293
Staples, 207
Starlight Casino, 160
Starling Lane Winery, 331
Stationery, 220–21
Stawamus Chief, 277, 296
Steamworks Brewing Co., 114–15, 258
Steamworks TransContinental, 114–15
Stella's Tap and Tapas Bar, 115
Steve Nash Sports Club, 30
Steveston, 157–58, 269
Steveston Bicycle, 269

Steveston Pizza Co., 115–16
Stock Market, The, 218
Stray animals, 31
Suasion, 326
Subeez Cafe, 116
Suite 400 Executive Offices and Secretarial Services, 27
Suki's, 213–14
Sumac Ridge, 372
Summer Night Market, 178
Summerhill, 373
Summerhill Pyramid Winery, 370
Summerhill Sunset Bistro, 377
Summit, The, 353–54
Sun Run, 292
Sun Sui Wah Seafood Restaurant, 95, 116
Sunset Victoria Symphony Splash, 327–28
Sunshine Coast, 274, 278
Sunshine Coast Festival of the Written Arts, 240
Sunwolf Outdoor Centre, 361
Supervalu, 29
Surrey, 43
Sushi, 50
Sushi on the Sea, 329
Sushi Village, 350
Sutton Place Hotel, The, 132–33, 135
Sutton Place Wine Merchant, 223
Suvai Restaurant, 116–17
Sweat Co., 277
Sweet Obsession Cakes & Pastries, 265
Swimming, 299–300
Sylvia Hotel, 133, 135–36

T

Taco Shack, The, 117
Tally-Ho, 309
Tangled Vines, 371
Tantalus Range, 275–76
Tantalus Vineyards, 373
Tapastree Restaurant, 117
Tapioca Express, 75
Tauca Lea Resort and Spa, 323
Taverns, 254–58
Taxes, 12
Taxis, 3, 25, 309
Taylorwood Wines, 223
TBC Indoor Kart Racing, 271
Tea, 74–75, 118–19, 243, 263–66
Tearoom T, 265
Tech 1 Hair Design, 214
Telephone numbers, 37–38
Television stations, 35–36
Temperature, 10
Ten Ren Tea & Ginseng, 188, 265
Tennis, 300
Terminal City Tower Hotel, 136

Terra Breads, 197
Terrace, The, 377
Theatre, 226–30
Theatre Under the Stars, 228
Theo's, 377–78
Therapy Vineyards, 371
32 Books, 199
Thistledown House, 137
Thomas Haas Patisserie and Café, 117–18, 201
Thomas Hobbs Florist by Maureen Sullivan, 204
Thompson River, 292
Thornhaven, 372
Three Dog Bakery, 17
3 Vets, 220
Tickleberry's, 371
Tilford Gardens, 173–74
Time, 10
Times Square Suites, 136
Tinhorn Creek, 369, 371
Tinland Cookware, 217
Tla-Ook Cultural Adventures, 335
Toasted Oak Wine Bar and Grill, 371, 378
Tofino, 334–36
Tofino Botanical Gardens, 335
Tojo's, 118–19
Tom Lee Music, 208
Tomahawk Restaurant, 119
Tomato Fresh Food Café, 120
Tommy Africa's Bar, 358
Tonic, 254
Toshi Sushi, 120
Touchstone Theatre, 226
Tourism Vancouver, 18
Tourism Victoria Visitor Info Centre, 308
Toybox, The, 222
Toys, 221–22
Tracey Lawrence Gallery, 172
Trafalgars Bistro, 120–21
Trains, 8, 27, 341
Tramonto at the River Rock Casino Resort, 121
Translink, 4, 8, 22
Transportation
    airplane, 2–4, 308, 341, 364
    bicycle, 25–26
    bus, 5, 22, 306, 340
    car, 8–9, 23–24
    ferry, 5, 8
    limousines, 25
    seabus, 23, 152–53
    seaplanes, 4–5, 308
    skytrain, 22–23
    taxi, 3, 25, 309
    train, 8, 27, 341
Trattoria di Umberto, 350
Trattoria Italian Kitchen, 121
Travel Bug, The, 199

Travel with Taste, 310
Trolley tours, 183
Tropika, 121–22
Trout Lake Farmers Market, 179
Truck Farmers Market, 188
True Confections, 265–66
True Grain Bread, 332
True Value Vintage, 211
Truffles Bistro, 261
T&T Supermarket, 188, 217
Tugwell Creek Honey Farm & Meadery, 329
Tung Fong Hung Medicine Co., 188
Turnabout Collections Ltd, 203
Turtle Express, 322
2010 Olympic Winter Games, 302–3, 354

U

UBC Bookstore, 200
UBC Botanical Garden, 145
UBC Farm Market, 179
Udder Guys Ice Cream Parlour, 332
Umbrella Shop, The, 211
Unique Lives & Experiences, 235
Unitarian Church of Vancouver, 29
University Golf Club, 281
University Hospital, 30
University of British Columbia, 21, 36, 226, 286, 300
Uno Langmann Ltd, 190
Urban Fare, 219
Urban Ink Productions, 226
Uva Wine Bar, 122

V

Vagabond Players, 226
Value Village, 326
Vancouver All-Terrain Adventures, 184
Vancouver Animal Emergency Clinic, 31
Vancouver Aquarium, 154–55
Vancouver Aquatic Centre, 300
Vancouver Art Gallery, 156–57, 186, 234
Vancouver Bullion and Currency Exchange, 16
Vancouver By Cycle, 26
Vancouver Canadians, 302–3
Vancouver Canucks, 303–4
Vancouver East Cultural Centre, 228, 236
Vancouver General Hospital, 30
Vancouver Giants, 304
Vancouver International Airport, 2
Vancouver International Children's Festival, 180

Vancouver International Dance Festival, 236
Vancouver International Film Festival, 238
Vancouver International Fringe Festival, 229
Vancouver International Writers (& Readers) Festival, 240
Vancouver Jewish Film Festival, 238
Vancouver Law Courts, 149
Vancouver Maritime Museum and St. Roch, 169, 180
Vancouver Museum, 154, 180
Vancouver New Music, 232
Vancouver New Play Festival, 229
Vancouver Opera, 232–33
Vancouver Pen Shop, The, 221
Vancouver Playhouse, 230
Vancouver Police Centennial Museum, 169
Vancouver Pride Parade, 16
Vancouver Public Library, 239
Vancouver Queer Film + Video Festival, 238
Vancouver Recital Society, 233
Vancouver Symphony Orchestra, 233
Vancouver Taxi, 14, 25
Vancouver TheatreSports League, 230
Vancouver Tourist Info Centre, 21
Vancouver Trolley Company, 183
Vancouver Veterinary Hospital, 31
Vancouver Whitecaps, 304
Vandusen Botanical Garden, 144–45
Vanier Park, 132, 179–80, 287, 293
Vanity Fair Antiques and Collectibles Mall, 325
Varsity Theatre, 238
Venturi-Schulze Vineyards, 332
Via Rail, 8
Victoria
    attractions, 309, 318–25
    Cowichan Valley, 332–33
    Duncan, 333
    festivals, 327–28
    lodgings, 315–18
    Long Beach, 334–36
    Malahat, 331–32
    map of, 307
    nightlife, 304
    orientation of, 308
    parking, 309
    performing arts, 326–27
    restaurants, 311–15
    Saanich Peninsula, 331
    Salt Spring Island, 333–34
    shopping, 325–26
    Sidney, 331

Sooke, 328–31
Tofino, 334–36
tours, 310–11, 319
transportation to, 306, 308
traveling in, 309
visitor information, 308
Victoria Bug Zoo, 320
Victoria Carriage Tours, 309
Victoria Fringe Festival, 327
Victoria Harbour Ferry Company,
309, 318
Victoria Operatic Society, 327
Victoria Regional Transit System,
309
Victoria Summer Music Festival,
328
Victoria Symphony Orchestra, 327
Victoria Tea Festival, 327
Victorian Hotel, 136
Vida Wellness Spa, 214
Video In/Video Out, 170
Vij's, 122–23
Vij's Rangoli, 122–23
Vineyard Terrace, The, 377
Vista d'Oro, 219
Vogue Chinese Cuisine, 123

W

Waazubee Cafe, 261
Walkabout Historic Vancouver,
183
Walking, 292–93
Walking tours, 183
Wanderlust, 200
Waterfront Park, 153
Waterfront Wines, 378
Waves Coffee, 266
Wear Else?, 195
Weather, 9
Web information, 17–18
Wedge Rafting, 361
Wedgewood Hotel, 136–37
West, 59, 123
West Coast Air, 4, 308
West Coast City and Nature
Sightseeing, 183
West Coast Dental Clinics, 30
West Coast Express, 27
West Coast Railway Heritage
Park, 340
West End, 20
description of, 163–64
lodgings, 130–37
nightlife, 242
restaurants, 43–44

West End Farmers Market, 179
West End Guest House Bed &
Breakfast, 137
West End Veterinary Clinic, 31
West Side, 44
West Vancouver, 44, 190
West Vancouver Transit, 8
Westbeach, 220
Western Canadian Opera Society,
235
Western Front, 170, 234
Western Institute for the Deaf and
Hard of Hearing, 13
Westin Resort and Spa, The, 354
Westjet, 364
Westworld Computers, 28
Whale-watching, 291
Wheely Clean, 28
Whip Restaurant & Gallery, The, 263
Whistler
exploring in, 355–56
lodgings, 351–55
map of, 339
nightlife, 357–58
orientation of, 341–42
recreation, 358–62
restaurants, 344–50
shopping, 357
transportation to and from,
338, 340–41
traveling in, 343–44
visitor information, 343
Whistler Activity and Information
Centre, 356, 360
Whistler Cigar Company, 357
Whistler Express, 4
Whistler Film Festival, 239
Whistler Mountain, 358
Whistler Mountain Bike Park, 361
Whistler Museum & Archives
Society, 356
Whistler Olympic Park, 355
Whistler Outdoor Experience
Company, 362
Whistler Pinnacle, The, 355
Whistler River Adventures, 361
Whistler Transit System, 344
White Rock, 44
White Spot, 124
Whitewater Kayaking Association,
272
Whytecliff Marine Park, 278
Wickaninnish Beach, 291
Wickaninnish Inn, 336
Wild Goose, 371

Wild Rice, 124
Wilderness tours, 183–84
William Tell Restaurant, The,
124–25
Williams Sonoma, 189, 203
Win Store, 326
Winchester Cellars, 331
Windsure Windsurfing School, 300
Windsurfing, 300–1
Wine, 222–24
Wine bars, 245
Wine Country (Okanagan Valley),
368–73
Winter Farmers Market, 179
Winton's Social Stationery, 221
Women, 14
Womyns' Ware, 15, 161
Won More Szechuan Cuisine, 125
Woodman's Cleaners, 28
Word on the Street, 240
Workspace, 27
World Gym, 30
World/Club 816, 249
Wreck Beach, 15, 159

Y

Yale, The, 254
Yaletown, 44, 164–65, 186, 242
Yaletown Brewing Company, 258
Yaletown Farmers Market, 179
Yellow Cabs, 309
YEW Restaurant + Bar, 59, 125
Yoga, 33–34
Yoshi Japanese Restaurant, 125–26
Yuen Yuen Cafe, 75
Yuji's Japanese Tapas, 126
Yuk Yuk's, 254
YVR Airporter, 3–4
YWCA, 277
YWCA Hotel, 137

Z

Zakkushi Charcoal Grill Diner,
107, 126
Zambri's, 315
Zanatta Winery, 332
Zen Fine Chinese Cuisine, 126–27
Zen Japanese Restaurant, 127
Zest Japanese Cuisine, 127–28
Zing Paperie & Design, 221
Ziptrek Ecotours, 362
Zonda Nellis, 196
Zoo, 290
Zulu Records, 209

Best Places Vancouver Report Form

Based on my personal experience, I wish to nominate the following restaurant, place of lodging, shop, nightclub, sight, or other as a "Best Place"; or confirm/correct/disagree with the current review.

_____
_____
_____
_____

(Please include address and telephone number of establishment, if convenient.)

REPORT

Please describe food, service, style, comfort, value, date of visit, and other aspects of your experience; continue on another piece of paper if necessary.

_____
_____
_____
_____
_____
_____
_____
_____

I am not associated, directly or indirectly, with the management or ownership of this establishment.

SIGNED
_____

ADDRESS
_____
_____

PHONE_____**DATE**_____

Please address to *Best Places Vancouver* and send to:
SASQUATCH BOOKS
119 SOUTH MAIN STREET, SUITE 400
SEATTLE, WA 98104
Feel free to e-mail feedback as well: **BPFEEDBACK@SASQUATCHBOOKS.COM**

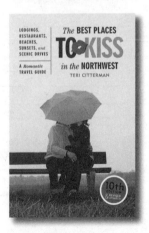